Giuseppe Veltri
Alienated Wisdom

Studies and Texts in Scepticism

Edited by
Giuseppe Veltri

in cooperation with
Rachel Aumiller

Editorial Board
Heidrun Eichner, Talya Fishman, Racheli Haliva, Henrik Lagerlund, Reimund Leicht,
Stephan Schmid, Carsten Wilke, Irene Zwiep

Volume 3

Giuseppe Veltri
Alienated Wisdom

Enquiry into Jewish Philosophy and Scepticism

DE GRUYTER

The series Studies and Texts in Scepticism is published
on behalf of the Maimonides Centre for Advanced Studies

ISBN 978-3-11-071054-0
e-ISBN (PDF) 978-3-11-060449-8
e-ISBN (EPUB) 978-3-11-060368-2
ISSN 2568-9614

Library of Congress Control Number: 2018946720

Bibliographic information published by the Deutsche Nationalbibliothek
The Deutsche Nationalbibliothek lists this publication in the Deutsche Nationalbibliografie;
detailed bibliographic data are available in the Internet at http://dnb.dnb.de.

© 2020 Walter de Gruyter GmbH, Berlin/Boston
This volume is text- and page-identical with the hardback published in 2018.
Cover image: Staats- und Universitätsbibliothek Hamburg, Ms Cod. Levy 115, fol. 158r:
Maimonides, Moreh Nevukhim, Beginn von Teil III.
Printing and binding: CPI books GmbH, Leck

www.degruyter.com

Foreword

It is customary for an author to explain the meaning of his or her title at the beginning of a book. Giuseppe Veltri, however, is rarely caught doing what is customary. He writes at the beginning of the present book that the meaning of its title will be explained "in the conclusion of the book."[1] What's this like? *Mashal le-mah ha-davar domeh?* It's like a book of puzzles in which the solutions are given at the end. Do the puzzles first, get the solutions afterwards!

The Jewish tradition, Veltri teaches, is a tradition of puzzles, a tradition of questions. In this way, Veltri continues, the Jewish tradition is similar to Greek scepticism. The Greek word "*skepsis*," he observes, means "enquiry," and the "sceptic/enquirer is whoever continues to raise questions."[2] The analogous Jewish view, he explains, is illustrated by the midrashic text about "four pupils" or "four sons," well-known from its inclusion in the *Haggadah* of Passover. According to this midrashic text, there are four different kinds of pupils: "the wise, the wicked, the simple, and the one who doesn't know how to ask." Veltri notes that the youngster in the last place is not the wicked youth nor the simpleton, as you might expect, but the one who doesn't know how to ask. The pupil who has no questions is the most disappointing. The wise pupil is the one who knows how to ask the toughest questions. The wicked pupil may ask obnoxious questions and the simple pupil naïve questions, but they are at least part of the debate, and thus are preferable to the dumbbell who questions nothing. Veltri astutely sums up the educational theory of classical Judaism as follows: "In the Talmudic and subsequent periods, the goal of learning was to ask the rabbi the (right) question that forces him to find the weak point in his argumentation." The aim of study is not to memorise but *to question* what the teacher says. In other words, the aim of study, according to classical Judaism, is *skepsis*.[3]

The difference between the dogmatist and the sceptic is that the former prefers answers, while the latter prefers questions. This sceptical love of questions is found in the positive Talmudic attitude toward *maḥloqet* ("debate," "division," "controversy," or "difference of opinion"). Veltri quotes a famous dictum of the Mishnah, *Avot* 5:17: "Every debate (*maḥloqet*) that is for the sake of Heaven will in the end endure [*sofah lehitqayyem*]." He explains that this means that a true, disinterested scholarly debate ("for the sake of Heaven") "ends with an *aporia*, i.e. [an] endless contradiction," and thus "will never cease." Debate is eternal. Questioning is eternal. *Skepsis* is eternal.[4] However, Veltri takes this Mishnaic dictum one big step further: following a clever interpretation mentioned by Rabbi Obadiah di Bertinoro in his Commentary on *Avot*, according to which the word "*sofah*" ("end") may be rendered as "purpose,"

---

1 Below, p. XX.
2 Ibid.
3 Ibid., p. XXI.
4 Ibid., p. 273 and passim.

Veltri suggests that the Mishnaic dictum may mean: Every debate that is for the sake of Heaven has *as its intended purpose* its eternal endurance.⁵ *Maḥloqet* is itself the purpose! It is *debate* that endures eternally. Questions are not designed for answers, but answers are means to questions.

The medieval Jewish philosophical book that most influences Veltri's text is probably Rabbi Judah Halevi's dialogue, the *Kuzari* (1140). The genre of the dialogue, Veltri explains, is an excellent vehicle for questioning, debate, and *skepsis*.⁶ Halevi's hero in the history of philosophy is the ever-questioning Socrates, not the more dogmatic Plato and Aristotle. Socrates is mentioned four times in the *Kuzari* (I, 1; III, 1; IV, 13; V, 14) and is quoted twice (at IV, 13, and V, 14) as saying: "O people, I do not deny this divine wisdom of yours, but I say that I do not understand it" (*Apology* 20de).⁷ Moreover, Halevi is important for Veltri because he criticises the alleged universality of philosophy and argues for "the genealogy of knowledge." According to Halevi's version of the genealogy of knowledge (I, 63), philosophy was developed among the children of Shem, including the Chaldeans, was still later transmitted to the Persians, who were children of Japheth, and finally was appropriated by the Greeks after they conquered the Persians.⁸ Therefore, according to Halevi, philosophy is not universal, natural, or purely rational, but depends on tradition, translation, and transmission. It has a history and a genealogy. In this sense, Veltri reads Halevi's *Kuzari* in conjunction with Nietzsche's *Genealogy of Morals* (which reclaims the historical value of the past) and Foucault's *Archaeology of Knowledge* (which refutes the totality of knowledge).⁹ If philosophy depends on tradition, translation, and transmission, it is also subject to forgetfulness, error, and transformation—and a reasonable individual will approach its pronouncements with no little scepticism.

The modern Jewish philosophical text that most influences Veltri's text is clearly Rabbi Simone Luzzatto's dialogue, *Socrates* (1651). Luzzatto's role in the present book is considerable. As Veltri himself puts it: "Simone Luzzatto is the pillar of this book because he offers enlightened definitions of Jewish philosophy, religion, cultural ghettos, monotheism, and, first and foremost, the sceptical attitude."¹⁰ Despite their boldness and originality, Luzzatto's works have been largely ignored throughout the centuries. Veltri has been seeking to correct this situation: he is currently supervising the publication of critical editions of Luzzatto's Italian and Hebrew writings, together with new English translations, in collaboration with Anna Lissa, Michela Torbidoni, and other scholars. The full title of Luzzatto's *Socrates* is revealing: *Socrates or On Human Knowledge: The Serious-Playful Exercise of Simone Luzzatto, Venetian Jew*. Why did Luzzato call his exercise "*seriogiocoso*"? Which aspects of the

---

5 Ibid., p. 273.
6 Ibid., pp. 70–71.
7 Ibid.
8 Ibid., pp. 38–39.
9 Ibid., p. XIII.
10 Ibid., p. 144.

book are serious and which playful—or perhaps it is impossible to disentangle one from the other.[11] Luzzatto describes himself as an "academic sceptic."[12] Is scepticism *seriogiocoso?* Veltri remarks that Luzzatto was the first author "in the history of Jewish philosophy" who "proclaimed himself a sceptic," and his *Socrates* is "the first extant treatise on scepticism written by a Jew."[13] One motif that occurs in Luzzatto's scepticism, as explored by Veltri, is that of "the naked truth" (*nuda veritas*). Luzzatto writes that truth is "simple" and "she takes the greatest delight in her very nakedness." Adam and Eve were created nude by God but obstinately preferred to ornament their bodies. The lovers of truth extol *nuda veritas*, but the vulgar deem it "indecent" for Lady Truth to appear "without any ornament." Luzzatto concludes his *Socrates* by quoting Ecclesiastes 7:29: "God made man upright, but they have sought out many cogitations." By "cogitations" (*ḥishevonot, cogitationes*), Luzzatto refers to immoderate thoughts and senseless quibbles that are the opposite of simplicity and nakedness. He seems to presume that we post-Edenic human beings can never wholly free ourselves from such cogitations. How can one see the naked truth if *la bella Verità* is always adorned with gaudy and ostentatious *cogitationes?*[14]

Before I conclude this Foreword, I must say some words about the book's curious title, *Alienated Wisdom*.

In 1975, the classical historian Arnaldo Momigliano published an incisive little book, *Alien Wisdom*, that treats Hellenistic civilization. Momigliano sought to understand the cultural relationships between the Greeks and the peoples they conquered, in particular the Persians, the Romans, the Jews, and the Celts. "Alien wisdom" refers both to Greek wisdom (what the Jews called *ḥokhmah yewwanit*) in the eyes of the barbarians, and barbarian wisdom in the eyes of the Greeks. Momigliano found that some cultures, like the Romans and the Jews, were good at learning the secrets of "alien wisdom," while other cultures, like the Greeks, were bad at it. This skill of the Romans and Jews helps explain the uncanny success of Christianity in Europe. Veltri tells us that Momigliano's term inspired his own term, "alienated wisdom."[15]

However, Veltri's concept of "alienated wisdom" is somewhat different from Momigliano's "alien wisdom."[16] The difference may be explained as one of focus: Momigliano was primarily interested in the relationship between different cultures, while Veltri is primarily interested in the attitude of different cultures toward knowledge. Veltri's concept is similar in an odd way to the post-liberal notion of "cultural appropriation." For example, if Jews or Muslims studied Aristotle, they ostensibly *alienated* his philosophy and turned it into "*alienated* wisdom." However, if Judah Halevi is right in his genealogy of knowledge, and Aristotle himself *alienated* Semitic

---

11 Ibid., p. 238.
12 Ibid., pp. 90 and 144.
13 Ibid., p. 213.
14 Ibid., pp. 233–234.
15 Ibid., p. 282.
16 Ibid., pp. 282–283.

philosophy, then his philosophy is itself "*alienated* wisdom" (cf. Marx's concept of "alienated labour"), and those Jews or Muslims who utilized Aristotle's philosophy were Semites reclaiming what was originally theirs. The question of what is or is not "alienated" depends on one's narrative. What does one say about an American hamburger bar in Hamburg?

In Veltri's analysis, the concept of "alienated wisdom" is related to that of "stolen wisdom" (*sapientia capta*).[17] According to an ancient belief, the Greeks plagiarised the sciences and philosophy from the Jews. Writing in the second century BCE, Aristobulus of Alexandria charged Pythagoras, Socrates, and Plato with appropriating ideas from the Law of Moses.[18] Alienated wisdom becomes "stolen" wisdom or "plagiarism" when the appropriators claim that the wisdom originated with them.

In order to consider wisdom "alienated," one must, like Judah Halevi, deny the universality of knowledge. Maimonides did not consider either his own philosophy or Aristotle's philosophy to be "alienated." In his *Guide for the Perplexed*, I, 71 and II, 11, he taught that the sciences and philosophy had flourished in ancient Israel, but were lost when the Jews were exiled and subjugated by the ignorant nations. Maimonides uses the Arabic term "*jāhiliyya*" to designate the ignorant nations who subjugated the Jews. This is the same charged term used by the Muslims to designate the Age of Ignorance before the advent of Islam. If Momigliano wrote about the relationship of the conquerors with the barbarians, Maimonides referred to the relationship of the conquered with the barbarians.

Veltri's *Alienated Wisdom* is a tour de force. It is exciting and challenging to read. At a dizzying pace, issuing insight after insight, Veltri leaps from the Hebrew Bible, to the Greek tomes of Philo of Alexandria, to the Aramaic Gemara, to Saadia Gaon's Arabic *Beliefs and Opinions*, to Obadiah Sforno's Latin *Light of the Nations*, to Sara Copio Sullam's Italian *On the Immortality of the Soul*, to Leopold Zunz's German books on Jewish history, and many more. Remarkably, he is entirely at home with all of these diverse sources. There is no trace of alienation in his wisdom.

Warren Zev Harvey
The Hebrew University of Jerusalem

---

17 Ibid., p. 20.
18 Ibid., pp. 11–12.

Contents

Preface —— XIII

Documentation Style —— XVII

Introduction —— XIX

PART ONE ALIENATED WISDOM

Synopsis: How the Written and Oral Torah Became Alienated Wisdom —— 3

1	Between Myth and History of Knowledge —— 5
1.1	The Christian Use of an Alexandrine Myth —— 6
1.2	Antiquity as the Premise for Authority —— 9
2	The "Theft" of Written and Oral Wisdom —— 21
2.1	Strengths and Weaknesses of "Writing" vs. "Orality" —— 22
2.2	He Who Did Not Write but Published: Ezra the Scribe —— 25
2.3	The Publication of the Greek Torah —— 26
2.4	The Record of Oral Wisdom —— 28
2.5	The Transmission of Wisdom —— 33
3	Between "Theft" and Genealogy of Knowledge: The Middle Ages —— 35
4	Primordial Wisdom and Historical Consciousness —— 43
4.1	Arcane Wisdom in a Bookshop —— 43
4.2	Galatino, Lusitanus, and Azariah de' Rossi —— 44
4.3	Method and Reader —— 49
4.4	The Sources of Wisdom —— 56
4.5	Polemic Anthropology and Religious Ontology —— 58

PART TWO JEWISH PHILOSOPHY: HISTORY OF DEFINITIONS

Synopsis: How Jewish Tradition Became (Philosophy of) Religion —— 67

1	From *Philosophia Hebraeorum* to Jewish Religion —— 69
1.1	Reducing Jewish Tradition to "Ceremonial Laws" —— 69

| 1.2 | Jewish Tradition as Religion —— 89 |
| 1.3 | A Turning Point? Moses Mendelssohn: Between *Caerimonialia* and Religion —— 101 |

| 2 | **Philosophy between Jewish Studies and Theology —— 105** |
| 2.1 | Jewish Philosophy: History of Wisdom —— 106 |

| 3 | **Leopold Zunz: The "Scientific" Creation of Jewish Studies —— 121** |

| 4 | **Abraham Geiger: Jewish Theology as Institution —— 127** |

| 5 | **Philological Demythologisation as a Premise of New Dogmatisms and Ethics —— 133** |

PART THREE (JEWISH) SCEPTICISM

Synopsis: On Jewish Philosophy and Scepticism in the Early Modern Period —— 143

1	**Research on (Jewish) Scepticism —— 146**
1.1	Research on Scepticism(s) —— 146
1.2	Research on Jewish Scepticism —— 151

2	**At The Eve of Modernity: Scepticism in-between —— 157**
2.1	From Scholasticism to Sceptical Attitudes —— 158
2.2	Three Sceptical Strategies: De' Rossi, the Maharal, and Sforno —— 167

3	**Spaces of Dialectic Exchange: The Academies and the Venetian Ghetto —— 185**
3.1	Italian Academies and Scepticism —— 186
3.2	Jewish Academies —— 188
3.3	The Ghetto and Dialectic Strategies: The Philosopher Sara Copio Sullam —— 194

4	**Socrates, the Jew: The Scepticism of Simone Luzzatto —— 213**
4.1	Apologetic Strategies, Scepticism, and Empiricism —— 214
4.2	The Politics of Scepticism: Luzzatto's *Socrate* —— 233

5	**Sceptical Judaism: A Protestant Strategy —— 265**
5.1	Negotiating the Principle of Contradiction: Johann Frischmuth on Rabbinic Dialectical Discussion —— 265
5.2	The "Sceptic" Solomon: Halle's Protestant Vision —— 276

Conclusion —— **281**
  Alienation and Philosophies —— **281**

Appendix I —— **297**
  Johannes Frischmuth (1619–1687) Guido Bartolucci —— **297**

Appendix II —— **303**
  Johann Frischmuth & Johann Leonhard Will —— **303**

Bibliography —— **325**

Index —— **357**

Preface

According to a medieval Jewish tradition, the soul along the path of its metamorphosis must traverse successive stages that entail a loss of memory provoked by the soul's shock at finding itself in abruptly new situations. In the first stage, within the heavenly world, the soul's state of tranquillity shields it against disturbances as it pursues its divine mission: to merge in procreation with the female bosom. Despite the soul's laments and supplications, an appointed angel acting with divine instructions delivers a blow to the soul and obliterates all memory of that tranquil state. In the womb, the soul takes shape in a setting that gradually becomes familiar, agreeable, and serene. The idea of departing is not only unwelcome but objectionable. The angel's blow brings about birth into the new human world, where the soul crafts another space of tranquillity through self-absorption, *amor sui*. At the end of its time on earth, the soul again has no interest in leaving the world willingly, or at least quietly, and so the angel is compelled to strike it once more so that it can forget the human realm as it returns to the peace of the divine.

This picture of creation as one that comes about through a series of events, partitioned by gaps of memory, is a metaphor for the modern mindset that systematically disregards the past in its constant quest for new stimulation. Perhaps it is precisely these memory gaps that lead to optimism, which drapes a merciful veil of ignorance over past experiences.

The idea of a cultural memory, as it is called (not without a postmodern inflection) by the Egyptologist Jan Assmann, must incorporate the understanding that such reminiscence needs to be actualised in our society if it is to play any useful role. Otherwise we might well be condemned to relive the past. Intellectual progress cannot be accomplished if the study of the past is preemptively selective, only incorporating prevalent principles—the so-called mainstream—while overlooking the marginal, muted experiences that nonetheless contribute to the formation and growth of thought in general. Such an acknowledgement of influences and interconnections can be uncomfortable, because it questions and often openly threatens truths and certainties that are foundational for the dominant culture. Nevertheless, such an acknowledgement can also open new intellectual spaces, opportunities for learning, and methods for the disclosure of fresh insights because the future can only come about through a dialectical appropriation of the past, even if that appropriation is not a fully conscious one.

That is also the main reason why the history of philosophy necessarily involves both Foucault's *Archaeology of Knowledge* (for its refutation of the totality of knowledge) and Nietzsche's *Genealogy of Morals* (for its reclamation of the un-conscious or forgotten historical value of the past), at the same time that it transcends them because of its conscious appropriation of the past in order to ground the present. It is for this reason that for years I have concentrated my studies on the genesis of the historical and contemporary Jewish conception of their own distinct philosophy as well as the genesis of a love for Jewish wisdom that has both manifested itself *in time* but is also a product *of* that time. Additionally (and here with a stronger claim to novelty), I have focused on the Jewish tendency of opposition to systems in philosophy, which is a tendency that is—in my humble view—dialectically sceptical *in nuce*.

Let me also make clear from the start: the study of Jewish philosophy is not simply a historical effort to systematically research origins and influences, *volens nolens*, through generations of (Greek, Islamic, and European) philosophy and cultural history. It primarily entails confronting the issue of philosophies in the plural: asking ourselves about the status of a philosophy—its existence and essence—when it is defined by an adjective that is fundamentally an *aporia*. To put it another way: is it possible to modify a philosophy with an adjective without undermining the philosopher's central claim to universality? Does this adjectival qualification limit the philosopher from freely participating in philosophy as such? In this case, Jewish philosophy can become Daniel's rock of biblical prophecy, hurled at the statue of the world's ages. The idea of Jewish philosophy itself brings into question the legitimacy of the idea of a universal philosophy.

That is the subject of following book. It is conceived as an aporetic journey into a world that can most accurately be described as unexplored despite the fact that we have lived in it for centuries. Both concentration on something and the inner experience of the particularity of that thing do not *prima facie* include an awareness of its confines: the limits are visible obviously only from outside and/or in the consciousness of "others." Our voyage through the history of Jewish philosophy and scepticism —understood in an a-systematic and asymmetrical way—will therefore be accompanied by questions about the denomination and characterisation of the field of the research, i.e. the "calculation" of the *fines* (boundaries) and *limes* (limits) as *defini*tion and de*limit*ation. It is a philosophical phenomenon that's difficult to circumscribe because of its dual nature—universal but modified by an adjective—and because of the unique circumstances of Judaism, a precise and historically defined culture and experience despite its geographical, cultural, and linguistic dispersion.

I hope that the reader will grasp the meaning of "alienated wisdom" at the end of this volume as a result of my exploration. I will briefly explain the subtitle, *Enquiry into Jewish Philosophy and Scepticism*, which is consciously challenging. Jewish philosophy is, indeed, a question mark appended to general philosophy, but, at the same time, it is an object of investigation. According to Sextus Empiricus, ancient Greek "scepticism" (σκέψις) means "enquiry" and sceptics are students who always venture to scrutinise dogmatism(s). The sceptic/enquirer is whoever continues to raise questions. They are a student of a school in which the main object, the "enquiry," is paradoxically at the same time the method and the intent of knowledge and research. "Enquiry into Jewish Philosophy" will consequently explore the foundations of an *alienated* wisdom, the history of definitions, and sceptical strategies.

This book is an introductory contribution to the history of Jewish philosophy and scepticism as a result of my studies at the *Maimonides Centre for Advanced Studies,* created in 2015 at the University of Hamburg thanks to the generous financial support of the German Research Foundation (*Deutsche Forschungsgemeinschaft*). This volume is a preface to other books I have planned on the history of Jewish scepticism, which will offer a platform for newly emerging explorations of this currently underrepresented field.

In closing this preface, I would like to thank Stanley Levers, who translated the first part of the book from Italian to English, and Anthony Paletta and Patricia Grosse for the language editing of the entire book and especially for the parts written originally in English. I would like to thank Dr. Giada Coppola for the compilation of bibliography and indexes and some improvements, Dr. Anna Lissa and Dr. Michela Torbidoni for their long-standing contributions to the project concerning the work and the philosophy of Simone Luzzato, Dr. Guido Bartolucci for his precious additions, Dr. Valentina Decembrini for the transcription of Latin and Hebrew texts of Johann Frischmuth, and Dr. Rachel Aumiller for her careful editorial supervision. I also am indebted to Dr. Albrecht Döhnert, editorial director at the publishing house Walter De Gruyter, Berlin-Boston, for his support, and Dr. Sophie Wagenhofer, acquisitions editor at De Gruyter, for her helpful advice in all production matters.

My special thanks to my colleagues and the fellows of the *Maimonides Centre* for reading former drafts, Guido Bartolucci, Emidio Spinelli and Dirk Westerkamp for their note and comments, and especially Dr. Warren Zev Harvey for his scrutiny of the entire book, for suggesting several important and learned improvements, and his brilliant and admirable preface.

The reader will obviously find weak points if not errors and mistakes in my arguments and observations. Yet, the Andalusian philosopher Ibn Rushd (Averroes) wrote in his *Tahāfut al-tahāfut* that the man of learning "is under obligation to choose the best religion of his period, even they are all equally true for him, and *he must believe that the best will abrogated by the introduction of a still better*" (my italics).[1] His thought is valid for every philosophy, system of thought, and commentary and of central importance for this book.

Hamburg-Altona, 30 April, 2018

---

[1] Averroes, *Incoherence of the Incoherence*, 16, 4th discussion; in Averroes' *Tahafut al-Tahafut*, translated by Simon van den Bergh (Cambridge: Gibb Memorial Trust, 1954), 360. I thank Steven Harvey for the reference to this quotation.

Documentation Style

The documentation system of this text follows the Chicago Manual of Style with the exception of the format for subsequent references to the same work, for which I preferred adding one or two words from the title of the book, article, or part of the book. The transliteration of Hebrew words follows the *Encyclopaedia Judaica* (1972) and the transliteration of Greek words retains the common rules of classicists (for example, υ in the diphthong is "au," "ou," and when standing alone "y") with exception of the tonic accents, which are not necessary for the reproduction of Greek letters.

Quotations from the Bible are taken from the New International Version unless I expressly quote from an English translation of a rabbinic text. Slight changes to the quotation are not mentioned provided there is no distortion of the original meaning. No abbreviation of biblical, Rabbinic, Jewish-Hellenistic or other Jewish or Christian literature is adopted.

If not expressed otherwise, all other translations of Rabbinic, Christian, and Jewish medieval and modern authors are my own.

The text and translation of Latin and Greek authors follow as a rule the digital library of Perseus (http://www.perseus.tufts.edu/hopper/), unless other editions and/or translations are expressly referred to.

Texts of Luzzatto are mainly taken from forthcoming translations by Giuseppe Veltri, Anna Lissa, and Michela Torbinoni.

Introduction

In studying the nature of Jewish thought, the modern scholar continually confronts the Socratic injunction of knowing what one does not know, a principle that is both the method and the object of Jewish philosophy. The qualifying adjective makes clear from the start that our field is not an analytical philosophy that is focused on linguistic systems and employs a method that works, at least according to ancient Greek philosophy, totally outside the world of the contingent (even though it is a product of that world). The modifier "Jewish" limits our field of investigation instead to a historical and cultural experience, whereas the term "philosophy" operates within a space that is (potentially) logical and cognitive in itself and steps at least hypothetically outside the limitations of the contingent world of history and cultures.

The task is always the same, a categorical imperative that every student of Jewish philosophy finds inscribed on the tables of the law at the beginning and end of the curriculum: to demonstrate that Jewish philosophy is different in its method and object from universal philosophy. Attempts to respond with simple references to the ethnicity, geography, and culture of a given philosopher do not resolve the question. The moment we do so, we expose ourselves to questions on the "Jewishness" of thinkers whose contributions to philosophy are of a scale that renders limiting adjectives problematic: Isaac Israeli and Solomon Ibn Gabirol in the Middle Ages, Simone Luzzatto and Baruch Spinoza in the modern era. Even trickier to delimit are the roles of Karl Marx, Ernst Bloch, Walter Benjamin, Ludwig Wittgenstein, or Jacques Derrida in modern (Jewish) philosophy and to determine whether their work can ever be dissociated from the more general context of contemporary thought.

Scholarship in the last century looked to resolve disputes on the nature and goal of Jewish philosophy, postulating a discipline between theology (defined as the study of a predetermined canon connected to a denominationally specific public) and philosophy (the study of the means and foundation of reason). Generally characterised as a religion without dogmas, Judaism looks into the very nature of the Law, seeking to understand its unique foundation and in so doing to establish its identity. Introductions to Jewish thought tend to justify this intrinsic goal while investigating the paradigms (in the plural) of philosophy, or those of the neighbouring field of (Neo)Platonic and Christian theology.

The modification of philosophy by this adjective raises not only the question of the status of Jews who throughout history dedicated themselves to philosophy, but also the question of the very idea of "thinking Jewishly," that is, the history of the notion that there exists a *specifically* Jewish philosophy on which general philosophy has occasionally drawn. A further question is whether Jewish philosophy is nothing more than a *theology* of which neither the method nor the scope nor the intended audience are known. These topics, which in recent years have stirred lively debates, also have deep roots in Jewish-Hellenic antiquity (with all its reverberations in Christianity).

The following study addresses problems of an epistemological nature that hinge on the question of how to define Jewish thought. The question of qualification by adjectives is not merely a preliminary conceit, but something that highlights a central problem in the theory of consciousness: whether we are limited by our cultural context in knowledge and science and—if the response is in the affirmative—whether or not such limitations prejudice the nature of philosophy, which (at least in the ancient and medieval understanding) aims to be a universal explanation of truth and reason. As will become clear, it was precisely the plurality of definitions associated with Judaism between the Enlightenment and the modern era that produced its "borrowed" identity. These definitions did not arise from a process of internal reflection among Jews, but are rather the fruit of the environment in which they lived.

This study will begin with an ancient question, that of the relationship between Jewish culture, Greek philosophy, and Greco-Roman (and Christian) thought in connection with a query about the history and genealogy of wisdom and knowledge (the first part of *Alienated Wisdom*). The expression "history of wisdom and knowledge" may seem oxymoronic to modern readers, since knowledge transcends time and the "wisdom" contained in the word "philosophy" (*sophia*) falls outside of any chronological aspect. However, the concept of wisdom has an origin and it recalls a historical process of entelechy, having (almost) actualised all the potentialities hidden and implied in that origin. In addition, it is on this point that the idea of ancient philosophy as "theft" (*sapientia capta*) revolves. Not only philosophy but also the theoretical and practical sciences have raised the question of the *primus inventor*, the figures who first invented ideas, concepts, and sciences. This is not a question of the authorial rights of that *inventor*, as it is today, but rather about claims of primacy in the sequence of influence on a given culture's formation and education and, subsequently, its influence on other cultures. The accusations of Greek plagiarism of Jewish texts, levelled above all by Alexandrine Judaism, have a dynamic that lies outside of the Jewish propaganda against the empire of the *logos hellenicos*. Nevertheless, this claim is also an apology *ad intra* aimed at preventing the destruction of Jewish culture by Greco-Roman Hellenism, with its refined allure lying somewhere between science and wisdom. The central problem here, which we will confront, is whether the discussion of Jewish philosophy should itself be interpreted as a process of alienation *ad extra* and *ad intra*. That is, we seek to determine if the Jewish tradition was exploited by others (in particular Christianity) and if philosophical and theological Judaism itself alienated concepts that did not originate within its own tradition (see the conclusion of this book).

Our journey into the history of the denomination "Jewish philosophy" will include a leg that will lead us to certain declarations of political, moral, and scientific principles, and then on to the birth of what is called *philosophia perennis* or, in Christian circles, *prisca theologia*. Objectively, perennialism amounts to an assertion of the possession of all wisdom, a theological and apologetic holism that leads to dogmatic absolutisms. It is undeniable that the holistic Christian tradition—which saw and sees in Christ the sum of all truth, past, present, and future, and its mooring in biblical revelation—had a decisive role. The harmony that existed between the Christian and Jewish traditions—reinforced above all by Kabbalistic theorisations—will come to an end at the very moment of its apogee. We see this especially in the Renaissance when Lutheran thinkers deny the Jews any claim to authority over the wisdom of their own tradition. They thus reduced biblical and post-biblical Judaism to a mass of ceremonial rites. *Philosophia perennis* will become Christian *in toto*.

At the very moment when the appeal of Jewish wisdom largely dissipated for Christian writers, a new kind of research was born within the academies and the private circles of the so-called "science of Judaism," *Wissenschaft des Judentums* (a form of research that also stems from the Enlightenment and its Jewish equivalent, the *Haskalah*). This study of particular authors, currents, ideas, and concepts has been called by many, though not all, "Jewish philosophy" (see the second part: *Jewish Philosophy, History of Definitions*). Various theses exist on the genesis of this concept, and the one sustained in this study is that it acquires multiform denominations precisely because it is not a Jewish concept but a Christian one, adopted for the purposes of simplification and emancipation. Our subject of enquiry will thus be the birth of the *concept* of Jewish philosophy. We will confront the question of the application of Jewish theology on the part of reformed Judaism, and, ultimately, we will investigate the motives and premises that led to the birth of a *Jewish philosophy of religion*. These are the stages of definition designed to limit and standardise the concept of Jewish thought, the import of which was not certain, nor well-understood, nor perhaps even desired.

As such, a special emphasis will fall on the topic treated in the last part of this study: *(Jewish) Scepticism*, which is a theme that involves the philosophical attitude founded in dialectical "enquiry," as the etymology of the Greek word *skepsis* properly means. Two significant research methodologies can be identified in the research on scepticism: a philosophical approach based in an analytical and diachronic-historical perspective and a cultural approach based on an analysis of elements of sceptical strategies, contents, and attitudes (to be called "cultural expressions of scepticism"). Although scepticism is essential to the Jewish epistemological understanding of reality, as well as sources and systems of knowledge, it is rather surprising to note that it is still largely excluded from, or at least underrepresented in international research and debates on scepticism and Jewish philosophy. The lack of interest in the intricacies of Jewish scepticism within Jewish studies may be rooted in the modality of Jewish philosophy, given that it is a concept that is, as already stated above, notoriously in-between, one that subsumes and affects traditional wisdom, philosophy, theology, Jewish and general *Weltanschauung*, as well as cultural history. It is a hazardous bridge between orthopraxy and orthodoxy. Yet, Jewish philosophy—and to an even greater extent Jewish scepticism—are dialectical struggles against the authority of a universal dogmatic reason.

If, on the one hand, scepticism makes a forceful case for the limits of our knowledge, on the other, it refuses every delimitation of "reality" and implication of authority, because it precludes other possibilities. This is why the sceptic was viewed with hostility in the ancient, medieval, and modern worlds: her/his activity was a thorn in the flesh, considered dangerous to society. Socrates, most notably, was called a "corrupter of laws and of the youth," primarily because he was a thinker who ventured beyond the limits of authority.

In the last part of this book, we will ask why scepticism was rarely discussed within academic Jewish philosophy as well as what happens when this current of enquiry is placed at the centre of all speculation about philosophy's theme and system. We will discover that intriguing discussions on the sceptical "nature" of Judaism originated in two different areas contemporaneously: in Northern Italy (particularly in Venice) and in some German Protestant universities. While the focus of the Protestant scholars mainly concerned the goal of disavowing the oral and written tradition, the main question among Jewish intellectuals was the authority of reason and human knowledge, a question naturally intertwined with authority.

According to the Midrash *Mekhilta de-Rabbi Yishma'el* (*bo', pisḥa* 18), "there are four types of pupils: the wise, the wicked, the simple, and the one who doesn't know how to ask." The most disappointing pupil is the one who doesn't know how to ask. Hence, the goal of learning is to ask the Rabbi the (right) question, to find the weak point in his argumentation—to be sceptical. I am conscious that questions are fundamental while every answer can be only temporary. They are dependent on time and space and at best only provide a possible or probable premise for other questions. I hope, then, that I have posed the right questions.

PART ONE ALIENATED WISDOM

Synopsis: How the Written and Oral Torah Became Alienated Wisdom

Jewish philosophy is a history of concepts, beliefs, and (borrowed) identities. We will begin with a scrutiny of the origin of the concept of an alienated wisdom, the first concept of a Jewish ancestral philosophy. The word alienation is used here in a typically philological sense, an alleged or real process of estrangement of ideas, concepts, and traditions of philosophical fundaments. According to Jewish-Hellenistic and Christian scholars the claim of an illegal appropriation of the Jewish biblical tradition by Greek philosophers is not an apologetic demand for copyright, but rather one concerning the lack of an acknowledgment of the Hebraic and Jewish biblical contributions to philosophy and science in ancient times.

The first chapter of the first part of this book is devoted to the creation of a (Jewish) perpetual wisdom. First from Greco-Roman and then Christian Late Antiquity, through the Middle Ages, and, to some extent, beyond the early modern period, an idea of a divine knowledge and science was created and perpetuated. This idea was epitomised in the delivery of the Torah to Moses on Sinai, and then, of course, passed down from generation to generation. As early as the second century C.E., Christian claims to possess the entirety of wisdom had become common. The Greek monopoly on *sophia* was not haphazard or episodic—as is maintained by Alexandrine Judaism, which claims that they only selected certain ideas, concepts, and laws—but total, a full investment in the idea that all wisdom and science was Christian *in nuce* and *de principio*. This belief pervades Christian Late Antiquity, the Middle Ages, and the modern era, making metaphysical wisdom one of its foundational pillars.

The second chapter of part one is mainly devoted to the dynamic of the "first discoverer" (*Prōtos Heuretēs*) in a literary context. The attribution of the very origins of knowledge to a single group is an invention and a product of the creativity of the ancients. This concept is at base a declaration of the primacy of a genealogy of wisdom in which the ascendancy of the *primus* is explained as *a priori* a matter of right. This logic is followed by Jewish-Hellenistic and then Christian apologetics that take up the task of explaining the presence of similar doctrines in the Bible and Greek philosophy, arguing on grounds of historical-literary dependence. It is a correspondence, in fact, that would come to be associated with claims of plagiarism, the "theft" of doctrines. In Judaism the problem of how the Torah became publicly known is a question that stems from an apologetic imperative, resulting from the outer world's *de facto* ignorance of Jewish culture and literature. In the context of this chapter, the question will also be posed *a posteriori*, asking, that is, if it was the very publication and translation of the Torah in Greek that led to the "theft" of Jewish thought.

The third chapter is dedicated to the tradition of the "alienation" and of genealogy of wisdom in the Middle Ages, mainly due to the theft of books. The loss of books from libraries or their destruction by fires, wars, or purposeful destruction is a *topos* that we find throughout the Middle Ages and the modern period, not to mention our current era. Beyond placing an emphasis on an issue of great historical significance, this *locus communis* is also consequential to the history of Jewish literature's canonisation. There is more to it: according to medieval Jewish tradition, the scientific and mystic-magical writings of the legendary Solomon may also have been lost in this manner.

The fourth chapter will delineate the way in which the first traces of this practice evolved in the historical consciousness of the Renaissance by following certain figures who played decisive roles in the history of Jewish thought. The Renaissance's adoption of methods of historical analysis—the first steps that will eventually lead to a routine analysis of textual sources—came about from an interest in the restoration of the past and an awareness, more or less conscious, of a certain ascendancy of the *iuniores*, the recent scholars, over the *antiqui*, the old wise men. The *querelle des anciens et des modernes*, which began before the Renaissance, is the turning-point that will lead to a new epistemology of the rationalist and sceptic critique of the sources of knowledge.

1 Between Myth and History of Knowledge

Like all learning and technical knowledge originating in or developed by Greece over the course of Alexander's three-pronged conquest (military, political, and cultural), philosophy provided a horizon of thought for the ancient world. It suffused the civilised world with new concepts and new tools of discourse for logical and empirical methods, organising knowledge and creating new theories of perception and communication for the tasks of explaining and interpreting reality and its components. Taking full advantage of the Macedonian's success, Greek philosophy began to weave itself into the world of that epoch,[1] such that it began to change the very bearings of thought and expression throughout other cultures, which would subsequently be compelled to measure themselves by means of the logic and dialectic of the Athenian schools. It is well known that philosophy in this age was not seen as mere speculation but as what we would today call a "science of knowledge," where "science" is understood in the sense of "ordered knowing" (from the Latin *scientia*) as expressed in the words *epistēmē* and *technē*.[2] These two words furnish the foundation, according to Xenophon's Socrates, for the *kaloskagathos*, the ideal of an elegant, cultured, morally irreproachable individual.

Hellenisation aroused other reactions from peoples not directly involved in the diffusion of the new culture, groups that largely felt robbed of their own modes of thinking and traditions of knowledge. Among these, certainly, was Judaism, the apologetic defences of which have been transmitted by both Jews and Christians. From the first Greco-Roman and then Christian centuries through the Middle Ages and, above all, in the epoch spanning the Renaissance and the early modern period, an idea of a divine knowledge and science was created and perpetuated, an idea epitomised in the delivery of the Torah to Moses on Sinai, and then the concept of its passing-down from generation to generation. The genealogy of knowledge aims to situate this idea in history and as such render it communicable beyond the confines of religion, culture, and language.

Horace's famous saying, *Graecia capta ferum victorem cepit* ("Vanquished Greece conquered its own crude conqueror")[3] also applies in a uniquely illustrative manner to the phenomenon of the Hellenisation of the Mediterranean and its neighbouring territories. Greek culture also conquered, paradoxically, the conquerors of the Greco-Roman empire, who in turn would rise up and level accusations that the Greeks had copied and counterfeited their knowledge. This accusation is prominent in Alexan-

---

[1] A phenomenon best understood through the analysis of concepts of fusion and diffusion, a dichotomy made emblematic by Moses Hadas, *Hellenistic Culture. Fusion and Diffusion* (New York: Columbia University Press, 1959).
[2] Cf. Rudolf Löbl, *Technē: Untersuchungen zur Bedeutung dieses Worts in der Zeit von Homer bis Aristoteles* (Würzburg: Königshausen & Neumann, 2003); Richard Parry, *Episteme and Techne*, in *The Stanford Encyclopedia of Philosophy*, ed. Edward N. Zalta.
[3] See Horace, *Epistulae* II, 1, 156.

drine Judaism, which reacted defensively to the Greek (and Greco-Roman) predominance across the spectrum of culture, education, science, and even quotidian pastimes: thermal baths, theatres, imperial games. Jewish apologists of the first century C.E. often imputed to the Greek philosophers, rhetoricians, and statesmen of the past a knowledge of the Torah of Moses, insinuating that they had lifted from it in various ways and presented its ideas as their own. In the next section of this chapter, I will address this peculiar aspect of Jewish "conquered" thought; indeed, these Jewish apologists formed the first comparative cultural, philosophical, and linguistic study.[4]

By the second century C.E., the framing of Christian thought as encompassing all wisdom was commonly accepted by Christian theologians. Jesus Christ was held to be its incarnation—"word made flesh"[5]—both font and culmination of the world's knowledge. The Greek monopoly on *sophia* was not haphazard or episodic—as is sustained by Alexandrine Judaism, claiming that they only selected certain ideas, concepts, and laws—but total, a full investment in the idea that all wisdom and science was Christian *in nuce* and *de principio*. This belief pervades Christian Late Antiquity, the Middle Ages, and Modernity, asserting metaphysical wisdom as one of its foundational pillars. Renaissance Humanism added to this conception of wisdom as Christian through its focus on the esoteric and hermetic traditions, following the discovery and Latin translation of the *Corpus Hermeticum* and the Chaldean Oracles. Yet another decisive element was the Christian discovery of the Kabbalistic traditions, additional testaments to the primordial wisdom delivered to Abraham in Chaldea. This passing-down of wisdom is at the heart of Perennial Philosophy (or Perennialism),[6] itself a persistent esoteric tradition in Western thought.

1.1 The Christian Use of an Alexandrine Myth

In the third century C.E., writing in defence of early Christianity, Tertullian cites the Jewish origins of the sect's beliefs as an argument for the juridical legitimacy of the Christian community as it tried to become a *religio licita*. In the rhetorical construction of his *Apologeticum*, Tertullian evokes two commonplaces that speak to the importance of Judaism in the history of ideas:

---

[4] On this chapter, see the contribution of Abraham Melamed, *The Myth of the Jewish Origins of Science and Philosophy* [Hebrew] (Jerusalem: Magnes Press, 2010). For antiquity, see 3–65.
[5] John 1:1–3.
[6] On the Western developments in the conception of perennial philosophy, see the monograph of Wilhelm Schmidt-Biggemann, *Philosophia perennis. Historische Umrisse abendländischer Spiritualität in Antike, Mittelalter und früher Neuzeit* (Frankfurt am Main: Suhrkamp, 1998): English version: *Philosophia Perennis. Historical Outlines of Western Spirituality in Ancient, Medieval and Early Modern Thought* (Dordrecht: Springer, 2004).

1) The Christian sect or "path" had its roots in Judaism, which, in turn, possessed illustrious ancient texts on philosophy and Greco-Roman law.[7]
2) The Jewish written tradition, now cleansed of elements refuted by the new sect, should itself now be considered Christian, restored to the moment before the Jews concealed their prophecies, abandoned divine law to live like pagans, and were condemned to wander the world.[8]

In his first statement on the roots of Christianity, Tertullian evokes an ancient dispute over the origins of *sophia*,[9] certainly a literary-mythical problem, but one with significant juridical import. In the end, Christianity's legal recognition would itself follow Tertullian's example and invoke the lengthy history of the sect's origins.[10]

An insistence on the antiquity of Jewish texts appears early on in the Greek apologetics[11] of Alexandrine Judaism. They allege plagiarism of Jewish texts, attributing to the Greek philosophers an indirect awareness of original biblical truths. The Christians who also employ this *topos* distance themselves from the Jewish apologetics, framing the correspondence between their beliefs and core points of pagan philosophy as a kind of evangelical *preparation*, traces of the God that the Athenians venerated without knowing it.[12] In casting Jewish and Greek thought as prefiguration

---

7 Tertullianus, *Apologeticum* XIX 1 *Corpus Christianorum*, series Latina, I and 2, ed. Eloi Dekkers, et al. (Turnhout: Brepols, 1954), 119–120; see XLVII 1: Adhuc enim mihi proficit antiquitas praestructa divinae litteraturae, quo facile credatur, thesaurum eam fuisse posteriori cuique sapientiae."
8 Ibid., XXI 4–5: "Totum Iudaeis erat apud Deum gratia ubi et insignis iustitia et fides originalium auctorum [...]. Sed quanta deliquerint fiducia patrum inflati ad declinandum disciplinam in profanum modum, etsi ipsi non confiterentur, probaret exitus hodierni ipsorum. Dispersi, palabundi, et soli et caeli sui extorres vagantur per orbem sine homine, sine Deo rege, quibus nec advenarum iure terram patriam saltim vestigio salutare conceditur."
9 Ibid., XIX 15: "Adeo respici potest tam iura vestra quam studia de lege deque divina doctrina concepisse. Quod prius est, hoc sit semen necesse est. Inde quaedam nobiscum vel prope nos habetis. De sophia amor eius philosophia vocitatus est, de prophetia affectatio eius poeticam vaticinationem deputavit"; LXV 4: "Dum tamen sciatis ipsas leges quoque vestras quae videntur ad innocentiam pergere de divina lege, ut antiquiore forma, mutuatas. Diximus iam de Moysi aetate."
10 Ibid., XIX 1: "Primam igitur instrumentis istis [scl. thesauris litterarum] auctoritatem summa antiquitas vindicat. Apud vos [scl. Romanos] quoque religionis est instar, fidem de tempore adserere."
11 For the reference to Moses' antecedence over Plato, see Iustinus, *Apologia* I: 44, 59, 60; Clemens Alexandrinus, *Stromata* I: 1–166; V: 92, 1–4; *Protrepticus* 70: 1; Origenes, *Contra Celsum* IV: 39, 43–66; Pseudo-Iustinus, *Cohortatio ad Graecos* 14: 20.22; Eusebius, *Praeparatio Evangelica* XI 8,1; see also the opposing position of Lactantius, *Institutiones Divinae* IV: 2,3–5, according to whom a plane of divinity impeded Plato from knowing the wisdom of Judaism. For an analysis of these sources see Heinrich Dörrie, *Der hellenistische Rahmen des kaiserzeitlichen Platonismus* (Stuttgart: Fromann, 1990), 198–219; 488–505.
12 New Testament, *Acts of the Apostle* 1 7:23. A parallel example can be found also in the so-called *Letter of Aristea to Filocrates* e16. Here, however, the issue would be more the translatability of the Greek pantheon within Jewish categories than the issue of other cultures as unconscious cultivators of the true God. A similar tendency is encountered in Aristobulus, the philosopher, and in Eusebius, *Praeparatio Evangelica* XIII: 12,7.

of the "true religion," Christianity paves the way for the concept of "Perennial Philosophy" as a method of establishing primacy.

Having established the antiquity of Judaism, Tertullian distances himself from the Jewish religion itself in his second argument and evokes a common anti-Jewish *topos:* Jewish customs and traditions, like the observance of Shabbat and circumcision (mocked in the Greco-Roman world),[13] are refuted by the principles of the new, preeminent religion. These points resist all appeals to the chronological order of prophecy and revelation as the new sect insists that they are the "true religion" of Moses himself. The Christian apologists certainly acknowledged that their sacred texts came from the Jews, but they framed this as a bequest of scriptures from one party (Jews) who did not understand these texts to another party (Christians) who discovered their true meaning. The Jewish nation, so privileged by God, would be brought low not only by their own failures of scholarship, in their failure of recognising the *true* Messiah, but also by their pride: "Dispersed, wandering, exiled from their own land and sky, they stray the world over, without man or God for their king."[14]

This tract, polemical with regard to Judaism but apologetic concerning the Christian appropriation of the Scriptures, is also mentioned as early as the *Epistle of Barnabas*[15] and in greater detail in the anonymous *Exhortation to the Greeks* (*Cohortatio ad Graecos*).[16] The fact that the Jews received (from Moses) and kept the sacred books does not disprove the Christians' claim of ownership. According to the *Cohortatio*, the Scriptures should simply be considered to have been Christian all along.[17] One can see in these statements a vicious hermeneutic circle: the old tradition of Jewish sacred texts is denied and subsumed by the Christian claim to sole ownership because they (the Christians) own the true (prophetical) meaning of the Jewish text.[18]

---

13 On the observance of the Shabbat, see Robert Goldenberg, *The Jewish Sabbath in the Roman World up to the Time of Constantine the Great*, in Aufstieg und Niedergang der römischen Welt, vol. II, ed. Wolfgang Haase (Berlin: De Gruyter, 1979): 414–447. On circumcision see Strabo, *Geographica* XVI: 2.37 and 4:9 in *Greek and Latin Authors on Jews and Judaism*, ed. Menahem Stern (Jerusalem: Magnes, 1974), vol. I, no. 115 and no. 118, 295 and 312; Petronius, *Satyricon* 68, 4–8 in ibid., no. 193: 441–443. A satire of both can be read in Persio, *Saturae* V: 176–184 in ibidem, no. 190: 435–437.
14 Idem, *Apologeticum* XXI: 4–5 (Corpus Christianorum, 123): "dispersi, palabundi, et soli et caeli sui extorres vagantur per orbem sine homine, sine deo rege".
15 *Barnabas* 4, in Schriften des Urchristentums. 2. Didache (Apostellehre), Barnabasbrief, Zweiter Klemensbrief, Schrift an Diognet, ed. Klaus Wengst (Munich: Kösel, 1984): 146–148.
16 *Cohortatio* o13 in Iustini Philosophi et Martyris Opera quae feruntur omnia, vol. 2, ed. Johann Carl Theodor von Otto (Ienae: G. Fischer, 1879), 56–58. On this writing, once attributed to Iustinus, see Robert Grant, "The Cohortatio of Pseudo-Justin," *Harvard Theological Review* 51 (1958): 128–134; Paolo Siniscalco, "Caratteri espressivi ed estetici della profezia vetero-testamentaria secondo la *Cohortatio ad Graecos*," *Studi Storico-Religiosi* 4 (1980): 29–44.
17 Cf. Juda Bergmann, *Jüdische Apologetik im neutestamentlichen Zeitalter* (Berlin: Reimer, 1908), 61.
18 See my monograph, *Libraries, Translations, and 'Canonic' Texts. The Septuagint, Aquila, and Ben Sira in Jewish and Christian Tradition* (Leiden: Brill, 2006).

Simply on the grounds of their acquaintance with the Torah, the "nations of the world" (in the terminology of the rabbis), can claim to be the *verus Israel*. This is the last stage of the appropriation of *sophia:* incorporating past phases by negating their (Jewish) origin. If the contents of ancient scripture are re-cast as prophecies of Christian events, by the logic of the church fathers, rabbinical Judaism cannot lay any intellectual or theological claim to biblical thought. For this reason, the Mishnah—the tradition that, according to the rabbis, constitutes the very substance of the scriptures ("instruction by repetition")—is derided as an "expedient," a man-made artifice. Politically, Justinian's *Novella 146* is the first document to use such premises to prohibit rabbis from expounding on the Hebrew Bible, holding their instruction to be in competition with the Christian interpretation of these texts.[19]

The rabbinical traditions that we will consider later define themselves in relation to the *querelle* on the origins of the Torah and Jewish thought, classifying all development in rabbinical consciousness in relation to the God-of-Israel concept, a development of the constitutive elements of the *verus Israel* and of the perceived value of the oral tradition (with regard to the importance of the oral Torah, the *torah she-be'al peh*). The foremost concern of the rabbis is not merely the legitimacy of these books, the tradition that acts as a guarantor of truth, but also the process of their interpretation itself: the hermeneutical tradition that is the foundation of the oral Torah.

The aim of this chapter is to trace the coordinates of the debates on the origin of Jewish wisdom, debates that came out of Ptolemaic Egypt, where a strong Jewish community sought to affirm its own independence from Greek culture, an effort that continued into the Roman Empire and the early stages of the Christianisation of the "European" world.

1.2 Antiquity as the Premise for Authority

The question of the Jewish tradition's age in relation to Greek thought is undoubtedly Alexandrine in origin as it is indicative of this place and the major encounters between Hellenism and Judaism that occurred there. This is clear even in the absence of many of the names and precise dates of the Jewish apologetics that flowed from Alexandria.

Evidence of tension with Greek culture is found in the Sibylline oracles,[20] which cast Homer as a falsifier of the Sybil's verses.[21] Demetrius, whose identity is uncertain

---

19 For a treatment of this aspect of the *Novella 146*, see my monograph, *Gegenwart der Tradition: Studien zur jüdischen Literatur und Kulturgeschichte* (Leiden: Brill, 2002), 104–119.
20 On the historical and literary problem, see Emil Schürer, *The History of the Jewish People in the Age of Jesus Christ*, vol. 3/1. Edited by Geza Vermes, Fergus Millar, and Martin Goodman (Edinburgh: T. & Clark, 1986), 618–654.
21 *Oracula Sibyllina* 3: 419–432. See Valentin Nikiprowetzky, *La troisième Sibylle*, (Paris, La Haye: Mouton, 1970), 310–312. Cf. Lactantius, *Divinae institutiones* I: 6,9; see also Jean Pépin, "Le 'chal-

and to whom Clement of Alexandria attributes the treatises "On the Kings of Judea" (*Peri tōn in tēi Ioudeai Basileōn*),[22] is said by Eusebius of Caesarea to number among the first Jewish-Hellenistic authors who sought to prove the "antiquity" (*antiquitas*) of Moses, basing his argument above all on chronological evidence.[23] The historian and chronologist Eupolemos, to whom Clement attributes *On the Kings of Judea*,[24] states that Moses was "the first knower, the first who transmitted the scripture to the Jews." Through the Jews, Eupolemos believes, Moses's works arrived among the Phoenicians, who in turn transmitted them to the Greeks.[25]

The historian-storyteller Artapanus, who employs far more fantasy than the preceding authors, identifies Moses as Musaeus, master of Orpheus,[26] inventor of navigation, military science, and military philosophy. He believes that Moses divided Egypt into thirty-six provinces and gave the priests their sacred characters (the so-called hieroglyphs). He says that Moses was admired by the Egyptians for his political and religious prowess, honoured as a god by their priests, who called him Hermes, considered by Iamblichus as the "inventor" of wisdom, associating him with the practice of interpreting Holy texts.[27]

If we look past the thorny questions of dating that surround Philo of Alexandria, the first Jewish author to focus his attention on Greek philosophy's direct borrowing from Jewish texts would be Aristobulus,[28] a philosopher whose work unfortunately

---

lenge' Homère-Moïse aux premiers siècles chrétiens," *Revue des sciences religieuses* 29 (1955): 105–122; Rieuwerd Buitenwerf, *Book III of the Sibylline Oracles and Its Social Setting* (Leiden: Brill, 2003); Jane L. Lightfoot, *The Sibylline Oracles. With Introduction, Translation, and Commentary on the First and Second Books* (Oxford: Oxford University Press, 2007).
22 Clemens Alexandrinus, *Stromata* I: 141, 1–2.
23 *Historia Ecclesiastica* VI, 13,7. See Elias J. Bickerman, *The Jewish Historian Demetrios. Studies in Jewish and Christian History* (Leiden: Brill, 1980), 347–358.
24 *Stromata* I: 153, 4.
25 Eusebius, *Praeparatio Evangelica* IX: 26,1 in *Fragmenta pseudepigraphorum quae supersunt graeca*, ed. Albert-Marie Denis (Leiden: Brill, 1970), 179; cf. Clemens Alexandrinus, *Stromata* I: 23,153. On this passage see Ben Zion Wacholder, *Eupolemos. A Study of Judaeo-Greek Literature* (Cincinnati: Hebrew Union College, Jewish Institute of Religion, 1974), 71–96; *Fragments from Hellenistic Jewish Authors*, vol. 1, ed. Carl R. Holladay (Chico: Society of Biblical Literature, 1983): 137–138, notes 5 and 6.
26 Cf. René Bloch, *Orpheus als Lehrer des Musaios, Moses als Lehrer des Orpheus*, in *Antike Mythen. Medien, Transformationen und Konstruktionen*, eds. Ueli Dill and Christine Walde (Berlin: de Gruyter, 2009), 65–82.
27 Eusebius, *Praeparatio Evangelica* IX: 27,6 in *Fragmenta pseudepigraphorum*, 187–188; cf. Holladay, *Fragments from Hellenistic-Jewish authors*, 209–210, 232–255, notes 45–55. In this passage there is a nod towards a popular etymology according to which *hermēneia* derives from "Hermes." On the Thoth-Hermes identification, see Plato, *Phaidros*, 274c; Martin Hengel, *Judentum und Hellenismus* (Tübingen: Mohr, 1969). Hermes comes to be considered by Iamblichus as the "inventor" of wisdom: Iamblichus, *De Mysteriis Aegyptiorum* 1: 3–5; cf. Edouard des Places, *Les mystères d'Égypte* (Paris: Belles Lettres, 1989), 38.
28 Cf. Nicholas Walter, *Der Thoraausleger Aristobulos. Untersuchungen zu seinen Fragmenten und zu pseudoepigraphischen Resten der jüdisch-hellenistischen Literatur* (Berlin: Akademie-Verlag, 1964);

survives only in fragments cited by Clement of Alexandria and Eusebius of Caesarea. Confronted with the problem of how Plato could have known Jewish thought, living as he did before the Torah was translated in the era of Ptolemy II Philadelphus, Aristobulus states:[29]

> There is no doubt that Plato followed our legislation. There is no doubt that he carefully studied even the details. And before others, indeed, i.e. before Demetrius Phalereus, and prior to the conquest of Alexander and the Persians—he translated a summary of Exodus of our countrymen, the Hebrews, out of Egypt, and the reports of all that had happened to them, the conquest of the land, the exposition of the whole of the Law. So that it is manifest that many things have been borrowed by the previously mentioned philosopher [i.e. Plato], for he is very learned, as also Pythagoras who plagiarized many of our teachings and inserted them into his own system of doctrines.[30]

The historically unverifiable claim that the Torah was translated into Greek even before Alexander's conquest[31] is treated here as indisputable fact: Plato "followed" Moses. Another fragment by Aristobulus re-states this position on Greek thought and Mosaic literature, going into greater detail on the theory of Greek plagiarism, even providing concrete examples:

> For we must understand the "voice of God" not as words spoken, but as construction of works, just as Moses in the Law has spoken of the whole creation of the world as "words of God." For he constantly says of each work, "And God said, and it happened so." Now it seems to me that he has been very carefully followed in all by Pythagoras, and Socrates, and Plato, who said that they heard the voice of God, when they were contemplating the arrangement of the universe so accurately made and indissolubly combined by God.
> Moreover, Orpheus, in verses taken from his writings in the On the Sacred Word, thus sets forth the doctrine that all things are governed by divine power, and that they have had a beginning, and that God is over all.[32]

Aristobulus firmly believes that the three philosophers knew the Mosaic doctrine of creation. He emphasises that Pythagoras, Socrates, and Plato each interpreted Moses, and that, in forming their interpretations, they exemplified the contemplation of the form of the universe as a means of hearing the voice of the universe's creator and sustainer. Aristobulus, in his interpretation of *Genesis*, says that the seventh day

---

Paul Pédech, *Historiens, compagnons d'Alexandre: Callisthène, Onésicrite, Nèarque, Ptolémée, Aristobule*, (Paris: Les Belles Lettres, 2011).
29 Eusebius, *Praeparatio Evangelica* XIII: 12,2, in *Fragmenta*, 222–223.
30 Eusebius, *Praeparatio Evangelica* XIII: 12.1–2. Cf. Étienne Nodet, "Editing the Bible: Alexandria or Babylon?" in *The Bible and Hellenism. Greek influence on Jewish and Early Christian literature*, eds. Thomas L. Thompson and Philippe Wajdenbaum (Durham: Acumen, 2014): 36–55. For an English translation see Eusebius, *Evangelicae Praeparationes. Liber XVI*, ed. Edwin Hamilton Gifford, vol. 3 (Oxford: Ex Typographia Academica, 1903), 663.
31 Cf. Nicholas Walter, *Der Thoraausleger Aristobulos*, 45.
32 Eusebius, *Praeparatio Evangelica* XIII: 12 in *Fragmenta*, 224.

of the creation "can also be called the first day, according to its nature, since the first day is the genesis of light, the moment when the *all* can first be contemplated." On the seventh day, God does not rest but acts: the meaning of Genesis 2:2 is not that God refrained from doing things, but only that he ceased to *create* so that he could give order to the universe. Having ordered it He maintains it. Aristobulus's God cannot rest or the world would perish. For him, to "order" and "maintain" are parts of the creative act itself. God's "word" not only gave form to the universe but also sustains it. The instant the divine creative presence ceases to be, the world returns to non-existence.

My view here is not exactly in line with Heinrich Dörrie, who believes that Aristobulus had no knowledge of Pythagoras or Plato at all. Dörrie's view is not reflective of a close reading of the passage in question. He claims that Aristobulus identifies the contemplation of the form of the universe as the task of the three great philosophers, instead of the "annunciation of the divine voice" (*"die 'Stimme Gottes' zu verkünden"*).[33] However, Dörrie neglects Aristobulus's view that through the act of contemplation, owing to the nature of things, the world cannot fail to recognise that "voice" ("let it be and it is") that created and sustains it.[34] If this interpretation is wrong, one would have to conclude that Aristobulus violates and even openly contradicts his own principles. As he states, at the beginning of the fragment: "For we must understand the 'voice of God' not as words spoken but as the construction of works, just as Moses in the Law has spoken of the whole creation of the world as 'words of God.'" If a word is not enunciated it cannot be physically heard, but only perceived "conceptually." In short, Aristobulus affirms that Pythagoras, Socrates, and Plato "followed Moses" because they *understood* the creative act of God as both performing and constituting the universe.[35]

These fragmentary affirmations of the Greeks' philosophical debt to Jewish doctrine are reported to us exclusively by the Fathers of the Church. On the basis of such incomplete evidence, it is not easy to know where to locate the theory of this debt in the whole of Aristobulus's *oeuvre*. Nicholas Walter considers the comments to be cursory, exaggerated later by Christian apologists.[36] This position is reinforced by the place that the "theft" occupies in the Philonian *oeuvre:* Philo never mentions a direct Platonic dependence on Jewish thought, despite his repeated citations of Moses, whom he parallels with Plato.[37]

This point is even more significant given that Philo was unquestionably aware of the legend of Greek plagiarism. *In Specialibus Legibus IV* he defends the very texts

---

[33] Heinrich Dörrie, *Rahmen*, 482.
[34] Pseudo-Longinus recognises precisely in this formula, taken from Genesis, a speaking proper and suited to divinity, a thing that Homer himself could not have produced, cf. Menahem Stern, *Greek and Latin Authors*, 364.
[35] See the sources listed in Dörrie, *Rahmen*, 278.
[36] Cf. Nicholas Walter, *Der Thoraausleger Aristobulos*, 45.
[37] Cf. the sources in Madeleine Petit, ed., *Quod omnis probus liber sit* (Paris: Édition du Cerf, 1974).

that claimed the Greeks had "copied" Exodus 23:1 ("Do not diffuse any defamatory claims"), saying that one need not grant as much credence to spoken words as to visual evidence ("that which one hears said is not at all trustworthy"). The principle of *akoēn martyrein* is, in effect, attested by the Attic rhetoricians as a principle of Athenian jurisprudence.[38] In the *De Confusione Linguarum* 141, Philo refers to the same principle and to the verse purportedly taken from Exodus 23:1, but he does not report the borrowing to the Attic legislators.

In *Quaestiones in Genesim VI §167*, referring to Genesis 25:28, Philo inveighs against the recent Greek philosophers who had taken from Moses ("*nonnulli imitantes Mosen*") the principle as it is presented in the Armenian version of the Latin text ("*solum esse bonum propter se amandum placendumque*").[39] More often, he refers to Heraclitus' doctrine of contraries as unquestionably a plagiarism that was falsely held to have originated in Ephesus.[40]

His attitude towards the claims of plagiarism is not, however, always polemical. *In Quod omnis probus liber sit §57* he softens his tone considerably when talking about Zeno, who had supposedly borrowed the story of the two brothers from Jewish texts (Genesis 27:40). In *Quaestiones in Genesim II §6*, regarding Socrates, he is uncertain: Socrates might have borrowed from Moses ("*sive a Moyse edoctus*"), or he could have been genuinely "moved" by the true nature of things ("*sive ex rebus ipsis motus*"). In the case of Philo, I am in agreement with Harry A. Wolfson that the great Jewish philosopher of Alexandria did not believe that Greek philosophy borrowed from Jewish writings: for him philosophy was a revelation to the Greeks, just as the Torah was to the Hebrews.[41]

The historiographer Josephus, in his *Contra Apionem*,[42] mentions Megasthenes and Clearchus (among others) regarding the fame of the Jews as philosophers, ad-

---

38 Demostenes, *Contra Eubuliden*, 1300, §§6,7; Demostenes, *Contra Stephanum* II, 1130.8; source references in *Philo: in ten volumes*, vol. IV, ed. Francis H. Colson (Cambridge: Harvard University Press, 1932, reprinted 1985), 556–557; cf. *A Dictionary of Greek and Roman Antiquities*, ed. William Smith et al. (London: John Murray, 1890); *The Cambridge Companion to Ancient Greek Law*, ed. Michael Gagarin et al. (Cambridge: Cambridge University Press, 2005), 153.
39 "Sicut et nonnulli iuniorum novissimorumque ab ipso Mose tamquam a fonte acceptantes sententiam virtutis studiosam asseruere, solum esse bonum propter se amandum placendumque, quod vero non tale est, ob utilitatem." The *Quaestiones* were transmitted only fragmentarily in Greek. The Armenian version was published in 1826 by Johannes B. Aucher. See Philo Supplement I: *Philo Quaestions and Answers in Genesis*, ed. Ralf Marcus (Cambridge: Harvard University Press, 1953, reprinted 1993), 452–453.
40 *Legum allegoriae* I: §108 (Genesis 2: 17); *Quis divinarum rerum heres sit* 214; see *Quaestiones in Genesim* III: §5.
41 Cf. Harry A. Wolfson, *Philo* (Cambridge: Harvard University Press, 1962), 138–143.
42 Cf. *Contra Apionem* II: §§165–169 and §§255–257 (in Heinrich Dörrie, *Rahmen*, 194–197 and 484–488). On this tract see Lucio Troiani, *Commento storico al Contro Apione di Giuseppe* (Pisa: Giardini, 1977); Louis H. Feldman, John R. Levison, eds., *Josephus Contra Apionem. Studies in its Character and Context with a Latin Concordance to the Portion Missing in Greek* (Leiden: Brill, 1996); Christine Gerber,

dressing the claims of Greek plagiarism in an apologetic tone. Josephus cites Pythagoras, Anaxagoras, Plato, and the Stoics as cultivators of a concept of divinity (the foundation of theocracies like that of Moses),[43] holding that every good, unique and immutable, is knowable through its *dynameis*, but is not reachable in its essence. According to Josephus, Plato[44] seems to follow the Mosaic injunctions in particular when he excludes Homer from his "city-state" because his myths represented a threat to monotheistic doctrine. Plato's principle of protecting citizens from external dangers and his proposal to make citizens memorise the state's laws seemed, to Josephus, proof of the fact that the philosopher was a steadfast admirer of Mosaic laws. In Josephus's view, Moses provided Greek thinkers with certain key theological points. The Jewish laws are therefore not to be considered philosophical treatises lifted by Greek intellectuals but rather directives that influenced the course of Greek thought.

In direct response to and in argument against Apion and Apollonius Molon—who held that the Jews produced no original technical or cultural innovations[45]—Josephus employs a principle which the Eupolemus and Artapanus also believed to be well-diffused and commonly accepted in antiquity: *Prōtos Heuretēs* ("First Discoverer").[46] The antiquity and abiding integrity of the Jewish tradition guarantee this tradition's quality. The Greek debt to Jewish texts is not one of direct borrowing but of intellectual and historical influence. In the first paragraphs of the *Contra Apionem*, Josephus looks to support this by emphasising the foundation of Jewish texts in historical events, thus contrasting them to the multiform abstractions of Greek writings.[47] His aim here is to underscore the *antiquitas* of Judaism and the reliability of the accounts handed down by its priestly class.

Christian thought itself, then, follows the plagiarism claims, establishing its doctrine out of the debate, adhering to a theological and metaphysical argument that harkens back to Tertullian, who understood the concept of *Prōtos Heuretēs* as a prin-

---

Ein Bild des Judentums für Nichtjuden von Flavius Josephus: Untersuchungen zu seiner Schrift 'Contra Apionem' (Leiden: Brill, 1997).
43 Cf. Jürgen C.H. Lebram, "Der Idealstaat der Juden" ein *Josephus-Studien. Untersuchungen zu Josephus, dem antiken Judentum und dem Neuen Testament, Otto Michel zum 70. Geburtstag gewidmet*, ed. Otto Betz et al. (Göttingen: Vandenhoeck & Ruprecht, 1974): 233–253; René Bloch, *Moses und der Mythos. Die Auseinandersetzung mit der griechischen Mythologie bei jüdisch-hellenistischen Autoren* (Leiden: Brill, 2011), 41–43.
44 *Contra Apionem* II §§256–257.
45 *Contra Apionem* II §182; *Contra Apionem* II: §§135, 148; cf. Lucio Troiani, *Commento*, 58 and ff.
46 Cf. Adolf Kleingünther, *Protos heuretes: Untersuchungen zur Geschichte einer Fragestellung* (Leipzig: Dieterich, 1933); Klaus Thraede, "Erfinder," *Reallexikon für Antike und Christentum* 5 (1962): 1191–1278; Floris Overduin, *Nicander of Colophon's Theriaca. A literary commentary* (Leiden: Brill, 2015), 109–112.
47 Cf. my article "Canone, Scrittura e contesto immanente in alcuni testi del I secolo," *Laurentianum* 30 (1989): 17–24.

ciple not just of historical origin but metaphysical foundation.⁴⁸ What is temporally prior did not just come first: it is also an ontological point of origin. This allows them to cast the matter not simply as a question of sequential ordering, which will preoccupy the Alexandrine Jews, but as a question of how Greek theology and philosophy were derived from what turned out to be Christian revelation.⁴⁹

Temporal priority establishes truth ontologically, though not always historically.⁵⁰ The beliefs of the Gentiles are divided by Christian apologetics into three categories: false; plagiarism of Christian doctrine; and things that are "close" to Christianity ("*prope nos*"). Following this, Tertullian holds that philosophy derives from "sophia," poetry from "prophecy," and the Greek laws from the Mosaic Laws; the rest is mere corruption.⁵¹

The Jewish-Hellenistic traditions are thus to be considered from a historical and literary point of view as apologetic *topoi:* one simply cannot speak of Jewish "propaganda" in the way that Heinrich Dörrie does, and not take into account the theses of Nicholas Walter.⁵² The apologetics that the word "propaganda" suggests are always turned *outward:* a group "propagates" its polemical version of the truth, exaggerating its import.⁵³ Walter, however, believes that the Jewish-Hellenistic apologetics were in reality directed towards Judaism's *own* ranks to safeguard its patrimony from the dominant culture.⁵⁴ In this sense we would not, strictly speaking, call it Jew-

---

48 *Apologeticum* XIX: 15: "Quod prius est, hoc sit semen necesse est. Inde quaedam nobiscum vel prope nos habetis. De sophia amor eius philosophia vocitatus est, de prophetia affectatio eius poeticam vaticinationem depuravit. Gloriae homines, si quid invenerant, ut proprium facerent, adulteraverunt; etiam fructibus a semine degenerare contigit. Multis adhuc de vetustate modis consisterem divinarum litterarum, si non maior auctoritas illis ad fidem de veritatis suae viribus, quam aetatis annalibus suppetisset."
49 Cf. Klaus Thraede, "Erfinder," 1247, where the author speaks of a spiritualization of the principle of dependence ("Spiritualisierung des Abhangigkeitstopos").
50 Cf. *Ibidem*, 1248: "Die ganze Argumentation, aus der die Vorstellung einer 'Antike' allererst entstanden ist, will besagen, daß man sich zum Heidentum ebenso zu verhalten gedenke wie ehedem zum A.T."
51 Cf. Mark S. Burrows, "Christianity in the Roman forum," *Vigiliae Christianae* 42 (1987): 209–235. Andreas Schwab, *Thales von Milet in der frühen christlichen Literatur: Darstellungen seiner Figur und seiner Ideen in den griechischen und lateinischen Textzeugnissen christlicher Autoren der Kaiserzeit und Spätantike* (Berlin: De Gruyter, 2011), 104–105.
52 "Schon früh hat sich die jüdische Propaganda des, wie es schien, unanfechtbaren Faktums bedient, daß Platon sein Wissen in den entscheidenden Stücken bei den Weisen des Ostens erworben habe" in *Rahmen*, 480; cf. Nicholas Walter, *Thoraausleger*, 50: "nicht gerade schüchterne jüdische Propaganda."
53 Even in the apology of Josephus, which could well have had a non-Jewish readership, the term "propaganda" is not claimed. On this, see the article of Arnaldo Momigliano, "Un'apologia del Giudaismo: il *Contro Apione* di Flavio Giuseppe," in *Pagine ebraiche,* (Turin: Einaudi, 1987): 63–71. The author sees in the *Contra Apionem* a Hellenising presentation of Judaism rather than a defence of its principles, traditions, and religiosity.
54 Cf. Nicholas Walter, *Thoraausleger* 44, and ff.

ish "propaganda." Walter modifies this position, taking up the theses of Victor Tcherikover, who casts the Jewish-Hellenistic apologetic literature as a form of panegyric.[55]

It is a matter of apologetics turned inward: the persistence of Greece—the culture that tried, after Alexander's conquest, to Hellenise every "barbarian" group—was not to be underestimated by Jewish culture.[56] Only an all-out counterattack aimed at subverting the authority of the fathers of Greek culture might have succeeded, something that would question the priority of Greece's cultural foundations: an attack like an accusation of plagiarism. This was so, at least in the eyes of the Alexandrine Jews, who were facing the possible loss of the identity and autonomy of their traditions and roots[57]. Their labours evince above all a desire to locate a historical priority and chronological supremacy in their ancient traditions, the self-protective effort of a people living in a context that was by turns hostile, distrustful, and altogether indifferent.

Nevertheless, among themselves they knew that the situation was altogether different. One commonplace, found in the Hellenistic writer Aristeas and the philosopher Philo of Alexandria,[58] asserts the total absence of any trace of Jewish thought or writing in pagan culture. According to §312 of the *Letter of Aristeas to Philocrates*—an apology of Jewish culture and wisdom—the king Ptolemy Philadelphus marveled when the Torah was read to him in Greek (only recently translated by the 72 scholars coming out of Palestine), and wondered "'How is it that none of the historians or the poets have ever thought it worth their while to allude to such

---

[55] Cf. Nicholas Walter in *Jüdische Schriften aus hellenistisch-römischer Zeit*, vol. 3: *Unterweisung in lehrhafter Form. Das Buch Baruch. Der Brief Jeremias. Testament Abrahams. Fragmente jüdisch-hellenistischer Exegeten: Aristobulos, Demetrios, Aristeas* (Gütersloh: Gütersloher Verl.-Haus Mohn, 1980), 125, citing Victor Tcherikover, "Jewish apologetic literature reconsidered," *Eos* 48 (1956): 169–193. Cf. Steve Mason, "Of Audience and Meaning. Reading Josephus' *Bellum Judaicum* in the Context of a Flavian Audience," in *Josephus and Jewish History in Flavian Rome and Beyond*, ed. Joseph Sievers, Gaia Lembi (Leiden: Brill, 2005): 71–100.
[56] See also Guy G. Stroumsas, *Barbarian Philosophy: The Religious Revolution of Early Christianity.* (Tübingen: Mohr, 1999).
[57] On the problem of the Hellenization of Judaism, see Louis Feldman, "The Orthodoxy of the Jews in Hellenistic Egypt," *Jewish Social Studies* 22 (1969): 215–217; Martin Hengel, *Judentum und Hellenismus*; idem, *Aspekte der Hellenisierung des Judentums in vorchristlicher Zeit* (Stuttgart: KBW Verlag, 1976); Jonathan Goldstein, "Jewish Acceptance and Rejection of Hellenism," in *Jewish and Christian Self-Definition*, vol. 2, *Aspects of Judaism in the Graeco-Roman period*, ed. E. Parish Sanders (Philadelphia: Fortress Press, 1981): 64–87; Louis H. Feldman, "Torah and Secular Culture: Challenge and Response in the Hellenistic Period," *Tradition* 23 (1988): 26–40.
[58] Cf. Paul Wendland, "Zur ältesten Geschichte der Bibel in der Kirche," *Zeitschrift für alttestamentliche Wissenschaft* 1 (1900): 65–66; Giuseppe Veltri, *Eine Tora für den König Talmai. Untersuchungen zum Übersetzungsverständnis in der jüdisch-hellenistischen und rabbinischen Literatur* (Tübingen: Mohr, 1994); Giuseppe Veltri, *Libraries, Translations, and "Canonic" texts. The Septuagint, Aquila, and Ben Sira in Jewish and Christian Tradition*.

a wonderful achievement?"⁵⁹ Aristeas explains the omission by citing the sacredness of the text:

> Because the law is sacred and of divine origin. And some of those who formed the intention of dealing with it have been smitten by God and therefore desisted from their purpose." He said that he had heard from Theopompus that he had been driven out of his mind for more than thirty days because he intended to insert in his history some of the incidents from the earlier and somewhat unreliable translations of the law.⁶⁰

Aristeas' emphasis on the Torah's apotropaic character⁶¹ conceals, in any case, his embarrassment in the face of historical fact. It was the conviction of Alexandrine Judaism that the Torah's tradition in Greece was meant to fill the void that Ptolemy Philadelphus cites. However, this was not the case in reality.⁶²

It is significant that Philo, with his vehement polemics against the plagiarism of the pre-Socratics and the Athenian legislators, affirms the exact opposite in *De Vita Mosis II*.⁶³ According to him, the Law, written in "Chaldean" (Hebrew/Aramaic), "remained in this form for a long time, not being translated into any other tongue, and as a consequence retained its beauty while not being revealed to other men (§26)." It was a scandal, Philo commented, that only half of humanity—the "barbarians"— could study the Torah, while the other half remained completely shut off from it (§27). Yet, the translated Torah failed to accomplish the effect that Philo expected. The Alexandrian, who writes at least two centuries after the translation of the Torah into Greek, bemoans the lack of awareness of the text among contemporary writers and rulers. In response to the pagan polemic on the inferiority of Jewish law codes, he says: "That which concerns a people no longer at its [political] apogee, lives in the shadows."⁶⁴ It is doubtful that Judaism was ever politically and militarily at the apogee of the Mediterranean world between Egypt and Babylonia. Philo notes, in any case, that even the legendary age of David and Solomon was distant in time and hazy in memory.

The important question, at this point, is whether the position of Alexandrine Judaism—contradictory in itself—was born completely out of the desire (perhaps the fantasy) of defending itself against Greek usurpation. The answer must be no—

---

59 Cf. Raffaele Tramontano, *La lettera di Aristea a Filocrate* (Naples: Ufficio Succursale della Civiltà Cattolica, 1931), 247.
60 Aristeas, §§313–314 in the translation of Robert H. Charles.
61 Babylonian Talmud, *Ḥullin* 60a. *The Apocrypha and Pseudepigrapha of the Old Testament*, ed. and trans. Robert H. Charles (Oxford: The Clarendon Press, 1913).
62 On this aspect see Arnaldo Momigliano, *Alien Wisdom. The Limits of Hellenization* (Cambridge: Cambridge University Press, 1975), 91 and ff. On the pagan world's familiarity with the Jewish and Christian bible, see Giancarlo Rinaldi, *Biblia Gentium. Primo contributo per un indice delle citazioni, dei riferimenti e delle allusioni alla Bibbia negli autori pagani, greci e latini, di età imperiale* (Rome: Libreria Sacre Scritture, 1989).
63 Philo, *De Vita Mosis* II: §25 ff.
64 Philo, *De Vita Mosis* II: §43.

once the claims of plagiarism find a hospitable setting, as they do among second century Christians—if only because of the nature of the premise debated, i.e. the non-originality of Greek thought.[65] The idea that Pythagoras and Plato acquired their wisdom from the Orient, and especially from Egypt, is an ancient one.[66] References to this idea being applied to Pythagoras, Democritus, and Plato are made by Isocrates,[67] Diodorus Siculus,[68] Cicero,[69] and Quintilian.[70] The claim hinges on the antiquity of Egyptian culture compared to Greek culture. The Egyptians, after all, exemplified the *Prōtoi Heuretai*, the "first discoverers," with regard to virtually all thought in their epoch: there was no branch of ancient knowledge they had not treated. The attribution of the invention of writing to them, in particular, provoked a kind of inferiority complex in the Greeks. It is for this reason that Artapanus makes a point to trace writing back to Musaios/Moses, trying in this way to "steal" a myth from the Egyptians by way of the Jewish tradition.

Furthermore, the Jews were known for being philosophers.[71] If we believe, along with Josephus,[72] the testimony of Clearcus, then we would hold that Aristotle considered the Jews "the philosophers among the Syrians" (*hoi philosophoi para Syrois*).[73] The fourth century B.C.E. Greek writer Megasthenes, author of the *Indica*[74], asserts that a commonality of ideas—if not an outright causal dependence—existed between the Greeks, Brahmans, and Jews. "All the ancients' opinions on nature are found among philosophers outside of Greece, some among the Indian Brahmans and others in Syria among them called Jews."[75] Hermippus of Smyrna, who lived in the last half of the third century, was convinced that Pythagoras was influenced by the Jews and the Thracians.[76]

---

65 Elias J. Bickerman, *The Jews in the Greek Age* (Cambridge: Harvard University Press, 1988), 219: "[…] the Greeks were unable to antedate the beginnings of their history," and 220: "[…] the Greek were persuaded that wisdom is at the beginning and that descendants must be like the ancestors." In the footnotes he cites Plato, *Epinomis* 987e and Iulianus, *Misopogon* 348b.
66 Moses Hadas, "Plato in Hellenistic Fusion," *Journal of the History of Ideas* 19 (1958): 3–13; Hans Lewy, "Aristotle and the Jewish Sage According to Clearchus of Soli," *The Harvard Theological Review* 31 (1938): 205–235.
67 Isocrates, *Busiris* 28.
68 Diodorus Siculus, Book I:98,1–4.
69 Cicero, *De finibus bonorum et malorum* 5,50, 5,87; *De Republica* 1,16; *Tusculanae disputationes* 4,44.
70 Quintilian, *Institutio Oratoria* I:12,15, see Heinrich Dörrie, *Rahmen*, 168–170, 427 and following.
71 Arnaldo Momigliano, *Ebrei e Greci*, in idem, *Pagine ebraiche*, 20–21.
72 Josephus, *Contra Apionem* I: 179.
73 Hans Lewy, *Aristotle and the Jewish sage*, 205–235.
74 On this see Arnaldo Momigliano, *Alien Wisdom*, 83–87; Schürer-Vermes, *History*, vol. 3/1, 85, n. 100.
75 Text and translation in Menahem Stern, *Greek and Latin Authors*, vol. 1, no. 14, 94.
76 Josephus, *Contra Apionem* I: §§164–165, Menahem Stern, *Greek and Latin Authors*, no. 25, 93–96); see also Nicholas Walter, *Thoraausleger*, 46; see also Bezalel Bar-Kochva, *The Image of the Jews in Greek Literature: The Hellenistic Period*.

After the entrance of Christianity into Mediterranean history the only pagan author who continued to argue for the thesis of Plato's borrowing from Moses is Numenius of Apamea.[77] His interest in Jewish "sophia" is demonstrated by Clement of Alexandria, Origen, Porphyry, Eusebius of Caesarea, Theodoret, and the lexicon of Souda. He is believed to have coined the axiom: "Who is Plato if not a Moses who speaks Attic?"[78] He asserts, further, the existence of a harmony between the ethical positions of Plato, Pythagoras, and ancient peoples like the Brahmans, the Jews, the Magi, and the Egyptians. Like Artapanus, he identifies Musaios as Moses.[79] Given the fragmentary character of the texts, one must acknowledge that even taking into consideration the arguments of Numenius it is difficult to fully understand the context in which the dependence of Greek thought on the Torah (or even the more general consonance of Greek philosophy with some points of oriental thought) had been professed.

It is clear now that it was almost exclusively the fathers of the church who handed down to us texts that make reference to Moses. Numenius, following Eusebius, refers to the whole of Eastern knowledge as the source of Greek thought. Origen, who likely relies on the same source, cites Numenius but speaks only of Jewish thought. Iamblicus, for his part, cites Egyptian writings as the primary font of knowledge but never states this with respect to the Jewish traditions. We should not forget that the fathers of the church tended to exaggerate in their reports on the works of Numenius, making false claims about the philosopher's interest in the question of source borrowing.[80] Numenius's primary aim was likely to bring Eastern philosophy into harmony with Platonic thought, a precursor to a commonplace among Neoplatonists: the search for points of synthesis between Greek philosophy and foreign thought (or at least the interrelation of elements from the two).[81]

In concluding this section, we can posit that, from the end of the fourth century B.C.E. through the beginning of the third, a particular attention was given to so-

---

[77] John Whittaker, "Moses Atticizing," *Phoenix* 21 (1967): 196–201; see also John Whittaker, *Studies in Platonism and Patristic Thought* (London: Variorum, 1984), 196–201; John G. Gager, *Moses in Greco-Roman paganism* (Nashville: Abingdon Press, 1972), 63–69; Menaham Stern, *Greek and Latin Authors*, vol. 2, no. 363–369, 209–216; Rinaldi, *Biblia Gentium*, no. 18, 187; no. 118, 264–265; Mark J. Edwards, "'Atticizing Moses?' Numenius, the Fathers and the Jews," *Vigiliae Christianae* 44 (1990): 64–75; Daniel Ridings, *The Attic Moses: The Dependency Theme in Some Early Christian Writers* (PhD dissertation, University of Gothenburg, GUPEA, Gothenburg University Publications Electronic Archive, 1994).
[78] See Clemens Alexandrinus, *Stromata* I 22, 150, 4. For the other patristic references see Menaham Stern, *Greek and Latin Authors*, vol. 2, no. 363a–e, 209–210.
[79] Numenius, *De Bono*; Eusebius, *Praeparatio Evangelica*, IX: 7,1, in Menaham Stern, *Greek and Latin Authors*, vol. 2, no. 364a–b, 211–212.
[80] Numenius, *De Bono*; Eusebius, *Praeparatio Evangelica* IX: 8,1–2, in Menaham Stern, *Greek and Latin Authors*, vol. 2, no. 365, 212–213.
[81] John G. Gager, *Moses*, 67.

called "barbarian" writings.[82] This does not mean that the pagans had read the Greek translation of the Torah—the Septuagint—much less the original Hebrew. Their awareness was likely derived from spoken traditions passed on by the Jews themselves. We have no evidence of any Jews reading the Greek Torah before the first century C.E. (and this dating too is not beyond doubt).

The status as philosophers that is bestowed on the Jews, which we find in Megasthenes and perhaps in Aristotle, takes as a given both their wisdom and the antiquity of their traditions. Likewise, in Jewish culture there exists no caesura between "mythos" and "logos," between philosophy and religion: their "philosophers" were for the most part both priests and amateur philosophers, something that would have fascinated the Platonic schools and that went on to definitively influence Neoplatonism. The appellation "alien wisdom" is in essence a respectful attribution in the face of the unknown and the untried, in the face of things that come from cultures ancient and thus full of mystery. The theory of Greek source borrowings reveals a sensitivity in Greek philosophy towards foreign thought. The Greeks had been "civilised" relatively late—they were almost the last civilisation to arise in the Mediterranean basin. The Egyptians, Phoenicians, and Jews, for example, could boast far more ancient traditions.

The Jewish claim to primacy was a modern-era misinterpretation. To the extent that the enduring fragments of apologetics preceding Philo of Alexandria can tell us anything conclusive, it seems that the plagiarism theory is not about the affirmation of principles (as among the Christians), but about the establishment of fact and propriety: the doctrine of contraries, monotheism, etc., are Jewish discoveries repurposed by Greek thinkers. The basic paradox here—the idea that the pagans somehow came to know Jewish traditions even though the Torah had not yet been translated—interests only Aristobulus, who postulates that access to the translations originated with the Septuagint translators. For most other thinkers it does not represent a problem. In fact, according to the principle of the "first discoverer," what counts is temporal priority—something that is grounded, as far as concerns biblical history, on the antiquity of their genealogy (Eupolemus, Demetrius) and on the veracity of their tradition (Josephus).

---

82 On the thesis of the Jewish origin of Numenius, see Henri-Charles Puech, "Numénius d' Apamée et les théologies orientales au second siècle," *Annuaire de l'institut de philologie et d'histoire orientales* 2 (1934): 745–778, and for the challenge to this thesis Eric R. Dodds, "Numenius and Ammonius," in idem, *Les sources de Plotin* (Geneva: Fondation Hardt, Vandœuvres, 1960), 4–32.

2 The "Theft" of Written and Oral Wisdom

The attribution of the very origins of knowledge to a single group as if it were particular to a people, the hereditary property of a specific nation or culture, is an invention and a product of the creativity of the ancients, the consequences of which, in the history of European thought, nonetheless expand well beyond the dynamics of the "First Discoverer" examined above. This concept is at base a declaration of the primacy of a genealogy of wisdom in which the ascendancy of the *primus* (the aforementioned Tertullian also calls it "seed") is explained as *a priori* a matter of right. Whatever does not belong directly to the group that advanced the claim of primacy is labelled as posterior and irretrievably historically situated in a relation of dependence on the former (as with Greek philosophy and the sciences). This logic is followed, as discussed in the preceding section, by the Jewish-Hellenistic (and then Christian) apologetics that take up the task of explaining the presence of similar doctrines in the Bible and Greek philosophy as due to a historical-literary dependence: this correspondence would come to be associated with the claims of plagiarism, the "theft" of doctrines.

It is logical, therefore, that alongside the questions of intellectual genealogy and debt we should discuss when and how the foundational, "canonical" writings of the Jewish world were themselves published. Apart from Aristobulus, this aspect was not dealt with by those who lamented the antiquity of their own traditions in the Hellenic-Egyptian world, at least according to the extant fragments of the Jewish apologetics. The determination of the historical epoch of the Torah's publication for non-Hebrews (and thus its translation out of Hebrew) turned into an outright dilemma the moment it became known that the Septuagint was in circulation in Ptolemaic Egypt and subject to the politics of acquisition in the library of Alexandria. It is commonly known that, in antiquity, the dissemination of texts occurred primarily by means of the diffusion of scripture, access to which was often not assured for all the peoples and nations of the Mediterranean, due to the difficulties, both practical and economic, of publishing a text in a wide radius of circulation.[1]

In Judaism, the problem of how the Torah became publicly known is a question that is apologetic and imperative. As the aforementioned Aristeas and Philo report, an effort must be made to understand this exception to the outer world's *de facto* ignorance of Jewish culture and literature. The Jews were an ancient people, relatively small in number, weak in political influence, and, perhaps above all else, in possession of a literary heritage written in a language that was far from common. Indeed, this language is quite distant from the logic of the κοινὴ διάλεκτος (*koinè diàlektos*), the language that conquered the world of that period. However, the question as to

---

[1] See Christopher A. Rollston, *Writing and Literacy in the World of Ancient Israel: Epigraphic Evidence from the Iron Age* (Leiden: Brill, 2010), and regarding the successive period see Cathrine Hezser, *Jewish Literacy in Roman Palestine* (Tübingen: Mohr, 2001).

the circumstances under which the Torah was publicised must also be considered *a posteriori:* is it possible that it was the very publication and translation of the Torah in Greek that led to the "theft" of Jewish thought?

The advent of certain Jewish sects as well as enormously diffuse religious and cultural movements like the Gnostics of the Greco-Roman era presented the problem from just this point of view, that is, they posed the question of the precise appearance of the original Jewish traditions, ideas, and philosophical and political concepts that subsequently retained specifics of Jewish history and literature but were disseminated by others as if they were their own heritage. The idea of the "theft" of wisdom acquires, therefore, a new dimension, that of the apologetics *ad intra:* the goal of demonstrating that a *proprium hebraicum* exists that other groups, though reading, citing, and appropriating its texts, have no claim to by priority or right.

A correlative aspect that is rarely if ever cited in this context is the issue of the origins of the oral Torah and its relation to the written Torah: the debate, in other words, on the function of oral tradition in biblical scripture[2] and its transmission through subsequent generations. This topic likewise produces its own genealogy of wisdom that is certainly secondary but also parallel and in certain ways antagonistic. The oral Torah arose, according to Jewish tradition, simultaneously with the written Torah. The former is the latter's vehicle and means of interpretation, a faithful sister but also the font of authority on the meaning of the written Bible's letter. However, the oral Torah could also be stolen and plagiarised, for which reason the rabbis of the classical age emphasised its esoteric aspects, prohibiting its free circulation in writing. Regardless, the principle of orality did not prevent, at a certain historical moment, a radical change that resulted in the oral tradition being set down in writing. This perhaps arose out of a fear that the traditions would become the fodder of oblivion, a fear that likely explains the emergence of the tendency, from Late Antiquity onward, to privilege the written forms of the Mishnah, the Talmud, and the Midrash, not to mention the Masorah (the infratext tradition that accompanied the consonant text of the Hebrew Bible, the *miqra'*). Before confronting the problem of the "theft" of wisdom in the rabbinical world, therefore, we must map out the dynamics of scripture and orality, publication and spoken tradition.

2.1 Strengths and Weaknesses of "Writing" vs. "Orality"

Let us begin by turning to Greek philosophy and the question of writing proposed in the Platonic corpus. In the *Phaedrus*, Socrates recounts (274c–d) that the Egyptian god Theuth invented not only numbers themselves, arithmetic, and geometry, but also, first and foremost, the letters of the alphabet. Theuth demonstrates his inven-

---

[2] See the discussion of the distinction between *traditum* and *traditio* in Michael Fishbane, *Biblical Interpretation in Ancient Israel* (Oxford: Clarendon, 1985).

2.1 Strengths and Weaknesses of "Writing" vs. "Orality" — 23

tions, interweaving them with panegyrics, to Thamus, king of Thebes, saying of letters that "'This invention, O king,' said Theuth, 'will make the Egyptians wiser and will improve their memories; for it is an elixir of memory and wisdom that I have discovered.'" The King of Thebes, at this announcement, reacts by denying it:

> But Thamus replied, "Most ingenious Theuth, one man has the ability to beget arts, but the ability to judge of their usefulness or harmfulness to their users belongs to another; and now you, who are the father of letters, have been led by your affection to ascribe to them a power the opposite of that which they really possess. For this invention will produce forgetfulness in the minds of those who learn to use it, because they will not practice their memory. Their trust in writing, produced by external characters which are no part of themselves, will discourage the use of their own memory within them. You have invented an elixir not of memory, but of reminding; and you offer your pupils the appearance of wisdom, not true wisdom, for they will read many things without instruction and will therefore seem to know many things, when they are for the most part ignorant and hard to get along with, since they are not wise, but only appear wise."³

In his analysis of this passage, Jan Assmann underscores the peculiar reception of the written Platonic works: "It deals with the preserved wisdom of the Egyptians, with the use of this technique to put the known into writing, with the usefulness of conserving the very experience of making known the new and unknown."⁴ Assmann cites further the testimony of Diodorus Siculus⁵ regarding the doubleness of writing (hieratic and demotic) that would have bearing on the double dimension of the written thereafter: demotic for the masses, and hieratic for the priests. One asks oneself, however, what Plato refers to: the known and its relationship to the unknown (the question, that is, of esotericism in the written medium), or the double nature of the written (demotic and hieratic) with regard to class distinctions? Or perhaps he refers to both doubled issues.

Whatever the answer to this question, I do not believe this interpretation of Plato to be a decisive point in his philosophy. I do not think, that is, that Socrates-alias-Plato had such a distinction in mind because it is not consonant with the dialectic of his thought. Assmann undervalues the sentence: "Their trust in writing, produced by external characters which are no part of themselves, will discourage the use of their own memory within them" (ἅτε διὰ πίστιν γραφῆς ἔξωθεν ὑπ'ἀλλοτρίων τύπων, οὐκ ἔνδοθεν αὐτοὺς ὑφ'αὑτῶν ἀναμιμνῃσκομένους). The key words of the text are undoubtedly ἔξωθεν ("external" versus ἔνδοθεν ("internal"), which delimit the meaning of ὑπ'ἀλλοτρίων τύπων and ὑφ'αὑτῶν ἀναμιμνῃσκομένους, that is, the distinction between external letters and that which is carved into one's internal memory. Assmann, unfortunately, makes a false distinction between "internal" and

---

3 *Plato in Twelve Volumes*, vol. 9 transl. Harold N. Fowler (Cambridge: Harvard University Press, 1925).
4 Cf. Jan Assmann, *Weisheit und Mysterium: das Bild der Griechen von Ägypten* (Munich: C.H. Beck Verlag, 2000), 65–66.
5 Diodorus Siculus, *Book* I. 81. 1.2, and III. 3.4.

"external" knowledge with regards to Plato's discussion of the two modes of Egyptian writing (since Plato deems the external and material as incompatible with human memory). In fact, in his reprimand regarding the *Prōtos Heuretēs* (the above mentioned "First Discoverer")—on the issue of who first invented letters— king Thamus takes note that the benefit of writing is not so much as an external memory as it is a reference: one thing pointing to another. It is not, in this way, a question concerning the essence of the thing but of reminding: "You have invented an elixir not of memory, but of reminding; and you offer your pupils the appearance of wisdom" (οὔκουν μνήμης ἀλλὰ ὑπομνήσεως φάρμακον ηὗρες. σοφίας δὲ τοῖς μαθηταῖς δόξαν, οὐκ ἀλήθειαν πορίζεις). According to Plato, awareness is internal and the external can only act as a directional reference, far from complete and certainly no replacement for memory. He continues:

> Writing, Phaedrus, has this strange quality, and is very like painting; for the creatures of painting stand like living beings, but if one asks them a question, they preserve a solemn silence. And so it is with written words; you might think they spoke as if they had intelligence, but if you question them, wishing to know about their sayings, they always say only one and the same thing. And every word, when once it is written, is bandied about, alike among those who understand and those who have no interest in it, and it knows not to whom to speak or not to speak; when ill-treated or unjustly reviled it always needs its father to help it; for it has no power to protect or help itself.[6]

The notion that the written letter lacks strength, is silent, and relies on the interpreter/father to articulate its meaning and to bring it back to life is not a novel or random concept but one common in classical antiquity and revived in medieval and modern literature. This idea receives exemplary exposition in the writings of the archdeacon Pierre de Blois, who lived in the twelfth century (mostly on British soil) and is known as the author of numerous letters. In one of these letters (92) he comments on Bernard of Clairvaux's axiom "we are dwarfs on the shoulders of giants" (*nos quasi nani super humeros gigantum*)[7] adding to it a note of acuity that elevates the reader to the role of a divine force insofar as, with the energy of his reading, he resuscitates dead words (*quasi iam mortuas in quamdam novitatem essentiae suscitamus*).[8] Plato

---

6 Ibid.
7 See the bibliography of my own "The Humanist Sense of History and the Jewish Idea of Tradition: Azaria de' Rossi's Critique of Philo Alexandrinus," *Jewish Studies Quarterly* 2 (1995): 372–393, to which must be added Jeffrey R. Woolf's "Between Diffidence and Initiative: Ashkenazic Legal Decision-Making in the Late Middle Ages (1350–1500)," *Journal of Jewish Studies* 52 (2001): 85–97. Robert K. Merton's fascinating study, *On the Shoulders of Giants. A Shandean Postscript* (New York: Free Press, 1965), should be cited not only for the author's magnificent prose, but also for the book's panoramic perspective, which includes Judaism among its themes.
8 Pierre de Blois, "Epistula XCII ad Reginaldum Episcopum," in *Patrologia Latina* vol. 207, 290: "[...] quorum beneficio longius, quam ipsi, speculamur, dum antiquorum tractatibus inhaerentes elegantiores eorum sententias, quas vetustas aboleverat, hominumve neglectus, quasi jam mortuas in

spoke of the author as father of a given written work, whereas the successive tradition will speak of interpreters as authorities of the text.

For Platonic philosophy, the etching of words (in stone or drafted on papyrus) implicitly led to writing's association with immutability, harkening back above all to the phase of publication and the dangers inherent to that phase, as, once the word is codified in writing, every discourse ends up in the hands of everyone. It is not important at this moment to ascertain if this is a sign of Platonic esotericism or something else that has no impact on the fundamental question of the relationship between writing and interpreting. This last point is crucial for the discussion, because it introduces an element of mediation between text and audience, the figure, that is, of Plato the "father" who defends the text and helps it to successfully reach its audience.

Perhaps it is no mistake that the Rabbi of ancient rabbinical literature comes to be called "Father" (*Av*), being author of generations of traditions and the proponent of a transfer from father to son, a transfer which arises, as in Plato, with the dynamics of orality, although in Plato the function of the "father of the letters" is rather negative.[9] Regardless, here the issue is writing, not orality, as a form of disclosure. This is one of the central themes of Jewish literature, as can be deduced from the earliest historical documents of Ezra and Nehemiah from the time of the Babylonian exile, which we will consider in the following section.

2.2 He Who Did Not Write but Published: Ezra the Scribe

According to Deuteronomy 31:9, the written Torah was entrusted to the priests, the sons of Levi, and to the ancients of Israel so that they would organise a public, oral reading of it every seven years for the Israelites gathered in assembly. According to biblical pronouncement, all this comes about "so that they will listen, learn, and fear the Lord our God, and so that they will take care to put into practice all the words of this law" (Deuteronomy 31:12). This verse alludes to the mandate that the Law should be read publicly every seven years, a necessity since the literacy rate was not high and, more importantly, written texts did not often circulate.

The (re)discovery of the book of laws at the time of King Josiah's religious reforms in the seventh century B.C. represents something like a historical recurrence of Deuteronomy's commandment. In this case, however, it seems that it was the king and not the Levites who ordered the public readings.

---

quamdam novitatem essentiae suscitamus." For a hermeneutical assessment of this principle see my own *Gegenwart der Tradition*, XIV–XVI, and my *Libraries, Translations, and Canonic Text*.
9 *Phaedrus* 275a: "and now you, who are the father of letters, have been led by your affection to ascribe to them a power the opposite of that which they really possess." See further in *Phaedrus* 275a: "when ill-treated or unjustly reviled it always needs its father to help it; for it has no power to protect or help itself."

This book is read in front of the assembly of the Israelites in order to be understood by all, thus adhering to Deuteronomy. Then the king seals an alliance with God so that they can follow "His commands, His laws, and His decrees [...] and [...] put into practice the words of this alliance written in this book" (2 Kings 23:3). The scene repeats itself, historically, several centuries later, at the time of the repatriation of (some of) the tribes of Israel from the Babylonian exile. According to Ezra 7:12–26, it was a foreign king, Artaxerxes of Persia, who ordered the introduction of the Torah, thus inaugurating its legitimisation.[10] His decree was met with favour from Jews: the political goal was to reconstruct the wall, the temple, the city and to publicly restore the Torah and its substantiality as a document, effectively making it the Law, which would be in the hands (Ezra 7:14) of Ezra the scribe (Ezra 7:6).

The public reading of the Torah at the Gate of the Waters performs a role that is central to classical Jewish literature, passing beyond the stage of mere "reading and listening" of the text, bestowing on it a position statelier than Ezra could have foreseen. It is in this case that one can note how the reconstruction of a text, which is read and explained "in front of the assembly of men, women, any who were able to understand,"[11] becomes the *deus ex machina* of a political reform.

2.3 The Publication of the Greek Torah

The same constellation of elements is echoed several centuries later in Alexandria, Egypt, where, according to the legend, 72 Jewish translators had rendered the Torah into Greek over the course of 72 days in the famous library of Ptolemy. According to Aristeas, the first witness to this legend in the above-cited letter to Philocrates, the translating event took place under the guidance of Demetrius of Phalerum, who would then have delivered the translation of Jewish Law to Ptolemy II Philadelphus.

Aristeas recounts that after Demetrius of Phalerum recited the Greek text of the Torah in the library of Alexandria, the priests and the translators proclaimed to the representatives of the politico-social complex of the *politeuma* and to the people themselves that the translation was accomplished with great care and accuracy. For this reason, any subsequent changes would have been strictly forbidden. The translators accepted this injunction, proclaiming that, "following their customs,"

---

10 Cf. Abraham Berliner, *Targum Onkelos: Einleitung und Register* (Frankfurt: Kauffmann, 1884), 74; Hans Heinrich Schaeder, *Esra der Schreiber* (Tübingen: Mohr, 1930), 39–59; Klaus Koch, "Ezra and the Origins of Judaism," *Journal of Semitic Studies* 19 (1974): 173–197; Antonius H. J. Gunneweg, "Zur Interpretation der Bücher Ezra-Nehemia. Zugleich ein Beitrag zur Methode der Exegese," *Vetus Testamentum Supplement* 32 (1981): 146–161; Luis D. Merino, "Philological Aspects in the Research of the Targums," *Proceedings of the Ninth World Congress of Jewish Studies* (Jerusalem: 1985); Panel Sessions: Bible Studies and Ancient Near East, ed. Moshe H. Goshen-Gottstein (Jerusalem: World Union of Jewish Studies, 1988), 87–97.
11 Nehemiah 8:2.

they would condemn anyone who attempted to modify the body of the text through addition, omission, or any other form of alteration.[12]

That the translators themselves were there at the Greek Torah's public reading seems to indicate the significance of the event, an incorporation of their presence into the text's epiphany. This aspect is emphasised by the quasi-liturgical scene of the public recitation,[13] even if the text's reader was a "pagan." The presence of both the sovereign and Demetrius underscores the political dimension of the recitation. According to Aristeas, God and the king would work together towards the production of a text for both pagans and Jews, and in this act would remain in accord with the manifest project of Alexandrine Judaism to openly position itself in the Greco-Egyptian context.

Nevertheless, the liturgical aspect is foregrounded from the moment when, in the description of the public recitation, Aristeas overtly voices the refrain of the text's inalterability, claiming that it was safeguarded by curses against those who tried to modify it. This is likely a reference to the Deuteronomic curses and blessings.[14] And it is perhaps for this very reason that the text includes the expression "following their customs": Aristeas had presumably read Deuteronomy 4:2 and the parallel passage in Deuteronomy 13:1 from this perspective. If this hypothesis is exact or at least plausible, the Greek Torah becomes *ipso facto* a substitution of the original.[15]

The texts examined from 2 Kings 23, Ezra 7, and Aristeas' legend of the 72 translators share one aspect: they all tell stories of texts recuperated, reconstructed, or translated, and are all read aloud at a community gathering. They tell of documents that must be treated, from that moment on, like binding tools of law. Authority—be it Jewish or not—constitutes a decisive factor: it is a guarantor of the text that enters into force and, ultimately, acts like an organ that controls its eternity, its inalterability.

---

12 For the text of the so-called "letter" of Aristeas, see *Aristeas ad Philocratem epistula*, ed. Paul Wendland (Leipzig: Teubner, 1900); *Aristeas to Philocrates*, ed. Moses Hadas (New York: Harper and Brothers, 1962); *Lettera di Aristea*, ed. Francesca Calabi (Milan: Biblioteca universale Rizzoli, 1995). For a bibliography of the secondary literature, see my *Gegenwart der Tradition*, 14–16.
13 Cf. Harry M. Orlinsky, "The Septuagint as Holy Writ and the Philosophy of the Translators," *Hebrew Union College Annual* 46 (1975): 110–113; Daniel R. Schwartz, "The Priests in Ep. Arist. 310," *Journal of Biblical Literature* 97 (1978): 567–571.
14 Cf. Charles Fensham, "Malediction and Benediction an Ancient Near Eastern Vassal-Treatises and the Old Testament," *Zeitschrift für die Alttestamentliche Wissen-schaft* 74 (1962): 1–9.
15 The version of the story of the 72 that involves the recurrence of Deuteronomy 4:2 merits a deeper reflection, considering the various modifications in the verse, as it was interpreted by the translators. In the two versions the word *phylassein* means "to supervise," "to observe," or "to guard" (Deuteronomy 4:2 and in Aristeas §311), and is correlated with the terms *nomos* and *rhema*. Aristeas uses the word with reference to a written text: the Greek Torah, whose words must be preserved and protected. The word *phylassein* thus does not mean only the observation of a law, but also—through an alteration of meaning—the watchful custody of a text. There is no reference here, however, to a strategy for ensuring the immutability of the text or to any statement for the prohibition of altering or translating the sacred writings of the Torah, which became regarded as substitutions of the original.

The stress on the publication of the Torah in both Hebrew and Greek pursues a double end: the pinpointing of the historical moment when the founding document of Judaism was made public through official presentation to the (Jewish) people, and the open divulgation of the collective memory of the people of Israel, making it known and accessible to all (in principle at least). The first element is about the establishment of the community with its laws and its traditions, and the second is about documenting the ancient foundations of Jewish knowledge in its chronological precedence over other cultures and languages. This last aspect is especially valid for the Jewish Egyptian community still in the midst of its Diaspora. This *topos* will reappear in the rabbinical literature, however, when, despite a partial return to their homeland, the Jews find themselves living under foreign rule. Their enduring condition will be that of foreigners in their own land, first under the yoke of the Romans and then the Byzantines and then the Arabs.

There is one other aspect to be discussed that led the theme of the "theft" of wisdom. With the advent of various heretical currents, among them Christianity, and with the Jewish community's separation into powerful groups representing varied religious and political interests (Rabbis against the Pharisees and Sadducees, the intellectual world of Palestine against that of Babylon, the Gnostics, and the agnostics, etc.), and now that the written Torah has become *de principio* and *de facto* the patrimony of all, the question of which is the true Judaism emerged with a new force. Moreover, the deliberate opening of Alexandrine Judaism, putative progenitor of Christianity, became a danger to cultural identity.

The discussion of the earliest records of oral wisdom becomes a point of urgency for the reconstruction of the tradition's unity and the effort to avoid its loss in the multifaceted world of the Common Era.

2.4 The Record of Oral Wisdom

The *topos* of the Torah's lack of recognition that we have encountered in Jewish-Hellenistic literature and philosophy is echoed also in rabbinical literature, though the discussion's form and content differ from those in the Hellenistic theses of the Egyptian Jews. The Torah would not have been an exclusive gift to the people of Israel if the "pagans" had accepted it. From the beginning, on Sinai, the divine offering was directed towards the "nations of the world" (*'ummot ha-'olam*), who would prove disinterested and even spurn the offering outright.[16]

The intended function of this Midrashic tradition must be approached as an exegesis rather than a form of direct polemic against a fixed audience. In fact, the exe-

---

16 Mekhilta de-Rabbi Yishma'el, Ba-ḥodesh Yitro § 5. Cf. also Ephraim E. Urbach, *The Sages. Their Concepts and Beliefs* (Jerusalem: Magnes, 1975), 532 and ff.; Peter Schäfer, "Israel und die Völker der Welt. Zur Auslegung van Mekhilta de Rabbi Yishma'el, bahodesh Yitro 5," *Frankfurter Judaistische Beiträge* 4 (1976): 32–62.

getical problems that were posed are first, how to explain the direct connection between the revelation on Sinai and the divine epiphanies at Seir and on mount Paran (Deuteronomy 33:2)[17] (probably in the Arabian desert) and second, why the epiphany on Sinai and the gift of the Torah did not originate in the land of Israel itself.[18] However, we cannot ignore how this emphasis on the exclusivity of the revelation to the Jewish people also generated polemics.[19] The Midrash gives a direct answer to the query, suggesting that the exclusivity does not represent a particularity on God's part, but rather an appropriate response on the part of the Jews to the gift of the Law.

According to the *Mishnah* (*Soṭah* 7:5), the Torah would be written in seventy languages on the stone of the altar (basing this on Joshua 4:2–8 and 20–24): "After they [the twelve tribes] carried the stones and constructed the altar, the recovered it with limestone and carved atop it all the words of this Law in seventy languages, doing so 'very clearly,' as it is written [Deuteronomy 27:8]. They took the stones, putting them in their places as they left." The Torah is, therefore, property of the twelve tribes in all their complexity, a property nonetheless open to all, as suggested by the metaphorical evocation of the 70 languages.[20] The tradition of the *Tosefta* (*Soṭah* 8:6) limits this geographically universalist feature of the *Mishnah*, and to the question of how the nations of the world came to know the Torah, Rabbi Yehudah responds[21]: "The Most Holy, blessed be He, granted wisdom[22] to the nations of the world and they all sent scribes to record the inscriptions on the altar stones in seventy languages. In that moment, the condemnation of the nations of the world into the deep

---

17 This is not the place to identify geographical locations, but only to reveal the difference in the locations and therefore differences in the revelation itself.
18 This theme is taken up in the rabbinical literature again and again and serves as the opening for the Midrash *Mekhilta de-Rabbi Ishmaʻel*.
19 Cf. Eugene Mihaly, "A Rabbinic Defence of the Election of Israel," *Hebrew Union college Annual* 35 (1964): 103–143.
20 On the parallels to this tradition see *Der Tosefta-Traktat Sota. Hebräischer Text mit kritischem Apparat, Übersetzung und Kommentar*, ed. H. Bientenbard (Berlin: Lang, 1985), 160–161, note 48.
21 *Die Mischna. Seder 3, Naschim, Traktat 6, Sota (Die des Ehebruchs Verdächtige). Übersetzung, Erklärungen, textkritischer Anhang* (Berlin: Töpelmann, 1956), 116, VII, note 3. The author does not take into account the symbolic aspect of the scene and states: "Sie nahmen den Altar wieder auseinander. Damit wird aber die ganze Sache illusorisch: Wie hatten die 70 Weltvölker in so kurzer Zeit Kunde von dieser Sache bekommen?" This is not a historical text—how could they have in truth been able to write the totality of the Law on the surfaces of 12 stones—but rather a symbolic one. The Torah belongs to all of Israel (Mekhilta de-Rabbi Yishmaʻel, *Baḥodesh* 5; cf. Peter Schäfer, "Israel und die Völker der Welt: Zur Auslegung von Mekhilta deRabbi Yishma'el, baḥodesh Yitro 5," FJB4 (1976): 32–62, 51–52. Another tradition holds that Moses wrote thirteen Torot, twelve for the twelve tribes of Israel, one to be left in the arc so as to prevent anyone from falsifying the complete Torah (Midrash Tehillim 90:3; cf. Midrash Devarim Rabbah 9, *Wayelek*.
22 The Hebrew *natan be-libbam* literally means "it gave, it instilled in their hearts," semantically underscoring the aspect of the divine initiative rather than inspiration in the mantic sense of divine possession; on this see my own study, *Eine Tora für den Konig Talmai*, 160

wells[23] was declared." According to the version in the Tosefta, the "condemnation of the nations" results from their failing to recognise the value of the gift they received, rejecting the Torah as they did. This condemnation was declared the moment the Torah was inscribed on the stones in seventy languages. In that moment, the condemnation of the nations of the world into the deep wells of the Law. A law is, in fact, valid from the moment it is published. A law's publication comes in multiple languages when it contains a universal message, one for all the world's inhabitants and one for all the provinces of a realm "to the satraps of the king and the governors of all the provinces according to their modes of writing and to all the people of their language," as it is put in Esther 3:12.

The principle of divine election is therefore not a belief in an arbitrary decision, but something decided by a group's awareness of the awesome gift represented by the bestowal of the Torah on Sinai. The very constitution of the people of Israel is in this way based on the principle not only of God's gift but also its acceptance on the part of the Jews.

The cultural horizon changes diametrically when the "nations of the world" begin to consider themselves the rightful owners of the Torah, which—from the rabbinical viewpoint—is a question about the formative elements of the concept of the "true Israel" defined in relation to the gift of the two Torot. Two traditions were passed down, ones that differ notably, however, with regard to the mode in which the nations—the Gentiles—went about appropriating the Torah. The traditions converge substantially on one basic point: that which distinguishes Israel is not the possession of the sacred books so much as the possession of the oral tradition. The first tradition focuses on the political aspect, contending that "the nations of the world" would subjugate Israel and would take the Torah; the second tradition addresses pagan proselytism in more cognitive and liturgical terms. The *Midrash Tanḥuma* (version B), *kī tissa* § 17,[24] reports the following tradition:

> After Moses had learned it [the Torah], the Most Holy, blessed be he, said to him: "Go and teach it to my son." Moses responded: "I could have given it [the oral Torah] also in writing if, it is manifest that the nations of the world will subjugate [the Jews] and steal it [the written Torah] from them, and [in this case] my son would become like the nations of the world. The Bible gift it in writing, whereas the Mishnah, the Haggadah, and the Talmud render it unto them orally."
>
> And God said to Moses: "Write it for yourself [*ktav lekha*],[25] that is, the Bible, since the mouth [*ki 'al peh*],[26] that is, the Mishnah and the Talmud, is what constitutes the difference between Israel and the nations of the world.

---

23 Psalms 55:24.
24 *Midrash Tanḥuma*, ed. Solomon Buber, 2 vol. (Vilnius: Romm, 1885), 58b–59a.
25 Exodus 34:27.
26 Ibid.

Although the sense of this passage is clear in context, insofar as it defends the orality of the Mishnah's transmission, when it is analysed in greater detail certain interpretive difficulties arise. Indeed, the subject of the request here is not clear. In the parallel tradition, which we will examine later, a similar phrase is attributed to God, who, as in the passage above, speaks of "my son."[27] The expression "the *miqra'* [the written Hebrew Bible] gift it in writing" suggests that Moses is the subject, even if the subject might also be God, as it seems to me it must ultimately be understood (following the translation used here). The sentence "the nations of the world will subjugate [the Jews] and steal it [the written Torah] from them" could refer to the written Torah, and in this case would allude to the seizure of the Torah like a victor's trophy; or it could refer to the oral Torah, for which case we might offer a hypothetical construction: "If I gave the Mishnah in writing, it could be taken from them by the nations of the world."

Regardless of these exegetical problems, the structure and the significance of the Midrash underscore that the feature most fundamental to Israel's identity is its oral tradition. The elements that contribute to the formation of this rabbinical exegesis do not have a significance in and of themselves, but are only structural necessities. Notice in this passage that there is no mention of the Torah's appropriation by the "nations of the world," nor of theft or political dominion. The parallel tradition is elaborated differently. In *Pesikta Rabbati* § 5 (Friedmann 14b):[28]

> R. Yehudah, pupil of R. Shalom, said:
> Moses prayed [that God] would deliver the Mishnah in writing.
> The Most Holy, blessed be he, foretold of a day when the nations would translate the Torah and would have it recited in Greek and for this would proclaim "They [the Jews] are not Israel."
> The Most Holy, blessed be he, said to him: "Oh Moses! One day the peoples will say, 'We are the sons of God.' Israel will respond, 'We are the sons of God!' This will hold the scales in balance!"
> The Most Holy, blessed be he, said to the nations: "Why do you say that you are my sons? Only I know that it is my son who possesses my secrets." The nations responded: "What are your secrets?" He said unto them: "They are the Mishnah."

The central question of the Midrash is the orality of the Mishnah in its relation to the written Torah. The Mishnah is the foundation of Israel's distinct identity amidst the nations of the world.[29] Beyond this fact, it is difficult to extract from the Midrash anything more precise regarding the historical circumstances of its generation. In all cases, it is problematic to cite such passages, as one so often does, as mere docu-

---

27 On this name see *Mishnah Avot* 3:14; *Aggadah Bereshit* (cf. Solomon Buber, 2 vol. (Vilnius: Romm, 1925), chapter 12 on Psalm 27:1); Juda Bergmann, *Jüdische Apologetik im neutestamentlichen Zeitalter*, 143.
28 See also *Midrash Tanḥuma wa-yera* §5 (26), *Tanḥuma wa-yera* (44b) and *Tanḥuma ki tissa* 34 (127).
29 Peter Schäfer, *Studien zur Geschichte und Theologie des rabbinischen Judentums* (Leiden: Brill, 1978), 173–178.

mentation of the controversial arguments for and against the Torah's translation into Greek, or as proof of a direct conflict between Judaism and Christianity stemming from the Torah's unacknowledged appropriation.³⁰

More problematic still is identifying in this passage a rabbinic condemnation of the translation of the Bible into Greek.³¹ I have worked elsewhere³² to demonstrate how rabbinical Judaism's position regarding the Greek Bible is largely positive. Even in this passage, there is no trace of denunciation of the Torah's appropriation. The fact that the nations of the world translated and recited the Torah in Greek is representative of the element of the text that unites Jews and non-Jews. This expression—"they translated the Torah and recited it"—is a liturgical one, where *liqro'* indicates the typical rabbinical mode of recitation and *le-targem* signifies the oral translation of the Torah in the synagogue.³³ On the other hand, the rabbis knew quite well that the Torah was not translated by the "nations of the world" themselves, but by Jewish masters and sages, as is attested to in the introductory rabbinical formula used to cite the 72 scholars: "Our Rabbis [or: "our Sages," ḥakhamim] wrote [the following verse] for King Ptolemy." According to the rabbinic terminology, therefore, the passage above is *not* making reference to the 72 scholars' Greek translation.

The rabbis, furthermore, do not contest the fact that the nations read the written Torah. The Jews' identity as the *verus Israel*—a claim based on the possession of the Torah—is not questioned: the balance of the scales is maintained. The most important point, for the rabbis, is that the possession of the written Torah is inadequate evidence for a claim to identification as the true Israel ("my son"). The status of Israel is based on the oral Torah, transmitted by God on Sinai and conserved orally in the

---

30 George F. Moore, *Judaism in the First Centuries of the Christian Era*, vol. 2 (Cambridge: Harvard University Press, 1927), 68, note 6; Dominique Barthélemy, "L'Ancien Testament a mûri à Alexandrie," *Theologische Zeitschrift* 21 (1965): 364–365; Idem, *Études d'histoire du texte de l'Ancien Testament*, *Éditions universitaires* (Göttingen and Fribourg: Vandenhoeck and Ruprecht, 1978), 133–134; see also Juda Bergmann, *Jüdische Apologetik*, 61; Ephraim E. Urbach, "Halakha we-nevu'a," *Tarbiz* 18 (1946–1947): 1–27, 6–7, note 50; Juda Bergmann, *The Sages. Their Concepts and Beliefs* (Jerusalem: The Hebrew University Magnes Press, 1979), 305–6; Marcel Simon, *Verus Israel. Ètude sur les relations entre Chrétiens et Juifs dans l'empire romain (135–425)*, (Paris: Boccard, 1964), 225; Leo Baeck, "Haggadah and Christian Doctrine," *Hebrew Union College Annual* 23/1, (1950–1951): 557–558; Marcel Simon, "La Bible dans les premières controverses entre Juifs et Chrétiens," in *Le monde grec ancien et la Bible*, ed. Claude Mondésert (Paris: Beauchesne, 1985), 111; Johann Maier, *Jüdische Auseinandersetzung mit dem Christentum in der Antike* (Darmstadt: Buchgesellschaft, 1982), 184–185.
31 Cf. Nicholas de Lange, *Origen and the Jews. Studies in Jewish-Christian Relations in Third-Century Palestine* (Cambridge: Cambridge University Press, 1976), 50.
32 Giuseppe Veltri, *Eine Tora für den Konig Talmai*.
33 See Mishnah, *Megillah* 4.

rabbinical school. It is based, in other words, on a more profound sense of the Torah and its mysteries.[34]

This last point indicates the decisive element of the discussion. The oral tradition represents a point of distinction, a sign that cannot be understood in its totality. The ascription of a privileged access to wisdom is certainly a hermeneutical matter, insofar as it is part of an effort to establish an interpretation of the written Torah (its inner teachings). The Torah itself, however, bases the essence and the status of the people of Israel on criteria that elude simple cognition and understanding. In affirming that the possession of the oral Torah constitutes the "mysteries" of God, rabbinical Judaism signals a decisive step in the esoteric conception of wisdom: wisdom as a form of knowing that is mystically revealed and passed down.

2.5 The Transmission of Wisdom

Let us recall, in concluding this section, that claims to esotericism found in several Platonic doctrines were born out of an effort to valorise certain Eastern cultures, which, in the eyes of the Greeks, had been obscured by temporal distance and the veils of mystery. Rabbinical Judaism returns continually to the same categories to affirm that wisdom, the existential ground of the *verus Israel*, transcends knowledge: it cannot be attained independently per se, but through the mystery of tradition. In this way, we arrive at the threshold of the Middle Ages, the first conceptual attempts to form a doctrine of the *Torah Nistarah*, the secret Torah whose concealed lessons are not the domain of all people, but must be reached esoterically. In this sense, the claims of Greek plagiarism and the idea of the *verus Israel* are notions that presuppose the same conceptualisation: that true *sophia* can only be reached hermeneutically, by means of tradition. The principle of scripture is a particular one because it entails both the dissemination of the text and its protection from alterations. This applies especially to the religious and legal texts of a community eager to continually adapt the tradition in the light of scriptural paradigm shifts. Yet, changes to the transmitted text would only be possible if the text remained oral. Hence, in the case of written records, only the hermeneutic tools can smooth out odd, old-fashioned, antiquated passages of the traditional text.

Like the writing of a "sacred" text, hermeneutics itself can represent the discordant motifs that arise between different schools of thought, differences of both practical and legal gravity. The discussions between Christians themselves, in their multifaceted communities, and between Christian and Jews (starting in the third century) arise and become contentious typically around questions of texts, translations, and

---

[34] See Talmud Yershalmi, *Pe'a* 2.6 (17a/43–50) and Talmud Yerushalmi, *Ḥagiga* 1.8 (76d/17–24), 94. Cf. Gerd A. Wewers, *Geheimnis und Geheimhaltung im rabbinischen Judentum* (Berlin: De Gruyter, 1975), 87–90.

interpretive variations. When hermeneutics elevates itself to the level of tradition, its official status is legitimised in writing. In Judaism, this second proposition is not accepted without contention. The treasure of tradition, according to a broadly resonant Jewish attitude, is not a textual corpus but rather a method of continual study. In this sense, to fix a single element as stable, predetermined, and universally recognised forsakes the very processes that provided the basis of tradition. It is perhaps because of this that even up to the ninth century C.E., the time of Sherira Ga'on, there was still an effort to establish the definitive history of the oral Torah's inscription in written form, the Torah's definitive form being neither clear nor secure (another topic altogether).[35]

An element that must be underscored in this chapter is the growth of esotericism in the study of Jewish identity, the *proprium* that constitutes the tradition of Judaism. At first there were challenges to the claims of the written Torah's theft and plagiarism, thanks largely to the diffusion of the Greek version, making it common domain and therefore not particular to or characteristic of the Jews. Rabbinical Judaism seeks refuge in the mystery of the oral Torah, something distinctive of the *verus Israel*. It will be this element that becomes the ground of the medieval and modern conversation between Jewish intellectuals who lament the loss of their own intellectual and scientific identity, a loss that occurred precisely because of renewed attempts at appropriation on the part of foreign nations.

---

[35] Cf. Giuseppe Veltri, "Über die Anwendung christlicher Terminologie auf die rabbinische Tradition: Einige Anmerkungen zum Fall Suksession", in *Sukzession in Religionen. Autorisierung, Legitimierung, Wissenstransfer*, ed. Almut-Barbara Renger, Markus Witte (Berlin: De Gruyter, 2017), 221–230.

3 Between "Theft" and Genealogy of Knowledge: The Middle Ages

The tradition of the "theft" of ancient wisdom extends itself also into medieval philosophy. Certain tendencies surrounding this tradition developed in Arab philosophy, which through its own *translatio sapientiae* justified the study of Greek philosophy that rests at the heart of both Jewish and Arabic thought. In this way, the doctrine of the "theft" becomes, apologetically, a reappropriation of what had been taken *ab antiquo*.

The philosopher, Moses Maimonides, known by the acronym RaMBaM (Rabbi Moshe ben Maimon), immersed himself in this deep-rooted tradition, enriching it with other elements. In the seventy-first chapter of the first part of the *Moreh Nevukhim* (*The Guide for the Perplexed*), he makes reference to the Talmud, according to which "That which God has communicated to you orally, you are not permitted to put into writing."[1] According to Maimonides, this Talmudic passage alludes to metaphysical instruction, i.e. the esoteric element contained in the oral Torah. His comment is, therefore, pertinent: metaphysical instruction is conceded only to the elect few, following the Talmudic principle that "[t]he secrets of the Torah must be transmitted only to the prudent and the wise,"[2] and then that "[...] our nation lost its awareness of these important disciplines. All that remained were allusions enclosed in the Talmud and the Midrashim."[3]

In the eleventh chapter of the second part of *The Guide*, Maimonides affirms that biblical and rabbinical instruction are in perfect harmony with the sciences, seeing as how "our people is a knowing people." How do we explain, though, how the sciences, among which philosophy was queen, did not have Jewish followers? Maimonides attributes the decline of Jewish wisdom to the "barbarians" (*jāhiliyya*):

> We have already explained that all these views do not contradict anything said by our prophets and the sustainers of our Law. For our community is a community that is full of knowledge and is perfect, as He, may He be exalted, has made clear through the intermediary of the Master who made us perfect, saying: "Surely, this great community is a wise and understanding people" (Deuteronomy 4:6). However, when the wicked from among the ignorant communities ruined our good qualities, destroyed our words of wisdom and our compilations, and caused our men of knowledge to perish, so that we again became ignorant, as we had been threatened because of our sins—for it says: "And the wisdom of their wise men shall perish, and the understanding of their prudent men shall be hid" (Isaiah 29:14); when, furthermore, we mingled with these communities and their opinions were taken over by us, as were their morals and actions—for just as it says regarding the similarity of actions: They mingled themselves with the communities and learned their works, it says with regard to the adoption by us of the opinions of the ignorant: And they please themselves in the children of strangers, which is translated by Jona-

---

1 Babylonian Talmud, *Gittin*, 60b.
2 Babylonian Talmud, *Hagiga*, 13a.
3 My translation of the Hebrew text.

than ben Uziel, peace be on him: And they walk according to the laws of the gentiles; when, in consequence of all this, we grew up accustomed to the opinions of the ignorant, these philosophic views appeared to be, as it were, foreign to our Law, just as they are foreign to the opinions of the ignorant. However, matters are not like this.[4]

The absence of the sciences from the Jewish world of his epoch was, according to Maimonides, attributable to the annihilation of so many of its members. That is, the annihilation of the Jews themselves, a tragic history that would deliver into ignorance the very people who were the intended beneficiaries of the sciences. Two elements here must be underscored: that Judaism did indeed experience an epoch of scientific development destined for them alone (philosophical and scientific esotericism) and that this period was ended by the eradication of its sages and the influence of "the ignorant nations" (*jāhiliyya*).

That the Sephardic master makes reference to the esoteric character of philosophy and the sciences is not itself unusual. Aristotle had already made reference to his own doctrine as a science reserved to a restricted circle. Yet, in referring to wisdom and the nations of the world, he changes important details: Maimonides does *not* say that Jewish wisdom was usurped or stolen. It is of interest that he uses the Arabic term *jāhiliyya* to designate the ignorant nations who subjugated the Jews.[5] The Muslims used this term for the pre-Islamic ignorant pagans.[6]

What was new in Maimonides's account, however, was the "homicide" of the Jewish sages perpetrated by the nations of the world. The Egyptian rabbis likely made reference to the raiding and looting of synagogues (as well as Christian abbeys) and communities, and in this same context there are clear, albeit symbolic references to the destruction of the temple, where according to Jewish and Christian tradition the Torah and other texts were conserved. According to rabbinical tradition, it was this destruction that constituted the end of prophecy.[7] Maimonides uses the same image to explain the link that relates the "loss" of the sciences within Jewish circles and the prohibition of Jews from studying "Greek wisdom." The expression "Greek

---

[4] Moses Maimonides, *The Guide for the Perplexed*, transl. Shlomo Pines, Chicago: University of Chicago Press, Chicago 1963, 1,71, 175: "Know that the many sciences devoted to establishing the truth regarding these matters that have existed in our religious community have perished because of the length of the time that has passed, because of our being dominated by the pagan nations, and because, as we have made clear, it is not permitted to divulge these matters to all people."
[5] William E. Shepard, "Sayyid Qutb's Doctrine of Jāhiliyya," *International Journal of Middle East Studies* 35, no. 4 (2003): 521–545. According to Shepard, the term in the Qur'an indicates "barbarians." It may be a reference to the polytheists as well as the opponents of Islam (Shepard, 522). Also see Qur'an 48:26.
[6] My gratitude to Warren Zev Harvey who contributed to this paragraph.
[7] Babylonian Talmud, *Baba Batra* 12b.

wisdom," imprecise though it may seem, denotes both the *epistēmē* and *technē* of philosophy and science.[8]

Aside from apologetics—which are unquestionably present in Maimonides and appear in Jewish literature especially when the neglect of historical or intellectual essentials becomes too prevalent—the reader will wonder how Judaism was able, in the end, to avoid becoming entirely appropriated by the Greek culture that in turn became a heritage of all peoples of the Mediterranean world. In explaining how this was avoided we would need to specify that the Jewish community of Late Antiquity—the Rabbinic-Talmudic period to which Maimonides refers—did not directly contribute to the establishment of the contemporary philosophical panorama, as the Alexandrine Jews did between the third and first centuries B.C.E. The reasons for this are many and varying. Importantly, the loss of political and cultural autonomy after the destruction of the temple led to a great weakening of cultural centres: there were no longer the means to acquire books, nor probably the possibility of re-writing or copying them. This is a plain consequence of endemic societal poverty at the time. To combat these problems and to preserve their cultural autonomy, the rabbis permitted some classes to learn Greek and Hellenic culture, thereby cultivating contact with first the Roman and then the Byzantine Empires.

All this does not mean, however, that the rabbinical and popular epoch was otherwise isolated from the culture of Late Antiquity. Greek influxes pervaded every aspect of the knowable in this period, from the architectural arts to the maritime, popular medicine to agricultural techniques, visual art to music, technology to written cultures. Even the spheres of leisure and recreation became infused with Greco-Roman culture. Thermal baths and stadium games were frequented by Jews, Roman soldiers, and Christians alike, with and without the approval of the rabbinical class or the episcopacy.

One thing that the Greek influx did not change, however, was Jewish philosophical thought. We can advance only a few hypotheses to explain this lack of effect. The available sources on this question are only in Hebrew and Aramaic while the official language and *lingua franca* of the epoch's schools and academies was Greek. Even if the Jews had contributed to the debates of the time, there would still be no traditional means for their texts to be passed down. Let us remember that the legacy of Alexandrine Judaism was preserved by the Fathers of the Church for reasons of theological consequence. Disinterest in this question in rabbinical circles can be explained either due to scepticism concerning the Greek language or to the absence of a culture of textual transmission within the Jewish community. Every community is the carrier

---

[8] *Mishnah*, Soṭa 9.14, cf. Saul Lieberman, *Hellenism in Jewish Palestine. Studies in the Literary Transmission, Beliefs and Manners of Palestine in the I Century BCE–IV Century CE* (New York: Jewish Theological Seminary of America, 1962), 100–114; Giuseppe Veltri, *A Mirror of Rabbinic Hermeneutics. Studies in Religion, Magic and Language Theory in Ancient Judaism* (Berlin: W. De Gruyter, 2015), 99–114.

of a literary legacy, but in the case of the Greek-speaking Jews this does not seem to be the case.

A further element helps to explain the lack of open philosophical discussion: the situation (between the first and the sixth centuries C.E.) of the schools and the philosophical academies, did little to cultivate classical philosophy and, rather, sought refuge in other forms that we might describe as more sceptical. In the Roman Empire the centres of philosophical interest were numerous, and for the most part of a Stoic or Epicurean orientation.[9] It is no surprise that Stoicism and Epicureanism can be found in rabbinical sources (although almost always with negative connotations) and that the most prevalent school of thought was that of the sceptics.[10]

But if the encounter with classical philosophy did not involve rabbinical Judaism in Late Antiquity, it became, by contrast, a fixed point in the medieval schools. The study of philosophy became a rite of passage for the reacquisition of that lost wisdom, known and esteemed, from the matrix of Judaism.

The same sort of argument is found, *mutatis mutandis*, in the Islamic world, where philosophical study is grounded expressly in this element of classical influence. Muslim scholars from Muhammad al-Shahrastānī (twelfth century) to Quṭb ad-Dīn Maḥmūd ibn Masʿūd aš-Šīrāzī (seventeenth century) underscore how in the Islamic world Greek learning was acquired from the "cave of the lights of prophecy."[11] Even if this assertion were deemed ahistorical, or simply a fiction based on apologetic premises, the fact would remain that philosophical study, like science, subsequently functioned as a bridge between Christianity (in its Alexandrine version), Judaism, and Islam, a fact that became a common refrain in the period of Renaissance Humanism. The foundation of this *topos* of classical influence—the columns that hold up this construction—are the principle of the chain of tradition (the principle of historical plausibility), the rejection of Aristotelian instruction (the polemic-philosophical principle), and the notion of harmony (believed in, desired, sought after) between biblical instruction and non-Jewish wisdom (theological argument). Let us examine some of the sources of these principles.

In his famous *Sefer ha-Kuzari*, the philosopher Judah Halevi describes his version (1.63) of the genealogy of science and knowledge, and how the latter emerged from Greece and then travelled widely.

---

9 In saying this it is not my intention to deny the diffusion of the Platonic schools and, for certain reasons, the Aristotelian schools, especially in the Christian theological academies after the third century. My aim is only to highlight that philosophical study had acquired certain characteristics linked specifically to groups in the classical Greek world. Moreover, the Greco-Roman world between the first and sixth centuries was largely guided by Neoplatonism in its broad diffusion, neither purely Platonic nor of a purely Aristotelian orientation. For the most part stoicism reigned and scepticism was affirmed by the writings of Cicero and Sextus Empiricus and the intensely personal critique of Augustine.
10 On this aspect, see the third part of this book.
11 Henry Corbin, *History of Islamic Philosophy* (London: Kegan Paul International, 1993), XV.

> [...] the Greeks did not inherit science, nor the Torah. They are Greeks and Greece makes up part of the descendants of Japheth, inhabitants of the North. Science is an Adamic inheritance, reinforced by the divine energy and found only among the progeny of Shem, who represents the unicity of Noah's successors. This did not cease and it will not cease from the lineage of Adam. The Greeks did not possess the sciences until they had taken political power and translated the divine wisdom of Persia that they received from the Chaldeans. The famous [Greek] philosophers made their appearance [in history] not before this period. But once political command turned back to the hands of the Romans, they did not produce philosophers worthy of the name.[12]

Certain differences emerge with regards to this traditional partitioning of knowledge in the *Sefer ha-Kuzari* (which I read in Ibn Tibbon's Hebrew text): the sciences and the Torah are cast as two distinct elements resembling, in principle, *epistēmē* and *technē*. The claimed absence of wisdom among the Greeks is explained by geographic realities, with their descendants having lived in the north while Adam lived in the south. Another essential hinge is philosophy's link to centres of political power: once Rome became the maker of fortunes, philosophy ceased to reside in the tents of Japheth. Judah Halevi provides a typical example of the plausibility of a genealogy of wisdom and science that did not remain with the Greeks but only resided with them as long as their power lasted before passing on to the Romans

One defender of the genealogy of knowledge is Shem-Tov ibn Falaquera,[13] who in his *Sefer ha-Ma'alot*[14] reports on a tradition that claimed its origins in Shem, Eber, and Abraham, which would make them the sources of Greek philosophy. According to Falaquera, the genealogical chain was grounded in a concept of diligent translation of the scientific and philosophical books of other peoples in their languages, as Halevi had already contended. Thus it was, also, with the Greeks. Falaquera cites as an example King Ptolemy, who tasked the priests of the temple of Jerusalem with the translation of the "Wisdom of the Jews" (the Torah) in Greek.

It is certainly not a novelty that recourse is made to the legend of the 72, which from the already mentioned Letter of Aristeas onwards was broadly popular among Jews, Christians, and Muslims. This legend is at base an apologetic response to Greek culture's rule over its subjugated peoples. What's unusual is Falaquera's use of this particular episode, where king Talmai ("Ptolemy" in Hebrew) acts as protagonist to justify the practice of translation in the Middle Ages. The Jews had permission, even the obligation, to translate works of philosophy because philosophy belonged to them and was then copied and plagiarised by the Greeks. According to the logic

---

12 Cf. *Sefer ha-Kuzari: Das Buch Kusari des Jehuda ha-Levi*, ed. David David (Leipzig: F. Voigt, 1869).
13 On his work cf. Colette Sirat, *A History of Jewish Philosophy in the Middle Age* (Cambridge: Cambridge University Press, 1985), 234–238; cf. Mauro Zonta, *La filosofia antica nel Medioevo ebraico* (Brescia: Paideia, 1996), 204–212, and 219–220.
14 See Shem-Tov ibn Falaquera, *Sefer ha-Ma'alot*, ed. Ludwig Venetianer (Berlin: Verlag von S. Calvary &. Co., 1894), 12.; See the bibliography on Falaquera in Steven Harvey, "Shem Tov Ibn Falaquera," *The Stanford Encyclopedia of Philosophy*.

of *The Guide for the Perplexed*, Falaquera affirms in his *Iggeret ha-Wikuaḥ* (*Letter on the Dispute between a Ḥasid and a Ḥakham*)[15] that the philosophical and scientific books of the Jews were destroyed, therefore creating the need to read the subsequent copies found in the works of non-Jews.

The theoretical premises of these literary associations, which for a student of our times would be considered pure antihistorical apologetics, should be evaluated in the context of the ancient and medieval desire to establish a genealogical harmony between secular wisdom and Jewish wisdom, one in which the latter must by necessity take precedence. This is the same method employed in a book of medicine, the so-called *Sefer Asaf*, a work of the early Middle Ages. In this book it is hypothesised that Shem, son of Noah, wrote a book of medicine that was the source of knowledge for Greek physicians, and thus was translated into their language.[16] The same line of logic is followed in the *Sefer Yareaḥ* (ca. 1305) by Abba Mari ben Moses ben Joseph, a Provencal rabbi born in Lunel, according to whom the Greeks had stolen the science of the Jews.[17]

The genealogical principle of scientific knowledge is to be qualified as anti-Aristotelian because it is grounded in a heteronomous principle that does not satisfy common criteria for scientific proof or even for logical inference. At the beginning of the thirteenth century, Rabbi Menaḥem Recanati passed on a legend of the consonance of philosophy in more ancient times, a harmony shattered by the arrival of Aristotle. Dissonances with the Torah thus become attributable to Aristotle and his "evil disciples," who made substantial alterations to it, before "[...] the masters of the Kabbalah revealed [his] illusions (*aḥizat 'enayim*)."[18] Very close to this position was the Renaissance philosopher Leone Ebreo,[19] who asserted that Plato was fundamentally influenced by the Mosaic revelation and that his disciple Aristotle simply did not understand his master's teachings.[20]

---

15 Shem-Tov ibn Falaquera, *Iggeret ha-wikuaḥ: Dialog zwischen einem Orthodoxen und einem Philosophen*, ed. Adolf Jellinek (Vienna, 1875: reprinted in Jerusalem, 1970), 14; cf. Steven Harvey, *Falaquera's Epistle of the Debate: An Introduction to Jewish Philosophy* (Cambridge: Harvard University Press, 1987).
16 Ludwig Venetianer, *Asaf Judaeus. Der älteste medizinische Schriftsteller in hebräischer Sprache*, (Strasbourg: Karl J. Trübner, 1916–1917), part one, 6–8; cf. Moshe Idel, "The Journey to Paradise: The Jewish Transformation of a Greek Mythological Motiv" [Hebrew], *Jerusalem Studies in Jewish Folklore* 2 (1982): 7–17.
17 *Sefer Yareaḥ*, 6; Abba Mari of Lunel, *Sefer Minḥat Qena'ot* (Pressburg: A. von Schmid, 1838), 126; Norman Roth, "The 'Theft of Philosophy' by the Greeks from the Jews," *Classical Folia* 32 (1978): 53–67.
18 *Perush 'al ha-Torah* (Venice: Bomberg, 1523; reprinted in Jerusalem, 1961), fol. 15a; cf. Moshe Idel, "Jewish Kabbalah and Platonism in the Middle Ages and Renaissance," in *Neoplatonism and Jewish Thought*, ed. Lenn E. Goodman (Albany: SUNY Press, 1992), 321.
19 See Julius Guttman, *Philosophie des Judentums* (Munich: Reinhardt-Verlag, 1933), 271.
20 Leone Ebreo, *Dialoghi d'amore: Hebräische Gedichte*, ed. C. Gebhardt (Heidelberg: Curis Societatis Spinozanae, 1929), Dialogue III, fol. 125b: "Come ch'io sia mosaico ne la Theologale sapientia m'abbraccio con questa seconda via, però che è veramente Theologia Mosaica, e Platone

In the first half of the fifteenth century, Azaria de' Rossi emerged as the most prominent mouthpiece of this tradition. He makes reference to Greek philosophy's dependence on Jewish philosophy, a dependence penetrating down to its deepest roots. In his work, the *Me'or 'Enayim*, he posits the creation of the perceptible world, as it is presented by Philo of Alexandria, as a Kabbalistic emanation,[21] constructing a bridge between the world of Plato and that of the Middle Ages and the Renaissance. Carrying on in this vein over the course of the work, the author reveals a certain interest in the figure of Marsilio Ficino, designated as "the great Christian sage,"[22] but also an interest in the works of Symphorien Champier,[23] the French mediator of Ficino's Platonism.[24]

These learned men believed in the concept of a true and proper continuity within the esoteric traditions, the foundation of which was to be identified in the Mosaic Torah and then transmitted as an emanation from Hermes Trismegistus through the mediation of Plato and Philo of Alexandria until reaching the Kabbalists.[25] For Azaria, there is nothing unorthodox; he synthesises all:

> The abstract idea of God, divided in our limited awareness [of the divinity], possesses in truth the principle of unicity. For this reason is it perhaps not simply a problem of terminology when one speaks of "Son," "Emanation," "Light," "Sephirot" or "Idea" as Plato calls it? Galen states, in a few passages in his writings, that we do not perceive the difference between individuals by means of their names.[26]

It is plausible that Azaria had also read Nicolas of Cusa's theory of names according to which the letters of the name of God change but the content of the named thing remains invariable.[27] Nicolas of Cusa reports the opinion of (some) Jews who interpreted the doctrine of the Trinity as a triad of divine attributes (*quae in eorum libris exprimitur tres proprietates intelligi debere*). These properties, according to Azaria, would be considered *kinnuyim* (attributes).[28] For Azaria, the *Prisca Theologia* could

---

come quel che maggior notitia haveva di questa antica sapientia che Aristotile la seguito."
21 See my "The Humanist Sense of History and the Jewish Idea of Tradition."
22 Azaria de' Rossi, *Sefer Me'or 'Enayim*, 100, ed. David Cassel (Vilnus: Romm, 1884–1886).
23 Cf. Symphorian Champier, *Symphoriani Champerii De quadruplici vita. Theologia Asclepii, Hermetis Trismegisti discipuli cum commentariis eiusdem domini Simphoriani*, Lugdunum, 1507 (Berlin: Staatsbibliothek Berlin, Ai 951); Symphorian Champier, *Simphoriani Champerii De Triplici disciplina, cuius partes sunt: philosophia naturalis, medicina, theologia, moralis philosophia integrantes quadruvium*, Lugdunum, 1507 (Berlin: Staatsbibliothek Berlin, Ai 953).
24 Cf. Daniel R. Walker, *Ancient Theology: Studies in Christian Platonism from the Fifteenth to the Eighteenth Century* (London: Duckworth, 1972), 64ff.
25 Brian P. Copenhaver, "Lefèvre d'Etaples, Symphorien Champier, and the Secret Names of God," *Journal of the Warburg and Courtauld Studies* 40 (1977): 189–211.
26 Azaria de' Rossi, *Sefer Me'or 'Enayim*, 100.
27 Wolf P. Klein, *Am Anfang war das Wort* (Berlin: Akademie-Verlag, 1992), 36.
28 *Excitationes* I: "Verum Judaei volentes trinitatem evadere dicunt per trinitatem, quae in eorum libris exprimitur tres proprietates intelligi debere, scilicet divinam sapientiam, bonitatem et potentiam,

be retained as a Jewish concept, and it was thus possible to use Christian terminology to explain Jewish philosophy. In this Azaria exudes the Renaissance spirit of a Pico della Mirandola or a Ficino, who saw the advent of Trinitarian doctrine (*vestigia trinitatis*) in Plotinus.

Historiosophic research was at base modelled on a hermeneutic that excluded logic and historical proof. It passed on that tendency in its understanding of human perception and knowledge. Later centuries, however, would abolish the aforementioned genealogy of knowledge and wisdom, replacing it with a scientific conception that posits phenomenology as the sole point of reference for its epistemology. The problem of sources and their critical examination by the prudent reader—he who knows how to distinguish the false from the authentic, the plagiarised from the true—is an ancient debate that is renewed in the Renaissance, there constituting the beginnings of modern criticism.

---

per quas proprietates dicunt creata. Et hoc Nicolaus de Lira destruit in libello quodam contra Judaeos pluribus ostendens auctoritatibus veteris testamenti trinitatem. Ego etiam aliquando disputando deprehendi sapientes Judaeos ad credendam trinitatem inducibiles, et hoc non est eis difficile persuadere. Sed quod filius in divinis sit incarnatus, hoc est, in quo sunt indurati, nec rationes nec prophetas audire volunt." Cited from Jacob Guttmann, *Die Scholastik des dreizehnten Jahrhunderts in ihren Beziehungen zum Judenthum und zur jüdischen Literatur* (Breslau: Marcus, 1902), 170, footnote 1.

4 Primordial Wisdom and Historical Consciousness

The debates surrounding the topic of primordial wisdom—the *alpha* and *omega* of all human knowledge—were not settled by the duelling claims of propriety. It was the Renaissance that brought about an interesting admixture of Judaism and Christianity, just at the moment when the Protestant world inaugurated its tendency to devalue the Hebrew Bible and its claims to eternal wisdom, to which we will turn in this next chapter. This was not the only important factor in the historicisation of wisdom, however. In the humanist period and the Renaissance another problematic process began, one historicising ancient Jewish wisdom in order to accomplish its negation: namely the Christian appropriation of the Kabbalistic traditions, arguing for their origins in an ancient Adamic genealogy, transmitted by Abraham during his time in Chaldea.

The following section will delineate the way in which the first traces of this practice evolved in the historical consciousness of the Renaissance by following certain figures who played decisive roles in the history of Jewish thought. The Renaissance's adoption of methods of historical analysis—the first inroads that will lead to a routine analysis of textual sources—came about from an interest in the restoration of the past and an awareness, more or less conscious, of a certain ascendancy of the *iuniores*, the recent scholars, over the *antiqui*, the old wise men. The *querelle des anciens et des modernes*, which began before the Renaissance, is the turning-point that will lead to a new epistemology of the rationalist and sceptical critique of the sources of knowledge.

4.1 Arcane Wisdom in a Bookshop

In 1548 or 1549, the Jewish doctor Amatus Lusitanus[1] and an unnamed friend met in a bookshop in Mantua and chanced upon *De arcanis catholicae veritatis contra obstinatissimam Judaeorum nostrae tempestatis perfidiam*,[2] a polemic by Pietro Galatino, published in 1518 by Gershom Soncino. While the two friends admired the elegance of the work and the erudition of its author, Azariah de' Rossi arrived, who Lusitanus introduced to his friend as an expert of Hebrew and Latin. Lusitanus describes the encounter thus: "Azariah de' Rossi took part in our conversation and made known in particular his opinion on the Jesuits, who in the work come to the

---

[1] Harry Friedenwald, "Two Jewish Physicians of the Sixteenth Century. The Doctor, Amatus Lusitanus, the Patient, Azariah dei Rossi," in *The Jews and Medicine. Essays*, ed. H. Friedenwald, vol. 2 (Baltimore: Johns Hopkins Press, 1944), 393.

[2] Pietro Galatino, *Opus toti christianae Reipublicae maxime utile, de arcanis catholicae veritatis, contra obstinatissimam Iudaeoru[m] nostrae tempestatis p[er]fidiam: ex Talmud, aliisq[ue] hebraicis libris nuper excerptum: & quadruplici linguarum genere eleganter congestum* (Suncinus, Orthonae Maris, 1518).

defence of the famous Reuchlin, who in that moment found himself under arrest. The two Jesuits not only rejected the false accusations levelled against Reuchlin, but also hazarded to stand behind him." Let us clarify the historical inaccuracies of this short and curious report: in the year of the appearance of Galatino's book (1518), Reuchlin was neither in danger nor under arrest. Furthermore, Galatino was a Franciscan friar and Jacob van Hoogstraten a Dominican. Finally, Hoogstraten was not Reuchlin's defender, but his inquisitor. Galatino's book was directed towards an erudite public and discussed theological convictions and Jewish traditions that were circulating in the late fifteenth century into the sixteenth.

To present Galatino, Lusitanus, and Azariah de' Rossi as such is not meant to correct shortcomings of a minor episode of Jewish life, but to explain an aspect of the intellectual history of the Jews in the Renaissance and their *Weltanschauung*. They are—so to speak—figures that are symbolic of a world shifting from medieval systems of thought to modern epistemologies founded on history and sciences.

4.2 Galatino, Lusitanus, and Azariah de' Rossi

The book of the Apulian friar Pietro Galatino[3]—which had considerable success and was reprinted—is an apologetic defence of Reuchlin. Conceived as a dialogue between Galatino, Reuchlin, himself, and Jakob van Hoogstraten, it focuses on the principal points of the controversy regarding Reuchlin.[4] The polemical works of apologetic Christians were certainly not a novelty for the Jews, but the Jews did not read them unless expressly obliged to do so. Over the centuries the Christians had adopted new apologetic methods, perhaps noting that the old exegetical and moral invectives against the Jews were unsuccessful in converting them, or perhaps simply because the literary genre of the *Contra Iudaeos*, directed at a Christian public, sought new and coercive methods of diffusion in order to convert the Jews.[5] The

---

[3] On Galatino's text, see Benigno F. Perrone, "Pietro Colonna Galatino, O.F.M. (1465–1540). In un testo di Mariologia francescana condotto con metodo 'filologico-cabbalistico'," *Studi francescani* LXXX (1983): 127–164; François Secret, *Les Kabbalistes Chrétiens de la Renaissance* (Milan: Arché, 1985), 102–105; Sharon A. Leftley, "A Millenarian Thought in Renaissance Rome with special reference to Pietro Galatino (c. 1464–c. 1540) and Egidio da Viterbo (c. 1469–1532)" (PhD dissertation, University of Bristol, 1995).

[4] On the controversy surrounding Reuchlin, see J. H. Overfield, "A new look at the Reuchlin affair," *Studies in Medieval and Renaissance History* VIII (1971): 165–207; Marianne Awerbuch, "Über Juden und Judentum zwischen Humanismus und Reformation. Zum Verständnis der Motivation von Reuchlins Kampf für das jüdische Schrifttum," and Julius Schoeps, "Der Reuchlin-Pfefferkorn-Streit in der jüdischen Historiographie des 19. und 20. Jahrhunderts," in *Reuchlin und die Juden*, ed. Arno Herzig and Julius H. Schoeps (Sigmaringen: Jan Thorbecke, 1993), 189–200 and 203–212; Frank D. Smith, "The Reuchlin Controversy," *Journal of Progressive Judaism* 4 (1995): 77–88.

[5] Regarding this point see the literature on the public disputes, or *wikuḥim*, which begins with the disputes of Paris and Barcelona: Yitzhak Baer, "The Disputations of R. Yeḥiel and R. Moses ben

Jews were compelled to listen to sermons and take part, *volens nolens*, in public debates.

The situation regarding Galatino is different than that, *mutatis mutandis*, of Reuchlin. These two had not only advocated for Jewish literature but defended it against others within their own faith. Following Reuchlin's school and with the help of Raimund Martín's *Pugio fidei*, Galatino had come to the defence of Jewish authority. Galatino did not attack Jewish *stultitia*—the wilfulness with which the Jews persisted in their traditions. His primary interest was to appropriate the Jewish tradition for Christian ends. In his view, the Talmud and the Kabbalah are not a "secret Jewish science" (*scientia secreta iudaica*) but an argument *ex parte alterius* that lays the foundation for the truth of Christian revelation.[6] Galatino's text is certainly not inspired by an ideal of tolerance toward those of different religions—an ideal foreign to Renaissance culture—but rather a desire to appropriate the cultural patrimony of the Jewish tradition, a logical consequence of which is valuing it positively.

João Rodriguez de Castelo Branco,[7] known by the pseudonym Amatus Lusitanus, was a Marrano, the son of a Jewish family from Portugal forced to convert to Chris-

---

Naḥman" [Hebrew], *Tarbiz* 2 (1930–1931): 172–187; Judah M. Rosenthal, "The Talmud on Trial," *Jewish Quarterly Review* 47 (1956–1957): 58–76; and 145–169; Martin A. Cohen, "Reflections on the Text and Context of the Disputation of Barcelona," *Hebrew Union College Annual* 35 (1964): 157–192; Haim H. Ben-Sasson, "Jewish-Christian Disputation in the Setting of Humanism and Reformation in the German Empire," *Harvard Theological Revue* 59 (1966): 369–90; Robert Chazan, "The Barcelona 'Disputation' of 1263: Christian Missionizing and Jewish Response," *Speculum* 52 (1977): 824–842; *Idem*, "From Friar Paul to Friar Raymond: The Development of Innovative Missionizing Argumentation," *Harvard Theological Review* 76 (1983): 289–306; *Idem*, "The Condemnation of the Talmud Reconsidered (1239–1248)," *Proceedings of the American Academy of Jewish Research* 45 (1988): 11–30; *Idem*, "In the Wake of the Disputation," *Hebrew Union College Annual* LXI (1990): 185–201; *Idem, Barcelona and Beyond. The Disputation of 1263 and its Aftermath* (Berkeley: University of California Press, 1992); *Idem, Medieval Stereotypes and Modern Antisemitism* (Berkeley: University of California Press, 1997); Marvin Fox, "Nahmanides on the Status of Aggadot: Perspectives on the Disputation at Barcelona, 1263," *Journal of Jewish Studies* XL (1989): 95–109; Jeremy Cohen, *The Friars and the Jews. The Evolution of Medieval Anti-Judaism* (Ithaca: Cornell University Press, 1982; Haim Maccoby, ed., *Judaism on Trial. Jewish-Christian Disputations in the Middle Age. With a New Introduction* (Oxford: The Littman Library of Jewish Civilization, 1993); Ora Limor and Guy G. Stroumsa, ed., *Contra Iudaeos. Ancient and Medieval Polemics between Christians and Jews* (Tübingen: Mohr, 1995); Fausto Parente, "La Chiesa e il 'Talmud.' L'atteggiamento della Chiesa e del mondo cristiano nei confronti del 'Talmud' e degli altri scritti rabbinici, con particolare riguardo all'Italia tra XV e XVI secolo," in *Storia d'Italia. Gli Ebrei in Italia*, vol. 11: *Dall'alto Medioevo all'età dei ghetti*, ed. Corrado Vivanti (Turin: Einaudi, 1996), 521–643; Israel J. Yuval, *"Two Nations in your Womb." Perceptions of Jews and Christians* (Tel Aviv: Am Oved, 2001).

6 See the *Praefatio* in Pietro Galatino, *Petri Galatini opus de arcanis catholicae veritatis*, s.p. "Talmud ipsum, veluti in multis bonum, atque catholicae veritati ad conterendam durissimam Iudaeorum cervicem maxime proficuum, commodum ac necessarium summo studio tutari nititur."

7 On Amatus Lusitanus, see Aaron J. Feingold, *Three Jewish Physicians of the Renaissance: The Marriage of Science and Ethics* (New York: American Friends of Beth Hatefutsoth, 1994); Aaron J. Feingold, *The Marriage of Science and Ethics: Three Jewish Physicians of the Renaissance*, in *Jews and Medicine. Religion, Culture, Science: Based on the Exhibit at the Beth Hatefusoth*, ed. Natalia Berger

tianity. Lusitanus was one of the most famous doctors of his time: several important discoveries in anatomy are attributed to him. He was the author of various medical works, which reflect the cultural ties between Jews and Christians of the time.[8] His 1553 commentary on Dioscorides (*In Dioscoridis ennarationes*) garnered much praise but also provoked envy and criticism from the likes of Pietro Andrea Mattioli,[9] botanist and doctor at the court of Vienna, who accused Lusitanus of heresy. In the events that followed—resulting from Pope Paul IV's 1555 decree against the Marranos of Ancona, as well as the accusations levelled by Mattioli—Lusitanus's rich library was destroyed along with manuscripts of his own works. Lusitanus managed to escape, first living in Pesaro and then in the Republic of Ragusa (today Dubrovnič), where he lived for several years. In 1568 he died in Thessaloniki, having returned to the Jewish faith there. Lusitanus also authored an oath of professional conduct which he modelled after that of Hippocrates, a masterpiece of medical ethics. In this oath he endeavours—in keeping with his responsibilities to the God who revealed Himself on Sinai—to conscientiously practice medicine in the same fashion on Jewish, Christian, and Muslim patients: not a given in this period when knowledge was subordinated to religious affiliation. On this point, historian of medicine

---

(Philadelphia: The Jewish Publication Society, 1995), 89–111; Dov Front, "The Expurgation of the Books of Amatus Lusitanus: Censorship and the Bibliography of the Individual Book," *Book Collector* 47 (1998): 520–536; George H. Tucker, "To Louvain and Antwerp, and Beyond; the Contrasting Itineraries of Diogo Pires (Didacus Pyrrhus Lusitanus, 1517–1599) and Joao Rodrigues de Castelo Branco (Amatus Lusitanus, 1511–1568)," in *The Expulsion of the Jews and Their Emigration to the Southern Low Countries (15th–16th C.)*, ed. Luc Dequecker and Werner Verbene (Leuven: Leuven University Press, 1998), 83–113.

8 On this author see the preliminary but very detailed study by Eliezer Gurwirth, "Amatus Lusitanus and the Location of Sixteenth Century Cultures," in *Cultural Intermediaries. Jewish Intellectual in Early Modern Italy*, ed. David Ruderman and Giuseppe Veltri (Philadelphia: Pennsylvania University Press, 2004): 216–238.

9 Author of the *Compendium de plantis omnibus, una cum earum iconibus, de quibus scripsit suis in commentariis in Dioscoridem editis: in eorum studiosorum commodum, atque usum; qui plantis conquirendis, ac indagandis student* (Venice: Valgrisius, 1571). The fame of Pietro Andrea Mattioli (Siena, 1500–Trent, 1577) stems from his commentary on Dioscorides, *Il Dioscoride con gli suoi discorsi aggiuntovi il sesto libro degli antidoti contra tutti i veleni*, (Venice, 1544), composed in Italian, since the book was addressed to specialists who for the most part did not know Latin. See Pietro A. Mattioli, *Di Pedacio Dioscoride Anazarbeo libri cinque della historia, & materia medicinale tradotti in lingua vuvlgare italiana da M. Pietro Andrea Matthiolo Sanese medico. Con amplissimi discorsi, et comenti, et dottissime annotationi, et censure del medesimo interprete. Da cui potra ciascuno facilmente acquistare la vera cognitione de' semplici non solamente scritti da Dioscoride, ma da altri antichi, & moderni scrittori, & massimamente da Galeno. La cui dottrina intorno à tale facultà tutta fedelmente interpretata si ritrova posta ne' proprj luoghi. Con due tavole alphabetiche da poter con prestezza ritrovare cio che vi si cerca [...].*" (Venice: Niccolo Bascarini, 1544). Later, a Latin translation would appear with minor variations (*Commentarii, in libros sex Pedacii Dioscoridis Anazarbei, de medica materia. Adiectis quam plurimis plantarum & animalium imaginibus eodem authore* [Venice: Vincenzo Valgrisi, 1554]). Mattioli's commentary enjoyed great success and was reprinted many times up through the middle of the seventeenth century.

Winfried Schleiner defines the *medicus prudens*[10] as someone who applies his expertise case by case and follows only his own conscience.

The new appreciation for Hebrew sources promoted by Galatino, in the wake of Reuchlin's tradition, was also connected to the Franciscan's clear support of the diffusion of awareness of the Hebrew language itself. There was, moreover, awareness at that time of the importance of Hebrew in the field of natural sciences. The classicist Petrus Mosellanus, for example, when he became a rector at the University of Lipsia, stressed in his 1517 inaugural lecture that the Hebrew sources—and by extension the language in which they were written—should enjoy a higher esteem in the medical community than other languages.[11]

Galatino's interest in the Hebrew language and tradition stemmed not so much from scientific motives as a conviction that there was a primordial wisdom to be found in the Talmudic and Kabbalistic writings. This conviction found nourishment in the apologetic literature of the Renaissance and in authors like Leone Ebreo and the already mentioned Azariah de' Rossi.

De' Rossi was born in Mantua around 1514 to an affluent family, judging from the richness of their library, and died in Ferrara in 1577. He spent parts of his life in Venice, Ancona, and Bologna. After the expulsion of the Jews from the Papal States in 1569 at the decree of Pope Pius V, Azariah moved to Ferrara. He found himself there during the earthquake of 18 November 1570, an event that, judging from his own writings, spurred him to literary activity. The description of the earthquake became, in effect, the first part of his work *Me'or 'Enayim*, "*The Light of the Eyes.*"[12] In these tragic days, a Christian scholar friend of Azariah's asked him for information about the existence of a Hebrew version of Aristeas's letter. Surprised by Azariah's response in the negative, the Christian scholar invited him to translate the letter into Hebrew. I think there is no doubt that the earthquake served as a literary expedient that served to rhetorically introduce Azariah's interest in ancient literature, especially that of the Jewish-Hellenistic tradition. His awareness of the ancient Greek, Roman, and Hebrew world was, in fact, immense, even disregarding the intrinsic and extrinsic references he makes to contemporary works.

---

10 Winfried Schleiner, *Medical Ethics in the Renaissance* (Washington, D.C.: Georgetown University Press, 1995); cf. D. W. Amudsen's review in *The New England Journal of Medicine* 334 (1996): 1206.
11 Cf. Natalia Berger, "Doctors in the House," *Hadassah* 79 (1999): "In the libraries of the Jews a treasure of medical science lies hidden, a treasure as scarce as is to be found in any other language. Nobody [...] will be able to get access to this treasure without intimate knowledge of the Hebrew grammar." The text was published in Lipsia in 1518. See Petrus Mosellanus, *Oratio de variarum linguarum cognitione paranda Petro Mosellano Protogense authore Lipsiae in magna eruditorum corona pronunciata* (Leipzig: Valentini Schumann, 1518). For a biography of Mosellanus and a bibliography see Achim Krümmel, "Mosellanus, Petrus (Peter Schade)," *Biographisch-bibliographisches Kirchenlexikon VI* (1993), col. 169–171.
12 See the beautiful translation and erudite commentary in *Azaria de' Rossi, The Light of the Eyes*, ed. Joanna Weinberg (New Haven: Yale University Press, 2001).

The *Me'or 'Enayim* is not a homogenous treatise, but rather has the literary form of a book of essays, a collection of diverse writings modelled on medieval literary and humanistic genres. The description of the earthquake and the Hebrew translation of Aristeas's letter are followed by treatments of various matters. Azariah first focuses on the question of why he makes recourse to non-Hebrew authors and sources to confirm, or in some cases refute, Hebrew sources. He continues with a critical analysis of the work of Philo of Alexandria. Azariah then turns his investigation to the problem of translations of the Bible and dedicates five chapters to questions concerning the outward appearance of priestly vestments. Six further chapters are dedicated to diverse topics, among them the Hebrew alphabet and grammar, and synagogue poetry (*Piyyuṭ*). The core of his work (sixteen chapters from 29 to 44) is nevertheless dedicated to the problem of chronology. This section is controversial due to its polemical thesis on the historical irrelevance of the classical account of the rabbinical tradition, the Haggadah.

Azariah's interest in Galatino's work derives from the use the Franciscan forms of Talmudic and Kabbalistic sources, which he considered to constitute the original Hebrew traditions. During his treatment of Philo of Alexandria, as already reported above, Azariah renews the discussion of the expression "Son of God," adopted both by the author of the hermetic texts and by Philo himself to connote "Light." Azariah cites, to this end, the expression "qaddisha abba," which he believed to be Kabbalistic, and which he might have taken from Galatino. It reads:[13]

> Indeed, Rabbi Yonatan expressed it in the Chaldaic (i.e. Aramaic) language: *qadish abba, qadish bera, qadish ruḥa qadisha*, that is: holy is the Father, holy is the Son and holy is the holy spirit (*Rabbi vero Ionathan ita caldaice inquit qadish abba, qadish bera, qadish ruḥa qadisha.*[14] *Id est sanctus hic est pater, sanctus hic est filius, sanctus hic est spiritus sanctus*).[15]

In Azariah's view there was no doubt that this was a passage taken from the Targum Yonatan,[16] as Galatino had suspected. Yet, Galatino believed that the Jews had modified their ancient, original traditions, which bore witness to the Christian truth, in a way that devalued Christianity.[17] If the tradition had really been that clear, that man-

---

13 Avraham Farissol had already uncovered the falsification of this passage in his *Magen Avraham* (Ferrara, 1514); Azariah nonetheless made use of it since, in his view, all the denominational forms of God represent but one terminological question.
14 Printed in Hebrew letters.
15 Galatino, *Opus toti christianae Reipublicae maxime utile, de arcanis catholicae veritatis*, xxxi/r, 51 (in the 1550 Basilea edition).
16 In Galatino's own times he was beset by accusations of falsification and plagiarism of past traditions. Galtino defended himself against these claims in a letter to Pope Paul III (MS. Vat. Libr., cod. Ottob. Lat. 2366, fol. 300–308). On this, see Thomas Plassmann, "Pietro Colonna Galatino," in *Catholic Encyclopaedia* (New York: Robert Appleton Company).
17 "Est, in his Ionathae libris quos nunc ipsi frequentius prae manibus habent, hoc (ut ipse nosti) non haberi, cum illud inde maiores eorum deleuerint, eoque in loco ita scripserunt, ut libri quos post-

ifest, then why, following the objections made against Galatino by Leone Modena in his 1613 book *Magen wa-ḥerev*, did the rabbis of that period not convert to Christianity?[18] Galatino had given a very simple explanation: these rabbis had passed down the Catholic truth without having understood it.[19]

Galatino's attitude is a sign of respect towards the contribution of the ancients, retaining nonetheless a certain autonomy of judgement in the field of experiential knowledge. The *topos* to which Galatino indirectly alludes is the famous adage "nos qui nani super humeros gigantum" ("we, who are dwarfs on the shoulders of giants"),[20] interpreted, however, in a Christian light. The ancients were temporally closer than us to the truth, but we can see further because we are able to add to the revelation of antiquity our own personal experience.

Even in Judaism, this logic of the tradition is voiced whenever new knowledge renders the theses of the ancients no longer sustainable. Exemplary in this is the methodological training and planning of Azariah de' Rossi.

4.3 Method and Reader

The recourse to non-Jewish authors to confirm or refute Jewish sources was a revolutionary method, probably one introduced by Azariah. The violent reactions that followed are thus no surprise. Little time passed before his book was called heretical, a charge levelled by Halakhist and Kabbalist Yosef Caro. In the end, a compromise was struck: the book was allowed but with strict limitations imposed to guide those readers who, in the judgement of the rabbis, might be negatively influenced by it. Thirty years after the appearance of the book, the polemic had still not settled. The famous Rabbi Löw, known as the Marahal di Praga, sensing the book's explosive potential, attacked its author with unusual vehemence and branded his method as a danger to the effort to preserve the Jewish tradition:

> And today, in this generation—wrote Rabbi Löw—which is marked by imperfection and ignorance, one man rises who speaks against the Saints, those who lived for over a thousand years and said "Behold my method: be wise!" In some passages, he makes use of profane

---

modum scribi contigit, continent. In vetustissimis tamen libris, qui rarissimi sunt, ita prosus habetur, ut ego retuli." *Opus toti christianae Reipublicae maxime utile, de arcanis catholicae veritatis*, xxxi/r, 51 (Basilea edition).

18 Leone Modena, *Magen wa-Ḥerev* (*Clipeus et gladius: tractatus antichristianus*), ed. Shlomo Simonsohn (Jerusalem: Mekitse Nirdamim, 1960), 51.

19 "Veteres [...] Talmudistae infinita prope arcana figuris et aenigmatibus tradiderunt, quae iis qui ea non intelligunt, fatuitates atque absurditates videntur", in *Opus toti christianae Reipublicae maxime utile, de arcanis catholicae veritatis*, V, 23b (Basilea edition), V (23b). Cf. Fausto Parente, "La Chiesa e il 'Talmud,'"579–581.

20 Ibid.

and idolatrous writings to sustain his thesis, rendering vain and null the words of our wise men, holy and faithful to God![21]

We will come back to the debate between Azariah de' Rossi and the Maharal in the third part of this book. Here it is sufficient to emphasise that the method of Azariah that Rabbi Löw points to was that of proposing alternative sources to the "illuminated reader," with the conscious goal of developing a faculty of independent judgement by means of pondering previously settled matters that did not touch on the essence of Judaism. Rabbi Löw had rightly noted that the question of this method would have significant repercussions for intellectual history: the method is the path itself, the way to the discovery of truth across a kind of gap in the tradition.

Rabbi Löw also rightly highlighted, however, that there was a generational change underway, a change poised to alter the traditional vision of the ancient rabbinical period. In reality, the Mantuan was bringing into question the reliability of ancient Hebrew sources and authors, and in so doing conferring reliability on the new sciences (geography, chronology, astronomy, etc.). According to Rabbi Löw these were not marginal aspects, as Azariah had proclaimed, but essential elements, foundations upon which Judaism was founded historically and theologically.

Azariah's novelty consisted in proposing to the "enlightened reader" (*qore maskil*) a means of forming one's own judgements by examining previously studied material. This freedom of critical discernment regards, however, only the "marginal aspects," not things at the nucleus of the tradition, those that according to Azariah constituted the Halakhah. That Judaism is fundamentally a praxis-oriented[22] religious community was already recognised in the Talmudic era. In Maimonides we find for the first time a canon of laws which *inter alia* contains dogmas (*Mishneh Torah*) and a list of 13 principles of Jewish beliefs (in the *Commentary on the Mishnah*). Echoes of these are nowhere to be found among those Jewish scholars who were his contemporaries, however. The list became a sort of confessional act which later found a place in the prayer books.

Only in the Renaissance with Azariah de' Rossi do we see an effort to distinguish the essence of Judaism from its formal aspects. This effort is comparable to the attempts in Protestant contexts—principally due to Melanchthon in the fourth decade of the sixteenth century—to reduce Christianity to certain fundamental principles, tenets which could be accepted by both Protestants and Catholics.[23] This is a matter

---

[21] Cf. my own "Science and Religious Hermeneutics: The 'Philosophy' of Rabbi Loew of Prague," in *Religious Confession and the Sciences in 16th Century*, ed. Jürgen Helm and Annette Winkelmann (Leiden: Brill, 2001), 119–135, se also part three of this book.
[22] The commonly used word orthopraxy is deceptive because it was coined after orthodoxy. In classical rabbinic Judaism there is the Halakhah according to the majority which cannot be per definitionem the "right".
[23] See the 1577 *Formula of Concord*, art. 10: *De ceremoniis ecclesiasticis quae vulgo adiaphora seu res mediae et indifferentes vocantur*; See Abraham Angermannus, *Forum adiaphororum h. e. sententia ec-*

of the so-called "adiaphora" (a Stoic term denoting "undifferentiated things"), which, interpreted theologically, deals with things not pertinent to the essence of the faith. Melanchthon took his departure from a Pauline aphorism,[24] recalling the dictum attributed to Augustine: "in essential things unity; in doubtful things freedom; in all things charity" (*In necessariis unitas, in dubiis libertas, in omnibus caritas*).

Although Azariah certainly might have been aware of the debate first between Protestants and then between Catholics and Protestants, his invocation of the essence vs. marginality dichotomy aims at something else. If he directed his entire system of definitions of Renaissance historical-philological knowledge toward the goal of elucidating Judaism's past it was only to re-establish the tradition on a more secure and neutral historical foundation. The importance of Azariah's work does not consist, however, in its methodological novelty, but rather in applying Christian methods to the Jewish tradition (and also in the opposite sense, making use of Jewish sources to confirm or refute Christian traditions and historical reports). From a traditional Jewish perspective, this method represented a danger given the Christian intellectual world's frequent profoundly radical anti-Jewish sentiments. The infiltration of technical expressions from the Christian tradition was regarded in some quarters as an implicit recognition of the anti-Jewish critique.

Azariah thus justified his method, which presupposed a *qore maskil*, just like the Hebrew tradition of the Latin *lector prudens*—the "enlightened reader" to whom he submitted diverse opinions so that reader could learn to form his own judgements. At the end of his analysis of the writings of Philo of Alexandria, Azariah states:[25]

> In my view, this was a man who had fallen between two stools, so that it is impossible to form a clear opinion about him. Based what was discussed in this chapter, I tell the children of Israel: I will not pass judgment on this Yedidya, or Philo—as he is called in Greek—on his purity or impurity, as regards the importance or respect that is due to him. [...] We well mention him in the same manner as the other sages of the world [Christians] in order to clarify side aspects (*milleta be-'alma*), but not regarding the essence (*u-be-may de-la shayyeke be-gawwe*). With regard to the rest of his ideas and books, the reader should be able to form his own judgment, in keeping with his own opinion.

---

clesiæ reformatæ, veram, orthodoxam & perpetuam scripturæ sacræ, sanctorum patrum, & totius catholicæ & apostolicæ ecclesiæ doctrinam de ritibus & ceremonijs ecclesiasticis, breviter complectens & perspicuè proponens: explicata ab authoribus, quorum nomina & scripta paginæ præfationem proximè sequentes, & præsens liber exhibebunt, Matthæus Welack excudebat (Witebergæ 1587); Karl A. von Hase, *Libri symbolici Ecclesiae Evangelicae, sive concordia* (Leipzig: Johannes Suehring, 1827), 614–616. On the *Adiaphora*, see Thomas F. Mayer, "Starkey and Melanchthon on Adiaphora: A Critique of W. Gordon Zeeveld," *Sixteenth Century Journal* 11/1 (1980): 39–49; Jay Irwin, "Hamilton, Music, and the Doctrine of Adiaphora in Orthodox Lutheran Theology," *Sixteenth Century Journal* 14 (1983): 157–172.

24 Cf. James L. Jaquette, *Discerning what Counts: The Function of the Adiaphora Topos in Paul's Letters* (Atlanta: Scholars' Press, 1995).

25 Azaria de' Rossi, *Sefer Me'or 'Enayim*, 129.

Before Azariah, Jerome had already voiced a goal of cultivating the critical judgement of his readers. He responded to Rufinus's reproach that he had abandoned the Christian tradition and made recourse to Hebrew *veritas*—to the Hebrew drafting of the Bible rather than the canonical drafting of the Septuagint—by introducing heretical ideas into his statements. Jerome justifies his actions by looking back to the commentaries of Origen, Didymus, and Apollinaris (which were not always in agreement). Even he, like his predecessors, wanted merely to propose *opiniones*.

It is left to the reader to judge between the true and the false, as the money changer distinguishes between genuine and counterfeit currency.[26] In the same context, Jerome makes reference to Donatus's comment to Terrence. In the Renaissance, the same *topos* is employed by Filippo Beroaldo in his commentary on Properzio.[27] That Donatus, Jerome, and then later Beroaldo return to this *topos* does not mean that one should linger—to use the modern terminology—on questions of textual fluctuation or diversity within the textual tradition. "False" textual interpretations are offered so that the reader may learn to distinguish between them. Even on the title page of the Bible edited by Santes Pagnini in 1528 the reader is admonished by the *lector prudens* formula.[28] Pagnini clearly meant this to refer to Jerome, and for

---

26 St. Jerome, *Contra Rufinum* I, 16: "Ego enim in commentariis ad Ephesios sic Origenem et Didymum et Apollinarem secutus sum, qui certe contraria inter se habent dogmata, ut fidei meae non amitterem veritatem. Commentarii quid operis habent? Alterius dicta edisserunt, quae obscure scripta sunt plano sermone manifestant, multorum sententias replicant et dicunt: Hunc locum quidam sic edisserunt, alii sic interpretantur, illi sensuum suum et intelligentiam his testimoniis et hac nituntur ratione firmare, ut prudens lector, cum diversas explanationes legerit, et multorum vel probanda vel improbanda didicerit, iudicet quid verius sit et, quasi bonus trapezita, adulterinae monetae pecuniam reprobet. Num diversae interpretationis, et contrariorum inter se sensuum tenebitur reus, qui in uno opere quod edisserit, expositiones posuerit plurimorum? Puto quod puer legeris Aspri in Virgilium et Sallustium Commentarios, Vulcatii in Orationes Ciceronis, Victorini in Dialogos eius et in Terentii Comoedias, preceptoris mei Donati aeque in Virgilium, et aliorum in alios: Plautum videlicet, Lucretium, Flaccum, Persium atque Lucanum. Argue interpretes eorum, quare non unam explationem secuti sint: et in eadem re quid vel sibi, vel aliis videatur, enumerent."

27 Venice edition, 1491, f. 1r: "Sed iam enarrationem auspicemur, in qua non solum quid nobis placeat, sed quid aliis etiam videatur explicabimus. Nam, ut inquit divus Hieronymus, commentatoris officium est multorum sententias exponere, ut prudens lector, cum diversas explanationes legerit, iudicet quid verius sit: et quasi verus trapezita, adulterinae monetae pecuniam reprobet, et probam sinceramque recipiat [...]"[in Anthony Grafton, "On the Scholarship of Politian and its Context," *Journal of the Warburg and Courtauld Institutes* 40 (1977): 150–188, 187, footnote 137.

28 Santes Pagnini, *Biblia: habes in hoc libro prudens lector utriusq[ue] instrumenti novam tranlatione [m] / aeditam à reverendo sacre theologiae doctore Sancte Pagnino Luc[c]esi concionatore apostolico praedicatorii ordinis, necnon & librum de interpretamentis hebraicorum, arameorum graecorumq[ue] nominum, sacris in litteris contentorum in quo iuxta idioma cuiusq[ue] linguae, propriae ponuntur interpretationes, derivationes ac eor[um] compositiones adamussim disquiruntur, citantur loca, & codicu[m] latinoru[m] varietates subnotantur, & corrupta ac depravata propriae restituu[n]tur scriptioni, acce[n]tus quo[que] per impositas virgulas com[m]ostrant singulis in capitibus quot sint versus in hebraeis codicibus, rece[n]setur ut pauca sint desideranda : [...] abbreviationem librorum historialium veteris in-*

this reason he was criticised by Luther and accused of literalism and acquiescence to the "Jewish influx." The *lector prudens* here is he who leaves the traditional path and honours the opinion of the third party: the perspective of Judaism.

The term *lector prudens* brings to mind a second rhetorical figure: the quest for a text's esoteric meaning, the trajectory of which the editor lays out for any reader expert in the material at hand. Hrabanus Maurus makes reference to his *De rerum naturis*, [29] where the author attends not to the variety of the text's possible explanations, but to the rhetorical preparation it grants the reader, inviting him to develop his own singular interpretation. The text's mystical meaning is, plainly put, the sense beyond the literal, the meaning that transcends the word's dictates through an effort to reach the nous, the essence of the *verbum*.

We should not take Azariah's principle of the autonomy of judgement as a declaration of the freedom of the will, nor of the autonomy of the individual. In his address to the *lector prudens* he makes clear, rather, that scholars had intervened in past traditions, even in well-founded and important traditions. These scholars dared to juxtapose their own theses with those of translated texts and recognised authorities. They dared to make recourse to other sources, ones not cited in preceding commentaries. Their gnoseology did not stem from the exegetical tradition given once for all eternity but rather in the reception and valuation of different sources, sometimes-contradictory ones. The terms of the discussion are not "collective tradition" and the "rational individual," but the tradition of *opiniones*, which comment on the tradition. If Jerome or Azariah grant human beings the freedom of judgement, this means that from context and from the way *opiniones* are presented it should be clear which opinion contains the truth. Opinions restore the clarity of truth.

We find a much different attitude in the Jewish doctor and encyclopaedist Avraham Portaleone, who took up the question of the appraisal of the erudition of the ancients and ultimately delivered a prudent response. In his main work, *Shilṭe ha-Gibborim*, published shortly before his death in 1612, Portaleone writes thus:

> I cannot pass silently over, O reader, the fact that all that I have written regarding these beams [of time] came to me from the heart and was expressed in the form of a logical reflection there, where the commentators touch rather than speak. Also as a result of the well-noted impediment[30] I was not able to ascertain if this point regarding the *Gemara* says something. And if God in his goodness and mercy should permit that you sip the milk and honey of our masters' words, blessed be their memory, and may God will that with the consent of our sovereigns and

---

strumenti & erratorum castigationes quas (Lyon: Antoine du Ry, Francesco Turchi, Dominique Bertus and Jacques Giunta, 1528).

29 *Prohemium* I (1b): "Sunt enim in eo plura exposita de rerum naturis, et verborum proprietatibus, necnon etiam de mystica rerum significatione quod idcirco ita ordinandum estimavi, ut lector prudens continuatim positam inveniret historicam et mysticam singularem rerum explanationem" in Hrabanus Maurus, "De Universo Libri Viginti Duo, Praefatio Ad Ludovicum Regem Invictissimum Franciae," *Patriologia latina* vol. 111 (Paris: J. P. Migne, 1852), col.9b.

30 I.e. the injunction against possessing the Talmud.

princes—may God watch over them—then you, blessed by God, you will hold only their words alone and this explanation of mine will be considered nothing. It is in fact only on this condition that I have written what I have here. You well know that I, God as my witness, would never ever sustain a view different from that of our masters, blessed be their memory, since they are the truth and their words are the truth. Blessed is he who has chosen and will choose their words, their teachings and their outlook.[31]

The reader notes here the posture of respectful obedience that tries to avoid contradicting the opinions of the ancient wise men. He/she has the freedom to choose only when the masters are of diverse beliefs on a matter. In one passage Portaleone is in almost total agreement with the critique advanced by Rabbi Löw to Azariah de' Rossi:

Regardless you must never abandon the words of our Ge'onim, sources of the water of life, to construct them from fractured cisterns, and my opinion is not sufficient to contain the water of wisdom and reason and I do not say to you (may the Merciful One be my witness!): Follow my opinion! The decision is, after all, yours and not mine to make.[32]

Portaleone's thought, like that of his contemporary Rabbi Löw, is inspired by the doctrine of Plotinus: wisdom was perfect in the beginning. From the Fall, the original sin, up through our own times, all is merely ongoing decadence. The fonts of wisdom are by now dried up. Following this notion, the ancients would be closer to the truth than the moderns, rendering unthinkable the privileging of individual opinion over the wisdom of old. The author works to put his reader on guard against setting out on this false path.

We must bear in mind, however, that this hermeneutical stance on the past should not be identified with a conservative attitude, an opposition to every new development of significance. Its reverence towards antiquity is in effect a mantle of humility *ad extra* that conceals within itself implicit and explicit attacks on its own tradition. One recalls that the mystic Joachim of Fiore, first ratified but later deemed heretical, declared his obedience to the Church, a fact that did not prevent the Fourth Lateran Council from deeming his work contrary to the Church's magisterial tradition.[33]

The question, as raised by Rabbi Löw, is one of method: the recognition *de principio* of the superiority of the ancient tradition, something that is *de facto* sup-

---

31 Avraham Portaleone, *Shilṭe ha-Gibborim* (Mantua: Elieser d'Italia, 1612), 14 (13a).
32 Ibid., 87 (92b–93a).
33 The text of the letter, Joachim's defence of his own orthodoxy that is now the preface to almost all his writings, can be found in Antonio Crocco, *Gioacchino da Fiore* (Naples: Empireo, 1960). Even a preliminary bibliography on the Calabrian abbot would be over-ambitious here: for a general introduction see Bernard McGinn, *L'abate calabrese. Gioacchino da Fiore nella storia del pensiero occidentale* (Genoa: Marietti, 1990). See also *Gioacchino da Fiore tra Bernardo di Clairvaux e Innocenzo III*, ed. Roberto Rusconi (Rome: Viella, 2001). Also consulted were the Joachimite studies on http://www.gioacchino.it/ (accessed 26 November, 2016).

pressed. It will be this very rabbi of Prague, favoured by some conservatives, who will go on to advocate the study of the new sciences.

De' Rossi, instead, was thoroughly convinced that truth (including philological truth) is reached the moment when uncertain and unsustainable basic premises are completely eliminated. His position is best illustrated by an episode from his life. A few years before De' Rossi's death, the inquisitor of Ferrara attempted to convert him to Christianity. Ultimately, in the inquisitor's resigned report to the ecclesiastical authorities, he wrote:

> I have not, however, neglected for years to make every effort to turn this Jewish Bonaiuto de Rossi into a Christian, but in vain all along, since yesterday morning finally he prayed that I should write to you, telling how he resolutely desires to remain Jewish, though not a foolish Jew—one, that is, who would cease to tell the truth in favour of every other religion [...].[34]

Azariah did not wish to maintain an acritical attitude towards the new scientific concepts of the day. Judaism remained the stable point in his life, one that historical events and scientific progress did not undermine. Certainly he was not the first to affirm this—we must take into account the poet Manuello (Immanuel/Immanuello) Romano, who harboured a certain tolerance which, seen in its own context, can be nothing other than a desire *ad extra* for the Christian world, unable as it was to tolerate other religions:[35]

---

34 Joanna Weinberg, "Azaria de' Rossi: Towards a Reappraisal of the Last Years of his Life," *Annali della Scuola Normale di Pisa VIII* (1978): 511; cf. Robert Bonfil, "The Historian's Perception of the Jews in the Italian Renaissance. Towards a Reappraisal," *Revue des Études Juives CXLIII* (1984): 81–82.
35 In steso non mi conosco, ogn'om oda,
che l'esser proprio si è ghibellino:
in Roma so' Colonnes' ed Ursino,
e piacemi se l'uno e l'altro ha loda.

Ed in Toscana parte guelfa goda;
in Romagna so' ciò ch' è Zappetino;
mal giudeo sono io, non saracino:
ver' li cristiani non drizzo la proda.

Ma d'ogni legge so' ben desiroso
Alcuna parte voler osservare:
de' cristiani lo bever e 'l mangiare,

e del bon Moisès poco digiunare,
e la lussuria di Macón prezioso,
che non ten fé de la cintura in gioso

Cf. Vatican City, Vatican Library, MS Barb. Lat. 3953 in *Poeti giocosi del tempo di Dante*, ed. Mario Marti (Milan: Rizzoli, 1956), 313–321; On Immanuel see *Maḥberot Immanuel ha-Romi*, ed. Dov Yarden, 2 vols. (Jerusalem: Mossad Bialik, 1957); Jacqueline Genot-Bismuth, "Philosophie et Poétique dans

> Myself I do not know extensively—everyone hear—
> that the very being is Ghibelline:
> In Rome I am a Colonnese and Ursino,
>
> And I am happy whichever one receives praises.
> And in Tuscany let the Guelph party enjoy favour;
> In Romagna I know what is a Zappetino;
> I am a bad Jew, not a Saracen:
> I do not raise my bow to the Christians.[36]
>
> But of every religion I am desirous
> Of wishing to observe some part:
> Of the Christians the eating and drinking,
>
> And little fasting from the good Moses,
> And the licentiousness of precious Macon,[37]
> Which has no religion below the belt.[38]

Azariah de' Rossi is representative of a historiographical conception typical in the Renaissance, one grounded in erudite debate about historical events. Historiography is not to be identified with *narratio*, reportage, chronicling. It is, rather, the realm of revelation and historical unfolding. In this *historia* the Jews play a relevant role as a people, the group from which wisdom is derived and through whom God is revealed, a people that continues to guard the true tradition.

4.4 The Sources of Wisdom

One of the most-debated epistemological questions in the Renaissance concerned the reliability of sources of knowledge. The question was born out of the cult of classical antiquity, one whose zeal was nourished by the conviction that the writings of classical authors represented a kind of *praeparatio evangelica*, as discussed above. The test of a source's reliability is the first premise for the conception of a genesis of wisdom, which, in the image of a Plotinian inverted pyramid, is born out of a variety and multiplicity of knowing and flows into the unity of Christian revelation.

This theorem had *prima facie* an apologetic character, but it established at the same time the utility of the adoption of new scientific disciplines, seen as elements of a kind of primordial wisdom. Even certain Jewish intellectuals remained fascinated by this vision of the development of the sciences, although, naturally, they were

---

l'oeuvre d'Immanuel de Rom" (PhD dissertation, Université de Paris III–Sorbonne Nouvelle Paris, 1977).
36 I.e. I do not convert to Christianity.
37 I.e. Mahomet
38 The first English translation was begun by Ed Emery on a website that no longer exists. I revised the translation because of some errors.

not able to share the vision's implicit conclusions. Ethical-religious truth, for them, had been handed down once and for all on Mt. Sinai. However, this was not the case for pagan wisdom, which, following the original sin, could not be further transmitted. By consequence, their idea of knowledge came to coincide with the capacity for judgement of propositions.

Let us return to the library of Mantua. Galatino, Azariah, and Lusitanus had something in common: they were attentive readers. Galatino proposed to render the truth contained in the Jewish sources doctrinally useful and to harmonise the different strands of wisdom born over the course of centuries and millennia. The study of Jewish "truth" is none other than the study of one's own identity from the viewpoint of Christian posterity looking back upon Jewish antiquity. Like Reuchlin, Galatino was moving on dangerous terrain, where the authority of Christianity could easily be called into question.

Galatino's thesis—according to which the Jews did not fully comprehend the things that they transmitted—could have been shared without major problems by Renaissance scholars, seeing as how the point could so easily be inverted. Did Christianity truly understand the things that Judaism had transmitted? This, in fact, was Azariah de' Rossi's position. For him, any recourse to Christian sources is a confirmation of Judaism's truth, though not without being acquainted with the limits of the Jewish tradition. They consist in the Halakha, which constitutes the essence of Judaism, while the rest of the literary tradition (including the Haggadah, despite its antiquity) is marginal, of arguably secondary importance. The *lector prudens* is granted freedom of judgement only with regards to this last aspect of the Jewish tradition. However, once the individual is permitted even this narrow critique, who can prevent them from questioning the whole of the tradition? This was the fear of contemporary rabbinical circles.

Lusitanus indirectly follows a different rabbinical teaching: that the shared intellectual community of Jews and Christians can be maintained only on the practical plane, in realms like medicine, where Jews, Christians, and Muslims can be treated in the same way, and doing so indeed becomes a moral obligation. Here we can recognise the traditional attitude of diffidence, if not complete rejection of fields of learning that were prospering at that time, as documented, for example, in a letter of Ya'aqov ben David Provenzale to David ben Yehudah Messer Leon: according to the Talmud, individual judgement is only legitimate in practical sciences like medicine, botany, and agriculture. Philosophy and the speculative sciences are forbidden.[39] Both of these stances on knowledge (be it theoretical or practical) have some-

---

[39] On this point, see Gianfranco Miletto, "The teaching program of David ben Abraham and his son Abraham Provenzali in the Historical-cultural Context of the Time," in *Cultural Intermediaries Jewish Intellectuals in Early Modern Italy*, 127–148, and my own article, "Jüdische Einstellung zu den Wissenschaften im 16. und 17. Jahrhundert: Das Prinzip der praktisch-empirischen Anwendbarkeit," *Judentum zwischen Tradition und Moderne*, ed. Gerd Biegel and Michael Graetz (Heidelberg: C. Winter,

thing in common, however: the *lector prudens*, who like the *medicus prudens* is able to gather every affirmation and sign and submit it to the analysis of his own experience and judgement. The *lector prudens* can reach the nucleus of the truth, even if the truth does not always deliver the "remedy" one might hope for.

It would be illusory, however, to think that the Renaissance preoccupation with the truth—which sets one onto rarely travelled paths of esoteric wisdom, towards fantastical worlds—was an indication of tolerance between emerging denominations and established religions. The same world that gave us an esteem for the *homo universalis*, the *vir perfectus*, also gave rise, paradoxically, to a denominational and religions anthropology that defined man ontologically on the basis of creed.

4.5 Polemic Anthropology and Religious Ontology

Reading the most important and deservedly-cited works on the notion of the "Renaissance man"—those of Jacob Burkhardt,[40] Ernst Cassirer,[41] and Eugenio Garin[42]—one notes how the almost romantic and idealist enthusiasm for the authors of this period leads scholars to attribute to them concepts and beliefs that are, in my modest judgement, products of the age of Enlightenment. In this period when sculpture and painting began to stress the humanity, the corporality, the beauty and ugliness of *homo sapiens*—masculine and feminine, hetero- and homosexual, Lord or Lady of the court, divine being or goddess—one should not succumb to the temptation to see in everything the exultation of *homo universalis*, stemming as this notion does from the Christian context in which it was developed and where it was later interred. Advancing concurrently with scepticism (which we will discuss in the third part of this monograph) was an ever-strengthening notion of the pervasiveness of the divine throughout the created world—the idea of the individual being defined, aesthetically, by religious credo.

Religion is the source of the new human; the way he/she aspires to this idea. It is through this relation that the aesthetic is deemed to lead to virtue and virtue to contemplation.[43] The torsos and eroticised bodies of angels and saints—not to mention

---

2002): 149–159. For an ampler treatment, see my *Renaissance Philosophy in Jewish Garb: Foundations and Challenges in Judaism on the Eve of Modernity* (Boston: Brill, 2009), 97–127.

40 Jacob Burckhardt, *Die Kultur der Renaissance in Italien* (Leipzig: Seemann, 1869), Jacob Burckhardt, *The Civilization of the Renaissance in Italy*, trans. Samuel George Chetwynd Middlemore (Vienna: Phaidon Press, 1937).

41 Ernst Cassirer, *Individuum und Kosmos in der Philosophie der Renaissance* (Darmstadt: Wissenschaftliche Buchgesellschaft, 1987). The notion of the individual as the matrix of humanism is found in his book, first published in 1906: *Das Erkenntnisproblem in der Philosophie und Wissenschaft der neueren Zeit*, vol. 1 (Darmstadt: Wissenschaftliche Buchgesellschaft, 1994), 23.

42 See Eugenio Garin, *L'uomo del Rinascimento* (Bari: Laterza, 1988).

43 Cf. Agnolo Firenzuola, "Delle bellezze delle donne," in *Opere*, ed. Delmo Maestri (Turin: UTET, 1977), 725: "[. . .] perciò che la donna bella è il più bello obietto che si rimiri, e la bellezza è il maggior

4.5 Polemic Anthropology and Religious Ontology

Jesus, Mary, the apostles, and God himself—are not intended as praise of man, but rather as an exultation of man as a specifically Christian creation. This principle is behind the near-nudes depicted in Renaissance churches, something that today, in our supposed secular times, is less prevalent. The Renaissance made divinities out these creations (the aesthetic renderings of the bodies of Christ and the saints), such that that if one were separated from God one would not have had access to places where the divinity is adored, i.e. the Church. This all served to create a new idea altogether of the human essence (ontology) one formed principally by religion or confession.

We will need to explain in detail the genesis of this concept of "confessional ontology," one which undergirds the religious philosophy of the Renaissance. In a provocative article, German scholar Friedrich Niewöhner challenges his reader not to marry the terms of Humanism and Judaism: "Judaism, as a religion, is essentially anti-human, anti-humanistic, and un-humanitarian." He cites, in axiomatic fashion, the Christian religion as a *terminus comparationis:* "While Christianity should be considered anthropocentric, Judaism must be labelled theocentric."[44]

For non-German readers we must specify that the concept of "Humanismus" used by German literature is an altogether ambiguous one, certainly because in the German sense it signifies both a philological movement, one that sought to restore a Greco-Roman past, as well as the German movement of the nineteenth and early twentieth centuries under the banner of Johann Wolfgang von Goethe, Friedrich Schiller, and Alexander von Humboldt, who advocated the concept of the freedom of the will, the unassailability of human dignity, and the tolerance (even if only in theory) of contrary opinions. It is Goethe's idealistic Humanism, described as such in 1949 by Ernst Simon,[45] which I apply here to Jewish culture. This concept prevails, however, in the modern discussion that over-emphasises elements that were certainly not predominant in the period of Renaissance Humanism.

Niewöhner's negative view of Judaism[46] is not unique, but on the contrary is born out of what we might call "ideological realism," the movement, from both within and outside of Israeli Judaism that implies an ideological reality born from the political situation within the country. Among this view's proponents, the Israeli biologist and philosopher Yeshayahu Leibowitz excels in particular, a man who draws on the same interpretive angle when he argues against the application of the term Humanism to (contemporary) Judaism, believing the modern Jew to be none of the tri-

---

dono che facesse Iddio all'umana creatura; con ciò sia che per la di lei virtù noi ne indirizziamo l'animo alla contemplazione e per la contemplazione al desiderio delle cose del cielo."
44 Friedrich Niewöhner, "Anmerkungen zum Begriff eines 'jüdischen Humanismus'," *Archiv für Begriffsgeschichte* 34 (1991): 214–224.
45 Ernst Simon, "Goethe und der religiöse Humanismus," in *Brücken. Gesammelte Aufsätze (mit einem Geleitwort von Martin Buber),* ed. Ernst Simon (Heidelberg: Schneider, 1965), 220–245; cf. Friedrich Niewöhner, "Anmerkungen zum Begriff eines jüdischen Humanismus," 214.
46 I am speaking here only of this context and not on the whole activity of the German scholar.

une adjectives implied by the term Humanism: neither "cosmopolitan" nor "pacifist" nor "anarchist."[47] What Leibowitz means by "Humanism" is perhaps only a popular philosophical vision, one which does not correspond at all (to put it magnanimously) to the Berlin-Jerusalem debate that the term presupposes, a debate beginning in the 1800s. It is neither the project that the German Idealists hoped to carry out (a re-awakening of the classical man, albeit as a slave to the Prussian system) nor the issue of the beloved Renaissance father whom we are discussing.

Nevertheless, to avoid irrelevant generalisations we will turn directly to that foundational work of Renaissance anthropology, Giovanni Pico della Mirandola's *De hominis dignitate*, a work that Jacob Burckhardt called "one of the noblest inheritances from that cultural epoch" ("[...] eines der edelsten Vermächtnisse jener Kulturepoche"),[48] a hymn for humankind and human freedom. My task will not be to deconstruct the Pichian system, but simply to specify what this great thinker meant.

In Pico's view, mankind is a multiform composite,[49] a historical construct:[50]

> From its birth, mankind was provided by God the Father with the seeds and germs to generate every form of life. Men were to be able to grow and produce only when taught to do so: when they fix their minds on vegetables, they bring plants into being; if they become sensitive beings, they rise to the level of animals; if they plant germs of reason they develop into vital celestial beings; if they merge with the spiritual they become angels or the son of God.[51]

Based also on the Neoplatonic philosophy of Iamblichus,[52] this genre of anthropology is decidedly infused with Christian philosophy. According to Pico, the seeds and germs received by God the father can be adopted by man in his freedom:

> If you see someone reduced to crawling on the earth on their stomach, it is not a man that you see but a plant; If [you see] someone blinded as by Calypso with vain mirages of fantasy, overtaken by seductive enchantment, made a slave to the senses, it is a beast that you see and not a man.
> If [you see] a philosopher discerning all things with rigorous reason, venerate him; he is not an earthly animal but a celestial one.
> If [you see] a pure contemplative, heedless of the body, banished to the inner recesses of the

---

47 Yeshyahi Leibowitz and Michael Shashar, *Gespräche über Gott und die Welt* (Frankfurt: Insel Verlag, 1990), 209–216 (translated from Hebrew in Jerusalem, 1987).
48 Jacob Burckhardt, *Die Kultur der Renaissance in Italien, mit einem Geleitwort von Wilhelm von Bode* (Berlin: Knaur Nachf, 1928), 354.
49 Cf. Giovanni Pico della Mirandola, *Oratio De hominis dignitate*, ed. E. Garin (Pordenone: *Edizioni* Studio *Tesi*, 1994): In German as *Über die Würde des Menschen*, ed. A. Buck (Hamburg: Meiner, 1990).
50 See my "'Dannare l'universale per il particolare?' Colpa individuale e pena collettiva nel pensiero di Rabbi Simone Luzzatto," *Rassegna Mensile d'Israele LXXVII*, 1–2 (2012): 65–81.
51 Giovanni Pico della Mirandola, *De hominis dignitate*, 7.
52 Iamblicus, *Protreptikos* 5.

4.5 Polemic Anthropology and Religious Ontology — 61

mind, it is neither a terrestrial animal you see, nor a celestial one: this is a more august spirit, cloaked in human flesh.[53]

We must not deceive ourselves with respect to this text's account of the levels of human existence because at the end of the ontological pyramid there is only the *homo christianus*. The philosopher is, rather, the first stage of human being: "He who does not take pains to make an expression literally elegant is not a humanistically educated man. He who does not consider philosophy necessary is not a living being."[54] Note here Pico's emphasis on the passage from the *studium humanitatis* to philosophy as a prerequisite for *humanitas*. As for Christian philosopher Thomas Aquinas, philosophy for Pico is a premise (a "necessity") for theology (read *Christian* theology). After a process of purification, Pico teaches us, one must inundate one's cleansed soul with the light of natural philosophy (*philosophia naturalis*), in order to then arrive at a state of perfection in the consciousness of divine things. If theology is the innermost chamber of the temple of the individual, philosophy represents the temple priest. If one is mindful of the predominance of Christianity in the Renaissance—an era which, although attending to and appropriating the categories of Perennial Philosophy, was ultimately a fundamentally Christian one that refuted opposing interpretive approaches—one can see past this predominance and affirm that man need not be reduced to *homo christianus*, that the forms of vegetable, animal, and philosophical being simply represent the forms and levels of being that deliver one to true Christianity.

It is easy to forget that the anthropological conception of the Renaissance Man as *homo naturaliter christianus* will have tragically fatal consequences in later centuries. Examining the art and literature of the period, one finds—as I have demonstrated elsewhere—that with rare exceptions Jews are described and depicted with the characteristics of animals, with accolades for human beauty reserved only for Christians.[55]

---

[53] "Si quem enim videris deditum ventri, humi serpentem hominem, frutex est, non homo, quem vides; si quem in fantasiae quasi Calipsus vanis praestigiis cecucientem et subscalpenti delinitum illecebra sensibus mancipatum, brutum est, non homo, quem vides. Si recta philosophum ratione omnia discernentem, hunc venereris; caeleste est animal, non terrenum. Si purum contemplatorem corporis nescium, in penetralia mentis relegatum, hic non terrenum, non caeleste animal: hic augustius est numen humana carne circumvestitum." On the larger project that Pico envisioned, see note 330, par. 3.2 in the same volume.
[54] Eugenio Garin, *Filosofi italiani del Quattrocento* (Florence: Istituto nazionale di studi sul Rinascimento, 1942), 440.
[55] Against the mainstream on Pico is also Brian P. Copenhaver, "Pico risorto: cabbalà e dignità dell'uomo nell'Italia post-unitaria," in *Giovanni Pico e la Cabbalà*, ed. Fabrizio Lelli (Florence: Olschki, 2014): 1–18.

The response to polemic is, generally, more polemic, and the denominational anthropology of the Renaissance finds an echo in the Jewish context of Prague in the form of the aforementioned mythical figure Rabbi Yehudah Löw.[56]

The title of "philosopher" is not commonly accepted for Rabbi Löw. His life remains as legendary as his intellectual formation—only once, in fact, does he give veiled hints as to who his teachers were; he never names them outright. In citing only a few contemporary authors, the Maharal (Rabbi Löw) did not mean to distance himself from others but rather to highlight his own character as *homo novus* of his generation. Apart from his brother, Rabbi Löw makes reference only to Azariah de' Rossi, Eliezer Ashkenazi, and Don Issac Abravanel. Moses Isserles and his work, *Torat ha-'ola*, are not directly cited but are implicitly present. With this approach—in contrast to his disciple David Gans, for example—Rabbi Löw mounts an incisive critique of the world around him, reproaching it as "ignorant."

According to the Maharal, knowledge forms a Plotinian pyramid, the summit of which stands for absolute knowledge—unique and perfect, but it, like a brook, thins as it descends, drying out at the lowest point. As he sees it, the springs that once filled the well of wisdom have by his time run dry. The only hope is that true wisdom can be revived: a *tiqqun 'olam*, "the healing of the world," that would restore the primordial state. The new sciences, which the Rabbi repeatedly deems to be at odds with the Torah and rabbinical wisdom, are in truth in agreement with that wisdom, even if our awareness is too impoverished to fully understand it. One cannot, therefore, impugn ancient wisdom with an argument based in the makeup of modern consciousness. The modern exegete's task is to find the true sense, or as the Maharal affirms, the *sibbat ha-sibbot* (*causa causarum*) of the text or event, and that truth will be found by whoever does not stop at the level of the accidental, the proximate cause (*sibba qeruva*), which would be the literal sense.[57]

In his *Gevurot ha-Shem*, Rabbi Löw explains the relationship between Israel and the Gentiles. The gift of the Holy Spirit, he says, was granted only to Israel. The prophecy was handed down to no other people on earth. This distinction did not develop *a posteriori*, but is part of God's creation, implicit in the nature of man and Jewish man. Only to Jewish individuals was a superior intellect gifted by means of the Torah,[58] as the Maharal of Prague phrases it in a commentary on the Haggadah. It is as a result of this that there can be no community of goods and property between Jews and the other peoples of the world—there can only be opposition, like that be-

---

[56] On the Maharal see my own contribution, *Renaissance Philosophy in Jewish Garb*, 110–128, where the reader will find a relevant bibliography.
[57] On this element that one could well call "sceptical," see "my Maharal against Azaria de' Rossi", 65–76.
[58] Cf. Jacob Katz, *Exclusiveness and Tolerance. Studies in Jewish-Gentile Relations in Medieval and Modern Times* (Oxford: Oxford University Press, 1961), 140–141; cf. Julius Guttmann, *Philosophie des Judentums*, 144–148.

tween form and matter. The *homo perfectus*, in the Maharal's view, must also thus be *homo iudaicus*.

The emphasis on the qualification that "confession" or "religion" is what defines the human being—confessional anthropology or a divine ontology that is denominationally determinate—is the best indication of how the traditional categories of *homo naturaliter christianus* and *homo iudaicus* were problematic, that the variety of denominations posed a problem regarding the virtue of religion *vis à vis* philosophy. Both Pico and the Maharal participate in a debate that will continue over successive centuries and up to our own current day. The fundamental question—whether religion is an essential component of philosophy, or instead an assemblage of the traditional rites and symbols that distinguish one people from another—remains open.

In the next part we will set out to trace the decidedly Christian trajectory of reducing Judaism to *caerimonialia*—customs and rites—so that the shared parts of the Torah and the commandments cannot be considered *qua definitione* Jewish. They are Christian, or simply belong to all humankind. The Renaissance becomes, as such, the crossroads that marks the divergence of philosophy and Judaism.

PART TWO JEWISH PHILOSOPHY: HISTORY OF DEFINITIONS

Synopsis: How Jewish Tradition Became (Philosophy of) Religion

The crucial turning point of western thought and philosophy occurs, as we know, in the late medieval and early modern period. During this era, philosophy changed its focus from a (meta)physically centred study dedicated to establishing the existence and the essence of sub- and superlunary worlds as well as matter and form to an epistemological preoccupation with questioning the consistency, truth, and falsity of our knowledge through and beyond the senses. In the case of Jewish philosophy, a new kind of consciousness was introduced, one which reduced the mystery of creation in Jewish narrative philosophy (*arcana mundi*) to a simple account of rites and symbols, that is, religion. This new consciousness invoked a historicisation and demythologisation of the Jewish tradition. It is this period that gave birth to the concepts Jewish Philosophy (*Philosophia Hebraeorum*) and Jewish Religion (*Religio Hebraeorum* or *Iudaeorum*), which concepts were subsequently summarised in German-speaking countries as *Jüdische Philosophie:* i. e. a definition that includes both Judaism's historical contribution to "philosophy" and its mysticism, called "Jewish wisdom." This second part of my book consists of five chapters that orbit around the elements (or ingredients) of Jewish philosophy: cults vs. religion, philosophy vs. theology. Let us summarise the steps that led to the nineteenth-century concept of Jewish philosophy.

The first phase, treated in the first chapter, is the Christian practice of describing Jewish tradition as solely a set of customs, ceremonies, and rituals. Despite its grounding in the Bible, this practice was typically intent on making clear that these customs and rituals were rendered obsolete by Christ's "true religion." Connected and perhaps in contrast to the formation of the idea of "true religion," it is remarkable that the term "religion" was applied also to Judaism by Christians since the fifteenth century (with Ficino) and by Jewish scholars only beginning in the seventeenth century—an obvious consequence of the historical crisis of universal belief and power between the Renaissance/Humanism and the Early Modern periods.

However, a change in understanding must be noted: the emphasis is less on the primeval foundations of universal wisdom than on the historical development of Jewish philosophers. In the second chapter, we will deal with the origin, conception and development of a Jewish philosophy by the name of "*Philosophia Hebraeorum/Iudaeorum*," "*Jüdische Philosophy*," or "*philosophie/pensée juive*." In German publications of nineteenth century, Jewish philosophy first appeared in Leopold Zunz's manifesto of the *Wissenschaft des Judentums*. The selection of the adjective "Jewish" instead of "Hebrew" or "Judaic" is, of course, not casual: it is explicitly political in nature. Although Hebrew was commonly known as the language of the Jewish people according to the literary tradition of the Bible and the language of the creation, Christians also considered the Hebrew language to be a part of their own heritage, often labelling themselves Israelites. The terms "Jewish" and "Jew," by contrast, were applied to the "unconverted" Hebrews after the coming of Christ. The main task of the second chapter is to delve into the labelling of philosophy as Hebrew, Jewish, "of Judaism" or "of Hebraism," and into the implications of this labelling.

As new concepts arose, they often continued utilising this distinction, although each new concept had a character of its own, including "Jewish Studies" (third chapter) and "Jewish theology" (fourth chapter), which were programs of philology and cultural history explicitly concerned with religion but which often were not primarily concerned with dogma. Jewish scholars adopted the entirely new term of "philosophy of religion" to describe a rising preoccupation with philosophical topics within Judaism as well as attempts to merge Jewish philosophy into philosophy of religion after the model of Christian counterparts like Georg Wilhelm Friedrich Hegel.

Philosophy is, of course, an inspirational craft that motivated many known and unknown Jewish scholars to use the label "philosophy of religion" (*Religionsphilosophie*) to describe, characterise, and to, at times, dogmatise Jewish religion and religious thinking. The tendency to use philology as a historical methodology for the comparative analysis of Jewish philosophy was generally popular. Indeed, Jewish scholars were the first to study Islam as a philosophy and culture in a particular philological manner (e. g. engaging with different editions of texts, analysing word and concepts, comparing philosophical ideas and coinages, and so on).

An analysis of the origin and consolidation of a philosophy of Jewish religion (fifth chapter) is not expressly the object of this book. That topic will be explored in a future work on the dogmatisation of Jewish thought and philosophy, which followed the same tendency in Christian theology and philosophy. The most relevant aspect of the growth of the Jewish philosophical tradition in the nineteenth and twentieth centuries is the concentration on what we can call the "dogmatisation" of Judaism, the movement focused on emphasising the *Geist* of the Jewish past: its ideas, concepts, dogmas, all of the things that make Judaism a religion can be compared to Christianity.

After the rise of assorted scepticisms in the sixteenth to eighteenth centuries, the crisis of authority of the Enlightenment and the scientific elaboration of Jewish literature (*Wissenschaft des Judentums*), the next turning point was the construction of a philosophy of religion (*Religionsphilosophie*). The purpose of this second part is more specifically to sketch the frame of the phenomenon of the history of concepts, denominations, and ideas in Jewish philosophy between the sixteenth and the nineteenth centuries, in the epoch of which it served to provide the foundation of a *philosophia perennis* at the same time as it disappeared from Christian philosophy because of philological and historical demythologisation.

1 From *Philosophia Hebraeorum* to Jewish Religion

The Mantuan bookshop where we left Lusitanus, Azariah, and their friend was both a meeting place and the symbolic location of a larger sixteenth century shift in mentality, a convergence between the Christian search for the *Philosophia Hebraeorum* (the Kabbalah or mystical tradition), the German interest in Judaism and the Jewish tradition (Reuchlin and the Protestant movement), and a more general attention to the way in which the world of customs and rites was constitutive of identity. From the sixteenth century onwards, the river of Jewish history runs between the banks of the reduction of Jewish tradition to a question of ceremonial law on the one side and the new definition of religion, superstition, and true religion on the other. Jewish philosophy had become almost totally ignored by Christian scholars by the eighteenth and nineteenth century when a renewed consciousness of a Jewish philosophical attitude was born in the emerging *Wissenschaft des Judentums*. In this chapter, we will concentrate on the origins and development of the concepts of ceremonial law and "Jewish religion" as a necessary premise and background to the development of a "Jewish philosophy" and "philosophy of religion," which will be the focus of the following chapters.

1.1 Reducing Jewish Tradition to "Ceremonial Laws"

The realities of foreign cultures and philosophies (*Weltaschauungen*) are almost invariably more complicated than external perceptions of their customs and rites.[1] Throughout the Middle Ages, it was almost solely Jewish *customs* that attracted the focus of Christian curiosity, with little attention given to the beliefs undergirding those practices. As evidence, we need think only of Tacitus's polemical notes on Jewish customs and traditions and the numerous tractates against Judaism written by Church Fathers and Christian scholars in the Middle Ages. With few exceptions, knowledge of Jewish texts, language, and traditions was both limited and faulty, based mostly on second-hand sources; that is, either polemical reports by converts to Christianity or by other Jewish informants such as those referred to by the Church Father Jerome. Given both the difficulties of language and the prohibitions of watchful Church authorities, the reading of actual rabbinic texts or the visiting of local synagogues was neither possible nor desired.

---

[1] The first part of this chapter follows in the main my *Renaissance Philosophy in Jewish Garb: Foundations and Challenges in Judaism on the Eve of Modernity* (Leiden: Brill, 2009): 169–194. In addition to the bibliographical notes offered there, see Yaacov Deutsch, *Judaism in Christian eyes: Ethnographic descriptions of Jews and Judaism in early modern Europe* (Oxford: Oxford University Press, 2012).

The emergence of Jewish mystical texts and the increasing recognition of Jewish expertise in biblical grammar and exegesis gradually gave rise to a new attitude among Christian scholars in the Humanist and Renaissance periods. Humanist schools such as those initiated by Giovanni Pico della Mirandola and Johannes Reuchlin openly professed an appreciation of Jewish mystical traditions and literature. Suitability to Christian purposes was established by explaining that ancient (or purportedly ancient) Jewish mystical methods, texts, and traditions were Christian in either *origin* or *intention*. The result was that a number of scholars—either followers of the Kabbalistic discourse or opponents of this new intellectual fashion—wrote a large number of books, booklets, tractates, and chapters on Jewish grammar, traditions, and texts. The representation of Jewish mystical traditions contained in these works is often of good quality, frequently based on sources authored by converted Jews or created with the active cooperation of Jewish scholars. Rabbinic prohibitions against teaching Hebrew to Gentiles did not inhibit Jews from helping Christian Hebraists who wished to concern themselves with the Kabbalah.

In the Christian vision of humanity, at least in that of its more enlightened scholars, a place could be found for the toleration of non-Christian ("pagan") religions and customs. The status of Judaism and of Jewish laws as a legal institution posed a more serious problem because Judaism, in the Christian view, could not be simply categorised as a *natural* religion. Its place in the conception of humanity *more Christiano* was not clear. Judaism was seen as something anachronistic, not a valid and vital religion but an antiquated faith. The discussion of the rites of the Jews was often chiefly concerned with confirming their outdated and antiquated character.

Sources of the Discussion

The source of this view was, throughout the Middle Ages and up until the enlightenment, the Thomist vision of the law of the Old Testament. The source the theologian and philosopher Thomas Aquinas drew on was in part the Vulgate translation of Deuteronomy 6:1 (*haec sunt praecepta et caerimoniae atque iudicia*),[2] which translates *mishpaṭim* as *iudicia*, *miṣwot* as *praecepta*, and *ḥuqqim* as *caerimoniae*. However, there was a long tradition of the categorisation, cataloguing, canonisation, and Christian interpretation of Old Testament law in the Latin West dating back at least as far as Augustine. In the Scholastic period, there was a revival of the discussion in the so-called dialogue-literature, such as Peter Abelard's *Dialogus inter Philosophum, Iudaeum et Christianum* and Judah Halevi's *Sefer ha-Kuzari*.[3]

---

2 Cf. also Deuteronomy 7:11 and 11:1, 2 Ezra 9:13, 3 Kings 2:3 where all the three terms occur.
3 Leo Strauss, "The Law of Reason in the Kuzari," *Proceedings of the American Academy of Jewish Research* 3 (1943): 47–96.

According to Aquinas, "[…] we must distinguish three kinds of precept in the Old Law; viz., *moral* precepts, which are dictated by the natural law; *ceremonial* precepts, which are determinations of the Divine worship; and *judicial* precepts, which are determinations of the justice to be maintained among men."[4] The first precepts, *moralia*, are of universal value because they belong to the law of nature, while the cultic system of Israel, the *caerimonialia*, and the civil code of the nation, the *iudicialia*, were additions to the expressions of natural law found in the Old Law and summarised in the Decalogue.[5] Moral precepts derive their binding force from reason. Both ceremonial and judicial precepts, on the other hand, derive their binding force "not from reason alone, but by virtue of their institution." The distinction is very important because it introduces the category of the "institution," which gives both philosophical and political expression to Thomas's explicit goal of demonstrating the historical contingency of Jewish judicial and ceremonial law. The *iudicialia* and the *caerimonialia* are considered as having unquestionably been handed down not merely in but particularly *for* their particular historical context. By making this distinction, Thomas makes it clear that judicial and ceremonial laws point forward to the coming of Christ, who brought them to fulfilment,[6] while the natural law is a product of reason.

Aquinas displays little originality in his vision of the "Old Law" (*vetus lex*); he is indebted to the Church Fathers, including, among others, Jerome, Augustine, Albert the Great,[7] the Franciscan John of La Rochelle,[8] and the Latin version of Aristotle's *Politics*, first translated in 1262 by William of Moerbeke. Thomas is also arguing against the *Moreh Nevukhim*,[9] in which Maimonides maintains the rationality of revelation without Christ. Aquinas responds by emphasising the pedagogical role of the Torah for the Jewish people—but only prior to the coming of Christ. In his view, the Messiah's arrival rendered most of the Torah obsolete.

---

4 *Summa Theologica*, 1a, 2a–e. 99, 4. Translated by Stephen B. Casselli, "The Threefold Division of the Law in the Thought of Aquinas," *Westminster Theological Journal* 61 (1999): 175–207, here 185.
5 Ibid., 185.
6 Thomas *Summa Quaestio* 47, 2; 48: "Quia in morte Christi lex vetus consummata est, potest intelligi quod patiendo omnia veteris legis præcepta implevit: moralia quidam, quæ in præceptis caritatis fandantur, implevit in quantum passus est et ex dilectione patris et eliam ex dilectione proximi, cæremonialia vero praecepta legis, quæ ad sacrificia et oblationes præcipue ordinantur, implevit Christus sua passione, in quantum omnia antiqua sacrificia fuerunt figuræ illius veri sacriticii, quod Christus obtulit moriendo pro nobis. […] Præcepta vero judicialia legis, quæ præcipue ordinantur ad satisfaciendam injuriam passis, implevit Christus sua passione, permittens se ligno affigi pro pomo quod de ligno homo rapuerat contra dei mandatum."
7 On this question, see Aloysius Obiwulu, *Tractatus de Legibus in 13th Century Scholasticism. A Critical Study of Law in Summa Frati Alexandri, Albertus Magnus and Thomas Aquinas* (Münster: Lit Verlag 2003).
8 Cf. Beryl Smalley, "William of Auvergne, John de la Rochelle, and Thomas Aquinas on the Old Law," in *St. Thomas Aquinas Commemorative Studies*, vol. 2, ed. Armand Mauer (Toronto: Pontifical Institute of Medieval Studies, 1974): 11–71.
9 Cf. John Y.B. Hood, *Aquinas and the Jews* (Philadelphia: University of Pennsylvania Press, 1995), 41.

The first reaction to Aquinas's categorisation of the law is found a century later in the Spanish philosopher Joseph Albo's well-known *Sefer ha-'Iqqarim* (*Book of the Principles*).[10] First published in 1485, it was one of the first works of Jewish philosophy to reach a printing press. Albo was involved in the so-called Dispute of Tortosa, the main topic of which was the validity of Jewish law. In chapter XXV of part three, he quotes the opinion of a Christian scholar on this question.[11] The sages had argued that the Law was comprised of three elements:

1) the *caerimonialia*[12] are commandments relating to divine worship (i.e. relations between man and God);
2) the *iudiciales* are rules and principles relating to business transactions between man and his fellow man (i.e. relations between man and man) and finally
3) the *morales* are precepts relating to the relationship of the individual to himself (i.e. virtuous living, humility etc.).

The "Christian scholar" had attacked, in particular, the *ceremonials*, that is, Jewish divine worship, because it "commands the slaughter of animals, the burning of flesh and fat, the sprinkle of blood, all of which are unclean form of worship."[13] Albo follows the line taken by Maimonides, whom he quotes expressly, claiming that the Temple ceremonies are nothing other than stimuli for prayer and divine love. The sacrifices of the Temple service are exclusively symbolic in nature, intended to protect Israel from idolatry. Contrary to the common Christian opinion of his time, Albo argues that the Torah (the *Old* Testament, in Christian parlance) is perfect,[14] as expressly stated in Psalm 19:8: *Torat Yhwh temimah*. Hieronymus had erroneously translated *temimah* as *immaculata* (immaculate) giving rise to suspicion that the Torah was unclean. This interpretation, claims Albo, is totally unfounded, as *temimah* is nothing but a synonym for the adjective *shelemah*.[15]

Although Albo's stance was known,[16] there is little or no mention of it within later commentaries on Thomas's division of the law.[17] In the subsequent treatments

---

10 Joseph Albo, *Sefer ha-'Ikkarim* III, 25; see Sina Rauschenbach, *Joseph Albo. Jüdische Philosophie und christliche Kontroverstheologie in der Frühen Neuzeit* (Leiden: Brill, 2002), 142–156.
11 My English summary is linguistically based on the translation in Isaac Husik, ed., *Sefer ha-'Ikkarim. Book of Principles by Joseph Albo*, 4 vols, vol. 3 (Philadelphia: The Jewish Publication Society of America, 1946): 217–245 (part III, chapter XXV–XXVI).
12 All three technical terms are in Latin with Hebrew transliteration.
13 Translated by Isaac Husik.
14 *Sefer ha-'Iqqarim* III,25: On the subject of law and Torah in Albo see Sina Rauschenbach, *Josef Albo*; Dror Ehrlich "A Reassessment of Natural Law in Rabbi Joseph Albo's 'Book of Principles,'" *Hebraic Political Studies* 1 (2006): 413–439.
15 By way of proof he quotes *Numeri* 19,2 and the Midrash *Sifre Numeri* 123.
16 Cf. Michela Andreatta, *Il trattato sui dogmi ebraici (Sefer ha-'Iqqarim) di Yosef Albo. Il codice miniato dell'Accademia dei Concordi di Rovigo* (Treviso: Antilia, 2003), especially 9–64 (general introduc-

of the subject, such as that of Francisco de Vitoria, the *caerimonialia* and *iudicialia* are deemed no longer valid:

> All the commands of the Old Law which are not matters of natural law have ceased, and especially "judicial" commands, for "ceremonial" ones have certainly ceased. But with regard to judicial commands, everyone admits that they have all ceased, and for this reason a blasphemer is not now killed. It is very true that those same judicial commands could be re-instituted, so that a robber be condemned to seven-fold restitution. But in that case it would not be a command of the Old Law, but rather human law, which would prescribe this. Therefore, the fact that it is now lawful to kill a murderer is not because of an exception to the law, because that exception has ceased and in the same way that command about killing has ceased, since all judicial commands have ceased.[18]

The discussion continues in the seventeenth century. In his *Colloquium*, the lawyer, historian, and philosopher Jean Bodin[19] divides divine law into three branches: *lex*

---

tion and translation of chapters xxv–xxvi of the third part) and 65–78, which is by Giuliano Tamani and which can be found on the manuscript and print tradition of the book.

17 Chapter XXV of part 3 of Sefer ha-'Ikkarim was separately translated into Latin in 1566 by the Benedictine Gilbert Genebrard, *R. Iosephi, R. Davidis Kimhi, et alius cuiusdam Hebraei anonymi argumenta, quibus nonnulos fidei Christianae articulos oppugnant* (Paris: Martinus Iuvenis, 1566); on this translation with the correspondent polemical commentary of the author see Sina Rauschenbach, *Josef Albo*, 178–198.

18 Commentary on *Summa Theologiae IIa-IIae Q. 64* in John P. Doyle, *Francisco de Vitoria OP. On Homicide, and Commentary on Thomas Aquinas: Summa theologiae 2a 2a–e 64* (Milwaukee: Marquette University Press, 1997), 143: "Secundo dico de adultera, quod in Hispania solum permittitur occidi, non tamen in aliis provinciis ut Aragonae, Italia, Gallia. Sed bene faciunt Hispani, utuntur enim jure communi, quia leges videntur illud permittere. Et ad argumentum Scoti quo probat illud esse revocatum in lege nova, miror quidem de illo. Ideo dico quod omnia praecepta veteris legis quae non sunt de jure naturali, cessaverunt, et praecipue judicialia, quia caeremonialia etiam cessaverunt. Sed de judicialibus omnes fatentur cessare omnia, et ideo blasphemus modo non occiditur. Bene verum est quod possent eadem illa praecepta judicialia iterum institui, ut quod latro condemnetur ad septenas; sed tunc non esset praeceptum veteris legis, sed lex humana quae hoc praeciperet. Ergo quod liceat occidere nunc homicidam, non est propter illam exceptionem legis, quia illa exceptio cessavit; et ita illud praeceptum de occidendo cessavit, quia omnia judicialia cessaverunt. Sed tamen quia rex et imperator potest illa civilia jura nunc imponere et tenebunt, hinc est quod si licet occidere homicidam, non est quia sit exceptio in veteri, lege, sed quia nunc est lex imperatoris quae praecipit hoc."

19 Joannes Bodinus, *Colloquium heptaplomeres de rerum sublimium arcanis abditis e codicibus manuscriptis bibliothecae academicae gissensis cum varia lectione aliorum apographorum nunc primum typis describendum*, ed. Ludwig Noack (Schwerin: F.G. Baerensprung, 1857): "SALOMO: Nihil in majestate Bibliorum antiquius aut sacratius est lege divina, cujus divisio triplex est. Nam praeter historiarum libros praecipua est lex moralis, secunda ritualis, tertia politica. Moralis iterum duplex: altera pars ad Dei cultum, altera ad hominum inter ipsos mutua officia spectat. Dei cultus quatuor decalogi capitibus primis continetur, caetera sex capita ad tuendam hominum inter se fidem ac societatem pertinent. Politica vero diffusius eadem complectitur, quae secunda tabula brevissime continet, scilicet leges judiciales, connubiales, praetorias, quibus Hebraeorum respublica fundata est et constituta, sine quibus licet et viro bono in desertissima solitudine et ubique terrarum salutem adipisci. Ritus

divina, *lex ritualis*, and *lex politica*. Divine law exists in two varieties: that relating to the cult (the first four commandments of the Decalogue), and that relating to social behaviour (the other six commandments); the *politica* on which the Hebrew republic was founded are the laws that order common, everyday life (judicial laws, civil code, etc.); the *lex ritualis* is concerned with ceremonies, sacrifices, etc. For Bodin, the *lex politica* is not temporary; it stands as a foundation for Christianity.[20]

The "Ethnography" of the Jews

The growth of interest in Jewish rites and ceremonies at this time was, to be clear, not principally a manifestation of an effort to create an "ethnology" of the Jews, as some scholars maintain. It was the result, rather, of explicitly political efforts whose aim was the denial of any authoritative value of Jewish law. The publications are not a (polemical) peephole into life in the ghetto and the Jewish community (ethnography). They are an exposure of Jewish "acts" and "beliefs" as anachronistic religious practices. They were not a careful and accurate presentation of the life of the Jews but a listing of their disgraceful and outmoded customs and prayers.

The first example of an ethnography of the Jews is a booklet by Johannes Pfefferkorn, a converted Jew from Moravia, entitled: *Ich heyß ain buchlein der iuden peicht*.[21] In this text he describes the rituals and ceremonies proper to two Jewish holidays, *Rosh ha-Shanah* (New Year) and *Yom Kippur* (Day of Atonement). Perhaps in the same year, another converted Jew, Victor von Carben, published a description of Jewish holy days, customs, and ceremonies, entitled: *Hierinne wirt gelesen, wie Her Victor von Carben, Welicher eyn Rabi der Iude gewest ist zu Christlichem glawb komen*.[22] Both Pfefferkorn and von Carben wrote with the intention of converting

---

vero et sacrificia a Deo instituta, ut Israëlitae, qui ab Aegyptiis et finitimis populis sacra daemonibus et animalium statuis facere didicerant, ab iis deinceps abstinerent, quod fieri non potuisset ob inveteratum daemonibus sacrificandi morem, nisi eadem sacra Deo facere juberentur."

20 For a different conception that goes beyond Thomas's triune division of Jewish law, see for example John Calvin, *Institutio Christianae religionis* 4:20.

21 *Ich heyß ain büchlein der iuden peicht. In allen orten vindt man mich leicht. Vil newer meren seind mir wol bekannt* (Cologne: Johannes Landen, 1508); Latin: *Libellus de judaica confessione sive sabbato afflictionis* (Nuremberg: Jo. Weyssenburger, 1508); see Hans-Martin Kirn, *Das Bild vom Juden im Deutschland des frühen 16. Jahrhunderts dargestellt an den Schriften Johannes Pfefferkorns* (Tübingen: Mohr, 1989); Yaacov Deutsch, "Von der Juden Ceremonien," in Bell, ed., *Jews, Judaism*, 338–340.

22 Ortuin Gratius or de Graes, together with Victor von Carben, seems to have written an anti-Jewish tractate as early as 1504: *De vita et moribus Iudaeorum* (quoted in his history of the Jews by Graetz and others). In the Reuchlin-Pfefferkon's dispute, Ortuin played a fairly significant role. In 1509, de Graes translated Victor von Carben's *Opus Aureum ac Novum in quo Omnes Judæorum Errores Manifestantur*, in which he dealt with the life and customs of the Jews. On the works of von Carben see Wolfgang Schmitz, *Die Überlieferung deutscher Texte im Kölner Buchdruck des 15. und 16. Jahrhunderts*, (University of Cologne, Habilitationsschrift, 1990); see further Hava Fraenkel-Goldschmidt, "On the Periphery of Jewish Society: Jewish Converts to Christianity in Germany During the Reformation,"

Jews "from their wickedness" (Pfefferkorn: "von yrer böshait"). Both present a nearly accurate account of Jewish rituals, as Yaacov Deutsch argues;[23] their purpose, of course, was to expose the "ludicrousness" and "absurdity" of Jewish rituals and, above all, the anti-Christian nature of certain prayers and ceremonies.

Somewhat friendlier in aim is the work of François Tissard,[24] author of the first text on Hebrew grammar and of the first work in Greek characters to appear in France. Tissard was a student of Avraham Farissol, who taught him Hebrew over a period of several years.[25] He appended the tractate *De Iudaeorum ritibus compendium* to his Hebrew grammar (1508) with the intention of furnishing the French public with information about Jewish rites and costumes hitherto unknown because Jews did not commonly reveal them to strangers:[26] "I strongly desired to witness their rites, to hear their singing and to comprehend their mysteries."[27] In his view, it was only through an understanding of Jewish literature and rituals, not compulsion, that it would be possible to convert them to Christianity.

After the Lutheran Reformation, the literary genre of descriptions of Jewish rituals and ceremonies made a new and more successful beginning. The first comprehensive treatise on Jewish customs and rites, including the first translation of a Hebrew prayer book into a European language, was composed by the converted Jew Anthonius Margaritha. The work was entitled *Der gantz Jüdisch glaub*[28] (*The Entire*

---

in *Culture and Society in Medieval Jewry* [Hebrew], ed. Menahem Ben Sasson, Robert Bonfil, and Joseph R. Hacker (Jerusalem: Magnes, 1989), 623–654; Maria Diemling, "'Christliche Ethnographien' über Juden und Judentum in der Frühen Neuzeit" (PhD dissertation, University of Vienna, 1999). The Berliner library owns a book listed under the call number Um2059/100, *Ricoldi, Ordinis praedicatorum, Contra sectam Mahumeticam non indignus scitu libellus. Cuiusdam diu captivi Turcorum provinciae septemcastrensis, de vita & moribus eorundem alius non minus necessarius libellus. Adjunctus est insuper Libellus de vita & moribus Judaeorum* (Paris: Stephanus, 1511). In the first edition, dated 1509, there was no mention of the *Libellus*, which is probably to be attributed to Ortuin.
23 Yaacov Deutsch, "Von der Juden Ceremonien," 338–342.
24 François Tissard, *Dialogus: Prothymopatris kai Phronimos [...] De Judaeorum ritibus compendium. Tabula elementorum Hebraicorum. Documenta ut debeant illa elementa proferri ac legi. Ut Hebraei numeros signant. Oratio dominica Hebraicis characteribus impressa. Genealogia beatae Mariae: una cum aliis plusculis eisdem characteribus impressioni mandata. Iesus Nazarenus Rex Iudaeorum Latine, Graece et Hebraice. Grammatica Hebraica succincte tradita. Tabula elementorum Graecorum cum diphtongis et pronunciandi regulis et pluribus Graecis orationibus et Hyppocratis iusiurando. Abbrevationes Graece. Ut Graeci numeros signant amplissima descriptio. Operoso huic opusculo extremam imposuit manum Egidius Gourmontius integerrimus ac fidelissimus primus duce Francisco Tissardo Graecarum et Hebraearum litterarum* (Parrhisiis impressor, 1508).
25 On the humanist Tissard and his attitude towards Judaism, see David B. Ruderman, *The World of a Renaissance Jew. The Life and Thought of Abraham ben Mordecai Farissol* (Cincinnati: Hebrew Union College Press, 1981): 98–106 and footnotes 215–217.
26 Fol. 1b–2b.
27 Fol. 17b; English translation by David B. Ruderman, *The World of a Renaissance Jew*, 100–101.
28 Peter von der Osten-Sacken, *Martin Luther und die Juden: Neu untersucht anhand von Anton Margarithas "Der gantz Jüdisch glaub" (1530/31)* (Stuttgart: Kohlhammer, 2002); Maria Diemling, "Anthonius Margaritha on 'Whole Jewish Faith': A Sixteenth-Century Convert from Judaism and his Depic-

Jewish Faith)[29] and had a marked influence on generations of Christian scholars. As such, it is central to any research on "Jewish rites." In the first part of his book, Margaritha outlines Jewish rituals and customs; the second part contains translated daily prayers. Despite the existence of the earlier works by François Tissard, Johannes Pfefferkorn, and Victor von Carben, "it was *Der gantz Jüdisch glaub,* which became the first example of a new literary genre,"[30] as Maria Diemling has pointed out. The purpose of the book was to de-authorise the rabbinic tradition and present it as non-Biblical, even as an active contradiction to the Bible. As Steven Burnett puts it, the "goal was not to satisfy the curiosity of Christians, but to expose Judaism as an unbiblical religion that posed a danger to Christian faith."[31] Martin Luther found Margaritha's book "so great a solace that he had it read to him for a time regularly at his table; he compared the several rites and ceremonies therein described with the idolatrous worship of the Papists,"[32] as Louis I. Newman notes.

Towards the end of the sixteenth century, a number of other works on the subject appeared: the *Tractatus de imposturis et ceremoniis Iudaeorum nostri temporis,* by Conrad Huser, alias Lombardus Marcus,[33] was published in 1575. Some years later, Rudolf Wirth, alias Rudolf Hospinian, issued two works on Jewish festivals and ceremonies: *De Festis Judaeorum et Ethnicorum, hoc est de origine, progressu, ceremoniis et ritibus festorum dierum Christianorum*[34] and *De origine progressu ceremoniis et ritibus festorum dierum Judaeorum, Graecorum, Romanorum et Turcarum.*[35] In 1603, Johannes Buxtorf published his well-known *Juden-Schül,* which went through a number of printings, in Latin, Dutch, and English translation under the title *Synagoga Judaica;*[36] this text quickly became the single most popular book on Judaism availa-

---

tion of the Jewish Religion," in *Jews, Judaism, and the Reformation,* ed. Dean P. Bell and Stephen G. Burnett (Leiden: Brill, 2016): 303–333.

29 Antonius Margarithus, *Der ganz Jüdisch Glaub mit sampt ainer gründtlichen und warhafften anzaygunge aller Satzungen, Ceremonien, Gebetten, haymliche und offentliche Gebreuch* (Augsburg: Heinrich Steyner, 1530).

30 Maria Diemling, "Margaritha," 308.

31 Stephen G. Burnett, "Distorted Mirrors: Antonius Margaritha, Johann Buxtorf and Christian Ethnographies of the Jews," *Sixteenth Century Journal* 25 (1994): 275–287, here 276.

32 Louis I. Newman, *Jewish Influence on Christian Reform Movements* (New York: Columbia University Press, 1925), 627.

33 *Tractatus de imposturis et ceremoniis Iudaeorum nostri temporis, antea quidem ab authore Germanice editus: nunc vero in gratiam Reipublicae Christianae Latine redditus a Conrado Husero Tigurino* (Basileae: Per Petrum Pernam, 1575); Herzog August Library, Wolfenbüttel A: 177.4 Theol. (6); see Gaby Knoch-Mund, *Disputationsliteratur als Instrument antijüdischer Polemik. Leben und Werk des Marcus Lombardus, eines Grenzgängers zwischen Judentum und Christentum im Zeitalter des deutschen Humanismus* (Tübingen, Basel 1997).

34 Two volumes, Tiguri, 1592/93

35 Three volumes, Zürich, 1593.

36 German: (Basel, 1603; Hanau 1643, 1680; Frankfurt and Leipzig, 1728, 1729, 1737, 1738 Latin: Hanau, 1604, 1614, 1622, 1641, 1661; Basel, 1680, 1712 Hildesheim, 1989: Reprint of the 1680 Latin ed-

ble, at least in Protestant countries. The seventeenth and early eighteenth centuries saw additional contributions. Among these are the works of two Jewish authors: Simone Luzzatto's *Discorso* and Leone Modena's *Riti*. Works by Christians include Johannes Andrea Quenstedt's *Sepultura veterum sive tractatus de antiquis ritibus* (1660),[37] Georgius Sigimundus Strebel's *De antiquis Judaeorum Ritibus* (1664),[38] John Spencer's *De legibus Hebraeorum* (1685),[39] and other writings by less well-known students and scholars of Judaism at German and other European universities.

Between the beginning of the Protestant reformation and the end of the political seclusion of the Jews in ghettos, Christian literary production relating to Jewish rituals and ceremonies was undeniably vast, its expansion extending to nearly all countries in Northern Europe. Modern scholars face a difficult task in finding a plausible explanation for this interest as well as in elucidating why the phenomenon began in this period at all. Nevertheless, in coming to terms with this literary and polemical phenomenon, care must be taken to avoid modern religious, literary, and political categories that are unsuited to the period under examination. We especially should not consider this an early example of modern ethnography.

Current explanations suggesting "ethnographical" interests as the root of this scholarship, as proposed by Ronnie Po-chia Hsia,[40] or "polemical ethnography," as proposed by Yaacov Deutsch,[41] may possibly shed some light on popular interest in foreign rites and symbols. In my opinion, however, they are insufficient to explain the theological, philosophical and political foundations of that interest. I would even go so far as to argue that common theories of a "Christian ethnology" of non-Christian peoples are not applicable here. The central interest of this study was not a modern concern with expressions of human diversity as represented by ethnic divisions

---

ition. Georg Olms Verlag, Dutch: Amsterdam, 1694; Leiden, 1702 Rotterdam, 1731 English: London 1663, 1742.

37 *Sepultura veterum sive Tractatus de antiquis ritibus sepulchralibus graecorum, romanorum, judaeorum & christianorum,* [...] / *studio & opera Johannis Andreae Quenstedt* (Wittenberg: Sumptib, Haered, D. Tobiae, Mevii, & Elerdi Schumacheri, typis haered. Melchioris Oelschlegelii, 1660).

38 *Decas selecta positionum philologicarum de antiquis antiquis Judaeorum ritibus et moribus, unde quamplurimis ssae. locis lux aliqua affunditur August Pfeiffer* [Resp.:] Georgius Sigismundus Strebel August Pfeiffer; Georg Sigismund Strebel (Wittenberg: Henckel, 1664).

39 *De legibus Hebraeorum ritualibus et earum rationibus. Libri Tres* (Cambridge: Richard Chiswel, 1685); *De legibus hebraeorum ritualibus earumque rationibus libri quatuor. Praemittitur Christ. Matth. Pfaffii, Dissertatio praeliminaris qua de vita Spenceri, de libri pretio & erroribus quoque disseritur. Autoresque, qui contra Spencerum scripsere, enarrantur* (The Hague: Arnold Leers, 1686); see Jonathan M. Elukin, "Maimonides and the Rise and Fall of the Sabians: Explaining Mosaic Laws and the Limits of Scholarship," *Journal of the History of Ideas* 63 (2002): 619–637.

40 Ronnie Po-chia Hsia, "Christian Ethnographies of Jews in Early Modern Germany," in *The Expulsion of the Jews: 1492 and After,* ed. Raymond B. Waddington and Arthur H. Williamson (New York: Garland 1994): 223–235.

41 Yaacov Deutsch, "Representations of Jews in Sixteenth-Century Germany," in *Jews, Judaism, and the Reformation:* 347–356; Cf. Elisheva Carlebach, *Divided Souls: Converts from Judaism in Germany 1500–1750* (New Haven: Yale University Press, 2001).

and cultural and social cults and beliefs. Rather, at issue was the legal status of non-Christian peoples who came under Christian rule, either in the past or in the present. Judaism was a case unto itself because, although it was a separate ethnic group under Christian rule, it had deep connections with Christian origins and theology. To clarify this point, it will be useful to briefly look into Christian attitudes towards "Gentiles" in the Humanist period.

The Christian reaction to Gentile customs and beliefs initially took the form of apologies in defence of Christianity. At the core of this reaction was a concern with understanding the legal status of the Gentiles in Christian society. Christian interest in this issue can be observed in works dealing with the customs and beliefs of Turks and Native Americans. Aloysius de Crieva (Ludovicus Cervarius Tubero), a Ragusian historiographer writing at the turn of sixteenth century described Turkish customs and religious beliefs,[42] dwelling on their atrocities against prisoners. Bartholomeus Georgijevic published a book on Turkish customs in 1544.[43] Bartolome de las Casas and Francisco de Vitoria are well-known for their early reports on the "Indians" of the new world[44] and for their development of a new concept of natural law as international law.[45]

As noted by Victor Segesvary,[46] the Catholic Church was concerned with the danger of a return to paganism, as some contemporaneous scholars recognised in other religions and peoples a reflection of the *theologia* or *philosophia naturalis* that could serve as the basis for a Christian dialogue with non-Christian systems. For Raymond of Sabunde,[47] known not least from Montaigne's "Apology de Raymond Sebond,"[48] natural theology cannot be reduced to a religious text and thus can serve as the basis of all things, understandable to all. In Raymond's thesis we find enunciated for the first time the notion of a common *substratum* existing between all peoples and religions, a common premise and basis for all religion. His philosophy of nature,

---

[42] Ludovicus Cervarius Tubero, *De Turcarum origine, moribus et rebus gestis* (Florence: apud Antonium Patauinium, 1590).

[43] *De Turcarum moribus epitome* (Lyon: J. Tornaesius, 1555).

[44] Modern edition: Bartolomé de las Casas, *Historia de las Indias*, edición preparada por la Fundación 'Instituto Bartolomé de las Casas,' de los Dominicos de Andalucía (Madrid: Alianza Editorial 1994); Franciscus de Victoria, *De Indis recenter inventis et de jure belli Hispanorum in barbaros. Relectiones: Vorlesungen über die kürzlich entdeckten Inder und das Recht der Spanier zum Kriege gegen die Barbaren 1539*, ed. Walter Schätzel (Tübingen: Mohr, 1952).

[45] On this very important aspect see James B. Scott, *The Spanish Origin of International Law. Francisco de Vitoria and his Law of Nations*, (Oxford: The Clarendon Press, 1934).

[46] *L'Islam et la reforme: Étude sur l'attitude des reformateurs Zurichois envers l'Islam 1510–1550* (La Haye: Mikes International, 2005), 35.

[47] Raymundus de Sabunde, *Theologia naturalis, sive liber creaturarum* (Strassburg: Martin Flach, 21 Jan. 1496). See Jose Luis Sanchez Nogales, *Camino del hombre a Dios: la teología natural de R. Sibiuda* (See Granada: Facultad de Teología, 1995).

[48] There are a huge number of editions, see e.g. *Apologie de Raymond Sebond*, ed. Paul Mathias (Paris: Flammarion, 1999).

however, should not obscure the fact that the place of natural theology is, of course, fixed, in his view, within the bounds of Christian revelation.

Contrary to the irenic view of recent scholarship in this area, I remain highly sceptical towards attempts to discover an enlightened attitude toward other religions among Christian scholars of the Late Medieval and Humanist periods. The celebrated conception of Nicolas of Cusa, according to which there is one religion in a multiplicity of rites,[49] cannot obscure the fact that he saw every good, pious, and beautiful aspect of the Koran as having its origins the light of the Gospel.[50] Only the Christian religion can be seen as the basis or substratum of all humanity, which other religions fail to acknowledge, whether intentionally or otherwise. The variety of rites is not an expression of a variety of equivalent pieties but of relative ignorance and partial deviations from the one true divine plan for humanity.

Some decades later, the conquistadores took up the motif of the ignorance of the "Indians," specifically their seeming lack of any conception of morality, in order to justify war against them in keeping with Biblical precepts against idolatry and immorality. The Spanish royal chronicler Gonzalo Fernandez de Oviedo wrote the following "observations" in the first part of his *Historia general y natural de las Indias* (1535) on the Amerindians:

> [They are] naturally lazy and vicious, melancholic, cowardly, and in general a lying, shiftless people. Their marriages are not a sacrament but a sacrilege. They are idolatrous, libidinous and commit sodomy. Their chief desire is to eat, drink, worship heathen idols, and commit bestial obscenities. What could one expect from a people whose skulls are so thick and hard that the Spaniards had to take care in fighting not to strike on the head lest their swords be blunted?[51]

The original focus of this text was of course race, yet its possibly more important point is the classification of Amerindian "customs" within the catalogue of sins against "natural law" as iterated in the Bible. Commenting on this text, Thomas F. Gosse states: "In Spain a debate continued throughout the sixteenth century on the question of whether the Indians in the New World were really men, or whether they were beasts or perhaps beings intermediate between beasts and men. As in

---

49 "Una religio in rituum varietate," *De conjecturis* I, 13, written between 1440 and 1444; see Walter A. Euler, "*Una religio in rituum varietate*. Der Beitrag des Nikolaus von Kues zur Theologie der Religionen," *Jahrbuch für Religionswissenschaft und Theologie der Religionen* 3 (1995): 67–82; Angelo Marchesi, *Una religio in tritium varietate. Il pensiero ecumenico di Nicola Cusano* (Parma: Zara 1986).
50 Nicholas of Cusa, *Cribatio alchorani* I, 6: "[...] sid quid pulchri, veri et clari in Achorani repetitur, necesse est, quod sit radius lucidissimi evangelii."
51 Gonzalo Fernandez de Oviedo, *Historia general y natural de las Indias, Islas y Tierra Firme del Mar Oceano*, ed. José Amador de los Rios, 4 vols. (Madrid: Real Academia de la Historia, 1851–1855), part I: Lib. 2, cap. 6; Lib. 4, cap. 2; quoted from Lewis Hanke, *The Spanish Struggle for Justice in the Conquest of America* (Philadelphia: University of Pennsylvania Press, 1949), 11; see also Olive Patricia Dickason, *The Myth of the Savage, and the Beginnings of French Colonialism in the Americas* (Edmonton: University of Alberta Press, 1997), 31–32.

the case of the Jews, we find arguments that the Indians were an accursed people." [52]

Without becoming overly entangled in the details of a very complicated question, I would partially disagree. Oviedo's main purpose is to justify a colonial war by indirectly invoking the Bible, where in Kings 14:24 the destruction of the Canaanites is justified by exaggerating their obscene practices and idolatry. The negative qualities of the Amerindians are nothing but the inversion of natural law, as understood both by Christian and Jews, including, among other crimes, perverse sexual practices, idolatry, lying, and other "sins against nature."[53] In Oviedo's vision and description, the Amerindians are the subject of an ethical and ethnological *Wunderkammer* ("Cabinet of curiosities"). It is, incidentally, no accident that such museums were a product of this period.[54] Each cabinet of curiosity was a product of the (creative) imagination, a Christian fiction, aimed at depicting non-Christian peoples and their environments as scenes of fantasy, inhabited by monsters and animal rarities. As beautiful as these curious spectacles may seem, however, they are capable of brutality, indecent behaviour, nudity,[55] and cannibalism.[56] The invention of the "noble savage," by such thinkers as Montaigne, was a reaction to this phenomenon.[57]

One figure opposed to forcing the Amerindians into submission was the Spanish Dominican mentioned above, Francisco de Vitoria. In his *De Indis et Iure belli* (written in 1539/1540, published in 1557), de Vitoria states expressly that even the "Indians' sins against natural law" provide neither an absolute nor a legal reason for compelling them:

> Christian princes cannot, even by the authorization of the Pope, restrain the Indians from sins against the law of nature or punish them because of those sins. My first proof is that the writers in question build on a false hypothesis, namely, that the Pope has jurisdiction over the Indian aborigines, as said above. My second proof is as follows: They mean to justify such coercion either universally for sins against the law of nature, such as theft, fornication, and adultery, or particularly for sins against nature, such as those which St. Thomas deals with (*Secunda Secundae*, qu. 154, arts. 11, 12), the phrase "sin against nature" being employed not only of what is contrary to the law of nature, but also of what is against the natural order and is called uncleanness in II Corinthians 12, according to the commentators, such as intercourse with boys and with animals or intercourse of woman with woman, whereon see Romans 1.

---

52 Thomas F. Gossett, *Race. The History of an Idea in America*, New Edition, (Oxford: Oxford University Press, 1997), 12.
53 Thomas, *Secunda Secundae*, qu. 154, arts. 11, 12.
54 Cf. Oliver Impey and Arthur MacGregor, *The Origins of Museums: The Cabinet of Curiosities in Sixteenth- and Seventeenth-Century Europe* (Oxford: Clarendon Press, 1985); see also William C. Sturtevant, "Does Anthropology Need Museums?" *Proceedings of the Biological Society of Washington* 82 (1969): 619–650.
55 Cf. Rachel Doggett, *New World of Wonders. European Images of the Americas 1492–1700* (Seattle: University of Washington Press, 1992), 38–42.
56 Cf. Christian Feest, "Mexico and South America in the European Wunderkammer," in *The Origins of Museums: The Cabinet of Curiosities in Sixteenth- and Seventeenth Century Europe*, ed. Oliver Impey and Arthur Macgregor (Oxford: Clarendon Press, 1985), 237–244.
57 Cf. Rachel Doggett, *New World*, 52 and 91 and corresponding pictures.

Now, if they limit themselves to the second meaning, they are open to the argument that homicide is just as grave a sin, and even a graver sin, and, therefore, it is clear that, if it is lawful in the case of the sins of the kind named, therefore it is lawful also in the case of homicide. Similarly, blasphemy is a sin as grave and so the same is clear, therefore. If, however, they are to be understood in the first sense, that is, as speaking of all sin against the law of nature, the argument against them is that the coercion in question is not lawful for fornication; therefore not for the other sins which are contrary to the law of nature.[58]

According to de Vitoria there does exist a natural law, the law of reason, which must also be followed by the Amerindians. The subject of his discussion, however, does not relate to the conception and content of "natural law," but to the jurisdiction and legal authority, both Papal and royal, for enforcing that law. The legal argument against the subjugation of the Amerindians and the subsequent punishment for their "sins" is that the Pope, as guarantor and supreme authority of the Christian faith, does not have any political jurisdiction over the "Indians." Moreover, war against the Amerindians with the intent of subjugating and converting them is not permitted by Christian law.

And what about Judaism and the Jews living under Christian rule? On this question, which is of fundamental importance to the present study, de Vitoria displays a distinctly liberal attitude: although the Jews, like the Saracens, are enemies of Christianity, they are not compelled to embrace Christian faith.[59] In terms of their legal standing, they are to be dealt with like Christians: criminal acts of theft or robbery against them are to be treated no less seriously than when such acts are committed against Christians:

> Unbelief does not destroy either natural law or human law; but ownership and dominion are based either on natural or on human law; therefore, they are not destroyed by want of faith. In fine, this is as obvious an error as the foregoing. Hence it is manifest that it is not justifiable to take anything that they possess from either Saracens or Jews or other unbelievers as such, that is, because they are unbelievers; but the act would be theft or robbery no less than if it were done to Christians.[60]

De Vitoria's enlightened position on Judaism (and Islam) did not, of course and unfortunately, reflect the mainstream of thought, either in Roman Catholic academies

---

58 Francisco de Vitoria, *De Indis*, part 2, 10:16; English translation by John Pawley Bate quoted as appendix to James B. Scott, *The Spanish Origin*, 324.
59 See Francisco de Vitoria, *De Indis*, part 1, 24 and, above all, part 2, 10, 322: "Sixth proposition: Although the Christian faith may have been announced to the Indians with adequate demonstration and they have refused to receive it, yet this is not a reason which justifies making war on them and depriving them of their property. This conclusion is definitely stated by St. Thomas (*Secunda Secundae, qu. 10, art. 8)*, where he says that unbelievers who have never received the faith, like Gentiles and Jews, are in no wise to be compelled to do so."
60 Francisco de Vitoria, *De Indis*, part 2, 7; English translation by John Pawley Bate quoted as appendix to James B. Scott, *The Spanish Origin*, 301.

or in Protestant theology, as we will illustrate below. Jewish communities in the Christian world had a special status. Their position depended on the goodwill of the sovereign power. Their laws were considered "rites and ceremonies" that had been revealed to Moses at a specific time and which corresponded to their particular situation at that time, but which, in the intervening period, had been rendered void by the God of the New Testament.

A Lutheran Point of View

The controversy over the value of Jewish (biblical) ritual law is the central issue in the Jewish-Christian debate in fifteenth century Spain, which was subsequently exported into Ashkenazic lands.[61] The fact that Margaritha, although he deals only with Jewish customs, ceremonies, and prayers, entitled his book *The Whole Jewish Faith* should not be overlooked. On the other hand, the debate over the threefold division of Old Testament laws was the central point in the dispute between Protestants and Catholics. In his commentary on Galatians 2:16, a central text in Lutheran theology, Luther, the former monk, states:[62]

> For the sake of argument let us suppose that you could fulfil the Law in the spirit of the first commandment of God: "Thou shalt love the Lord, thy God, with all thy heart." It would do you no good. A person simply is not justified by the works of the Law.
> The works of the Law, according to Paul, include the whole Law, judicial, ceremonial, moral. Now, if the performance of the moral law cannot justify, how can circumcision justify, when circumcision is part of the ceremonial law? The demands of the Law may be fulfilled before and after justification. There were many excellent men among the pagans of old, men who never heard of justification. They lived moral lives. But that fact did not justify them. Peter, Paul, all Christians, live up to the Law. But that fact does not justify them. "For I know nothing by myself," says Paul, "yet am I not hereby justified." (I Corinthians 4:4.)
> The nefarious opinion of the papists, which attributes the merit of grace and the remission of sins to works, must here be emphatically rejected.

Luther continues this exposition in his commentary on Galatians 4:3:

> In calling the Law the elements of the world, Paul refers to the whole Law, principally to the ceremonial law which dealt with external matters, as meat, drink, dress, places, times, feasts, cleansings, sacrifices, etc. These are mundane matters which cannot save the sinner. Ceremonial laws are like the statutes of governments dealing with purely civil matters, as commerce, inheritance, etc. As for the pope's church laws forbidding marriage and meats, Paul calls them elsewhere the doctrines of devils. You would not call such laws elements of heaven.

---

61 I cannot here elaborate on this point in such detail as it merits.
62 All references to this text are quoted are from *Commentary on the Epistle to the Galatians (1535) by Martin Luther*, translated by Theodore Graebner (Grand Rapids: Zondervan Publishing House, 1949).

While Jews and Catholics follow ritual (ceremonial) laws, they do not have any foundation in revealed Biblical law, which Christ has fulfilled. This aspect is also stressed in a sermon discussing Matthew 21:12–13 Luther delivered in Leipzig on 12 August 1545.[63] In this passage, Jesus went into the Temple, and cast out all who sold and bought in the temple, overthrowing the tables of the moneychangers and the seats of those who sold doves: "and said to them, 'It is written, My house shall be called the house of prayer; but you have made it a den of assassins'" (in Luther's version). The Wittenberg Reformer interprets the scene not as a criticism of the Jewish people, who gained money by profiting from the presence and importance of the Temple, but rather of the priestly class, with their cults and ceremonies.

"Den of assassins" refers first and foremost to the bloody offerings of the Jewish priests, characterised as "proper liturgy" (*ordentlicher Gottesdienst*). Luther recognised this proper divine service as valid, although it was later abolished by Christ. His comments are aimed not at the Jews, of course, but at the Catholic Church, whose offering in the Holy Mass represents the "murder" of the son of God. These offerings should be seen as representing the traditional service to God, whereas Christ himself, according to Luther, speaks, like Jeremiah, only of prayer. In this context, Luther applies to "old" Jews and the old tradition of the Catholics the same reproach: that of *Seelenmörder* ("murderers of the souls"). He portrays the Pope, the friars, and the monks as priests of the old Temple, selling their services (ceremonial cults) and murdering the souls of the poor.[64]

Jewish Answers in Sixteenth-Century Venice

If the *caerimonialia* are an aspect of Biblical law that has been suppressed and abrogated by Christ as no longer valid, we may ask why the Venetian Rabbis Simone Luzzatto and Leone Modena chose such a paradigmatic term to describe Jewish life and customs. In the introduction to his *Riti*,[65] Leone Modena speaks of the under-

---

63 *D. Martin Luthers Werke. Krirtische Gesamtausgabe*, vol. 51, (Weimar: Hermann Böhlaus Nachfolger 1914), 22–41. I thank Dr. Beyse, University of Halle, for the reference to Luther's text.
64 "[...] das da sollte ein Bethaus sein (wie Christus as Jesaja lvi. sagt), machen sie zu einem schendlichen kauffhaus, ja zur Modgruben der Seelen" (31); "[...] Aber sie trieben allein auffs opffer on die lere und anruffen, Darüber ward das Haus zu nichts anderes denn zu einer Mordergruben. Denn damit verderbten sie die armen seelen [...] (33); "[...] dann sie nichts sind denn Seelenmörder (weil sie nichts recht leren, wie man gleuben und beten sol) [...]" (36).
65 Leone Modena, *Historia de riti Hebraici. Vita, & osseruanza de gl'Hebrei di questi tempi*, 2nd ed. (Venice: Benedetto Miloco, 1678); Leone Modena, *Les Juifs présentés aux chrétiens. Cérémonies et coutumes qui s'observent aujourd'hui parmi le Juifs*, ed. Jacques Le Bruns, Guy G. Stroumsa (Paris: Les belles Lettres, 1998); Cecil Roth, "Leone de Modena and the Christian Hebraists of his Age," in *Jewish Studies in Memory of Israel Abrahams* (New York: Press of the Jewish Institute of Religion, 1927): 384–401; Cecil Roth, "Léon de Modène, ses Riti ebraici et le Saint Office de Venise," *Revue des Études Juives* 7 (1929): 83–88; Mark R. Cohen, "Leone da Modena's Riti: A Seventeenth Century Plea for So-

lying purpose that motivated his tractate: to provide a response to the deficiencies of the Johannes Buxtorf's *Synagoga Judaica*.[66] This clearly apologetic work is aimed at correcting the vision of Christian scholars. The division of his book into 5 chapters, in imitation of the Torah, is a patent reference to the Biblical roots of Judaism. I do not know whether he was aware that Christian commentaries on *riti* no longer questioned their biblical foundations, but focused rather on their validity following the "Redemption" of Christ.

A more efficient use of the Christian terminology is to be found, however, in Simone Luzzatto's *Discorso*[67] on the state of the Jews of Venice and on Jewish Rites and Dogmas.[68] Luzzatto's intent is also apologetic: he attempts to respond to all arguments raised against the Jews both in the past and in the present. I believe, however, that the there is a fine line that separates the two rabbis of Venice. Luzzatto attempts to shift the focus of his arguments to an issue of recent relevance within Protestant-Catholic disputes: the argument that the Biblical ceremonies had lost their validity with the death of Jesus. I think it is worthwhile to look into this point in some detail, if for no other reason than that Luzzatto's contribution to this debate has thus far not received the attention it deserves in this text.

Luzzatto does not give a semantic distinction between "rites," "cults," and "ceremonies." In referring to the prohibition against celibacy, for example, he uses the term "rite."[69] In his usage, the process of salting meat for bleeding (and, thus, for conservation) is also a "rite."[70] "Rite" refers also to practices that provide an element of separation between Christians and Jews, such as the divergence of languages and dietary laws and the prohibition of mixed marriages.[71] "Cult" is used as a synonym for ceremonies.[72]

---

cial Toleration of Jews," in *Essential Papers on Jewish Culture in Renaissance and Baroque Italy*, ed. David B. Ruderman (New York; London: New York University Press 1992): 429–473.
66 See also Evelien Chayes's contribution in Giuseppe Veltri, Evelien Chayes, *Oltre le mura del Ghetto. Accademie, Scetticismo e Tolleranza nella Venezia Barocca* (Palermo: New Digital Frontiers, 2016), 89–90.
67 *Discorso circa il stato de gl'Hebrei et in particolare dimoranti nell'inclita Città di Venetia* (Venice: Calleoni, 1638). The English translation is from a forthcoming translation of the *Discorso*.
68 More on Luzzatto in the third part of this book, chapter 4.
69 *Discorso*, 18v: "Nela scola del disaggio sotto la rigorosa disciplina di esso bisogno, sono eruditi, ed instruiti li ebrei più che ogn'altra nazione, essendo privi di beni stabili, senz'essercizio delle arti mecaniche, lontani da proffitti del foro, e d'altri impieghi urbani, carichi di famiglia essendoli anco per loro riti proibito il celibato [...]."
70 *Discorso*, 30r: "[...] e si potrebbe ancor addurre certe minuzie, com'il consumo dal sale, che credo esser il quadruplo di quello adoperano li cristiani per il rito ch'osservano nell'insalare la carne per l'estrazzione del sangue a loro proibito, che non occorre farne raconto."
71 *Discorso*, 40v–41r: "In quanto alla prima instanza se li risponde, che non può succedere scandalo, e mal esempio per esser così poco comunicanti insieme gl'ebrei con cristiani, e tanto differenti de riti, ed anco per la varietà delle lingue, che li loro libri sono composti; vi s'aggiunge la proibitione, cosi all'uni come all'altri del convivere insieme, ed in particolare l'osservanza de gl'ebrei circa il gustare molti cibi, che non li sono leciti conforme a loro riti, come anco li comercii carnali, che oltre al divieto

In his explanation of the nature of the Jewish religion, Luzzatto reveals himself to be acquainted with the current Christian discussion of Jewish law. He draws a distinction between divine law "and the ceremonial precepts included in it."[73] The Thomist, triune division of the law is here clearly explained and adapted to the Jewish conception of the Law. The first and most fundamental level of the Law is populated by ceremonies and cults—that which is commonly termed "religion." The second level, on which the Law operates, promotes the social and amicable communion of human beings; the third level is that of natural morality, by which all humanity is bound together:[74]

> The commonness of religion is the greatest bond and most tenacious knot that keeps humanity closely united and even that pagan said "since life is upheld by religion."[75] And the most learned and eloquent Jew Philo wrote: "For the most effectual love-charm, the chain which binds indissolubly the goodwill which makes us one is to honour the one God."[76] This does not mean that for this reason the Jews consider all those outside of the observance of their rites or [outside of] assent to their particular beliefs thence completely free and unbound in terms of any obligation to humanity or reciprocal amity. For they believe that there are different degrees of connections among men. To the same extent [they also believe] that within one nation the obligations of compassion must be subordinated among them: the love of self obtains first place, followed by blood-ties, and last by the amity between citizens. They therefore believe that foreigners and aliens belonging to a different religion share the common ground of humanity that hence binds them to observing the precepts of natural morality and to having some cognition of a superior cause.

---

delle loro leggi, da editti del Principe parimente interdetti, e li transgressori severissimamente castigati; v'è ancora, che la impotenza, e soggezzione de gl'ebrei cagiona, che da qualunque fuori della loro religione si trova, sono scansati, e sfugiti, e di rado alla loro credenza si convertono." See also *Discorso* 49v.

72 *Discorso*, 43r–43v: and *Discorso* 64r.

73 *Discorso*, 48v–49r: "E quegli Hebrei dimoranti sotto il Dominio di Asuero re di Persia essendoli permesso per editto regale la vendetta nella vita de nemici, e svaligio della lor robba, eseguirono l'una, e si astenero dall'altro, li quali esempii devono essere cosi osservabili *da chi professa la Legge ebraica, come il mantenimento de preceti cerimoniali in essa contenuti*, che pure con tanta scrupolosità da ognuno di loro sono eseguiti [...]," italics is mine.

74 *Discorso*, 51v–52r: "La comunicanza della religione è il maggior vinculo, e più tenace nodo che conserva ristretta la società umana, ed insin quel etnico disse, *vita humana Religione constat*, e Filone ebreo dottissimo, ed eloquentissimo lasciò scritto, *nam unius Dei cultus est amoris mutuaeque benivolentiae vinculum insolubile*, non resta per ciò che appresso gl'Hebrei si tiene, che quelli si trovano fuori dell'osservanza de loro riti, ed assenso de loro credenze particolari, non siano però reputati affatto disciolti, e slegatti da qualunque legame de umanità, e reciproca amista: stimando essi che vi siano diversi gradi di connessione fra gli uomini, come ancora in un'istessa natione l'obligi di carità sono fra loro subordi|nati, l'amor di se stesso ottiene il primo loco, dopo v'è la congiunzione del sangue, poi l'amistà fra cittadini, e per ciò credono che gli esteri, ed alieni della loro religione partecipano con loro della comune umanità, che insieme li congiunge, osservando però li precetti della naturale moralità, ed avendo alcuna cognizione d'una causa superior."

75 Plinius, *Naturalis Historia* XIV:119.

76 Philo, *De specialibus legibus*, I: 52.

This corresponds to the logic of the "particular," according to which Judaism proselytises, as evidenced in the case of the Jews of Babylonia and the inhabitants of Nineveh (Jeremy 10:11–12),[77] who "did not convert to the Hebrew religion, but ceased from their thieving extortions and fraud, remaining Gentiles as before."[78] In explanation of the absence of proselytism in Judaism, Luzzatto has no other argument than that of absolute divine will, which is also the source and reason of creation and revelation.[79]

Laws, ceremonies and rites were given by divine will to the Jewish people without any obligation to universality. Hence, Luzzatto does not pretend to qualify Judaism as a universal religion, but only to legitimate its existence by demonstrating that its rites are "not dissonant from the universal." His intent is to qualify Judaism as a confession, which is the reason for his highly intriguing comparison of Jewish rites and the dogma with the Roman Catholic credo:

> For the most part, the Jews do not reside in the dominions separated from the Roman church. It is certain that in some matters the Jewish Nation inclines to the Roman opinion more than to their beliefs. The Jews maintain that in many places the Sacred Scripture is not intelligible without the light of tradition, placing great value on it, and relying on them, as I have already demonstrated. They also believe that meritorious deeds please God, and they practice them quite a lot, accompanied, however, with faith. They believe in free will, and they consider it to be a principle article of their beliefs; they likewise affirm that the merits of others can be of help to those who are less deserving, and the living [91r] pray for the souls of the dead. They say that the penance of the penitent is real, and not simply putative, that it bestows absolution, as Calvin believed. And even though their authors do not frequently mention the word purgatory, they divide the fate of the separated soul into three parts: beatitude, finite temporal punishment, and the eternal. For they believe that God absolves guilt, but He still exacts punishment. Their prayers are in the Hebrew language, not in the vernacular. All these things are discussed and examined in the treatise on dogmas and rites.[80]

---

77 *Discorso*, 52r.
78 *Discorso*, 53r.
79 *Discorso*, 55r: "[...] ciò stà involto nelli profondi secreti della divinità, siccome non si può conprendere n'anco qual sia stato la cagione che gia pochi mille anni solamente ebbe principio il mondo e che tanto ritardasse Iddio diffondere la sua benignità alle future creature, com'anco non si può arrivar a sapere perché creò tal numero d'uomini, e tale d'angioli."
80 *Discorso*, 90v–91r: "[...] certa cosa è che la nazione ebrea in alcuni articoli inclina alla romana più che alla loro opinione; tengono gli ebrei la scrittura sacra in molti lochi non esser intelligibile senza il lume delle tradizioni, facendo gran stima e fondamento sopra esse, come ho già dimostrato; credono ancora che grande sia il valore dell'opere meritorie appresso Iddio, ed in esse grandemente si essercitano, accompagnandoli però con la fede; asseriscono il libero arbitrio, e lo stimano essere articolo principale delle loro credenze; affermano parimente, che li meriti altrui possino coadiuuare alli imperfetti, e li vivi pre|gano per l'anime de morti, dicono la giustificazione del penitente esser reale, e non putativa, ed assolutoria, come ha tenuto Calvino, e se bene non hanno il nome di purgatorio frequente nelli loro auttori tripartiscono gli avvenimenti delle anime separate alla beatitudine, alle pene temporali finite, ed alle eterne, tenendo ch'Iddio assolva la colpa, ma tuttavia esige la pena; le loro orazioni si fanno in lingua ebraica, non in volgare; le qual cose nel trattato delli dogmi, e riti sono discussi, e ventilati."

Luzzatto's comparison of Jewish and Christian dogmas and rites must be interpreted as a *captatio benevolentiae:* he defines Judaism as a world parallel to that of Roman Christianity. It goes without saying that any perceived proximity to the conceptions of the Protestant confession(s), even if only theoretical, could easily have been his undoing. Practically, as Rabbi of Venice, his tendency was conservative, denying, for example, all legitimacy to Karaite Judaism, which was seen as a prototype of Protestantism.[81]

We will turn back to the topic of religion addressed by the Venetian rabbi. Here it is enough to emphasise that, in his "Discorso," Luzzatto does not explicitly mention any argument for or against the assertions of Christian theology that claimed to be the fulfilment of divine law; he writes only that Jewish customs are no different from those generally observed (i.e. the Christian), as he states in the preface: "I proposed to compose a concise but truthful account of this nation's principal rites and most commonly shared opinions, which are not dissonant or discrepant from the universal ones."[82] In his conception of political thought, the rites are a particular element of the Jewish identity, based mostly on the oral law. They are a constant over time: "To these learned men (the Rabbis), all the Hebrews in every place and time have given punctual assent in that which relates to the fulfilment of rites and precepts, and especially *ceremonials* which are considerable and evident observances and do not change with the times."[83] The logic of such a proposition is clearly to be interpreted as an indirect refutation of Christian claims of temporally-bounded absolutes: what God had transmitted to Jews as law cannot be temporary; it is an eternal commitment to his people and a task to be fulfilled (an interpretation that John Toland, a reader of Luzzatto, clearly acknowledged). The Rabbi of Venice turns the tables, so to speak.

The Borrowed Identity and Baruch Spinoza

The conception of Judaism as a religion based on ceremonies and rites is of Christian origin. There is no trace in the literature of ancient or early medieval Judaism of a division between natural, judicial, and ritual law. This partitioning is the result only of Christian attempts to create a theoretical and practical basis for accepting the novelty of the Revelation and grounding its importance in the fulfilment and perfection of the Law, while also stigmatising the Old Testament as anachronistic, obsolete, and imperfect. As part of this process, Christianity's initial dependence on Jewish tradition, although theoretically and logically coherent, must be invalidated. This

---

[81] See Valerio Marchetti, "The Lutheran Discovery of Karaite Hermeneutics," in *Una manna buona per Mantova. Man tov le-Man Tovah. Studi in onore di Vittore Colorni per il suo 92° compleanno*, ed. Mauro Perani (Florence: Olshki, 2004), 433–459.
[82] *Discorso*, 4r.
[83] *Discorso*, 77v.

can only be achieved by declaring the rites of the Torah—among them the observance of the Sabbath and circumcision—as antiquated, obsolete, and non-binding. The entire development, of course, reflects a Pauline vision of Christianity, which later also influenced Jewish understandings of their own traditions. According to Luzzatto (and later also Moses Mendelssohn), natural and political laws follow a paradigm common to both Christians and Jews; ceremonies are a distinctive element of the Jewish religion.

The reaction of Baruch Spinoza in the fifth chapter of the *Philosophical-Theological Treatise* is well known: the Jewish ceremonies are of historical and material value because they represent the temporal prosperity of the historical kingdom of Israel. The Temple cult has political meaning only because its purpose was to preserve the state. The role played by Moses is to be understood from the same perspective:

> His sole care was to teach moral doctrines, and distinguish them from the laws of the state; for the Pharisees, in their ignorance, thought that the observance of the state law and the Mosaic law was the sum total of morality; whereas such laws merely had reference to the public welfare, and aimed not so much at instructing the Jews as at keeping them under constraint.[84]

According to Spinoza, the abolition of the rites did not follow from the destruction of the Temple but from the loss of national independence and the exile; the "state law" of the Jews was intended to be observed only in the Jewish state (*imperium*).[85] The Pharisees, of course, continued to practice these rites even after the destruction of the kingdom, more "with a view of opposing the Christians than of pleasing God." Spinoza seems here to follow the Protestant interpretation of Jewish rites, quoting Paul's letter to the Galatians 5:22–23: "But the fruit of the Spirit is love, joy, peace, patience, kindness, goodness, faithfulness, gentleness and self-control against which there is no law." The Pharisees embody the separation between religious practice and a moral way of life, identifying themselves with ceremonial law.

The process that began with Aquinas ends here with a Jewish identity derived from the Christian definition of Jewish law—a borrowed identity—coupled with a criticism of the image of the Pharisees as presented in Christian scholarship. The main points of this dispute have remained topical to the present day in all religious and confessional discussion of the foundations of Jewish precepts, rites, and customs, even as the political and philosophical significance of such debates fades into the background.

Yet, an intriguing aspect of the history of the description of Jewish legal and religious tradition as *caerimonialia*—excluding any relevance for the development of moral and legal patrimony of European thought included in the Torah—is the historically parallel creation of the term "Jewish religion." *Religio Hebraeorum* or *Iudaeo-*

---

[84] *The Collected Works of Spinoza*, ed. and trans. Edwin Curley (Princeton: Princeton University Press, 1985).
[85] See Warren Zev Harvey, "Spinoza's Counterfactual Zionism," *Iyyun* 62 (2013): 235–244.

rum is mostly meant as social-historical category, namely as a group with its own history, concepts, and beliefs, while the word "nation" (also a concept from the Baroque period) is concerned with the ethnic aspect as an attribute of Judaism as a whole or as characteristic of the separate entities of the Levantines, Ashkenazim, Sephardim, etc.

1.2 Jewish Tradition as Religion

Recent publications have advanced the thesis that Judaism became a "religion" through the work of Moses Mendelssohn in the period of the Enlightenment, culminating in the Romantic and Idealistic age.[86] I would like to claim that the expression *Religio Hebraeorum* or *Iudaeorum* appears much earlier in European languages, first among Christian and then Jewish authors. The general concept of "religion" in its multifarious facets existed previously and has a long tradition, of course. In the present book, however, there is no need to retrace the steps of the history of the concept "religion" back to Lactance.[87] Many publications and monographs have deeply researched the manifold world of applications of the term "religion" in its philosophical and theological implications.[88] My interest here is much narrower: I seek to trace several important developments in the understanding and use of the idea of the *Jewish* religion among *Jewish* scholars in the sixteenth through eighteenth centuries.

We will first address the concept of true (Jewish) religion and its impact on Judaism and then devote ourselves to Rabbi Simone Luzzatto's framing of Jewish monotheism as critical for Jewish society. We have to outline at the outset that the Venetian Rabbi was not only the first to use the concept "Jewish Religion" as focusing on history, rites, and symbols of the Jewish people, but was also the first to develop the doctrine of monotheism as a modern category to define Jewish dogmas, as I try to demonstrate in the following.

The True Religion and the Superstition

The concept of Jewish religion was born in fifteenth-century Italy where interest in Jewish tradition, ancient doctrine, and "secret revelations" was lively among human-

---

[86] Leora Batnitzky, *How Judaism Became a Religion: An Introduction to Modern Jewish Thought* (Princeton: Princeton University Press, 2011). Cf. Guy G. Stroumsa, *A New Science: The Discovery of Religion in the Age of Reason* (Cambridge: Harvard University Press, 2010).
[87] Lactantius, *Institutiones Divinae* IV: 28: vinculo pietatis obstricti Deo et religati sumus, unde religio nomen cepit.
[88] Cf. the four volumes of Ernst Feil, *Religio. Forschungen zur Kirchen- und Dogmengeschichte* (Göttingen: Vandenhoeck & Ruprecht, 1986–2012).

ist scholars.[89] Marsilio Ficino did not coin the term; in fact, he translated it from the Latin *Religio Hebraeorum* or *Iudaeorum*. However, he was probably the first to understand religion as a search toward the fundamental elements of the *philosophia perennis*, the *everlasting wisdom* that formed or was present at the creation of the world. His concept of religion is imbued with philosophical ideas such as the eternity of primeval wisdom as the origin of the world. By the same token, religion became a universal concept beyond every custom, cult, and ceremonial law, a conception already present in the quoted Nicolas of Cusa's principle of "One religion in a variety of rites" (*una religio in rituum varietate*).[90]

The modern concept of Jewish religion first appeared in Judaism most likely with the *Discorso* (1638) of the above mentioned Venetian Rabbi Simone Luzzatto.[91] He utilises this concept within the context of the plurality of religions (*rituus varietate*) and their nature as representing "humanity." He is conscious of the difficulty of the quest for a "true religion" as well of the complexity in distinguishing it from impiety and superstition. In his *Discorso*, Luzzatto is an academic sceptic who encourages the eternal enquiry into true religion, but in his later work, *Socrate* (1651), he considers true religion as tantamount either to enlightened knowledge or, on the contrary, to a Pyrrhonian suspension of judgment and, like a Pyrrhonian adept, he left open the question of the political function of religious morality and policy. We will shortly analyse these important points.

In his *Discorso* (34r), he speaks of the Joseph of Pharaoh's time, who is characterised by "a different religion." To him, a difference of religion is no justification for making war on one's neighbours when all "share the common ground of humanity."[92] In the Humanist and Renaissance period, the concept of humanity is intrinsically related to *humanitas Christiana*, as already discussed. From the Renaissance onwards, *humanitas Christiana* tended to be replaced by *humanitas politica*, according to the research of Mihai-D. Grigore.[93] The concept of a *political humanity* seems to be

---

89 I am referring to Guido Bartolucci, *Vera religio: Marsilio Ficino e la tradizione ebraica* (Turin: Claudiana, 2017); see his "Il De Christiana religione di Marsilio Ficino e le 'prime traduzioni' di Flavio Mitridate," *Rinascimento* II 46 (2007): 345–355.
90 See above, p. 79.
91 Cf. Abraham Melamed, *Dat: From Law to Religion: A History of a Formative Term* [Hebrew] (Tel Aviv: ha-Kibbutz ha-meʾuḥad, 2014), who refers to Simone Luzzatto as the first source of the term "religion" in Judaism.
92 Luzzatto, *Discorso*, 51v–52r: "To the same extent [they Jew also believe] that within one nation the obligations of compassion must be subordinated among them: the love of self obtains first place, followed by blood-ties, and last by the amity between citizens. They therefore believe that foreigners and aliens belonging to a different religion share the common ground of humanity that hence binds them to observing the precepts of natural morality and to having some cognition of a superior cause."
93 See Mihai-D. Grigore, "Humanism and its Humanitas: The Transition from Humanitas Christiana to Humanitas Politica in the Political Writings of Erasmus," in *Humanity. A History of European Concepts in Practice from the Sixteenth Century to the Present*, ed. Fabian Klose and Mirjam Thulin (Göttingen: Vandenhoeck & Ruprecht, 2016), 73–90.

attested in seventeenth-century Venice when Luzzatto refers to the entire world's population as "humanity" (*Discorso*, 8v). He also holds that humanity is what commerce transfers to every people, together with customs, arts, and doctrines. Central for the comprehension of the concept of humanity is the already quoted text of Luzzatto's *Discorso* (51v–52r) where he listed the connection between men: "This does not mean that for this reason the Jews consider all those outside of the observance of their rites or [outside of] assent to their particular beliefs thence completely free and unbound in terms of any obligation to humanity or reciprocal amity. For they believe that there are different degrees of connections among men." Religion is a particular form of existence of particular groups and humanity provides a broader connection based on natural morality and the cognition of a superior cause. Natural morality is, according to Luzzatto, the avoidance of larceny, extortion, and fraud. It essentially consists of acting in accord with the precepts of Noachide origins (see *Discorso*, 53v).

Luzzatto characterises Judaism as a religion firmly convinced by its own doctrines, perseverant in its rites: the distinctive element is "a firmness and inexpressible tenacity in the observance of their faith and a uniformity of dogma regarding their beliefs during the course of 1,550 years[94] of dispersion in the world. This is a remarkable steadfastness, if not in encountering dangers then at least in bearing calamities."[95] The Rabbi of Venice attributes to them a uniformity of religion and rites (38r):

> With regard to carnal vices, [they practice] great abstinence. They are careful and mindful to preserve their lineage, unmixed and uncontaminated. They are able to deal with any [38v] difficult business whatsoever. They usually display submission and respect towards anyone not belonging to their religion. Their errors and offences are almost always more spineless and wretched than atrocious. When it happens (as it often does with any nation) that one of their members commits a crime, and transgresses the edicts of the Prince, the remedy and relief are very simple.

However, their persistence in these customs and rites made them an object of hatred and contempt:

> Yet, in the narration of the customs and rites of the Jews, he was so overcome with hatred for the Jewish religion and contempt for the Jewish nation that he was eventually excessively neglectful [58r] in investigating their true origins and events from their history. Nonetheless, if by the word superstition he intended to refer to a tenacious cult, an inviolable reverence to a superior cause, and the postponement of any human interest in this cause, and if by religion he wanted to sig-

---

94 If the figure of the years is precise, by adding to it the year of the destruction of the Temple, the result indicates the years 1620/1622 as a date for the writing of the treatise, or at least its possibility.
95 *Discorso*, 38r.

nify a *lesbia* rule,⁹⁶ which was fixed and yet pliant to every human occurrence, then no doubt he did not wander far from impiety, calling religion superstition, and atheism faith and devotion.

According to the zealots pursuing the expulsion of the Jews form Venice (40v), it is "contemptuous of their own religion to allow those who do not practise the commonly approved religion into the state" and "politicians say that it is not beneficial to tolerate a multitude of religions in the same city both because of the scandal and the bad example that one group makes for another, as well as the dissent, disunity, and hatred that can arise among the inhabitants of the city."

Luzzatto introduces the idea of the secret of the true religion by making a comparison to the market:

> The world resembles a great market; God dispenses some coins to buy that which is displayed and available. The most current [coins] are prudence and strength, forged in God's mint, since He is [the source of] both science and power. With these [coins] everything subject to human will can be bought. True religion is that which begs from God an abundance of the aforementioned coins. For without this abundance it cannot hope to achieve anything important. Solomon, in Proverbs Chapter 17 [states]: "to what advantage does a fool possess riches, seeing he hath no understanding."⁹⁷

The metaphor of the market is intriguing because it familiarises the (Christian and Jewish) reader with the parable of the three rings⁹⁸ in a masked manner. The "true religion" is not that which possesses science and power because it is of divine origin. The true religion is not that which possesses science and power because it is of divine origin, but rather, "religion is that which begs from God an abundance of" prudence and strength. These virtues were used in the answer to Saladin's question regarding which of the three religions is true in Lessing's *Nathan the Wise*: specifically, *the virtue of prudence not to answer the question by means of avoiding every statement concerning it.*⁹⁹

The most fascinating aspect of Luzzatto's concept of (Jewish) religion appears in *Socrate*, where he addresses the differences between philosophy and religion, on one hand, and superstition and impiety, on the other. He returns to the concept of the "cognition of superior cause" that he first discusses in the *Discorso* (52r), but here

---

96 Aristotle *Ethica Nichomachea* V, 10 (1137b29–b33): "For when the thing is indefinite the rule also is indefinite, like the lead rule used in making the Lesbian moulding; the rule adapts itself to the shape of the stone and is not rigid, and so too the decree is adapted to the fact."
97 *Discorso* 67v.
98 See Roberto Celada Ballanti, *La parabola dei tre anelli: Migrazioni e metamorfosi di un racconto tra Oriente e Occidente* (Rome: Edizioni di Storia e Letteratura, 2017); Iris Shagrir, *The Parable of the Three Rings and the Idea of Religious Toleration in Premodern European Culture* (in Hebrew) (Jerusalem: The Hebrew University Magnes, 2017).
99 See Marc Shell, *Money, Language, and Thought: Literary and Philosophic Economies from the Medieval to the Modern Era* (Baltimore: John Hopkins University Press, 1982), 160–161.

considers it to be the monocausal reason of the true religion. A difficulty with Luzzatto's *Socrate* is that the distinction between his position and the other opinions with which he is dealing is at times unclear. The discussion of religion is introduced in Luzzatto's book with a discussion of Hippias, the Sophist and dialogic partner in Plato's dialogue of the same name. In this section,[100] which is composed theatrically, Luzzatto is considering the idea of cognition of the supreme cause.[101]

Note that in the *Discorso* this was Luzzatto's opinion and here it is presented as a logical consequence of the observation of "the regulated motion of the skies, the ordered government of sublunary things," "whose knowledge we admire, whose power we revere, and whose goodness we love." However, this is a scholastic (and definitely not a sceptical) view of the *causa causarum*, reinforced by an argument about the wonders and memories of miracles which found the Tradition.[102] Only philosophy can remove and eradicate "useless and excessive fertility" caused by superstition and impiety (*Socrate*, 274):

> Primarily, philosophy destroyed that damned and wicked impiety, as a solicitous nurturer of every vice, in order to prepare the human soul for the sense of true religion. Moreover, it [i.e. philosophy] was attempting to refute mad superstition, which, like germinating weeds, oppresses the refined harvest of venerable religion. Once wisdom cuts off and mutilates those deformed rags and attachments joined and attached to it [i.e. wisdom] by insane superstition, it [i.e. wisdom] induced sage men to have the due respect for the Supreme Author and Architect. Indeed, superstition unworthily supposed Him to be sometimes too flexible and indulgent, and therefore less revered, and sometimes represented Him as extremely rigorous, implacable, and inexorable because of every minute transgression, and thus feared rather than loved.

The idea of an "excessive fertility" is probably based on a quotation from the Gospel of Matthew 13:24–25:[103] "The kingdom of heaven is likened unto a man which sowed good seed in his field: But while men slept, his enemy came and sowed tares among the wheat, and went his way."[104] In the Gospel there was some resonance to the image of tares and weeds in the Greek-Roman world,[105] the addressee of Luzzatto

---

100 Here I am referring to our edition and English translation of *Socrates or On the Human Knowledge (1651). A Sceptical Essay by Simone Luzzatto Venetian Jew*, bilingual Edition, edited, translated and commented by Giuseppe Veltri and Michela Torbidoni (Berlin: De Gruyter 2018). I am quoting from Socrates, 273 of the original.
101 *Socrate*, 273: "[prudence] has provided us with the cognition of that very eminent cause which disposes and directs the whole to the best aim."
102 Luzzatto does not explain what the meaning of "Tradition" is in this context. I suppose that he is speaking of Revelation based on wonders and miracles and—as he maintains—can be destroyed by time and unbelievers.
103 Thanks to Dr Guido Bartolucci for referring me to this source.
104 King James Version.
105 See Diogenes, *De vita et moribus philosophorum libri X*, VI,6 and Seneca, Epistulae Morales 73,16, mentioned by Craig A. Evans, *Matthew* (Cambridge: Cambridge University Press, 2012), 281.

is the world of contemporaneous political[106] and philosophical thought. There are some important differences, indeed. The parable of the weeds and the tares was a Christian text useful against either heretics or heresies, or both. The trick question is that, according to some exegetes, the parable allowed the extermination of heresies, and, according to others, the parable allowed the extermination of the *heretics* themselves. What for the some was an act of toleration was for others an encouragement to the complete intolerance of heretics. The first gloss follows the injunction of the Lord to *wait* for the harvest: "But he said, Nay; lest while ye gather up the tares, ye root up also the wheat with them. Let both grow together until the harvest: and in the time of harvest I will say to the reapers, Gather ye together first the tares, and bind them in bundles to burn them: but gather the wheat into my barn."[107] The latter emphasised the pure harvest.

Remarkable in the observations of Luzzatto is the fact that the "inquisitor" function is played by the philosopher and not the *religio*; additionally, the philosopher must hold the concept of a "flexible and indulgent" supreme author *together with* the concept of a "extremely rigorous, implacable, and inexorable" supreme author. That is, the philosopher must balance between two opposing conceptions of divinity. Philosophy, then, is the tool, or *organon*, of the in-between. Even so, according to the Hippias of Luzzatto's text, "wisdom" becomes like a vigorous warrior, defeating both impiety and superstition. The curious reader will ask how he intends to conciliate both functions, the balancer of social order and the warrior. No answer is to be found.

Hippias' plea for a true religion of philosophic origin does not convince Socrates-alias-Luzzatto, but "Socrates" does not actively contest the idea, preferring instead to suspend judgment. However, the reader of Luzzatto's *Socrate* will surely ask why Hippias claims that Socrates, with his criticism of the human capacity to attain knowledge, is destroying the "great theatre of the universe," described by Hippias as

> [...] open and gaping to the senses and intellect of all human beings, the nobles as much as the plebeians, the rich as much as the poor. With liberal indifference, it [i.e. the theatre of the universe] shows and offers its admirable performances, and it pleases and instructs at any time by altering its aspects. Many of its mysteries are disclosed to our ancestors, which have been somewhat revealed to us in the present time, but a greater quantity will be shown to the world to come.[108]

The vision of Hippias is typical for a philosophy according to which (divine) knowledge is accessible to all people and mysteries are disclosed to one's ancestors, revealed partly in the present time and shown in their totality in the world to come. This vision of the *theatrum mundi*, as Luzzatto calls it, is an irenic and ludic dimen-

---

106 See James D. Tracy, *Erasmus of the Low Countries* (Berkeley: University of California Press, 1996), 163–174 ("the parable of the tares").
107 *Gospel of Matthew* 13:29–30 (King James Version).
108 *Socrate*, 275.

sion of the life "which continuously provides and puts forth many pleasures and delights to such a great multitude of human beings." The presentation of Hippias in Luzzatto's rendition makes this clear: the sceptic claim of the "weakness of human judgment" causes "[...] no little damage to good morality which keeps mankind together. Wicked people can easily avoid the public laws through keeping their crimes secret; and the false opinion of impious people concerning the connivance of God, and [that of] libidinous people concerning His indulgence, makes the latter confident and the former daring in clandestinely committing wickedness and vileness."[109] The vision of religious life focused on the certitude of knowledge in this and next life could be interpreted as description of religion (and superstition) sustained by ancient historians and intellectuals such as Polibius in his *Histories*[110] and, in the Renaissance, by Niccolò Machiavelli.[111] However, Hippias is not speaking of political power, but of "conscience namely reason," with the help of the metaphor of the (inner) magistrate, who is the origin of "terror": "Yet the terror imposed by the strict magistrate [located] in the innermost recess of us, appointed by Nature itself, is so effective that it holds us back not only from [committing] evil deeds, but also pulls us away from malicious thoughts."[112] The sceptical view of Socrates alias Luzzatto intends to destroy the peaceful world by introducing doubt of (human) knowledge. The reader can observe here the switch from human knowledge to revelation: because *conscientia seu ratio* includes truths to be clarified in the world to come. Luzzatto's Socrates is a sceptic, but he does not directly respond to Hippias, perhaps because in Hippias' irenic vision of humanity there is a hidden Luzzattian criticism: knowledge (whether philosophical, religious, or superstitious) is a narcotic:[113] "Undoubtedly the pretension that every man has concerning his own knowledge is that powerful narcotic which anaesthetises by making [every man] unaware of his

---

109 *Socrate*, 276.
110 *Historiae* VI: 52 "But the most important difference for the better which the Roman commonwealth appears to me to display is in their religious beliefs. Regard to religion. For I conceive that what in other nations is looked upon as a reproach, I mean a scrupulous fear of the gods, is the very thing which keeps the Roman commonwealth together. To such an extraordinary height is this carried among them, both in private and public business, that nothing could exceed it. Many people might think this unaccountable; but in my opinion their object is to use it as a check upon the common people. If it were possible to form a state wholly of philosophers, such a custom would perhaps be unnecessary. But seeing that every multitude is fickle, and full of lawless desires, unreasoning anger, and violent passion, the only resource is to keep them in check by mysterious terrors and scenic effects of this sort. Wherefore, to my mind, the ancients were not acting without purpose or at random, when they brought in among the vulgar those opinions about the gods, and the belief in the punishments in Hades: much rather do I think that men nowadays are acting rashly and foolishly in rejecting them."
111 There is no consensus on Machiavelli's use of religion in political matters, see Maurizio Viroli, *Machiavelli's God* (Princeton: Princeton University Press, 2010), 5–7.
112 *Socrate*, 276.
113 Ibid.

own miseries and that fascination which subverts judgment and causes each person to be satisfied with himself."

The everlasting refrain of Luzzatto's philosophy is the emphasis on the feeble character of our knowledge. There is something new in Luzzatto's *Socrate* that makes his approach closer to "modernity": the novelty and originality of his approach consists of the criticism not only of human but also revealed knowledge. With his commitment to philosophy as an investigator of impiety and superstition as well as with the introduction of the concept of true religion, together with his veiled attack against tradition and prophecy (in the *Socrate*, not in the *Discorso*), he opens the door for Spinoza's criticism of superstitions and Mendelssohn's definition of Judaism as a practical-pragmatic religion.

Excursus: Jewish Monotheism: Luzzatto on the Aristotelian Antiperistasis

To the best of my knowledge, Simone Luzzatto was the first to explain the phenomenon of the disinterest in proselytising in Judaism as a divine commandment with a social-military argument. However, should anyone ask a Jew why God did not care to have his religion and the observance of his rites propagated in antiquity among the Gentiles, he would respond that such information remains enveloped in the profound secrets of the divinity.

> If any human reason could access the secrets of His Divine Majesty, the Jews would reply that God, wanting to preserve religion among them, did not wish their [55v] rites to spread to the neighbouring Gentiles, a possible reason for this being something similar to the *antiperistasis*. The *antiperistatic* motion reinforces the qualities of natural things and strengthens them. The cold surrounding the hot increases its heat. This led the stoics to believe that the cold air suddenly assailing the new-born baby breathes life into it by summoning up heat within it. So too the threat of the enemy and terror makes people fierce and infuses them with military spirit. In the same way, the repugnance of religion professed by the surrounding neighbours rendered the faithful people more fervent in their own beliefs and more militant in the defence of their native rites.[114]

---

[114] "Ma s'alcuno ricercasse all'hebreo qual fosse la cagione ch'Iddio non si curò di far propagare anticamente la sua religione, et osservanza di riti nella gentilità, risponderebbe che ciò sta involto nelli profondi secreti della divinità [...] E se a gl'arcani di Sua D.M. può giunger alcuna humana ragione si potrebbe ancor replicare conforme a gl'hebrei ch'Iddio volendo conservar la religione fra loro, non curò che agli confinanti gentili si dilatasse il [55v] rito hebraico, e la ragione di ciò fu, che siccome l'antiperistasi rinforza la virtù alle cose naturali, e l'invigorisce, et il freddo circondando il caldo l'accresce virtù, tanto che li stoici dissero che l'aere freddo ch'assale repentinamente il novello parto riconcentrandoli il calore lo fa divenire vivo, così ancor il soprastar del nemico, et il terrore aguerisce li popoli, e l'infonde spiriti militari, nell'istesso modo la repugnanza della religion de circonvicini rendeva più vivo il popolo fedele, nella propria credenza, e più militante alla difesa de suoi patrii riti."

1.2 Jewish Tradition as Religion — 97

The usage of the word *antiperistasis* here merits a close examination. As a widespread explanation of meteorological events resulting from "warm and cold" phenomena and their application to physical movement, sixteenth- and seventeenth-century thinkers returned to the Greek doctrine of the *antiperistasis*, which briefly (and therefore imprecisely) can be described as the reaction of opposing forces which reinforce themselves the closer they come together. An article on *antiperistasis*, written by Kirstine Meyer (born Bjerrum) in 1903 and almost forgotten today,[115] explains in an illuminating way the steps of the construction and impact of this doctrine from ancient philosophy, starting from the tractate by a later contemporary of Luzzatto, the famous Robert Boyle. Boyle criticised *antiperistasis* as popular yet unproven in his *New Experiments and Observations Touching Cold, [...] to which are Added an Examen of Antiperistasis*, published in 1665.[116] Boyle's criticism is the endpoint of a belief and doctrine introduced by Greek philosophy; as an explanation for projectile motion, the *antiperistasis* becomes a theory

> [...] that denies that there is a void, and denies the existence of any force except impulsion. The idea is to eliminate mysterious "attractions" from nature. In nature there can be "pushes" but no "pulls." The flight of projectiles, magnetic attraction, and the suction of fluids are among the phenomena the theory must explain. The view goes back to Empedocles, and is adopted by Plato in the Timaeus.[117]

Although Aristotle did not oppose the doctrine of the *antiperistasis* as a type of locomotion in water and air (*Physics* VIII, 10, 267a15–20), he contended that it can explain a projectile motion, as Plato put it (*Timaeus* 79e10–80a6).[118] Kristine Meyer notes that in Greek philosophy the doctrine had been used to explain different aspects of human life such as fever and remedies against sneezing, or to provide a cause of growth in plants and maturation of fruits in botany (as determined by Theofrast in *De Causis Plantarum*). There was no criticism of the doctrine in the Middle Ages, Meyer notes,[119] which, in my view, was self-evident, since most of the authors during this period—at least most Christian authors—were interested in logic and Ar-

---

[115] Kirstine Meyer born Bjerrum, "Zur Geschichte der Antiperistatis," *Annalen der Naturphilosophie* 3 (1903): 413–441.
[116] *New experiments and observations Touching Cold, or, An experimental history of cold begun to which are added an examen of antiperistasis and an examen of Mr. Hobs's doctrine about cold.* (London: John Crook, 1665).
[117] Simon Blackburn, *The Oxford Dictionary of Philosophy* (Oxford: Oxford University Press, 1996), 20.
[118] On this aspect I follow Theokritos Kouremenos, *The Proportions in Aristotle's Phys. 7.5* (Stuttgart: Steiner, 2002), 38–50, here p. 44.
[119] Kirstine Meyer born Bjerrum, "Zur Geschichte der Antiperistatis," 424–425.

istotle's commentary on the sciences but were not in the habit of carrying out experiments. Peter King also notes this in reference to *antiperistasis*.[120]

Not until the sixteenth century do we have any criticisms or specifications of the Aristotelian doctrine, as exemplified in Telesius's *De natura rerum*.[121] There is also some criticism in Bacon's *Novum organum*, where he emphasises the difference between the reaction in the human body and in meteorology.[122] In the seventeenth century, the concept became a *topos* in medicine as well, as reflected in Sir Thomas Browne's commentary *Religio Medici* (1642),[123] which was probably influenced by Galen, who explained some medical phenomena with the help of *antiperistasis*.[124]

Nevertheless, the reader of Meyer's article will miss an important point in the development of the doctrine in the sixteenth and seventeenth centuries, namely, the

---

120 Peter King, "Mediaeval Thought-Experiments: The Metamethodology of Mediaeval Science," in *Thought-Experiments in Science and Philosophy*, ed. Gerry Massey and Tamara Horowitz (Lanham: Rowman & Littlefield, 1991), 43–64. On *antiperistasis*, see 47.
121 Argument: a large amount of warm and cold air causes only (and correspondingly) rejection.
122 *Novum Organum* II, 48:10: "Sit Motus Decimus, Motus Fugae; motus scilicet motui congregationis minoris contrarius; per quem corpora ex antipathia fugiunt et fugant inimica, seque ab illis separant, aut cum illis miscere se recusant […] Veruntamen etiam in aliis locum habet iste motus. Conspicitur enim in antiperistasibus nonnullis; ut in aeris media regione, cujus frigora videntur esse rejectiones naturae frigidae ex confiniis coelestium; quemadmodum etiam videntur magni illi fervores et inflammationes, quae inveniuntur in locis subterraneis, esse rejectiones naturae calidae ab interioribus terrae. Calor enim et frigus, si fuerint in quanto minore, se invicem perimunt; sin fuerint in massis majoribus et tanquam justis exercitibus, tum vero per conflictum se locis invicem summovent et ejiciunt."
123 Thomas Browne, *Religio Medici: Hydriotaphia: And, the Garden of Cyrus*, ed. Rossel H. Robbins (Oxford: Oxford University, 1972) 78, Questia, Web, Dec. 30, 2010: SECT. 10 "For my conversation, it is —like the sun's—with all men, and with a friendly aspect to good and bad. Methinks there is no man bad, and the worst, best; that is, while they are kept within the circle of those qualities wherein they are good. There is no man's mind of such discordant and jarring a temper to which a tuneable disposition may not strike a harmony. Magnae virtutes nec minora vitia—it is the posy of the best natures, and may be inverted on the worst; there are in the most depraved and venomous dispositions certain pieces that remain untouched, which by an antiperistasis become more excellent, or by the excellency of their antipathies are able to preserve themselves from the contagion of their enemy vices, and persist entire beyond the general corruption. For it is also thus in nature. The greatest balsams do lie enveloped in the bodies of most powerful corrosives; I say, moreover—and I ground upon experience—that poisons contain within themselves their own antidote and that which preserves them from the venom of themselves; without which they were not deleterious to others only, but to themselves also. But it is the corruption that I fear within me, not the contagion of commerce without me; 'tis that unruly regiment within me that will destroy me. 'Tis I that do infect myself; the man without a navel yet lives in me: I feel that original canker corrode and devour me; and therefore Defenda me Dios de me—Lord deliver me from myself—is a part of my litany and the first voice of my retired imaginations."
124 See Galen, *De placitis Hippocratis et Platonis libri novem*, 8, 8–9; see also see Keimpe Algra, "Aristotle and the Aristotelian Tradition," *Phronesis* 50 (3): 250–261.

application of *antiperistasis* when referred to moral behaviour and social contexts.[125] The changes, new stresses, and applications of Aristotelian doctrine in the seventeenth century are important to an understanding of Bacon's premise as well Luzzatto's, for they begin a new era in which this theory of motion becomes a doctrine to explain social phenomena and moral attitudes. In his *Apologie de Raymond Sebon* (1580),[126] Montaigne utilises the concept of *antiperistasis*, applying it to morality and education, but he does not explicitly refer to the term.[127] In 1585, Giordano Bruno utilised it in a non-physical or meteorological context, applying it to human psychology (in a humanist sense):

> See how impossible it is for the heart to persuade itself that from one contrary cause and principle proceeds the force of a contrary effect; it goes so far as to refuse to admit any such possibility, even by way of *antiperistasis*. This word refers to the vigour acquired by one contrary while it flees the other contrary and becomes united, self-enveloped, condensed, and concentrated toward the individual substance of its own virtue, which gains in efficacy what it loses in extension. [128]

As mentioned above, the doctrine occupies a central place in the thought of Francis Bacon.[129] However, it doesn't solely function as an acceptance of the Aristotelian doctrine and/or its pale criticism. A clearly applied mention of this doctrine appears in Bacon's opus as an explanation for virtuous and vicious moral behaviour[130] (as in Montaigne), and last but surely not least in the reference to politics: "'The force of an agent is increased by the reaction of a contrary,' is a rule in *Physics*. The same has wonderful efficacy in *Politics*, since every faction is violently irritated by the en-

---

125 Cf. Simon Blackburn, *The Oxford Dictionary of Philosophy* 20: "In the 17th century the term [antiperistasis] became used more for the equally Aristotelian doctrine that contrary qualities 'repel,' tending both to intensify one another, and to flee from one another." The author does not specify what is meant by "qualities."
126 I owe thanks to Dr. Jean-Marc Mandosio for this reference.
127 Terence Cave, "La logique de l'antipéristase dans l'Apologie de Montaigne," in his book *Pré-histoires: textes troublés au seuil de la modernité* (Geneva: Droz, 1999), 39.
128 Giordano Bruno, *Degli eroici furori* (Paris: Baio 1585), 3,10: "Vede, come non possea persuadersi il core di posser da contraria causa e principio procedere forza di contrario effetto, sin a questo che non vuol affirmare il modo possibile, quando per via d'antiperistasi, che significa il vigor che acquista il contrario da quel che, fuggendo l'altro, viene ad unirsi, inspessarsi, inglobarsi e concentrarsi verso l'individuo della sua virtude, la qual, quanto più s'allontana dalle dimensioni, tanto si rende efficace di vantaggio." English translation by Paulo Eugene Memmo, Jr. (1964).
129 As Charles Crawford states in the *The Bacon-Shakespeare Question*, 20.
130 Francis Bacon, *De Sapienta Veterum, Of the Wisdom of the Ancients*, in *The Works of Francis Bacon*, ed. James Spedding. (London: Longman, 1857–1870): "For as to the first, every passion flourishes and acquires vigour by being resisted and forbidden, as by a kind of antiperistasis; like the ivy by the cold of winter. As to the second, the master passion spreads itself like ivy about all human actions and resolutions, forcing itself in and mixing itself up with them."

croachment of a contrary faction."[131] This application of the doctrine to social inferences and political "irritations" is the core of the interpretation of Luzzatto's presentation of Jewish beliefs as quoted above (*Discorso*, 55r–v). Luzzatto's argument is carefully constructed. He begins with the absence of missionary activities of Judaism in antiquity, here explained as a divine secret; God did not care to spread Jewish religion into neighbouring lands and peoples. Luzzatto is speaking only of "antiquity" and "Gentiles." For the Rabbi of Venice knows that missionary activity in Judaism in his time was punishable by death. But how should we explain the absence of something that must be considered the core of divine religion but unfortunately has not spread to the Gentiles? Christianity has, of course, the Pauline argument that the advent of Christ permitted the expansion of belief in a true God and his rites; the Rabbi of Venice, by contrast, has recourse to the argument of the secrets of God.

The second point is much more important and of salient significance for the rabbis. We may ask: How can we explain the persistence of beliefs, rites and monotheism in Judaism in the wider context of the pagan world? Luzzatto refers to the doctrine of "*antiperistatic* motion" which "reinforces the qualities of natural things and strengthens them." He mentions its physical application, the medical observation— or better speculation on—birth and respiration as attributed to Stoic philosophy,[132] and repugnance towards the religion practiced by surrounding neighbours. The persistence of monotheism is not a gift from heaven but a product of contrast with surrounding religions.

The strange thing in this debate is the influence of Christianity on the controversial topic of the definition of Judaism as Jewish faith or religion, while emphasising its nature as a religion of rites and customs. These two elements are clearly in opposition: the first defining Judaism as a religion with dogmas, rites and customs, the other reducing it merely to the ceremonial laws, a legal system without any claim to dogmatic beliefs. Dogmatic beliefs are, according to Moses Mendelssohn, even present at the origin of the enchainment of reason.

---

131 Francis Bacon, *The Works of Francis Bacon* (London: Adamant Media, 2000), *De Augumentis Scentiarum*, III. chap. 1: 338–339.
132 Luzzatto is probably referring to Plutarch, *Moralia* V, 15: "Diogenes, that infants are bred in the matrix inanimate, yet they have a natural heat; but presently, when the infant is cast into the open air, its heat draws air into the lungs, and so it becomes an animal." English translation from *Plutarch, Plutarch's Morals*. Translated from the Greek by Several Hands. Corrected and Revised by William W. Goodwin, with an Introduction by Ralph W. Emerson. 5 Volumes (Boston: Little, Brown, and Co., 1878), vol. 3.

1.3 A Turning Point? Moses Mendelssohn: Between *Caerimonialia* and Religion

Moses Mendelssohn's philosophy of Judaism can be considered a decisive point in which all prior definitions of Judaism as a "religion of ceremonial laws" converged. Indeed, Mendelssohn's work marks the beginning of a Jewish philosophy, although Mendelssohn probably would not have used that term. Born in Dessau (Anhalt) on 6 September, 1729 (12 Elul, 5489), he moved to Berlin following his teacher David Fränkel, where he learned German, Latin, Greek, French and English. He also privately studied philosophy and mathematics.[133]

Mendelssohn as author is connected with numerous works, among others *Phaedon, or On the Immortality of the Soul* (*Phädon oder über die Unsterblichkeit der Seele*, 1767), *Jerusalem or on Religious Power and Judaism* (*Jerusalem oder über religiöse Macht und Judentum*, 1783), *On the Question: What Does "To Enlighten" Mean* (*Über die Frage: was heißt aufklären*, 1784); *Morning Hours or Lectures on the Existence of God* (*Morgenstunden oder Vorlesungen über das Daseyn Gottes*, 1785).[134]

Our interest will be concentrated on *Jerusalem*, a work which displays a clear connection with our topic.[135] He starts his treatise with the German translation of Menasseh ben Israel's *Vindiciae Iudaeorum*,[136] a Portuguese Jew in Amsterdam with whom Hugo Grotius and Pierre-Daniel Huet, among others, corresponded. Menasseh also wrote the famous successful petition to Oliver Cromwell in support of the readmission of the Jews in England. Manasseh's had several pointed goals in this text: to

---

[133] On his life, see Alexander Altmann's classical study, *Moses Mendelssohn: A Biographical Study* (Tuscaloosa: University of Alabama Press, 1973).
[134] For a short presentation of his philosophical world, see Daniel Dahlstrom in the *Stanford Enyclopedia of Philosophy* (2006), https://plato.stanford.edu/archives/fall2008/entries/mendelssohn/.
[135] Cf. Allan Arkush, *Moses Mendelssohn and the Enlightenment* (Albany: State University of New York Press, 1994). For the literature on the subject "Ceremonial laws" see Daniel Krochmalnik, "Mendelssohns Begriff 'Zeremonialgesetz' und der europäische Antizeremonialismus. Eine begriffsgeschichtliche Untersuchung," in *Recht und Sprache in der deutschen Aufklärung*, ed. Ulrich Kronauer and Jörn Garber (Tübingen: Niemeyer, 2001), 128–160; *idem*, "Das Zeremoniell als Zeichensprache. Moses Mendelssohns Apologie des Judentums im Rahmen der aufklärerischen Semitiok," in *Fremde Vernunft. Zeichen und Interpretation*, ed. Joseph Simon and Werner Stegmaier (Frankfurt: Suhrkamp, 1998); see further Jakob J. Weil, "Über die Personification in der hebräischen Poesie und das Ceremonialgesetz in der hebräischen Religion," *Sulamith* 3/1 (1810): 162–182; Anonimous, "Die jüdischen Zeremonialgesetze," *Jeschurun* [old series] 2 (1854–1855): 70–76; ed. W. Gunther Plaut, *The Rise of Reform Judaism* (New York: World Union for Progressive Judaism, 1963).
[136] *Vindiciae Judaeorum, Or A Letter in Answer to Certain Questions Propounded by a Noble and Learned Gentleman, Touching the Reproaches Cast on the Nation of the Jevves: wherein all Objections are Candidly, and yet Fully Cleared* (Amsterdam: R.D., 1656); *Menasseh ben Israel's mission to Oliver Cromwell: Being a Reprint of the Pamphlets Published by Menasseh ben Israel to Promote the Re-Admission of the Jews to England, 1649–1656*, ed. Lucien Wolf (London: Macmillan & co., 1901). See also his "To His Highnesse the Lord Protector of the Common-Wealth of England, Scotland, and Ireland, the Humble Addresses of Menasseh ben Israel" (1655), also republished by Lucien Wolf.

unmask and disprove the common and old Christian accusation of the Jewish use of blood within their rituals; to assert the Jew's obedience to political authorities; and to deny the accusation of blasphemy and address the possibility of conversion to Judaism. The reason for introducing "Jerusalem" with Manasseh ben Israel's petition was clearly the success of this petition, which was also examined by the deist John Toland.[137] Perhaps Mendelssohn was acquainted with the source of Manasseh's presentation of the Jews as useful for Christian society,[138] an argument that the Rabbi of Amsterdam plagiarised from the above-quoted Simone Luzzatto.[139]

For Mendelssohn, doctrines (e.g. the existence of God, reward and punishment, immortality) are always universal, but historical truths (e.g. the sacrifice of Isaac, the splitting of the Red Sea) may be particular. Ceremonies (e.g. the dietary laws, the laws of the Sabbath) are wholly exclusive to Israel. With this emphasis, the enlightener of Dessau displays his proximity to Luzzatto, who appealed precisely to this element to highlight the non-proselytical nature of Judaism, which is not a religion but a revealed law:[140]

> The Israelites have a divine legislation: laws, precepts, commandments, rules of life, instruction that comes from the will of God, [i.e.] how should we behave so that temporal and eternal happiness is attained. These laws and commandments were communicated to them through Moses in a marvellous and supernatural way. However [It has not been revealed] neither doctrinal opinions, nor saving truths, nor general rational propositions.

And more specifically:

---

[137] John Toland, *Reasons for Naturalizing the Jews in Great Britain and Ireland, on the Same Foot with all other Nations. Containing also, a Defence of the Jews against all Vulgar Prejudices in all Countries* (London: J. Roberts, 1714).
[138] Alexander Altmann in his introduction to Jerusalem cites Luzzatto's work and notes: "Es wäre reizvoll, die von Mendelssohn angeführten Argumente für die, Nützlichkeit' der Juden mit denen Luzzattos, Manassehs und Tolands im einzelnen zu vergleichen. Was schon bei einer flüchtigen Gegenüberstellung ins Auge fällt, ist der neue Zugang zur Frage, den Mendelssohn in der populistischen Theorie findet. Diese Lehre, die in seiner Zeit viel Anklang fand, sieht in der Bevölkerungszunahme das wesentliche Gut und den Reichtum des Staates, und Mendelssohn macht sich diesen Gesichtspunkt völlig zu eigen," in *Moses Mendelssohn, Gesammelte Schriften. Jubiläumsausgabe*, vol. 8, ed. Alexander Altmann (Stuttgart: Fromann, 1983): XVIII.
[139] Isaac Barzilay, "John Toland's Borrowings from Simone Luzzatto: Luzzatto's Discourse on the Jews of Venice (1638) the Major Source of Toland's Writing on the Naturalization of the Jews in Great Britain and Ireland (1714)," *Jewish Social Studies* 31(1969): 75–81.
[140] Moses Mendelssohn, *Gesammelte Schriften*, vol. 8, ed. Alexander Altmann (Stuttgart: Frommann-Holzboog, 1983): S. 157: "Die Israeliten haben göttliche Gesetzgebung. Gesetze, Gebote, Befehle, Lebensregeln, Unterricht vom Willen Gottes, wie sie sich zu verhalten haben, um zur zeitlichen und ewigen Glückseligkeit zu gelangen; dergleichen Sätze und Vorschriften sind ihnen durch Mosen auf eine wunderbare und übernatürliche Weise geoffenbart worden; aber keine Lehrmeinungen, keine Heilswahrheiten, keine allgemeine [sic] Vernunftsätze."

1.3 A Turning Point? Moses Mendelssohn: Between *Caerimonialia* and Religion

> Both written and oral laws have, as practical commandments and rules of life, public and private happiness as the immediate goal. They have to be considered for the most part as a way of writing and have as ceremonial laws sense and meaning. These lead the enquiring intellect to the understanding of divine truths; partly to the eternal ones, partly to the historical truths that are based on the religion of the people.[141]

The first element emphasised is the nature of the commandments: they are communicated with the help of miracles and marvellous phenomena (*eine wunderbare und übernatürliche Weise*). These phenomena are a sign of their divine origin. Revelation is not simply communication (that is the work of Moses), but a communication through wonders, something that enforces its origin. The second element is that the *halakhot* are not dogmas or saving truths, as in Christian churches, nor are they accessed through reason as general rational propositions, as in philosophy or rational theology.

Mendelssohn goes into greater detail on the nature of the commandments and rules of life, or ceremonial laws. They are in the main to be considered an art of writing (*Schriftart*). The meaning of this word is illuminated in another context, in the letter of Mendelssohn to Herz Bomberg, from 22 September 1783,[142] where he speaks of the utility (*Nutzen*) of the meaning and art of writing of the ceremonial law. He uses the words "meaning" and "letter" in a manner which refers to the previously quoted text from Paulus, which is also referenced by Spinoza. According to Mendelssohn, the ceremonial laws are a propaedeutic tool to perfect knowledge, now obscured by polytheism, anthropomorphisms, and religious usurpation. He called the ceremonial laws *Band der Vereinigung* (bound of assembly/unification) that cannot be dogmatic beliefs because they are the origin of reason. The revealed *caerimonialia* are meaningful acts (*bedeutende Handlungen*). The special meaning of such acts is "the understanding of divine truths" (*göttliche Wahrheiten*).

This is not the place for deep explorations of the enlightened and pedagogical character of Mendelssohn's concept of commandment.[143] My interest here is only to stress the turning point of a philosophy of Judaism that refers to the pragmatic nature of Jewish law as a premise to its truth. The sceptic Luzzatto saw in the commandment and ceremonial law only a divine will detached from any explicit goal for exploration, while the enlightened Mendelssohn acknowledges in the Halakhah the

---

[141] *Gesammelte Schriften*, vol. 8, 193: "Sowohl die geschriebenen, als auch die ungeschriebenen Gesetze haben unmittelbar, als *Vorschriften der Handlungen und Lebensregeln*, die öffentliche und Privatglückseligkeit zum Endzwecke. Sie sind aber auch größtentheils als eine Schriftart zu betrachten, und haben als *Zeremonialgesetze*, Sinn und Bedeutung. Sie leiten den forschenden Verstand auf göttliche Wahrheiten; theils auf ewige, theils Geschichtswahrheiten, auf die sich die Religion des Volkes gründete."
[142] I am reading here the edition of Moses Mendelssohn, *Gesammelte Schriften*, vol. 5 (Leipzig: Brockhaus, 1844), 669.
[143] See Chad Hillier, "The Rationalism of Jewish Law in Moses Mendelssohn," *Canadian Theological Review* 2/1 (2013): 87–106.

divine plan, which is rational in its nature. Both of them see dogmatic Christianity as the real enchainment of reason.

This discussion will advance by addressing the topic of a Jewish philosophy and theology, which is the premise for a philosophy of religion. The task of nineteenth- and twentieth-century Judaism will be to adapt Jewish tradition to the category of modern (Christian) theology by developing a philosophy of its essence. That is the topic of the following chapters.

2 Philosophy between Jewish Studies and Theology

The idea of a "Jewish philosophy" emerged in Judaism at a specific moment in time in German-Jewish history: the assumptions underlying the contemporary debate developed during the nineteenth-century emancipation of the Jews. Until this time, the perception of Judaism and Jewish religion in Christian circles had been quite different. Judaism had defined itself until the end of the eighteenth century first and foremost through its own written and oral tradition, considering the Torah to be both a book and a mnemonically transmitted heritage complete with its own hermeneutic tradition.

In the nineteenth century, however, the Jewish self-image went through a serious crisis. The gradual process of political emancipation made it possible for Jews to reflect upon their own identity in ways that had been unimaginable within the confines of the ghetto. This gave rise to a new Jewish self-image which must constantly struggle to overcome its own past. On the one hand, Jewish scholars from Leopold Zunz onward felt it their duty to try to lend distinction to their own intellectual tradition by treating it as the object of serious philological, historical, and cultural analysis. On the other hand, these scholars simultaneously propagated the theory that there had been periods of darkness in the history of Judaism that were somehow responsible for the state of intellectual "poverty" that characterised contemporary Jewish culture. Magic and mysticism (and above all the Kabbalah) were barred from this renaissance of Jewish culture, while Maimonides rose once again to pre-eminence, a status that, even in his own lifetime, was considered questionable.

Israel Scheftelowitz, and, indeed, all other representatives of the *Wissenschaft des Judentums* from Leopold Löw onward, saw in Maimonides the beginnings of the process of enlightenment that would, in the nineteenth century, finally put an end to spiritual belief.[1] Maimonides, he wrote, "had striven to liberate the core of the religion from the shroud that had enveloped it through centuries of folk belief run rampant, and thus to present in all clarity the true essence of the religion."[2] This reverence for Maimonides as the personification of enlightenment, together with the desire for a scientific philosophy—that is, the desire for a critical-historical analysis of their own tradition—led the first proponents of the *Wissenschaft des Judentums* to constitute "Jewish philosophy" as an academic discipline. It is worth remembering, however, that from Isaac Israeli to Maimonides, from Leone Ebreo to Spinoza and Mendelssohn, no Jewish scholar had ever referred to himself as a Jewish philosopher or even considered himself as such. It seems that, in reality, the philos-

---

[1] On the influence of Maimonides on the Berlin *Haskalah* see Isaac E. Barzilay, "The Ideology of the Berlin Haskalah," *Proceedings of the American Academy of Jewish Research* 25 (1956): 4–7.
[2] Isidor Scheftelowitz, *Alt-palästinensischer Bauernglaube in religionsvergleichender Beleuchtung* (Hannover: Lafaire, 1925; reprint Osnabrück: Biblio, 1975), 171.

ophy of Judaism first evolved as a by-product of the *history* of Jewish philosophy.³ It seems that in reality, the philosophy of Judaism first evolved as a by-product of the history of Jewish philosophy. In other words, "Jewish philosophy" was created by nineteenth-century Jewish historians, not by Jewish philosophers. The first published use of the term, as we shall see, was by Zunz in 1818.

2.1 Jewish Philosophy: History of Wisdom

History of Jewish Philosophy

The first sketch of Jewish philosophical history that clearly demonstrates the problem of research in this area was carried out by Simone Luzzatto.⁴ In his *Discorso*, Luzzatto explains to his Venetian audience the advantages of integrating Jews into the general commerce of the city and maritime freight to the East; to do so, he refers to the Jewish history of culture and Jewish traditions in order to present the Jews as an essential part of Venetian society. Although his audience was urbane and sophisticated, they were not willing to conceptualise the presence of Jews in Venice in a favourable light. The *Discorso* begins first with a description of Hellenistic thought and an introduction of thinkers such as Saadia Gaon, Abraham Ibn Ezra, Maimonides, Levi ben Gershon, Ḥasdai Crescas, and Joseph Albo. Luzzatto does not describe the Kabbalists individually; rather, he explains their theories in detail. He presents them not as thinkers but as a class of intellectuals.⁵ This first treatise on the history of Jewish philosophy is not a long one—it only covers eight octavo pages—but it is important inasmuch as it points to two peculiarities of Jewish thinking in the Middle Ages: first, to a discussion concerning the Arabic origin of Jewish

---

3 Cf. *The Cambridge Companion to Medieval Jewish Philosophy,* ed. Daniel H. Franck and Oliver Leaman, (Cambridge: Cambridge University Press, 2003), 5.
4 To my knowledge, there is no earlier text available that discusses the evolution of philosophy in ancient and medieval Judaism in such a (more or less) systematic manner.
5 The entire subdivision of the intellectura has been taken from the *Apologia* of Giovanni Pico della Mirandola see, *Opera Omnia* (Basilae: per Henricum Petri, 1557), 180–181; see Saverio Campanini, "Talmud, Philosophy, Kabbalah: A Passage from Pico della Mirandola's Apologia and its Sources," in *The Words of a Wise Man's Mouth are Gracious. Festschrift for Günter Stemberger on the Occasion of His 65th Birthday,* ed. Mauro Perani (Berlin: De Gruyter, 2005), 429–447. On this subject, see further François Secret, "Un texte mal connu de Simon Luzzato sur la cabbale," *Revue des Études Juives* 118 (1959/1960): 121–128, and Moshe Idel, *Kabbalah: New Perspectives* (New Haven: Yale University Press, 1988), 5. I also refer to my own "Von der 'philosophia giudaica seu ebraeorum' zur 'jüdischen Philosophie': (Ver)wandlungen eines Begriffes im Kontext der Kabbala Denudata," *Morgen-Glantz: Zeitschrift der Christian Knorr von Rosenroth-Gesellschaft* 16 (2006): 323–341. See especially the discussion concerning Luzzatto on 334–340; Bill Rebiger, "Sceptical Strategies in Simone Luzzatto's Presentation of the Kabbalists in his Discorso," *Yearbook of the Maimonides Centre for Advanced Studies* 2 (2017): 51–69.

philosophy, and second, to the Arabic and Judeo-Arabic historical identity of Jewish philosophers.

Following Luzzatto's introduction of Philo of Alexandria and Josephus Flavius as the main representatives of the Judeo-Hellenistic philosophy, there is, surprisingly, no reference whatsoever to rabbinic teachings, the Talmud or the Midrashim. The most essential element Luzzatto puts into the foreground is the *translatio sapientiae*, i.e. the fact that "after the fall of the Roman Empire its teachings were transferred to the Arab nation." After the disintegration of Roman hegemony, the knowledge of the philosophers found a new refuge in the Moslem-Arabic academies; it is also there that Jews found a new cultural home. Luzzatto particularly reveals in this sketch his conviction that philosophy is a universal teaching that is unrelated to the special rights of one particular nation (e.g. biblical revelation). From a philosophical perspective, which he develops further in his 1651 *Socrate*, Luzzatto understands this *dottrina umana* (human doctrine) to be the result of the mind and, therefore, essentially treacherous.

If Luzzatto associates philosophy with brittle knowledge, why does he dedicate an entire sophisticated chapter to prominent figures of ancient and medieval Judaism? The reason is, as I see it, that Luzzatto wishes to exercise a veiled yet identifiable criticism: he turns against all those who want to harmonise philosophy with revelation. It is not a coincidence that he refers to the intellectuals he discusses not as philosophers but as *teologi filosofanti* ("philosophising theologians"). The term *philosophantes* is not a neutral one; it invokes the difference that the Scottish theologian and scholastic Johannes Duns Scotus emphasised in the twelfth century: the difference between those philosophers who do not necessarily demand the existence of revelation, such as Aristotle and Averroes, and those intellectuals who want to solve the seeming incongruity between philosophy and revelation through mutual appreciation.[6] When Dante Alighieri referred to himself as one of the *philosophantes* in his *Quaestio de aqua et terra*, he wrote, "*inter vere philosophantes minimum.*" He did so because he demanded of himself what Thomas Aquinas had denied poets in general: that he be a philosopher.[7] In the age of humanism and the Renaissance, the *De Dignitate* of Giovanni Pico della Mirandola showed that the word took on an esoteric meaning.[8] In Christian rhetoric another hundred years later (the sixteenth century), *philosophantes* were those intellectuals who were unaware of true philosophy.[9]

---

[6] See Johannes Duns Scotus, *De primo principio* III. See also Etienne Gilson, "Les 'Philosophantes,'" *Archives d'Histoire doctrinale et littéraire du Moyen Âge* 19 (1952): 135–140.

[7] See the beginning of the tractate in Dante Alighieri and Giambattista Giuliani, *Le opere latine: Reintegrate nel testo con nuovi commenti* (Florence: Le Monnier, 1882). Thanks to the work of the *Bibliotheca Augustana* in Augsburg, Bavaria, the text is accessible online: Dante Alighieri, "Quaestio de aqua et terra [le opere latine]," *Bibliotheca Augustana*, http://www.hs-augsburg.de/~harsch/Chronologia/Lspost14/Dante/dan_aqte.html; Aquinas, *Summa theologica* I, 1, 9.

[8] Giovanni Pico della Mirandola wrote: "Once we, inspired by the Cherubic spirit, have reached this point through the art of speaking or of reasoning, that is, philosophizing according to the grades of

According to Luzzatto, philosophy is a universal science common to all cultures that should be separated entirely from revelation. In his philosophical treatise *Socrate*, Luzzatto refers to neither Jewish nor Christian authorities, although he does make indirect references. Rather, he spoke of the Socratic academy that had to be addressed from a historical standpoint separately from all Jewish or Christian influences. The subject of the treatise was mostly the relationship between authority and religion, between the treacherous mind and the school of Athens. In *Discorso*, Luzzatto refers to this paradigmatic separation as standing at the core of his thinking. In his description of Jewish philosophy, he criticises the *teologi filosofanti* because "[…] the philosophizing theologians reduce the sayings and claims of the old to generally accessible science; and as they are convinced that one special truth might not necessarily preclude another, and that the opinions of the old scholars do not contradict the apparent truth, they believe their authority might compensate for the flaws of Judaism and the human mind."[10] In the view of the sceptical Venetian rabbi-philosopher Luzzatto, philosophy indicates a weak and errant human mind. Interestingly, however, Luzzatto does not discuss in this treatise either the topic or the truth of revelation. Spinoza would later adapt such sceptical categories in order to question the objectivity of the Jewish concept of revelation.

The second element that Luzzatto considers in his brief treatise is the function of Egypt as the central school of the mind. In this regard, Luzzatto refers to a *topos* of Christian origin, of Egypt possessing a role in salvation due to it being the place of Moses' revelation, the place of the seventy translators of the Torah, and the place of refuge for Jesus of Nazareth from Herod Antipas's persecution.[11] Luzzatto takes up this *topos* from a Jewish point of view: Egypt is the homeland of the lawgiver of the Jews, Moses, the Platonising philosopher Philo of Alexandria, and the philoso-

---

Nature, penetrating the whole from the center to the center, we will then descend, dashing the one into many with Titanic force like Osiris, and ascend, drawing together with Apollonian force the many into one like Osiris's limbs until at last, resting in the bosom of the Father Who is at the top of the ladder, we will be made perfect in theological bliss." The original Latin is translated into English and made accessible online through the Pico Project of the Department of Italian Studies at Brown University and the Università di Bologna. Pico della Mirandola, *De Dignitate* 15, § 87, *Pico Project/Progetto Pico*.

9 See the *Bulla Apostolici Regiminis* from 1513 (DH 1440): "de natura praesertim animae rationalis, quod videlicet mortalis sit, aut unica in cunctis hominibus, et nonnulli temere philosophantes secundum saltem philosophiam verum id esse asseveren." Heinrich Klee, *Katholische Dogmatik*, 2nd ed. (Mainz: Kirchheim Schott & Thielmann, 1840), 289.

10 "[I teologi filosofanti riducono] li detti e pronunciati de gl'antichi in conformità delle dottrine comunemente abbracciate, e ben che tengono per fermo che le verità non s'oppongono l'una l'altra, e che la semplice openione delli antichi dottori non si deve opponere all'evidenzia, così la loro autorità supplisce a gl'ebrei, ove che la ragione umana è manchevole e difettosa di potere con si suoi argomenti arrivarvi." Luzzatto, *Discorso*, 80v.

11 Giuseppe Veltri, *Libraries, Translations, and 'Canonic' Texts*, 62–63.

pher-theologian Maimonides.¹² In this statement, it is easy to identify the function of Arabic culture and geography as the source of Jewish thinking. It is easy to identify, too, the role of Egypt as the land of revelation. It is surely not a coincidence—as the Rabbi Luzzatto likely would phrase it—that one Midrash transmitted in the *Mekhilta de-Rabbi Yishma'el* poses the question of why revelation took place outside of the land of Israel.

The Jewish experience in lands under Islamic rule played a central role in the development and solidification of Jewish identity during the nineteenth century. In that century, the edicts of emancipation granted Jews access to German schools and universities, though the edict was one that all German sovereigns implemented at their own pace. The remembrance of Egyptian Alexandria, once considered the ideal cultural centre, as well as the history of the Jewish community in Muslim Spain and Cairo, the city of Jewish rebirth, became markers of identity for German Jews, as evidenced most visibly through the new Moorish revival architecture of synagogues. German Jews were now enabled to discuss through scholarly-philological means their own antiquity and culture.

At the beginning of the nineteenth century, Leopold Zunz wrote that the new science of the time should also include the scholarly and historical study of Jewish philosophy and the related influence of Arabic philosophy.¹³ It is not a coincidence that Zunz researched the ideas of Spanish philosopher Shem Tov Falaquera in his own doctoral thesis.¹⁴

"Jüdische Philosophie" and "Wissenschaft des Judentums"

Three hundred years after the Lutheran Reformation, new theses were nailed to the gate of science, and one of them concerned so-called Jewish philosophy.¹⁵ The nov-

---

12 See Simone Luzzatto, *Discorso*, 79r: "Et è notabile che siccome l'Egitto diede esordio alla celebrità della natione hebrea per cagione de protenti e miracoli ch'a favor suo occorsero, così anco produsse et educò li tre piu famosi uomini ch'in la natione fiorirono; Moise profeta sommo legislatore nel principio della loro solevatione, Filone eloquentissimo oratore mentre ancor'erano appresso le nationi in alcuna stima; Rabi Moise ora sopranominato, egregio et eccelentissimo. Dottore nella loro caduta et oppressione."
13 Leopold Zunz, *Etwas über die rabbinische Litteratur*, in *Gesammelte Schriften* (Berlin: Curatorium der 'Zunzstiftung,' 1875).
14 Leopold Zunz, "De Schem-Tobh Palkeira, imprimis de ejusdem libro, qui inscribitur Sepher-ha-maaloth" (PhD dissertation, University of Halle, 1821); Material in relation to Zunz's dissertation has been published in Giuseppe Veltri, Annette Winkelmann, "'[...] daß er in Rabbinischer und in der Talmudischen Litteratur ziemlich bewandert ist.' Leopold Zunz und die Universität Halle–Wittenberg," in *Jüdische Bildung und Kultur in Sachsen–Anhalt von der Aufklärung bis zum Nationalsozialismus*, ed. Giuseppe Veltri and Christian Wiese (Berlin: Metropol Verlag, 2008): 239–260. This thesis was begun in Berlin and presented in Halle.
15 My starting point is the *Wissenschaft des Judentums* und the concept of a Jewish philosophy it developed. See also Thomas Meyer, "Die Einheit von Wissenschaft und Religion. Die Herausforder-

elty of the approach is evident in the new literary coinage, the term "Jewish philosophy."[16] In Leopold Zunz's manifesto of the *Wissenschaft des Judentums*, "Etwas über die rabbinische Litteratur," published in 1818, the German expression *Jüdische Philosophie* first made its appearance in a Jewish publication. Zunz writes:

> Above the halls of science, above the entire playground of human endeavour, rules Philosophy in unrivalled majesty, ever invisible, devoting herself with invulnerable self-reliance to all that is humanly knowable. And that is why we have not wished to see her as a separate science, as the epitome of Jewish wisdom alone; for she is also the higher, historical awareness of how this wisdom spread over centuries, put down in writing to be treated and mistreated by Jews and non-Jews; she is the loftiest guide when we ourselves undertake to know the intellectual greatness of our people and to transmit that knowledge. In this manner, each historical date discovered through industry, deciphered with acumen, employed by philosophy, and arranged with discernment, becomes a contribution to human knowledge, the sole, worthiest end of all inquiry. But it is also only this higher notion that behoves Science, who survives states and nations, exalted over all earthly pettiness; she alone can lead us one day to a true history of *Jewish philosophy*, in which the lines of thought pursued by great minds need be discerned and comprehended, and retraced in parallel with the comprehensive teachings of the earth, according to the strict prescripts of history.[17]

Zunz's text is very peculiar in this genre. His at times very convoluted style contains some declarations on the history and nature of (Jewish) philosophy, presents philosophy as Jewish wisdom and not a separate science; it also includes "the higher, historical awareness of how this wisdom spread over centuries, put down in writing to be treated and mistreated by Jews and non-Jews."

With this statement, Zunz is attempting to meld together two concepts, one of which refers to Jewish wisdom, while the other strives for, or presupposes, a "higher, historical awareness" of this Jewish wisdom. Or is he, in fact, trying to say that the latter historical awareness should completely replace the former Jewish wisdom? One thing seems to me to be beyond doubt: Zunz refuses to accept Jewish philosophy's reduction to mere Jewish wisdom. He has no wish to deny the latter its identity as characteristically Jewish, but at the same time he proposes a new concept, Jewish philosophy, in which it is precisely the historical dimension that plays a decisive, unifying role.

---

ung einer Wissenschaft des Judentums," in *Die "Wissenschaft des Judentums." Eine Bestandaufnahme* (Wilhelm Fink: Paderborn, 2015), 159–175.

16 The coinage "Jewish philosophy" or "Jüdische Philosophy" is, of course, older than the Jewish usage of it. For the German literature see the valuable, standard study of Dirk Westerkamp, *Die philonische Unterscheidung. Aufklärung, Orientalismus und Konstruktion der Philosophie*. The interested reader can find some lines of Westerkamp study in his English article, "The Philonic Distinction: German Enlightenment historiography of Jewish Thought," *History and Theory* 47 (2008): 533–559.

17 Leopold Zunz, *Etwas über die rabbinische Litteratur*, vol. 1, 30–31. All of the quotations from Zunz in this section are ibid. Emphasis mine.

This historical awareness plays, of course, a major role in research on the Jewish study of philosophy and how Jews have contemplated it. For "In this manner, each historical date discovered through industry, deciphered with acumen, employed by philosophy and arranged with discernment, becomes a contribution to human knowledge, the sole most worthy end of all inquiry." Zunz's real problem is not defining what philosophy is, nor is it historically integrating Jewish philosophy into general philosophy. His principal concern is how to identify Jewish philosophers in a historical sense—within the axes of time and place—and to situate their scientific knowledge amidst other contemporary achievements. He stresses: "it/she [this higher notion, the higher historical awareness] alone can lead us one day to a true history of Jewish philosophy, in which the lines of thought pursued by great minds need be discerned and comprehended, and retraced in parallel with the comprehensive teachings of the earth, according to the strict prescripts of history."

The historical perception, listing, and study of all of the writings concerned with these topics is a key problem because of the lack of research on the topics themselves. The second problem is in defining what Jewish wisdom is or, more specifically, what it *was*.

Jewish Philosophy in its Historical Awareness

Although Zunz had not attended Hegel's lectures at the University of Berlin,[18] there can be no doubt that he is referring to the Prussian professor when he defines the element of intellectual development in the history of philosophy as a product of higher historical awareness. This sentence is first a plea against those that deny any contribution of the Jewish people to universal intellectual history. Second, it constitutes a kind of lament about the lack of scholarly awareness of Jewish historical heritage. I will emphasise this aspect by quoting several Christian authors, beginning with an account of how Christians have generally dealt with Jewish philosophy.

The first occurrence of the expression *philosophy of Judaism* in English I have encountered in my research is in the title of Shaw Duncan's *The History and Philosophy of Judaism: Or, A Critical and Philosophical Analysis of the Jewish Religion*, published in 1787 in Edinburgh.[19] Duncan, minister of the parish church of Elgin (Moray, Scotland), writes in apologetic answer to the opinion of David Hume on the absurdity of

---

[18] This can be clearly seen from his study records. On this, see my contribution, "Altertumswissenschaft und Wissenschaft des Judentums: Leopold Zunz und seine Lehrer F. A. Wolf und A. Boeckh," in *Friedrich August Wolf. Studien, Texte, Bibliographie*, ed. Reinhart Markner and Giuseppe Veltri (Göttingen: Steiner, 1999), 32–47.

[19] Duncan Shaw, *The History and Philosophy of Judaism: Or, A Critical and Philosophical Analysis of the Jewish Religion. From which is Offered a Vindication of its Genius, Origin, and Authority, and of the Connection with the Christian, against the Objections and Misrepresentations of Modern Infidels* (Edinburg: C. Eliott, 1787).

Jewish religion. In his *Of Superstition and Enthusiasm* (1741), Hume writes: "Modern Judaism and popery (especially the latter), being the most unphilosophical and absurd superstitions which have yet been known in the world, are the most enslaved by their priests."[20]

In quoting Hume's essay, the clergyman omits any mention of the Catholic Church, the very focus of Hume's attack, and furthermore questions the adjective "modern." In his view, the Jewish religion of post-biblical, Talmud, Mishnah, and Gemara, "will justify the severest epithets that could be bestowed upon it,"[21] while the Old Testament itself fully exemplified the quality of philosophical rationalism.

Duncan's argument follows a discussion that began properly in the sixteenth century in Wittenberg and involved both Judaism and Catholicism; in the eyes of the Lutheran leaders of the Reformation, both were old-fashioned and outdated religions wedded to indurate tradition. "Jewish tradition," in this case, was deduced archeologically from "canonical" sources and theologically based on the rational attitude to modernity. These "canonical" sources, of course, are simply and solely selected from the Old Testament according to the Lutheran vision of New Testament: the only valid law is the natural law written on the Tablets of the Ten Commandments. The customs and ceremonial laws of the Jews, in this view, are devoid of any and all validity.

It is very curious to observe that this negation of the validity of the Torah of Moses became a very real stimulus for the study of Jewish customs, rites, and post-biblical traditions. Interest in Jewish practices, both in the liturgy and in everyday life, was, of course, not entirely new. Novel, however, was the relatively high number of publications such as those we discussed above.

Of some interest as well is a further phenomenon which demonstrates the focus of attention on Judaism in Protestant academies in the seventeenth and eighteenth centuries; this focus is evident from the sheer number of dissertations from the

---

20 The entire text is: "Modern Judaism and popery, (especially the latter) being the most unphilosophical and absurd superstitions which have yet been known in the world, are the most enslaved by their priests. As the Church of England may justly be said to retain some mixture of Popish superstition, it partakes also, in its original constitution, of a propensity to priestly power and dominion; particularly in the respect it exacts to the sacerdotal character. And though, according to the sentiments of that Church, the prayers of the priest must be accompanied with those of the laity; yet is he the mouth of the congregation, his person is sacred, and without his presence few would think their public devotions, or the sacraments, and other rites, acceptable to the divinity." *The Philosophical Works: Essays Moral, Political, Literary, Edited and with a Foreword, Notes, and Glossary by Eugene F. Miller, with an appendix of variant readings from the 1889 edition by Thomas H. Green and Thomas H. Grose*, revised edition (Indianapolis: Liberty Fund, 1987). The essay appeared in 1741 in the first volume of Hume's *Essays, Moral and Political* (Edinburgh: R. Fleming & A. Alison, 1741). This paragraph disappeared in successive editions. Either the philosopher changed his mind or—more plausibly—the reaction of Roman Catholic Church caused it to be erased.
21 Ibid., 26.

era concerning Hebrew and Jewish studies.[22] In the libraries of German universities, we can find carefully stored more than 100,000 dissertations on almost every aspect of academic life. Approximately 5 to 10% of them are concerned with Jewish topics of various themes, starting with biblical theology, philology, rabbinic literature, and Jewish philosophy from the Middle Ages and Humanist period, ending with subjects of modern life such as the political condition of the Jews, etc. The philosophical texts and ideas of the Jewish medieval tradition played a large role in the Protestant concern with Judaism. The classical works of Maimonides, Joseph Albo, and Isaac Abravanel were read, partly translated into Latin, and extensively quoted. Contemporary authors such as Azariah de' Rossi and Rabbi Löw of Prague were also the object of translation and study.

The interest in locating Judaism within the compass of Christian history was probably the origin of the historical study of medieval and modern Jewish authors on philosophy and ethics. This interest definitively ended with the second half of the eighteenth century. Only biblical Judaism maintained a place in academic teaching; the so-called "later Jewish literature" from then on appeared but rarely, having been polemically silenced or "underquoted." Nineteenth- and early twentieth-century concerns with Jewish literature, such as the work of August Ferdinand Dähre, Hermann L. Strack, Paul Billerbeck, Gustav Dalman, and others, are the exception rather than the rule; they tend to focus only on ancient literature as an explanation for facets of the New Testament. This lack of interest has a likely reason behind it: namely, the critical historicisation of Jewish wisdom.

Jewish Philosophy as Wisdom

In his 2008 article on "Philosophy and Kabbalah," David Myers[23] writes: "One literary genre whose significance Zunz did *not*[24] herald in this essay was Kabbalah."[25] He is right: it isn't mentioned in the text of the essay, only in the footnotes. I can concede that Zunz's note is not a plea for the study of a genre, but it is very significant for the succeeding study of Jewish mysticism that is situated against the negative vision of mysticism among the advocates of the *Wissenschaft des Judentums* (which Gershom Scholem believed himself to have unmasked). Zunz was indeed conscious of the Christian and Jewish use and misuse of Kabbalistic texts.

---

22 See Giuseppe Veltri, "Academic Debates on the Jews in Wittenberg. The Protestant Literature on Rituals, the Dissertationes and the Writings of the Hebraists Theodor Dassow and Andreas Sennert," *European Journal of Jewish Studies* 6 (2012): 123–146.
23 David N. Myers, "Philosophy and Kabbalah in Wissenschaft des Judentums: Rethinking the Narrative of Neglect,'" *Studia Judaica (Cluj-Napoca)* 16 (2008): 56–71.
24 Italics by the author.
25 David N. Myers, "Philosophy," 60.

It isn't surprising that Zunz's thesis on Jewish philosophy also takes the Kabbalah into consideration and says nothing either good or bad about the pre-Kabbalistic "Book of Creation" the *Sefer Yeṣirah*, apart from the laconic remark,

> The *Yeṣirah* is a little book that is neither as clever nor as silly as partisans of either view would have it. This is what has confused the majority of those who have attacked the Kabbalah; honest Reuchlin is still the one who manages best with it. Very much to the point is Andreas Sennert (*exercitt. phill. hept. alt.* 139): *Kabbalah nobis alia est verior, indubitata atque divina; alia sequior hac, media et humana, quae et Judaica dicitur vulgo; alia denique falsa, superstitiosa, immo daemoniaca.*

Although Zunz praises the scholarly honesty of Johannes Reuchlin, it is the opinion of Andreas Sennert that he quotes. Sennert was a Hebraist from Wittenberg who devoted several chapters of his *Exercitationes Philologicarum*[26] to Jewish mysticism. The treatise appeared in 1678 and is largely ignored today. In it, Sennert addresses the names of God, the Masorah, the Kabbalah, the *Musica Hebraeorum*, Jewish schools and studies and the like, up to and including hieroglyphics. His vision of the Kabbalah is clear: there is one version that is divine and indisputable; a second that is human, the so-called Jewish Kabbalah; and a third that is unquestionably false, a superstitious and devilish invention. Judaism is no longer considered the bearer of the *Philosophia kabbalistica divina*.

The Wittenberg Hebraist had no personal interest in Kabbalistic practices. He treats the matter as a subject of enquiry, judging the extent of its relevance by the fact that it was considered important to Christianity by the illustrious likes of Pico della Mirandola and Johannes Reuchlin, as well as by Petrus Colonna Galatinus. He deals extensively with the ways in which the Kabbalah is designated and the synonyms applied to it, compares it with the *allegoria patrum*, examines in detail the practical Kabbalah as *technē* (of Pythagorean origin), and thus shows some appreciation for it as a useful "scientific" instrument. He closes his treatise with the remark that the study of the *Kabbalah artificialis sive technica* is a worthwhile occupation that ought to be engaged in with caution (*caute*) and moderation (*moderate*). It is worthwhile, even a duty, in order to avoid bringing guilt upon oneself, either through excess (*per excessum*) or deficiency (*per defectum*). For there are, he adds, two groups that failed to follow this golden rule (*ne vel in excessu, aut defectu quoque peccetur*): the Valentinians, that is, the Gnostics, who misused Holy Scripture for heretical purposes; and the Karaites, who abhorred the Kabbalah and advocated only a literal in-

---

[26] *Exercitationes philologicarum Heptas altera: quarum I. De Div. Nom. Elohim. add: Mantissa de Jehovah; II. De Masorah; III. De Cabbalah; IV. De Musica Ebræor.; V. De Scholis, studiis, &c. &c. eorundem. ; VI. De Mendis Codicum Apographorum V. Intr. Ebr. Hodiernor. VII. De Sceptro Judah, &c. ex Genes. c. XLIX. comm. 10, Cui additur Hierographicum Sinaicum Kircher &c. &c.* (Wittenberg: Joh. Sigismundi Ziegenbeins, 1678).

2.1 Jewish Philosophy: History of Wisdom — 115

terpretation of the Bible.[27] Drawing a direct comparison between these two groups was something of a novelty.

There is, however, a second author whom Leopold Zunz quotes, someone who had dealt with the subject of Jewish philosophy before him: Franz Budde. It is worth considering this quotation more closely and in context. Part of Zunz's objective in his quest for "a true history of Jewish philosophy" is that "the line of thought pursued by great minds need be discerned and comprehended, and retraced in parallel with the comprehensive teachings of the earth, according to the strict prescripts of history." He criticises the fact that Jewish authors had thus far all been treated as representatives of the Jewish people, without distinction as to time or place of origin and without taking into account the intellectual influence of their surroundings. On this subject, he remarks, "Buddeus provides only an introduction, and a sparse one at that." This remark and its implications has not received much attention from modern scholars. Who was Budde?

Among the accomplishments of Wilhelm Schmidt-Biggemann is his ability to clearly formulate philosophical theories and to clarify the historical context of intellectual developments. Moreover, he did this while venturing into fields where representatives of modern philosophical discourse famously fear to tread. One such case was his recognition of the *philosophia perennis* as a spiritual and intellectual dimension of Western philosophy.[28] Another was his interest in the origins of the *Philosophia Hebraeorum* as an historical concept that doubtlessly played a role in the formation of the tradition of archaic/eternal Philosophy. According to Schmidt-Biggemann, the eclectic Johann Franz Budde historicises the Christian philosophical Kabbalah in

---

27 *De Cabbalah. IV*, 177: Ita vicissim tamen, ut moderate eadem atque caute item adhibeatur, ne vel in excessu, aut defectu quoque peccetur. In excessu, cum Valentinianis atque Gnosticis jam olim, quorum Haeresi, teste Irenaeo & Epiphanio, originem dedisse creditur non absimilis prorsus modus, & ipsis jam tum Quoque usitatus, interpretandi Scripturam S., dum discussis inter sese varie elementis lacerabant verius eam, quam examinabant aut exponebant, in lucem expositis ab ipsis miris inauditisque haereseon portentis. In defectu vicissim tamen, & ipso quoque cum Judaeis hodie nonnullis, quae apud ipsos factio ideo קראים sive Caraitae vocantur, et in Polonia, Russia atque Turcia praesertim satis frequens est, quibus (maxime propter Cabbalae abusum) nihil sapit nisi unice litera textus, quam mordicus ideoque tenent, nec ab ac vel latum unguem discedunt. ("Again, however, in such a way that it be approached with both moderation and with caution, lest one sin either through excess or deficiency. Through excess, along with the Valentinians and the Gnostics of long ago, whose heresy, according to Irenaeus and Epiphanius, is, in short, believed to have had its origin in a not dissimilar method of interpreting the Holy Scriptures, which they, too, even then made use of. When discussing various elements [of Scripture], they tended to mangle it rather than investigate or interpret it, professing miracles and unheard of heretical portents. Or through deficiency, on the other hand, and this along with not a few contemporary Jews, among whom there is a faction called the קראים, or Caraites, which is quite popular in Poland, Russia, and especially Turkey, who—largely because of the misuse of the Kabbalah—acknowledge nothing but the letter of the text, to which they cling tenaciously, not departing from it by a finger's breadth.")

28 Wilhelm Schmiddt-Biggemann, *Philosophia perennis. Historische Umrissse abendländischer Spiritualität in Antike, Mittelalter und Früher Neuzeit* (Frankfurt: Suhrkamp, 1998).

his *Introductio ad Historiam Philosophiae Ebraeorum*.²⁹ This process takes place in specific stages and in accordance with certain assumptions, of which Schmidt-Biggemann provides us with a very precise list. He distinguishes three historical periods that specify the inclusion and exclusion of Judaism from the general (Christian) philosophical discourse. The first is represented by Pico della Mirandola and Johannes Reuchlin and is characterised primarily by speculation with numbers and Pythagorean theory. The second is represented by Knorr von Rosenroth. The third by Budde under the influence of Wachter's criticism of Spinozan pantheism. It is not my intention here to treat, or even to question, each of these points. Instead I will focus on rethinking Schmidt-Biggemann's framing of Budde's thought.

According to Schmidt-Biggemann, the premises underlying the *Introductio* can be condensed into three main arguments: 1) the philosophical-historical bases of the Kabbalah are disputable; 2) the linking of Pythagorean philosophy with Kabbalah (as proposed, for example, by Henry More) is closer to *philosophia perennis* than Knorr's interpretation; and 3) Wachter's identification of Kabbalah with Spinozan philosophy renders the Kabbalah as a prelude to pantheism and atheism. Budde's "contribution" is, according to Schmidt-Biggemann, more of a destructive nature, or, to let the author speak for himself: "His particular, and lasting, contribution to the discussion consists in his having been the first to connect the Pythagorean interpretation of the Kabbalah with late antique, anti-Christian Gnosis. In this, Budde's intent, with respect to the Kabbalah, is destructive. Christian apologetics has long since refuted the Gnosis. The anti-Gnostic arguments are thus equally applicable to the Kabbalah." Therefore, "[t]he Kabbalah, as a serious object of Christian speculation, has been expelled from the realm of academic Protestant theology."³⁰

While the approach taken by Schmidt-Biggemann is admirable, there is some question as to whether the process of estrangement of Jewish tradition did, in fact, first emerge as a consequence of Budde's *Introductio*. As for the turning point in the level of esteem attached to the Christian Kabbalah, there can be no doubt that Knorr von Rosenroth was still an adept. He was perhaps the last of those who still adhered to the tried and true Christian theory of the Kabbalah as a manifestation of divine, archaic wisdom and who tried to support that theory with new arguments.

Knorr's conception of the *philosophia iudaica sive hebraica sive Hebraeorum* clearly revolves around the Zohar.³¹ Beginning with the title of his monumental work, he provides a clear indication as to what the reader is—or at least should

---

29 Johann Franz Buddeus, *Io. Francisci Buddei [...] Introductio ad Historiam Philosophiae Ebraeorum: Accedit Dissertatio de Haeresi Valentiniana. Editio Nova eaque Multis Accessionibus Auctior* (Halle: Orphanotropheum, 1720).
30 Wilhelm Schmidt-Biggemann, "Die Historisierung der 'Philosophie Hebraeorum' im frühen 18. Jahrhundert. Eine philosophisch-philologische Demontage," in *Historicization— Historisierung*, ed. Glenn Most (Göttingen: Vandenhoeck & Ruprecht, 2001), 103–128.
31 On Knorr, I have followed the highly detailed analysis of his work by Andreas Kilcher, "Synopse zu Knorr von Rosenroths *Kabbala denudata*," *Morgen-Glantz* 10 (2000): 201–220.

be—avidly seeking: *doctrina Hebraeorum transcendentalis et metaphysica atque theologica opus antiquissimae philosophiae barbaricae*. In the *loci communes* that constitute a kind of philological-philosophical-theological *apparatus* to the Zohar, the word "philosophy" does not, of course, appear. In its stead, there is an entire arsenal of conceptual terminology that the reader is free to use for his own purposes.

Knorr clearly proceeds from the assumption that the Kabbalistic tradition of the Zohar is meant to be understood as being Adamitic and thus as universal knowledge. He does so in spite of, or perhaps because of, the fact that he had included in the first volume of his *Praefatio ad lectorem philebraeum* a translation of the story of the cave of Rabbi Shim'on ben Yoḥay. There he also mentions doubts as to the truth of the Kabbalah, based on there being no reference to it in the Talmud.[32] By bringing up the cave of Shim'on, Knorr alludes implicitly to Plato's "Allegory of the Cave" and its implications for the philosophy of being, the theory of revealed knowledge and the epistemology of appearance. In treating the Hebrew term "wisdom," he characterizes it not as something specifically Jewish, but equates it rather with philosophy, or, more specifically, with ontology.[33]

The divine wisdom of Scripture is the equivalent of the central question of the Presocratics: *ti esti*, which is the equivalent of Adam, according to the Gematria: מה = 45, אדם = 45. In treating archaic knowledge, Knorr defines it as being of Oriental origin; divine knowledge is clearly equated with theology in keeping with the definition offered by Maimonides:[34]

> חכמה קדומה: *Oriental Wisdom* as an indication of the antiquity of this notion, which is in proximity to the Crown, which is called קדמון, or anterior. One speaks moreover of חכמת אלהים *The Wisdom of God* (I Kings 3:28), that is, as Rabbi Moses would have it, that [wisdom] that is given to those who can be measured, those who are called אלהים [God in plural].[35]

Knorr's interest in the Zohar derives from his view of it as being an archaic source of philosophic discourse (*ti esti*). He maintains this view in spite of the criticism aimed

---

32 Christian Knorr von Rosenroth, *Kabbala denudata*, 2 vols. (Sulzbach: Frankfurt a.M.: Abraham Lichtenthaler, 1677–1684 (reprint, Hildesheim: Olms, 1974). *Vol. 1*: 3: *Dubium tamen quibusdam exortum est, an etiam vera sint ista, quae in Sohar traduntur, de sapientia ipsius Cabbalistica; ex eo, quod in Talmudis Codice, ubi saepe eius est mentio, nihil unquam de Cabbala eius commemoretur.* ("Some have had doubts as to whether the things transmitted in the Zohar are even true, as to its its Kabbalistic wisdom; this because in the codex of the Talmud, to which it often refers, there is no mention at all of the Kabbalah.")

33 Knorr von Rosenroth, *Kabbala Denudata. Tomus primus, pars prima: loci communes*, p. 343: חכמה: Sapientia, Est sephirah secunda, quae sic vocatur, quia est sapientia entis. Deque ea dicitur Ijobh 28,12: *Est sapientia ab* אין *invenietur*. Est autem חכמה quasi כח מה ist est vis מה qui est numerus אדם…".

34 Ibid.: "חכמה קדומה : *Sapientia Orientalis*, ut indicetur anterioritas notionis eius, quae vicina est coronae, quae vocatur קדמון anterior. Dicitur etiam porro חכמת אלהים *Sapientia Dei. I. Reg 3,28.* id est, ut vult R. Moscheh, illa, quae datur mensuris illi, quae vocantur אלהים."

35 Translated by Hal Wyner.

at him by his contemporaries with respect to both the age and the veracity of the Zohar. Reading his *Excerpta ex Epistola quadam Compilatoris de utilitate Versionis Libri Cabalistici Sohar*,³⁶ one has the impression that he considers the Kabbalistic text less an object of philological or philosophical debate than a defence of an article of faith. The important thing for him is the *vetustas* and, especially, the great wisdom that Judaism, like a river, bears along with it in its flow. Certainly, Pythagorean and Platonic philosophy have also left behind traces of archaic philosophy (*amica responsio:* [...] *multa occurrere philosophiae huius barbaricae vestigia*).³⁷ These, however, are mere brooks as compared with the fountain (*fons*) of Jewish philosophy. In this, Knorr's intent was to refute Henry More's thesis, according to which the *philosophia perennis* had been best preserved in Pythagorean philosophy and of which the Jewish Kabbalah was, by comparison, a mere distortion. Knorr treats the Kabbalah with the conviction of a believer. He was, perhaps, the last to argue for the recognition of Kabbalistic theology as the archaic precursor of Greek philosophy. That he had few if any followers was due to the fact that Protestant theology was by that time well on its way toward de-Judaising the theological canon.

As Schmidt-Biggemann would have it, Jarig Jelles's reading of Spinoza³⁸ and, more particularly, Georg Wachter's subsequent work *Spinozismus in Judenthumb* (1699), which treated Spinozan philosophy as pantheism, equated with atheism, played a role in the de-Judaisation of the *philosophia perennis*. There is not, for the moment, sufficient evidence to satisfactorily judge whether this was in fact the case. It is clear, however, that the process of de-Judaising philosophy and theology was, at this time, already under way, as other scholars have shown. The work of Valerio Marchetti is particularly instructive in this regard.³⁹ As his studies on the *dissertationes* in Protestant universities of the period confirm, the question of the Jewish or Christian origins of Pythagoras, Aristotle, and Plato was actively debated in the academic world of the period. It is thus not surprising that there, once again, we encounter the name of Budde, and this even before he had written his *Introductio*. As early as 1702, a certain Johann Jacob Borsch wrote a *Dissertatio historica de peregrinationibus Pythagora* ("Historical Dissertation on the Peregrinations of Pythagoras"), under the direction of Budde, who also led the discussion thereof. Both student

---

36 Ibid., *pars secunda*, 3–5.
37 Ibid.
38 Jelles was the author of a foreword to the *Opera Posthuma* of Spinoza, published by Rieuwertsz, Amsterdam, 1677. Neither the place of publication nor the author's name is noted in the edition.
39 See Valerio Marchetti, "Sulla degiudaizzazione della politica. In margine alla relazione di Horst Dreitzel," in *Aristotelismo e ragion di stato*, ed. Enzo A. Baldini (Florence: Olschki, 1995), 349–358; Valerio Marchetti, "An Pythagoras proselytus factus sit," in *Dimensioni e problemi della ricerca storica* 2 (1996): 111–131; Valerio Marchetti, "'Aristoteles utrum fuerit Iudaeus.' Sulla degiudaizzazione della filosofia europea in età moderna," in *Anima e paura. Studi in onore di Michele Ranchetti*, ed. Bruna Bocchini Camaiani (Macerata: Quodlibet, 1998), 249–266; Valerio Marchetti, "Il teologo luterano Johann Franz Budde (1667–1729) e la filosofia ebraica," in *Interculturalità dell'ebraismo*, ed. Mauro Perani (Ravenna: Longo, 2004), 299–314.

and master principally attacked French scholar Pierre-Daniel Huet,[40] who, in his *Demonstratio evangelica* (1679), mounted an impassioned defence of the idea of the Mosaic origins of philosophy. Borsch and Budde reject the idea of Pythagoras having been a student of the Prophets Daniel or Ezekiel. The very real travels of Pythagoras, they argue, had taken him to both Egypt and Babylonia, and thus expanded his philosophical horizon. However, they had in no way contributed to a mastery of Jewish philosophy on his part. A similar point had already been made two years earlier by Daniel Bandeco, a student from Berlin, who in 1700 defended his thesis, *Pythagoras utrum fuerit Judaeus, Monachusve Carmelita*[41] ("Whether Pythagoras was a Jew and a Carmelite Monk"), in Hamburg under the direction of Johann Friedrich Mayer. Mayer and Bandeco thoroughly analysed the ancient belief that Pythagoras was a student of Daniel or Ezekiel, concluding that, although there might be some concordance between Hebrew and Pythagorean thought, there is no evidence of a direct relationship.[42]

In the opening of his *Introductio*, Budde addresses the fact that there are different uses of the word philosophy. He makes clear in his book that when he employs the term Jewish philosophy he is utilising the definition of philosophy as the "study of wisdom and love for it" (*sapientiae studium atque amor*).[43] With his brief statement regarding the beginnings of a Jewish philosophy in Budde, Zunz refers to the Halle pietist's work concerning the Bible, rabbinic literature (that is, the schools), Jewish mysticism (such as that of Rabbi Johanan ben Zakkai), as well as medieval and renaissance literature and philosophy. He lists authors and works and tries to put them in historical context. Most of the 800 pages of Budde's treatise are devoted to the ideas and concepts of the Kabbalah. There are, of course, mistakes; however Zunz provides, as he claims, a first step towards a history of Jewish philosophy. One has to note here that in the *Wissenschaft des Judentums* of the nineteenth century, a history of Jewish philosophy was never written. It was only a scholarly *desideratum*.

Between the second half of the eighteenth and the first decades of the nineteenth century,[44] Jews experienced a quiet dramatic revolution: they were released from the

---

40 On Huet see now, Suzanne Guellouz, ed., *Daniel Huet (1630–1721): Actes du colloque de Caen (12–13 novembre, 1993)* (Paris, Seattle and Tübingen: Romanisches Seminar, 1994).
41 Daniel Bandeco, *Pythagoras utrum fuerit Judaeus, Monachusve Carmelita*, (Hamburg: Reumann, 1700).
42 My interest here is not to determine who was the first to question the presumed derivation of Pythagoras' *philosophia antiqua* from archaic Jewish philosophy, but rather to establish the fact that this question had already been raised before the publication of Budde's *Introductio*.
43 Johann Franz Buddeus, *Io. Francisci Buddei [...] introductio ad historiam philosophiae Ebraeorum. Accedit dissertatio de haeresi Valentiniana. Editio nova eaque multis accessionibus auctior* (Halae Saxonum: Orphanotropheum, 1720), 2. See also Dirk Westerkamp, *Die philonische Unterscheidung*, 34–38.
44 This chapter is a, substantially reworked part of my book *Language of Conformity & Dissent. The Imaginative Grammar of Jewish Intellectuals in the Nineteenth and Twentieth Centuries* (Boston: Aca-

hated inhuman ghetto into free bourgeois society—they went from a condition of unjust confinement forced upon them by Christian society into the realm of enlightenment and emancipation. At long last, Jews were permitted to participate in public life, although that participation was still subject to restrictions. The removal of constraints is, to be sure, quite different from the actual achievement of equality, however. As late as 1832 Leopold Zunz was still viewing emancipation and equality of rights as goals that Jews needed to achieve: "It is high time that Jews in Europe, especially in Germany, were granted justice and freedom instead of rights and freedoms: not a measly humiliating privilege, but the full, uplifting bourgeois status."[45]

The full, uplifting bourgeois status also implies the recognition of Judaism as a religion, culture, philosophy, history, literature, all that what later authors will call "Jewish civilisation,"[46] and, for Leopold Zunz, more humbly, Jewish Studies. Following the origins and developments of Jewish studies in the nineteenth century, in the next chapter I will turn to two attempts to create academic disciplines that aimed to investigate and teach to Jews and non-Jews the Jewish culture and heritage in its manifold aspects. These attempts are important as a cultural thermometer for the history of Jewish philosophy because they also developed the coordinates of what Jewish studies represents for Jewish theology: a philological and methodological workshop.

We will begin with an introduction to Jewish Studies according to Leopold Zunz and continue with an introduction of Jewish theology according to Abraham Geiger. The knowledgeable reader is acquainted with the successive history and knows why there was no Jewish theological faculty at German universities until 2014. Here I would like instead to analyse the premises of a process which was fertile but also fatal for German and European Jewry.

---

demic Studies Press, 2013), 41–60 and 89–98. The paragraph dedicated to the Jewish theology is totally new. But see my "'Tochter der Zeit'—Zur Geschichte der Jüdischen Theologie in Deutschland."
45 Leopold Zunz, *Die gottesdienstlichen Vorträge der Juden, historisch entwickelt. Ein Beitrag zur Alterthumskunde und biblischen Kritik, zur Literatur- und Religionsgeschichte* (Berlin: Asher, 1832; repr. Hildesheim: Olms, 1966), 7.
46 The expression Jewish culture or Jewish Civilization goes back to Mordecai Kaplan, see Ken Koltun-Fromm, "Abraham Geiger—kulturwissenschaftliche Reflexionen," in *Jüdische Existenz in der Moderne: Abraham Geiger und die Wissenschaft des Judentums*, ed. Christian Wiese, Walter Homolka, and Thomas Brechenmacher (Berlin: De Gruyter, 2013): 37–69, 38. On this concept and his modern usage, see von Shmuel N. Eisenstadt, *Jewish Civilization: The Jewish Historical Experience in a Comparative Perspective* (New York: State University of New York Press, 1992).

3 Leopold Zunz: The "Scientific" Creation of Jewish Studies

Leopold Zunz, whose Hebrew name was Jomtob Lipmann, was born in Detmold, the capital of the German principality of Lippe-Detmold, on August 10, 1796.[1] Following the death of his father, Menachem, in 1803, Zunz entered the Samsonsche Freischule in Wolfenbüttel, Brunswick. The Samsonsche Freischule was the most important house of learning for the Jewish community in the area.[2] As mentioned above, one of Zunz's schoolmates was Isaak Markus Jost. Zunz was the first Jewish student accepted to the *Prima* of the *Gymnasium* in Wolfenbüttel; in other words, he was the first Jewish student ever to enter the high school there. He graduated in 1811.

He left Wolfenbüttel in the fall of 1815 and relocated to Berlin. He commenced his studies at the newly established Friedrich-Wilhelms-Universität, today's Humboldt University of Berlin. According to Zunz's *Curriculum Vitae*, which he included in his application for the PhD examination procedure in Halle, he read in Berlin with renowned scholars such as the theologian Wilhelm Martin Leberecht de Wette, with whom he was friends, and the professor of jurisprudence Friedrich Carl von Savigny.[3] Concerning his teachers, Karl Wilhelm Stolger (for logic), Friedrich Rühs (ancient history), August Boeckh, and Friedrich August Wolf, Zunz noted that "I leave Stolger for he his boring, and Rühs for he is against the Jews. Boeckh instructs [*belehrt*]. Yet it is Wolf alone who attracts me [*zieht mich an*]."[4]

Following the lectures of Wolf and Boeckh, Leopold Zunz outlined his ideas of Jewish studies in his first treatise, "Notes on the Rabbinical Literature" [*Etwas über die rabbinische Litteratur*]. Published in 1818, this treatise would become the

---

[1] On Zunz's biography, see, for instance, Nahum N. Glatzer, *Leopold Zunz: Jude, Deutscher, Europäer, ein jüdisches Gelehrtenschicksal des 19. Jahrhunderts in Briefen an Freunde* (Tübingen: Mohr, 1964), 1–72. See also Michael A. Meyer, *Von Moses Mendelssohn zu Leopold Zunz: Jüdische Identität in Deutschland 1749–1824* (München: Beck, 1994).

[2] On the Samsonsche *Freischule* see, for instance, Mordechai Eliav, *Jüdische Erziehung in Deutschland im Zeitalter der Aufklärung und der Emanzipation* (Münster and New York: Waxmann, 2001), 132–139.

[3] In the original Latin, the information on his years in Berlin reads "Quum vero Anno MDCCCXV Berolinum me contulissem, ibique per quadriennium universitati ascriptus fuerim, praelectionibus philosophicis mathematicis historicis et philologicis celeberrimorum | virorum Dr. Boeckh, Dr. Grueson, Dr. Ruehs, Dr. Solger, Dr. Tralles, Dr. Wilken, et Dr. F. A. Wolf interfui, – Doctores etiam praeclaros Savignium et de Wettium, quorum alter juris romani historiam, alter introductionem in Scripturam Sanctam disserebat audivi." Universitätsarchiv Halle, Rep. 21 II Nr. 15, Bl. 132. See also Zunz's letter to Samuel Meyer. Ehrenberg, dated July 11, 1817, in Glatzer, *Leopold Zunz*, 86.

[4] Leopold Zunz, *Das Buch Zunz: Eine Probe*, ed. Fritz Bamberger (Berlin: Officina Serpentis, 1931), 19. In 1816, Friedrich Rühs published his pamphlet *Die Rechte des Christenthums und des deutschen Volks, vertheidigt gegen die Ansprüche der Juden und ihrer Verfechter.* (Berlin: Realschulbuchhandlung, 1816).

manifesto of his *scientia nova*.⁵ In it, Zunz distanced himself from the contemporary approach of the rabbis; he ventured into the study of Jewish traditions without any considerations regarding "if their entire content should or would be *normative for our own judgment*."⁶ He outlined this creed in a letter to his teacher in Wolfenbüttel, Samuel Meyer Ehrenberg, when he wrote that "*nothing is to be achieved before the downfall of the Talmud.*"⁷ With that he referred to the primacy of the "cursed swashbuckling [*Klopffechten*, an exhibition fight of fencing]" as he called it in his treatise: the *pilpul* (the sharp analysis) of the "common tormentors of the Talmud [*gemeine Talmudquäler*]."⁸

The point of reference and departure for the *Wissenschaft des Judentums*, the "Science of Judaism," was the Reformation, when "a lively study of the biblical books" commenced as a result of the classical education, the *studia humanitatis*.⁹ Consequently, the study of the Jewish tradition was then directed by theological interests. Zunz wrote that

> [...] the theological knowledge of Hebrew was therefore limited to the Bible. When they [the theologians] graced with their attention later Jewish writings, they merely did so because they needed them for their understanding of the Bible: the theologians' gaze and love was reserved for the words of God, not the Jewish author. The non-theological world did not take any notice of Hebrew.¹⁰

According to Zunz, there was but *one* way to be occupied with "our" science, and that was in a critical and scholarly manner. He did not differentiate between Jews and non-Jews,¹¹ although he noted that the latter had often made Judaism the subject

---

5 Leopold Zunz, *Etwas über die rabbinische Litteratur, nebst Nachrichten über ein altes bis jetzt ungedrucktes hebräisches Werk* (Berlin: Maurer, 1818). I refer to the 1876 reprint: Leopold Zunz, "Etwas über die rabbinische Litteratur," in *Gesammelte Schriften*, vol. 1 (Berlin: Gerschel, 1876): 1–31. See also Hans-Joachim Bechtoldt, *Die jüdische Bibelkritik im 19. Jahrhundert* (Stuttgart: Kohlhammer, 1995), 64–83. Also refer to the rather undervalued Luitpold Wallach, "The Scientific and Philosophical Background of Zunz's 'Science of Judaism,'" *Historia Judaica* 4 (1952): 51–70.
6 Ibid., 5, fn. 1. Emphasis in the original.
7 Leopold Zunz to Samuel Meyer Ehrenberg, October 13, 1818, in Nahum N. Glatzer, *Leopold and Adelheid Zunz: An Account in Letters, 1815–1885* (London: East and West Library, 1958), 13.
8 Leopold Zunz, *Etwas über die rabbinische Litteratur*, 29, fn. 1.
9 Ibid.., 4.
10 German: "[...] die theologische Kenntniss des Hebräischen beschränkte sich demnach auf die Bibel, wenn sie gelegentlich späteren jüdischen Schriften Aufmerksamkeit schenkte, so geschah es lediglich, weil sie ihrer zum Verständniss der Bibel bedurfte: der Blick der Theologen und ihre Liebe galt dem Worte Gottes, nicht dem jüdischen Autor. Die nichttheologische Welt nahm vom Hebräischen gar keine Notiz." Leopold Zunz, "Die jüdische Literatur [1845]," in *Gesammelte Schriften*, vol. I, 48.
11 Cf. Nahum N. Glatzer, *Leopold Zunz: Jude, Deutscher, Europäer, ein jüdisches Gelehrtenschicksal des 19. Jahrhunderts in Briefen an Freunde, herausgegeben und eingeleitet von Nahum N. Glatzer* (Tübingen: Mohr, 1964), 10.

of their research for improper reasons. He concludes that a shameful collapse in the study of Jewish tradition occurred during the period after the Reformation:

> How can it be, one is inclined to ask, that at a time when a great gaze sets its magnificent eyes on all sciences, when even the most deserted corners of the world are travelled to, the unknown languages are studied, how can it be that our science alone is left barren? What is holding us back from knowing the entire content of the rabbinical literature, from understanding it properly, from happily explaining [it], from correctly judging [it], and comfortably surveying [it]?[12]

The young author explains the desolate condition of Jewish literature as due to the political situation of the "Hebrew" nation: "This nation, fallen from its political and intellectual height, appears to have lost the strength of reproduction over a long period. It has settled for the more or less successful exegesis of the rare writings from a better time"[13] The idea that the impoverished state of Jewish literature reflects the impoverished state of the Jewish nation is indeed an old one, having been heard at least since the days of Philo of Alexandria.[14] Zunz, however, had an additional idea that may be new: the Jewish focus on exegesis (of the Bible, Talmud, etc.) is a result of this impoverishment and reflects the Jew's desire to draw strength from those ancient and richer periods in Jewish history.[15]

That Zunz's treatise is intended to be provocative becomes evident in its closure:

> Indeed, it is not our talent but only our fiery will to strive for the good and noble that might excuse our bold entry into the midst of the authors' world in the eyes of readers capable of reason and leniency. Thus, we welcome the understanding treatise of this criticism so we do not have to consider it not noteworthy because it remained unnoticed.[16]

Zunz, therefore, preferred harsh criticism over *damnatio memoriae* ("condemnation of memory"); he wanted to step into a discussion with the "authors' world," and

---

[12] German: "Wie geht es zu, könnte man fragen, dass zu einer Zeit, wo über alle Wissenschaften, über alles Thun der Menschen ein grossartiger Gesammtblick seine hellen Strahlen verbreitet, wo die entlegensten Erdwinkeln bereist, die unbekanntesten Sprachen studirt, und kein Material verachtet wird, dem Baue der Weisheit zu dienen, wie geht es zu, dass allein unsere Wissenschaft danieder liegt? was hindert uns den Inhalt der rabbinischen Litteratur ganz zu kennen, gehörig zu verstehen, glücklich zu erklären, richtig zu beurtheilen und bequem zu übersehen?" Zunz, *Etwas über die rabbinische Litteratur*, 5.
[13] German: "Diese, von ihrer politischen Höhe wie von ihrer intellectuellen herabgesunken, schien die Reproductionskraft auf lange Zeit verloren zu haben, sich begnügend mit der bald mehr bald weniger gelungenen Exegese der sparsamen Schriften aus der bessern Zeit." Ibid., 3.
[14] See Philo's *De Vita Mosis*, II:43.
[15] My sincere thanks to Warren Zev Harvey for contributing to this section.
[16] German: "Wahrlich, dass wir so dreist instrauss die Mitte der Schriftstellerwelt treten, können unsere Talente nicht, kann nur unser feuriger Wille, das Gute und Schöne zu erstreben, in den Augen urtheilsfähiger und nachsichtsvoller Leser rechtfertigen. Drum sei eine verständige Kritik dieser Abhandlung uns sehr willkommen, dass wir sie nicht *desswegen für nicht bemerkenswerth* halten müssten, weil sie *unbemerkt blieb*." Leopold Zunz, *Etwas über die rabbinische Litteratur*, 31.

again make "our science" the subject of scholarly research the way it had been in the Renaissance. He was right, insofar as the "rubble [...] of the Hebrew canon" as the "foundation of the Christian states" had become an "industry of the mind" that was "more admirable than the Greek [one] because it had created its wealth from fewer resources."[17] Zunz paid tribute to the performance of the construction of a Christian culture from the ruins of that of the Jews. Humboldt had only acknowledged Greek antiquity. Zunz's interest in classical studies, the reason he delved into them, was apparently not influenced by Humboldt's ideal of *Bildung*, which assigned to Greece the designation of the peak of human culture. It was not Humboldt's Greek cult but Wolf's philological fervour that set its imprint on Zunz. In his programme for delineating a science of Judaism, Zunz followed Wolf's concept of classical studies.

This fact is evident in Zunz's concept of critique, which entails three levels: the "doctrinal" level, i.e. the explanation of Jewish tradition according to theology and humanities; the "grammatical" level, i.e. lexicography and philology, which had been utterly neglected; and finally the "historical" level, i.e. the overall recording and creation of inventories of the tradition.[18] By and large, Zunz follows Wolf's approach. In his lectures, Wolf emphasised that critique includes "a great part of the art of explanation," meaning hermeneutics. He subdivides critique into two main aspects: the philological, involved with the evaluation of words (*Wortkritik*) on the one hand; and the historio-philological (or higher) analysis on the other. Wolf states,

> [...] the one [critique] entails rules according to which it is possible to conclude authenticity, age, and author of the ancient writings. This part belongs to historical critique [or Realkritik]. The second [critique] entails principles according to which it is possible to learn how to examine, judge, and recreate the accuracy of the texts in their words, either for the entirety of the texts or for only parts of them.[19]

The increase of philology's autonomy as *critica*, which Wolf pursued, was an important stimulus for Zunz, because the "tormentors of the Talmud" pursued their exegesis for the sole purpose of the religious standardisation of Judaism. Zunz sought something clearly distinct from that. He considered philology to be independent from judgment. This idea echoes the concept of Boeckh, who considered that the scientific natures of philology and philosophy made them worthy of comparison to the "exact" sciences. Boeckh wrote that

---

17 Ibid., 3.
18 Ibid., 7.
19 German: "Der eine enthält diejenigen Regeln, wonach man Aechtheit, Alter und die Verfasser von den Schriften des Althertums erforscht. Dieser Theil gehört zur historischen [oder Realkritik]. Der zweite enthält die Grundsätze, wonach man die Richtigkeit der Texte in den Worten, theils im Ganzen, theils auch in einzelnen Stellen beurtheilt, prüfen und wiederherstellen lernt, wo es möglich ist." Friedrich A. Wolf, *Vorlesungen* (Leipzig: JD. Gürtler, 1839), 305.

[...] philology is as little connected to Christian conscience as are mathematics, chemistry, or astronomy. It has its essence in itself; a philologist could be Christian, and, the other way around, a Christian could be a philologist. Yet both are what they are for themselves. Is it not true that most men are Christians without being philologists, and Jews and Mohammedans had been skilled philologists; one does not have to mix all matters among themselves.[20]

The influence of Wolf and Boeckh on the new *Wissenschaft des Judentums* is a dual one: it is manifested in its comprehensive and "critical" approach and in its emphasis on its independence and autonomy. Critique is at the centre of Wolf's classical studies. Not surprisingly, Wolf the author placed himself in importance behind Wolf the editor. The professor mostly invested his extraordinary knowledge and assiduity into the thorough composition of critical editions. One is inclined to see in this fact a reflection of Protestant heritage, inasmuch as critical work is necessarily connected to questioning tradition. Leopold Zunz, too, believed that the first necessary task in the scholarly research of Jewish literature was the editing and production of reliable texts. The urgency of the task was evident, as the corpus of Jewish literature was virtually unknown.

The critical work was carried out free from any doctrine. Wolf and Zunz concurred that philology must not be utilised in the service of interests outside of the subject, whether theologically or politically motivated. Literature was to come into its own through studying it in its own right and identifying its contribution to the *Bildung* of the (European) man. The importance of the task becomes apparent if the historical and social coordinates of the emancipation of Jewry is considered. The journey from the ghetto to society had not been entirely concluded, and the prejudices of the Christian milieu and criticism from the Orthodox members of Jewish society posed equal risks to the acceptance of the new science. Boeckh's influence is visible in Zunz's aim of leading the Jewish history of ideas into general philosophy. This aim might be seen as a reaction to the then common philosophical perception of Judaism as a distant point of departure for the Christian idealistic *Weltanschauung*.

While Jewish Studies had at the beginning an academic character and recognition and acknowledgment from Christian society, the goal of Jewish theology based on the principle of the new science, the *Wissenschaft*, was first and foremost to educate a new generation of rabbis in new methods of enquiry and study of Jewish sources. The practice of the *Wissenschaft* differed, then, from what Zunz planned for the *Wissenschaft des Judentums:* "[...] their entire content should or would be *normative*

---

20 German: "So wenig als die Mathematik, die Chemie oder Astronomie etwas mit christlichem Bewusstsein zu thun haben, ebensowenig die Philologie. Sie hat ihr Wesen in sich, der Philologe kann ein Christ sein und umgekehrt ein Christ ein Philologe, aber beide sind jedes für sich. Sind ja doch die meisten Menschen Christen ohne Philologen zu sein, und Juden und Muhamedaner tüchtige Philologen gewesen; man muss nicht alle Dinge unter einander mischen." August Boeckh, *Encyklopädie und Methodologie der philologischen Wissenschaften* (Leipzig: B.G. Teubner, 1877), 29.

for our own judgment."[21] The next chapter will concern the difference between Jewish Studies and Theology.

---

[21] Ibid., 5, fn. 1. Emphasis in the original.

4 Abraham Geiger:
Jewish Theology as Institution

Born in Frankfurt on 24 May, 1810, Abraham Geiger was a rabbi, philologist, and theologian who was rightly considered a pillar of the Reform Judaism movement.[1] He began his study of philology, philosophy, and ancient languages and cultures at the University of Heidelberg, but he soon moved to Bonn where he studied Arabic at the school of the orientalist Georg Wilhelm Friedrich Freytag. In his dissertation, published in 1833, he treated the theme of "What Did Mahomed Borrow from Judaism?"[2]

At the beginning of his career as a rabbi in Wiesbaden, he launched and chiefly edited the *Scientific Journal for Jewish Theology* (*Wissenschaftliche Zeitschrift für Jüdische Theologie*), which published between 1835 and 1847. As early as in the first issue (1835), the journal developed topics of interest related to the creation of Jewish theology as an institution. One of the first articles of the journal, authored by the pedagogue and theologian Michael Creizenach, focused on the basic teachings of Jewish belief[3] and contested the common opinion that Judaism lacked systems of principles of faith. Creizenach questions the principle of (rabbinic) authority as basis of the Mitzvoth[4] and quotes the well-known text from Babylonian Talmud, *Baba Meşia* 59b,[5] to defend the principle that there is no authority from heaven in the Halakhah,[6] suggesting that rabbis do not receive their authority from the divine will.

---

[1] This is not the place to offer a detailed bibliography on Abraham Geiger; I would like only to refer to *Jüdische Existenz in der Moderne: Abraham Geiger und die Wissenschaft des Judentums*, ed. Christian Wiese et al. (Berlin: De Gruyter, 2012); Hartmut Bomhoff, *Abraham Geiger: Durch Wissen zum Glauben. Through Reason to Faith: Reform and the Science of Judaism*, 2nd edition (Berlin: Hentrich und Hentrich Verlag, 2015).
[2] Abraham Geiger, *Was hat Mohammed aus dem Judenthume aufgenommen? Eine von der Königl. Preussischen Rheinuniversität gekrönte Preisschrift* (Bonn: Selbstverl. des Verf. 1833); see also *"Im vollen Licht der Geschichte": die Wissenschaft des Judentums und die Anfänge der kritischen Koranforschung*, ed. Dirk Hartwig (Würzburg: Ergon-Verlag 2008). The writing has been translated into English as *Judaism and Islam. A Prize Essay. Translated from the German by a Member of the Ladies League in Aid of the Delhi Mission* (Madras: M.D.C.S.P.C.K. Press, 1898).
[3] Michael Creizenach, "Grundlehre des israelitischen Glaubens," *Wissenschaftliche Zeitschrift für jüdische Theologie* (1.1835): 327–339
[4] "Die israelitische Glaubenslehre unterscheidet sich ihrer Natur nach von der israelitischen Pflichtenlehre wesentlich darin, daß bei ihr von geistlicher Autorität keine Rede sein kann" (42).
[5] "Again he said to them: 'If the halachah agrees with me, let it be proved from Heaven!' Whereupon a Heavenly Voice cried out: 'Why do ye dispute with R. Eliezer, seeing that in all matters the halachah agrees with him!' But R. Joshua arose and exclaimed: 'It is not in heaven.' What did he mean by this? —Said R. Jeremiah: That the Torah had already been given at Mount Sinai; we pay no attention to a Heavenly Voice, because Thou hast long since written in the Torah at Mount Sinai, After the majority must one incline." Soncino Talmud.).
[6] Creizenach, "Grundlehre," 43.

The uneasy reality of being a Jew in a Christian world is dramatised by the struggle of the Christian theologians against the emancipation of the Jews.[7] We have to stress that the reaction against the emancipation of the Jews was pervasive and also prevailing in the "high society" of the epoch. An episode of Goethe's life[8] illustrates this attitude. In 1823, the Grand Duke of Saxe-Weimar-Eisenach issued a new decree concerning the Jews. Jews were granted the right to practice their religion freely and to attend *Gymnasien* (university-track high schools) and universities, as well as the freedom to enter the skilled trade of their choice. Jews were also allowed to marry Christians, albeit with the stipulation that the children of such unions be raised as Christians. Considerable other restrictions and special regulations were imposed on them, however, including the requirement that German was to be the language of their worship services, and that rabbis were to be paid by the members of the Jewish community. According to Chancellor von Müller, Goethe had expressed "his passionate indignation over our new Jewish law" in a conversation on September 23, 1823. "He expected the worst and shrillest consequences, claimed that if the general superintendent had any character, he should have to resign from his position rather than marry a Jewess in the name of the Holy Trinity in the Church. All moral feelings within the families, which after all rested entirely on religious ones, would be undermined by such a scandalous law."[9]

Given the references to Holy Trinity and the Church, Goethe's reaction is to be understood as a common Christian political reaction against the amalgam of Jewishness and Christianity. The theological response to the emancipation was to reject the close study of the Old Testament because it constituted "piety" and not "science." Against the passion of former theologians for the study of Hebrew and the prophecies of the Old Testament, a theologian of the Königlichen Friedrich-Wilhelms-Universität in Berlin, such as Friedrich Schleiermacher, wrote in his *"Zweite(n) Sendschreiben über die Glaubenslehre an Dr. Lücke"* in 1829:

> I am convinced that the vital Christianity in its development does not need any support from Judaism this conviction is as old as my religious consciousness itself. [...] I fear that the more we feel bound to the Old Testament instead of working in the reach pits of the new one, the more extreme the separation between piety and science will be.[10]

---

[7] Abraham Geiger, "Der Kampf christlicher Theologen gegen die bürgerliche Gleichstellung der Juden, namentlich mit Bezug auf Anton Theodor Hartmann," *Wissenschaftliche Zeitschrift für Jüdische Theologie* (Frankfurt: J. D. Gauerländer, 1835): 52–67; 2 (1836): 78–92; 446–473. On Hartman see Gustav M. Redslob, "Hartmann, Anton Theodor," *Allgemeine Deutsche Biographie* 10 (1879): 680–681.
[8] For the whole question see Giuseppe Veltri, *Language of Conformity & Dissent*, 100–123.
[9] Quoted from Goethe's *Gedenkausgabe der Werke, Briefe und Gespräche* Vol. 2, ed. Ernst Beutler (Zurich: Artemis, 1948–1954), 23, 298.
[10] "Diese Überzeugung, daß das lebendige Christentum in seinem Fortgange gar keines Stützpunktes aus dem Judentum bedürfe, ist in mir so alt, als mein religiöses Bewußtsein [...] Ich fürchte, je mehr wir uns, statt die reichen Gruben des neuen Bundes recht zu bearbeiten, an das alte halten, um desto ärger wird die Spaltung werden zwischen der Frömmigkeit und der Wissenschaft." Friedrich Schleiermacher, "Zweite(n) Sendschreiben über die Glaubenslehre an Dr. Lücke," *Theologische Stud-*

The main point of this discussion is that the attitude towards the Old Testament as a "transitional phenomenon" (*Übergangserscheinung*), as Schleimacher calls it,[11] is "piety" and not "science." Although "piety" plays a big role in Schleiermacher's theology,[12] it is clear that in this context it is an opposite to the "science" of Christian "positive" theology[13] based on the New Testament. For Schleiermacher, the theodicy of the Old cannot compete with that of the New Testament. As Geiger points out: "God of the Old Testament is a God of vengeance—so many Christian theologians often express it—and ought to be ashamed of himself before the God of the New Testament because the he is present as mercy and love."[14] By reading the theological literature of the nineteenth century, the reader gets the clear impression that an emancipation of the Jews cannot take place, among other factors, because they construct their religion around documents which are old-fashioned, and which have been surpassed because they are not amenable to "science," which Christian theology and dogma are.[15]

The task of the "science of Judaism" (*Wissenschaft des Judentums*) as Jewish theology (*Jüdische Theologie*), was, therefore, of a double nature: to explain and confirm itself as science through critical, philological, and dogmatic research into the source of Judaism and to create a generation of rabbis and theologians capable of understanding and fulfilling this task on the one hand and transmitting this "science" to Jewish community on the other. It was a Sisyphean task because the *Wissenschaft* was only the start of a critical analysis of Jewish sources and there was still no faculty of theology in Judaism, and, more troublingly, there also existed an Orthodox movement that denied both the value of a dogmatic approach to these sources and the necessity of a theology at all.

Geiger develops his vision of a faculty of Jewish theology in the second issue of the *Wissenschaftliche Zeitschrift* in 1836: "The Foundation of a Jewish-Theological

---

ien und Kritiken 2 (1829): 481–532; 497. This sentence is, of course, object of vivid discussion until today, cf. Matthias Wolfes, "Schleiermacher und das Judentum. Aspekte der antijudaistischen Motivgeschichte im deutschen Kulturprotestantismus," *Aschkenas* 14 (2007): 485–510.

11 Sources in Hans-Joachim Kraus, *Die biblische Theologie. Ihre Geschichte und Problematik* (Neukirchen-Vluyn: Neukirchener Verlag, 1970), 21 and A.A.A. (Ad) Prosman, "Nietsches's 'The Antichirst': an Anti-Christian and Anti-Jewish Document," in *Strangers and Pilgrims on Earth: Essays in Honour of Abraham Van de Beek,* ed. Eduardus van der Borght and Paul van Geest (Leiden: Brill, 2012): 147–160; 154.

12 Cf. Christian Albrecht, *Schleiermachers Theorie der Frömmigkeit. Ihr wissenschaftlicher Ort und ihr systematischer Gehalt in den Reden, in der Glaubenslehre und in der Dialektik* (Berlin: De Gruyter, 2011).

13 On this concept, see Christian Albrecht, *Schleiermachers Theorie der Frömmigkeit.*

14 Abraham Geiger, "Der Kampf christlicher Theologen," 61: "Der Gott des Alten Testaments, so sprechen oft die christlichen Theologen, ist ein Gott der Rache und muß sich vor dem Gotte des neuen Testaments schämen, wie da ist ganz Barmherzigkeit und Liebe."

15 On the concept of a dogmatic as science see Christian Albrecht, *Schleiermachers Theorie der Frömmigkeit,* 195–205.

Faculty: An Urgent Necessity of Our Time."¹⁶ The catch-word of his vision is at first not theology but science, *Wissenschaft*, which he highlights from the outset, employing imagery from Genesis 1: "The original stuff, available to it [science] in a disordered chaos, will be untangled. A perfectly clear coordination of all the parts will be come out of the crude matter. This will be transmitted to us, in turn, as ordered system."¹⁷ The highly embellished preface is full of dualistic rhetoric: light vs. darkness, chaos vs. creation of systems, cobwebs vs. threads, and, finally, concluding on the "spaces of the *Wissenschaft*" leading to the "marketplace of the life." If science (Jewish theology) is the key to the marketplace of life, it is even more important for, even the core of, humanity; according to Geiger, science induces our ennoblement and human improvement (*Veredlung und menschliche Vervollkommung*). Geiger laments the state of affairs caused by the former Jewish conception of "theology" that revolved exclusively around the study of the Talmud and ignored the exegesis of biblical texts, focusing only on the Halakhah (the practical side of life in which rabbinic authority played a large role).

However, the conditions of the time had changed basic claims about life, and the student of the time liked to ask questions and required answers *before* their study of the Talmud could begin. The details of the Talmud (as Geiger calls the rabbinic discussions, the question and answers) are not really important at the beginning of a rabbinic study; what is more important are questions as to the validity, origins, and stature of the Talmud (*Gültigkeit, Entstehn und Gestalt*). That is, it is better to begin rabbinical study with a philosophic and historical proof of the biblical revelation according to the "high and higher criticism" (*niedre and höhere Kritik*).¹⁸ The reader recognises here the typical language of Zunz,¹⁹ the student of Wolf who distinguished between a real analysis of the words (*Realkritik* or *niedre Kritik*) and the historical-philological (hermeneutical) approach called higher criticism (*höhere Kritik*). In Geiger's view, the Talmud should be an object of study with reference to its language and historical period.

It is at this point that there is a decisive divergence between Zunz's first writing on "Jewish Studies" and Geiger's approach. The science, Geiger adds, is something other than a natural development: it requires extremely vigilant care. Scholars must be dedicated to their craft with restless zealousness (*rastloser Eifer*). Geiger's

---

16 "Die Gründung einer jüdisch-theologischen Facultät, ein dringendes Bedürfniß unserer Zeit," *Wissenschaftliche Zeitschrift für Jüdische Theologie* (2.1, 1836), 1–22.
17 Abraham Geiger, "Die Gründung einer jüdisch-theologischen Facultät," 1: "[...] der zuvor in ihr in ungeordnetem Chaos vorliegende Stoff wird entwirrt, und aus der rohen Masse wird eine übersichtlich klare Zusammenfügung verschiedene Theile, die sie uns wiederum als ein wohl geordnetes ganzes überliefert."
18 Abraham Geiger, "Die Gründung einer jüdisch-theologischen Facultät," 4.
19 Cf. my contribuition in *Friedrich August Wolf: Studien, Dokumente, Bibliographie*, eds Reinhard Markner, Giuseppe Veltri (Stuttgart: Franz Steiner, 1999), 32–47, 44 and Zunz also referring to the Massorah in "Beurtheilung von Sach's Psalmen-Übersetzungen," in *Wissenschaft Zeitschrift für Jüdische Theologie* 2 (1836), 500.

aim is the education of rabbis and cantors who will serve as guides for their perplexed communities; a job, he claims, which will require perennial care. The rabbinical imperative is to turn from life as a nomadic wanderer to one as an attentive gardener. Geiger is shaping the figure of a new (Reform) Rabbi, a new Jewish minister or pastor who should "bring to the attention (of the children souls) the oft oppressed feeling of the human dignity and the dependency from a higher guide."[20]

According to Geiger, the real problem is not the contents and aims of theology, but its dignity: for "as soon as it, the theology, enters into the set of the sciences, it ties an indissoluble and indivisible knot, a covenant with its sisters."[21] Yet, the dignity of the theological science is in contrast with the actual situation of the Jewish community, that is, the real state of young people who lacked the means to pursue an education in theological sceinces. There is indeed a necessity for suitable sources from which to learn "Jewish theology." Geiger's lament about the state of sources and the lack of scholars is, of course, not directed against the movement of the "science of Judaism," but a passionate plea for lasting and sustainable structures to build up an institution: "and as long the science cannot put down deep roots, the fruits of our enlightenment will be remain stale."[22]

Geiger's main interest is the topic of rabbinical training and education and how to constitute a lasting structure, a "Jewish-theological faculty," [23] capable of teaching and studying science and method. It was not the task of his plea to shape the contents of theological education for the younger generation, but only to stress the necessity of an institution as such.

Discussion of the contents of Jewish theology advanced further in the nineteenth and twentieth centuries.[24] It is not my intention to deal with all such subsequent as-

---

[20] Abraham Geiger, "Die Gründung einer jüdisch-theologischen Facultät," 6: "[...] zur Erkenntnis zu bringen das oft niedergedrückte Gefühl der Menschenwürde und des Abhängigkeitsverhältnisses von einem höhern Lenker."
[21] Abraham Geiger, "Die Gründung einer jüdisch-theologischen Facultät," 6: "Denn sobald sie eintritt, die Theologie, in die Reihe der Wissenschaften, da hat sie einen Bund geschlossen mit ihren Schwestern, aunauflöslich, unzertrennlich."
[22] Abraham Geiger, "Die Gründung einer jüdisch-theologischen Facultät," 12: "Und solange die Wissenschaft nicht ihre Wurzeln tiefer zu schlagen vermag, werden auch die Früchte unserer Aufklärung schal bleiben."
[23] Abraham Geiger, "Die Gründung einer jüdisch-theologischen Facultät," 16.
[24] For discussions from the beginning of the last century, see Kaufmann Kohlers, *Grundriss einer systematischen Theologie des Judentums auf geschichtlicher Grundlage* (Leipzig: Fock, 1910); Eduard Strauss, "Eine jüdische Theologie?" *Der Morgen* 8 (1932): 312–314; Max Wiener, "Begriff und Aufgabe der jüdischen Theologie," *Monatsschrift für Geschichte und Wissenschaft des Judentums* 77 (1933): 3–16; Alexander Altmann, "Zur Auseinandersetzung mit der "dialektischen Theologie," *Monatsschrift für Geschichte und Wissenschaft des Judentums* 79 (1935): 345–361; Hans J. Schoeps, "Kritischer Idealismus und jüdische Theologie," *Monatsschrift für Geschichte und Wissenschaft des Judentums* 82 (1938): 73–85. A look into the status quaestionis is offered by Walter Homolka, "Jüdische Theologie. Zur Institutionalisierung eines Faches im Haus der Wissenschaft, "*Theologische Literaturzeitung* 140 (2015): 164–180. See also Thomas Meyer, *Vom Ende der Emanzipation. Jüdische Philosophie und The-*

pects of this topic, but only to stress the existence of this attempt to define Jewish theology as science, an attempt similar to developments in Protestant theology at the time.

If Protestant faith is to be fully identified with truth, there might very well be no conceivable place for other confessions or religions. This was essentially the stance of the Prussian government in answering a petition of Leopold Zunz to institutionalise a chair for Jewish history and literature. The aim of creation of this chair was not to offer a Jewish dogmatic parallel to Christian theological chairs but to provide a political foundation for the scientific study of Judaism:

> The Science of Judaism does belong to the other subjects that are strangers to the universities. There is no instruction of the future civil servants and future law givers [of Prussia] in the history and literature of the Jews from the last two thousand years as they receive their education. [...] Thus strangers to the field are forced to turn to outdated books or living acquaintanceships. This way, they are not protected from the oracle of ignorance or ill will whose influences will leave their traces in the decrees or laws.[25]

A tragic element of Christian-Jewish history consists in the conscious German ignorance of the philological developments of the *Wissenschaft des Judentums*. This period of the widespread perception of Jewish philosophy as a worthy realm of historical wisdom among Jewish scholars prompted almost no Christian interest in the topic. The Jewish philological revolution had no impact in Christianity and especially not in its political elements. The mythological time shifted away from stories about the Patriarchs towards those from Greek Antiquity. After and at times during the period of the historicisation of the Jewish philosophy, a new phenomenon occurred: a philological demythologisation that carried on the discourse of the de-authorisation of Jewish tradition in its entirety. The next chapter is devoted to the premises of a historical reconstruction of this dogmatic history of Jewish thought.

---

ologie nach 1933 (Göttingen: Vandenhoeck & Ruprecht, 2008); Ulrike Kleinecke, "Theologien des Judentums im jüdisch-amerikanischen Diskurs des 20. Jahrhunderts," *Pardes* 20 (2014): 117–131.

25 German: "Zu den auf Universitäten fremden Fächern gehört die Wissenschaft des Judentums. Über Geschichte und Literatur der Juden aus dem Zeitraum der letzten zweitausend Jahre wird da, wo die künftigen Beamten und Gesetzgeber ihre Vorbildung erhalten, keine Belehrung gegeben. [...] so sind die Fremdlinge auf diesem Gebiet gezwungen, sich an veraltete Bücher oder an lebende Bekanntschaften zu wenden, nicht geschützt vor dem Orakel der Unwissenheit oder des bösen Willens, deren Spuren alsdann Verfügungen und Gesetze tragen." Ludwig Geiger, "Zunz im Verkehr mit Behörden und Hochgestellten," *Monatsschrift für Geschichte und Wissenschaft des Judentums* 60 (1916): 258–259.

5 Philological Demythologisation as a Premise of New Dogmatisms and Ethics

In this chapter, I consciously use the denomination "demythologisation" while describing the process of historicisation of the myth of an *arcana philosophia* ("hidden philosophy") of Christian origins as well as the process by which the allegedly divine Hebrew language was re-characterised as profane by Christians, who also disavowed the Jewish genealogy of wisdom. Although this development is mainly philological, it affects other branches of knowledge as well. To understand this demythologisation, we must return to the teachers of Leopold Zunz and their works.

In his lectures held at the University of Halle in 1798–1799 and transcribed by S.M. Stockmann, Friedrich August Wolf exclaims, "[…] the oriental peoples differ entirely from the most excellent peoples of antiquity. The Hebrews had never evolved in such a way that they might be seen as a nation of scholars, and are thus too dissimilar to the Greeks and Romans. It is thus self-explanatory that we have to exclude the works of such peoples like the Hebrews." Only the most learned nations are worthy objects for systematic research, he felt. Wolf writes, "[…] the Greeks and Romans especially belong to this category. Both [peoples] were the most intellectual in antiquity—even according to Jewish judgment. These [Jews] parroted the Greeks in everything; they educated themselves according to them. Before the Greeks, and next to them, no other people had enlightened itself."[1] The humanistic education of a scholar, which was understood as *vir trilinguis* during the Renaissance, was reduced now to a *vir bilinguis*. One has to note, however, that Wolf defines only the Greek language as original. Between Athens, Jerusalem, and Rome, Athens was victorious on all fronts.

What, however, is the paradigm of this "victory"? There is no room for doubt that from the nineteenth century onward, classical studies referred to a methodology and curriculum that went beyond the scope of theology. The study of "Oriental" languages and cultures (also having deep roots in Halle, Leipzig, and Jena) gradually moved away from the missionary and Christian preconditions that were so prevalent in the most prominent school of Pietism; eventually scholars of this period founded secular literary studies. The incompatibility of the Semitic culture with the Greek was accepted as a fact in the twentieth century. Greek rather than Jewish culture was praised for

---

[1] German: "Die orientalischen Völker weichen gänzlich von den vorzüglichsten Völkern des Alterthums ab. Die Hebräer haben sich nie so ausgebildet, daß man sie für eine gelehrte Nation halten könnte, und daher sind sie zu verschieden von den Griechen und Römern. Es versteht sich also, daß wir Werke solcher Völker, wie die Hebräer waren, ausschließen müssen." Friedrich A. Wolf, *Encyclopädie der Philologie: Nach dessen Vorlesungen im Winterhalbjahre von 1789–1799*, ed. S. M. Stockmann (Leipzig: Expedition des europäischen Aufsehers, 1831), 9, quoted in Anthony Grafton, "Juden und Griechen bei Friedrich August Wolf," in *Friedrich August Wolf: Studien, Dokumente, Bibliographie*, ed. Reinhard Markner and Giuseppe Veltri (Stuttgart: Franz Steiner, 1999), 28.

having universalised Christianity. Gerhard Kittel is the author of the rightly still-praised and still-used *Theological Dictionary of the Old Testament* (*Theologisches Wörterbuch zum Alten Testament*) in which he poses as the foundational hypothesis of his scholarship the antinomy between Athens and Jerusalem as that between logos and myth.[2] Where did this rapidly spreading tendency originate?

Anthony Grafton came to surprising conclusions on the basis of an extensive discussion of the premises that guided Friedrich August Wolf in the composition of his philological encyclopaedia. According to Grafton, Wolf can be seen as having made a clear distinction between "classical studies" and "Jewish-Semitic studies." The latter, however, were no longer seen as solely adequate for the education of mankind. Wolf had employed the theories of Romanticism in order to solidify the position of classical studies at the expense of Semitic and especially Hebrew studies. Jewish culture was no longer perceived as worthy of a place in the curriculum of classical studies.

This hypothesis is intriguing because Wolf is depicted as a revolutionary of the academic and cultural environment, while his views led to tragic results concerning the *Bildung* of European individuals who were stripped of their Jewish tradition. Wolf was a scholar of his times, an "antiquarian" of knowledge, and an educated, very talented, and skilful philologist—but surely not a revolutionary ideologue.[3] There is a tendency in modern scholarship to overemphasise the consequences of Wolf's work, with, as Hermann Patsch has already noticed, the accomplishments of his students, friends, and acquaintances frequently attributed to him.[4] Indeed, Wolf referred to theories and ideas interesting to him without caring about or checking whether they were in accord with or in contradiction with other theories and ideas to which he had referred earlier. One of his students, August Boeckh, was merciless in his verdict concerning the *Meister:* philologists cannot create ideas. He had in mind especially Wolf, whose propaedeutic realisation of his encyclopaedia was unsound when viewed through the eyes of a philosopher.

The basic approaches of Wolf's philology—long known but almost forgotten—derived from the *critica sacra*, as mentioned above. What Jean Morin and Richard Simon had employed in respect to the New Testament, the latter in his *Histoire Critique* (1678), Wolf employed in the Homeric critique, according to the *Lectures* of Johann Gottfried Eichhorn.

Biblical criticism and philological critique rely on exactly this element that is advocated by Wolf: the exclusion of the author's inspiration ("divination" in Schleiermacher's terminology). The only aspect that matters is the literature of one particular

---

[2] See James Barr, *The Semantics of Biblical Language* (Oxford: Oxford University Press, 1961), where he addresses the ideological startpoints of Kittel's dictionary.
[3] On this subject, see the classical work, Arnaldo Momigliano, "Ancient History and the Antiquarian," *Journal of the Warburg and Courtauld Institutes* 13 (1950): 67–106.
[4] Hermann Patsch, "Friedrich August Wolf und Friedrich Ast: Die Hermeneutik als Appendix der Philologie," in *Klassiker der Hermeneutik*, ed. Ulrich Nassen (Paderborn: Schöningh, 1982): 76–107.

people, and not its ancestry, or the philosophical, religious, "divinatory" adaptation of knowledge, as Schleiermacher would phrase it. It this sense, Wolf writes,

> Before the Greeks, we have not witnessed one nation, and apart from them no Oriental one, that knew the art of oratory. This was rooted in the fact that they were not allowed to address important issues. The reason Oriental people did not have prose is the fact that they did not orate. They never succeeded in the felicitous connection of sentences, which is the art of writing.[5]

The superiority of the Greeks is not based in their inspiration, but on an aesthetic dimension, that is, on their literature and their "beautiful art." Wolf is aware that this conception of superiority in aesthetics is agreed on among Jews as well; indeed, from the Jews of the times of the Alexandrian Library to Isaak Markus Jost and Leopold Zunz, his students in Berlin. The Palestinian Talmud includes the opinion that the Greek language was suitable for poetry and songs, Hebrew only for everyday life, Latin for the Empire, and Aramaic for wailing.

Wolf had not separated classical from oriental studies. He had, however, decided that philology should exist independent from hermeneutics. The separation of philology from theology was the result of the work of others; Professor Wolf merely presented the outcomes. The fact that he mentions the Masoretes and biblical criticism alludes to little more than parallel development in biblical studies. The significance for literature, according to the principles of historical and critical philology, is the basis for classical studies, which are liberated from the burden of hermeneutics and the poetics of Platonic ancestry. However, Wolf cannot be blamed for the rising interest in the national/nationalist character of German culture in the nineteenth century: the logical step is simply too short between the adoration of an ancient people's superiority and German *Bildung* and the German spirit.

The demythologisation of ancient Hebrew literature was also the reason why Jewish scholars concentrated their efforts on reconstructing a Jewish philosophy of religion. This philosophy of religion was based not on the hidden mystery of a *philosophia perennis* or ancient hidden wisdom, but on the philosophical literature of the ancient Hellenistic time (Philo of Alexandria and the apologetics of Hellenistic Judaism). It included major works of Medieval philosophy between Islamic and Christian empires, as well as early modern work beginning with Abravanel, with new editions, commentary, and drafts of philosophical systems. That was the concern of groups of Jewish scholars, their pupils, their schools, and all those who had any chance to enter the Christian university, as an acknowledgment of the contribution of Jewish thought to "universal" philosophy was not to be found in a university syllabus.

By the end of the eighteenth century, a new term for this nascent discipline began to appear in German intellectual circles: "Philosophy of Religion" (*Religionsphilosophie*). The new coinage was mostly considered the substitution of *theologia*

---

5 Friedrich A. Wolf, "Vorlesungen," vol. 1, 33.

naturalis, for a branch of theology that tried to explain the nature of God and the world without resorting to revelation. To the best of my knowledge, the first person to use the term in a German publication was the Jesuit Sigismund von Storchenau in his *The Philosophy of Religion*,[6] an apology of the Roman Catholic practice of confession. Nonetheless, the most influential author writing on the argument was the Protestant philosopher Georg Friedrich Wilhelm Hegel; indeed, the most read work among intellectuals of this period was his *Lectures on the Philosophy of Religion*.[7] While Immanuel Kant and Friedrich Daniel Ernst Schleiermacher were also involved in the study of the definition, contents, and goals of the philosophy of religion, Hegel offered the structured vision of the new branch of intellectual study that identified religion with philosophy (and vice versa) and considered history to be the development of the spirit (*Geist*).

My aim is not to provide a discussion of the validity and consistency of this philosophical occupation with religion, rather to outline the use of a coinage in that century of philosophical research between the 1740s until the Shoah, the cruel and tragic years of Judaism in Europe. The coinage was, naturally, a consequence of speculations on religion in the eighteenth and nineteenth centuries that were critically directed against the ceremonial dimension of religion, instead concentrating on the project of universalising religious thought (Kant and Hegel) or feeling or divination (Schleiermacher) such that it could represent the general human experience as well as the history of the development of ideals. Jewish thought on religion became then a balancing act between the past and the present, between the tradition of customs, ceremonies, laws, and legal ordinances and the need to have a philosophy *beyond* the particular experience of the Jewish people.

To briefly summarise a lengthy question: the medieval Jewish author presented Judaism as a universal philosophy, the Renaissance and early modern period concentrated on its peculiarity, the eighteenth and nineteenth centuries made of this peculiarity a system.

An interesting aspect in the growth of the Jewish philosophic tradition in the nineteenth and twentieth centuries is the concentration on what we can unconcernedly call the "dogmatisation" of Judaism, the movement directed to emphasise the *Geist* of the Jewish past (its ideas, concepts, dogmas) that make Judaism a religion comparable to Christianity in popular and intellectual culture. After the scepticism of the sixteenth to the eighteenth centuries, after the crisis of authority of the

---

6 Sigismund von Storchen, *Die Philosophie der Religion*, 7 vols. (Augsburg: Veith, 1773–1789). See Matthias J. Fritsch, "Ansätze zur Religionsphilosophie bei Sigismund von Storchenau," *Verbum. Analecta Neolatina* 1 (1999), 105–116.

7 Lectures were held in 1827 and following years. For the reader not acquainted with the enormous bibliography of and on Hegel see for example Georg Wilhelm Friedrich Hegel, *Werke, in zwanzig Bänden. 16. Vorlesungen über die Philosophie der Religion*, 3rd ed. (Frankfurt: Suhrkamp, 1995); For an English translation, see Peter C. Hodgson, *Hegel: Lectures on the Philosophy of Religion. The Lectures of 1827* (Oxford: Oxford University press, 2006).

Enlightenment and the scientific elaboration of Jewish literature (*Wissenschaft des Judentums*) the turning point is the construction of a philosophy of religion (*Religionsphilosophie*) as a comparable identity to Christian elaboration of what Jean-François Lyotard calls "les grand narratives."

At the beginning of the twentieth century, a new shift in the mentality of Judaism occurred. Throughout almost its entire existence until its closure by the National Socialists in 1942, Berlin's Higher Institute for Jewish Studies, the *Hochschule für die Wissenschaft des Judentums*, which owed its fame to the gathering of Jewish intellectuals there, did not have a chair for Jewish philosophy. This was the result not only of a lack of interest, but a lack of means. Jewish philosophy was taught as a history of philosophy, according to the old classical-philological method, and because the golden age of Jewish philosophy was the Muslim-Arabic Middle Ages, Jewish philosophy was predominantly taught by Arabists such as Fritz Bamberger, the student of Julius Guttmann.[8] Subjects of study also included, of course, Arabic philosophy, Muslim theology and its schools, and the relationship between Arab philosophy and Jewish thought. Prominent scholars in the field were Manuel Joël and Saul Horowitz.

During the early years of the last century, the connection to the classical-pedagogic tradition disintegrated entirely. On January 6, 1904, Hermann Cohen made a speech before the trustees of the *Hochschule* proposing the introduction of a chair for ethics and religious philosophy.[9] According to Cohen, it was not enough to teach the history, and thus the exterior, of Jewish ethics, because the singularity of Judaism consists of the correlation between ethics (*Sittenlehre*) and theodicy (*Gottesidee*, concept of God). The concept of God refers to the unique and exclusive idea of the ethicality of man. Cohen argued that Jewish philosophy did not form a part but instead the essence of critical philosophy and that this essence could not be grasped without philosophy in general.[10] He attacked anyone who wished to reduce the study of philosophy to philological studies and called for putting the study and teaching of theology and Arabic philosophy into the hands of specialists. The independent study of ethics and religious philosophy, supervised by specialists, should rest at the centre of science and education.[11]

Hermann Cohen did not present a clear stance on Arabic philosophy in his work. This might be rooted in the fact that he was not sufficiently familiar with the classical writings and philosophers such as Avicenna, Averroës, or the movement of the Kalam. The only reference to these philosophers and their writings is included in his treatise on Jewish philosophy, *Die Religion der Vernunft aus den Quellen des Ju-*

---

8 Fritz Bamberger, "Julius Guttmann: Philosopher of Judaism," *Leo Baeck Institute Year Book* 5 (1950): 3–34.
9 Hermann Cohen, *Jüdische Schriften*, vol. 2, ed. Bruno Strauss (Berlin: Schwetschke, 1924), 108–125.
10 Fritz Bamberger, "Julius Guttmann," 10.
11 Ibid., 11.

dentums (*Religion of Reason from the Sources of Judaism*).[12] The references there, however, are largely confined to clichés that were apparently influenced by Maimonidean thought. The Talmud, for instance, whose philosophical property Simone Luzzatto had rejected, was presented in Cohen's work as harbouring traces of "independent philosophy."[13] Cohen himself rejects any influence of Muslim-Arabic philosophy on the concepts of monotheism and prophecy, which had been *en vogue* in medieval Jewish academies. Any possible similarities between the two religions, Judaism and Islam, should be ascribed to a mother-daughter-relationship, as Cohen a-historically notes.[14] Cohen sees the role of Islam (and Christianity) according to the perspective of Maimonides' *Hilkhot Melakhim*, that is, in a functional-saving manner, although Islam clearly has the advantage of having spread the idea of monotheism.[15]

We owe it to Hermann Cohen (and Ismar Elbogen) to recognise that he exercised his influence over the board of trustees of the Hochschule regarding the introduction of a chair for philosophy. We further must note that he called Julius Guttmann to this chair in 1919. Guttmann was the son of Jacob Guttmann, a specialist of medieval and Jewish philosophy, and Cohen's interest in him might be the result of mutual philosophical interests. In 1903, Guttmann presented his dissertation on Kant and the conception of the divine.[16] He is among the most important historians of Jewish philosophy of all time. I think it is important to emphasise that his contributions to Jewish scholarship remain consequential today. In his history of Jewish thought, published in 1933 as *Philosophie des Judentums*, he describes this history as "reality" and identified monotheism as the core of Judaism. As a complete authority on Arabic philosophy, Guttmann argued that medieval Jewish philosophy had originated in the Islamic world, under whose influence it stood entirely.[17]

Julius Guttmann summarised this aspect of the discussion in his well-known introduction to his *Philosophie des Judentums*: He denies the existence of Jewish philosophy as a separate entity by qualifying it as philosophy of religion. "It is philosophy of religion in the specific sense, given through the distinctive feature of the monotheistic religions of revelation, which through the energy of their claim to truth and the depth of their intellectual content, placed themselves over against philosophy as a power of their own." At the conclusion of this process, Jewish philoso-

---

[12] Hermann Cohen, *Die Religion der Vernunft aus den Quellen des Judentums* (Leipzig: Fock, 1919).
[13] Ibid., 34.
[14] Ibid., 108.
[15] See Maimonides, *Mishneh Tora, Sefer Shoftim, Hilkhot Melakhim* 11,4; Hermann Cohen, *Die Religion der Vernunft*, 281–282; see also Avraham ibn Migas, *Kevod Elohim* (Constantinople: 1585), fol. 128r–v; reprinted, (Jerusalem: Chaim Hillel Ben-Sasson, 1976).
[16] Julius Guttmann, "Der Gottesbegriff Kants" (PhD dissertation, University of Breslau, 1903); later revised and published as Julius Guttmann, *Kants Gottesbegriff in seiner positiven Entwicklung* (Berlin: Reuther & Reichard, 1906).
[17] Julius Guttmann, *Die Philosophie des Judentums*, 56.

phy and the Jewish philosophy of religion exist as two separate entities without direct cooperation. In fact, they contrast with one another. Leo Strauss could not abide this solution as, for him, (medieval) philosophy cannot be anything other than the philosophy of religion.[18] For Guttmann, on the other hand, "modern philosophy is superior to medieval philosophy, because it distinguishes religion and philosophy as 'spheres of different validity.'" Division against unity or instead of unity? That is the question.

The process of demythologising ancient Judaism did produce new "philosophies" of Judaism and philosophies of Jewish religion based on its claim to be a particular form of philosophy. This development rose in response partially to the dogmatic development of Christianity. But that is an argument for another book.

Important to the conclusion of this chapter as well as the second part of this book is the fact that the historicisation of the Christian conception of a *Philosophia Hebraeorum* together with the demythologisation of the Hebrew language led into a new process of philological reappraisal of Hebrew and Jewish literature (*Wissenschaft des Judentums*), a development which built on the premises of a new discussion on Jewish philosophy of religion as well as on the theological debate on the "essence" of Judaism, which we have already addressed. All of these definitions have something to do with Christianity, either as borrowed developments of Christian theology and philosophy or as responses to them. However, the history of scepticism in Judaism has another story which will be told in the third part of this book. This story developed in the early modern period as a reaction to the incipient interest in epistemology and the science of cognition as well as the cessation of interest in the *philosophia prima*, metaphysics and theology.

---

18 Strauss held that there is a contradiction between philosophy and religion. He claimed that medieval Arabic and Jewish philosophy (e.g. Alfarabi, Averroes, Maimonides) was primarily political philosophy, while medieval Christian philosophy (e.g. Augustine, Aquinas) was primarily theology. (My thanks to Warren Zev Harvey for this note).

PART THREE (JEWISH) SCEPTICISM

Synopsis: On Jewish Philosophy and Scepticism in the Early Modern Period

It is perhaps no surprise that the period in which the concept of a "Jewish philosophy" originated also included the origin of the idea of a Jewish scepticism. In this part of my book, I will address the many elements that created the Jewish sceptical tradition, which occurred in active parallel to Christian efforts to dogmatise the Jewish philosophical tradition of integrating the genealogy of wisdom and mystical Kabbalistic tradition. I will thematise the contraposition between wisdom and scepticism both in the Jewish tradition (i.e. Simone Luzzatto's sceptical attitude towards the Jewish intellectual class) and in Protestant theology (i.e. Johann Frischmuth's writings on the Oral Torah and the debate between Jakob Friedrich Reimmann and Reinhard Heinrich Roll on biblical scepticism).

This crucial part of my investigation begins with a *status quaestionis* on scepticism, which will bring us to our field of research. The first chapter of the third part offers an initial look into the question of modern studies and research on (Jewish) scepticism. The study of scepticism has undergone a vivid revival in recent decades not only in the field of history, pioneered by Richard H. Popkin, but also in institutes of analytic and theoretical philosophy all around the world. In addition, studies on the cultural impact of scepticism in literature, historical studies, tolerance research, law and society, etc. gained a new dimension with the integration of innovative perspectives of research on the perception of sceptical strategies. Jewish and Arabic scepticism were first thoroughly researched only recently. Our concern is explaining the reasons for this delay in scholarly attention.

The centrality of the early modern period to the development of Jewish philosophy does not require repeated substantiation here. The reader has been introduced to the field of research already in the preceding chapters where I dealt with the path from *Philosophia Hebraeorum* to the Jewish philosophy of religion, as well as the path from the Christian abandonment of Jewish fundamentals of Wisdom to the Jewish re-appropriation of the paradigms of philosophy and mysticism.

The sixteenth and seventeenth centuries are foundational for several aspects connected both with the Jewish consciousness of attitudes towards scepticism. At the end of the Humanist period and the Renaissance, we can observe the first changes in the perception and formulation of philosophical questions. After some seminal beginnings, mirrored by 'Ovadyah Sforno, there could be no hesitation in recognising that the use of *dubitatur/dubium* and *quaestiones dubitatae* is more than a rhetorical tool. They became a dialectical strategy that played an important role in the Late Renaissance (*Accademia dei Dubbiosi*) and early modern period (*Accademia degli Incogniti*, Simone Luzzatto). The "doubts" (*dubitationes*) are not primarily a literary instrument to introduce the dogmatic opinion of teachers, masters, or opponents, but a dialectical strategy to introduce very delicate questions that could have dangerous results for the majority. The topics handled involve the usual themes of sceptic origins and tradition: authority, morality, theodicy, collective society and individuality, immortality of the soul as a social and moral problem (doctrine of remunerations), etc. Of particular interest to this topic is my discussion of Sara Copio Sullam (3.3).

The strategy used by Jewish scholars against increasing prevailing "dogmatism" in the sense used by ancient sceptics relies on arguments of historical value that mostly originated in scientific and geographic discoveries. This strategy also relies on historical-philological examinations of sources. It is no surprise that Azaria de' Rossi as well as his opponent Rabbi Yehudah of Prague used the same or similar tactic in rejecting the literal sense of the canonical literature (the Oral and Written Torah), indirectly implying a linguistic scepticism. The objective of the Maharal was obviously to substantiate the written and oral Torah by creating a meaning beyond the literal meaning; he did so by using similar sceptical strategies. "Dogmatic" writers also found the sceptical arsenal useful.

A further step was the necessary osmotic encounter between the more liberal parts of Christian intellectual society and Jewish scholars. The participation of Jewish intellectuals in the new social and cultural phenomenon of the academies was decisive in the development of new ideas about Judaism, its place in world history, and its sceptical "vein," which I discuss in the third chapter. These developments were possible despite the seclusion of the Jews in a narrow space, the Ghetto. The residents of the Ghetto of Venice, the first official Ghetto fenced in by walls and closed off by a door, experienced a vivid intellectual life that overcame political fences and influenced the entire city. The reason for such freedom was the relatively liberal Venetian atmosphere that provided oxygen for Jewish life. Obviously, any situation featuring a walled Ghetto was not ideal, but the Ghetto of Venice was free enough for Jews to participate (with restrictions) in the intellectual and cultural events of the *Serenissima*. Without this environment and the inducements of the intellectual life of the Ghetto, the lives of Sara Copio Sullam, the first female philosopher of Judaism, and Simone Luzzatto, the Rabbi of Venice whose speculations provoked a clergyman's reaction and became a public debate, would have been impossible.

In these final chapters we will elucidate a phenomenon that has been left totally unexplored and largely unacknowledged: the origin and consciousness of a *sceptical* definition of (a Jewish) philosophy. The fourth chapter is an analysis of a Jewish philosopher who called himself an academic sceptic. Generally speaking, Simone Luzzatto is the pillar of this book because he offers enlightened definitions of Jewish philosophy, religion, cultural ghettos, monotheism, and, first and foremost, the sceptical attitude. A curious element that will be analysed in the fifth chapter is that the discussion of the sceptical "nature" (or, if we employ the sceptical category, "attitude") of Judaism originated in two different areas contemporaneously: in Northern Italy (especially Venice) and in German Protestant universities (first among them Jena and Halle). Nevertheless, this part of the book is not an answer either to the question of the primary reasons for the origin of scepticism nor to the question of why this tradition mostly disappeared in the nineteenth and in the beginning of the twentieth centuries. The reader will find here only examples of the sceptical attribution of identities and sceptical strategies in discussion that created a philosophical tradition.

In the conclusion of the book, I will return to the main themes of the text: the alienation of wisdom, the nature of Jewish philosophy, and, finally, the characterisation of sceptical strategy in the body of Jewish philosophy and literature.

1 Research on (Jewish) Scepticism

From the twentieth century until today, the study of scepticism has enjoyed a lively academic interest.[1] Ancient Eastern and Western schools of sceptical thought and philosophy have been the subjects of tractates, books, articles, and comments. The traditions of both Pyrrho and the Academics have already been explored, analysed, and elaborated upon. Likewise, there is no lack of studies on the development of sceptical methods and the sceptical tradition.[2] However, this volume of academic study is very much lacking in the case of the relationship between sceptical thought, Judaism, and Jewish philosophy.

To understand and situate Jewish scepticism within a wider context, a few examples regarding the state of current research on general scepticism will follow. Considering the number of relevant publications and numerous complex debates on various related topics, the outline below is far from comprehensive.

1.1 Research on Scepticism(s)

Two significant research fields can be distinguished in the research on scepticism: a philosophical approach based on an analytical and diachronic-historical perspective, and an approach featuring elements of sceptical strategies, contents, and attitudes (here called "cultural expressions of scepticism"). Both fields relate to ancient scepticism and its transformation and reception during the Renaissance. There are several studies that are concerned with the Platonic, Middle and New Academies.[3] Some scholars have examined different forms, such as medical tracts, of the dissemination of sceptical knowledge.[4] Furthermore, a number of monographs, surveys, and editions of key texts, especially those relating to Pyrrhonism by Sextus Empiri-

---

[1] A perusal of the publications on scepticism from the nineteenth twenty-first century would exceed by far the goal of this chapter, which is only concerned with the phenomenon as a whole. The reader will find here some bibliographical information that can help her/him with further research on this topic. This is only a beginning, not the core and the extension of a possible research.

[2] The vivid interest in the topic can also be inferred from numerous recent publications like the *International Journal for the Study of Skepticism*, which began in 2011 and is published by Brill, websites, online forums and blogs like *Aporia* (http://blogaporia.blogspot.de/), and the creation of a Centre for the study of (Jewish) scepticism in Hamburg (www.maimonides-centre.uni-hamburg.de).

[3] James Allen, "Academic Probabilism and Stoic Epistemology," *Classical Quarterly* 44 (1994): 85–113; Charles Brittain, *Philo of Larissa: The Last of the Academic Sceptics* (Oxford: Oxford University Press, 2001).

[4] Cf. James Allen, *Pyrrhonism and Medicine*, in *The Cambridge Companion to Ancient Scepticism*, ed. Richard Bett (Cambridge: Cambridge University Press, 2010): 232–248.

cus[5] (*Outlines of Pyrrhonism*[6]) and Diogenes Laertius (*Lives of Eminent Philosophers*),[7] have recently been re-published and re-translated.[8]

Other studies have focused on Philo,[9] Cicero,[10] and Augustine,[11] examining their sceptical and anti-sceptical positions. The work of the Jewish philosopher Philo of Alexandria is an obvious starting point of every history of ancient scepticism. His epoch, the first centuries B.C.E. and C.E., is also crucial for the study of scepticism. Indeed, it is probably at this time that the term *skeptikos* was coined, or at least commonly expressed: the term came into widespread use during this time as an archetypal and philosophical denomination of a scholar, student, or intellectual who used sceptic strategies. Philo is the first known to us who introduced the "modes," the sceptical "*tropoi*," in his tractate *De Ebrietate* 169–202. It is difficult to determine whether he directly read the *tropoi* of Aenesidemus or took them from an intermediate source.

Augustine's critique of sceptical philosophy is especially relevant to the study of ancient Jewish scepticism.[12] The Bishop of Hippo offered a topical and typological

---

5 Cf. *Sextus Empiricus. Outlines of Scepticism*, 2nd edition, ed. Julia Annas and Jonathan Barnes (Cambridge: Cambridge University Press, 2000).
6 Cf. Emidio Spinelli, *Questioni scettiche. Letture introduttive al pirronismo antico* (Rome: Lithos, 2005); also see the book he authored with Mario de Caro, *Scetticismo: Una vicenda filosofica* (Rome: Carocci, 2007).
7 *Diogenis Laertii Vitae philosophorum*, trans. Miroslav Marcovich (Stuttgart: Teubner, 1999); *Diogenes Laertius. Lives of Eminent Philosophers*, ed. Robert D. Hicks (Cambridge: Harvard University Press, 1979).
8 Cf. Diego E. Machuca's "Bibliography on Skepticism" on his personal website, *Diego E. Machuca*, https://sites.google.com/site/diegomachuca/bibliography-on-skepticism (accessed 3 May, 2018); see also Katja Vogt's "Ancient Skepticism" in *The Stanford Encyclopedia of Philosophy*, http://plato.stanford.edu/archives/win2011/entries/skepticism-ancient/ (accessed 3 May, 2018); Peter Klein, "Skepticism," *The Stanford Encyclopedia of Philosophy*, http://plato.stanford.edu/archives/sum2013/entries/skepticism/ (accessed 3 May, 2018); and Charles Bolyard, "Medieval Skepticism," *The Stanford Encyclopedia of Philosophy*, http://plato.stanford.edu/archives/spr2013/entries/skepticism-medieval/ (accessed 3 May, 2018).
9 Carlo Lévy, "Le scepticisme de Philon d'Alexandrie, une influence de la Nouvelle Académie?" in *Hellenica et Judaica. Hommage à V. Nikiprowetzky*, ed. André Caquot, Mireille Hadas-Lebel, and Jean Riaud (Leuven: Brill, 1986): 29–41; Carlo Lévy, "Le concept de doxa des Stoïciens à Philon d'Alexandrie. Essai d'étude diachronique," in *Passions and Perceptions. Studies in Hellenistic Philosophy of Mind. Proceedings of the Fifth Symposium Hellenisticum*, ed. Jacques Brunschwig and Martha C. Nussbaum (Cambridge: Cambridge University Press, 1993): 250–284. Carlo Lévy, "La conversion du scepticisme chez Philon d'Alexandrie," in *Philo of Alexandria and Post-Aristotelian Philosophy*, ed. Francesca Alesse (Leiden: Brill, 2008): 103–120. See also my book, *Dialectic and Doubt. Hellenistic, Rabbinic, and Jewish Medieval Sceptic Strategies* (working title, to be published in 2019).
10 Cicero, *On Academic Scepticism*, trans. Charles Brittain (Indianapolis: Hackett, 2006).
11 Augustine, *Contra Academicos, De Beata Vita, De Ordine*, ed. Therese Fuhrer and Simone Adam (Berlin: De Gruyter, 2017).
12 Cf. Therese Fuhrer, "Das Kriterium der Wahrheit in Augustins Contra Academicos," *Vigiliae Christianae* 46 (1992): 257–275; Gonzalo Soto Posada, "La muerte del escepticismo o san Augustín y los académicos," *Estudios de Filosofía* 26 (2002): 277–292; Brian Harding, "Skepticism, Illumination

description that prevailed throughout the fourth and fifth centuries C.E.. He particularly elaborated on sceptical thought and strategies using the classical literary dialogic system.[13] He also argued against the principles of authority and truth. Doubt and methods of enquiry into the truth as well as silence and the suspension of judgement are obviously highly relevant for rabbinic literature. Augustine's strong arguments against scepticism turned out to be centrally important for medieval anti-scepticism.[14]

After decades of neglect, the status of medieval (anti-)sceptical philosophers has recently received greater scholarly attention.[15] Traces of ancient scepticism are evident during this period when strong anti-sceptical currents prevailed. Adherents of the latter include well-known authors such as John Buridan and Thomas Aquinas.[16] Similarly, established, sceptical learning is prevalent in the works of Henry of Ghent, Duns Scotus, William of Ockham, and Nicholas of Autrecourt.[17]

Contrary to these well-researched texts, the field of (Arabic-)Islamic philosophy and theology has only been partially studied and examined with respect to Scepticism.[18] Al-Ghazālī,[19] who is often regarded as the precursor of Cartesian doubt, has been a focus of scholarly attention on this subject.[20] Ibn al-Haytham's *Kitāb*

---

and Christianity in Augustine's Contra Academicos," *Augustinian Studies* 34, no. 2 (2003): 197–212; Giovanni Catapano, "Quale scetticismo viene criticato da Agostino nel Contra Academicos?" *Quaestio* 6 (2006): 1–13; Luca Castagnoli, *Ancient Self-Refutation. The Logic and History of the Self-Refutation Argument from Democritus to Augustine* (New York: Cambridge University Press, 2010).

13 On this theme, see the text and bibliography in Daniel Boyarin, *Socrates and the Fat Rabbis* (Chicago: University of Chicago Press, 2009); cf. also Jacob Howland, *Plato and the Talmud* (Cambridge: Cambridge University Press, 2010).

14 Cf. Henrik Lagerlund, *Rethinking the History of Skepticism. The Missing Medieval Background* (Leiden: Brill, 2010).

15 The turning point is Richard H. Popkin's "Amos Funkenstein and the History of Scepticism," in *Thinking Impossibilities. The Intellectual Legacy of Amos Funkenstein*, ed. Robert S. Westman and David Biale (Toronto: Toronto University Press, 2008): 281–288.

16 Han T. Adriaenssen, *Representation and Scepticism from Aquinas to Descartes* (Cambridge: Cambridge University Press, 2017).

17 Charles Bolyard provides a good outline with an updated bibliography in his "Medieval Skepticism."

18 Abdel M. Turkī, *Théologiens et juristes de l'Espagne musulmane: Aspects polémiques* (Paris: Maisonneuve et Larose, 1982), especially concerning the refutation of scepticism in Ibn Ḥazm (159–198); Fuat Sezgin, *Greek Philosophy and the Arabs: Texts and Studies* (Frankfurt: Institute for the History of Arabic-Islamic Science, 2000); Paul L. Heck, *Skepticism in Classical Islam: Moments of Confusion. Culture and Civilization in the Middle East* (Hoboken: Taylor and Francis, 2013); Fatemeh C. Azinfar, *Atheism in the Medieval Islamic and European World: The Influence of Persian and Arabic Ideas of Doubt and Skepticism on Medieval European Literary Thought* (Bethesda: Ibex Publishing, 2008).

19 Leor Halevi, "The Theologian's Doubts: Natural Philosophy and the Skeptical Games of Ghazali," *Journal of the History of Ideas* 63, no. 1 (2002): 19–39.

20 Sami M. Najm, "The Place and Function of Doubt in the Philosophies of Descartes and Al-Ghazali," *Philosophy East and West* 16, nos. 3–4 (1966): 133–141; Syed R. Zamir, "Descartes and Al-Ghazali: Doubt, Certitude and Light," *Islamic Studies* 49, no. 2 (2010): 219–251.

al-Manāẓir (*Book of Optics*) and *Al-Shukūk ʿalā Batlamyūs* (*Doubts Concerning Ptolemy*) should also be mentioned in this context. Nevertheless, there are still vast areas of uncharted territory, such as the influence of scepticism on the schools of Muʿtazila and Ashʿariyya.[21] The sceptical outlook of al-Rāzī, Ibn Ḥazm, and the Jewish philosopher Saadia Gaon are also under-researched; the influence of Pyrrhonism on Arabic writers "is still to be fully explored."[22] Also important to mention is Taqī al-Dīn Abū al-ʿAbbās Aḥmad ibn Taymiyyah and his "rejection of the idea of universals, the confutation of the distinction between Existence and Quiddity, the reduction of the Syllogism to Analogy."[23] The research in this field is still nascent.

One of the most popular research areas is the development of sceptical philosophy and cultural history during the Renaissance.[24] Henri Estienne's 1562 Latin translation of Sextus Empiricus' *Outlines of Pyrrhonism* was certainly one of the cornerstones of Renaissance scepticism: it strongly influenced the dissemination of humanism throughout Europe. Richard Popkin[25] and Charles Schmitt[26] have foregrounded this period in the history of scepticism by analysing numerous authors, some less well-known, and introducing their contributions to present academia. Additionally, modern studies includes a large range of philosophical, political, and social theories emerging from scholars such as Machiavelli in Italy,[27] Montaigne in

---

[21] Cf. Josef van Ess, "Skepticism in Islamic Religious Thought," *Al-Abhath* 21 (1968): 1–17.
[22] Cf. Luciano Floridi, "The Rediscovery and Posthumous Influence of Scepticism," in *Cambridge Companion to Ancient Scepticism*, ed. Richard Bett (Cambridge: Cambridge University Press, 2010): 264–287. 274: "A final remark must concern the coeval influence of Pyrrhonism on Arabic writers. The field is still to be fully explored however, in this case too, there seems to have been a wider availability of original texts than in Western countries. A philosopher like al-Ghazzali, with his *The Incoherence of the Philosophers*, exercised a direct influence on the work of the Hebrew philosopher Judah Halevi—a key figure in twelfth-century Jewish thought, whose *Kuzari* displays an interesting use of sceptical arguments against Aristotelian philosophy and in favour of religious faith—and some conjecture that he might have acted as a cultural bridge between Greek scepticism and the later critical philosophy of Nicholas of Autrecourt, especially as far as the analysis of the notion of causality is concerned."
[23] Stefano Malfitano, "The Ways of Skepticism: An Arabic-Islamic Detour? Notes on Ibn Taymiyyah's Rebuttal of Logic and the Developments of Ancient Skepsis," unpublished, https://goo.gl/MfLhBA (accessed 3 May, 2018). Cf. also Jon Hoover, *Ibn Taymiyya's Theodicy of Perpetual Optimism* (Leiden, Boston: Brill, 2007), 69, 129–130.
[24] Cf. Gianni Paganini and José R. Maia Neto, eds., *Renaissance Scepticisms* (Dordrecht: Springer, 2009).
[25] I quote here only Richard H. Popkin, *The History of Scepticism. From Savonarola to Bayle*, Revised and Expanded (Oxford: Oxford University Press, 2003).
[26] Richard H. Popkin and Charles B. Schmitt, *Scepticism from the Renaissance to the Enlightenment* (Wiesbaden: Harrassowitz, 1987).
[27] Aryeh Botwinick, *Participation and Tacit Knowledge in Plato, Machiavelli and Hobbes* (Lanham: University Press of America, 1986); Aryeh Botwinick, *Skepticism and Political Participation* (Philadelphia: Temple University Press, 1990); Aryeh Botwinick, *Skepticism* (Philadelphia: Temple University Press, 2010); Michelle Zerba, *Doubt and Scepticism in Antiquity and the Renaissance* (Cambridge: Cambridge University Press, 2012).

France,[28] Pedro de Valencia in Spain,[29] Francisco Sanchez in Portugal and later in France,[30] Sir Francis Bacon in England, Baruch Spinoza in the Netherlands, and, finally, Descartes, author of the sceptical turning point, in France,[31] just to chart a few stages in the development of scepticism in Europe.

Whereas the humanist influence on this development originated in Italy, the religious impetus was provided by Humanism and the Reformation in Germany. Not only did newly founded academies display traces of stoic and sceptical thinking, but they also played a crucial role in the development and conceptualisation of literature[32] and drama during that time.[33] The notion of "scepticism" in the general and diffuse meaning we give it today certainly derived from the debates and developments in arts and literature so prevalent during the Renaissance and early modern period. However, what freshly emerged during the fifteenth and sixteenth centuries were sceptical positions against the rapidly developing sciences.

It would certainly be too bold, and in fact would compromise the aims of this *status quaestionis*, to claim the ability to provide a comprehensive overview of the developments of sceptical philosophy since Descartes. After all, alter to methodological doubts and critiques for and against the reconstruction of dogmatic philosophical systems as well as the (im)possibilities of metaphysical theories (see David Hume)[34] are always at the core—and at stake—in those areas of philosophy where metaphysical notions and epistemology have to be negotiated. This certainly involves a balance between the world of ideas and the methods of securing historical approaches that verify or falsify "truths" and "beliefs."

The Enlightenment is a very complex phenomenon based on freedom of thought and political emancipation,[35] because or perhaps in spite of the insight that Socrates had not offered a solution to the problematic issue of authority.[36] In contrast to En-

---

28 Cf. Nicola Panichi, "Montaigne and Plutarch: A Scepticism that Conquers the Mind," in *Renaissance Scepticisms:* 183–212.
29 Cf. John C. Laursen, "Pedro De Valencia's Academica and Scepticism in Late Renaissance Spain," in *Renaissance Scepticisms:* 111–124.
30 Cf. *Francisco Sánchez. Quod Nihil Scitur. Dass nichts gewusst wird*, ed. Kaspar Howald (Hamburg: Felix Meiner, 2007).
31 Cf. Richard H. Popkin, *The History of Scepticism.*
32 Cf. Graham Bradshaw, *Shakespeare's Scepticism* (Brighton: Harvester Press, 1987).
33 Cf. the humanist reception of Theophrastus' doctrine of the characters and Seneca's ethical teachings; Giuseppe Veltri, "'Dannare l'universale per il particolare?' Colpa individuale e pena collettiva nel pensiero di Rabbi Simone Luzzatto," *Rassegna Mensile d'Israele* 77, no. 1–2 (2012): 65–81.
34 David F. Norton, *David Hume: Common-Sense Moralist, Sceptical Metaphysician* (Princeton: Princeton University Press, 1982); Paul Stanistreet, *Hume's Scepticism and the Science of Human Nature* (Aldershot: Ashgate, 2002).
35 Cf. Jonathan I. Israel, *Radical Enlightenment. Philosophy and the Making of Modernity 1650–1750* (Oxford: Oxford University Press, 2001).
36 Cf. Richard H. Popkin, *Scepticism in the Enlightenment* (Dordrecht: Kluwer, 1997); Petr Lom, *Scepticism, Eclecticism and the Enlightenment. An Inquiry into the Political Philosophy of Denis Diderot* (San

lightenment ideas prevalent in Christian Europe, thinkers such as Moses Mendelssohn[37] were much less likely to receive recognition for their endeavours. Likewise, Salomon Maimon, the harshest and most sceptical critic of Kant, was largely ignored by his contemporaries.[38] In this context, the sceptical perspective can be viewed as a reaction to attempts to universalise "reason" and knowledge. The responses to conflicts in issues such as assimilation, acculturation, and the preservation of identity in many circles of eighteenth-century society and in the Jewish communities themselves were highly ambiguous and always vehement. The emergence of a *critical* scientific philology during the nineteenth and twentieth centuries was crucial for keeping the sceptical method of doubt towards dogmatic systems alive.

Between the end of the twentieth and the beginning of the twenty-first century, the emergence of Postcolonial Studies has inspired ongoing debates on whether "Western" philosophy and academic science, with their Eurocentric notions of knowledge production, are in a position to apply a just and appropriate stance towards the research of non-Western cultures. Doubt about the concept of "reason" per se generated doubt about the transferability of this concept between cultures and continually challenged the question of whether the so-called postcolonial systems of knowledge did or did not obscure their use of methods generated by colonialist views.[39] This also applied and still applies to the notable absence of Jewish thought and thinkers in the study of philosophy.

Yet, if the Jewish tradition has barely been considered in the general field of philosophy or within the history of philosophy, it remains to be examined whether Jewish scepticism makes an appearance in the area of "Jewish" philosophy at all.

1.2 Research on Jewish Scepticism

The sceptic is always viewed with suspicion, as a kind of "malicious genius,"[40] because she/he doubts and mistrusts every belief. The sceptic asks questions and these

---

Domenico: European University Institute, 1998); *Scepticism in the Eighteenth Century: Enlightenment, Lumières, Aufklärung*, ed. Sébastien Charles and Plínio J. Smith (Dordrecht: Springer 2013).

37 Mendelssohn's theory of probability is very important in this context; see the contribution of Edith D. Sylla, "Mendelssohn, Wolff, and Bernoulli on Probability," in *Moses Mendelssohn's Metaphysics and Aesthetics*, ed. Reinier Munk (Dordrecht: Springer 2011): 41–64.

38 Cf. Gideon Freudenthal, *Salomon Maimon. Rational Dogmatist, Empirical Skeptic. Critical Assessments* (Dordrecht: Kluwer, 2003); Gideon Freudenthal, "Maimon's Subversion of Kant's Critique of Pure Reason. There are no Synthetic a priori Judgements in Physics" Berlin: Max-Planck-Institut für Wissenschaftsgeschichte, 2001).

39 I will omit a detailed bibliography on the topic and instead refer you to Sandra G. Harding, *Is Science Multicultural? Postcolonialisms, Feminisms, and Epistemologies* (Bloomington: Indiana University Press, 1998).

40 Markus Gabriel, "The Art of Skepticism and the Skepticism of Art," *Philosophy Today* 53/1 (2009): 59–69.

questions may upset and disconcert firm opinions and alleged insights, especially if there are no ready-made responses to the sceptic's questions and if there exists in the opinion-holder a fear of losing her/his certainty about the world. This mistrust and suspicion is frequently applied to Judaism (which can be highly disconcerting) because one of its essential features is to critically interrogate every aspect of life.

This is manifest in the Talmud: the Talmudic art of teaching is primarily aimed at invoking pleasure in the close studying of objects and situations and in finding gratification in the acquisition and use of knowledge. In Judaism, the art of learning entails continually raising doubts about what the teacher thinks and says. There is no doctrinal theology at the core of studying the Torah. It is not a question of learning something by heart nor of endlessly repeating a teacher's lessons.

The rabbinical school was vehement in opposing such commonplace views, which is manifest in many didactical anecdotes where the rabbi makes fun of the ignorant pupil. According to Tractate *Soṭa* 22a of the Babylonian Talmud, a *tanna*[41] was hardly different from a magician (*magush*) because both repeated and learned by heart words they did not properly understand. In this sense, teaching also entails understanding rather than mere repetition. As previously observed, the Midrash Mekhilta de-Rabbi Yishma'el (*Pisḥa, Bo'* 18) states: "There are four types of pupils: the wise, the wicked, the simple, and the one who doesn't know how to ask."[42] In the Talmudic and subsequent periods, the goal of learning was to ask the rabbi the (right) question that forces him to find the weak point in his argument.

The topic of scepticism in Judaism has already been a focus in biblical studies. The book of Kohelet (Ecclesiastes) was already an object of discussion in Rabbinic antiquity because of its contradictions and cryptic criticism of the philosophy of everyday life with its repetitions, failures, and endless difficulty. We will see that the logical inconsistency of this text was also noted in Protestant faculties of theology in the seventeenth century. In the past few decades, a new debate reopened the question of whether the biblical book of Kohelet should be included in the history of scepticism.[43]

Although scepticism is essential to the Jewish epistemological understanding of reality, as well as sources and systems of knowledge, it is rather surprising to note

---

[41] *Tanna* means "repeater" or "transmitter" of the entire Tannatic tradition. As a rule, the term is translated as "teacher," but it can also include the pupil who is a transmitter of the teachings of the transmitter.
[42] Giuseppe Veltri, "Freche Schüler vs. gescheite Rabbinen. Die Kunst des Lernens im antiken Judentum," in *Meister und Schüler in Geschichte und Gegenwart. Von Religionen der Antike bis zur modernen Esoterik*, ed. Almut-Barbara Renger (Göttingen: Vandenhoeck & Ruprecht Gmbh & Co, 2012): 135–145.
[43] Cf. James L. Crenshaw, "The Birth of Skepticism in Ancient Israel," in *The Divine Helmsman. Studies on God's Control of Human Events. Presented to Lou H. Silberman*, ed. James L. Crenshaw and Samuel Sandmel (New York: KTAV Publishing House, 1980): 1–19; Bernon Lee, "Towards a Rhetoric of Contradiction in the Book of Ecclesiastes," (PhD dissertation, University of Calgary, 1997); William H. U. Anderson, "What is Skepticism and Can it Be Found in the Hebrew Bible?" *Scandinavian Journal of the Old Testament* 13, no. 2 (1999): 225–257.

that it is still largely either excluded from or, at least, underrepresented in international research debates on scepticism and Jewish philosophy.⁴⁴ As an example, the entry of Alvin J. Reines in both the old and new editions of the *Encyclopaedia Judaica* only refers to the question of the unreliability of reason by quoting Judah Halevi and Ḥasdai Crescas on the inadequacy of the Neoplatonic and Aristotelian conception of the knowledge of physics and metaphysics as naturally acquired⁴⁵—a standpoint recently and uncritically adopted by the *Stanford Encyclopedia of Philosophy*.⁴⁶ Significantly, Reines's article mentions some important studies of the Breslau scholar Saul Horovitz without integrating them into his outline of Jewish scepticism.

Horovitz addressed the study of Jewish scepticism as an important objective of medieval philosophy in 1912; in 1915, he returned to the topic and published an essay on the familiarity of medieval Muslim and Jewish authors with scepticism.⁴⁷ The neglect of Horovitz's contribution to Jewish philosophy⁴⁸ is all the more regrettable as he introduced the concept of a "sceptical (under)current" (*skeptische Geistesströmung*),⁴⁹ referring to ideas and tropes that survive as fragments in various authors' texts and within movements of sceptical interest.

Horovitz's studies are now outdated and his analysis of Saadia's reception of sceptical philosophy does not adequately engage with many of the philological and philosophical difficulties intrinsic to the book of the *Emunot we-deʻot* (*Kitāb al-amānāt wa-al-iʻatiqādāt*).⁵⁰ Saadia dedicated much effort to opposing sceptical

---

44 Cf. Jack Goody, "A Kernel of Doubt," *The Journal of the Royal Anthropological Institute* 2, no. 4 (1996): 667–681.
45 Alvin J. Reines; "Skepsis and Skepticism," in *Encyclopaedia Judaica*, vol. 18, 2ⁿᵈ edition, ed. Michael Berenbaum and Fred Skolnik (Detroit: Macmillan, 2010): 657–658.
46 Charles Bolyard, "Medieval Skepticism."
47 Saul Horovitz, *Über den Einfluss der griechischen Philosophie auf die Entwicklung des Kalam* (Breslau: Th. Schatzky, 1909); Saul Horovitz, "Über die Bekanntschaft Saadias mit der griechischen Skepsis," in *Judaica. Festschrift zu Hermann Cohens siebzigstem Geburtstage*, ed. Ismar Elbogen, Benzion Kellermann, and Eugen Mittwoch (Berlin: Bruno Cassirer, 1912): 235–252; Saul Horovitz, *Der Einfluss der griechischen Skepsis auf die Entwicklung der Philosophie bei den Arabern* (Breslau: Th. Schatzky, 1915).
48 On the impact of Horovitz in recent studies of Arabic philosophy, see Carmela Baffioni, "Per l'ipotesi di un influsso della scepsi sulla filosofia islamica," in *Lo scetticismo antico*, Atti del Convegno organizzato dal Centro di Studi del pensiero antico del CNR, Roma 5–8, vol. 1, ed. Gabriele Giannantoni (Napoli: Bibliopolis, 1981): 417–434; Josef van Ess, *Die Erkenntnislehre des ʻAḍudaddīn Al-Īcī. Übersetzung und Kommentar des ersten Buches seiner Mawāqif* (Frankfurt: Universität Frankfurt Habilitations-Schrift, 1964; Wiesbaden: Steiner, 1966); Horovitz, *Über den Einfluss*; and Horovitz, *Der Einfluss der griechischen Skepsis, auf die Entwicklung der Philosophie bei den Arabern*, 21–112.
49 Shaul Horovitz, "Über die Bekanntschaft Saadias," 239.
50 Harry A. Wolfson, *Repercussion of the Kalam in Jewish Philosophy* (Cambridge: Harvard University Press, 1979): 151–162. See also Israel Efros, "Saadia's Theory of Knowledge," *The Jewish Quarterly Review* 33/2 (1942): 133–170; Abraham J. Heschel, "The Quest for Certainty in Saadia's Philosophy," *The Jewish Quarterly Review*, 33, no. 3 (1943): 265–313. Although dealing with the same texts as Horovitz, Harry H. Wolfson does not mention him; perhaps this slight is because he was not convinced by the arguments of Breslau's teacher.

ideas in his treatise *Emunot we-de'ot*, a work which raises some questions regarding the nature of both his philosophy and his intended audience. Yet, it is difficult to ascertain whether his interest in the topic ought to be interpreted as evidence of the presence of sceptical circles, movements, or groups in his time and, accordingly, whether his offensive posture was determined by the pedagogical and apologetic necessity of disavowing the authority of the sources used by contemporaneous sceptics. A second explanation is possible: namely, that his extensive dealings with sceptical ideas, movements, and concepts can be explained as a strategy of reinforcing his arguments for true knowledge by aiming them against theoretical enemies in an imagined controversy. Nevertheless, Saadia is the primary source for the idea that prior sceptical opinions and strategies were known to Jewish and Muslim scholars and intellectuals of his time and, perhaps, that there were sceptics in his own time.[51]

Relying on publications such as those mentioned, it might seem as if the question of sceptical thinking had seldom been addressed in Jewish academies or among Jewish scholars. Aryeh Botwinick[52] is one of the few scholars who has attended to the topic of Jewish scepticism; however, he overemphasises the role of negative theology in the development of sceptical thought. In his book, Botwinick draws a connection between the negative theology of Maimonides and the negative vision of the godhead in Nietzsche. He interprets monotheism as both a criticism of and as a sceptical attitude towards knowledge due to its attempts to describe God by negation (*via negativa*).

Different still is Josef Stern's approach to the problem of whether Maimonides was a sceptic.[53] According to him, the Egyptian physician and Rabbi challenged the belief that it is humanly impossible to achieve (scientific) knowledge, specifically that variety concerned exclusively with metaphysics and cosmology. I do not seek here to debate the validity of Stern's point. However, his clear philosophical commitment to the scepticism of Maimonides is representative of an old debate as to whether the great Sephardic Rabbi was also an advocate of an elitist knowledge reserved only to a few.[54] The possibility of knowledge is, perhaps, not totally negated but only limited. I will return to this claim in a future publication.

---

[51] I thank Warren Zev Harvey for his contribution to this section. He adds: "The question of why Saadia was preoccupied with the problem of doubt is a fascinating one. Here it may be relevant to mention Heschel's important essay, 'The Quest for Certainty in Saadia's Philosophy' (1943). According to Heschel, Saadia's interest in scepticism was not motivated by the doubts of others, but by *his own doubts*—by 'quandaries knocking at his own heart' (265)."

[52] Aryeh Botwinick, *Skepticism, Belief, and the Modern: Maimonides to Nietzsche* (Ithaca: Cornell University Press, 1997).

[53] Josef Stern, *The Matter and Form of Maimonides' Guide* (Cambridge: Harvard University Press, 2013).

[54] Harvey has provided the following comment: "This is true in an obvious sense. However, Maimonides dedicated his life to making knowledge known to the many. Not one of his works was written for professionals or experts. The *Mishneh Torah*, his greatest work, was a Code intended for *every* Jew,

There are some rare examples of studies on Jewish scepticism from a later period that are concerned with the Jewish convert[55] Uriel da Costa[56] and Salomon Maimon.[57] Furthermore, studies on expressions of religious (or rational) and linguistic criticism (Eliezer of Eilburg),[58] doubts,[59] literary genres, and different social configurations (conversion strategies)[60] require mentioning.

The important contribution of David Ruderman regarding Simone Luzzatto's *Socrate*[61] is particularly worth mentioning here. Ruderman devotes a detailed chapter of his 1995 monograph *Jewish Thought and Scientific Discovery in Early Modern Europe*[62] to Luzzatto's work. He summarises its contents and focuses on the problem of Luzzatto's use of sources as well as Luzzatto's position within early modern and Jewish scholarship and the sceptical tradition. Two years later, Richard Popkin edited an insightful book, *Skepticism and Irreligion*, that lacked a single contribution on Jewish thought.[63]

---

learned or unlearned. Even his *Guide* was not written for accomplished philosophers, but for young beginning students (i.e. undergraduates) like Joseph ben Judah."

55 On Francisco Sánchez and whether he converted from Judaism to Christianity, see Elaine Limbrick's introduction to Sánchez, *That Nothing is Known*, (Cambridge: Cambridge University Press, 1988), 6; Cf. José Faur, "Sánchez' Critique of Authoritas: Converso Skepticism and the Emergence of Radical Hermeneutics," in *The Return to Scripture in Judaism and Christianity. Essays in Postcritical Scriptural Interpretation*, ed. Peter Ochs (New York: Paulist Press, 1993): 256–276; cf. Martin Mulsow, "Skepticism and Conversion to Judaism. The Case of Aaron d'Antan," in *Secret Conversions to Judaism in Early Modern Europe*, ed. Martin Mulsow and Richard H. Popkin (Leiden: Brill, 2004): 123–182.
56 Sanford Shepard, "The Background of Uriel Da Costa's Heresy: Marranism, Skepticism, Karaism," *Judaism* 20 (1971): 341–350.
57 Nathan Rotenstreich, "The Problem of the 'Critique of Judgment' and Solomon Maimon's Scepticism," in *Harry A. Wolfson Jubilee Volume on the Occasion of His Seventy-Fifth Birthday*, vol. 2, ed. Saul Lieberman, (Jerusalem: American Academy for Jewish Research, 1965): 677–702.
58 Cf. Joseph Davis, "The Ten Questions of Eliezer Eilburg and the Problem of Jewish Unbelief in the 16th Century," *The Jewish Quarterly Review* XCI, no. 3–4 (2001): 293–336; Joseph Davis, "The Ten Questions of Eliezer Eilburg," *Hebrew Union College Annual* 80, no. 173 (2009): 244.
59 Gideon Freudenthal, "The Remedy to Linguistic Skepticism. Judaism as a Language of Action," *Naharaim—I Zeitschrift für deutsch-jüdische Literatur und Kulturgeschichte* 4, no. 1 (2011): 67–76.
60 Cf. Martin Mulsow, "Skepticism and Conversion to Judaism. The Case of Aaron d'Antan."
61 Cf. Jehuda Bergmann, "Sokrates in der jüdischen Literatur," *Monatsschrift zur Geschichte und Wissenschaft des Judentums* 80 (1936): 6–10.
62 David B. Ruderman, "Science and Skepticism. Simone Luzzatto on Perceiving the Natural World," in *Jewish Thought and Scientific Discovery in Early Modern Europe* (Detroit: Wayne State University Press, 1995): 153–184.
63 Richard H. Popkin and Arjo J. Vanderjagt, eds., *Skepticism and Irreligion in the Seventeenth and Eighteenth Centuries* (Leiden: Brill, 1993); see also Popkin's *History of Scepticism* where he refers to some Jewish sceptical thinkers like Halevy and Crescas without mentioning the question of Jewish scepticism. Asher Salah is preparing an edition of some letters of Popkin which will provide another picture of his vision of Jewish scepticism.

It should be clear from this chapter that the research on Jewish philosophical scepticism is still nascent. Although the situation has been improving,[64] a history of Jewish scepticism is still a desideratum. This also holds true for a history of Jewish cultural expressions of scepticism, i.e. the modes of sceptical strategies present in Jewish literature, culture, history, societies, and education. The lack of interest in the intricacies of Jewish scepticism in Jewish studies may be rooted in the modality of Jewish philosophy as such, a concept that is notoriously in-between and that subsumes and affects traditional wisdom, philosophy, theology, Jewish and general *Weltanschauung*, as well as cultural history, being a hazardous bridge between orthopraxy and orthodoxy. The invisibility of the particular (i.e. Judaism) due to its immersion in general philosophy could be one reason for the lack of interest. The focus on enquiry and doubt as a kind of Platonic *motor mobilis* will thus be a solution (and, paradoxically, the reason) for the *aporia*. Here, the need for an "imaginative grammar" in the language of scepticism within the history of Jewish philosophy and cultural history (as well as that of the adjacent cultures) becomes apparent.

Subsequent chapters will try to provide an answer to how the process of the particularisation of Jewish philosophy came about. In the first two parts of this book, I demonstrated that Christian intellectuals and philosophers made the Jewish biblical tradition into a universal *philosophia perennis*. Later, in the sixteenth and seventeenth centuries, Christian philosophers were the initiators of a historicisation and demythologisation of the fundaments of such a philosophy as well as a temporal concretisation of Jewish mysticism. The (Jewish) sceptical tradition has something to do with this process because it contributed to undermining other dogmatic certainties.

In the following chapters, we will examine the origin of a sceptical, anti-philosophical, and anti-dogmatic attitude in Jewish philosophy since the Humanist early modern period. The first timid steps occur at the end of the Middle Ages, the next developments at the beginning of the seventeenth century, and, finally, the crucial change between the seventeenth and eighteenth centuries, by means of two German Protestant theologians and the Venetian Rabbi Simone Luzzatto.

---

64 The Maimonides Centre for Advanced Studies at the University of Hamburg focuses on this topic. See the homepage for more information on this topic as well as the Centre's fellowship program (www.maimonides-centre.uni-hamburg.de). An entire issue of issue of *Melilah* (12 [2015]) of has been devoted to the topic.

2 At The Eve of Modernity: Scepticism in-between

Henri Estienne's 1562 Latin translation of Sextus Empiricus' *Outlines of Pyrrhonism* was obviously a very important, decisive step, but surely not the sole force that steered Renaissance scholarship toward scepticism and methodological doubt.[1] Sceptical strategies and methods were already known in the Latin medieval period: John Buridan, Henry of Ghent, Duns Scotus, William of Ockham, and Nicholas of Autrecourt were philosophically and theologically active and left their mark on the history of sceptical ideas and philosophy. It is necessary to look for the modes of transmission of philosophical ideas, concepts, and methods among European Jews and the offspring of Arabic Judaism (mostly of Sephardic heritage) in comparison with Christian Latin intellectuals. Jewish *literati* and scholars occupied a space between the Arabic and Latin traditions. Rather than a constraint, this in-betweenness was a stimulating challenge.

The aim of the following chapter is to highlight certain events, movements, and Jewish scholars in the Renaissance and early modern period up to Simone Luzzatto. In my opinion, some aspects of Jewish intellectual and literary life ought to be considered precursors of, or, perhaps more cautiously, implicit references either to Jewish scepticism or a Jewish sceptical dimension of life. To be clear, however, Jewish scholars during this time period did not directly thematise a sceptical consciousness even when their strategies were sceptical in nature. First we must clarify the concept of strategies before we concern ourselves with other important aspects of Jewish scepticism: these strategies are more or less formalised dialectic argumentations[2] aimed at finding weak points in the formulation of "dogmatisms," mostly terminating either in the suspension of judgment or in further enquiry. In our case, the dialectic arguments of the sceptics pertain to the (im)possibility of reaching the truth, the (un)certainty of the responsibility of the individual, doubts as to the immortality of the soul, etc. Although similar arguments can also be found in Christian texts, Christian authors were more cautious because of the Inquisition's activity in much of the Italian peninsula; the Jews were usually unaffected by punitive measures because their "heresies" were pertinent only to their "religion" and of no interest to Christian authorities.[3] This oversight of Jewish "heresy" was possible in Venice of the seventeenth century, where, over and against the attempts of the Roman Church, we have first in the Academies and later in the Universities a conscious sceptical tra-

---

[1] See Luciano Floridi, "The Diffusion of Sextus Empiricus's Works in the Renaissance," *Journal of the History of Ideas* 56, no. 1 (1995): 63–85.
[2] See Katja M. Vogt, *Belief and Truth: A Skeptic Reading of Plato* (New York: Oxford University Press, 2012), 137, 157 (with reference to Sextus).
[3] As a rule, the Inquisition attacked Jewish concepts and ideas primarily when they had something to do with Christianity (for example, regarding the Marranos, converts, etc.). Heretical movements among the Jews and direct questioning of the "Jewish" faith was of no interest. The Inquisition, of course, was not an institution to protect Jewish religion and faith.

dition that was indebted to Aristotelian metaphysics, systems of logic and anti-logic, Averroism(s) concerning the immortality of the soul and materiality, and scepticisms of philological, historical, and philosophical origins.

In the following chapter, we will search for the tiles of a mosaic which mirrors Jewish Northern Italian cultural society at the eve of modernity, which was affected by the crisis of metaphysics turning into epistemology, and, interestingly, by increasingly dogmatic views of religion. The sceptical vein in the Renaissance and early modern period is visible everywhere, although or perhaps because scholars of this period are very prudent in avoiding attacking and criticising religious ideas and doctrines. Scepticism is a symptom of the political and intellectual crisis of early modern period—it is obviously not the cause. A first step will be to trace the paradigms of a perceived revolution in terminology (e. g. psychology, the individual, individual perception, gnoseology, etc.). The next step will be in using sceptical strategies to disavow the authority of the past.

2.1 From Scholasticism to Sceptical Attitudes

Elements of the Movement and Jewish Scholars[4]

Joseph van Ess[5] claimed that medieval Islamic scepticism was a product of crisis, especially the crisis that formed when the three religions were in contact with each other, when their cultural and religious messages were focused, and their own particular religious, philosophical, and religious truths seemed to be at stake. In 1968, Van Ess adopted the paradigm of crisis for Islamic philosophy that Richard Popkin developed in the 1950s.[6] Popkin was the first to note the significant impact of the Reformation on the research and debate about the criterion of truth, which was seen as a sceptical topic of ancient origin.

However, there are also other reasons that explain the uncertainty and scepticism of the Humanist, Renaissance, and early modern period that also unquestionably undermine the criterion of authority and truth. New geographic and historical discoveries (such as those by the "discoverer of America," Christopher Columbus), the progress of the sciences (with new mechanical, scientific, and medical achievements), and the philological undermining of historical and religious certainty (by

---

[4] I thank Dr. Giada Coppola (a research assistant at "Project Sforno," which is funded by the German Research Council) for gathering some bibliographic material and ideas for this paragraph on Jewish scholasticism and ʿOvadyah Sforno.
[5] Josef van Ess, "Skepticism in Islamic Religious Thought," *Al-Abhath* 21 (1968): 1–18.
[6] Richard H. Popkin, "The Sceptical Crisis and the Rise of Modern Philosophy: I–III," *Review of Metaphysics* 7, no. 1 (1953): 132–151; 307–322; 7, no. 3 (1954): 499–510; see his book *The History of Scepticism from Erasmus to Descartes* (Assen: van Gorkum, 1960): 1–16.

philological scepticism, such as that the *Donatio Constantini* by Lorenzo Valla],[7] and the questioning of the biblical canon itself) are a few elements among the many fifteenth- to seventeenth-century challenges to the authority of holy and profane texts, universities, and churches. The increased interest in Averroistic philosophy at the universities prompted questions—particularly among Jewish scholars of the early modern period—about the concept of transcendentalism, that is, about the existence of the afterlife and the remunerability of our good and bad deeds in the next world. The problem of the (last) divine judgment after death was secondary to the morality of acts and the confession of "true" faiths and beliefs. In sum, of most philosophical interest were themes involving the responsibility of the individual to her/his religious and political community in *this* life.

Central to comprehending the phenomenon of the scattering of philosophical ideas in the Middle Ages, Renaissance, and early modern period is the proliferation of spatial entities of intellectual exchange, i.e. intellectual circles, cities, areas, and other spaces where the conception and diffusion of ideas took place. Whereas in the Early Middle Ages monasteries with their libraries and rabbinic academies with their *ratio studiorum* (plan of studies) played a crucial role in intellectual life, in the Later Middle Ages the universities became the suitable forum for cultural exchange.

A new element of not insignificant importance would still yet arise: the teaching system. History is known for its slow steps in overcoming large distances, and one of these slow steps occurred during the Humanist and Renaissance period, namely, the creation of scholasticisms on the duty of the universities, which was taken to be the task of summarising the whole of the philosophical tradition, including materials for teaching and learning,[8] and routinely outlining contrary opinions. In doing so, these historians of philosophy spread non-conforming (even heretical) ideas and concepts. The scholastic presentation of (almost) all opinions of *argumenta* became, obviously, a promotion of alternative philosophies. There was another change in the Humanist (fourteenth and fifteenth) centuries: the formulation of the *quaestiones* became much longer than the objections, i.e. the enunciation of the opposite argument became much shorter.[9] It is obviously a stretch to infer from these changes a larger turning point in philosophy itself; however it is a sign of change that the reinforcement of one's own position became prioritised over the presentation of alternate opinions: the authority in an argument switched from the school to the individual scholar.

---

[7] Lodi Nauta, "Lorenzo Valla and Quattrocento Scepticism." *Vivarium. A Journal for Medieval and Early-Modern Philosophy and Intellectual Life* 44, no. 2–3 (2006): 375–395; Letizia A. Panizza, "Lorenzo Valla's *De Vero Falsoque Bono*: Lactantius and Oratorical Scepticism," *Journal of the Warburg and Courtauld Institutes* 41 (1978): 76–107.

[8] See Paul O. Kristeller, "Der Gelehrte und sein Publikum im Mittelalter und in der Renaissance," *Medium aevum vivum. Festschrift Walter Bulst*, ed. Hans Robert Jauss ed. Dieter Schaller (Heidelberg: Winter, 1960): 212–230.

[9] Cf. John Marenbon, *Later Medieval Philosophy (1150–1350). An Introduction* (London: Routledge, 1991), 31.

The phenomenon of Late Scholasticism also affected Judaism between the Humanist period and the Renaissance as it shifted from Arabic to Latin Aristotelianism in Italy and Spain.[10] In the Renaissance, Aristotelianism survived only in particular intellectual and scholarly circles, such as the University of Padua, however it did survive, making Aristotle's later "renaissance" possible.[11] In the fifteenth and sixteenth centuries, Jewish authors composed philosophical treatises in which they discussed the same questions and used the same methods as contemporary Christian philosophers. This tendency seems to be in continuity with Averroes's interpretation of Aristotle, which had characterised the medieval period. Jewish philosophers, Averroists among them, represented a bridge between the old philosophy and the new.[12]

The Jewish intellectual elite experienced an educational programme very similar to Christian school and university instruction. This was the case with the academy of Judah ben Yeḥiel ha-Rofe, who known as Judah Messer Leon: classical Jewish religious teachings were combined with the study of the liberal arts, consisting of the *trivium* (grammar, rhetoric, and logic) and the *quadrivium* (arithmetic, geometric, music, and astronomy).[13] The Italian Rabbi and philosopher, born in Montecchio Maggiore (now in the province of Vicenza), was one of the most important promoters of Hebrew Scholasticism. He was well known as the author of a treatise on the art of rhetoric, the *Sefer Nofet Ṣufim* (*Book of the Honeycomb's Flow*),[14] and he also wrote commentaries on logic and the natural science: a supercommentary on Averroes's Middle Commentaries on the *Isagoge*, the *Categories*, and the *De Interpretatione*; a supercommentary on Averroes's Middle Commentaries on the *Prior Analytics* and

---

10 Mauro Zonta, *Hebrew Scholasticism in the Fifteenth Century: A History and Source Book* (Springer: Dordrecht: 2006).

11 Charles B. Schmitt, "Towards a Reassessment of Renaissance Aristotelianism," *History of Science* 11 (1973): 159–193; Luca Bianchi, "Continuity and Change in the Aristotelian Tradition," in *The Cambridge Companion to Renaissance Humanism*, ed. James Hankins (Cambridge: Cambridge University Press, 2007): 49–71.

12 Alfred Ivry, "Remnants of Jewish Averroism in the Renaissance," in *Jewish Thought in the Sixteenth Century*, ed. Bernard D. Cooperman (Cambridge: Harvard University Press, 1983): 243–265.

13 See the valuable contribution by Gianfranco Miletto, "The Teaching Program of David ben Abraham and His son Abraham Provenzali in the Historical–Cultural Context of the Time in Cultural Intermediaries," in *Cultural Intermediaries Jewish Intellectuals in Early Modern Italy*, ed. David B. Ruderman, Giuseppe Veltri (Philadelphia: Pennsylvania University Press, 2004): 127–148; and my article "Jüdische Einstellung zu den Wissenschaften im 16. und 17. Jahrhundert: Das Prinzip der praktisch–empirischen Anwendbarkeit," in *Judentum zwischen Tradition und Moderne*, ed. Gerd Biegel and Michael Graetz (Heildeberg: C. Winter, 2002): 149–159; and in enlarged version in my book, *Renaissance Philosophy in Jewish Garb: Foundations and Challenges in Judaism on the Eve of Modernity* (Leiden: Brill, 2009): 97–127.

14 Judah Messer Leon, *The Book of the Honeycomb's Flow. A Critical Edition and Translation*, ed. and trans. by Isaac Rabinowitz (Ithaca: Cornell University Press, 1983).

the *Posterior Analytics*; and a supercommentary on Averroes's Middle and Long Commentaries on the first three books of the *Physics*.[15]

The particular activity of this Jewish intellectual scholar during the Renaissance includes not only original works, but also the translation of classical texts with a special interest in Aristotle and the Peripatetic tradition. The *corpus Aristotelicum* recovered many materials that were unknown in the Middle Ages and grew still further with the gradual introduction of Greek, Latin, and Arabic commentators. As Alfred Ivry[16] has remarked, Averroism was a major vehicle of expression in Renaissance philosophy; Jewish scholars and translators worked in the "shadow of Averroes." Between the fifteenth and sixteenth centuries, it is possible to identify a first wave of translations,[17] among them Elijah Del Medigo, Calonymos ben David, called Calo Calonimo, Abraham ben Meir de Balmes, Jacob Mantino, Moses Alatino, and Moses Finzi.

The interest in these new tendencies among Jewish scholars turned towards a particular aspect of the Renaissance tradition. During the Middle Ages, translations of Aristotle focused overwhelmingly on the realm of logic and natural science; however, in the sixteenth century, philosophers' speculations revolved around questions about the nature of the intellect and the soul. Despite the inheritance of the topic of the immortality of the soul from medieval Scholasticism (suggested by Averroes), no other Arabic philosophical theory received comparable attention in the Renaissance.[18] Concerning the Averroes's Long Commentary on the *De Anima*, we are aware of a translation from Arabic into Latin usually ascribed to Michael Scot (ca. 1220); an Arabic-into-Hebrew version of this treatise translated by Zeraḥyah ben Isaac ben She'alti'el Ḥen (1284);[19] a Latin-into-Hebrew translation made by Abraham of Benevento in the late fifteenth century[20]; and the Hebrew-into-Latin Giunta edition of an alternative version of Book Three by Jacob Mantino (1562).

In addition to these translations of the book of the *De Anima*, many other philosophical works about the unity of the intellect and the immortality of the soul were translated and annotated. Calo Calonimo translated Averroes' *Libellus seu epistola de connexione intellectus abstracti cum homine* (1527) and Abraham de Balmes translat-

---

15 All of these notes are based on Mauro Zonta, *La filosofia ebraica medievale: storia e testi* (Rome: Laterza, 2002), 210 and following as well as 230 and following.
16 Alfred Ivry, "Remnants of Jewish Averroism."
17 Dag N. Hasse, "The Social Conditions of the Arabic-(Hebrew-) Latin Translation Movements in Medieval Spain and in the Renaissance," in *Wissen über Grenzen: arabisches Wissen und lateinisches Mittelalter*, ed. Andreas Speer, Lydia Wegener (Berlin: De Gruyter, 2006): 68–87.
18 Ibid.
19 Mauro Zonta, "Aristotle's *De anima* and *De generatione et corruptione* in the Medieval Hebrew Tradition," in *Studies in the History of Culture and Science: A Tribute to Gad Freudenthal*, ed. Resianne Fontaine, Ruth Glasner, Reimund Leicht, and Giuseppe Veltri (Leiden: Brill, 2011): 91–101.
20 Mauro Zonta, "The Autumn of Medieval Jewish Philosophy," in *Herbst des Mittelalters? Fragen zur Bewertung des 14. und 15. Jahrhunderts*, ed. Jan A. Aertsen and Martin Pickave (Berlin: De Gruyter, 2004): 474–492.

ed both al-Fārābī's treatise *De intellectu et intellegibili* (1522–ca.1523) and Averroes's Epitome of the *De Anima* (1552). The most interesting interpretation of Aristotelianism and Averroist theories is offered by Elijah Del Medigo, who should be considered the most important Jewish Averroist in Italy. Del Medigo was commissioned to translate works about logic, physics, psychology, and metaphysics for his Christian patrons;[21] for example, he translated Averroes' Epitome of the *De Anima* for Giovanni Pico della Mirandola. However, Del Medigo also wrote two Averroist treatises (1482) in Latin that were subsequently translated into Hebrew. The first treatise concerns the unity of the material intellect and the possibility of conjunction with the active intellect, and the second concerns the immortality of the soul, explaining in detail the incongruence of Averroes's positions on the *De Anima* part III, 36 in his Epitome and Long Commentary.

The interest in Aristotle's *De Anima* (and in Averroes' commentaries) is the real turning point in the Humanist early modern period, given that it was one the most commented upon texts at universities in the Late Middle Ages.[22] The fortunes of the Averroistic conception of the soul in the sixteenth and seventeenth centuries are obviously connected with the topics that constituted the intellectual turning point between the epochs. Some of these topics include the faculties of perception (the senses), and the sources of perception. Other topics include typical Averroistic principles like the denial of the immortality of the soul, its status as the only happiness in this life, the unity of the intellect, and the well-known doctrine of "double-truth." Each of these convictions could be interpreted in a sceptical way. However, this is not the place to explore the spreading of Averroistic theories in the Middle Ages and early modern period, a topic best treated by other scholars.[23] I seek here only to illuminate the elements of philosophical movements not directly connected with scepticism that prefigure the "crisis of scepticism," as Popkin called it.

'Ovadyah Sforno

One prominent Scholastic that merits mention here is 'Ovadyah Sforno.[24] He is considered the last Jewish scholastic authority.[25] The Scholastic tradition in the Renais-

---

[21] Cf. Michael Engel, *Elijah Del Medigo and Paduan Aristotelianism investigating the Human Intellect* (London: Bloomsbury, 2017).
[22] Cf. *Ancient Perspectives on Aristotles de Anima*, ed. Gerd Van Riel and Pierre Destree (Leuven: Leuven University Press, 2009).
[23] Dag N. Hasse, "Aufstieg und Niedergang des Averroismus in der Renaissance: Niccolò Tignosi, Agostino Nifo, Francesco Vimercato," in *"Herbst des Mittelalters?" Fragen zur Bewertung des 14. und 15. Jahrhunderts* (Berlin: De Gruyter, 2004): 447–473.
[24] Ephraim Finkel, "R. Obadja Sforno als Exeget," Universität Tübingen, Inauguraldissertation (Breslau: Theodor Schatzky, 1896); Robert Bonfil, "Torat ha-nefesh ve-ha-qedushah be-mishnat R. 'Ovadyah Sforno," *Eshel Beer-Sheva, Studies in Jewish Thought* 1 (1976): 200–257; Robert Bonfil, "La produzione esegetica di 'O. Servadio Sforno," in *La lettura ebraica delle Scritture*, ed. Sergio. J. Sierra

sance period, particularly in Italy, is considered an extension of the medieval philosophical tradition. However, this approach is entirely at odds with another contemporary trend aimed at assimilating renewed interests in Platonism, Kabbalah, Hermeticism, and Magic into the general currents of philosophy. In view of this fact, Mauro Zonta defines the period between 1450–1500 as: "the 'autumn' of Medieval Jewish philosophy in the sense that it was a time of change, one of the last stages of this historical phase of Jewish thought, but also one of its most innovative and fruitful periods"[26].

Sforno published only one philosophical work, entitled *Or 'Ammim* (1537), *The Light of Nations*, which he made available to a Christian Humanist readership through his own Latin translation under the title *Lumen Gentium* (1548). This work could be considered a kind of "Summa," although some precaution is necessary. Although the structure of *Or 'Ammim / Lumen Gentium* is similar, nonetheless a small aspect differentiates Sforno from previous scholars. Seen from the perspective of the deep spreading of Averroistic conceptions among the Jews, it is not surprising that the most important (twelfth) chapter of this book is devoted to the immortality of the soul, in marked contrast to that of his predecessors.

In the most general sense, this work presents itself as a *quaestio disputata* (disputed question). Sforno develops fifteen questions in order to refute Averroes and the Aristotelianism of the Peripatetics by using the Aristotelian method. For the reader, here a synopsis of the *quaestiones:*[27]

1. Whether the movement of generation and corruption is eternal?[28]
2. Whether the elements are eternal?[29]
3. Whether the first matter is eternal?[30]
4. Whether the heavens are eternal?[31]
5. Whether the movement is eternal?[32]
6. Whether there is creation, namely, creation in which both matter and form as well as their whole composite came from absolute nothingness?[33]

(Bologna: Edizioni Dehoniane, 1995): 261–277; Saverio Campanini, "Un intellettuale ebreo del Rinascimento: 'Ovadyah Sforno a Bologna e i suoi rapporti con i Christiani," in *Verso l'epilogo di una convivenza: Gli ebrei a Bologna nel XVI secolo*, ed. Maria G. Muzzarelli (Florence: La Giuntina, 1996): 98 –128; *Kitvei Rabbi 'Ovadyah Sforno*, ed. Ze'ev Gottlieb (Jerusalem: Mosad ha-Rav Kuk, 1983).

25 Mauro Zonta, *Hebrew Scholasticism*, 30.
26 Mauro Zonta, "The Autumn of medieval Jewish philosophy," 476.
27 This synopsis was compiled and edited by Dr. Giada Coppola.
28 ראשונה אם תנועת ההויה וההפסד קדמונית /1. Utrum motus generationis et corruptionis habuisset esse ab eterno.
29 שנית אם היסודות קדמונים /2. Utrum corruptibilium elementa habuissent esse ab eterno.
30 שלישית אם החמר הראשון קדמון /3. Utrum materia prima habuisset esse ab eterno.
31 רביעית אם השמים קדמונים /4. Utrum celum habuisset esse ab eterno.
32 חמישית אם התנועה קדמונית /5. Utrum motus habuisset esse ab eterno.
33 ששית אם יש נמצא קדמון בורא וממציא יש אחר האפיסות המוחלט והוא עשה אינו ישנו /6. Utrum detur creatio qua scilicet tam materia et forma quam totum compositum habuisset esse post merum non esse.

7. Whether, if there is creation and consequentially a Creator, this Creator is corporeal or incorporeal?[34]
8. Whether He is only one or not?[35]
9. Whether He is omniscient or not?[36]
10. Whether He has equal power over two contraries to choose one of them with His free will?[37]
11. Whether He has providence over individual human beings?[38]
12. Whether the individual intellectual soul of human beings is immortal or not?[39]
13. Whether good deeds are beneficial or even necessary for the perfection of the aforementioned intellectual soul?[40]
14. Whether the perfection of the soul is reached by means of human power alone or by means of divine or natural power?[41]
15. Whether[42] the final goal of celestial bodies and their movement is a necessary benefit for human perfection?[43]

Five of the questions are concerned with eternity (generation and corruption, first matter, elements, heavens, movement); one about the creation of the world (creation); five on theodicy (corporeality, unity, omniscience, free will, providence); two on individuality (immortality, merits), one on the soul (perfection of human soul) and finally one on the celestial bodies. The reader will be surprised to note the difference between the content of this list and that of the 13 principles of Maimonides: in the Sforno list there are very few questions about God and no question on the Messiah. The omnipresent topic in this list is the immortality of matter, the elements, and

---

34 שביעית אם הוא גוף או כח בגוף אם אין / 7. Utrum data creatione et per consequens Creatore idem Creator sit quid corporeum vel sit quid incorporeum.

35 שמינית אם הוא אחד בלבד אם אין /8. Utrum unus tantum detur Creator vel plures eque primi dentur creatores.

36 תשיעית אם הוא יודע כל / 9. Utrum idem Creator omnia sciat vel econtra.

37 עשירית אם יש לו יכולת בשוה על שני ההפכים ובוחר באחד מהם בכונה וברצון / 10. Utrum idem Creator habeat liberam ad utrumque contrariorum potentiam quorum alterum voluntarie eligat.

38 אחת עשרה אם הוא משגיח באישי ההוויים ונפסדים /11. Utrum de mortalium individuis habeat sollicitudinem sive curam.

39 שתים עשרה אם הנפש האנושית השכלית האישיית היא בלתי נפסדת / 12. Utrum intellectiva individui humani generis anima sit quid immortale vel econverso.

40 שלש עשרה אם המעשים הטובים הם מועילים או הכרחיים בהצלחת הנפש השכלית הנזכר / 13. Utrum pia intentio et conatus ad pia opera exequenda concurrat ad eiusdem anime perfectionem.

41 ארבע עשרה אם שלמות הנפש יושג בכח אנושי בלבד ולא יושג בכח אלהי או טבעי / 14. Utrum eiusdem intellective anime perfectio per humanam virtutem tantum non autem per naturalem vel divinam acquiri contingat.

42 חמש עשרה אם תכלית המכוון מן השמים וצבאם ומהעולם המוחש בכללו הוא המין האנושי ושלמותו /15. Utrum celestium horumque motuum finis sit mortalium oportunitas ad humanam perfectionem necessaria.

43 That is, whether the human species and its perfection is the intended purpose of the heavens and of the heavenly bodies and of the material world in its entirety.

2.1 From Scholasticism to Sceptical Attitudes — 165

the soul; the space devoted to other issues is not always proportionate to their importance.

Sforno's dialectical method obeys the classical methodological approach of medieval scholastic discussion. The author defines the contents of each single *quaestio* in the introduction of both translations and presents the *quaestio* in the classical *quaestio* format: statement of problem / argument / counterargument / solution.[44] Before the opening *quaestio*, Sforno stresses the importance of method in defining seven "assessments" (*na'arukhim*).[45]

It should be noted the Sforno translates the Latin term *quaestio* from *ḥaqirah*, which was also preferred by Gersonides. Sforno's choice moves away from the classical medieval school, which translated *quaestio* from *derush* or *she'elah*. Another aspect of interest is that, in the introduction of a philosophical question in the Latin version of *The Light of Nations*, we find *dubitatur utrum*[46] instead of the classical form *quaeritur utrum / quaesitum est*. Sforno presents another philological novelty: the standard *disputatio* becomes *dubium*. Generally, the *dubia* were a particular section of the *lectiones* in which scholars discussed particularly difficult points. Only in the fourteenth century, chiefly in England, did the *dubia* evolve into an autonomous literary genre, perhaps generated in the category of preaching.[47]

In the Hebrew version, Sforno does not use this kind of formula and hence he does not dissociate himself from other Jewish Scholastic authorities.[48] Sforno translates the Latin formulation, which introduces the last section of the *quaestio*—namely the solution—with a paraphrase: נשיב אם כן להתיר ספק החקירה הנזכרת (*Ad dubium ergo respondetur* etc.). The doubt (*dubium/safeq*) has a peculiar dialectical function, as a logical connective word that introduces the solution.

In the *Or 'Ammim* the doubt's function is not merely dialectical. Sforno follows the Maimonidean tradition[49] in which "doubt and perplexity"[50] are inherent to the quest for knowledge. An important text, extant only in the Hebrew version—because

---

44 Cf. John Marenbon, *Later Medieval Philosophy*, 31–34.
45 Hebrew Text: *Or 'Ammin*, 14; Latin text *Lumen Gentium*, 12.
46 I thank Warren Zev Harvey for his contribution to this section. He adds: "The 13th-century Latin translation of the *Guide* was often called *Dux dubiorum*, although it seems its original title was *Dux neutrorum*."
47 Cf. Marc Saperstein, "Problematizing the Bible in Late Medieval Jewish Exegesis," in *With Reverence for the Word: Medieval Scriptural Exegesis in Judaism, Christianity, and Islam*, ed. Jane Dammen McAuliffe, Barry D. Walfish, and Joseph W. Goering (Oxford: Oxford University Press, 2003): 133–156, 142.
48 Cf. Mauro Zonta, *Hebrew Scholasticism*, 30.
49 Cf. Warren Z. Harvey, "Maimonides' first Commandment, Physics, and Doubt," in *Hazon Nahum, Studies in Jewish Law, Thought, and History Presented to Dr. Norman Lamm*, ed. Yaakov Elman and Jeffrey S. Gurock. (New York: Michael Scharf Publication Trust of the Yeshiva University Press, 1998): 149–162.
50 Ibid., 161.

Sforno interestingly does not translate it into Latin—reveals important aspects of his philosophy: [51]

הן רבים עתה אמרו שמצוה עלינו להאמין כל שרשי תורתנו, ומהם הרמב"ם ז"ל בספר המורה מאמר ג' פרק כ"ח, גם שנראה שברח מזה בתחילת ספרו ספר המדע, עם היות בכמו אלה לב דופק עם ספק על ימין שהיא שמאל ותהי האמת והפכה בספק ספקא, אבל המון בני עמנו ואצל קצת תופשי התורה מן השפה ולחוץ, מבלי אין אצלם ראיה מספקת להעביר כל ספק משרשי תורתנו, עד היות אמונה כזאת בלתי בחיריית ובלתי נופלת תחת מצוה כלל, כי אמנם לא יוכל האדם להאמין כרצונו בהחלט, כל שכן כאשר יצווה, גם כי אולי יפצה פיהו ברצון ההמון ויבטא בשפתיו.	There are many now who say that there is a commandment on us to believe in all roots of our Torah, and among them is Maimonides—of blessed memory—in his book *The Guide for the Perplexed*, Part III, Chapter 28; although it seems that he fled from this in the beginning of his *Book of Knowledge*. Now, in those like him the heart pounds with doubt whether their right hand is their left, and the truth and its contrary are in gravest doubt. However, the multitude of our nation and some scholars of the Torah give this lip service. Yet they have no sufficient arguments to remove all doubt from the roots of our Torah, such that belief is involuntary and does not at all fall within the realm of the commandment—for a person cannot believe entirely at will, especially if commanded. This is the case even if one opens his mouth to appease the will of the multitude and makes utterances with his lips.

Sforno does not explain to us how to verify the principles of the Torah and why most lack the capacity to prove them. For Maimonides, there are two groups with the same, yet gradual objective

> These commands will enable the throng and the elite to acquire moral and intellectual qualities, each according to his ability. Thus, the godly community becomes pre-eminent, reaching a two-fold perfection. By the first perfection I mean, man is spending his life in this world under the most agreeable and congenial conditions. The second perfection would constitute the achievement of intellectual objectives, each in accordance with his native powers.[52]

The real question arises when the mass does not achieve the intellectual qualities of the elite and therefore has no defence against the verification of the truth of the principles. However, what does *emuna bilti beḥiriyit*, translated as "a belief without free-

---

51 I thank Warren Zev Harvey for this English translation.
52 Ibid.

will," really mean? According to his commentary on Genesis 1:26, the difference between the angels and human beings consists in the freewill or free choice of the latter, while the former are acting under divine compulsion.⁵³ The human being is similar to God because of freewill, i.e. because acting "with knowledge and consciously." Hence, the mass of people who "have no sufficient proof to remove every doubt from the roots of our Torah" cannot be defined as human beings.

Sforno's position is very close to that of Saadia Gaon,⁵⁴ according to whom the liability of doubt (ספק) depends on the enquiring subject (מבקש המדע השכלי) either because he has an inadequate idea of the investigation (אופני הראיות) or because he is careless in his observation and too quick in his conclusion (הוא מקל על עצמו וממהר לגזור על הידוע קודם השלמת מלאכת העיון בו). In both cases, the responsibility lies with the subject because of his/her inadequacy or because of his/her carelessness. The only and decisive difference between both is that Saadia was discussing sense perception while Sforno was treating the Torah as if it were a book of anatomy. Such is the debate of the sixteenth through the seventeenth centuries on the veracity of the oral and written Torah and its comparison with the sciences. Sforno did not have a sceptical attitude—he was only exploring the different sides of a debate. His was the first step.

2.2 Three Sceptical Strategies: De' Rossi, the Maharal, and Sforno

The second step rests just beyond the first. Let me describe some of the ideas surrounding the first "sceptic" in Judaism: Simone Luzzatto, privileged subject of this third part of my book. In his *Discorso circa il stato degli Hebrei* (1638), repeatedly mentioned above, the Venetian introduces the non-Jewish audience to the intellectual subdivisions of Jewish intellectuals, enumerating among the elite the rabbis, the philosopher-theologians, and the Kabbalists. Referring to the second group, he comments:

> Although the Jews refer [for their decisions] to the [authority of the] doctors of the second class [i.e. the philosopher-theologians], they do not fail to conform the sayings and pronouncements of the ancients to the commonly held doctrines. And although they firmly hold that the truths do not contradict each other, and that the simple opinion of the ancient sages should not be op-

---

53 כדמותנו בענין המעשיות שידמה בם קצת לפמליא של מעלה בצד מה שהם פועלים בידיעה ובהכרה אמנם פעולתם היא בלתי בחיריית ובזה לא ידמה להם האדם

54 Saadia Gaon, *Sefer ha-nivḥar be-emunot we-deʽot. Maqor we-targum*, ed. Yosef Kafaḥ (Jerusalem: Defus ha-emunim, 1970); Saadia Gaon, *Sefer Emunot we-Deot* (Constantinople: 1562); Saadia Gaon, *Kitāb al-amānāt wa-al-iʽatiqādāt*, ed. Samuel Landauer (Leiden: Brill, 1880). English translation: *The Book of Doctrines and Beliefs*, ed. Alexander Altmann, and Daniel H. Frank (Indianapolis: Hackett, 2002), 25.

posed to the evidence, so that their authority compensates the Jews, when human reason, deficient and defective of power, does not attain it with its argument.⁵⁵

In this short text, Luzzatto refers to two different controversies: one concerning the authority of ancient traditions and the other regarding authority in general. The first question focuses on the problem of the authority of the ancient sages whose sayings and pronouncements are dependent upon the doctrines of their time (i.e. conformity with "the generally held doctrines"). Here Luzzatto cryptically refers to the opinion of some rabbis and philosophers that both the opinion of the sages and the (scientific) evidence *cannot* be opposed ("they firmly hold that the truths do not contradict each other, and that the simple opinion of the ancient sages should not oppose the evidence"). The reader cannot overlook Luzzatto's commitment to the *obligation* of the theological and dogmatic view according to which Revelation cannot be imperfect, although it may not comport with (scientific or historical) evidence.

The second necessary question is the primacy of the authority of the sages, that is, the Revelation of the written and oral Torah, over human reason if, "deficient and defective of power," human reason cannot "attain it with [their] argument." With this expression, he introduces his later treatise on the failure of human reason, his book *Socrate overo dell'humano sapere* where he denies the authority of the sciences, the knowledge of the senses, logical inferences, and appeals for systematic doubt.

The first question is addressed in the controversy between Azaria de' Rossi and the Maharal of Prague, to which I turn in the next section.⁵⁶ The second question concerns the topic of two scholars of the Renaissance and early modern period: Judah Moscato and Simone Luzzatto, which we will deal with later.

Azariah de' Rossi and the Maharal: The Other Side of Scepticism

While neither the Mantuan intellectual Azariah de' Rossi nor his opponent Yehudah Löw are qualified as sceptical philosophers, they are important to the history of scepticism because both of them adopt some sceptical strategies in order to directly (the former) and indirectly (the latter) undermine the authority of the Ancients in scientific and historical matters. Let us examine those texts.

---

55 *Discorso*, 80r: "E con tutto che tanto si riportano gl'hebrei alli dottori della seconda classe, non mancano però di ridurre li detti e pronunciati degl'antichi in conformità delle dottrine comunemente abbracciate, e benché tengono per fermo che le verità non s'oppongono l'una all'altra, e che la semplice openione delli antichi dottori non si deve opponere all'evidenzia, così la loro auttorità supplisce agl'hebrei, ove che la ragione umana è manchevole e diffetosa di potere con suoi argomenti arrivarvi."
56 This section is an updated version of my "Maharal against Azaria de' Rossi: The Other Side of Skepticism," in *Rabbinic Theology and Jewish Intellectual History. The Great Rabbi Loew of Prague*, ed. Meir Seidel (Oxford: Routledge, 2012): 65–76.

The topic of the controversy between Rabbi Löw, the Maharal of Prague, and the physician and scholar Azariah de' Rossi is well-known: the reliability of the *Aggadot*, the rabbinic "stories." To reach a better understanding of de' Rossi's opponent, the Maharal, I would like to provide a summary of the many theses of his philosophy, partly based on my previous works on the topic,[57] as well as a revision of my former interpretation of the controversy and a greater elaboration of the arguments of both the Maharal and de' Rossi.

The literary genre of the "story" was the subject of rabbinic controversies as early as the ancient and classical period. Rabbinic academies were, of course, not as "rational" as modern scholars are; they were, however, critical enough to question the authority of some biblical texts and to believe that some expressions would qualify as exaggeration;[58] the divine opinion expressed by the *Bat Qol* (the voice from heaven) was considered as good and authoritative as the opinion of a rabbi and/or a school.

The famous philosopher and theologian Maimonides expressed doubts as to the historical credibility of the non-legal rabbinical literature, interpreting it in a rationalist-literary way. In his *Moreh Nevukhim*, he described the Aggadot as "poetic parables."[59] Critics regarded this attitude as dangerous, not only because of reservations about Maimonides' rationalist slant, but also because of the danger of Christian exploitation of internal Jewish quarrels. One need only mention that the evaluation of rabbinical storytelling art, the Aggadah, was one of the main subjects of the disputations of Paris in 1240 (Nicholas Donin vs. Rabbi Yeḥi'el ben Yosef), Barcelona in 1263 (Fray Pablo Christiani vs. Moses ben Nachman), and Tortosa in 1413–1414 (Geronimo de Santa Fe vs. Joseph Albo).[60] In any case, rabbinical writings were spoken of in denigrating terms, sometimes as *"diabolici libri."*[61]

Not until the Renaissance, however, did the subject of Judaism's critical attitude towards its own traditions lead to an open dispute: the Mantuan scholar Azariah de' Rossi, also influenced by the thinking of Christian contemporaries, dismissed the Aggadot as unreliable, considering them an invention whose significance was primarily ethical. Azariah was of the opinion that the Aggadot could not be considered history

---

57 Cf. Giuseppe Veltri, *Renaissance Philosophy in Jewish Garb*, 97–128.
58 Cf. "Zur jüdischen und christlichen Wertung der Aggada," in my *Gegenwart der Tradition. Studien zur jüdischen Literatur und Kulturgeschichte* (Leiden: Brill, 2001): 264–279.
59 William G. Braude, "Maimonides' Attitude towards Midrash," in *Studies in Jewish Bibliography, History and Literature in Honor of I.E. Kiev*, ed. Charles Berlin (New York: Ktav, 1971): 75–82; see also my article: "Zur jüdischen und christlichen Wertung der Aggada," *Frankfurter Judaistische Beiträge* 22 (1995): 61–75, which is now in my book *Gegenwart der Tradition. Studien zur jüdischen Literatur und Kulturgeschichte* (Leiden: Brill, 2002): 264–282.
60 Cf. Hyam Maccoby, *Judaism on Trial. Jewish-Christian Disputations in the Middle Ages* (Oxford: Littman, 1982).
61 Hans Schreckenberg, *Die christlichen Adversus-Judaeos-Texte (11.–13. Jh.)* (Frankfurt: Lang, 1991), 186.

and ought not to be taken literally [62] since they consisted of "fabricated conjectures." His opinion, however, was reached through a comparison of pagan, Christian, and Jewish sources. One of the most famous examples that he cites as proof that the Aggadah is a fabrication is its treatment of the death of the Emperor Titus. The Aggadah, which regards Titus as deserving of punishment for the destruction of the Temple, attributes his death to a mosquito that had entered his nose and bored into his brain after the First Jewish Roman War. The Babylonian Talmud claims that the insect had grown to the size of a bird in the seven years in which it was there. The creature was found during the autopsy that Titus himself had ordered. Azariah disputed this myth/fairy tale, not only on the grounds of its physiological impossibility, but also—and this was something new—on the basis of non-Jewish descriptions of the death of Emperor Titus occurring because of a fever, possibly malaria (which as we know stills had a certain connection with the deadly insect).[63]

In the sixth section of his *Be'er ha-Golah*, the Maharal deals with the criticism of rabbinical literature formulated in scholarly circles that the Sages had hardly any idea or knowledge of the human sciences. Although the Sages were, in their intellectual focus, not so far away from the sciences, they spoke about them as if they were completely foreign pursuits. The criticism was even more scathing: the scholars alleged that the rabbis had attributed completely inaccurate causes to natural occurrences. The Maharal replied that the critics had failed to recognise the truth. What they regarded as the cause was merely the visible, i.e. natural reality. This could satisfy only physicists and mathematicians, but not the Sages. The latter had spoken of supernatural causes, *causa causarum* (*sibbat ha-sibbot*). It may be interesting to note that the interpretation of biblical texts as "jumping" quickly to the *causa causarum* was already elaborated upon by Maimonides (*Moreh* II, 48).

The Maharal saw Azaria's ideas as contrary to Jewish tradition; thus, he sharply attacked them in the sixth chapter of his apology of Judaism, "Fountain of Exile" (*Be'er ha-Golah*), which appeared in 1600:

> I would have already ended what I had to say, if a book from someone belonging to our people had not reached my hands. I was told that the book contained some new ideas. When I saw it, I was very pleased, as a bridegroom is very pleased when he looks at his bride. While reading it, however, my heart broke and my spirit poured out in my insides. Woe unto the eyes that have seen it! Woe unto the ears that have heard such words! Cursed be the day that these things were published and made known! A man who is not in a position to understand the words of the Sages, not even one of the most minor points, much less the deeper ones? How does he dare to speak out against them and to discuss with them as if they were men of his generation or even his fellows?

---

[62] See Joanna Weinberg, "The Me'or 'Enayim of Ayariah de' Rossi: A Critical Study and Selected Translations" (PhD dissertation, Oxford University, 1982), 219.
[63] Joanna Weinberg, "Me'or 'Enayim," 224; see also my article: "Wertung der Aggada," 73 and following.

2.2 Three Sceptical Strategies: De' Rossi, the Maharal, and Sforno

First, note the erotic language applied to reading a book.[64] There is, of course, a Biblical reference to the delusion and disappointment of the bridegroom in seeing his bride for the first time (Jacob and Leah, for example). The comparison of a book to one's spouse is a familiar one.[65] Yet, the erotic comparison cannot hide the fact that the attack refers less to the disappointment caused by reading a book (because it did not satisfy his expectation) but rather to the fact that the author belongs to "our people" and, in his opposition to the sayings of the sages, finds the "support of worldly and idolatrous writings." The Maharal vehemently denies any alleged supremacy of the new scholarly disciplines over the rabbinical authorities. In his view, even the mere mention of foreign authorities was to be rebuked:

> Each generation has its scholars, each its sages. Have we had anything to compare with them? If you look attentively at them, you will find that the *Amora'im* did not contradict their predecessors (*rishonim*), the *Tanna'im*. Also the successors of the *Amora'im* did not contradict them, being well aware of their worth. Indeed, those who follow are not the equals of those who have lived earlier, who were close to the Prophets. And now, in our generation, which is characterized by imperfection and stupidity, someone stands up and speaks out against the holy ones who lived more than a millennium before us, saying: 'Observe my method and be wise!' In several places, he has drawn upon the support of worldly and idolatrous writings and treated the words of our sacred Sages, who were faithful to God, as trivial and inconsistent speeches.

The ideas that the Maharal would obviously like to combat are contained in Azaria's work:[66]

> [...] Moreover, there is a second thing [to take into account], which is a matter of course for every honest person, and that is, that what is found in their [the Rabbis'] works about science, e.g. astrology, the form of heaven and earth, comes entirely from their human comprehension. For they devoted themselves to their inquiries, each according to his intellectual gifts or on the basis of what he received as tradition from the Sages of the preceding generations, from whatever nation. All this occurred with the gifts of the Prophets or their help. In this area [of science] we are permitted, with their consent, to listen to those who wrote against them and to investigate the issues according to our knowledge. [...] Truly, after what the predecessors (*rishonim*) accomplished has come (down) to the descendants (*aharonim*) and gone beyond what they (the descendants) themselves achieved, does it not seem that the parable of the dwarf riding on the shoulders of giants applies to these very attainments, a parable that the author of the *Shibbole ha-Leqet* mentions in the name of an ancient Sage in his introduction? In this way one can rightfully claim that the superiority, which the First possess over the Last with respect to prophecy—because they were closer to the Prophets—corresponds to that which the Last possess over the First in the newly sprouting branch of science and experimentation.

---

64 On the erotics of reading see Michael McKeon, "Literary and Graphic Images of Intimacy in Seventeenth and Eighteenth-Century England," *Interfaces* 28 (2008): 95–114.
65 Cf. Maria L. Radosav, "The Metaphor of the Book. The Hebrew Book and its Perception in the Jewish Communities of North Transylvania," in *Essays in Honor of Moshe Idel*, ed. Sandu Frunza and Mihaela Frunza (Cluj-Napoca: Editura Provopress, 2008): 243–252.
66 *Me'or 'Enayim*, Imre Bina 14, ed. David Cassel, 196.

Azariah clearly gives us to understand that in his study of the past he foregrounds the principle of individual judgment. He is a scholar who refers to the achievements of scientific analysis. Thus, his work is an echo of the *Querelle des anciens et des modernes*,[67] which took place during the Renaissance, despite, or probably precisely because of, the cult of reverence for Antiquity. Following the aphorism of Bernard of Chartres, he also states that we are "dwarfs on the shoulders of giants," (*nos quasi nani super humeros gigantum*) and that, although our predecessors are greater than we, we can see farther.[68]

The hermeneutical and epistemological value of the aphorism lies less in the acknowledgment of the grandeur of its predecessors than in the height of the point of view, in the narrowest meaning of the expression. Paradoxically, the dwarfs are better equipped than the giants.[69] That is the first epistemological observation which provoked the sharp reaction of the Maharal for its "arrogance" to belittle the wisdom of the ancient sages. If Azariah is firmly convinced that the rabbinical Aggadah "comes entirely from their human comprehension," then he is proverbially biting the hand which feeds him. For there is no longer a chain of tradition but only a void of knowledge between the Revelation and the present, filled by the science of the Gentiles. Azariah introduces a *tertium comparationis* by weakening the Jewish past. That is the core of the problem.

The Maharal draws the attention of his reader to the main point in question, i.e. the methodology: "Someone stands up and speaks out against the holy ones who lived more than a millennium before us, saying: 'Observe my method and be wise!'" The question of the method will be the core of the philosophy of the seventeenth century, the method of obtaining knowledge as a clear and distinct idea; a clear idea in the logical exposition compared to mathematics, astronomy and geometry; a distinct idea accepted by the other scholars, as are the sciences of the Gentiles. Yet, the results of modern sciences are commonly considered in opposition with the teachings of the Sages.

The Maharal knows that "words of our sacred Sages" are plainly not in agreement with the sciences; however, the sages were "faithful to God," and God cannot delude his people without putting at risk the foundations of the Revelation, a conclusion which therefore could not be endorsed by a Renaissance man. That means

---

67 Cf. Hans Baron, "Querelle of Ancients and Moderns," in *Renaissance Essays*, ed. Paul Kristeller and Philip W. Weiner (New York: Harper and Row, 1968): 95–114.
68 Cf. Forster E. Guyer, "The Dwarf on the Giant's Shoulders," *Modern Language Notes* 45 (1930): 398–402; Robert K. Merton, *On the Shoulders of Giants. A Shandean Postscript* (New York: Free Press, 1965); Edouard Jeauneau, "'Nani gigantum humeris insidentes': Essai d'interpretation de Bernard de Chartres," *Vivarium* 5 (1967): 79–99. Abraham Melamed, *On the Shoulders of Giants: A History of the Debate between Moderns and Ancients in Medieval and Early Modern Jewish Thought* [Hebrew] (Ramat Gan: Bar-Ilan University, 2003); David Faleck, "Immovable Giants? Rabbinical Approaches to Science and Jewish Law," *Kedma* 3 (2007): np.
69 Cf. Jacob Teicher, "Il principio 'Veritas filia temporis' presso Azaria de' Rossi," *Rendiconti della reale Accademia Nazionale dei Lincei. Classe Morali, Storiche e Filologiche* 6, no. IX (1933): 268–275.

that the reader must locate the cause of the discordance between rabbinical stories and modern sciences. If the profane sciences, where we can use them, contradict the texts of the Sages, then it is our fault, according to the Maharal. We have to search for the alleged contradiction, for an accounting of the discrepancy that incorporates a meta-level capable of integrating the truth of the past with the truth of modern sciences.

The argument of the Maharal is similar to the conclusion of Thomas Kuhn on modern science developing the theory of paradigms and revolution.[70] A revolutionary theory can be of lasting significance only if it includes all the evidence of former investigations, providing an explanation for all of them. The Maharal's view is to include all the literary/aggadic past of Judaism in the explanation of reality, although a plain meaning of their contents (with relevance for sciences and history) is not possible.

The famous example is the aforementioned legend about Titus: the Maharal claims that Azariah has not understood anything. The story is the expression of a deeper science. *Of course* the Sages do not speak of a mosquito in the *physical* sense, rather about the force that penetrated Titus' brain. Titus, the destroyer of the Temple, the arch-villain of Jewish history who wanted to drive a wedge between God and Israel, was vanquished by one of the smallest creatures of Divine Creation. Note the Maharal's concessive sentence: although the plain meaning is not true, the verity of the story is to be trusted. We are miles away from the PaRDeS, the medieval teaching of the four senses of the Scriptures, because the plain or the literal meaning (*sensus literalis*, *Peshat*) is not to be considered as a historical account. The only extant meaning is the intention of the sages, the real meaning, and the cause of the causes.

Doubts as to the reliability of Antiquity would destroy the holistic nature of the system of the tradition that was based on the assumption that the Revelation had taken place once and was intended for all eternity. For this reason, the rabbinical authorities are not to be reproached nor are their utterances to be decried as mere worldly wisdom. The search for the "real meaning" or, as the Maharal expresses it, the *sibbat ha-sibbot* (*causa causarum*), should be the task of exegetes. The fact that rabbinical sayings are occasionally rejected due to their alleged incompatibility with reason only means that people have not understood the logic of the tradition. The truth always lies beyond the *sibbah qerovah* (*causa proxima*), the literal meaning. It is hidden.

To explain this meaning, Rabbi Löw cites an example from the Babylonian Talmud, tractate *Sukkah* 29a:

> Eclipses of the sun occur for four reasons: because a head of the Sanhedrin (*Av Bet Din*) was not properly eulogized; because of the lack of aid to a betrothed maiden who has cried out for help in the city when she was about to be raped; because of homosexuality; because of the simulta-

---

[70] Thomas Kuhn, *The Structure of Scientific Revolutions* (Chicago: University of Chicago Press, 1962).

neous murder of two brothers. Eclipses of the moon and sun are also due to four reasons: because of those who falsify records (or signatures); because of those who allow false witnesses to step forward; because of those who breed small animals in the land of Israel; because of those who chop down trees in good condition.

These causes of eclipses of celestial bodies named by the Rabbis according to their knowledge are rejected by human understanding (ha-ḥush ha-nigleh). For it is known that eclipses of celestial bodies depend on the paths of these bodies, on their conjunction and opposition, on their remoteness or closeness, on their length or width. Thus, how can they say that eclipses depend on such things when we know the exact point of time based on a calculation? How is it that the Rabbis want to make these things dependent on certain sins? The question is put wrongly. For it was not in the interest of the Rabbis to determine the causa proxima (ha-sibba ha-qerovah)—for it is a truism that eclipses of celestial bodies are influenced by their paths—but they named the *causa causorum*. If there was no sin in the world there would be no eclipses of celestial bodies. For there is no doubt that the eclipse of a celestial body is an imperfection and a flaw in the universe. If there were no sin, the order of creation would not permit eclipses to happen, because they constitute an imperfection and a flaw in the universe, as everyone realises.

The core of the discussion is that the perfect universe and world was a paradisiacal condition destroyed by sin. The Rabbi plays on the word *lqh*, at first as the *terminus technicus* for eclipses of the sun and celestial bodies and then as a verb and noun meaning "fault," "defect," and "punishment."[71] The answer to the question why certain sins cause eclipses of the sun and celestial bodies exceeds the limits of human understanding, the Maharal affirms. Only the Rabbinic comprehension permits a look into the relationship between celestial events and human conduct.

A very similar position is taken by the Maharal in his interpretation of the episode of Joshua[72] and the miracle of the sun.[73] The opposition between the evidence of the sun and its (alleged) orbit and the biblical text about its standing is still evident. The motionless presence of the sun is not scientifically proven. The miracle rests not in its staying still in general but rather in its stopping only for Joshua and those who required miracles. The others, who did not need miracles, "experienced the natural course" of the sun.

In this way, the Maharal reaffirms the main concern of his studies, namely to prove that the knowledge of the rabbis is on a different plane than that of the scholars of the world. Mentioning (Christian) sages in connection with rabbinical literature is therefore inappropriate.

Philological developments and scientific discoveries are rightly considered coordinates of the interpretative world of the Renaissance and the early modern period.

---

[71] The theory of a connection between sins and atmospheric events is very old. Hesiod maintains that famines and infectious diseases exist because of the sins of a specific evil person or persons (*Erga*, 240–245); on this connection, see Giuliana Lanata, *Medicina magica e religione popolare in Grecia fino all'età di Ippocrate* (Rome: Edizioni dell'Ateneo, 1967), 30–31.
[72] Tamar Ross, "The Miracle as an Added Dimension in the Thought of the Maharal of Prague" [Hebrew] *Daat* 17 (1986): 81–96; Benno Gross, "Faith and Trust in the Maharal's Teaching" [Hebrew] *Sinai* 101 (1988): 138–147; Ruderman, *Jewish Thought*, 78–79.
[73] Cf. Maharal, *Gevurot ha-Shem* (New York: Judaica Press 1969), 17 and following.

2.2 Three Sceptical Strategies: De' Rossi, the Maharal, and Sforno

Philology was at first an art of discerning the better edition of a text and of historically determining the origin of a tradition, while scientific discoveries found many problems in the interpretation of the revealed text because of the faults, errors, mistakes, and incongruities of the ancient authors.

Renaissance philology and the methodology of the sciences have something in common:[74] They are both searching for evincible proof of the fact or of the text. The Protestant priority of the text over tradition (explanation, authority, etc.) takes the philological search for the original text into account, at least the reformer had the intention of incorporating that search. Going back to the Hebrew original was a pre-condition. Returning to the sources of revelation, the *ad fontes*, was the fundamental feature of Humanism and, of course, of the Renaissance. The tendency to go back to the sources did not hide the fact that the methodology sat outside the traditional interpretation of Scriptures. For Protestant theology, the text must possess an unambiguous meaning, an original significance. The Reformers of Wittenberg introduced the concept of the literal meaning as one of absolute historical value. Their aim was not only to follow the Humanist preoccupation with original truth and texts but also and primarily to reach a state of certainty beyond the corruption of history.

Furthermore, the new sciences were searching for a new literal interpretation of the Creation, for a language caring for the real understanding of the figures and the characters of the letters which compose the universe. As Galileo Galilei puts it,

> Philosophy is written in this grand book, the universe, which stands continually open to our gaze. But the book cannot be understood unless one first learns to comprehend the language and read the letters in which it is composed. It is written in the language of mathematics, and its characters are triangles, circles, and other geometrical figures without which it is humanly impossible to understand a single word of it.[75]

Galileo displays an interesting point of view in conceiving of the building of the universe as language, as a precise shape which can be understood as basis of the "language of mathematics, and its characters are triangles, circles, and other geometrical figures." Galileo is also searching for the language with which one can read and interpret the whole universe, the *sibbat ha-sibbot* or, mathematically, the *figura figurarum* that explains the universe.

The most intriguing aspect of the controversy between the Maharal and Araziah de' Rossi lies in the fact that both of them refused to accept the literal meaning of the Aggadah. They maintained that, first and foremost, the literal meaning misguides the real, proper meaning of the text either because it is dependent on the common

---

[74] Cf. Charles P. Snow, *The Two Cultures and the Scientific Revolution* (Cambridge: Cambridge University Press, 1959).
[75] Galileo Galilei, *The Assayer*, in *Discoveries and Opinions of Galileo*, trans. Stillman Drake (New York: Anchor, 1957), 237 and following: quoted by Peter Harrison, "Fixing the Meaning of Scripture: The Renaissance Bible and the Origins of Modernity" *Concilium* 294 (2002): 102–110.

knowledge of the world in which the authors were living (Azaria) or because it is only a superficial dimension of the complex entity of meaning (the Maharal). The real meaning extends beyond its literal sense. We have to carefully read the abundantly literal and almost always polemical text of the Maharal, which constantly speaks of literal and hidden meanings[76] that have little to do with Kabbalistic speculation, as some authors maintain. While the literal sense, the plain meaning, can be regarded as "far-fetched by ordinary human standards,"[77] the hidden meaning is the sign of a hidden science that can be reached only through divine (i.e. non-human) knowledge. The error of Azariah (but also of his teacher Maimonides) was—according to the Maharal—to have considered the teaching of the Sages as human knowledge.

Yet, both Azariah de' Rossi (as well as Maimonides) and the Maharal are critically engaged in rejecting the text as it is written. In some ways, they are both rejecting the literal meaning because they do not accept as a truth the pure meaning of the text as it is: according to Azariah, because the Aggadot are not Halakhah, but "invented suppositions,"[78] and, according to the Maharal, because the text of the Aggadah is only a reference to a deeper (ethical) meaning. The difference between them is "only" that for Azariah de' Rossi the Aggadot are "fictitious inventions," originating in the cultural environment of the rabbis, while the Maharal sees in them a literary form intended to introduce the reader to the deeper layers of a profound science. For both of them—and this is a very intriguing aspect—the Aggadot have a moral value: according to Azariah, the Aggadah is morally used to implant "in the minds of the people the virtues which were the aim of their instructions."[79] According to the Maharal, the moral value of the episode of Titus is evident: whoever destroyed the temple of the God of the Jews, sowing division between them, merits a correspondingly harsh punishment.

The tendency to search beyond the text is nothing but a sceptical attitude towards the truth of the text. Concessive and parenthetical sentences such as "Yet, they did not mean it literally, of course not," or, more critically, "Only foolish people take it as it sounds," testify to the gap in meaning between the past and the present filled for Azariah by some information acquired through the reading the Sages of the Gentiles, whereas, in the Maharal's view, this gap is bridged by a de facto acknowledgement that the Sages did not mean what they wrote. For the Maharal, the text has an eternal meaning (mostly of ethical value) which lies beyond the literal meaning; for Azariah the text of the Aggadah has a meaning which is dependent on the understanding of the Rabbi, relying on the *veritas temporis*.

The question of whether the past as history, revelation, and text has a meaning at all is the main occupation in/of the Renaissance and the early modern period. The

---

[76] Cf. Jacob Elbaum, "Rabbi Judah Loew of Prague and His Attitude to the Aggadah," *Scripta Hierolomitana* 22 (1971): 28–47.
[77] *Be'er ha-Golah*, 49.
[78] Joanna Weinberg, "The Me'or 'Enayim of Azariah de' Rossi," 222; and *Me'or 'Enayim*, 210.
[79] Ibid., 225.

answer is only a commitment to the past of the revelation ending with the *credo quia obscurum,* not *absurdum:* the Renaissance man believed that the past has a meaning that the modern scholar has to investigate. Yet, the question is whether, after investigating the sources of the past, we can trust them as reliable. We can adopt the story of the mosquito and Titus as an explanation of this "dangerous" tendency, i.e. the spirit of a sceptical search for the truth can be dangerous and destroy the foundations of the faith. Azariah de' Rossi tried to find the real essence of tradition in the Halakah, because the plain meaning of the Aggadah is not reliable while the Maharal explained that every story is apparently inconsistent because it refers to the essence which is behind the plain meaning. Logically, he infers that the plain meaning has no apparent meaning.

The Maharal's attack against the "new" methodology of Azariah de' Rossi might be rooted in a quasi-Socratic approach to the sciences as it requires a perception of ignorance and leads to an understanding of the characteristic of truth as an esoteric doctrine. The perception of ignorance is an aspect of the *theologia negativa* of which, for example, Maimonides (but above all Crescas) was a preeminent exponent. A century earlier, Nicolas of Cusa expressed the central idea of sceptical thinking in his famous *De docta ignorantia:* knowledge is only pure knowledge if it is without comprehension (*visio sine comprehension*). Put another way, sceptical thinking is speculation because we cannot (fully) comprehend the knowledge we acquire.

Although the Maharal of Prague is notoriously an opponent of the philosopher Maimonides, he claims the same approach to real/hidden truth, for he shares Maimonides' elitist conception of knowledge that few people can understand the real meaning of the tradition. The Maharal speaks openly of a measure of divine revelation to hide the real meaning in order "to prevent wisdom becoming something to be trodden underfoot by every ignoramus, for that would be the opposite of wisdom."[80] The Maharal admits that the plain text (at least that of the Aggadot) has a far-fetched meaning, abstruse to common understanding, while it has a real, hidden meaning known (only) to the Sages. If we consequently acknowledge that the present generation is ignorant *per definitionem*—for we are extremely distant from the sources of knowledge—we have to accept the conclusion that the truth is inaccessible. The consequence of the Maharal's philosophy is a pure scepticism about human knowledge in approaching the text and tradition of the Revelation. His position is very similar to the Italian scholar Judah Moscato, who lived before him. We do not have any proof that the Maharal read his sermons, but we cannot exclude the possibility.

---

80 *Be'er ha-Golah* 87, translation of Jacob Elbaum, "Rabbi Loew," 36–37.

The Religious Scepticism of Judah Moscato

Judah Moscato is well-known as the author of a collection of sermons called *Nefuṣot Yehudah* (*The Dispersed of Judah*)[81] and of a commentary on Judah Halevi's *Sefer ha-Kuzari*, entitled *Qol Yehudah*.[82] *Nefuṣot Yehudah* belongs to the very core of his important oeuvre. Composed in Mantua and published in Venice in 1589, the collection of fifty-two sermons addresses the subject of Jewish festivals as a kind of liturgical platform for addressing issues in philosophy, theology, mysticism, culture, history, and other arguments important to the speaker and his audience. Moscato's philosophical positions stem from the rabbinical tradition, classical and contemporary authors, and Neoplatonic thought. He readily quotes non-Jewish authorities when they seem to confirm his positions, such as his use of Heraclitus in his sermon about the validity of the sciences, a topic of Renaissance philosophy and scepticism.

In Sermon XIV,[83] he addresses the topic of the validity of the human sciences.[84] He notes that this sermon "will magnify the Torah and glorify its essence as being superior to the seven arts, by making clear the latter's intrinsic deficiency" (XIV:1). Moscato will "show how vain[85] the human sciences are as long as they do not keep a covenant of concord with the divine Torah with respect to two differences [between them and the Torah]" (XIV:8).

The preacher of Mantua bases his argumentation on two premises: the first one concerns methodological meaning. The sciences prevent us from attaining truth in relation to the precious things (החכמות מקצרות מהשיג האמת בדרושים היקרים). He explains further,

> For while demonstration is found in most of the mathematical sciences, namely, geometry, arithmetic, music,[86] and to some extent also astronomy, the same does not apply to ethics or to physics, and even less so to metaphysics, [87]which is called "first philosophy" or "divine philosophy"

---

[81] Giovanni di Gara, Venice, 1589.
[82] Giovanni di Gara, Venice, 1594. Cf. Adam Shear, *The Kuzari and the Shaping of Jewish Identity, 1167–1900* (Cambridge: Cambridge University Press, 2008), 135–169.
[83] All of the quotations from Judah Moscato's main text and footnotes are taken from the edition and English translation, *Judah Moscato's Sermons*. Vol. Two, ed. Gianfranco Miletto and Giuseppe Veltri (Boston: Brill, 2012). For the first volume, see *Judah Moscato's Sermons*. Vol. One, ed. Gianfranco Miletto and Giuseppe Veltri (Boston: Brill, 2011).
[84] Here I am following the summary of Moscato's sermons which I cowrote with Gianfranco Miletto; This summary is primarily mine.
[85] The Hebrew verb *lehavhil* literally means "to emit steam" (or, in this context, "to turn into steam"). Yet here the expression is to be interpreted also in the light of the term *havel*, i.e. "vanity."
[86] In Italian or Latin in the text. For music, see the Sermon I in the first volume of Moscato's Sermons.
[87] Warren Zev Harvey notes, "See Maimonides, *Guide*, I:31: much perplexity exists in metaphysics, some in physics, none in mathematics."

by the philosophers. Surely mistakes are to be found in all of them, and particularly in metaphysics for, without a doubt, philosophers fall amazingly short of attaining the truth.[88]

The process explained here is the Neoplatonic or Plotinic pyramid, where the almost perfect sciences, mathematics, geometry etc. are at the beginning and metaphysics at the end of the chain of logical probability. Moscato illustrates it with a famous example taken from the Midrash Kohelet Rabbah 1:3:[89]

> [24] This provides a correct elucidation of the midrashic epigraph to our sermon. For the passage first posits how it is that *man*, in himself, when he relies solely on philosophizing, *is like unto steam*.[90] Then it explains the nature of the "steam" which it treats on the basis of the statement of Kohelet, *Steam of steams*, etc.,[91] by stating that there are the seven steams that lift up steam through the seven sciences. The subject of these sciences is likened to seven pots piled one on top of the other.[92] For the pot on the bottom melts the vapours and lifts up the steam through the power of the fire burning under it. But since the second pot lifts up steam by power of the vapours rising from the first pot, its steam is certainly diminished. The same holds true for the third pot in relation to the second, and thus it is for all the seven pots, each in relation to the one immediately below it. This extends up to the seventh pot, which, since it is very far removed from the fire; and because of the fact that the heat of the vapours that rise to it from the sixth pot is faint, it indeed cannot raise steam endowed with any substance.[93] [25] And lo, the same law also applies to the seven sciences. For each of them is sustained by another according to an ordering [like the one] we mentioned that proceeds from the mathematical sciences to the ethical [sciences], from the ethical [sciences] to the physical [sciences], and from the physical [sciences] to the divine [sciences]. Besides, the mathematical sciences are themselves sustained by one another, for geometry is sustained by arithmetic, and so is music, as [the calculation of] the intervals between its sounds requires; and astronomy is sustained by both geometry and arithmetic. Thus, mathematical sciences direct the intellect and accustom it to understanding and to intellection.

The Plotinic pyramid of the arts refers to the nature of human sciences and arts which are sustained by one another according to an inner ordering. They possess some truth, but not enough to reach and attain perfect knowledge. It should be noted that the doctrine of successive vapours or fumes induces the reader to conclude that there is a chain of logical inferences from the mathematical sciences to metaphysics. At the top of the chain (or at the bottom of the pots), there is mathemat-

---

88 Isaiah 50:2.
89 Rabbi Samuel ben Nahman taught in the name of Rabbi Joshua ben Korah. He wrote, "It may be likened to a man who sets on the fire seven pots, one on top of the other, and the steam from the topmost one has no substance in it" (*Kohelet Rabbah* 1:3). Translation from Christopher P. Benton, "In Search of Kohelet," *The Maqom Journal for Studies in Rabbinic Literature* V (2003). Online: http://www.maqom.com/journal/paper9.pdf (accessed 3, May 2018).
90 Psalms 144:4. The JPS translation has been modified to fit the context.
91 Ecclesiastes 1:2. The JPS translation is "Vanity of vanities."
92 *Kohelet Rabbah* 1:3.
93 Ibid.

ics, which can be considered an almost perfect science. I emphasise the adverb *almost*, i.e. not *entirely* perfect, for perfection is reserved solely for the Torah, with the help of which human beings may obtain their joyful purpose. The imperfection of mathematics rests in its abstract nature, while the natural sciences in their general meaning cannot be reliable because their subject is constantly changing, as Moscato states in Sermon XIV:7:

> You can see that mathematical sciences cannot provide suitable nourishment for the life and sustenance of the intellective soul because their subject depends solely on things that are envisioned in the intellect and do not exist outside of the soul, since the intellectually recognized objects are abstracted from matter, both ontologically and categorically.[94] For, such things do not exist and were not created. Nor can the natural sciences [provide suitable nourishment for the life and sustenance of the intellective soul], since they concern things that are constantly changing. Even the sciences that the philosophers call "divine"[95] cannot [provide suitable nourishment for the life and sustenance of the intellective soul], since speculation by means of them relies on farfetched estimates and very doubtful pretexts as their practitioners themselves admit.[96]

The claim of the profane sages (the object in Sermon XIV) is that the sciences and arts can help to obtain perfect knowledge. And that is the very question of the second error attributed by Moscato to the philosophers of sciences (XIV:27):

> [...] for by their philosophizing, philosophers will never attain any happy or joyful end. Even though they scheme about divine things, they will not raise steam endowed with any substance. That is, the cloud of incense of their soul shall never rise up[97] to the upper bliss of everlasting immortality, since the attainment of unitive conjunction (*devequt hitaḥedut*) with the Agent Intellect is prevented from them, even according to their own position, as has been said.

The postulation addressed here was explained at the beginning of Sermon XIV:10,

> And yet this conjunction has to be understood as a process of assimilation whereby one becomes like to Him through the attainment of all of the intellectually cognized objects. And this is impossible as Gersonides pointed out in his *Sefer ha-Milḥamot* (part I, chapter 12).[98] It is also stated in Kohelet: *All the things toil to weariness*, etc.[99] It is also said there: *Also He hath set the world in their heart, yet so that man cannot find out [the work that God hath done from the beginning even to the end]*.[100] This being the case, what is contingent on impossibility is impossible, wherefore they will never be able to make their soul enjoy the benefit of their labour.[101]

---

94 Literally, "in being and in definition."
95 I.e. metaphysics and theology.
96 Babylonian Talmud, *Bava Meṣiʻa* 3b; cf. *Sefer ha-Kuzari* 4:25.
97 Ezekiel 8:11.
98 Gersonides actually denies this theory in *Sefer Milḥamot ha-Shem* 1:4.
99 Ecclesiastes 1:8.
100 Ecclesiastes 3:11.
101 Ecclesiastes 2:24.

Moscato sees only one way to reach perfection: occupation with the Torah, the sure path to holiness, namely one's own "happy and joyful purpose" (XIV:21). The preacher of Jewish Mantua follows a perfectly constructed stylistic and rhetorical scheme which consists of constantly repeating a thesis as a refrain, adding more elements each time in order to confirm it. He quotes the Babylonian Talmud[102] to underscore the view that, if man relies only on himself, he cannot attain true knowledge. The latter is, of course, to be achieved by means of the study of the Torah.[103]

Regarding the fideist principle, he commits himself to a kind of argument which I would call "affirmative conviction." The only perfect science is the Torah, the only one capable of attaining felicity. And if there seems to be a contradiction with the natural sciences, it is due to defective human knowledge. Further, he quotes Solomon, traditionally the father of every science, who was able to gather together the sum of his great knowledge. He refers to Solomon and his seven names as an allusion to the seven arts, which Solomon declares void whenever they do not agree with and are not crowned by the Torah (XIV:70–73). Returning to his interpretation of the Midrash *Kohelet Rabbah* 1:3, Moscato comments (XIV:75):

> You have also heard my words concerning the explication of this passage with regard to the seven sciences that are organized one on top of the other until they reach the seventh one, which they call "divine," as it is the fruit of all of their speculation. And in the end, they give rise to a steam that has no substance. And all their wisdom will be swallowed if those who master them are not firmly grounded upon the foundations of the Torah.

The "divine" seventh art is of course the *philosophia prima*, addressed already in Sermon XIV:9: "[...] even less so to metaphysics, which is called 'first philosophy' or 'divine philosophy' by the philosophers. Surely mistakes are to be found in all of them, and particularly in metaphysics, for without a doubt, philosophers fall amazingly short of attaining the truth."[104] The *philosophia prima* or *divina* as a denomination of metaphysics delivers us back to the division of the sciences proposed among Arabic as well as Latin schools (Avicenna and Thomas). As a representative thinker in Western philosophy, it is useful here to recall Roger Bacon, who speaks of the *metaphysica* as *divina scientia*, *sapientia* and *philosophia prima*.[105] Moscato is of the opinion that the human sciences, because they have been produced by human thought, cannot grasp the Divine without conjunction with the divine intellect; that is an axiomatic position whose truth is notoriously taken for granted. The almost deductive conclusion is that they cannot *per definitionem* attain the truth. The sciences historically collect their knowledge from generation to generation (XIV:78) as a mirror of

---

102 Babylonian Talmud, *Bekhorot* 8b–9a.
103 Sermon XIV:34.
104 Isaiah 50:2.
105 *Quaestiones alterae supra libros primae philosophiae. Opera Hactenus Inedita Rogeri Baconi* 11 (Oxford: 1936), 30, in Ulrich Köpf, *Die Anfänge der theologischen Wissenschaftstheorie im 13. Jahrhundert* (Tübingen: Mohr, 1974), 231 and corresponding footnotes.

the natural order of nature, created in seven days by God (note the repetition of the number seven). Two elements of their nature speak against the seven arts as "(divine) science," for they are contingent (the factor of time) and related to the *natura creata* (the factor of space/matter in the creation).

Speaking of created nature (*natura creata*), it is obvious that Moscato is discussing here the trustfulness of the organs of perception, the senses, a chief argument of scepticism, dealt with some decades later by Luzzatto in detail. I will discuss Luzzatto in the fourth chapter. For Moscato, the point, in short, is that the senses are incapable of attaining truth:

> Nevertheless, *all things toil to weariness*, for [Fol. 70b] in there is great toil in attaining such things. *Man cannot speak*[106] by giving them a perfect definition because he cannot grasp its essence by means of their existence. This corresponds to the saying, *The eye is not satisfied with seeing*, since, indeed, knowledge commences with what the senses attain. *And there are ten parts belonging to*[107] the sense of sight, for it is able to determine several distinctions, more so than the other senses. And it does not depend on the study of that which is other than it. This is the meaning of that which is written: *Nor will the ear be filled with hearing.*[108] [80] These two senses[109] are mentioned because they are the most subtle and the most apt for the attainment of science; for [it is written] *the hearing ear, and the seeing eye, the Lord hath made even both of them.*[110] Their activity shall be related to the Creator of all, more than that of the other senses, since by means of them man reaches intellection, which is the most perfect activity for him. [This] accords with the elucidation put forward by the author of *Sefer 'Iqqarim*.[111]

If the senses are not adequate for the attainment of knowledge, he asks, "If the son of the king[112] had so weak a perception of natural things, which are to be attained through the senses, then what is to be done by the musk [that grows] on the wall,[113] who strives to reach the sublime things, which the senses cannot master in the least?" The impossibility of formulating any sure statement concerning reality is also confirmed by the philosopher Heraclitus (XIV:86), who is expressly mentioned by Moscato:

> [86] Do not keep your ears from hearing that which I am accustomed to interpret regarding some of the verses mentioned above, namely, that it was the opinion of the ancient philosopher Heraclitus[114] that one can make decisive statements concerning the truth of sensible objects only through things that are imagined and only through the appearance of things. [Heraclitus ex-

---

106 Ecclesiastes 1:8. The JPS translation has been modified to fit the context.
107 2 Samuel 19:44. The JPS translation has been modified to fit the context. The expression has an idiomatic meaning which could be rendered: "And the lion's part is played by [...]."
108 Ecclesiastes 1:8.
109 Viz. hearing and sight.
110 Proverbs 20:12.
111 Joseph Albo, *Sefer ha-'Iqqarim*, 3:2.
112 I.e. Solomon.
113 I.e. "the weak."
114 Judah Moscato writes the name in the Italian "Eraclito," though in Hebrew letters.

pressed this] by saying that everything flows at a uniform and constant velocity, and that there is nothing about which we can say: "That is x," for while one is still glancing at it, it is no longer that thing in its substance. [87] He explicitly said that something that is one in its substance cannot appear twice, and he even went so far as to state that it is impossible to indicate anything through speech. Thus he would indicate things by hinting at them with his finger, thinking that the motion of his finger would be faster than putting things into words. His heart urged him to say that if he were to begin to indicate something with his words, then while he was still speaking about it, that thing would pass and would change into something with a different nature, before he could complete a statement about it.

Aenesidemus had already interpreted Heraclitus as a proto-sceptic;[115] his scepticism was a *locus communis* in the Middle Ages[116] and was developed further in Humanism[117] and the Renaissance as the picture of Donato Bramante of the laughing philosophers (*Heraclitus flens: Democritus ridens*) shows.[118] Moscato appeals to Heraclitus in order to reinforce his stance against the validity of the sciences, contradicting himself because he affirms at the beginning that—following its metaphor of science/wisdom as pots—the first pot of the chain of steam is *on the fire:* according to the metaphor, the sciences are created through the fire of the (true) knowledge. How can we explain that everything is relative by quoting Heraclitus? His answer is as unambiguous as it is logically problematic:

> [90] Therefore, my heart lifted me up to think and to say that perhaps Solomon meant to allude to this opinion when he referred to mundane things and the human sciences that derive from them as the vanity of steams. For by saying, *All the rivers run into the sea, yet the sea is not* [Fol. 71a] *full; unto the place whither the rivers go, thither they go again*,[119] he alluded to the metaphor of the stream mentioned by that philosopher, who wanted to point out the course of all natural things and their constant change. [91] Afterwards, he referred to that image with *one language and one speech*[120] in accordance with the words of the philosopher that we have mentioned, when he said, *All things toil to weariness; man cannot utter it, the eye is not satisfied with seeing, nor the ear filled with hearing.*[121] And the meaning has been elucidated.

The metaphor of steam describes the volatile nature of the sciences, which cannot rest on eternal results because they change in time and space; they are constantly changing and are susceptible to weariness. The fire (of knowledge) is no longer a

---

115 Roberto Polito, *The Skeptical Road: Aenesidemus' Appropriation of Heraclitus* (Leiden: Brill, 2004).
116 Martin Pickavé, "Henry of Ghent and John Duns Scotus on Skepticism and the Possibility of Naturally Acquired Knowledge," in *Rethinking the History of Skepticism: The Missing Medieval Background*, ed. Henrik Lagerlund (Leiden: Brill, 2010): 61–96, 72.
117 Cf. Marcel Françon, "Petrarch, Disciple of Heraclitus," *Speculum* 11 (1936): 265–271.
118 Jill Pederson, "The Academia Leonardi Vinci: Visualizing Dialectic in Renaissance Milan 1480–1499" (PhD dissertation, Johns Hopkins Univiversity, 2007), 117–124.
119 Ecclesiastes 1:7.
120 Genesis 11:1.
121 Ecclesiastes 1:8.

focus because it does not fit in with his concept of philosophy. Quoting Genesis 11:1, Moscato suggests to the reader that he considers the alleged authority of the (new) sciences as an assault against the unity of God. That is, obviously, an apologetic argument that cannot explain why the sciences are the common heritage and achievement of the whole of humanity and for which reason revelation had to be added to them as the "core" of human science and knowledge.

Moscato's position is inherent in the system of fideist apologetics, which attacks the trustfulness of the sciences in its discourse (the logic of the pots and the vapours) and postulates another perfect language for revelation. The question is inherent in every revealed religion, which postulates a corrupt knowledge in order to justify an "added" doctrine that should supplant the core of the first one. The question is finally how to perceive a supplementary knowledge if the instrument of perception is corrupt. That is the problem of the trustfulness of the source of knowledge (the problem of authority), a question addressed by Simone Luzzatto (and later Baruch Spinoza).

The Venetian Rabbi Simone Luzzatto wrote his major work, *Socrate overo dell'humano sapere*, in 1651: it is a very important milestone in modern scepticism, and his detailed introduction to the question of human knowledge is a document of the Venetian reception of European scholarship.[122] However, before we engage with him, we must describe both the world of the Academy and of the Ghetto in order to encompass Venetian activity in this period.

---

[122] See my "Economic and Social Arguments and the Doctrine of the Antiperistasis in Simone Luzzatto's Political Thought: Venetian Reverberations of Francis Bacon's Philosophy?" *Frühneuzeit Info* 22 (2011): 23–32.

3 Spaces of Dialectic Exchange: The Academies and the Venetian Ghetto

Historical ghettos were limited spaces in which Jews were compelled to live. Much of the history of the Ghetto—its origin and spread across the whole of Europe, its political geography, its interaction with the ruling authorities, its inner life, and the impact of the exclusion on its environment—has been the object of a relatively large number of monographs, articles, and encyclopaedia entries.[1] Yet, up to the present, an intriguing aspect of its history has been almost completely unfamiliar to scholarship and therefore underestimated: the interaction between the academies of the sixteenth and seventeenth centuries and the Jews of the Ghetto. It's not just a simple deficiency in modern scholarship but a remarkable absence, because it is an important indicator of the cultural cooperation between two different social entities within a particular power dynamic: the ruling society that dictated the conditions of the seclusion and exclusion and the compelled group that was the victim of it. The question of how they could work together is both intriguing and the topic of this chapter.

It must be stressed that the state of subjection that the Jewish people experienced throughout the centuries obviously did not encourage cultural dialogue; however, it wasn't necessarily an impenetrable obstacle either. The only real obstacle was the impossibility of studying outside texts and traditions. As the Venetian rabbi Simone Luzzatto put it, although the Jews were notoriously in a state of subjection, they applied themselves to study, and it was this application which demonstrated their skill and industry. This study was possible because of the protection of the rulers, or, in his words,

> Certainly, the Jews, finding themselves in their present state of subjection and having no freedom whatsoever apart from applying their minds to study and doctrine, should devote themselves to these with all their skill and industry. They should be aware of the fact that the unity of dogmas, the patronage granted by the princes, and the protection from so much oppression were obtained over such a long period of time, humanly speaking, from the learning of a virtuous few. They acquired credibility and authority under those who ruled, since they were deprived of all other means for aspiring to the favours and graces of the great in any other way. [The Jews] should [therefore] rest assured that if they lacked the appreciation deriving from their command of humanist letters and the esteem of the virtuous, they would incur a considerable decline and a more despicable oppression than they have ever endured in the past.[2]

Luzzatto's description of the Jewish Ghetto as a source of cultural unity ("study and doctrine") in the midst of the Christian society is a novelty in the landscape of Jewish self-definition. Yet in Italy, Jews attempted to participate in the cultural life of their

---

[1] For example, see the article "Ghettos" on the website for the *United States Holocaust Memorial Museum*, https://www.ushmm.org/collections/bibliography/ghettos (accessed 3 May 2018).
[2] Simone Luzzatto, 85v.

environment, coming into dialogue with it and contributing to its scientific, philosophical, literary, and theological discourse. An illustration of this underestimated aspect is the relationship of Jewish intellectuals to the Italian academies: a phenomenon, cultural performance, and study that originated in the sixteenth century and reached its climax in the seventeenth century.

3.1 Italian Academies and Scepticism

Scepticism is an attitude to life that correspondingly implies the freedom to enquire into the root of knowledge; therefore, it requires a space to develop new theories as well as counter-theories. This space is necessary because sceptical thinking has often been regarded as dangerous to social and political stability and was hence heavily suppressed. That is the reason why the only location in seventeenth-century Italy where scepticism was relatively possible was in Venice, where there was some resistance to the politics of Roman Catholic Church and its Inquisition;[3] there was private initiative for creating cultural, artistic, religious, and philosophical circles and the academies proliferated.[4] These academies were among the institutions that featured strongly in the intellectual atmosphere of the Renaissance and Baroque in Italy in general and Venice in particular.[5] There were intellectual circles that gathered periodically in order to share their common interests and opinions about language, literature, art, philosophy, and theatre. The history of these institutions was retraced in the eighteenth century by Giacinto Gimma, an erudite man of letters from Bari, who in 1723 dated the origin of the academies back to Humanism and the Renaissance.[6] From Gimma's description, a typical and intriguing feature of the academies comes to light: the custom and convention of taking another name on the point of entering the academy. These new and sometimes pompous names were like masks that academy members used to wear.

---

[3] That is a *quaestio disputata*, at least for the Spanish Inquisition. Cf. Michael Alpert, *Crypto-Judaism and the Spanish Inquisition* (New York: Palgrave, 2001), 203: "The rise of the New Christians, often Judaizers, in Spanish society, coincided with the age of expansion, the maritime and commercial triumph of England and Holland, and the beginning of religious and scientific scepticism. Contrary to what is often asserted, the Inquisition did not isolate Spain completely from new currents of thought, nor did it destroy on principle characteristics which favoured economic expansion."

[4] For the Italian academies are still valuable; see the volumes of Michele Maylender, *Storia delle accademie d'Italia*, vol. 1, Abbagliati-Centini. vol. 2, Certi-Filotomi (Bologna: L. Cappelli Edit. Tip., 1926–1927); for the Venetian academies see Michele Battagia, *Delle Accademie Veneziane: Dissertazione storica* (Venice: G. Orlandelli, 1826).

[5] Cf. Giuseppe Veltri and Evelien Chayes, *Oltre le Mura del Ghetto: Accademie, Scetticismo e Tolleranza nella Venezia Barocca* (Palermo: New Digital Frontiers, 2016). See also the recent European project on the Italian Academies: "Italian Academies. British Library," http://www.bl.uk/catalogues/ItalianAcademies/GeneralBibliography.aspx (accessed 3 May, 2018).

[6] Giacinto Gimma, *Idea della storia della Italia letterata*, vol. 2 (Napoli: Felice Mosca, 1723), 459.

The study of the history of the academies very soon becomes a journey through the formation of a cultural mentality that has several features and extraordinary implications. I shall therefore list the most important ones:

- The humanistic sense of the *restauratio* of classical heritage and of its imitation. Gimma explains that the first model of the academy dates back to Cardinal Basilio Bessarione, who brought many Greek books to Venice and gathered several specialists in order to translate and study them. His library would later form the core of the Biblioteca Marciana;
- Distancing themselves from the universities controlled by the State and/or by the Church. Academies were born out of boredom with university teaching in law, for example;
- Academies were free spaces, like Boccaccio's *loci amoeni*, where it was possible to discuss all kinds of disciplines and liberal arts;
- Academy members used to change their names. This is a very intriguing feature, since in the fifteenth and sixteenth centuries it occurred mainly on two occasions: conversion or admission into a religious order. Although many academy members would choose their names from amongst those of Greek and Latin authors, some of these names were the product of their creative imaginations. In doing so, they were adopting masks not unlike those used in the theatre (which often interested the same thinkers).

If in the Italian territory, the academies were becoming more widespread wherever a group of intellectuals and a noble or ecclesiastical patron could be found, in Venice[7] they were an outstanding success, enabled by the tolerant atmosphere and the absence of any direct influence of the Inquisition, as was often the case elsewhere.

The *Accademia dei Dubbiosi*[8] was a noteworthy case. It was founded by Fortunato Martinengo in 1551 and closed when he died in 1554. Among its members were women, too, for example the poet Gaspara Stampa. This Academy shows the peculiar aspect of "doubt," doubting just about anything but above all else authority on questions of morality, dogmas, etc. There existed a list of the "doubts," according the re-

---

[7] I thank Warren Zev Harvey for his contribution to this section. He adds: "Isaac Abrabanel compared Venice to Jerusalem: 'the republic of Venice, the great dame among the nations, and princess among the provinces' (cf. Lamentations 1:1 כאלמנה רבתי בגוים שרתי במדינות). See Harvey's: "Anarchism, Egalitarianism, and Communism in Isaac Abrabanel," in *Al Da'at ha-Qahal*, Jubilee Volume in Honor of Aviezer Ravitzky, ed. Yosef Stern, Benjamin Brown, Avinoam Rosenak, and Menachem Lorberbaum (Jerusalem: Shazar Center, 2012): 213–229.

[8] Marco Faino, "Fortunato Martinengo, Girolamo Ruscelli e l'Accademia dei Dubbiosi tra Brescia e Venezia," in *Girolamo Ruscelli dall'accademia alla corte alla tipografia. Atti del Convegno internazionale di studi, Viterbo, 6–8 ottobre 2011*, ed. Paolo Marini and Paolo Procaccioli, vol. 2, (Manziana: Vecchiarelli, 2012): 455–519; Marco Faino, "A Ghost Academy between Venice and Brescia: Philosophical Scepticism and Religious Heterodoxy in the Accademia dei Dubbiosi," in *The Italian Academies 1525–1700. Networks of Cultre, Innovation and Dissent*, ed. Jane E. Everson, Denis V. Reidy, and Lisa Sampson (Cambridge: Legenda, 2016): 102–115.

port published in 1552 by Giolito de Ferrara.⁹ This list included many questions concerning morality, sexuality, and love, which was a typical topic of discussion during the Renaissance and early modern period (i.e. the phenomenon of the libertinism). The questions addressed are of such a variegated and, at times, arbitrary nature that they suggest the typical character of a play that illustrates human nature as afflicted by troubles and doubts at the same time that it is capable of resolving them; at least, this is what the title of Giolito's *Quattro libri* suggests. Nevertheless, these academic exercises suggest that a sceptical, or at least critical, atmosphere was present. The certainties of former centuries are missing and doubt, or at least an enquiry into the doubtful world of culture, religion, science, and morality, was at work.

It is not possible to trace and prove a historical link in the continuity of the tradition of the sceptical *Accademia dei Dubbiosi*. However, it is certain that the *Accademia degli Incogniti*,[10] founded in 1630 by the patrician Giovanni Francesco Loredano,[11] harboured ideas that were very close to classical and Renaissance scepticism. The Academy was mainly influenced by the Aristotelian Cesare Cremonini, who succeeded Jacopo Zabarella as the chair of philosophy and medicine in Padua. He was a materialist and to the same extent likewise an atheist; he also invoked the authority of Aristotle and Galileo against the Inquisition. Following Pomponazzi, Cremonini was of the opinion that reason cannot demonstrate the immortality of the soul, and that the active intellect cannot conjoin with the Agent Intellect because it is prevented from doing so by human nature in its materiality, a view much debated in his time. Some members[12] of the *Academia degli Incogniti* were also members of Jewish academies, as we will discuss in the case of the academy of Sara Copio Sullam below.

3.2 Jewish Academies

The spirit of the academies also penetrated and imbued the Italian Jewish culture of the Renaissance and Baroque period; it found there a very fertile ground because of the importance of teaching and education in rabbinic academies (*Yeshivot*). In fact, the education and training of children in the study of the Torah is part and parcel of Jewish culture. Teaching was mainly restricted to boys; at the moment, we do not

---

9 Ortensio Lando, *Quattro libri de dubbi con le solutioni a ciascun dubbio accommodate. La materia del primo è naturale, del secondo è mista (benché per lo più sia morale) del terzo è amorosa, & del quarto è religiosa* (Venice: Giolito de Ferrari, 1552).
10 Michele Battagia, *Delle accademie Veneziane: Dissertazione storica* (Venice: Orlandelli, 1826), 42–43; cf. Girolamo Brusoni and Giovanni Francesco Loredan, *Le glorie de gli incogniti o vero gli huomini illustri dell'Accademia de' Signori incogniti di Venetia* (Venice: Francesco Valuasense, 1647).
11 See the Bibliography in Ellen Rosand, *Opera in Seventeenth-Century Venice: The Creation of a Genre* (Berkeley: University of California Press, 1991).
12 Concerning music, cf. Ellen Rosand, *Opera in Seventeenth-Century Venice*, 37–40.

have reliable data concerning the education of women because research in this field is only just beginning.

The *yeshivah* (pl. *yeshivot*, Aramaic *metibta*, pl. *metibata*) was a typical Jewish institution.[13] The most renowned *metibata* were based in Babylonia, namely in Sura and Pumbedita. The beginnings of these institutions are still a matter of debate. Thus they must have been deeply rooted in Jewish tradition. Nonetheless, these schools/academies were not an exception. On the contrary, the Christian school/university of Nisibis was a "sister-institution,"[14] as was also the case for the philosophical and medical academies in Late Antiquity that were closed by Emperor Justinian in 529.

I will not attempt to provide a detailed discussion of the Jewish educational system. I will, however, point out that Jewish schools and academies based in Italy during the Renaissance tried to enhance and develop an educational programme based on openness to the non-Jewish surrounding culture. Accordingly, they introduced the liberal arts (*trivium* and *quadrivium*) into the academic curriculum. This programme was not very successful: it was adopted and spread only by the *Wissenschaft des Judentums* started by Leopold Zunz during the Enlightenment and Romanticism.

I have spoken of the *Yeshivot* and I have called them academies, but they should of course be kept separate from the academies the Jews established and attended during the Renaissance. The *Yeshivot* aimed to educate prospective rabbis, while these academies were the places where research and imitation of the past could be pursued. The universities where State and Church officials were educated and formed are the real innovation of the Renaissance. Simone Luzzatto described the task and the aim of these institutions in his *Socrate* (1651).

Although Simone Luzzatto was aware of the difference between the academy and the university—the universities were institutions created to teach future clerics and lawyers (in Judaism, rabbis)—he confused them at the end of the *Discorso*, 90v:

> In the Holy Land, and in particular Jerusalem, not only do a great number of Jews from all the countries of the earth arrive annually, they are also provided with a very great sum of annual revenue in order to maintain the poor and sustain academies. In Imperial Germany, there are a great number of them, but there are many more in Poland, Russia, and Lithuania. There are academies and universities for thousands of young people that are trained in civil law and the canon law of the Jews, since those regions allow the free judgement of all differences and controversies, both civil and criminal, that occur within the Nation.

Many Jewish intellectuals were attracted by the academies because of the spirit that inspired them and not because of their similarities to *Yeshivot*. There were few Jewish

---

13 Michael Sokoloff, *A Dictionary of Jewish Babylonian Aramaic of the Talmudic and Geonic Periods* (Baltimore: Johns Hopkins University Press; Ramat-Gan: Bar-Ilan University Press, 2002), 720–721.
14 Cf. Adam H. Becker, *Sources for the Study of the School of Nisibis* (Liverpool: Liverpool University Press, 2008).

intellectuals who attended the academies. Nonetheless, they are indicative of the cultural atmosphere of the time.

Leone Ebreo is considered the pre-eminent Jewish thinker of the sixteenth century. He was well acquainted, indeed imbued, with the Neoplatonic conceptions, ideas, and expressions then current in the Italian Renaissance. His *Dialoghi d'amore*,[15] a composition whose form was quite common in the Humanist period, is a celebration of cosmic love as the relationship between God, the universe, and man as the *intellectus agens*, in and of this world. Julius Guttmann maintained that Leone should be regarded as the "only truly Jewish Renaissance philosopher."[16] Leone was the first Jewish intellectual who failed to become an academic. It may have been a near miss, since he possibly had contacts with Giovanni Pontano, who was the president of the Accademia Pontaniana in Naples. The sources are still lacking.[17] Some suggest that Leone met the poet Iacopo Sannazzaro and Ambrogio Leone da Nola.[18] These acquaintances must be interpreted *cum grano salis*, because Leone remained a Jew, a member of an excluded minority. Furthermore, his works were only really appreciated during the seventeenth century and not before,[19] and almost only among a female audience.

Consider the following quotation from his autobiographical poem, the *Telunah 'al ha-zman* (*Complaint against the Times*),[20] where he presents his attitude towards the philosophical academies of his day:

> [110] I visited their schools of learning
> and there were none who could engage with me.
>
> [111] I vanquished all who rose in argument against me,
> and forced my opponents to surrender, putting them to shame.
>
> [112] Who would dare to argue with me on the secrets of creation
> and the mysteries of the chariot and its rider?

---

15 All quotations from the *Dialoghi d'amore* are from the first Blado edition reprinted by Carl Gebhardt, *Leone Ebreo. Dialoghi d'amore. Hebräische Gedichte* (Heidelberg: Curis Societatis Spinozianae, 1929). See *Leone Ebreo (Giuda Abarbanel). Dialoghi d'Amore*, ed. Santino Caramella (Bari: Laterza, 1929). Also see the new English translation by Cosmos D. Bacich and Rossella Pescatori (Toronto: University of Toronto Press, 2008).
16 Julius Guttmann, *Die Philosophie des Judentums* (Munich: Reinhadt, 1933), 271; *Leone Ebreo*, 4.
17 Cf. Angela Guidi, *Amour et Sagesse. Les Dialogues d'amour de Juda Abravanel dans la tradition salomonienne* (Leiden: Brill, 2011), 18–19.
18 Cf. Carlo Vecce, "I Dialoghi d'amore di Leone Ebreo: incontri di culture nella storia di un libro del Rinascimento," in *Autour du livre italien ancien en Normandie*, ed. Silvia Fabrizio-Costa (Berlin: Peter Lang, 2011): 321–331.
19 Giuseppe Veltri, *Renaissance Philosophy*, 69.
20 Cf. Angela Guidi, "Sapienza salomonica e sapere pagano: tradizione ebraica e neoplatonismo nei Dialoghi d'amore di Leone Ebreo," *Revue des Études Juives* 165 (2006): 313–130 for a commentary on the *Telunah 'al ha-zman*.

¹¹³ I have a soul which is higher and more splendid
than the souls of my worthless contemporaries.²¹

An important element, clearly perceptible in his complaint, is Leone's bitter observation that nobody takes him seriously as a philosopher: "nobody was ready to fight with me." Of course, we can interpret the text as a statement of victory over his adversaries who are "silent" before him, since this is also a biblical quotation about wisdom. On the other hand, it could also be a tacit comment on the impossibility of having an open and conclusive confrontation with his "adversaries." If we consult the Jewish and Christian testimony on Leone published by Carl Gebhardt at the back of his reprint of the Aldine *Dialoghi*, it comes as a surprise to find that there were no Christian writers interested specifically in Leone's philosophy. The reception of his work among Italian, Spanish, and French authors of the sixteenth and seventeenth centuries was limited to its treatment of the subject of love rather than of its philosophical themes. Only Jewish authors pointed out that Leone was indeed a Jewish philosopher.

Another example of cooperation with the academies took place in Venice. At the beginning of the sixteenth century, Aldus Manutius writes that a certain Nicolaus Iudecus was a member of the *Neoaccademia Aldina* in Venice.²² There should be no doubts concerning his Jewish origins, because Iudecus is the Greek form of Ἰουδαϊκός. We do not have much information about Nicolaus, although we do know that he corresponded with Janus Lascaris and Jérôme Aléandre, also known as Gerolamo Aleandro.²³

A few decades later, Azaria de' Rossi speaks about the Ferrara academy in his monumental work *Me'or Enayim*, where Greek and Latin culture merged with Christian and Jewish tradition. In the chapter about words stemming from Hebrew, Azaria mentions an academy that, according to his opinion, should be the *bet 'eked ro'im* from Kings 10:12. This short reference can only give an idea of the relationship with the academies of that period. It cannot, however, be evidence of a close relationship like Leone de' Sommi had in his participation in a musical and theatrical academy.

The first academy that seems to have accepted Jewish members was the *Accademia degli Invaghiti* in Mantua. It accepted the renowned *vir doctus* Leone de'

---

21 Translation by Dan Almagor, Barbara Gavin, and Dan Jacobson, "A Complaint against the Time," *Jewish Quarterly* Winter (1992–1993): 59.
22 *Aldi Pii Manutii scripta tria longe rarissima a Iacobo Morellio denuo edita et illustrata* (Bassano: Typis Remondinianis, 1806), 49: "Aldo quinam socii in Academia essent, apertius, quam scriptoribus etiam, de ea praecipuis ante hac innotuerit, modo constat: ac inter eos quidem, quantum video, annumerandi sunt Petrus Bembus, Angelus Gabriel, Paulus Canalis, Andreas Naugerius, Daniel Benerius, Baptista Egnatius, et Nicolaus Iudecu, qui Veneti omnes"; see also Ambroise Firmin-Didot, *Alde Manuce et l'hellénisme à Venise* (Paris: Firmin-Didot, 1875), 149.
23 Cf. John Lewis, *Adrien Turnebe (1512–1565): A Humanist Observed* (Geneva: Droz, 1998), 19–20.

Sommi.[24] In 1565, he presented his *Dialoghi in materia di rappresentazioni sceniche* to Cesare Gonzaga. As a Jew, Leone did not have the right to be accepted into an academy, since every member had to be a *cavaliere* and this office was incompatible with the status of Jew. He was thus accepted as a secretary of the academy,[25] although he complained about this. Federico Gonzaga attempted to lighten his burden by relieving him of the obligation of wearing the sign imposed on the Jews. This privilege was not granted spontaneously, but after his personal request.

Cecil Roth was the first scholar to uncover information about a Jewish academy in Venice, the *Accademia degli Impediti*.[26] The reference comes from Giulio Morosini's book *La via della fede*.[27] Morosini writes that the academy was founded in 1628 in Venice by some Jews who fled Mantua and who were musically talented. The Jews' interest in music is also confirmed by some records from Mantua in which Jews committed themselves to the study of music. The academy gathered around Leone Modena, but it lasted only for a short time. According to Cecil Roth, the Venetian Jewish academy came to an end because of the plague that broke out in 1630, which killed one third of the Jewish families in the Ghetto.

Cecil Roth was the first to reveal the existence of a Jewish academy founded in Venice, the Accademia degli Impediti.[28] The information does not come directly from any Jewish source, but from the work of a Jew who converted to Christianity, Giulio Morosini:

> I remember very well what happened in Venice in my times. It was around 1628, if I am not mistaken, when the Jews had to flee because of the war and took refuge in Venice. Since in Mantova many learned artistic skills flourished, the Jews too decided to devote themselves to music and musical instruments. When they came to Venice, they founded a musical academy in the Venetian Ghetto. They used to sing there twice a week in the evening and only the most important and wealthy in the Ghetto were allowed entry. They were financing this and I was among them. My master and Rabbi Leon da Modena was the choirmaster. In that year two wealthy

---

[24] Cf. Alessandro d'Ancona, *Origini del teatro italiano: Libri tre con due appendici sulla rappresentazione drammatica del contado toscano e sul teatro mantovano nel sec. XVI*, 2nd edition (Turin: Ermanno Loescher, 1891), 403.

[25] Cf. Anna Levenstein, "Songs for the First Hebrew Play *Tsahut bedihuta dekidushin* by Leone de' Sommy (1527–1592)," (PhD dissertation, Case Western Reserve University, 2006), 36.

[26] On this academy, see the Evelien Chayes's notes in *Oltre le Mura del Ghetto*, 106–108; She corrected Roth's errors of transcription as well as his description of the academy.

[27] Giulio Morosini, *Via della fede mostrata a'gli Ebrei, da Giulio Morosini Venetiano Scrittor della Biblioteca Vaticana nella Lingua Ebraica, e Lettor della medesima nel Collegio de Propaganda Fide* (Rome: Nella Stamparia della Sacra. Cong. de Prop. Fide, 1683), 793; See also Israel Adler, "The Rise of Art Music in the Italian Ghetto: The Influence of Segregation on Jewish Musical Praxis," in *Jewish Medieval and Renaissance Studies*, ed. Alexander Altmann (Cambridge: Harvard University Press, 1967): 321–364, 345.

[28] Cecil Roth, "L'accademia musicale del ghetto veneziano," *Rivista mensile d'Israele* 3 (1928): 160–162; Mark R. Cohen, *The Autobiography of a Seventeenth-Century Venetian Rabbi* (Princeton: Princeton University Press, 1988), 31; the reader can find a new, detailed trascription and interpretation by Evelyn Chayes in *Oltre le Mura del Ghetto*, 102–105.

and splendid persons had already made arrangements for the celebration of their marriage during *Shemini atzeret* and *Simḥat Tora*. One of them belonged to the Academy. Therefore, they organized two choirs in the *Scuola Spagnola* (richly decorated and adorned with silver and gems) to our advantage for the musicians. During the two evenings, i.e. the eighth day of *Shemini atzeret* and *Simḥat Tora*, they sang a portion in Hebrew of the *harbit*, some Psalms and the *Minchà*, i.e. the vespertine prayer of the final day, accompanied by solemn music. It lasted several hours into the night. Many noblemen and noblewomen came and offered great applause [for the choir's performance] They had to keep the doors open for guardians and policemen, so that everything might transpire smoothly.

Among the instruments, they also brought along an organ to the synagogue, which was, however, forbidden by the rabbis, since it was normally played in our churches. However, it all was but a flash in the pan, short-lived. The Academy did not last long, nor did the music, and everything returned to the usual routine [...].[29]

The passage is very interesting, although full of apologetic tones typical of a Jewish writer converted to Christianity, and obviously suffering from a syndrome of self-justification, as it would appear from his *excusatio non petita*. It is interesting to note that Morosini remains true to Leone Modena, whom he calls "my master and Rabbi." He also indirectly displays his appreciation for this group of academics in the synagogue, which was followed with the interesting passage, "Many noblemen and noblewomen came with great applause. They had to keep to the two doors open for guardians and policemen, so that everything could go on smoothly."

The information about the prohibition of organ use because it was played in the church is probably inaccurate. We must keep in mind that playing the organ involves engaging in a form of work, and this is what many rabbis forbade during the celebrations Morosini mentioned. There is also evidence from Mantua at the end of the sixteenth century and elsewhere according to which the Jews were very careful not to appear conspicuous with "many eccentric attitudes, such as fires, and other pleasant forms of entertainment, not envisaged by Jewish law for similar holy days." Thus is the comment as recorded by Leone Sommi on a sheet attached to a letter to Ottavio Lambertesco, Court valet of Donati, secretary of the prince Vincenzo I Gonzaga, and published by D'Ancona,[30] concerning the staging of a comedy or pastorale.

Also wrong, perhaps maliciously so, as Cecil Roth insinuates, is the information regarding the break-up of the academy because it was a "flash in the pan." The historical reason for the break-up actually stems from the fact that—according to some available evidence—the majority of the members died in the plague of 1630.[31] One third of the inhabitants of Venice (about 50,000 persons, according to Roth) perished

---

29 Giulio Morosini, *Via della fede mostrata a'gli Ebrei*, 793; Adler, "The Rise of Art Music," 345.
30 Alessandro d'Ancona, *Origini del teatro italiano: Libri tre con due appendici sulla rappresentazione drammatica del contado toscano e sul teatro mantovano nel sec. XVI*, vol. 2 (Turin: Ermanno Loescher, 1891), 426–427.
31 It seems pointless here to cite references to the numerous publications about the plague. See Giovanni Casoni's pamphlet, *La Peste Di Venezia Nel 1630 Origine Della Erezione Del Tempio A S. Maria Della Salute* (Venice: Tipografia Di Alvisopoli, 1830).

during this plague and in the Ghetto it wiped out several families (at least 170 individuals were victims during the first several months after the plague broke out). Unlike other coreligionists, who chose to flee, Leone Modena remained in the Ghetto and was not struck down by the disease.

But enough on the academy and Judaism, a topic of huge importance with which I have dealt elsewhere.[32] Central to this book is the fact that the Ghetto is a space of exchange between city and Jewish intellectuals, and that the topics handled in the academy (theatre, music, philosophy, literature, mathematics, dialectic argumentation), were also handled in the Ghetto.

3.3 The Ghetto and Dialectic Strategies: The Philosopher Sara Copio Sullam

Sara Copio Sullam[33] is a very interesting figure of the Venetian Ghetto, she was the initiator and mentor of an academy. In words of laudation for Sullam, poetess of the Ghetto, Giorgio Bassani wrote in his *Giardino dei Finzi Contini:* "She composed 'excellent' sonnets, whose beauty still awaits a person able to give it the prominence it is entitled to [...] A great woman [...] honour and pride of Italian Jewry at the peak of Counter-Reformation times."[34] Sullam's literary fortune is connected to a correspondence with a Genoese clergyman, Ansaldo Cebà, who in 1615 published his heroic poem "La Rheina Esther" (Queen Esther*)*.[35] As Cebà himself relates, his poem marked the beginning of a (Platonic) love affair, between himself, a Christian priest, and Sara the Jewish poetess: "My Poem [...] urged a noble Jewish lady to desire the friendship disclosed in these letters and I did not refuse to make love with her soul."[36]

It is undeniable that this love (and religious) contest may strike the reader as nothing but a literary fiction in accordance with all the *clichés* of the time: the learned Jewish lady,[37] conversion as a love dialogue between souls, the discussion of portraits (*imago* and *idolo*), the evaluation of Esther as a Jew and as queen at the court, etc. Therefore, the suspicion may arise that the whole issue is merely an

---

[32] Cf. Giuseppe Veltri and Evelyn Chayes, *Oltre le Mura del Ghetto.*
[33] Cf. Umberto Fortis, La *"Bella Ebrea." Sara Copio Sullam poetessa nel ghetto di Venezia del '600* (Turin: Silvio Zamorani Editore, 2003). There are several forms of her name in various the documents. I have privileged the name "Sara Copio Sullam."
[34] Giorgio Bassani, *Il giardino dei Finzi Contini* (Turin: Einaudi, 1962), 182; in Umberto Fortis, *La "Bella Ebrea,"* 7. The translation is mine.
[35] Ansaldo Cebà, *La Regina Ether. Astitit Regina* (Genua: Pavoni, 1615).
[36] Carla Boccato, "Lettere di Ansaldo Ceba, genovese, a Sara Copio Sullam, poetessa del ghetto di Venezia," *Rassegna mensile di Israel* 40 (1974): 169–191, 176.
[37] This issue was discussed again in 1719 in the German *Dissertationes* Johann K. Lufft's *De Rebecca Polona Eruditarum in Gente Judaica Foeminarum Rariori Exemplo Preside Gustavo Georgio Zeltner* (Altdorf: Iod. Guil. Kohlemsii, Universit. Typogr., 1719).

invention fashioned by a Christian (Cebà) and perhaps by Sullam's teacher, the Venetian Rabbi Leon Modena. I do not want to engage here in aimless discussion, although I am aware that in the past other scholars far more competent than the author of this book have doubted the authenticity of the dialogue. The sole work Sullam published, the so-called *Dispute on the Immortality of the Soul*, was printed by Giovanni Alberti in 1621.[38]

The Ghetto's Academy of Sara

Nonetheless, there is another interesting element whose purpose is relevant: the formation and foundation of an academy in Sullam's home. Involved in this academy were not only Leone Modena but also other nobles from Treviso, Padua, and Venice. Perhaps it is worth quoting at length the information Mandosio Prospero provides in the second volume of his *Bibliotheca Romana seu Romanorum Centuriae*,[39] on the basis of a handwritten letter of an Augustinian monk Father Angelico Aprosio Ventimiglia. He speaks of a Jewish Academy:

> He [Numidio Paluzzi] was more endowed with Nature's gifts than of fortune so that the aphorism *Ubi plurimum de ingenio, ibi minimum de fortuna* was not proven wrong for him. After leaving his homeland, he decided to move to another country. For he thought, that in Rome he could find a more benign abode. Nonetheless, as a learned man he would have to remember what Venusian (i.e. Horace) wrote *Celum non aninum mutant*, qui etc. [40] Alessandro Berardelli, who was also a Roman painter, accompanied him. After having visited the most renowned cities in Tuscany and Emilia, they settled in Venice, where fortune favoured him, and had he known how to use his fortune, he would not have fallen short of its favours.
>
> In the Ghetto of that city there happened to live Simone Copia, far wealthier than the other Jews. He had daughters from Ricca his wife, namely two girls Sara and Stella, both of them high-spirited; Sara, however, had more, for she took pleasure in reading books of poetry and other curious subjects. In order to please her, her father accepted that she open an Academy in his home.
>
> This Academy attracted people not only from all over the localities nearby but also from Trevigi, Padova and Vicenza and more faraway places where the more educated used to live. Paluzzi befriended her since she found herself in need of help, knowing that she could not equal the rumours of her renowned learning and value. She thought he had arrived at a convenient moment, since she knew he was poor. Then, not much effort is needed with such people, for those at risk of drowning would even hold on to a sword without fear of cutting their hands. He offered to serve her. In return she paid him not only the rent of the house but also provided

---

38 Sara Copio Sullam, *Manifesto di Sarra Copia Sulam Hebrea nel quale è da lei riprouata, e detestata l'opinione negante l'immortalità dell'Anima, falsamente attribuitale dal Sig. Baldassare Bonifaccio* (Venice: Giovanni Alberti, 1621).
39 Mandosio Prospero, *Bibliotheca romana seu Romanorum Centuriae*, vol. 2, (Rome: De Lazzaris, 1698), 113; I wish to thank Carla Boccato for bringing this text to my attention. Cf. Carla Boccato, "Lettere di Ansaldo Cebà," 172.
40 "Caelum, non animum mutant, qui trans mare currunt." Horace, *Epistulae* 1,11,27.

for his meals and attire, to such an extent that he had also funds left for his other activities. She acted in this manner because she did not want him to leave her.

In 1615, Ansaldo Cebà, a Genoese nobleman, published the poem Esther. After several years, a copy of this poem chanced to come into Sara's possession. This poem urged her to befriend Cebà. This intention is evident from the correspondence printed in Genova in 1623. It is possible there to read about the gifts they exchanged, and also the portraits. Again sonnets followed and other poetic works. Paluzzi had to play the part of the Jewish lady, nor could he give in to idleness. I happened to meet her and I know that she [Sara] was not endowed with much erudition.

At the Academy, they also had the possibility to discuss the immortality of the soul. Baldassarre Bonifacio, who was Arcidiacono of Trevigi at the time of Pope Innocent X and was afterwards installed as Bishop of Giustinopoli,[41] was under the impression that Sara inclined to believe in the mortality of the soul. Therefore, in 1621, he printed the book *Dell'immortalità dell'Anima Discorso di Baldassare Bonifaccio*. He wrote about it to Sara. She took offense and published in response against him the *Manifesto di Sarra Copia Sulam Hebrea nel quale è da lei riprovata, e detestata l'opinione negante l'immortalità dell'Anima, falsamente attribuitele dal Sig. Baldassare Bonifaccio*. It was published in Venice in the very same year. The former was eight pages long, the latter three. Nonetheless, in these three pages she attacked Bonifacio so vehemently that he would have lived better without them. However, it was not Sara's work but Paluzzi's that appeared under the name of this Jewish woman.

At a certain point Numidio misused Sara's kindness and started to be discourteous towards her, since men are never satisfied with the gifts of fortune. In the meanwhile, someone else happened to arrive to Venice. A man of quality from France. Having heard about the reputation of Sara's house, he decided to go there. He was very handsome. Therefore, although already married to Jacob Sullam, she said *ut vidi ut perii* ("As I saw [you] I lost [my heart]").[42] The Frenchman did not stay long in Venice. He possibly took no notice of her and after having finished his business, he returned to France.

Paluzzi noticed her love and thought he had found a way to entangle her in troubles. He had a letter to Sarra written from a Frenchman in the name of the other French gentleman. There he dropped hints of the gentleman's love for her, saying that he had had to keep it secret and begging from her a courteous answer. He also added that she should put her answer in the hand of the man who brought her his letter, so that he could receive it in less than 24 hours in Paris, for this man was very artful and he had already employed his clever services. It was not difficult for him to make her believe it, since the Jews cannot refrain from believing and practicing magic. This is how proposals and answers were made in Venice. However, since this practice was very common, after some months Sara happened to learn about the whole story.

Then, since Cebà was already dead, she did not need Paluzzi's skills any more in order to preserve her credit with him. Therefore, she chased him away and stripped him of every subsidy.

Although Mandosio should have told the story of Paluzzi's life and work, this report revolves not so much around Paluzzi but rather on Sara Sullam and the creation of her academy. This element is very palpable, and the seventeenth-century reader would have been more aware of this than any contemporary reader. Particularly revealing are the venue chosen for the meetings ("in his house," that is, her husband's house), Sullam's patronage, the fame that attracted nobles and intellectuals from all

---

41 Nowadays called Capodistria.
42 Virgil, *Eclogae* 8:41.

over the region, the disputes and the romantic contests (the invention of a "very handsome" French gentleman), and especially the betrayal of Paluzzi, who wanted to offend and hurt her.

In Aprosio's story, there are all the elements that used to feature in the life of the academies: inventions, masks, and intrigues. Unfortunately, in Sullam's case, this was not merely about literary fiction but also about the wickedness of a learned man who did not want to be cast into the shadows because everybody loved his own pupil more than him. Probably with the purpose of escaping ridicule after having been expelled from Sullam's house, he published accusations in *The Satires Sarreidi*, written together with Alessandro Berardelli, a Roman poet and painter. The dispute continued with explicit accusations of plagiarism formulated by Berardelli in his introduction to the *Rime del Signor Numidio Paluzzi all'illustre ed eccellentissimo Signor Giovanni Soranzo* (1626), to which Sullam herself replied.[43]

Obviously, the fact that a Jewish lady could be beautiful, rich, educated, and intelligent was unacceptable for Angelico and especially for those who, like Paluzzi, envied his pupil, while he himself was destined to remain in the shadows.

The argument has been put forward according to which Sullam would have had contacts with the *Academia degli Incogniti*, because some of the nobles she was acquainted with were also members of the Academy, including Cebà, and also because of the theme of immortality of the soul, which was a much-debated issue there.[44] Nevertheless, we must be cautious and avoid hasty conclusions. In fact, one of the spiritual founders of the *Academia degli Incogniti*, as we have already mentioned, was the philosopher Cesare Cremonini who denied that he rejected the concept of the immortality of the soul, a highly explosive subject at the time, not only for Judaism but also, and particularly, for Christianity.

How to be a Sceptic while Remaining Dogmatic: The Dialectics of the Immortality

The archdeacon of Treviso, Baldassarre Bonifaccio, was a participant in Sara Sullam's learned "academy" or "salon" in the Ghetto of Venice. He had also tried his

---

43 Cf. Carla Boccato, "Sara Copia Sullam: La poetessa del ghetto di Venezia: episodi della sua vita in un manoscritto del secolo xvii," *Italia* 6 (1987): 104–218.
44 Howard Tzvi Adelman, "Sarra Copia Sullam," in *Jewish Women: A Comprehensive Historical Encyclopedia. Jewish Women's Archive* (2009), http://jwa.org/encyclopedia/article/sullam-sara-coppia (accessed 2 March 2015); Howard Tzvi Adelman, "Leon Modena and Sarra Copia Sullam and l'Accademia degli Incogniti," in *Venezia, gli Ebrei e l'Europa (1516–2016)*, ed. Donatella Calabi (Venice: Marsilio, 2016): 284–286.

hand at drama, composing a tragedy entitled "Amata,"⁴⁵ but was principally known as *doctor utriusque juris* and was lauded as a man of letters blessed with a "clear intellect."⁴⁶ Until recently, it was only known that Sullam had written him a letter in which she expressed her doubts about the immortality of the soul. In reply, he published a small tractate, pillorying her heretical views. Sullam answered this attack with a "Manifesto," in which she sought to remove any doubts about her "orthodoxy." In it, she openly presents her views, censuring the brashness of a cleric who sought through effrontery to reap some profit from her fame and honour.

Modern and contemporary commentators add that the original letter by Sullam was merely a kind of philosophical exercise, and that her *Manifesto* was a panicked reaction fuelled by the fear that the Inquisition would accuse her of heresy and burn her at the stake—and that, in the worst case, it might also lead to the expulsion of the Jews from Venice. That was a horror scenario initially sketched by Heinrich Graetz⁴⁷ and supported in the literature by Moritz Levy, Leonello Modona, Carla Boccato, and Umberto Fortis.

To begin, it should be noted that, with the exception of a few brief notes, there is, to date, very little critical scholarship on the philosophical texts in question. The dispute between Sullam and Bonifaccio has been interpreted solely based on what is generally known. This philosophical-theological dispute is more than incidental, however. It is neither a literary exercise nor a panicked reaction. Rather, it reflects the sphere of the literary culture in that space and century that was open for public discussion and in which the Church still wished to play a didactic role. The Inquisition was still mostly interested in *Christian* heretical views, not those enunciated by *Jews* deviating from general *Jewish* opinion; there was never a tribunal for that.

However, the possible reasons that could have moved Bonifaccio to openly challenge Sullam in what had initially been merely a peaceful exchange remain something of a mystery. We know that it was Bonifaccio who initiated the dispute, with a letter to Sullam in early January, 1619. This letter had remained in manuscript form until 1988, when it was found and published by Carla Boccato.⁴⁸ The letter, which was contained in Bonifaccio's papers, is addressed to Sabba Giudea, who has been identified as Sullam.⁴⁹ The occasion appears to have been his desire to

---

45 Baldassarre Bonifaccio, *Amata, tragedia di Baldassare Bonifaccio* (Venice: Appresso A. Pinelli, 1622); *Lettere poetiche di Baldassare Bonifaccio, per difesa, e dichiaratione della sua Tragedia* (Venice: Antonio Pinelli, 1622).
46 For a bibliography on Bonifaccio, cf. Carla Boccato, "Una disputa secentesca sull'immortalità dell'anima—Contributi d'archivio," *La Rassegna mensile d'Israele* 45 (1988): 593–606, 593–594 and the corresponding footnotes.
47 Heinrich Graetz, *Geschichte der Juden von den ältesten Zeiten bis auf die Gegenwart*, vol. 10, 3rd edition (Leipzig: Leiner, 1897), 136; Graetz points here to the counter-example of Uriel da Costa "in libertarian Protestant Amsterdam."
48 Carla Boccato, "Una disputa," 593–606, text 603–604.
49 Carla Boccato attributes this obvious error to the poor state of the often-corrected manuscript of the author. It is also conceivable that the archdeacon is consciously associating and comparing Sara

wish her a happy New Year. At first glance, the letter seems like a harmless discussion of the immortality of the intellect, that part of the soul which avoids human decay and corruption. On closer examination, however, this New Year's greeting can be shown to be an astute Christian provocation on an eternal theme, conversion to Christianity, with the obvious aim of persuading Sullam to convert. I will review the main points of the argument.

Baldassarre Bonifaccio begins by noting that the year becomes younger while man grows older, because the former is constantly renewed (being a celestial body) while our life is limited in time, "[...] carved by the eternal God out of the eternity of being."[50] We cannot hope to preserve our being perpetually because, unlike the celestial bodies and spheres, our matter has a disposition only to one form.[51] Moreover, because of Adam's original sin, man has forfeited his initial immortality. Only that part of the soul which is reason and which was obedient to God had the supernatural ability to prevent the decay and corruption of matter, a faculty that was lost through the primal sin. Repentance made absolution from that sin possible, but the capacity for immortality was not restored. Since that juncture, matter cannot hope for immortality, as the woman of Tekoa says in II Sam. 14:14: "For we must die, and are as water spilt on the ground, which cannot be gathered up again."[52] Like water, man has a hybrid fate, because he belongs to the world above, like the

---

with the Queen of Sheba. According to Christian literature, a topic of the conversation between King Solomon and the Queen of Sheba was the immortality of the soul. This was the opinion of the monk Jacob Filippo Foresti in his book *De plurimis claris selectisque mulieribus opus prope divinum novissime congestum* (Ferrara: Laurentinus de Rubeis, 1497). His book was re-published in the Johannes Ravisius's collection, *De memorabilibus et claris mulieribus: aliquot diversorum scriptorium opera* (Paris: Simon de Colines, 1521), which enjoyed huge popularity in sixteenth and seventeenth century: The text reads: "Cui cum primo aenigmata et quaestiones quae ei prius insolubiles videbantur, atque ab ipso de agnitione veri dei, et de creaturis mundi, necnon et de immortalitate animae, et iudicio futuro: quod apud eam et apud doctores eius gentiles duntaxat philosophos incertum manebat, proposuisset, et earum solutiones ab eo velocissime audisset: ultro confessa est ipsius sapientiam, longe suam excessisse" (39b). The text is also available online: http://www.uni-mannheim.de/mateo/camenaref/muliers.html (accessed 3 May, 2007).
50 Carla Boccato, "Una disputa," 603: "[...] che standosi nell'interminabile dell'eternità in guisa ch'egli da lei non è circonscritto, cava il tempo dall'evo."
51 There is something skewed in the text of Baldassarre, which, according to Boccato in "Una disputa," reads: "[...] né possiamo sperare che l'essere nostro si conservi perpetuamente. Non essendo materia, salvo quella del cielo, che non habbia dispositione che ad una forma, sarebbe stato bisogno che i primi propagatori dell'humana generatione si fossero conservati nell'originale giustitia, se dovea la loro posterità conservarsi immortale" (Boccato, 603). According to Aristotle, the motion of the celestial bodies is eternal and circular (see Aristotle, *Physics* 12,7). See following note.
52 *Omnes morimur et quasi aquae dilabimur.* In Carla Boccato, "Una disputa," 603 uses the term *acquae*, which is probably a scribal error. This verse is a *topos* of Christian homiletics and sermons on the occasion of death (*Tractatus de Morte non Timenda*, etc.). Baldassarre quotes only the first part of II Sam 14:14, leaving out *in terram* (on the ground).

"small parts of water" which dissolve in the air,[53] and to the world below, like the "larger parts of water" that drain into the ground. The material part of man will dissolve and waste away in the grave, while the spiritual part enters the air and is there preserved.

This is the first, "innocent" part of the letter. Baldassarre makes use here of *philosophoumena* that presume a Christian reading of the Bible. It is worth noting that the reference to the woman of Tekoa, seemingly an allusion to the Old Testament, can also be construed as an indirect allusion to Christ on the cross. Jesus describes his condition with the words from the Psalm 21:15: "I am poured out like water" (*sicut aqua effusus sum*). Probably in keeping with an ancient Christian tradition, now in philosophical guise, Thomas Aquinas, here indirectly cited by Baldassarre, connects the two verses: the woman of Tekoa points to the mortality of man in the image of water spilt upon the ground, while Jesus symbolises the merging of the spirit with the air. The indirect reference to the cross has been included consciously, as the archdeacon later discloses in the letter, where his intention to convert Sara is clear. The body, because mortal, is also especially weak. The sole hope is salvation through Christ, who is the only one who can rebuild the temple of the body. Man is an ugly house that becomes a decrepit ruin. The cleric concludes his philosophical speculations with the sentence: "Only my Christ, the divine architect, who built the universe, can destroy and rebuild that temple in which human intellect resides like a god. And in this sense he spoke and confirmed with his work: *Possum destruere templum hoc et in triduo reaedificare illud* [Matthew 26:61]."[54]

Sara Sullam was lured into responding to these arguments and replied with a letter dated 10 January,[55] in which, in keeping with the patterns and usages of her time, she continued the philosophical discussion about the immortality of the soul, expressing her "doubts" concerning the construction of the cleric. We have seen that *dubitationes* is a technic term used in academic disputations to introduce problems, i.e. *quaestiones disputatae*.

But back to Sullam's letter. She said to have read the letter in her "academy" to her friends Paluzzi and Corniani. Her response to Baldassarre is very sophisticated in its formulation and logical in its philosophical structure, stringent in its conclusions

---

53 Cf. Thomas Aquinas, *In psalmos Davidis expositio a psalmo XXI ad psalmum XXX Reportatio Reginaldi de Piperno*, Ps. 21 (22): "Aqua leviter effunditur et proiicitur: sic ergo effusus sum."
54 Cf. Carla Boccato, "Una disputa," 604: "Solo il mio Christo, architetto divino ch'edificó l'universo, può distruggere e fabbricare quel tempio nel quale, com'una Deità, risiede l'intelletto dell'huomo. E però disse e confermò con l'opera: *Possum destruere templum hoc et in triduo reaedificare illud*." The Vulgata reads "templum Dei," which certainly does not fit in with Baldassarre's intentions. The King James' version is, "I am able to destroy the temple of God, and to rebuild it in three days."
55 The letter was published by Baldassarre Bonifaccio in his *Risposta al Manifesto della Signora Sara Copia del Signor Baldassare Bonifaccio*, Venetia: appresso Antonio Pinelli, 1621), fols. 5r–6v, in Umberto Fortis, *La "bella ebrea*," 145–147. The transcriptions of Baldassarre (and therefore of Fortis) are not free from errors: for example, "effects" instead of "affects" (5r); "language" (6r) instead of "lineage," and other spelling mistakes.

3.3 The Ghetto and Dialectic Strategies: The Philosopher Sara Copio Sullam

and very informative about the theses indirectly alluded to by Baldassarre. She immediately seizes on the first point, the comparison between the year, which through cyclic seasons becomes younger, and man, who grows ever older.

The fact that one year is followed by another, that the year is renewed (Baldassarre: "the year becomes younger"), also applies to mankind, although the life of a human being is longer than one revolution around the sun. Throughout the duration of a man's life, we see his identity as an individual. The biographical dates of a human life mark its individuality, as a fragment in time. Just as an individual year loses its essence to a number, a human being loses his individual essence through time. This sentence contains the main problem of the theory of human individuality (but also the problem of his moral responsibility and fate after death, which Sullam does not mention *expressis verbis*). The essential identity of the individual, Sara adds, is not due to his belonging to the species of "man," for,

> [...] if the essence of a single human being would not be distinguished from the others by dint of its individual essence, we would have to conclude that if the essence of Socrates were lost, then that of Plato, that is, of other individuals, would also be lost, so that the death of an individual would mean the death of the species.[56]

The idea that matter is corruptible, as held by the Peripatetics, is, in Sullam's view, easier to claim than to prove. In fact, if substance is an internal and external part of the composite and is eternal, how is it possible to assert that a thing can take on the quality of corruptibility from a part that is in itself eternal and non-corruptible? This conflicts with the general rules of logic.

It is evident that matter is immortal: this can be seen in the fact that, when any composite decomposes, its basic elements remain. If the Aristotelian composite of substance and form is mortal, which of the two components is eternal, which is doomed to decay? To solve this question, Sullam seizes on the substance and form of heaven. Before we continue, it is important to note that, according to Aristotle, here expressly mentioned, matter is eternal, but corruptible, while form is incorruptible, but not eternal, i.e. matter decomposes into its constituent elements, which then find a new form (the so-called "appetite of matter"). The substance of heaven longs for form, and although many forms are conceivable, only one is actually realised (*in actu*) for heaven and remains eternal. Heaven is actually finite, but eternal. If matter is eternal, only the form of heaven could be corruptible. However, this cannot

---

[56] Letter to Baldassare Bonifaccio (in Umberto Fortis, *La "bella ebrea,"* 145–146: "[...] se l'essenza di un uomo non si distinguesse essenzialmente dall'altra, ne seguirebbe che, mancando l'essenza di Socrate, mancasse anche quella di Platone, e cosí de gl'altri, in modo che nella morte di un individuo morirebbono tutti."

be the case concerning heaven, because it has only one form and one substance.⁵⁷ Thus, in Aristotelian philosophy, there is not an infinite number of heavens.

The situation is different in respect to human existence, since there are many human beings. Sullam reasons: if we follow Aristotle's notion and believe that the soul is passed on by procreation, one may ask why God did not create man immortal from the start, if he indeed intended to preserve him in this way? However, if the human being was created mortal, and we sink and are drained into the ground, as in the image of the woman of Tekoa, then we are only temporary human beings, not the same humans, although the species always remains one and the same. For that reason, neither the year nor any other transitory, short-lived being can bring about renewal and restoration, just as when a mason rebuilds a house that has been destroyed it will not be the same house as before, even if made from the same bricks.

Sullam is speaking in this text about the eternity of matter, *materia*, not about the mortality or immortality of the soul, and about the transitory nature of man, which is a function of number and, thus, of motion. She does not propose any clear alternative philosophy, but only asks questions about questions. One thing is certain: she rejects a direct connection between original sin and generation, because that would not follow logically from the idea of an original divine plan, and would, according to Baldassarre's logic, be the outcome of *ad hoc* planning (with God waiting until man sins). In particular, she rejected the notion of Christianity as some kind of a *reconstruction* of Judaism. If we suppose that the Jewish religion, or the Jew as such, since the time of Adam, is a destroyed house, then Christ erects a new building, since he cannot rebuild the old. *Ergo*, we would argue, Christianity cannot simply build upon Judaism. This is a subject richly reminiscent of philosophical discussions at the time of Mendelssohn, in which Judaism was defined as a sub-structure of Christianity.

Baldassarre goes beyond Sullam's courtly and discursive tone with the publication two years later, in 1621, of a small, 61-page volume entitled *Dell'immortalità dell'anima; Discorso di Baldassare Bonifaccio*, composed in the form of a public dispute.⁵⁸ One has the impression that he invested time and energy in writing a tractate for the public, and that its aim was to reduce the influence of Sullam's "academy," by endeavouring to depict her as an "Aristotelian." It thus becomes clear that

---

57 Aristotle, *Metaphysics*, Book XII, 8, ed. William D. Ross: "Evidently there is but one heaven. For if there are many heavens as there are many men, the moving principles, of which each heaven will have one, will be one in form but in number many. [...] So the unmovable first mover is one both in definition and in number; so too, therefore, is that which is moved always and continuously; therefore there is one heaven alone."
58 Baldassarre Bonifaccio, *Dell'immortalità dell'anima; Discorso di Baldassare Bonifaccio*, (Venice: Pinelli, 1621). The text I used is available online in the Herzog-August-Bibliothek in Wolfenbüttel, http://diglib.hab.de/drucke/83–12-quod-3/start.htm (accessed 3 May, 2018).

the first letter was conceived as a conscious provocation designed to incite Sullam to a response.

Baldassarre makes no secret of the fact that he views their dispute as a contest, and he embarks, without hesitation and armed with a "golden sword,"[59] into the battle against the "moon of the lady philosophers."[60] His bill of indictment is clearly a renewed provocation, since he accuses Sara of disrespect for the Jewish religion and obedience to the "poisoned" philosophy of Aristotle.[61] In order to demonstrate his knowledge of the Hebrew terms for "soul," he distinguishes between *neshamah* (*spiracolo di vita, animo ragionevole*), *nefesh* (*anima sensitiva dei bruti*) and *ruaḥ* (*spirito, sostanza incorporea*).[62] Baldassarre sums up Sullam's critique: immortality cannot be predicated on worldly things because their number is finite. Sullam's argument was: if all souls were immortal and infinite, they would be drawn into the world, which is eternal, and this would contradict the Aristotelian principle according to which nothing infinite can exist in nature, which is eternal but finite. Baldassarre replies: if we assume that Aristotle's theory about the eternity of the world is true (which he, Baldassarre, fervently denies) the doctrine of the immortality of the soul does not pertain to matter but only to things of the spirit (*cose spirituali come l'anima*),[63] so that the infinite would not remain in the finite (Baldassarre fails to say that for Aristotle, finitude (extension) and immortality (motion) are not the same!).

Another of Sara Sullam's arguments is as follows: if the soul were immortal, we would have an infinite number of souls, which would be a *contradictio*, because they would not be perceptible qua number, and thus not conceivable individually. Baldassarre replies: Since the soul is separate from matter and number is valid only for a divisible substance, it has no quantity. On the other hand, if the world is eternal for Aristotle, we would have an infinite number of days. Then immaterial souls would also be countable, because the infinitude of time is countable. Baldassarre suppresses the argument here that infinity of motion, which generates time, derives from the unmovable first mover, and that the "in-formed" matter is finite due to its extension. Moreover, the days do not differ from one another, as Sullam says, while the souls should differ as individual entities. Baldassarre is aware of the problem, because he sees the individual soul, in agreement with Thomas, as participating in the divine spirit, and not as identical with divine substance (which would be tantamount to a Spinoza's conception).

Sullam's second main argument runs: no agent can exist without action. Here Baldassarre does not appear to deal directly with the point Sullam is making. Her

---

[59] Baldassarre Bonifaccio, *Discorso*, 6: "[...] non ho bisogno dello scudo, ma solamente della spada [...] questa spada non è già di ferro per offender, ma d'oro per arricchire."
[60] Ibid., 5: "A gran torto Lucretio disse che Epicuro era il sole dei filosofi: ed io dirò con molta ragione che voi siete la Luna delle filosofesse."
[61] Ibid.: "pestifera dottrina del venenoso maestro."
[62] Ibid., 7.
[63] Ibid., 8.

assertion is that souls, as human essences, cannot be identical, otherwise the death of an individual would mean the death of the species. By contrast, Baldassarre directs his attention to the way in which the body is separated from the soul, since no matter can exist without actual concrete form. The soul perceives differently when it is within the body and when it is outside the body. The one process occurs through thought, the other through the species in which it participates. The first type of perception (within and *with* the body) is action, the second (without a body) is passion. This means that one comes about through the active intellect, the second through the passive intellect. Here, it would be appropriate to ask whether the passive soul, the participant in the species, does not indeed represent the entire species, if it is infinite in regard to time and, therefore, immortal.

The third argument is important for our thesis here. Sullam writes that if one speaks of corruption, the reference cannot intrinsically concern matter but only form, since matter dissolves into its elements, which are, obviously, never destroyed. In order to circumvent this problem, Baldassarre advances the concept of separation instead of corruption. He states that in the process of separation of soul and body, the body (matter) remains only a potentiality without existence. Baldassarre underpins his conclusions with a proof from the realm of sense perception:

> Would we need an additional proof, when we perceive with the senses that the substance of our fragile bodies wastes away every day? Would it not move irrevocably toward destruction if we did not maintain it each and every day with the food which we lose each day? Let us not be deceived—your gleaming eyes will become bleary eyes. Your breast will turn limp and flabby, your skin wrinkled. The body will become a corpse, decompose to putrescence and slime. But not the soul [...][64]

Baldassarre does not respond directly to Sara's philosophical question, preferring rather, in typically Baroque discursive style, the *ad hominem* argument of putrefaction, a topic important to him. At the end of his short book, he includes a poem:

> Sara, your beauty so beguiling,
>
> That it scorns being counted but second among the best,
> Is a thing far more transitory than a blossom,
>
> Is far more fleeting than a wisp of wind,
>
> And if I could say—peace be upon you—
> What is hidden, wrapped within your beauty,
> Then I would say that it is the grave,
> Where the impure soul lies buried because of Original Sin.

---

[64] Ibid., 11: "E che occore altra prova, se proviamo col senso che la materia di questo nostro corpo fra[gi]le ogni di si corrompe, e preciterebbe spacciatamente alla distruzione, tutte le colte che da noi non si ristorasse continuamente col cibo, quello che andiamo ogni giorno perdendo? Cotesti vostri occhi brillanti diverranno cispi, non ci inganniamo; vizze diverranno le poppe, e grinze le carni. Diverrà cadavere il corpo, e rimarrà finalmente putredine, e fango. Non cosi l'anima [...]."

3.3 The Ghetto and Dialectic Strategies: The Philosopher Sara Copio Sullam

That is the sin from whence sprang the body,
Which the immortal form of life pilfers and robs
And the image of Gods corrupts.

Run, run to the purifying fountain
Where life now springs forth: Christ is the pious bird
Who with his blood animates the dead children. [65]

The aesthetic theory reflected here is linked to religion. Baldassarre speaks of "feminine beauty" without referring to the corresponding tractates where beauty and virtue are seen as a divine composite that augurs and anticipates the beauty of the heavens. The true weakness of Sullam's letter, in Baldassarre's eyes, was not the theory of the mortality of the soul in general, but rather *her soul*, because she was a Jewess.

Having just recuperated from an illness, and surprised by the publication of the tractate, Sullam answered with a publication[66] that remained the only one in her life in which she attacked her opponent with vehemence, sarcasm, and a full command of all the rules of rhetoric, or, as Graetz puts it, "with mature dialectics, masculine courage and crushing force applied against her slanderous accuser."[67] That is perhaps the impression the reader might have initially. Yet a closer look reveals that Sullam does not really add any significant new arguments here, aside from two *ad hominem* remarks about Baldassarre's poor knowledge of Hebrew and an ironic comment that he should wish himself dead if indeed he so fervently desires the immortality of the soul after death. Sullam's rhetoric repeats clichés that are suitably Baroque, but it is hardly comparable to the logical speculations of her previous letter. Consider only

---

65 Ibid., 61:
Sara, la tua beltà cotanto audace
Che sdegna tra le prime esser seconda
E però più caduca assai che fronda,
E però più che vento assai fugace.

E, se potessi dir, ma con tua pace,
Ciò che la tua bellezza in se nasconda,
Io direi ch'ella tomba, ou'alma, immonda
Di colpa originale, sepolta giace

Questa è la colpa, onde quel colpo uscio
Che la forma immortal di vita priua
E corrompe l'imagine di Dio

Corri, corri al lauacro, ond'hor deriua
La vita: Christo è quel augel sì pio
Che col suo sangue morti figli auuiua.
66 Sara Copio Sullam, *Manifesto Di Sarra Copia Sulam Hebrea: Nel quale è da lei riprovata, e detestata l'opinione negante l'immortalitá deli' Anima falsamente attribuitale dal Sig. Baldassare Bonifaccio* (Venice: Pinelli, 1621).
67 Heinrich Graetz, *Geschichte der Juden*, 10:135.

her tone here: acrimonious, sarcastic, insulting, offensive, invidious. That is all. She begins with an avowal of faith that sounds like a statement of credo: "The human soul, Mr. Baldassarre, is incorruptible, immortal, and divine, created by God and breathed within our body at that time when what forms the organs is able to receive [the seed] in the womb."[68] This thesis is, in its tenor, as Christian as it is Jewish, and derived from her faith. Sara refuses to deal additionally with the topic. The reason becomes clear in the following sentences:

> If in a few conversations, I have raised philosophical or theological questions that should not be interpreted as doubt or fluctuation in my faith, but rather only as curiosity to hear, together with you, about the solution of difficulties even by means of strange and alien doctrines. I acted thus in the assumption that this is permitted to every person who is eager to learn, and thus also to a woman, a Jewish woman, who is constantly confronted with these topics by those who attempt, as you well know, to compel her to accept the Christian faith.[69]

It is clear that Baldassarre's letter to Sullam was meant as a provocation and that she allowed herself to be provoked to a response. In the society in which she had grown, it was customary to raise *dubitationes* and ask *quaestiones* in order to spark a discourse in its requisite acuteness. Sullam did this, and was now like a burnt child who dreads the fire because the archdeacon wanted to use the opportunity to force her, over and again, to deal with the topic of conversion.

Nonetheless, the question remains legitimate: why did she try to answer with a combination of sarcasm and a vehement profession of faith but without a foundation of philosophical argument? Was she really frightened about the Inquisition, and therefore decided to craft an avowal of her orthodoxy in order to avoid being accused of heresy, as others have argued? In my view, that is impossible, since the *Manifesto* is composed in a tone of voice so biting that she could have been accused of heresy simply due to that. Baldassarre was, after all, an archdeacon, accused by a Jewess of vanity, false zeal, ambition, and ignorance in the fields of philosophy, theology, and the Italian and Hebrew languages—and accused, most pointedly, of the cowardice of a knight who is content to measure his prowess against a woman! I do not see here any fear of the Church whatsoever!

---

68 "L'anima dell'uomo, Signor Baldassare, è incorruttibile, immortale e divina, creata e infusa da Dio nel nostro corpo in quel tempo che l'organizzato è reso abile nel ventre materno a poterla ricevere." In Umberto Fortis, La "bella ebrea," 150; according to *Vocabolario degli accademici della Crusca* (Venice: 1612), "organizzare" means "formare gli organi," which is a reference to Francesco da Buti's commentary on Dante.

69 Sara Copio Sullam, *Manifesto* (non-paginated), in Umberto Fortis, La "bella ebrea," 150: [...] "che se pure in alcun discorso io vi ho promossa alcuna difficoltà filosofica o teologica, ciò non è stato per dubbio e vacillamento che io abbia avuto nella mia fede, ma solo per curiosità d'intendere da voi, con la soluzione dei miei argomenti, qualcuna curiosa e peregrina dottrina, stimando ciò esser concesso ad ogni persona che professi studij, non che ad una donna, e donna Ebrea, la quale continuamente vien posta in questi discorsi da persone che si affaticano di ridurla, come voi sapete, alla Cristiana fede."

My thesis is as follows: the topic of the immortality of the soul was a highly explosive subject at the time, not only within Christianity but also acutely within Judaism. *That* is most likely why Sullam did not want to get involved, in such a public forum, in the vehement discussions then prevalent among rabbis, both in Venice and also in Amsterdam. It is no accident that this topic, which ranked among the most important theological, philosophical, and social issues of the time, was treated with the proper focus and attention by various Venetian Jews, such as Leone Modena, in his unpublished work of apologia *Magen va-Ḥerev*, or David del Bene, in his *Kissot le-vet David*.

After Sullam's debate with the priest, the topic of the immortality of the soul and eternal damnation was discussed with greater vehemence among the Jews. In 1622 to 1623, the Jewish physician Samuel da Silva published his *Tratado da immortalidade da alma*, a polemic against the now lost tractate of Uriel da Costa, the Portuguese Jew who had converted to Christianity and then returned to Judaism, entitled *Sobre a mordalidade da alma do homem*. Da Costa replied in 1623 with the tractate *Exame das tradições farisaicas conferidas com a lei escripta, contra a immortalidade da alma* (Amsterdam, 1623–1624), in which he denied the immortality of the soul. The question is further discussed by Menasse ben Israel (*Nishmat Ḥayyim*), Saul Levi Morteira, Isaac Aboab de Fonseca, and Moses Raphael d'Aguilar. This was not just a theological-philosophical discussion; it was also relevant for the question of the rehabilitation of the crypto-Jews who had been converted by force to Christianity.[70]

Sullam probably suspected that the Christian and Jewish discussion about the soul's immortality was only a subterfuge in order to discuss the place of the Jews and Judaism within Christian society. For the Christians, the most important objection was the honour and fame of a Jewish woman who had talent, beauty, and good manners but who did not follow the "true religion," and thus had no access to the world beyond. Her answer to that was clear and unambiguous:

> [...] the fact that I remain a Jew should eliminate any doubt about my viewpoint. For had I believed and, as you say, were not afraid of the loss of the happiness of the other life, there were indeed ample opportunities for me to improve my [material] situation by changing the law [the religion]. That is a fact known to many in authority, since they incessantly tried to bring it about.[71]

---

[70] Cf. Alexander Altmann, "Eternality of Punishment: A Theological Controversy within the Amsterdam Rabbinate in the Thirties of the 17th Century," *Proceedings of the American Academy of Jewish Research* 40 (1972): 1–88; Asa Kasher, Shlomo Biderman, "Why Was Baruch de Spinoza Excommunicated?" in *Sceptics, Millenarians and Jews*, ed. David S. Katz and Jonathan I. Israel (Brill: Leiden, 1990): 98–141.

[71] Sara Copio Sullam, *Manifesto* (no pagination): "[...] benché, a rimuovere ogni dubbio della mia opinione in questo, dovrebbe bastare il mio preservarmi Ebrea, perché, quando i credessi, come voi dite, e non temessi di perder la felicità dell'altra vita, non mi sarebbero mancate occasioni col

Her subsequent public silence until her death can serve as the best commentary on her avowal of faith because had she converted to Christianity it would have meant that she doubted the immortality of the Jewish soul.

In Judaism, the role of dogmatic issues is relative and absolute at the same time. It is true that there are no dogmas which can automatically exclude one from the Jewish community, as Jewishness is a condition of birth and not of confession. However, the question of the immortality of the soul is a multifarious topic that addresses many questions already present in rabbinic Judaism at the beginning of the rabbinic movement with the "sect" of the Sadducees, mentioned in the New Testament (Matthew 22:23 and Acts 4:1–2), which negated the doctrine of the resurrection and hence the immortality of the soul. Also, philosophers like Saadia Gaon refuted the conception of the immortality of the individual. What is the problem? The real problem is— as already referred to—the early modern discussion of Jewish society and its cohesion in the face of Christian attacks as well as the debate on the converts to Christianity and the status of their belonging to the Jewish community in this and next life, as it was a common conviction that the final redemption of the Jews was possible only as global unity (*kol Israel*). On the other hand, the negation of immortality definitely weakens the responsibility of the individual because of the doctrine of merits and retribution, also a topic of a debate but present in early modern Judaism, especially in Venice.

Sullam wielded arguments and doubts as a dialectical academic ploy, a provocation, a challenge taken by the clergyman who saw in it a chance to convert her to Christianity. The argumentation is similar for the same topic: the contingency of the individual. Sullam saw in it the eternity of the cosmic movement, Bonifacio the premise to the eternity of the (Christian) afterlife. Bonifacio responded to Sullam, accusing her of negating the immortality of the soul. She reacted vehemently to the charge, but in the end she preferred to confess her dogmatic belief in immortality without making any solid argument for it, perhaps because of her social commitment to the Jewish existence or perhaps because her doubts on immortality remained without an answer: an equipollence of arguments.

The Accademia of the Incogniti and the Ghetto

Before we deal with the sceptical philosophy of Simone Luzzatto, it is worthwhile to add a short paragraph on the relationship between the Ghetto, the *Academia degli Incogniti*, and the Rabbi of Venice. In the case of Luzzatto, the subject of next chapter, it cannot be ascertained whether he was a member of an academy. However, as is the case for Sara Copio Sullam and Leone Modena, some contact with the *Accademia*

---

cangiar legge, di migliorare il mio stato; cosa nota a persone di autorità, che l'hanno instantemente procurato e tentato."

degli Incogniti cannot be ruled out. Furthermore, he was acquainted with a French libertine, free thinker, and sceptic, Charles de Valliquierville, as Evelien Chayes has recently convincingly proved.[72]

A short look into the relationship between Luzzatto and the *Accademia* is important because of the topic we have already dealt with in the second part (the concept of religion and minorities), and the empirical arguments of an economic nature, used as an anti-dogmatic argument, which we will treat in the next chapter on the *Discorso* of Luzzatto.

Luzzatto's cooperation with the Venetian academies seems to be confirmed by the defence of Gian Francesco Loredan in 1659, founder of the *Accademia degli Incogniti*, in favour of the Jews; this defence was based mainly on Luzzatto's *Discorso*. The common attitude towards Jews in Europe during the period between the seizure of power by Constantine V in the sixth century and the emancipation in the eighteenth century, or even until 1945, was characterised on the one hand by oppression and religious and economic exploitation, and on the other the other hand the exploitation and abuse of biblical, rabbinical, philosophical, and Kabbalistic traditions in service of Christian belief.

With the exception of occasional personal contacts between rabbis and clergymen and intellectual figures, there's not much evidence of positive change in relations in this period. John Toland, the most prominent representative of Deism, wrote a treatise entitled *Reasons for Naturalizing the Jews* (1714),[73] where one can find a positive evaluation of Simone Luzzatto's arguments; nevertheless, there were no intellectuals, clerics, or Christian politicians who proved themselves more open to Judaism, as Gian Francesco Loredan was. The arguments he used in defence of Judaism are also intriguing within the broader history of scepticism.

Loredan chose to support the Jewish community in the struggle against Venice in his speech in favour of the Jews of the Ghetto, according to an unpublished document from the Archivio di Stato di Venezia, recently discovered and now just published.[74] This text is proof of an attempt to "*scazzar gli Ebrei*" (expel the Jews) from Venice in 1659 obstructed by Loredan[75] and is currently held by the special collection of "*Cinque Savi alla Mercanzia.*"[76] This remarkable document was probably kept in the

---

[72] René Pintard, *Le libertinage érudit dans la première moitié du xviie siècle* (Geneva: Editions Slatkine, 2000 [1943]), 370.
[73] John Toland, *Reasons for Naturalizing the Jews in Great Britain and Ireland* (originally published in London, 1714; Jerusalem: Hebrew University Department of Jewish History, 1963).
[74] Giuseppe Veltri, Gianfranco Miletto, "[...] per esser buon Catolico Cristian, è necessario esser perfettamente Ebreo." "Difesa inedita del senatore veneziano Loredan in favore degli ebrei nel 1659/60, basata sul 'Discorso' di Simone Luzzatto," *Henoch* 26, no. 2 (2014): 307–327.
[75] Clizia Carminati, "Loredan Giovan Francesco," in *Dizionario Biografico degli Italiani*, vol. 65 (Rome: Istituto dell'Enciclopedia Italiana, 2005): 761–770.
[76] Archivio di Stato di Venezia (ASVe), Collection "Cinque Savi alla Mercanzia," s. II b. 162, fasc. 165 first part.

Ghetto because a note in Hebrew appears at the foot of the page: "Great! Loredan is in favour of the Jews!"[77]

At the end of the nineteenth century, Luigi Arnaldo Schiavi became aware of such information[78] and quoted some passages of Loredan's speech in defence of a particular connection between limited space (meaning the Ghetto of Venice) and population growth. Schiavi refers to a speech in favour of the Jews[79] given in the Venetian Senate in 1659, and he suggests consulting the Archivio Frari "Ing. Eb." In the subsequent pages, Schiavi mentions a proposition at the Venetian Senate made by one Grimani in 1669, but this is perhaps a mistake or a misprint, because the same quotation has also been attributed to Gian Francesco Loredan. Schiavi quotes this speech based on the religious principles on which the Venetian Republic was built.[80]

The author of the speech was Gian Francesco Loredan, a member of the Venetian nobility, which was categorically opposed to the subordination of the Church, and he also claimed that the autonomy of the Venetian Republic followed a philo-semitic attitude.[81] The figure of Bartolomeo (Bartolo) Grimani, Loerdan's opponent, is hard to identify from an archival and historical point of view,[82] but he could possibly be identified as the Bortolo Grimani di Francesco mentioned in *Relatione dell'Eccellentissimo Signor Francesco Michael Cavaliere fu Ambasciator alla Corte Cesarea* in 1678.[83]

---

[77] " בן לורדאן א׳// פאוור יהודים. S[ine] Die. // Attione del N.H. quondam [...] Loredan a favor de Ebrei in Senato, acciò non venghino scacciati; C. Il. N.H. Grimani fece attione in contrario; e del contenuto fu dopo l'anno 1659."

[78] Luigi A. Schiavi, "Gli Ebrei in Venezia e nelle sue colonie. Appunti storici su documenti editi ed inediti," in *Nuova Antologia*, S. III, vol. 47 (1893): 309–333; 417–519; Brian Pullan, *Gli Ebrei d'Europa e l'Inquisizione a Venezia dal 1550 al 1670* (Rome: Il Veltro, 1985), 246, 263 e n. 60 and ASVe, Collection Luigo A. "Cinque Savi alla Mercanzia," busta 62, fasc. 165.

[79] Schiavi, "Gli Ebrei in Venezia," 507.

[80] Ibid.: "Religion! Quella che xe el fregio prencipal de questa Republica; quela che porta el nostro nome imortal sull'ali della fama; quela per la qual se cimentan i popoli, se profondono i tesori, se mette in compromesso el medesimo Stato? quella ch'è incontaminata in questo solo Stato; Quela per la quale non si son temude le inimicizie de' maggior Potentadi del mondo; quella che xe l'anima de questo Stato, quella che xè el sostentamento della nostra libertà. e se taxe!? E se sopporta!? E no i se scazza del tuto questi seguaci d'altra Legge, che de Cristo."

[81] Cf. Gaetano Cozzi, "Società veneziana, società ebraica," in *Gli Ebrei e Venezia secoli XIV–XVIII* (Milan: Edizioni di Comunità, 1987): 333–374; Gaetano Cozzi, *Giustizia "contaminata,"* Vicende giudiziarie di nobili ed ebrei nella Venezia del Seicento (Venice: Marsilio, 1996), 77.

[82] Cf. Marco Barbaro, "Arbori de Patritii veneti," ASV Miscellanee Codici—Storia Veneta 17—Miscell Codd. 894. From n. I to n. VII, 117–160, the author presents a genealogy of the Grimani family. We find a "Bartolamio" born in 1651 (128). There is no record of another Bartolomei or Bortolo.

[83] Francesco Michael Cavaliere, *Relatione dell'Eccellentissimo Signor Francesco Michael Cavaliere fu Ambasciator alla Corte Cesarea*. Biblioteca Italiana Online, http://ww2.bibliotecaitaliana.it/xtf/view?docId=bibit000471/bibit000471.xml&doc.view=print&chunk.id=0&toc.depth=1&toc.id=0 (accessed 3 May, 2018).

3.3 The Ghetto and Dialectic Strategies: The Philosopher Sara Copio Sullam — 211

Loredan attacks the argumentations of Bartolomeo Grimani and he appeals to Simone Luzzatto in support of his position. The most important argument taken from Luzzatto's *Discorso* is the conviction that the Hebrew nation is not able to initiate or to declare war on any other nation.[84]

Religion becomes the first argument raised by Grimani against the presence of the Jews in Venice. According to Grimani, religious difference inevitably leads to social division. As a counterargument, Loredan defends the idea that the Jewish religion has a divine nature and, for this reason, in spite of some deviation to the Christian path, must be held in high regard.[85] Loredan concludes his speech with an important sentence: being a good Christian is being a perfect Jew.[86] Using a specific *topos* of Christian literature,[87] Loredan refers to a traditional Thomistic idea by which the *caerimonalia* were suppressed by Jesus even if the central idea of the Torah had a divine origin.[88] He completes his sentence saying that those who condemn religious observance in Jewish law also condemn the law *tout court*.

In his *Discorso*, quoted by Loredan, Luzzatto seeks to vindicate the presence of the Jews and their value within Christian society. Yet he speaks in a tone that exceeds that of mere *petitio*, showing pride in his own attitudes and presenting reasons for valuing the Jewish presence in broader society, since he knows that the "Hebrew nation" currently has no other political possibility, as he himself argues: "Nonetheless, if someone still wishes to investigate which customs they share universally, one could say that they are a nation with an unusual and tired spirit, incapable in their present state of all political government, busy with their particular interests, quite—if not completely—unaware of their universal nature" (*Discorso* 36v–37r). Luzzatto was probably making an indirect reference to Cuso, who in *De pace fidei* wrote: "However, the presence of the Jews as residents does not prevent harmony, because they are few and they would be unable to disturb the peace of the world by the means of the force of weapons."[89]

Those who think that acknowledging their own weakness is an act of unconditioned submission are doubtlessly wrong here, at least in the logic of Luzzatto's treatise. In the dispersion of the Diaspora, the Jewish people preserve their unparalleled

---

84 "Non el timor de guerra, mentre questi non posson haver forza per sussitarne el Stato."
85 "E se ben in quelle parti alterade, o per la necessitudine de' tempi o per l'effetto delle mutation mondane, questo non ghe deve levar la veneration, questo no' ghe deve far perder la stima, questo non ghe leva quell'autentica che per esser certa, basta dir che sia divina."
86 "E questo tanto è vero quanto per esser buon Catolico Cristian, è necessario esser perfettamente Ebreo."
87 See Giuseppe Veltri, *Renaissance Philosophy in Jewish Garb*, 169–194.
88 "Mentre levati quei accidenti de tempio e de circoncision, da chi la Lezze, da chi insegnamenti, da chi le figure, da chi li prencipii se non da questa Lezze medesima che l'istesso ebreo venera, osserva, predica e professa."
89 Nicholas of Cusa, *De Pace Fidei*, in *Nicolai de Cusa Opera Omnia*, ed. Raymundus Kilibansky and Hildebrandus Bascour, vol. 7 (Hamburg: Meiner, 1959), 39: "Haec tamen Iudaeōrum resistentia non impediet concordiam. Pauci enim sunt et turbare universum mundum armis non poterunt."

ability for self-preservation through the awareness of a special identity, or, as Luzzatto argues, "The [Hebrew] nation [...] was broken, and divided into nearly infinite parts, dispersed and scattered in the whole universe, holding mainly onto the identity of its essentiality" (*Discorso* 89r). The political creed of the Venetian Rabbi was well received and understood by his followers and indirect disciples, whether with or without criticism. They saw in him the essential innovation which became a kind of Archimedean point, able to change the meaning the presence and usefulness of the Jewish minority in the Diaspora in the European or indeed the Western world. The issue at stake is not, the author claims, the antiquity of the lineage or a non-existing reverence for or recognition of a people who gave birth to the Christian faith. On the contrary, the *utilitas* and the *necessitas*, completely Machiavellian concepts, support the history of Western Judaism. The former strengthened its presence in society, while the latter elucidated and highlighted the virtues it acquired during its history. That is also the topic of following chapter dedicated to the first "sceptic" of Jewish philosophical history.

4 Socrates, the Jew: The Scepticism of Simone Luzzatto

Simone Luzzatto is the first Jew of the early modern period who, imbued with political philosophical ideas and a sceptical attitude, presented a new empirical concept of Judaism as an integral part of society while also remaining a sceptic intellectual who critically engaged modern sciences and philosophy. He is philosophically in step with the previously mentioned work of the rabbi, preacher, and philosopher Yehudah Moscato, who asserted the near perfection of mathematics against the weakness of the (new) sciences.[1]

For the first time in the history of Jewish philosophy, a scholar proclaimed himself a sceptic following the New Academy. Already in his first rather apologetic-political work, the *Discorso circa il stato degli Hebrei* (1638), Luzzatto qualifies himself as new academician:[2] "Political matters are full of alterations and contingencies, and in this *Discorso* I promised I would follow the probable and the verisimilar,[3] just as a new academician would, and in so doing [the academician] differs from the mathematicians that are used to following the absolutely verifiable and undeniable" (*Discorso*, 30r). Being a mathematician, as we can infer at least from some parts of his *Socrate* (1651),[4] Luzzatto was acquainted with axiomatic systems, demonstrably consistent because of their absence of contradiction *per definitionem*. He was, however, of the opinion that axiomatic logic does not work in the consideration of human affairs and political matters, and that the philosopher cannot reach a judgment on them with the sole help of probable and verisimilar argumentations because contradiction is here more often the rule than the exception. The adoption of the categories of plausibility and verisimilitude occurred first in the *Discorso*, the first field of his sceptical training, while in *Socrate* he presents very detailed strategies against dogmatic thought in almost every branch of human science and wisdom. To my knowledge, *Socrate* is the first extant treatise on scepticism written by a Jew.

The first emphasis of this chapter will be, therefore, to evince some subtle sceptical strategies Luzzatto used to substantiate the (right of) existence of the Jews de-

---

[1] This was also a topic of the Italian academies, in which the study of science and mathematics together with the liberal arts was both common and appreciated; see Michele Battagia, *Delle accademie Veneziane dissertazione storica* (Venice: Orlandelli, 1826), 35.
[2] For a bibliography of and on Luzzatto, see Giuseppe Veltri, *Luzzatto. Scritti*, 465–499.
[3] For a discussion on the term πιθανός as "verisimilar," see Pierre Gassendi in *Sintagma* (1658) I, *De logicae fine*, 5, *Opera* 1, 79b; cf. Robert Pasnau, *After Certainty: A History of Our Epistemic Ideals and Illusions* (Oxford: Oxford University Press, 2017); on the second volume of the *Exercitationes paradoxicae adversus Aristoteleos* II, VI,6 (1659), cf. Delphine Bellis, "*Nos in Diem Vivimus:* Gassendi's Probabilism and Academic Philosophy from Day to Day," in *Academic Scepticism in the Development of Early Modern Philosophy*, ed. Plinio Junqueira Smith and Sébastien Charles (New York: Springer, 2016): 125–152; on probable and verisimilar, see *Academic Scepticism*, 130–131.
[4] Cf. *Socrate*, 68, 158, 233–234.

spite and because of their differences in the face of the Venetian society and government; he weakened the arguments against Judaism and the Jews that were generated by their detractors and enemies. The second most important focus of this chapter will be the analysis of the keyhole like nature of Luzzatto's *Socrate*, as it provides a glimpse into a complicated world of modern sceptical philosophy and dialectic argumentation.

Although the *Discorso* and *Socrate* do have very different literary structures and therefore belong to different genres and address two different types of audience, it is my conviction that both of them follow the same sceptic logic: to counter dogmatic ideas and preconceptions with the intent to create at least an equipollence of arguments and culminate politically with the pragmatic issue of how to integrate the Jews into Venetian society. In the *Discorso*, Luzzatto defends the *integral* role of the Jews in the Venetian society against the alleged reason of political and religious *incompatibilities* between them and Christianity. In his philosophical work *Socrate*, he is in favour of the suspension of judgment for Socrates because of the impossibility of an impartial process and correspondent plausible judgment. In the first case, we have empiricism against dogmatism, in the second we observe the necessity of the *epoché*; all of them are sceptical strategies.

4.1 Apologetic Strategies, Scepticism, and Empiricism

According to some scholars, Luzzatto's *Discorso* falls into the category of the apology or "modern" apologetics of Judaism in Venice.[5] Because of my special research interest focused on sceptical strategies, it is worthwhile to explain some concepts surrounding the field of apology/apologia in modern (English) language.

The terms apology, apologia, and apologetics seem to philologically include the same concept, but philology does not play the decisive role here. Today the English word apology means "the act of declaring one's regret, remorse, or sorrow for having insulted, failed, injured, harmed or wronged another."[6] Yet, apologia derives from the same Latin word *apologia* and means what the Greek coinage ἀπολογία in substance addresses: "verbal defence, speech in defence." The first literary and philosophical occurrence known to me is the *Apologia of Socrates*.

By contrast, apologetics is systematic argumentative discourse in defence of a doctrine/ religion, as every dictionary confirms.[7] The method of the defence of apologetics may be similar to apologia but the goal is very different. Apologetics may and

---

[5] Cf. Francesca Trivellato, "Jews and Early Modern Economy," in *The Cambridge history of Judaism, Volume 7: The Early Modern World, 1500–1815,* ed. Jonathan Karp and Adam Sutcliffe (Cambridge: Cambridge University Press, 2018), 161.
[6] Quoted from Mihaela Mihai, "Apology," in *Internet Encyclopedia of Philosophy,* http://www.iep.utm.edu/apology/ (accessed 3 May, 2018).
[7] See, for example, https://www.britannica.com/topic/apologetics (accessed 3 May, 2018).

could have a missionary objective to convert people to the "true" religion, the "right" doctrine, while an apologia is primarily a defence designed to convince the judge of one's innocence in opposition to a prosecutor's arguments. The goal is to reach at least an equipollence of arguments. At any rate, an apologia is by no means an apology; it is not a remorseful speech or a term acknowledging wrongful or offensive action and it must also be properly located in the realm of jurisprudence and in philosophical/rhetoric dialectic discussions.

Further, it is well-known that in an accusatorial process the task of the defendant is to try to abate every charge of the accusation by using an arsenal of rhetorical tools, adducing evidence, (accurate) testimony, and (alleged or consistent) proof: all strategies in order to undermine the claim and argument of the (state) prosecutor. I will come back to this point later in my discussion of rhetorical logic and the results of a rabbinic discussion. At this point, I would like to confine myself only to written apologias by emphasising that *writings* in defence of individual or (political, religious, ethnic) groups against the charges of the majority or the ruling powers, are called "apologia" because they are defending their own point of view, behaviour, or identity which are different from that of the majority. The strategies involved in apologia and apologetics are similar: to produce evidence to counter the adversary, to reduce an accusation to a self-contradiction, and to disavow the charges, removing all legitimacy and plausibility from the construction of the prosecutor's indictment.

Luzzatto adopts this strategy for dismantling the accusation that the Jews are unsuitable to Christian society due to their identity as a different ethnic group and religion. He does not repeat ancient and traditional arguments of antiquity and (messianic) legitimacy in favour of the Jews, but he refers to the experiential, empirical argument of the socially cohesive nature and economic usefulness of the Jews of Venice. It is of course well known that empiricism and scepticism are not the same philosophical movement; however, they use very similar strategies and base their arguments on pragmatic facts based on experience.

A few words and notations should be addressed towards the topic of experience as a *philosophoumenon* both of the empiricism and scepticism.[8] The question of similarity between the two Greek schools is very old and goes back to Sextus Empiricus. Nevertheless, there is more. The discussion of whether Sextus, author of the main fonts of ancient scepticism, was an empiricist or not, as some ancient sources suggest,[9] does not obscure the fact that ancient empiricism did not admit a dogmatic vision of healing in its methods. Sextus recognises some validity to their strategies, when he affirms, "Some say that the sceptical philosophy is the same as the empiric school in medicine. But you must realise that if this form of empiricism makes affir-

---

[8] Cf. Emidio Spinelli, "L'esperienza scettica: Sesto Empirico fra metodologia scientifica e scelte etiche," *Quaestio* 4 (2004): 25–43.

[9] Cf. Alan Bailey, *Sextus Empiricus and Pyrrhonean Scepticism* (Oxford: Oxford University Press, 2002), 93–99; cf. Roderick M. Chisholm, "Sextus Empiricus and Modern Empiricism," *Philosophy of Science* 8, no. 3 (1941): 371–384.

mations about the inapprehensibility of unclear matters, then it is not the same as scepticism, nor would it be appropriate for Sceptics to take up with that school."[10] Although he seems to counter medical empiricism, he does seem to accept the medical method:

> They might rather adopt, as it seems to me, what is called the Method; for this alone of the medical schools seems to practise no rashness in unclear matters and (the empiricist school) does not presume to say whether they are apprehensible or inapprehensible, but it follows what is apparent, taking thence, in line with sceptical practice, what seems to be expedient.[11]

Independent from the question of the goals and of the approach to medicine, Sextus cannot negate the fact that empiricism and scepticism adopt very similar tactics.[12] Both of them back their strategies with experience (ἐμπειρία), a medical attitude of general significance, as an example of linguistic scepticism. To abate the grammarian's dogmatic vision of the "natural significance" of words, he bases his criticism on the experience with the "Barbarians" and comments, "If nouns exist 'by nature' and are not significant in each instance by reason of convention, then all men ought to understand the speech of all, Greeks that of barbarians and barbarians that of Greeks and barbarians that of (other) barbarians. But this is not the case; therefore, nouns are not 'naturally' significant."[13] The argument used here is from experience (that of the Barbarians and the Greeks), not from the realm of logic or metaphysics. Also well-known is his argument about the moral(s) of society: every people have different moral standards, ergo there is not a common morality "by nature." Furthermore, the argumentation "by nature" can be treacherous for the dogmatic because of the experience of good and bad, or according to his words: "For the man who opines that anything is by nature good or bad is for ever being disquieted: when he is without the things which he deems good he believes himself to be tormented by things naturally bad."[14]

Empiricism as a school and as a medical practice is not confined to ancient philosophy and medicine, it has a long history in the Middle Ages, Renaissance, and early modern period. Beginning with the schools of Roger Bacon and William of Ockham in Middle Ages, its apex occurred in the late Renaissance with Machiavelli and Guicciardini. Yet, from the *De rerum natura iuxta propria principia* (*On the Nature of Things According to their Own Principles*) of Bernardino Telesio in 1586 and Michel de

---

10 *Outlines of Pyrrhonism* I: 236, English translation in Sextus Empiricus, *Outlines of Scepticism*, ed. Julia Annas, Jonathan Barnes (Cambridge: Cambridge University Press, 2000).
11 Ibid.
12 It is not my intent here to deal with every aspect this topic involves. I refer the reader to the detailed study of Emidio Spinelli, "Sextus Empiricus," in *Dictionnaire des philosophes antiques*, ed. Richard Goulet (Paris: CNRS éditions, 2016): 265–300; "on empiricism", 279–282.
13 Sextus Empiricus, *Against the Professors*, I:VII, §144–145 (Loeb, 1949, 86–87).
14 *Outlines of Pyrrhonism* I:27; see also I:30. Cf. Michael Frede, "The Sceptic's Beliefs," in *The Original Sceptics: A Controversy* (Indianapolis: Hackett, 1997), 22.

Montaigne "Of Experience"[15] to Francis Bacon onwards, Empiricism experienced new modes of transmission and discussion. Luzzatto's acquaintance with it may derive from his study of Pierre Gassendi, a very probable source of his writing and perhaps a favourite reading.[16] Additionally, Francis Bacon was one of the sources of Luzzatto's attitude towards the sciences, mostly plausibly his first address for the doctrine of the induction. Francis Bacon is often indirectly quoted in the *Discorso*, as I have demonstrated elsewhere.[17]

Luzzatto's Strategies and the *Tropoi* of Sextus

Concerning the strategies of Luzzatto it is valuable to foreground some observations before we handle them in detail. In the *Discorso*, the rabbi uses some strategies to abate dogmatic principle (read: main, current, and influential opinions). The reader may be sceptical about my approach in this book on Luzzatto's language of scepticism and relative strategies. While it is true that the *tropoi* are indirect, they are the basic elements of the *Socrate*, as Michela Torbidoni has demonstrated,[18] and, in the *Discorso*, the Rabbi twice directly quotes Sextus Empiricus, on both occasions from the *tropoi*, which I would call strategies of scepticism.

In the first quotation, he speaks of moral scepticism, attacking Tacitus's calumny "to defame the Jewish Nation," painting it as dissolute in its carnal impulses: "and although as a race, they are prone to lust, they abstain from intercourse with foreign women; yet among themselves nothing is unlawful."[19] He adds:[20]

> But if this refers to the customs of the Jews, it could not be further from the truth, since there has never been a nation more restricted regarding carnal relationships than the Jews. The Egyptians, who were by no means barbarians, but in fact passed on many doctrines to the Greeks, took their sisters for wives, and the Ptolemaic kings set an example [of this habit] to the common people. The Persians, who enjoyed dominion over Asia and the subjugation of Greece, passed to a higher level of turpitude, permitting sons to wed their own mothers. Chrysippus, the propagator of Stoic philosophy, claimed that he was responsible for the reform of the human race. And yet he remained indifferent in the face of such a detestable practice; on the contrary, by means of

---

15 Michel de Montaigne, "Of Experience," ed. Patrick Madden, trans. Charles Cotton. (1588; 13 September, 2006). http://essays.quotidiana.org/montaigne/experience/ (accessed 3 May 2018).
16 *Luzzatto, Opera*, LXXX.
17 Giuseppe Veltri, "Economic and Social Arguments and the Doctrine of the Antiperistasis in Simone Luzzatto's Political Thought: Venetian Reverberations of Francis Bacon's Philosophy," *Frühneuzeit-Info* 23 (2011): 23–32.
18 Michela Torbidoni, "Il metodo del dubbio nel Socrate," in *Filosofo e Rabbino nella Venezia del Seicento. Studi su Simone Luzzatto (ca.1583–1663). Con un'appendice di documenti inediti dall'Archivio di Stato*, ed. Giuseppe Veltri (Rome: Aracne, 2015): 183–245.
19 Tacitus, *Historiae* V:5,7–8; *Historiae*, vol. III, 183.
20 *Discorso*, 59v–60r.

> some of his reasoning he sought toss describe it as almost honest, as one can read in the books of Sextus Empiricus.²¹

The argumentation is here highly imperative: Luzzatto's defence of Jewish custom neither takes into consideration the (im)morality of an act commanded by the God of the Jews (to refrain from intercourse with foreign women), thereby avoiding a return to the argument of a heteronomous moral act, nor does he found it on morality based on "nature." He infers the immorality from the discrepancy with the high esteem in which other peoples in the world community (Egyptian and Greeks) were held despite their incestuous and lascivious customs. With reference to the above listed sexual practices, Luzzatto states that the moral code of the Jews is more restrictive than that of Egyptian and Greeks, although they are judged as "barbarians" despite their probity. This is not a dogmatic argument, but a strategy taken from experience grounded in moral scepticism and relativism. The Sextian argument against natural morality was very similar: he quoted several examples of different customs in decisive moral acts like sexuality, which differed among Romans, Greek, Indians etc., an argument rooted in a multifaceted approach to law and custom.²² Luzzatto emphasises a particular element: the high esteem in which some cultures were held despite their even more radical difference in morality, e.g. the Egyptians enjoy our elevated cultural esteem despite their flagrant (according to our standards) immorality.

The second direct quotation is more complicated because he, speaking of the phenomenon of the Kabbalah, associates the 10 principles (the *sefirot*) and their flux to some ideas of the Platonic system of object and motion. He concludes:

> Plato, however, adhering in part to the said opinion, yet in a calmer manner, was not satisfied with entirely denying the existence and permanence of the being of whatever thing. For he conjectured that beyond the apprehension [82r] of our senses there were some firm and fixed substances. [According to his view,] these substances need neither a confrontation nor a relation to others, and thus could have a stable and firm existence in themselves. Furthermore, these [substances] were the origins of those apprehensions that we perceive and could be called shadows and unsubstantial appearances. This is the doctrine he affirms in his *Letters*,²³ which involves a great application of mind and a great force of intellect to apprehend a thing as pure, genuine, and bared of the commingling of relation and motion. For every object is burdened and wrapped up in these. This is what Sextus Empiricus demonstrated, i.e. that every phenomenon and object is mixed and involved in five kinds of relations. Proceeding in his examination, he even demonstrated that it is almost impossible to grasp anything about objects other than their relation. This thing [the relation] would be so feeble and slight that the Stoics, and after them the Nominalists, negated its existence, [by saying that] it was chimerical and imaginary, or even better, verbal.

---

21 Sextus Empiricus *Outlines of Pyrrhonism* III, I 14, paragraphs 152 and 160, *Outlines of Pyrrhonism*, 89 and 93 (the tenth mode).
22 *Outlines*, I:XIV, 152: "And we oppose habit to the other things, as for 152 instance to law when we say that amongst the Persians it is the habit to indulge in intercourse with males, but amongst the Romans it is forbidden by law to do so [...]" (trans. Loeb Library).
23 Luzzatto probably refers to the 7th Epistle of Plato.

The reference to Sextus in confirming a Platonic view of the system of the ideas and their relationship is tricky because Sextus does negate the existence of all fixed and firm substances. It is enough to refer here to *Outlines* III:3:

> Now, since some of the Dogmatists say that god is a body, other that he is incorporeal, some say that he is anthropomorphic, other not, and some in space, others not—and of those who say that he is in space, some say that he is within the universe, others that is outside—how shall we be able to acquire a conception of god if we possess neither an agreed substance for him, nor form, nor place where he is?[24]

But that is only one side of the question because Luzzatto connects the theory of the *Sefirot* to Plato's world of substances. Besides the tradition of this theory, already examined by Moshe Idel,[25] Luzzatto's strategic aspect cannot be concealed: fixed substances have a firm existence in themselves and therefore cannot be apprehended if not in their shadowy and unsubstantial appearances. According to Luzzatto's rendition of Sextus "every phenomenon and object is mixed and involved in five kinds of relations." He concludes "that it is almost impossible to grasp anything about objects other than their relation." As Emidio Spinelli wrote to me in a epistolary communication, Luzzatto may be referring here to the sceptic Agrippa. Sextus reported Agrippas' *tropoi*,[26] among them that of relativity, in his *Outlines*. The confusion has probably resulted, I imagine, because Agrippas' five modes are quoted by Sextus, as mentioned before.

Yet, as Spinelli comments, Sextus also speaks of the relativity in *Outlines* I:38–39 as a hierarchical submission of all *tropoi* to it. Expressly in *Outlines* I:140, he affirms, "So, since we have established in this way that everything is relative, it is clear then that we shall not be able to say what each existing object is like in its own nature and purely, but only what it appears to be like relative to something. It follows that we must suspend judgement about the nature of objects."[27] Ancient authors convey that Pyrrhonians were also relativists,[28] but an assimilation of their thoughts is not without problems, as Annas and Barnes sustain.[29] The *pros ti* of relations/relativity is also a topic of Stoic philosophy, as Luzzatto notes, which introduces or sustains the insubstantiality of relation in the cases of verbal definition, as "fa-

---

24 Sextus Empiricus, *Outlines of Scepticism*, 144.
25 That is, Isaac Abravanel; c.f. Moshe Idel, "Jewish Kabbalah and Platonism," in *Neoplatonism and Jewish Thought*, ed. Lenn E. Goodman (Albany: State University of New York Press, 1992): 319–352, 332–333. He speaks of the *Sefirot* as Platonic ideas (*sefirot*) and "separate universal forms." Yohanan Alemanno also speaks of the *Sefirot* as the primordial ideas of Plato.
26 Sextus Empiricus, *Outlines of Pyrrhonism III* I:15, 95–101, "The Five Modes."
27 English translation by Julia Annas and Jonathan Barnes, *The Modes of Scepticism: Ancient Texts and Modern Interpretations* (Cambridge: Cambridge University Press, 1997), 129.
28 Ibid., 97.
29 Ibid., 98.

ther" is father so long as he has a child, as Simplicius, in his *Commentary* on Aristotle's *Categories* comments.[30]

Luzzatto likes to demonstrate that a precise analysis of relations results in the conclusion that we cannot grasp the object of anything. The goal of his sentence is the negation of the dogmatic assertion of the existence of Plato's substances and, in this way, the *Sefirot*. From given relations we cannot infer a given substance.

It is important here to realise that sceptical strategies are at work in the *Discorso*, especially because Luzzatto considers himself in step with Sextus' scepticism, although he defines himself a New Academician and, therefore, not a Pyrrhonian. In the following section I will present some sceptical strategies present in Luzzatto's work, all of which are based on experience and achieved in history and society. Nevertheless, I suppose that Luzzatto is also using the *tropoi*, or strategy, of Sextus and Agrippa, using it as a political tool for describing, defending, and apologising for the Jews of Venice. I will select the political strategies of relation/relativity, recess, and necessity, and end with the argument concerning the "nude truth."

The Strategy of Relation/Relativity

Agrippa and Sextus Empiricus[31] agree—as I discuss above—that things are together by virtue of their relation and not due their nature. We will return to this idea with reference to usury. Here I would like to stress that the "relationship" between the elements of society is the backbone of its political structure, as well as the commitment of Luzzatto to the apologia. The presence of the Jews in Venice is due to their integration into every part of its fabric and life. Integration is not the deprivation of their factuality as Jews (i.e. conversion) but the recognition of their very clear position in society. This participation is not substantial but relative to the "state of the Jews in Venice." But first something on the *Discorso*.

Luzzatto's political thesis in the first part of the *Discorso* is simple and, at the same time, temerarious: Venice can put an end to its political decline, he argues, by offering to the Jews a monopoly on overseas commercial activity. This proposal recommends itself because the Jews are "well suited for trade," far more so than others (such as "foreigners"). The Rabbi opens his argument by recalling that trade and usury are the only occupations permitted to Jews. Within the confines of their histor-

---

30 "But when it is observed not in virtue of an internal difference but solely in virtue of its relation to something else, it will be a thing somehow in relation to something. Sons and people on the right require certain external things for theirsubsistence. That is why, even if no change takes place in themselves, a man may cease to be a father when his son dies and someone may cease to be on the right when what was next to him has changed position." *The Modes*, 134–135. The interpretation of Annas and Barnes does not take into account the oral element of stoic discourse.
31 A Pyrrhonis philosopher probably of the first century BCE and author of five tropoi, reported by Sextus, *Outlines*, I: 164–169.

ical situation, the Venetian Jews became particularly adept at trade with partners from the Orient. This talent could be put to the use by the Venetian government for maintaining—or, more accurately—recovering its political importance as an intermediary between the East and the West. Luzzatto was the first to define the role of the Jews on the basis of their economic and social functions, disregarding the classic categorisation of Judaism's (privileged?) religious status in world history.

Luzzatto prefaces his treatise with an *Introduction* (7r–8r), ostensibly intended to provide a theoretical outline of the political and economic aspects of his subject, a reflection also of his vision of the customs and ways of life followed by the Jews of the Diaspora. In this introduction to the "whole" tractate, he deals, in fact, with only *one* issue: the status of the Jews of Venice and their economic situation, which is, in turn, the topic to which the entire first part of the *Discorso* is devoted. Luzzatto clearly states his central thesis right from the outset: the ancient people of the Jews, present today in the illustrious city of Venice, are, in their constitution and way of life, a "fragment" of the God's original creation.[32] Nobody, he claims, can contest the proposition that Venetian Jews are a "reward" (*emolumento*) to the city of Venice and that they constitute an integral part of the common populace (*Discorso* 7v).

The Rabbi of the Ghetto of Venice avails himself of the fragment metaphor: the Jewish community of Venice is as a Democritian atom in the Milky Way of the Venetian *Res Publica* (*Discorso* 7r). Although the Rabbi has serious doubts as to the cosmological value of Democritus' philosophy, he seems to accept its usefulness as a source of metaphor: "And if this opinion was rightly condemned, what occurred to those men was more a result of the casual coupling of small bodies, which those philosophers proposed, rather than a result of the absurdity of the construction" (*Discorso* 7r).[33] The purpose of his treatise is not primarily to celebrate the antiquity of the Jews but rather to present some of the advantages they bring to the State. He considers the Jewish people as an integral part of city of Venice or, better, of the entire world. The function of the Jews, he claims, is similar to that of the atoms of Democritus that populate the "Lower World," which, in turn, feeds with its vapour the sun, the moon, and the other stars: a stoic idea. In this sense, every kingdom on the earth is comparable to the galaxy.[34]

---

32 *Discorso* 6v: "because the common consensus among men agrees that there was a time when this People took their form of government and social institutions from the Highest Artist."
33 Luzzatto seems here to refer to a criticism of atomistic theory, which was introduced into European intellectual circles by Gassendi. Luzzatto himself was a follower of sceptical theory. On Gassendi and scepticism, see Richard H. Popkin, *The History of Scepticism from Erasmus to Spinoza* (Berkeley: University of California Press, 1979).
34 Cf. Francis Bacon, *Essays XIX: Of Empire:* "Princes are like to heavenly bodies, which cause good or evil times; and which have much veneration, but no rest. All precepts concerning kings, are in effect comprehended in those two remembrances: memento quod es homo; and memento quod es Deus, or vice Dei; the one bridleth their power, and the other their will." On the classical origin of the idea, see A. I. Ellis, "Some Notes," *The Classical Review* 23 (1909): 246–247.

The metaphors he uses to describe the composition of society serve to draw attention to two specific points: that every element of society, and in particular that of Venice, should be fully integrated as a prerequisite to their contribution to the welfare of the whole. That is also the logic of the human body as Luzzatto expressly indicates, citing indirectly the fable of Menenius Agrippa:[35]

> [...] So too when our stomach suffers from lack of food, it lives on suitable humours with great pain and distress of other limbs.[36] But when the opposite occurs, and there is an abundance of nourishment, there is respite from the plundering, and this relief spreads to other parts of the body. Similarly, the preponderance of duties and passage taxes not only frees the populace from the burden of taxes and contributions—which they would be obliged to pay in emergencies and for the needs of the Prince—but also itself profits of this abundance of public money with not little advantage" (7v).

In sixteenth century, the metaphor of the stomach becomes more specific: in 1612 Francis Bacon writes in his *Of Empire* 11:

> For their merchants, they are vena porta; and if they flourish not, a kingdom may have good limbs, but will have empty veins, and nourish little. Taxes and imposts upon them, do seldom good to the king's revenue; for that that wins in the hundred, he leeseth in the shire; the particular rates being increased, but the total bulk of trading, rather decreased.

Luzzatto substantially agrees with Bacon. Taxes on imports and exports are lethal for an economy because they lead to a decrease in trade volume. In the end, the state treasury will end up with little more than usual. In addition, there is a moral aspect that should be also taken into consideration: the state should avoid imitating the ancient Romans who "ultimately imposed taxes on human excrement [...] and even disgraceful and obscene operations such as these helped enrich the treasury." In contrast to this depravity on the part of the ruling power, the Republic of Venice "has the custom of imposing taxes only on the industry of men, and not on their lives; to punish their vices, and not to profit from them." We have here, then, the principal ingredients of Luzzatto's political theory: 1) the Jews of Venice are an integral part of the Republic; 2) their function in commerce is vital and can be of true benefit only if the taxes imposed remain limited, since the taxes on imports and exports have a lethal effect on the general economy; 3) the Republic of Venice was founded on pragmatic ideas.

We can add that Luzzatto—if using the sceptic *topos* of relativity—argues that the relation of the Jews to the *Serenissima* is a profitable one and that changes to this

---

35 Livius, *Ad urbe condita*, II 32.
36 Galen thought that blood was produced in the liver from the food the stomach transported there via the portal vein. On the state of medicine at this time, based largely Galen, see Rudolph E. Siegel, *Galen's System of Physiology and Medicine. An Analysis of his Doctrines and Observations on Bloodflow, Respiration, Humors and Internal Diseases* (Urbana: University of Illinois Press, 1993).

4.1 Apologetic Strategies, Scepticism, and Empiricism — 223

relation (i.e. their expulsion from Venice) would also change the "state" of the Jews in Venice, and perhaps also Venice itself.

Another application of the political strategy of relation/relativity can be found in chapter 12 of the *Discorso* in which Luzzatto addresses the criticism of the Jewish presence as voiced by three different groups: religious zealots, politicians and statesmen, and the common people. The religious zealots claim that toleration of a religion that differs from the official faith is contemptuous; politicians argue that there is no utility to tolerating a diversity of religions in the same city, both because of the possibility of sacrilege and because of the bad example that one group may provide to the remainder of the population; and the common people simply believe and repeat any calumny and false slander invented out of hatred for the Jewish nation.

In response to the religious zealots, Luzzatto notes that the Pope himself admitted Jews into the city of his own residence, and that they have been living there for over 800 years. To the politicians he offers a very detailed response, stressing the physical separation between Jews and Christians, which is reinforced by Jewish law, according to which ritual contact and sexual relations with non-Jews are prohibited, as is proselytism. As for the crime of usury practiced by the Jews—he adds that it is only tolerated by their laws rather than expressly permitted, referring indirectly to Francis Bacon.

As for the denunciations of the common people, Luzzatto responds:

> Truth alone is harsh, and not very pleasing, whereas falsity is admired and delightful. The former is subjected to the occurrence of events; the latter free and wandering. The former is produced by the action of the object that impressed it in our mind, while the latter depends upon human judgments, and like our offspring, one brings them loving affection.

He then deals more specifically with the calumny of the Jews having been unfaithful, and with their purported friendship with pirates. Contrary to what his opponents maintain, Luzzatto describes the Jews as a harmonious part of society, living in reciprocal sympathy with their neighbours in keeping with the will of God, who "decreed that all humanity should conform together in unanimous amity, each man considering himself a citizen of one commonwealth" (46r). Religious differences, as he points out in chapter 14 and as we have analysed in the second part of this book, are by no means a good reason for war (51v).[37]

The perspicacious reader recognises here a typical strategy of referring to the successful integration of Jews into the Venetian city and their utility under the sky of the *Serenissima*. The reason given is not a dogmatic reference to the Revelation on Sinai, but rather the activity of the Jews, originating in historical necessity. Their success is dependent on the conservation of their status as Jews as well as

---

37 Cf. Isaac Abravanel, *Perush al nevi'im aaronim* (Tel Aviv, n.d.): 9; and Johann Maier, *Kriegsrecht und Friedensordnung in jüdischer Tradition* (Stuttgart: Kohlhammer, 2000), 403.

their utility for Venice;[38] that is, the key for the Jews' integration into Venetian society is to fill and to continue to fulfil the social position they already hold, a kind of political recess *ad infinitum*.

Strategy of Necessity, or, How to Explain Recess *ad infinitum* Politically

Luzzatto uses a typical political-economic category, "necessity." *Necessitas* as a category must not be confused with the Aristotelian logical concept of *necessitas*,[39] and it also occurs in sceptical philosophy: necessity is the reason, according to the sceptical philosophy of Sextus, to suspend every judgment.[40] The context of Sextus' use is totally different, but Luzzatto's logical use of necessity is very similar: to search for the major cause of necessity would regress to an analysis of animals, which do not possess reason. Luzzatto indirectly refers to regress to the causes of the situation of the Jews, because necessity *is* the situation into which humans are born and to which man can positively react, or, according to Luzzatto's wording,

> The majority of men claim that nature has thrust upon them and vexed them with obligations and necessities in greater abundance than other animals which are deprived of reason. But these men [the majority] complain of duty, because poverty and need are the true stimuli and incentives that result in the inventions and discoveries of the most worthy and excellent arts, which so ennoble the human race.[41]

The proverb *mater artium necessitas*, "necessity is the mother of invention," has a long tradition. In the Middle Ages, it was an operative concept of the political tradition, used in conjunction with other political terms such as *virtus* and *fortuna*.[42] There is of course a common use of the proverb which probably first appeared in print in 1519 in the *Vulgaria* of William Horman, "a book of aphorisms for the boys of the schools to learn by heart."[43] Yet numerous individuals and intellectuals

---

[38] On both categories during the Renaissance, see Paul-Erik Korvela, "The Machiavellian Reformation. An Essay in Political Theory" (PhD dissertation, University of Jyvaskyla, 2016), 119–120.
[39] Lambert Marie de Rijk, *Aristotle: Semantics and Ontology. Philosophia Antiqua*, vol. 91, no. 1 (Leiden: Brill, 2002), 569; Nathanael Stein, "Causal Necessity in Aristotle," *British Journal for the History of Philosophy* 20 (2012): 855–879.
[40] Cf. *Outline of Pyrrhonism* I:175–176, see Casey Perin, *The Demands of Reason: An Essay on Pyrrhonian Scepticism* (Oxford: Oxford University Press, 2010).
[41] *Discorso*, 18r.
[42] On the triad, cf. Felix Gilbert's chapter "Fortune, Necessity, and Virtù" in his *Machiavelli and Guicciardini: Politics and History in Sixteenth-Century Florence.* (Princeton: Princeton University Press, 1965): 191–200.
[43] It is very difficult to locate the origin of the proverb. Recent works refer it to Curtius Rufus's *Historia Alexandri Magni*, 4,3,24: "Efficacior omni arte imminens necessitas"; see Hubertus Kudla, ed. *Lexikon der lateinischen Zitate. 3500 Originale mit Übersetzungen und Belegstellen*, 3rd edition (Munich: Beck, 2007), n. 1439. I think that there is no precise Latin quote, but for a Latin sapiential tra-

were acquainted with this proverb and its inherent political-philosophical meaning. One such person was Leonardo da Vinci.⁴⁴ The category of necessity, however, did not become a political category with clear-cut criteria until Machiavelli's opus,⁴⁵ to which Luzzatto most likely refers.

According to the Rabbi of Venice and in agreement with the generally accepted history of the Jews since the Middle Ages, trade and money-lending were the only occupations permitted to the Jews. This historical necessity engendered in the Venetian Jews a highly developed capacity for these occupations. Consequently, they were considered by Luzzatto potentially capable of assisting the Venetian government in maintaining, or, to be historically more accurate, *recovering*, a position of political equilibrium between the East and the West. To put this briefly with respect to a very intriguing aspect of the political life of the Jews in Venice: the *Discorso* was published in 1638 in a period in which the political power of Venice was beginning to wane. His philosophical work *Socrate*, published in 1651, expressly refers to the Turkish threat against Crete and to the war in which Venice was involved. Hence, Luzzatto tried to offer the Governor of the *Serenissima* a political-economic prescription to restore the vital trade of Venice by offering the Jews more economic and social freedom.

Bacon's conviction was that "[i]t is against nature for money to beget money,"⁴⁶ echoing an Aristotelian-Thomistic conviction.⁴⁷ However, that is only a superficial read of Bacon's analysis, vision, and inferences.

An in-depth study of Bacon's conception of usury reveals a more complex attitude which, as we shall see, is similar to that of the Rabbi of Venice. Bacon is adamant in his opposition to usury, and it should be borne in mind that this activity as

---

dition of it, see all the proverbs on "necessity" quoted by the *Hoyt's New Cyclopedia of Practical Quotations* (New York: Funk & Wagnalls, 1922), 559; see also the collection of examples of this phrase at http://www.phrases.org.uk./meanings/necessity-is-the-mother-of-invention.html (accessed 3, May 2018).

44 "La necessità è tema e inventrice della natura, e freno e regola eterna," in *Scritti letterari di Leonardo da Vinci*, ed. Augusto Marinoni (Milan: Rizzoli, 1974), 7. See the very interesting philosophical evaluation of the maxim in Herr von Prantl, "Leonardo da Vinci in philosophischer Beziehung," *Sitzungsberichte der königlichen bayerischen Akademie der Wissenschaften zu München. Philosophisch-philologische Classe*. Jahrgang 1885 (Munich: Akademische Buchdruckerei, 1886), 17.

45 On the use of *"necessitas"* in Machiavelli, see *Machiavellism: The Doctrine of Raison D'Aetat and Its Place in Modern History*, trans. Douglas Scott (New Haven: Yale University Press, 1957).

46 Francis Bacon, "Of Usury," *Essays* (1625); see *The Merchant of Venice*, I, 3: "Antonio. Or is your gold and silver Eues and Rams? Shylock. I cannot tell, I make it breede as fast." See Francis Bacon, *The Essays or Counsels, Civil and Moral*, ed. Brian Vickers (Oxford: Oxford University Press, 1999), 94.

47 Thomas Aquinas, *Summa Theologica*, trans. Fathers of the English Dominican Province (London: R. T. Washburne, Ltd., 1918), 330–340, reprinted in Roy C. Cave & Herbert H. Coulson, *A Source Book for Medieval Economic History* (Milwaukee: The Bruce Publishing Co., 1936; reprinted, New York: Biblo & Tannen, 1965), 182. Walter S.H. Lim, "Surety and Spiritual Commercialism in *The Merchant of Venice*," *Studies in English Literature* 50, no. 2 (2010): 355–381, 371.

perceived by Luzzatto and Bacon was not only the act or practice of lending money at an exorbitant rate of interest, but rather simply the practice of lending money at any rate of interest at all.[48] However, the Lord of Verulam was well aware of the advantages of such activities. In his essay "Of Usury," he enumerated the advantages and disadvantages of usury, including the danger of capitalisation: "The fourth [disadvantage of usury is], that it bringeth the treasure of a realm, or state, into a few hands. For the usurer being at certainties, and others at uncertainties, at the end of the game, most of the money will be in the box; and ever a state flourisheth, when wealth is more equally spread." Luzzatto also refers to an ideal situation of greater equality, always desired but never attained. He states: "However, the aspiration to a rigorous reduction of one's possessions to a moderate size has been considered a desirable undertaking to this day, but it is hardly ever practiced, especially with regard to the equal distribution of moveable assets and cash. Whenever this was attempted with real estate, the result was for the most part unsuccessful."[49] Bacon's position is in fact very pragmatic: whoever thinks that one can lend money without profit belongs *ipso dicto* to the realm of utopian dreamers:

> It is a vanity to conceive, that there would be ordinary borrowing without profit; and it is impossible to conceive, the number of inconveniences that will ensue, if borrowing be cramped. Therefore, to speak of the abolishing of usury is idle. All states have ever had it, in one kind or rate, or other. So as that opinion must be sent to Utopia.[50]

Luzzatto also refers to Thomas More's *Utopia* as concretisation of the "*machinate repubbliche*" (ingenious republics) of Socrates and Plato, where the distribution of goods was the chief element of their political thought.[51] Bacon sums up his opinion on the re-integration of usury, stating that it should be reserved for a small group under government control: For "it is better to mitigate usury, by declaration, than

---

48 Cf. Benjamin Ravid, "Money Lending in Seventeenth-Century Jewish Vernacular Apologetica," in *Jewish Thought in the Seventeenth Century*, ed. Isadore Twersky and Bernard Septimus (Cambridge: Harvard University Press, 1987): 257–283, 262.
49 *Discorso* 25v: "Ma il volere con rigore ridure li haveri a segno di moderata proporzione, fu impresa sin ora desiderata, ma non giamai praticata, e massime l'uguaglianza de beni mobili, e danari contanti, e se fu alcuna volta attentata nelli beni stabili riuscì sempre con infelice successo." English translation by Ariella Lang.
50 Cf. *The English Renaissance: An Anthology of Sources and Documents*, ed. Kate Aughterson (London: Routledge, 1998), 548; Robert Appelbaum, *Literature and Utopian Politics in Seventeenth-Century England* (Cambridge: Cambridge University Press, 2002), 4.
51 *Discorso* 22r–v: "La massa degli huomini mentre non fosse stata dalla prudente diligenza di legislatori, e formatori di governi civili, distinta in varii ordini, e differenti classi rassembrarebbe maggior diformità che l'antico, e decantato cahos all'imaginatione de poeti giamai rappresentasse. Socrate, e Platone, nelle loro machinate republiche posero tal distribuitione, come principale elemento delle loro politie, e l'istesso osservò il moderno inventore della Utopia, ed il simile ancora eseguirono tutti li praticanti, come parimente Aristotile nel primo della Politica, ch'impiegò ogni suo spi|rito in riordinare, e correggere le divisioni fatte da quelli doi gran maestri dell'umanità."

to suffer it to rage, by connivance."⁵² In his response to some criticisms of money lending, made both by philosophers and statesmen, Luzzatto uses the same argument as advanced by Bacon, focusing on the stimulus generated by the moneylenders:

> [...] usury is a sin constantly condemned, but in every time and place practiced. For two stimuli of our fragility, contribute to it: the necessity of those who need the money and therefore give the interest, and the avidity of the moneylender. When such a transgression was not committed by a Jew, there was perhaps no lack of others, who with greater extortion of the poor and needy would practice such a contemptible profession, reducing the number of usurers. And I do not say this to defend such actions, but merely to demonstrate that such enormity, like some others, is not an essential property of the Jews, as many presume to assert; rather it is an accidental result that comes from the strictness of the life and conditions of the time.⁵³

The reader acquainted with sceptical strategies will have already recognised here the argument against an *essential* property of the Jews (that is, "is not an essential property of the Jews;" also see Sextus' usage of "by nature") and the recurrence of the strategy of infinite regress as factual relation used in political discourse: If agent A^1 does not do a practise P, there will be an A^2 which will do P. The argumentation does not presuppose a direct causality between A^1 viz. A^n and P, but it implies the experienced fact P which requited a non-essential but accidental relation to P. The only experienced fact is P, the agent A which/who produces P is only accidental and therefore theoretically infinite. The relation from P to A is not essential, therefore it leads to A^n.

Moral Scepticism, or, Stoic Teaching in Sceptical Dress: The Charakteres

Chapter 11 of the *Discorso* marks the beginning of its second part. Luzzatto begins by observing, with Socrates, that the human being is nothing but "a multiplicity of different animals, wrapped and entangled within themselves."⁵⁴ Luzzatto refers to to Seneca's letter CXIII *ad Lucilium* in which he purposely mentions the stoic doctrine of the multiple or animal soul in human beings, because virtues can only be animal

---

52 Francis Bacon, *Of Usury*, XLI.
53 *Discorso*, 42r–v: "[...] usura, peccato continuamente dannato, ma in ogni tempo e loco essercitato, concorrendovi due stimoli maggiori, ch'habbia la nostra fragilità, la necessità del mutuario che contribuisce l'usura, e l'avidità insaziabile del mutante, che la riceve, e quando non fusse commessa dall'hebreo tal transgressione, non vi mancarebbeno forsi altri, che con maggior estorsione dell'indigente, e bisogno, essercitassero tal prava professione, riducendosi a minor numero gl'usurarii." English translation by Ariella Lang.
54 *Discorso*, 35v: "(Socrate) pronunziò non sapere se egli fosse un solo animale, overo una moltiplicità di diversi in se stessi anodati, ed invilupati, talmente trovava in se medesimo confuse le virtù, e li vizii, li eccessi, e le moderazioni."

in nature: *virtutes esse animalia*.⁵⁵ The statement *virtutes esse animalia* goes back, according to the Stoic fragments, probably to Chrysippus.⁵⁶ Luzzatto wishes to find a philosophical connection to affirm that the human soul is a mixture. He indirectly cites the theory of *omomerie* (ὁμοιομέρειαι) by Anaxagoras, that is to say of the principles or roots of cosmological anthropological compositions forming a mixture in the body:

> And if Anaxagoras, who denied that natural things are generated and because of this he introduced a certain confused mass composed of all things, and who judged that in all things there is another one annexed and attached, an opinion considered as absurd, had a similar thing proposed about human soul, may be his opinion would have been received with more applause by the learned, because if one considered attentively the movements of the soul, it would appear as a universal mixture of infinite things.⁵⁷

Luzzatto's main objective is not so much contemplation about the composition of human personality, but rather discussion of the theme of virtue and vice in human beings. What follows is in fact a long passage on virtues and their obverse as individual characteristics in different moments and different locations:

> The courage of living an adventurous life often derives from the fear one has of vulgar whispers and gossips, as on the contrary Fabius, cowardly in attacking Hannibal but intrepid scorner of the tongue of the plebeians, the greediness of prolonging life and enjoying its pleasures putting the weak but durable avidities before the vehement and short ones, makes us tempered and moderate: whereas Socrates following Plato who discovered in his *Phaedo* this great arcane called morality that the moderates, "intemperantia quadam temperantes sint, e cosi timidatate forte sint," and Solomon in Ecclesiastes c. 4 said, "et contemplatus sum omnem laborem, et omnem rectitudinem operum, et ecce ipsa esse invidia hominis de socio suo," as in Hebrew; that is to say that the vulgar virtues are envy, competition and emulation keeping men close to one another, confusing in the way virtues and vices.
>
> [36v] Pleasure, the principal and most attractive object of our soul, is always mixed together with pain, its contrary, as Plato demonstrates in Philebus, hunger and thirst are the major condi-

---

55 Seneca, *Ad Luciulium espistolae morales*, liber XIX, CXIII,3: [2] "Animum constat animal esse, cum ipse efficiat ut simus animalia, cum ab illo animalia nomen hoc traxerint; virtus autem nihil aliud est quam animus quodam modo se habens; ergo animal est. Deinde virtus agit aliquid; agi autem nihil sine impetu potest; si impetum habet, qui nulli est nisi animali, animal est. [3] 'Si animal est' inquit 'virtus, habet ipsa virtutem.' Quidni habeat se ipsam? quomodo sapiens omnia per virtutem gerit, sic virtus per se. 'Ergo' inquit 'et omnes artes animalia sunt et omnia quae cogitamus quaeque mente conplectimur. Sequitur ut multa millia animalium habitent in his angustiis pectoris, et singuli multa simus animalia aut multa habeamus animalia.' Quaeris quid adversus istud respondeatur? Unaquaeque ex istis res animal erit: multa animalia non erunt. Quare? dicam, si mihi accommodaveris subtilitatem et intentionem tuam. [4] Singula animalia singulas habere debent substantias; ista omnia unum animum habent; itaque singula esse possunt, multa esse non possunt."
56 *Stoicorum veterum fragmenta*, vol. 3, ed. Hans F. von Arnim (Stuttgart: Tuebner, 1964), 75; Stobaeus Ecl. 64,18 and 65,1; see also Thomas G. Rosenmeyer, *Senecan Drama and Stoic Cosmology* (Berkeley: University of California Press, 1989), 96.
57 *Discorso*, 36r.

ments for out taste, tragic representations move us and produce in us indignation against tyrants, nevertheless we feel a certain hidden pleasurable itch and irritation, which amuses and captures us; the Jews express pleasure with the word תענוג which derives from the verb ענה which also means affliction and therefore confirms the above mentioned mixture.

The impulsive agitation of rage was commended by Homer as full of pleasantness and sweetness, in the same way in the fervour of love jealousy gets generated and therefore hate, as Tacitus said about Mount Lebanon mirum dictu tantos inter ardores opacum fidumque niuibus. Alexander, famous for his victories not less than for the virtues of his soul, so compassionate toward Darius and his women, was afterwards so inhuman against Parmenion and Clitus, who had put the dominion of the world in his hands, and also so cruel with Callisthenes, his master. Julius Caesar, ferocious and inhuman in Pharsalia but clement with Marcellus and indulgent with Brutus, his assassin. Nero, a monster for all times, sometimes was displeased by the fact that he was able to write, especially when he had to sentence criminals to death, even though he did not hesitate in applying it against his own mother [37r] and against Seneca, his master; he was a friend of virtue and doctrine but he hated those characters in others, and for that the most humorous of the poets who ever existed, Lucan, lost his life. At the time of the cruel proscription ordered by the triumvirate, where faith, charity and gratitude were exiled from the most eminent and well composed spirits of the republic, because these virtues could not be found in fathers, children and sibling, they took refuge among the abjections of the serfs and the obscenity of the harlots; among many, one of them suffered the last torments in order not to reveal the names of her dishonest friends. Socrates in the height of his wisdom found ignorance, and was therefore judged by the very wise oracle. Little irritated meekness becomes untamed haughtiness, and this, with masterful dexterity, converts itself in meek and flexible pleasantness.[58]

The careful reader has probably recognised part of the catalogue of the second book of Aristotle's *Rhetoric:* pleasure-pain, rage-meekness, friendship-hate, fear-courage, shame-shamelessness, compassion-disdain, envy-emulation. This list has a particular purpose: to demonstrate the multifaceted dimensions of the human soul. In the words of our character:

> The internal image of our soul is composed of a mosaic which apparently forms a single idea, but once it approaches, it shows how it is accompanied by various fragments and vile little and precious stones connected and committed together. In the same way, our soul is mostly composed by different and divergent pieces; in various occasions each one of them shows itself with a different appearance. Therefore, describing the nature and condition of a single man is very hard and difficult, and even more so is the will to refer his actions and ideas to a single norm.
>
> This explains why so many authors can be found [37v] who have written on the nature of horses, dogs and falcons, and who have devised with such an exactitude their customs and conditions, while very few have wanted to deal with men, and even so only in passing. The one who talked about them better was Theophrastus, Aristotle's disciple, who reserved the enterprise for the last years of his life as he was already eighty years old, and compiled a historical treatise about it with observations on the characters of the human soul; a fragment of his work made it all the way down to us, the rest was destroyed by the inclemency of times.[59]

---

58 *Discorso*, 36r and following.
59 *Discorso*, 37r and following.

Luzzatto refers here to Theophrastus of Eresos, author of *Charakteres*, a series of characterisations of the human soul. Angelo Ambrogini, nicknamed Poliziano, translated the first fifteen characters into Latin. These characters were published in Basel in 1532 by Andreas Cratander and did not feature Poliziano as the translator.[60] They were published again, this time with Poliziano's name, in Paris in 1583 by Frédéric Morel. Already in 1552 an edition of these works by Aldo Manuzio, with eight more characters added, had appeared thanks to the efforts of Giovanni Battista Camozza. In 1599, a second edition, titled *Caratteri*, was published in Leiden, including five more characters (21–28). This edition was discovered by Isaac Casaubon and copied once more by Marquard Freher. In 1620, Ansaldo Cebà[61] published an Italian version of the first fifteen characters, probably without taking into consideration Manuzio's edition, possibly because, as Romizi believes, he was too young to know of it. In any case, he does not utilise the 1552 edition. Cebà's book was, however, present in Venice, as the ancient catalogue of the Marciana Library reveals. This publication most likely circulated even in the Venetian Ghetto because at that time Cebà, a priest, had an epistolary love affair with a famous poet of Jewish origins, Sara Copio Sullam, who we have previously discussed.[62]

The Venetian Rabbi's objective is now evident: referring not only to Aristotelian rhetoric or to Theophrastus' composition, he underlines a very popular rhetorical device of that time: the use of typical characters of seventeenth-century theatre.[63] This representation of the affects of the human soul, and of its different characters, was a sign of distinction in a century of comedies and tragedies performed and sung on the stage. It will be exactly the above mentioned Cebà who publishes a detailed commentary to accompany Theophrastus' text. Something which does not escape the attentive reader is that emphasising the theatrical character of human soul also means negating objective responsibility: everyone is an actor on the *theatrum mundi* stage, always playing at a passion/affection or its reverse.

Conclusion: Reluctant and Nude Truth

At the end of this section of which the intent was to illustrate only some aspects of the *Discorso*, I would like to conclude with a central concept of Luzzatto's apologia of Jewish life in Venice: the "reluctant and nude truth."

---

[60] I refer the reader to my source for this paragraph, Andreas Cratander, *I caratteri Morali di Teofrasto*, ed. Augusto Romiti (Florence: Sansoni, 1899), which is the critical edition of the Greeek text with Italian translation and notes.
[61] Ansaldo Cebà., *I Charatteri morali di Teofrasto interpretati per Ansaldo Cebà. Al Cardinale Federigo Borromeo* (Genoa: Pavoni, 1620).
[62] Cf. Giuseppe Veltri, *Renaissance*, 226–247.
[63] Cf. Silvia Carandini, *Teatro e spettacolo nel Seicento* (Rome: Laterza, 1990).

4.1 Apologetic Strategies, Scepticism, and Empiricism — 231

Just at the beginning of the small treatise, the Rabbi ventures to present an image of Judaism that goes beyond prejudices and atavistic hatred. It is specifically addressed to the "*cultori dell'invita verità.*" Exactly what is meant by this expression, which was used in the dedication, is not clear at first sight. Earlier translators have preferred to consider it as a misprint and to amend the text to "*invicta verità*" (unconquerable truth). There is, however, no need to change the wording of the text, which in translation sounds.

> I dare to bring this work, neglected and stripped of ornate diction, to your noble attention, while indeed being aware that lovers of reluctant Truth appreciate simplicity. For [this reluctant truth] takes the greatest delight in [its] very nakedness. I do not claim [3v] undeserved favour, nor extorted applause from you, as I recognize how unworthy and unmerited it would be; but I plead for the most candid and honest judgment of the issues discussed[64].

The concept of "reluctant truth" fits very well into the system of Luzzatto's political. Lovers of the "reluctant/unwilling" Truth accept it, regardless of the form in which it may be propagated. In Luzzatto's own words (*Discorso* 5r–v):

> Therefore, with a minimum of talent that divine majesty granted me, I proposed to compose a concise but truthful account of this nation's principal rites and most commonly shared opinions, which are not dissonant or discrepant from the universal ones. In writing this text, I tried with all of my powers (even though I am from the same nation) to abstain from any emotionality or passion that could make me deviate from the truth. Thus I hope to meet discreet readers, who, void of any anticipation or troubled judgment, are not about to follow the vulgar custom of only approving and favouring happy and adventurous individuals, and always damning those who are disheartened and afflicted. Rather, with upright judgment they will balance their opinions on the subject, which my imperfection dictated to me, and in saying this I will omit an extended reflection on the antiquity of this race, on its unmixed blood, which has existed for such a long period of time, on the tenacity of this nation's rites and belief, and on its inflexibility during times of oppressions. I will only add to my aforementioned proposal a discussion of some of the profits that the Jewish nation that lives in Venice brings to this illustrious city. With this, I do not intend to offer any ambitious apparatus of profits and gains; rather I only wish to demonstrate that this nation is anything but a useless member of the general population of this city.

The author's commitment to his truth should not hide the fact that Luzzatto is not speaking of the Aristotelian principle of non-contradiction, but of the political perception of that condition. His intention is to provide as neutral a portrait of the Jews as possible, describing their presence in Venice and the (economic) advantages they bring. Although himself a member of the Jewish "nation," a *pars in causa*, he will nevertheless maintain his impartiality. In return for his unbiased presentation of the argument, he expects his readers to form their opinion on the subject without prejudice.

---

[64] A similar parallel appears in Francis Bacon, *The New Organon*, 14: "For a naked mind is the companion of innocence and simplicity, as once upon a time the naked body was."

The expression "nudity of the truth" is very intriguing. The reader of Luzzatto was acquainted with the concept of *nuda veritas* since Horace,[65] but also of its contradictory nature. For the nudity was, obviously, tantamount to purity and simplicity but also implied a lack of defences. The Florentine painter Sergio Botticelli recreated the *Calumny of Apelles*, a lost painting of the Greek painter Apelles, the story of which has been reported or perhaps invented by Lucian:[66] A slander, a rival of Apelles, accused the painter of revolt in front of King Midas:

> On the right sits a man with long ears almost of the Midas 5 pattern, stretching out a hand to Slander, who is still some way off, but coming. About him are two females whom I take for Ignorance and Suspicion. Slander, approaching from the left, is an extraordinarily beautiful woman, but with a heated, excitable air that suggests delusion and impulsiveness; in her left hand is a lighted torch, and with her right she is holding a youth by the hair; he holds up hands to heaven and calls the Gods to witness his innocence. Showing Slander the way is a man with piercing eyes, but pale, deformed, and shrunken as from long illness; one may easily guess him to be Envy. Two female attendants encourage Slander, acting as tire-women, and adding touches to her beauty; according to the cicerone, one of these is Malice, and the other Deceit. Following behind in mourning guise, black-robed and with torn hair, comes (I think he named her) Repentance. She looks tearfully behind her, awaiting shame-faced the approach of Truth. That was how Apelles translated his peril into paint.[67]

In the depiction of Botticelli, the Truth is naked, a nakedness which can have three possible meanings: 1) purity and simplicity, which causes or it is caused by innocence; 2) lack of defence; and 3) extreme difficulty in catching an adversary (e.g. in the Olympic games). While the first and the second possibilities are expressions of weakness and literary "imbecility" (incapability of fighting and defending oneself), the third one is almost the reverse, revealing the "sceptic" attitude of a bodily description.

Back to the picture: a very similar "translation" of a process of judgment into a piece of theatre has been presented by Luzzatto in his *Socrate*, where the theatrical figures of Defamation, Suspicion, Ignorance, Fame, and Custom (as ministers of Authority/Slander) appear.[68] In another passage of the *Socrate*, he comes back to the

---

[65] Horace, *Odes and Epodes*, ed. Paul Shorey and Gordon J. Laing (Chicago: Benj. H. Sanborn & Company, 1919), 1.24:
    cui Pudor et Iustitiae soror
    incorrupta Fides nudaque Veritas
    quando ullum inveniet parem?
[66] Cf. Rudolph Altrocchi, "The Calumny of Apelles in the Literature of the Quattrocento," *Modern Language Association* 36, no. 3 (1921): 454–491.
[67] *The Works of Lucian of Samosata*, ed. Henri W. Fowler and Francis G. Fowler (Oxford: The Clarendon Press, 1905).
[68] *Socrate*, 6–7: "Yet, as soon as the traitor [i.e. Authority] had achieved so noble a rank and become impudent through the simple obedience and easy credulity of the stupid folk, it began conspiring against me. Felony went so far that it chased me out of my royal seat and brought and relegated me to a dark and lonely prison. Hence, as I have indeed lost my freedom, it was forbidden to have

comparison between truth and nudity.⁶⁹ Here he is dealing with the consequences of his attitude to his enquiry "concerning the cognition of the truth, convinced to suspend and withhold [my] assent." His hesitation and perplexity lead him "to consider whether was a profitable decision to publicly discredit our alleged knowledge." Disclosing the truth, he maintains, does not always fulfil our interest, like the nudity of our body, although "the members were masterly constructed by the supreme Nature it often turns out to be indecent that the truth should appear to vulgar men without any ornament."

The truth of cognition is like nudity, appreciated by lovers but also likely considered indecent by common people. The indirect reference is obviously to Genesis 3 and the creation of the feeling of shame in seeing nudity after the primordial sin. For Luzzatto, this indecency is a feeling of vulgar men, provoked by the nudity of the truth. This indecency can also prompt scepticism concerning the effectiveness of the decision to "publicly discredit our alleged knowledge."

That is an extreme aspect of sceptical attitude: to be sceptical about one's own scepticism. It also contains the additional idea that scepticism can be politically dangerous, as we will see in the introduction of next paragraph.

4.2 The Politics of Scepticism: Luzzatto's *Socrate*

Luzzatto's *Socrate* begins and ends with quotations taken from the biblical book of Kohelet (Ecclesiastes). In the first quotation (9:16), the biblical author affirms that wisdom is better that strength. Luzzatto translates the Hebrew noun "strength" (גבורה) as "military arsenal" (*dicebam ego meliorem esse sapientiam, bellicis instrumentis*). The second passage at the end of the book is a direct quotation of Kohelet 7:29, a verse according to which God made the men righteous (ישר) but they have sought out many inventions. Luzzatto translates this passage with *Deus fecit hominem rectum, et ipsi requiserunt cogitationes multas* (God made man and they engaged in so many reasonings).⁷⁰

Timon in Luzzatto's *Socrate* comments, "The human being came from the hands of God, or Nature, as it is his servant, not only righteous, but unanimous and in

---

intercourse with my favourites and thus I became infertile and sterile [...] Indeed, it came so far only by means of sumptuous cloths, au thoritative bearings, frowning, intimidating glances, furrowing its brows, concise and ambiguous words, brief and reluctant conversations, contemptuous and delusory manners, obstinate and Custom, both of them promoters of its acclaims and commendations." Also *Socrate*, 65, "retinenza di giuditio, tanto da miei adversarii calunniata, et al Vostro spettabile tribunale acramente hora accusata," 74, 77, and 299 (of the Italian original).
69 *Socrate*, 256 (of the Italian original).
70 According to the interpretation of David B. Ruderman, *Jewish Thought and Scientific Discovery*, 171. According to the interpretation of Luzzatto, ישר cannot translated with "plain," as he does, but with "righteous."

agreement with himself. Yet, as he has been then corrupted by curiosity about immoderate knowledge and quibbling investigation, he became divided in himself, multiple, and in disagreement with himself."[71] As Ruderman already has stated, Luzzatto's *Socrate* accepts the negative vision of Timon.[72] In an inclusion bracketing the whole book, Luzzatto summarises his interest in the philosopher Socrates as an exemplum of peaceful learning and wisdom at same time as he is an expression of the danger of curiosity about immoderate knowledge and quibbling investigation. The reader has already recognised the rabbinic interest in the exegetical tradition of Genesis 3: the tree of knowledge and the nudity of the progenitors, Adam and Eve. To have eaten from the tree of knowledge is the premise for considering indecent their own nudity and also a paradox for Luzzatto because nudity is also synonymous with simplicity. Yet, the investigation of the truth may also be interpreted as a corrupted curiosity.

The quotations from the "sceptical" work of Kohelet express the contradiction of Luzzatto's book between wisdom and corrupted curiosity on investigation. We will deal in this chapter with the priority of the political danger of scepticism, deceitful sciences and deceptive perception, and the conclusion of Luzzatto's philosophy.

Kohelet, Socrates, and Scepticism

An oft-quoted opinion of scholars of ancient philosophy is that ancient sceptics showed no interest in politics. Indeed, no sceptical treatise on government or political utopia, or one displaying even slight political interest, has survived, if it was composed at all.[73] Yet I would like to avoid entering into the discussion of political engagement in ancient scepticism, because the adjective "political" includes many nuances and fields of research; it would be illusory to claim that ancient scepticism had no political dimension.[74] Furthermore, modern scholarship's hypothesis concerning the absence of political interest has shown itself to be too narrowly concentrated on philosophical systems, leaving out the narrative about philosophy that

---

[71] *Socrate*, 307 (of the Italian original).
[72] David B. Ruderman, *Jewish Thought and Scientific Discovery*, 171.
[73] Cf. John C. Laursen, *The Politics of Skepticism in the Ancients, Montaigne, Hume, and Kant* (Leiden: Brill, 1992), 1–3; John C. Laursen, "Escepticismo y política," *Revista de Estudios Políticos* 144 (2009): 123–142; John C. Laursen, "Skepticism, Unconvincing Anti-skepticism, and Politics," in *Scepticisme et modernité*, ed. Marc André Bernier and Sébastien Charles (Saint-Étienne: Publications de l'Université de Saint-Étienne, 2005): 167–188; Emidio Spinelli, "Stoic Utopia Reconsidered: Pyrrhonism, Ethics, and Politics," in *Philosophy and Political Power in Antiquity*, ed. Cinzia Arruzza and Dmitri Nikulin (Brill: Leiden, 2016): 148–163. Emidio Spinelli, *Questioni scettiche. Letture introduttive al pirronismo antico* (Rome: Lithos, 2005).
[74] In *A History of Western Political Thought* (London: Routledge, 1998), 81, John S. McClelland does speak of "Greek scepticism," but he does not mention any sources. Perhaps his use of scepticism is only the popular one.

4.2 The Politics of Scepticism: Luzzatto's *Socrate* — 235

philosophical ideas, concepts, and strategies are spread throughout literary and legal texts which bear witness to philosophical interests and debates. Nevertheless, it is undeniably true that there is only one area untouched by ancient scepticism, and this was kingship, the art of government. If a student of ancient philosophy looks into the political literature of the period between the third centuries before and after our common era, he will find many tractates on the art of kingship (*Perì Basileias*),[75] yet, to my knowledge, none of them are of sceptical origin.

With one exception: the book of Kohelet, the king of Jerusalem, which has a chapter dedicated to the area of the main occupation of kingship. Although no philosophical Hebrew treatise survives from the biblical period, it is a common opinion that the book of Kohelet has at least some traces of philosophical ideas and concepts. The precise localisation of this book in the sea of Hellenistic literature is not easy, and already in the ancient rabbinic period, scholars and students were debating its character and consistency because of its contradictions. Contradictory also is his idea of kingship. Being a king of Jerusalem, one expects from the narrator of this book a political philosophy, namely that of the philosopher king, an idea which informed the Hellenistic age. This text is nothing of the sort. Instead, Kohelet offers a concept of kingship that is completely full of pessimistic nuances, one totally devoted to the king's pleasure and wealth: a sceptic king dedicated only to his own bodily pleasure. We read in Kohelet that kingship consists of building houses, constructing reservoirs for irrigation, planting vineyards, building gardens, owing slaves, servants, flocks, and herds, and being rich in silver, gold, and everything that is a sign and symbol of magnificence. The conclusion is sceptical and pessimistic at first glance: all of this is folly. A second look reveals the real intention: all of this is folly because the king cannot do anything that will have lasting consequences, and furthermore, it is impossible for him to know what his successor will do.[76]

No wise words, no wisdom or political statements, no other source for the perfect life, no desire to improve the knowledge of the people. Nothing other than wealth and pleasure. In a period of the Hellenistic age when almost every king collected books for the enlargement of his knowledge and power, King Kohelet states (12:12), "And furthermore, my son, be admonished: of making many books there is no end; and much study is a weariness of the flesh." This is an antiheroic ideal of a

---

[75] Oswyne Murray, "Peri basileias: Studies in the justification of monarchic power in the Hellenistic world" (PhD dissertation, Oxford University, 1971).
[76] Kohelet 2: 4–12. "I did great things: I built houses and planted vineyards. I made gardens and parks and planted all kinds of fruit trees. I constructed reservoirs to irrigate the orchards. I bought slaves and servants and had slaves born in my household. I had flocks and herds in abundance more than anyone before me in Jerusalem. I acquired silver and gold—the wealth of kings and nations. I had choirmaster and singers and besides that, what most delights men. I became great, surpassing all my predecessors in Jerusalem without losing wisdom. I refused myself nothing that my eyes desired nor did I deprive my heart of any pleasure. I enjoyed all I undertook and that was my reward for my work. [...] I then decided to compare wisdom with folly and madness and I thought, 'What will my successor as king do?' We know what he did!"

king who is only preoccupied with the deeds of his successor. Doubt about a successor who could destroy everything he has done leads him to doubt all wisdom and knowledge, yet all things are folly and madness. To sum up: Kohelet created the image of a king as an antihero who, enclosed in his egoistical idea of power, was uncertain about what would happen after his own kingship and who arranged everything for his own pleasure. That is nothing but a parody of government.

Scepticism about kingship and government is deeply rooted in the Jewish tradition, where the supreme authority according to the Bible is not the king or the rabbi, but the law itself, the divine commandments issued by God on Sinai, as we will see later. Criticism of the monarchy is commonplace in the Hebrew Bible because of its incapacity to allow the people to follow the divine commandments expressed in the written and oral Torah. Scepticism is hence criticism of authorities which do not allow individual autonomous judgment in the study of the law. This is a common position very similar to the Socratic school, but also a danger and limitation due to its lacking an authority who supports the decisions of the individual in the collective community.

The trial and *Apology* of the Athenian philosopher Socrates has been idealised as an exercise of philosophy, rhetoric, literature, religion, politics, the science of education, and every other branch of the humanities in almost every period of European history. Prominent philosophers and scholars of former centuries associated his character, philosophy, and impact on world history and thought with an idealistic vision of freedom and peace, dialectical and pedagogical achievement, tolerance of ideals, and resistance to government and social constriction; everything an enlightened intellectual aspires to be or to become.[77] Socratic doctrines often became aporetically synonymous with everything from proving reason and scepticism, sophistic ability, dialectic sobriety to the obedience of laws, and subverting authority; Socrates' impact is more typical of a founder of a religion than a founder of a philosophy.

My interest here is the argumentation used in his commitment to epistemological scepticism and his political attitude. Hence, a very important aspect of his trial is the reason(s) why the jurors sentenced him to death. In the final part of *Crito* (53b–c), Socrates' friend summarises the case against him:

> And you yourself, if you go to one of the nearest cities, to Thebes or Megara—for both are well governed—will go as an enemy, Socrates, to their government, and all who care for their own cities will look askance at you, and will consider you a destroyer of the laws, and you will confirm the judges in their opinion, so that they will think their verdict was just [καὶ ὅσοιπερ κήδονται τῶν αὐτῶν πόλεων ὑποβλέψονταί σε διαφθορέα ἡγούμενοι τῶν νόμων]. For he who is destroyer of the laws [ὅστις γὰρ νόμων διαφθορεύς ἐστιν] might certainly be regarded as a destroyer of young [καὶ ἀνοήτων ἀνθρώπων διαφθορεὺς εἶναι] and thoughtless men. Will you

---

[77] For a famous example, see this enthusiastic piece by Adolf von Harnack, *Sokrates und die alte Kirche. Rede beim Antritt des Rectorates gehalten in der Aula der Königlichen Friedrich-Wilhelms-Universität am 15. October 1900* (Berlin: Buchdruckerei von Gustav Schade, 1900).

then avoid the well-governed cities and the most civilized men? And if you do this will your life be worth living? Or will you go to them and have the face to carry on—what kind of conversation, Socrates? The same kind you carried on here, saying that virtue and justice and lawful things and the laws are the most precious things to men? And do you not think that the conduct of Socrates would seem most disgraceful?[78]

Socrates is the διαφθορεύς of the law and of mindless men, commonly translated as "young people." In the *Apology*, he refuses to recognise the gods of the city and proclaims: "I shall obey God rather than you" (29d3), yet here he refuses to escape from prison, thus endorsing their authority.[79] The subverter of the law accepts the sentence of the jurors. Is this not a contradiction?

Although Socrates became the symbol of many ideas and concepts in the history of philosophy that are of sceptical origin, we cannot treat him as a sceptic in all matters related to freedom, authority, and agnostic visions of knowledge. However, in this scene in the Athenian jail, the reader will see the dual tendency of a sceptical philosopher: on the one hand, the critical refutation of authority, and on the other, the acceptance of the existing laws and therefore the acceptance of the judgment. The danger of being a sceptic rests in these two sides.

Both of these are also present in the seventeenth century, in Luzzatto's *Socrate*. Luzzatto writes that in its assembly in the Apolline Temple, the academy of Delphos debated whether to proceed against Socrates, indicted for trying to cancel the validity of the human sciences (*havere tentato l'eversione dell'humane scientie*).

Here is his lament in the first part of the book:

Throughout all my life, I have demonstrated to others that I am courageous and unafraid of dealing with the adversities of fortune. Yet I cannot deny that this charge, now brought against me by those malevolent to me, confounds my understanding, since I find it abrupt and unexpected. Who would ever have assumed that my suspension of judgement, my con-strained assent, my following of the simple and sincere probable as the only guide in life, and my obsequiousness to the signs and silent whispers of the gods would have suggested to my slanderers enough reasons to tear my fame and disfigure my name?

In the major philosophic work, the *Socrate*, Luzzatto attempts to shape the frame of a narrow dialectical criticism of what was considered authority, science, sense perception, and theoretical systems. The whole book can be considered an "impresa," an Italian variant of the emblem,[80] conceived as literary device of the *Accademia*

---

78 Plato. *Plato in Twelve Volumes*, vol. 1, trans. Harold North Fowler (Cambridge: Harvard University Press, 1966; London, William Heinemann Ltd. 1966).
79 Cf. Julius Tomim, "Socrates and the Laws of Athens," https://goo.gl/R7NJfV (accessed 3 May, 2018).
80 Cf. Evelyn Chayes, *Oltre le mura del Ghetto*, and "Language of Words and Images in the Rime degli Academici occulti 1568: Reflections of the Pre-conceptual?" in *Language and Cultural Change. Aspects of the Study and Use of Language in the Later Middle Ages and the Renaissance*, ed. Lodi Nauta (Leuven: Peeters, 2006): 149–171.

degli Incogniti. However, the main aim of the book is to write an apologia of Socrates as a sceptical essay against the certainty of human knowledge by adopting an arsenal of sceptic strategies, indirect quotations, summaries, and a discussion of the huge body of philosophical and literary readings with which he was familiar.

Socrate: The Sceptical Essay

Published in Venice in 1651 at the Tomasini printing house, the book is neither organised into different chapters nor into paragraphs. However, following the book fashion of this period,[81] Luzzatto included some marginal notations that act as guidelines pointing out the change of topic, interlocutors, and direction of speech (from direct to indirect). Luzzatto sometimes uses these marginal notations to highlight the exact sources of his quotations. The marginal notations also include a list of topics. This list contains references to numbered pages. Contrary to the *Discorso*, which is an essay organised into different considerations, *Socrate's* structure is uniform. The book also shows how the press progressed between 1638 (the publishing date of the *Discorso*) and 1651—the *Discorso* still used the recto/verso type of layout. The numbering in the *Socrate* is progressive and reflective of those in in modern books.

Socrates is the central character of the work. The principal argument that Luzzatto defends and suggests to his readers is that human reason must be led by divine revelation. This idea is also reflected in the title: *Socrates or on Human Knowledge. The Serious-Playful Exercise of Simone Luzzatto, Venetian Jew. A Work that Shows how Feeble Human Intelligence can be When it is not Led by Divine Revelation*) and a few times also through the text, where he replaces the expression "divine revelation" with "superior mind"[82] or "superior light."[83] David Ruderman[84] highlights the pragmatism of this text, which could meet the needs of both Christian and Jewish communities in Italy at the time of the Counter-Reformation. Therefore, by his careful research and planning, Luzzatto would meet with the approval of both.

After two pages of dedication to "the most serene Prince and the most excellent Council," namely the Venetian Doge Francesco Molino, there is a three-page note introducing the *errata corrige*, titled "the author and printer." This note suggests that Simone Luzzatto may have taken on the role of printer on this occasion. For this reason, he asks the benign reader for their indulgence for the text's large number of printing errors.

Luzzatto then provides a dedication to "the benign reader," explaining why he decided to write the *Socrate:*

---

81 Cf. Evelyn Tribble, *Margins and Marginality: The Printed Page in Early Modern England* (Charlottesville: University Press of Virginia, 1993).
82 *Socrate*, 1.
83 *Socrate*, 13.
84 *Jewish Thought*, 161.

> Every walk in this world which eventually remains traceless, is commonly considered as vain. In Proverbs, Salomon includes the snake among those four who leave any tracks in their passage: the snake, which slithers over tough stones, is not only futile but also harmful and enemy to mankind. Called by nature to walk this worldly path, I considered worthwhile leaving some traces, even if I think that the passage of others would delete them after a short while. However of this I don't care, since I have done my duty.[85]

According to Luzzatto, every man has to leave a mark of his own life on this world. Even if Luzzatto modestly states that he has done just his duty, we grasp here the echoes of the literary *topos* inaugurated by Thucydides in his *History of the Peloponnesian War* (I, 22, 4), where he considers his work as a "possession for eternity" (*ktema eis aiei*). Pliny in his *Epistulae* (III, 7, 14) and Horace in his *Odes* (III, 30, 6) have also taken up such a *topos*, with reference to the specific meaning of the literary work as living mark of themselves, guaranteeing their life after death. This *topos* alone is proof of Luzzatto's deep knowledge of classical literature. Finally, we should also remember Dante's gratitude to Brunetto Latini, who taught him "how a man becomes eternal" (*Hell*, XV, 82–85). Dante was one of Luzzatto's favourite authors. Nevertheless, Ruderman considers the reference to this literary *topos* poorly founded and vague, even if noble. In the dedication to the "benign reader," Luzzatto finally confirms the aim of his work: "Socrates confutes the human knowledge, but not that one inspired by divine mind, and goes further on this purpose recognising that the weakness of our native knowledge makes us yielding to emotions produced by sentences of the Holy Scriptures."[86] These lines repeat what he had already written in the title of the book. After the dedication, the author summarises in two pages the event that had led to the story, explaining why Socrates was on trial again (3–4). The real treatise starts only at page five.

Before getting to the core of the matter, it is important to point out the representation of the trial as a theatrical performance. The adjective "serious-playful" used in the title probably refers to the melodrama that flourished during the seventeenth century. The *Socrate* is a work defined by Luzzatto as serious and playful at the same time, namely, a work representing the varied nature of human soul; a topic already mentioned by Luzzatto in Consideration XI of his *Discorso*, which refers to Socrates. I do not want to explore here the relationship between music, theatre, and philosophy, but wish to point out that the topic of the theatre reminds Luzzatto's contemporary readers of the idea of *theatrum mundi* (literally, the world stage). This is a cosmological and encyclopaedic representation of the world widely held during the sixteenth and seventeenth centuries. At that time, the theatre, apart from Shakespeare's contributions, experienced a thorough reform thanks to the work of Lope de Vega and Calderon de la Barca. The idea of *theatrum mundi* resonated in the philosophical thought of the early modern period. The metaphor of *thea-*

---

85 *Socrate*, 1–2.
86 *Socrate*, 1.

trum mundi was widely held in theological literature, as demonstrated by the example of the probabilistic theologian Juan Caramuel. Not surprisingly, the metaphor of *theatrum mundi* is often used by Luzzatto in the *Socrate*.

Socrate is a philosophical work of Luzzatto's maturity. The book did not achieve any remarkable success until today. A very small number of scholars read, studied, or provided commentaries on it, even though the topic of scepticism has been widely studied in European and American universities. Luzzatto's approach to ancient, medieval and modern scepticism is both polyhedral and very detailed. Although he was the first Jew to examine such a philosophical topic, he didn't receive much attention from the erudite public. Instead, the public focused its attention on other contemporary authors, including Marranos, leaving out the Jewish thought of the seventeenth century altogether. This circumstance restricts the research field as well as the analysis I provide in this text, which cannot compensate *tout court* for such a wide gap in the literature. Nevertheless, I intend to provide here a first step in the study of this author.

Heinrich Graetz was among the first authors who offered a short summary of the *Socrate*, which he defined as a "parable" written by Luzzatto during his youth.[87] He describes Luzzatto's education, paying special attention to his mathematic skills and to his solid knowledge of ancient and modern literature, which are clearly evident in the *Socrate* itself. In his summary, Graetz focuses on one aspect, rightly considered the main one: during his long defence, Socrates states that reason and the authority of holy texts cannot pretend to have an exclusive power in human matters, although both of them contribute to human development. According to Socrates, the human being will be able to achieve all of his goals only if reason and revelation complete one another: this is the doctrine of the balance between *fides* and *ratio*. As Graetz rightly points out, such a doctrine has been a recurrent topic since Maimonides' time: the issue was formulated by him in order to contrast Averroes' doctrine, which separated reason and faith, considering them as two different fields of research and enlightenment that have to stay separate, like faith's truth and reason's truth.

The doctrine of balance between *fides* and *ratio* was reintroduced by Thomas Aquinas and became a fixture in Scholastic thought. Even if Scholasticism had a moment of decline after Luther's criticism, it flourished anew during the seventeenth century (the so-called Second Scholasticism), reaffirming the doctrine of balance between *fides* and *ratio* and at the same time introducing new elements. Some of its exponents thought that natural reason had to accept the "wonder of the probable," as Juan Caramuel writes.[88] We should point out such an important change in the direction of the speculation because it was part of Luzzatto's cultural context.

---

[87] Heinrich Graetz, *Geschichte*, 10, 150–151.
[88] *Le meraviglie del probabile: Juan Caramuel 1606–1682. Atti del convegno internazionale di studi, October 29–31, 1982*, ed. Pablo Passivino (Vigevano: Comune di Vigevano, 1990).

4.2 The Politics of Scepticism: Luzzatto's *Socrate* — 241

Graetz also focuses on another element, the spread of the Lurianic Kabbalah, which was supported by a greater and greater number of followers. However, even if the Kabbalah considered the doctrine of the balance between *fides* and *ratio* to be almost a heresy, Luzzatto succeeded in complying with this doctrine, as Graetz reported. The famous historian interprets the *Socrate* in the light of Judaism's concerns during those days, especially focusing on the contrast between the Kabbalah and rationalistic philosophy and pointing out that Luzzatto was inclined towards the latter.

Although Luzzatto addressed his work to the Italian public, nevertheless he was only more widely read after several generations had passed. Samuel David Luzzatto states that Simone Luzzatto was "less known than he deserved," but that he "had not only a wide rabbinical doctrine, but also a classical erudition and a political and philosophical knowledge."[89] He also provides a summary of the *Socrate* without a detailed discussion. He mentions in passing the topic of scepticism, to which he refers throughout the work with ill-concealed embarrassment and with a tone of indulgent justification. He concludes by pointing out that the work is written following "an easy style, but without any erudition and philosophical knowledge."

In accordance with the modern criterion of literary quality, this last remark is untrue. To the contemporary reader, Luzzatto's style appears pretentious because it follows the Latin structure of sentences and the rules of syntax and punctuation of seventeenth century. Nevertheless, we have to notice that the author uses a living Italian language that is characterised by a rich vocabulary, involving a highly cultured terminology, including words taken from the juridical context and Latinisms, words from the Venetian dialect, as well as some Spanish terms. It is still unclear whether the words of Spanish origin belonged to the Venetian spoken language of that time or were part of the lexicon introduced to Venice by Sephardi Jews who had escaped from Spain. Luzzatto's text proves that we should not assume so surely the theory of a "perfect diglossia" between the Tuscan dialect and the different spoken dialects during the seventeenth century.

The latest three studies concerning the *Socrate* and its *status quaestionis* were written by David Ruderman,[90] Ariel Viterbo[91] and the author of this book. Ruderman carefully discusses the scientific references in Luzzatto's work, paying special attention to the influence of Montaigne and of the sceptical thought of seventeenth century. He focuses on the following question: why does Luzzatto state in the title that

---

[89] Samuel David Luzzatto, *Autobiografia di S.D. Luzzatto preceduta da alcune notizie storico-letterarie sulla famiglia Luzzatto a datare dal secolo decimosesto* (Padova: Crescini, 1878), 15–16.
[90] David B. Ruderman, "Science and Skepticism. Simone Luzzatto on Perceiving the Natural World," in his *Jewish Thought and Scientific Discovery in Early Modern Europe* (New Haven: Yale University Press, 1995): 161–184.
[91] Ariel Viterbo, "La mitzwàh di studiare le scienze nell'opera di Rav Simchah (Simone) Luzzatto," *Segulat Israel* 4 (1997): 54–67; Ariel Viterbo, "Socrate nel ghetto: lo scetticismo mascherato di Simone Luzzatto," *Studi Veneziani* 38 (1999): 79–128.

revelation must lead human reason, but make no further reference to this matter in the text? Ruderman suggests that Luzzatto has an ambivalent attitude towards religion: on the one hand he paid a formal respect to its ceremonies, while on the other hand he rejected the concepts at their root.

Montaigne's interpretation of the relationship between *fides* and *ratio* deserves special attention because his point of view was very common in Libertine circles; it can be seen in Charron's *De la sagesse* as well as other such as La Mothe le Vayer, Gabriel Naudet, and Pierre Gassendi e Guy Patin, who were identified as the intellectual group of the *libertinage érudit*. Although he begins by stating the supremacy of *fides*, Montaigne focuses only on *ratio*, and by doing so reaches a positive and questioning scepticism. Such a position indirectly defends reason's prerogative in the same way it seems to happen in the *Socrate*. Does Ruderman think that Luzzatto could be considered a forerunner of Spinoza's thought? With such a hypothesis the American historian tries to answer to the most problematic questions of the *Socrate:* why did Luzzatto write such a work, to whom did he address it, and who actually read it? Indeed, the aim of the work is more laic than religious.

Ariel Viterbo accepts a similar interpretation, supporting the idea of Luzzatto's "disguised scepticism." According to his position, we should read the *Socrate* as Luzzatto's intellectual autobiography and, consequently, identify the Rabbi with the character of Socrates. Just as the Greek philosopher, the Venetian Rabbi was sceptical towards the human possibility of reaching firm knowledge. In accordance with Viterbo's opinion, such a mask was perhaps the only way for Luzzatto to spread his scepticism without fear of condemnation by Jewish religious authority, which was always directed against whoever doubted divine revelation's truth. However, such an interpretation is not well-founded, considering that Luzzatto clearly belongs to the current of religious scepticism, even if he leaves other alternatives open. Like Francisco Sanchez, Luzzatto refused to accept the primacy of human sciences and never criticised religious faith. Furthermore, there is no proof of the expulsion of any rabbi suspected of heresy during that time period.

In the *Socrate*, Luzzatto focuses only on human knowledge, as Sanchez and Montaigne have done, which explains why it is impossible to find any reference to revelation and Judaism in the text. Luzzatto intentionally leaves the issue of divine knowledge out of his essay and turns his attention purely to the possibilities of human knowledge. His question is how to combine the limits of the mind with the metaphysical truth that it might be able to reach. Therefore, the author develops his thinking on the topic without realising its destructive consequences in the context of revelation, as Spinoza later does.

Truth and doubt belong to the figure of the history and legend of the Athenian philosopher. Furthermore, Socrates has obviously been a source for several cultural movements in European thought and culture. The literary form of the dialogue is also a *trait d'union* with Judaism. Although Daniel Boyarin has recently attacked the *locus communis* of the research on the dialectic character of rabbinic writings, considering both the Greek and Rabbinic "dialogues" as actual "monologues,"[92] the literary form of dialogue remains valid and spread throughout rabbinic literature. We can discuss the historical significance of the dialogue, but not on the rhetorical importance of it.

Back to Luzzatto: Daniel Gerber has shown some parallelism between the "Jewish" Socrates, defined by Judah Halevi in his *Kuzari*[93] and Simone Luzzatto: both representations share the same sceptical aptitude.[94] Yet, we have to be cautious in parallelising: Luzzatto's *Socrate* involves a new trial, the actual intentions of which are not perfectly clear. Indeed, Luzzatto's Socrates states,[95] "I professed apathy and strict extraneousness of any affection, I was indifferent, immovable and regardless of any hit of the fortune, expression of my constant and free reasoning. However, as it was proper to the philosophical decorum, I snatched the hemlock out of the ill-intentioned hands of the judges." The reader may ask what the reason of Socrates' action is if he characterises himself as "indifferent immovable and regardless of any hit of the fortune." The reason may be the political atmosphere. We should not consider the *Socrate* as a rhetorical exercise, but as something beyond the supposed "philosophical imagination." It is the result of the doubtful atmosphere of the seventeenth century, deriving from philosophical analysis and an uncertain political and social situation. Without entering into a detailed discussion, we may say that, without the *Socrate* of the seventeenth century, it is difficult to understand the phenomenon of the French and German Enlightenment and the strong intellectual relationship between Venice and Berlin.

The frontispiece of the book contains the author's signature: "Venetian Jew." This signature demonstrates Luzzatto's belonging to both the Jewish nation and the Venetian Republic. While the *Discorso* was, beyond apology, Luzzatto's creative interpretation of the possible role of Jewish people in Venice, in the *Socrate* the author defines the relationship that he would like to see not only between the Jewish people and Venice, but also generally between Jews and all European cultures of his time. We may say that Luzzatto, at the height of his career and already of advanced age, was expressing a social and political project concerning European culture and the Jewish people. Therefore, we may suppose that Luzzatto wrote such a monumental work in order to show not only that the Jewish people have an active role in the Venetian economy, but also that they can have the same role in laying the foundations of the new modern culture. According to his point of view, the paradigm for a future Jewish instruction had to be the use of the Italian language, the

---

92 Daniel Boyarin, *Socrates and the Fat Rabbi* (Chicago: University of Chicago Press, 2009).
93 I thank Warren Zev Harvey for his contribution to this section. He notes that Socrates is mentioned four times in the *Kuzari*: I, 1; III, 1; IV, 13; V, 14 and that *Apology* 20de is quoted in IV, 13, and V, 14.
94 Gabriel Danzig, "Socrates in Hellenistic and Medieval Jewish Literature, with Special Regard to Yehuda Hallevi's *Kuzari*," in *Socrates from Antiquity to the Enlightenment*, ed. Michael Trapp (Cambridge: Routledge, 2007): 143–160.
95 *Socrate*, 14–15.

knowledge of Latin, and the knowledge of classic and modern literature. Obviously, this program was never realised.

Luzzatto's life and works are an example of the considerable potential of Jewish culture in Italy, which was comparable to the situation in Northern Europe. In the first salons in Berlin, where people met to talk about the political role of Judaism in culture, the cultural example of Venice was often recalled. Such a common sensibility explains why, in eighteenth century Prussia, the Jewish philosopher Moses Mendelssohn was called *"ein deutscher Sokrates."*

Summary of the Contents

The "serious-playful" philosophical exercise starts in Delphi on the occasion of the opening ceremonies of the Academy whose intent was the reform of human knowledge. During the first assembly, which takes place in Apollo's temple, a "receptacle created to collect all secret charges against the absurd theories going about some spread doctrines" is found.[96] The contents of the receptacle are revealed: A letter of *doléance and plaidoyer* from Reason to the assembly: it declares to be a prisoner of the authority and of its "two hard-working ministers, fame and custom,"[97] which have degraded it. Reason asks to be released to return to human doctrines their lost splendour and to grant a new dignity to mankind. Pythagoras and Aristotle, here identified with authority's principle of the *ipse dixit*, suggest denying this request consideration. However, the assembly decides to accept it, deliberating the temporarily rescue of Reason; Reason then places the secret "receptacle" in front of the Academy's door, where everyone could denounce doctrines and false opinion, "without running the risk of the author's disfavouring."[98] The "secret receptacle" was a famous instrument of the Inquisition and provides a reminder of the *bocche de leon* established in Venice to collect information. After that, they find a charge against Socrates, who is considered a "subverter of human doctrines" due to "his captious arguments, simulated irony, disappointing questions and inconclusive inductions deduced from carpenters, saddlers, shoemakers and similar workers," and is considered to be in favour of "suspension of judgment and withholding assent."[99]

The sole opponent of the trial is Xenophon, who tries to save his teacher from the charge with a pragmatic argument: he points out that a trial or a sentence would only increase Socrates' fame, while dropping the charge would silence Socrates' doctrine for the rest of time. However, Xenophon's recommendation was rejected and the accused was called to appear in court.

---

96 *Socrate*, 3.
97 *Socrate*, 6.
98 *Socrate*, 10.
99 Ibid.

Socrates begins his long defence[100] in the form of a monologue where he offers reminders of his various discussions about knowledge with wise men. After his defence, and also based on Plato's advice, the assembly decides to suspend judgement.[101] This suspension of judgement is the core of this sceptical essay. During his defence, Socrates explains to the judges the reason why he had decided to suspend his judgement, "I think now more than before that there is not any sure opinion in human mind that could resist to a good reasoning, so every object, by the intellect represented, assumes the appearance that the intellect decides to give it. So what is knowable exists just because our mind lends it shape and appearance."[102] Human beings have innately just opinions, which cannot contrast "good reasoning." Luzzatto's strong command of philosophical terminology is evident even in its first pages. For example, the term "discourse," often mentioned in the text, seems to hint at the *logos* of Greek philosophy. If what is "knowable" exists just because the "human mind lends it shape and appearance," it is possible to gather from such teaching the general lines of the proper aim of a real life:

> However, my teachings can appease human mind and also make men happy. One may consider that what usually upsets human mind, rises from wrong opinions, so my remedy is just to eradicate these opinions. So the only way to get this result is showing that is not sure our concept of right and wrong, as a base of these opinions by us strongly supported. [103]

According to Socrates' opinion, the suspension of judgement may appease the human mind and consequently lead to happiness. This peace of mind contrasts with the vertigo that he experiences after venturing into the study of philosophy: there he discovers that opinions concerning the "first principles of universal being of things" are various and often contradict one another:

> Going deep into philosophy, I encountered inextricable difficulties which made my mind confused and upset. The giddiness, produced by incompatible alternatives and opposite or incompatible opinions, blinded my reasoning, and almost extinguished it. I became even more upset when I observed that the opinions of the most distinguished philosophy experts, concerning the first principles of the universal being of things, are various and contrasting with each other.[104]

Moving from such premises, Socrates begins several discussions with different Greek philosophers in order to verify what knowledge is and whether the suspension of judgement is a reasonable solution. He takes into account varied theories concerning the composition of the universe; he engages with Cratylus, Protagoras, Anaximenes, Xenophon, Parmenides, Melissus, Heraclitus, Democritus, Tales, Empedocles, Pytha-

---

100 *Socrate*, 313–314.
101 *Socrate*, 314–316.
102 *Socrate*, 14.
103 *Socrate*, 15.
104 *Socrate*, 17.

goras, Anaxagoras, Orpheus, Plato, Aristotle and even the "blackened chemists," the alchemists. Socrates declares himself as confused as ever before and begins to apply methodical doubt: "I started to look with suspicion at the futility of human knowledge. I thought that so many disagreements concerning the principles make extremely hard the development of the argument [...].[105] Therefore, he starts with thinking about what knowledge is and what its early foundations are. Suddenly, external objects, the senses, the intellect, and knowledge itself begin to harshly dispute about "which of them had to be at first examined." After having examined the different arguments, Socrates cannot decide. His hesitation leads him to a long dialog with Gorgias, in which he hopes to obtain some clarification. However even Gorgias, pressed by the questions of Socrates, cannot help but come to the conclusion that that the only proper decision is the suspension of judgement:

> [62] All I can do now is just friendly advising you that, since we are in such inverted intricacy and tangled labyrinth, we lost the way to reach the truth about universal existence of things. For the future time you should abstain from any affirmative, resolute assertion or any negative one, since both need the expressions "is" and "is not." If you will follow such advice, I can foresee that, after long and inopportune oppositions of malevolent people, probably you will be not only appreciated by many of your fellow-citizens and by indefinite posterity, but you will be esteemed especially by the gods, because of your cautious modesty and discretion. The reason of it is that you have abstained from the treasures of Wisdom, reserved just to the gods, and you have not desired to put your profane hand on them, neither with your sacrilegious tongue you have dared to vainly boast about having the truth, which is their exclusive property.

The suspension of judgement, however, leads to a point which is morally unacceptable: idleness, a state that is not congenial to the *conditio humana*. Even facing such a deficiency, Socrates decides to continue with his philosophical research. He returns to examine the role of external objects, external senses (especially the sense of touch and the eyesight), internal senses, and the intellect, but all of them prove insufficient at providing a solid foundation for knowledge. Therefore, all Socrates can do is turn his attention to knowledge itself, but even in this case the results of his enquiry are unsure, namely they are incapable of resisting rigorous philosophical research. Socrates returns to the topic of what knowledge is[106] "as the final goal" of his "mental journey."[107] Having confuted all the fifteen hypotheses advanced by different philosophers, the only thing he can do is to support Cratylus's opinion that the starting point of human knowledge is the suspension of judgement, a sceptic refrain that returns to the same premises.[108]

The "probable" is the final goal and object of a long philosophical discussion. It is possible to find this aim in Luzzatto's *Discorso*, where the "probable" is mentioned

---

105 *Socrate*, 22–23.
106 *Socrate*, 166–167.
107 *Socrate*, 174.
108 *Socrate*, 235–236.

as a quest of his entire work.[109] Leaving out the origin and the development of the concept of the probable in scepticism, it is noteworthy that in the beginning of the seventeenth century the Catholic theologian Juan Caramuel focused his attention on the topic of the probable. It is important to point out that Caramuel was very interested in the topics discussed in the Spanish theatre, from the works of Calderon to those of Quevedo. Both artists tried to render life as an idea of the big theatre of the world. The Catholic world too, the ground of Luzzatto's speculation, was dealing with the disintegration of both the Thomistic system and its Aristotelian premises. Critical thought, supported by natural reason, had either to take shelter in scepticism or to look for other ways of being. Life's circumstances and history's urgency force you to make a choice, but if the being-in-itself of everything is unknowable; if natural law is not immediately accessible, you can only trust the probable. All one can do is to trust his own conscience, which decides in every situation what is most ethical. Although Caramuel's and Luzzatto's tendencies are very similar, it is not possible to ascertain if Luzzatto had read Caramuel.

In the *Discorso*, however, Luzzatto explains that the probable is not based on mathematical and incontrovertible truth, what we may call axiomatic truth, but on Aristotelian *phronesis*, namely the critical skill to judge in a meaningful way. In the *Socrate*, the context changes completely, since the discussion is solely philosophical and not economical-political. The sense of probable is here opposed to Aristotle's dogmatism as well as that of his followers. In accordance with Cratylus' opinion in the text, the concept of probable assumes a wider meaning: "I consider the probable as a momentary light, clear and evident for all mankind, which helps us in telling truth from falsehood without being corrupted and upset by the discourse [*logos*]."[110] Such "momentary light," an intuition more than a logical deduction, has to steer man towards the humility of a reduced view, as the example of Polyphemus' one-dimensional view: "Cratylus said: "If we cannot recognize the exact reality as Argus, with multiple eyes, does, we should be content with knowing just what is similar to it, just like Polyphemus does with his single eye. If we will be too much curious to know it, in the end we would become lacking of light and eyesight, as the blind Tiresias."[111] It seems like Socrates wants to abandon the issue and turn his attention to another topic "concerning the way to manage life customs and our own matters,"[112] hoping to find there a more solid knowledge. He continues his discussion, paying special attention to the definition of prudence. In this case, he succeeds in confuting all of the nine definitions provided in the discussion.

As the prudent reader might have already realised, Socrates' only aim was to prove the Delphic maxim. When he arrives at the end of "his long and difficult

---

109 *Discorso*, 30r.
110 *Socrate*, 236.
111 *Socrate*, 236–237.
112 *Socrate*, 237.

way," he finds himself "lacking of any sort of knowledge."[113] Nevertheless, he is not sad, because he is finally released from doubt. All that remains for him to do is decide whether he wants to spread what he has discovered and therefore publicly support the suspension of judgement, or if he prefers to take shelter in typical sceptic silence. After the last discussion with Hippias, who suggests that he remain silent, and with Timon, who invites him to express himself publicly, Socrates accepts Timon's advice to publicly talk about the suspension of judgement.

After a long and well-argued defence, the assembly faces a need to pass sentence, but is unable to deliberate. Most of the assembly's members are inclined to acquit Socrates of his charges and even to reward him for his doctrine on the suspension of judgment. Alcmaeon, "member of the Pythagorean sect,"[114] is peremptorily inclined to sentence him. Plato thinks of a more reasonable alternative:

> In order to solve such issue, we should choose the same method that Socrates uses while judging what is in front of him. As he withholds his assent, we should suspend our judgement about him. Suspending the verdict, we are not making now any peremptory decision, until we find an evident reason which leads us to acquit or sentence him.[115]

After Socrates' defence (rather, explanation of his convictions), the assembly, called to proceed against him, cannot make up its mind whether to pass judgment for his effort to deny the validity of the human sciences or to pronounce him innocent. Plato convinces the members of the academy to postpone judgment until a more opportune time.

Suspension of judgment, the avoidance of agreement, and sincere pursuit of the probable are Luzzatto's *dogmata*, which originate in his sceptical thought. The accusation against Socrates, in Luzzatto's view, shows that the opinion of human beings is of such firm certitude that it will not surrender to the torments of "importune discourse." The accused can be questioned on the basis of the same principle that the prosecutor uses against Socrates: by means of "importune discourse," namely, logic. Only with the help of logic, however, can the accused convince others that a judgment is impossible because we lack certain truths and because there exists no evidence beyond doubt.

This method to prove the uncertainty of human knowledge was of course motivated by the discoveries of Luzzatto's era that were attacked by some Church men and intellectuals. Luzzatto's argumentation is sometimes awkward, and it isn't free of *loca communia* and vicious circular reasoning, as I will I try to show in the following.

---

113 *Socrate*, 255.
114 *Socrate*, 315.
115 *Socrate*, 315–316.

The Sciences

While his earlier work, the *Discorso*, was a typical Jewish apologia, the aim of Luzzatto's book remains a puzzle because of its apparently "non-Jewish" content.[116] According to Ruderman, even the book's title is misleading, since Luzzatto does not deal with God and providence. Ruderman's conclusion on the position of Luzzatto departs from the path traced by Bernard Septimus, who, taking only the *Discorso* into account, sees Luzzatto as a Maimonides of the seventeenth century. Ruderman proposes to consider him as a kind of "foreshadowing of the lens-grinder of Rijnsburg."[117] In this way, he tries to locate Luzzatto's attempt to weaken and even subvert human knowledge by applying a radical scepticism within the lineage of sceptical philosophy and theology, leading all the way to Spinoza.

However, I do not think that a lack of theological discussion in the text automatically speaks against revelation and providence. Luzzatto is rightly concerned only with human knowledge, as "divine" knowledge wouldn't be very useful to a book titled *Socrate*. Other scholars before him, such as Abraham Portaleone, tried to resolve the conflict between science and religion, philologically reducing all aspects of knowledge, even recent techniques and discoveries such as gunpowder[118] to the Bible, an extreme consequence of the principle that all wisdom belongs to Israel, a notion also stated by Maimonides.[119] Azariah Figo's position is also relevant to this discussion:

> Someone cannot be an astronomer without prior knowledge of physics and mathematics, nor a doctor without prior knowledge of natural philosophy. Nor can a person acquire any knowledge unless he is accustomed to logic [...]. It follows, that one [field] justifies and prepares for the next, otherwise, the one which follows would have no foundation. But our Torah does not require any other wisdom nor any external knowledge, for everything is in her; she guides and informs herself with her own conclusions, principles, and ideas.[120]

---

116 A perusal of the concepts and ideas involved in the *Socrate* could show Jewish traditions in apparently non-Jewish garb.
117 David B. Ruderman, "Science," 184; Bernard Septimus, "Biblical Religion and Political Rationality in Simone Luzzatto, Maimonides and Spinoza," in *Jewish Thought in the Seventeenth Century*, ed. Isadore Twersky and Bernard Septimus (Cambridge: Harvard University Press, 1987): 399–434.
118 Cf. Gianfranco Miletto, "Die Bibel als Handbuch der Kriegskunst nach der Interpretation Abraham ben David Portaleones," in *An der Schwelle zur Moderne. Juden in der Renaissance*, ed. Giuseppe Veltri and Annette Winkelmann (Leiden: Brill, 2003): 78–89.
119 Maimonides, *Moreh Nevukhim* I, chapter I.71.
120 ʿAzaryah ben Efrayim Figo, *Sefer Binah le-ʿIttim*, vol. 2, sermon 43, 26b. I use here the translation of Isaac E. Barzilay, *Between Reason and Faith. Anti-Rationalism in Italian Jewish Thought 1250–1650* (The Hague: Mouton & Company, 1967), 201.

According to Figo, the secular sciences are interdependent and the "Torah is complete and stands on its own," as Gianfranco Miletto rightly summarises.[121] Yet, in this case we have little to no relationship between the sciences and the Torah, i.e. the absolute standard of the truth which cannot be exceeded by any science and art. Although Luzzatto seems to believe in the excellence of the Torah, he does not explain the reasons for its superiority.

The Venetian Rabbi deals with visual art in the contest over the validity of sense perception. After the examination of taste and its defects, Socrates takes a close look at sight.[122] He does not deny its excellent qualities (*egregie qualità*), which are in both its function as a mediator between human highlights and events and in its ability to bring human beings closer to the distant celestial bodies. Allusion is made here to the technical discovery of the telescope, which "proved the mistakes and defects which antiquity, following human discourse, retained as true and sincere doctrines."[123] The "defects" produced without or exposed by the telescope are here listed openly, following Galileo's *Sidereus Nuncius* (*Starry Messenger*), which offers a concise synopsis:

- The conviction that the galaxy was sublunary and consists of evaporation. Luzzatto already mentioned this first (false) conviction in his *Discorso*,[124] attributing it to the Stoics. That is indeed the doctrine of evaporation/nourishment of Zeno of Cittium, a conception which goes back to Heraclitus.[125] To the telescope of Galileo, however, the galaxy appears as congeries of tiny fixed stars in the higher parts of the sky.[126]

---

[121] Gianfranco Miletto, "Tradition and Innovation: Religion, Science and Jewish Culture between the 16th and 17th Centuries," in *Religious Confession and the Sciences in the 16th Century*, ed. Jürgen Helm and Annette Winkelmann (Leiden: Brill, 2001): 99–107, 105.
[122] *Socrate*, 94.
[123] Ibid.: "[...] e massime doppo che fu sufragato dall'egregio adminicolo del cannachialo che dimostrò l'errori e fallacie, che l'antichità normata dall'humano discorso giudicaua vere e sincere dottrine."
[124] *Discorso*, 7r: "one finds that among the famous ancient philosophers, the Stoics dared to declare that the Sun, the Moon, and other Stars nourish and feed themselves from the vapor of our low earthly sphere."
[125] *Stobaeus*, 1.213. 15–21. On the reception of Stoic philosophy in the seventeenth century, see *Le stoïcisme au XVIe et au XVIIe siècle: le retour des philosophies antiques à l'Age classique*, ed. Pierre-François Moreau (Paris: A. Michel, 1999).
[126] Galileo Galilei, *Nuncius Sidereus* (Venice: apud Thomam Baglionum, 1610): n.p. (after 16) "Est enim GALAXIA nihil aliud, quam innumerarum Stellarum coacervatim consitarum congeries: in quamcumque enim regionem illius Perspicillum dirigas, statim Stellarum ingens frequentia sese in conspectum profert, quarum complures satis magnê ac valde conspicuê videntur; sed exiguarum multitudo prorsus inexplorabilis est"; for an English translation, see Albert van Helden, ed., *Galileo Galilei, Sidereus Nuncius, or, The Sidereal Messenger* (Chicago: The University of Chicago Press, 1989).

- The telescope destroyed the belief that the moon was a clear and pure body, as it became evident that it was full of cavities and hills.[127]
- The conviction that only the moon has phases was corrected: Venus, like the moon, goes through regular phases, changing in appearance from crescent-shaped to a round disk.[128]
- The belief that Venus and Mercury were orbiting the earth was proven erroneous with its help, because they are satellites of the sun like the other planets. [129]
- This instrument discovered that four moons were revolving around Jupiter.[130]
- Saturn was described as one planet, a union of three bodies which, similar to the earth, revolve around it over a period of thirty years.
- The telescope informed us that the sun is full of hills and of volcanoes which emit fire and exhalations.

Luzzatto does not just mention the positive discoveries of the telescope however; he also regards it as a defective instrument. Its praiseworthy achievements are counterbalanced, even exceeded by its frauds and defects.[131] For it let "that which is big [appear] as little, something restless as motionless, one as two, something superior as inferior, the left as right, the square as round, the flat as deep, something close as distant."[132] Luzzatto's methodological inconsequence here is striking because he deals at length with the scientific achievements of the telescope and writes only a

---

127 *Nuncius Sidereus*, 5 and following, see for s. 5v: "Lunam superficie leni et perpolita nequaquam esse indutam, sed aspera et inêquali; ac, veluti ipsiusmet Telluris facies, ingentibus tumoribus, profundis lacunis atque anfractibus undiquaque confertam existere."
128 *Nuncius Sidereus*, 14 and following. "Quidam enim proprium esse ac naturalem ipsiusmet Lunê splendorem dixerunt; alii, a Venere illi esse impertitum; alii, a stellis omnibus; alii, a Sole, qui radiis suis profundam Lunê soliditatem permeet. Verum huiuscemodi prolata exiguo labore coarguuntur, ac falsitatis evincuntur [...]."
129 *Nuncius Sidereus*, 5v: "Verum, quod omnem admirationem longe superat, quodve admonitos faciendos cunctos Astronomos atque Philosophos nos apprime impulit, illud est, quod scilicet quatuor Erraticas Stellas, nemini eorum qui ante nos cognitas aut observatas, adinvenimus, quê circa Stellam quandam insignem e numero cognitarum, instar Veneris atque Mercurii circa Solem, suas habent periodos, eamque modo prêeunt, modo subsequuntur, nunquam extra certos limites ab illa digredientes."
130 *Nuncius Sidereus*, 28v: "nunc enim, nedum Planetam unum circa alium convertibilem habemus, dum ambo magnum circa Solem perlustrant orbem, verum quatuor circa Iovem, instar Lunê circa Tellurem, sensus nobis vagantes offert Stellas, dum omnes simul cum Iove, 12 annorum spatio, magnum circa Solem permeant orbem."
131 On the positive and negative reaction to the *Nuncius Sidereus* as well on the political aspects, cf. Mario Biagioli, *Galileo Courtier. The Practice of Science in the Culture of Absolutism* (Chicago: The University of Chicago Press, 1993), 103–157.
132 *Socrate*, 95: "[...] ma a questi suoi egregii suoi effetti mi conviene anco contrapporre le sue frodi et inganni, che equilibratti con le sue lodevoli conditioni triusciranno queste sopraffatte da suoi vitii e difalte, facendosi sovente apparire il grande piciolo, l'agitato immobile, l'uno duoi, il superiore inferiore, il sinistro destro, il quadro tondo, il piano profondo, il propinquo lontano, e tante altre fallacie [...]."

few sentences on the defects of this instrument, as if he were undecided whether to accept or refuse the discoveries of the telescope. If Socrates wants to prove the weakness of human vision, why spend so much time looking at the discoveries of a visual instrument? Perhaps because the instrument proves the defect of ancient observations of the sky attained solely with the aid of human vision.

The discreet critical reader here should note that the author apparently ends in a *contradictio in terminis:* how can we doubt the defect of the ancient optical vision of the stars through the telescope if that is even more defective? Luzzatto is perhaps quoting critics against this instrument, as reported by Simplicio's statement in Galileo Galilei's *Dialogo sopra I due massimi sistemi del mondo*[133]: "I have considered as defects and deceptions of the lenses those things which other people have admired as stupendous achievements."[134] Galileo and his "successors" in astronomic discoveries were aware of the technical troubles with this instrument, especially in reference to lenses, a problem known as spherical and chromatic aberration, later solved by Newton. I do not think that Luzzatto is addressing these technical aspects of the telescope—he does not speak of the distortion of colour because of refraction. Rather, he wants to locate weaknesses that confirm his thesis concerning the deficiency of the senses. Luzzatto's method of reasoning is, however, acceptable in one aspect: (the defect of) the telescope does convince him to conclude that the eye is defective, because the eye cannot realise and recognise reality.[135]

Note the increase in circular argumentation here: ancient optical visions of the firmament are defective because the telescope shows that optical vision is defective. The doubt about the lenses has, for Luzzatto, nothing to do with what is "scientifically" proven, i.e. technical observation, but rather with the analysis of sight as such and the formation of images in the human mind.

The Deceit of the Senses: Sight and the Mirror

According to Pyrrho, as it transmitted by Aristocles via Eusebius of Caesarea, knowledge acquired through the senses is neither true nor false: "Now he says that Pyrrho shows that objects are equally indifferent and unfathomable and undeterminable be-

---

[133] Galileo Galilei, *Dialogo sopra i due massimi sistemi del mondo*, ed. Fabio Attori (Milan: Sansoni, 2001), 349.
[134] Ibid., "[...] ho creduto esser fallaci e inganni de i cristalli quelle che altri hanno ammirate per operazioni stupende."
[135] Perhaps, Luzzatto is addressing the mechanical problem of scaling, which Galileo deals with in his last work *Discorsi e dimostrazioni matematiche* (1638); see the English version: *Two New Sciences*, trans. Stillman Drake (Madison: University of Wisconsin Press, 1974). On scaling, cf. Michael S. Mahoney, "Sketching Science in the Seventeenth Century," in http://www.princeton.edu/~hos/mike/articles/whysketch/whysketch.html (accessed 3 May, 2018).

cause neither our senses nor our judgements are true or false."¹³⁶ If our senses and therefore our judgments do not fulfil the criteria of the Aristotelian principle of contradiction being neither true nor false, they are either equipollent or insufficient for perception. The suspension of judgment is not only logical but also necessary.

According to the Pyrrhonian Sextus, the main argument for necessary invalidation of knowledge is "disagreement"¹³⁷ because of the difference of the senses (ἀπὸ τῆς διαφορᾶς τῶν αἰσθήσεων).¹³⁸ For it is obvious to Sextus that the senses differ from one another (ὁποῖον δὲ φαίνεται ἑκάστοτε δυνατὸν εἰπεῖν).¹³⁹ He also quotes some examples of discrepancies in perception. Sextus does not question the fact that an object could show the quality of what it is appears to be ("[...] it is possible to say what each thing at the moment appears to be").¹⁴⁰ However, the question is not the perception of the object in its appearance in a particular moment and particular space, but the perception according to its real nature (πρὸς τὴν φύσιν). For then the object does not "naturally" have any qualities: "Each of the phenomena perceived by the senses seems to be a complex: the apple, for example, seems smooth, odorous, sweet, and yellow. However, it is not clear whether it really possesses these qualities or whether it has but one quality that appears varied owing to the varying structure of the sense-organs, or whether, again, it has more qualities than are actually apparent to our senses."¹⁴¹

Besides the elusive impact of objects on our senses, there are also the illusions that can be provoked by them, as mentioned by Sextus in a peculiar point of the *Outlines*, often cited by modern scholars, in his reference to painting: "to the eye, paintings seem to have recesses and projections, but not so to the touch."¹⁴² Recesses and projections are a known element of geography¹⁴³ that painters often imitate in their works; they deceive the ocular senses but not the sense of touch.¹⁴⁴ Sextus returns to the topic of projection and the faculty of sight in *Outlines* I:120, also using the example of painting and its apparent rendering of objects that appear different if seen from one angle or another:

> Effects due to positions are such as these: the same painting when laid flat appears smooth, but when inclined forward at a certain angle it seems to have recesses and prominences. The necks

---

136 Aristocles in Eusebius, *Preparatio Evangelica*, trans. Julia Annas and Jonathan Barnes (Cambridge: Cambridge University Press, 1985), XIV, xviii, 2–4; *The Modes of Scepticism*, 11.
137 Cf. Markus Lammenranta, "The Role of Disagreement in Pyrrhonian and Cartesian Skepticism," in *Disagreement and Skepticism*, ed. Diego E. Machuca (New York: Routledge, 2012): 46–65.
138 Sextus, *Outlines of Pyrrhonism*, I, 91–92.
139 Ibid.
140 Ibid., 93.
141 Ibid., I, 94.
142 Ibid., I, 91–92; cf. *The Modes of Scepticism*, 69–71.
143 Both expressions are also in Strabo, *Geography*, 14, 2, 1.
144 While it is true that a painting cannot fool the sense of touch, it is not the case for bas-reliefs or impressions made on wax; Sextus does not discuss this kind of art.

of doves, also, appear different in hue according to the differences in the angle of inclination. Since, then, all apparent objects are viewed in a certain place, and from a certain distance, or in a certain position, and each of these conditions produces a great divergence in the sense-impressions (παραλλαγὴν περὶ τὰς φαντασίας), as we mentioned above, we shall be compelled by this Mode also to end up in suspension of judgement.[145]

The condition of the object produces divergence in the impression of senses, which necessarily leads to the suspension of judgment. Sextus attaches great importance only to the object which is responsible for the differences in perception. In this context, he does not attack the reliability of the eyes in their perception; rather, he stresses the divergence of the sources of the senses.

Luzzatto's argumentation is very similar in his long and complex discussion of the deceitful sense of sight and the correlating debate on the mirror, also a topic of Sextus. In his little history of ophthalmology,[146] which follows the topic of the discoveries and fallacies of the telescope, Luzzatto gives evidence of his acquaintance with ancient, medieval and modern theories of human eyesight.[147]

The reader is of course acquainted with the fact that ancient, medieval, and early modern discussions conducted on the senses mostly relied on Aristotle's *De Anima* in its multifaceted interpretations, receptions and commentaries from the ancient period, Arabic philosophy in general, the Middle Ages, the early modern period, and also Averroes.[148] In the second book, Aristotle discusses sense perception (II:5–6) and in II:7 (418a6–418a26) the sight. For Aristotle the problem is not whether perception is caused by the objects of perception, but *how* this is achieved[149] and *where* this perception takes place. It is no surprise then that both question are objects of Luzzatto's summary of visual perception. I emphasise the word summary, because he does not care to report on the development of the science of the ophthalmology; he only lists its theories.

Luzzatto is very precise, although his enumeration of varied opinions on human vision is very complicated. He notes that the discussion on the formation of images

---

145 Sextus, *Outlines of Pyrrhonism*, I, 120–122.
146 Cf. Waldemar Deonna, *Le Symbolisme de l'oeil*, fasc 15. (Paris: Broccard, 1965).
147 On ancient and medieval theories cf. David C. Lindberg, *Theories of Vision from al-Kindi to Kepler* (Chicago: University of Chicago Press, 1967); Gérard Simon, *Le regard, l'être et l'apparence dans l'Optique de l'Antiquité* (Paris: Edition du Seuil, 1988); Robert Nelson, *Visuality Before and Beyond the Renaissance. Seeing as Other Saw* (Cambridge: Cambridge University Press, 2000). On the echoes of ancient and medieval theory in poetry (Dante), cf. Burt Kimmelman, "Visionary Science in *Purgatorio* XVII and *Paradiso* XXX," *Comitatus* 26 (1995): 53–74.
148 For the reception of the *De Anima* in the early modern period, see Sascha Salatowsky, *De Anima. Die Rezeption der aristotelischen Psychologie im 16. und 17. Jahrhundert* (Amsterdam: Grüner Publishing Company, 2006).
149 *De Anima*, 417b18, 419a17; cf. Nicholas J. Wade and Michael Swanston, *Visual Perception*, 37; Thomas K. Johansen, *Aristotle on the Sense-Organs* (Cambridge: Cambridge University Press, 1998); and Scott M. Rubarth's Review of Johansen's text in *Bryn Mawr Classical Review* (1999.09.24): http://ccat.sas.upenn.edu/bmcr/1999/1999-09-24.html (accessed 3, May 2018).

4.2 The Politics of Scepticism: Luzzatto's *Socrate*

in optical perception is often very detailed and the conclusions reached are highly divergent. He lists the different opinions on the effusion of the image from the object to the eye as well as opinions on the place where the image is formed. First, he elucidates three theories on the modalities of sight, listing them as follows:[150]

- Some of them, as Crito already debated, considered vision to be carried out by the effluvium of rays extending to an object.
- Others excluded this remote ejection and considered that the rays first match the external light and then, once consolidated together, extend as far as the object.
- Furthermore, others argued against the emission of rays and rather asserted that some images and simulacra, once detached from the objects, enter into the eyes and that they are divided into two classes:
  - Some people thought that these images were the material remains of visible bodies, detached from the objects by the virtue and effectiveness of light.
  - Others thought that they were immaterial but proper instruments for leading us to acknowledge material objects, as they are their progenitors, although these simulacra are insensitive by themselves.[151]
- There were others who considered that sight may be carried out without the intromission of simulacra or the emission of rays, but that the presence of the object was sufficient for it [i.e. the sight] to be able to encounter the visual faculty.

An exploration of the many theories concerning sight throughout the ages is the project for another book. Here I simply seek to elucidate three theories that ancient theories were divided between: the theory that rays radiate from the eyes (emission theory), the theory that images come to the eye (intromission theory),[152] and, finally, the theory of which the important representative is Aristotle, which claims that the problem is how the object is received by the eyes via light and is then interpreted by the mind (reception theory).[153]

The first theory was split into two explanations of the process: the first, supported by Pythagoras, Euclid (in *Optics*), Ptolemy, and Leon Battista Alberti (in *De pictura*),[154] claimed that rays directly pass from the eyes to objects; the second, which was the Platonic conception of vision, claims that the rays emitting from the eyes have to meet with the light. This second explanation is also called the mixed theory

---

150 *Socrate*, 96.
151 Ibid.
152 Cf. Nicholas J. Wade and Michael T. Swanston, *Visual Perception*, 36.
153 Cf. *History of Ophthalmology: Sub auspiciis Academiae Ophthalmologicae Internationalis*, vol. 3, ed. Harold E. Henkes and Claudia Zrenner (Dodrecht: Kluwer Academic Publishers, 1990).
154 Leon Battista Alberti, *On Painting and on Sculpture*, ed. and trans. Cecil Grayson (London: Phaidon, 1972), 40–41. Cf. Jack M. Greenstein, "On Alberto's 'Sign': Vision and Composition in Quattrocento Painting," *The Art Bulletin* 79 (1997): 669–698.

because light has to been emitted both by the eyes and the objects. Plato wrote in *Timaeus* (45b–46a) that the "pure fire" within us compresses the central part of the eye in particular:

> [...] so that it kept out everything of a coarser nature, and allowed to pass only this pure element. When the light of day surrounds the stream of vision, then like falls upon like, and they coalesce, and one body is formed by natural affinity in the line of vision, wherever the light that falls from within meets with an external object. And the whole stream of vision, being similarly affected in virtue of similarity, diffuses the motions of what it touches or what touches it over the whole body, until they reach the soul, causing that perception which we call sight.[155]

Intromission theory postulates that tiny atoms or skins (*eidola, simulacra*) of the objects detach from the bodies of the objects while retaining object's image, coming to the eye and thereby generating vision. Democritus, Leucippus, Epicurus, Lucretius all ascribe to this theory.[156] According to Democritus, that is possible because of the interaction of the interaction of the *eidola* with the internal light of the viewer (doctrine of the efferent and afferent light).[157]

In Luzzatto's opinion, reception theory, which denies that rays emit from the eyes, can be divided into three groups: the first group of them assumes that images are material remainders of visible bodies, cut off from the objects by virtue of the light;[158] the second group maintains that images are immaterial, but permit recognition of the objects as their remote generators or emissions (for Luzzatto: *progenitors*).[159] The third group rejects all transmission through images and emission of rays, claiming that the presence of the object itself is adequate to meet the faculty of sight.[160]

He goes further:

- "The same opposition of opinions and positions concerns the location where vision occurs inside of ourselves, and whether this also happens through the intromission of simulacra.
- Some believed that it happens in the middle of the crystalline or glacial lens.
- Some others could not bear the idea that it could be produced in a simple humour [i.e. the glacial humour] lacking in life and perception and believed that

---

155 Plato, *Timaeus*, trans. Benjamin Jowett (Indianapolis: Bobbs-Merrill, 1949).
156 David C. Lindberg, ed. *Sciences in the Middle Ages*. (Chicago: University of Chicago Press, 1978), 340.
157 *History of Ophthalmology*, 60.
158 Ibid., "[...] alcuni giudicarno che tali imagini siano spoglie materiali di corpi visibili."
159 Ibid., "[...] altri che immateriali siano però idonei mezi per farci riconoscere l'oggetti materiali loro progenitori, ancor che essi simulacri per loro medesimi insensibili siano."
160 Ibid., "[...] altri vi furono che stimarono che la visione senza l'intermissione di simulacri di raggi possano ciò auvenire, essendo a ciò bastevole la presenza dell'oggetto all'incontro della facoltà visiva posto."

it is carried out in the retinal membrane, located in the innermost secret meanderings of the eye. Nevertheless, they attributed perception to this without paying enough attention to the fact that the images penetrating into it meet and cross, so that the right [image] becomes the left and the higher [image] becomes the lower.[161]
- Other people who cared even less about this believed that the images intruded as far as the optic nerves in order to avoid objects being duplicated because of the duplicity of those same eyes, as often happens to drunk and delirious people. They indeed do not consider the alteration of images which would necessarily result if they [i.e. the images] were passing through these very narrow meanderings [i.e. the nerves].
- Others did not agree with attributing this function to any solid part of the eyes, but rather to a spirit permeating the whole eye. [They supposed] that this spirit, which is of a very feeble and fluid condition, could stop and halt images, an [action] that is not even possible for water, naturally more solid than this—I am wrong if I mention water—indeed, it is not even possible for a crystal to do this.
- Others tried to accommodate all of the aforementioned opponents' opinions and they said that vision works through the encounter of simulacra with the heap of membranes, humours, nerves, and spirits located in the eyes. Thus, they thought to generously satisfy their mutual friends and were content with merely tolerating all the oppositions encountered for each of the aforementioned opinions.
- I [Luzzatto] believe that human curiosity will produce other dogmata concerning the way in which vision works, because it is pushed by a natural desire always inclined more to contradictions than to novelty."

In this list, Luzzatto presents a number of divergent opinions in reference to the inner place (*loco interno*) where sight takes place through an intermediary agency by images. Some opine that the intermediary is in the crystalline lens.[162] Others reject the idea that sight can take place in a humour which is lifeless and senseless and attribute it to the membrane of the retina (*membrana rettina*) located in the inner-

---

161 Luzzatto is referring to the projection of reversed images onto the retina, discovered by the Jesuit Christoph Scheiner during his research in Rome. He verified this phenomenon with anatomical dissections. Cf. Paolo Mancosu, "Acustic and Optics," in *The Cambridge History of Science: Volume 6, Modern Life and Earth*, ed. Peter J. Bowler and John V. Pickstone, (Cambridge: Cambridge University Press, 2008), 596–631; 616.

162 That vision takes place in the crystalline lens was the opinion of Galen. The lens was described as a round lens in the middle of the eye: "the crystalline lens is the principal instrument of vision, a fact clearly proved by what physicians call cataracts, which lie between the crystalline humor and the cornea and interfere with vision until they are couched" (*Galen and the Usefulness of the Parts of the Body*, ed. May M. Tallmadge (Ithaca: Cornell University Press, 1968) 463–464; cf. Julius Hirschberg, *The History of Ophthalmology*, vol. 1 (Bonn: Wayenborgh, 1985), §102 and §115. The anatomist Vesalius also reported the opinion of Galen and still believed that the lens is the center of the eyeball, see Hirschberg, Ibid. vol. 2, §305.

most interior of the eye.¹⁶³ Uninterested in the problem of how the images convert themselves optically, Luzzatto adds that an advocate of the last opinion assumes that the rays have to unify themselves in the optical nerves so that we do not see double, as the intoxicated do. The notion of the unification of these images in the optical nerve is attacked by Luzzatto: he argues that the supporters of this theory do not take into account the "corruption" (*depravatione*) of the images as they traverse the very tiny holes¹⁶⁴ (he leaves what he means by *depravatione* unexplained). A last group does not accept the attribution of this function to a solid material, and instead proposes a permeable spirit.¹⁶⁵ Luzzatto questions whether a permeable spirit that is fluid in nature can be impressed upon by images at all. With an argument *a maiori*, he doubts that a fluid spirit can "stop" images if water and even crystal cannot.

He disqualifies every scientific and philosophical attempt to explain the process of sight as "inclination to contradiction," a result of human curiosity. Against the Aristotelian principle of perception according to which "Each particular sense can discern these proper objects without deception,"¹⁶⁶ Luzzatto substantiates his conviction that the problem remains the contradiction of the images themselves and, of course, of the eyes as receivers:

> Yet which of these aforementioned opinions is the truest does not really concern my proposal. The reason for this is that I did not put forth these opinions to debate them, but I want to infer from this collection of various opinions only this: regardless of whether vision happens in this way or in other ways, it is necessary [to point out] that there is a great diversity between the appearance of objects and their true reality. Who may deny that the representation of what is visible would dramatically change if it happened through the emission of rays up to the object, or by these "rays" matching with the light, or rather by the intromission of images, or by the simple presence of the object, as well as whether it was carried out into the middle of the glacial or the

---

163 That was the postulation of Felix Plater, *De corporibus humani structura et usu* (Basel: 1583): 187, quoted by Hirschberg, *History*, vol. 2, §306 (290, note 179), perhaps in the appreciation of Kepler's *A Sequel to Vitello*, 1604; cf. Haim Z. Hirschberg, *History of the Jews in North Africa*, vol. 2, (Leiden: Brill, 1974–1980), §306, 294. The author of the idea seems to be Hieronymus Fabricius ab Aquapendente, a professor from the University of Padua, specifically in his *De Actione oculorum*, cf. *The History of Ophthalmology*, vol. 3, 66.

164 *Socrate*, 98: "[...] altri [...] tengono che insino alla unione di nervi optici convenga che s'introducano l'imagini, acciochè per la duplicità delli occhi non ci si rendono anco l'oggetti duplicati, come ad ubriachi & deliranti sovente accade; non facendo questi stima della depravatione dell'imagini che necessariamente occorerebbe, passando esse per l'anfratti d'ansiosissimi meati."

165 It is difficult to say what Luzzatto's reference to "spirito permabile" means. It may refer to Galen's theory of *pneuma*, which had a vivid reception in the Renaissance also with the help of Melanchthon, cf. Jürgen Helm, "Die Galenrezeption in Philipp Melanchthons *De Anima* (1540/1552)," *Medizinhistorisches Journal* 31 (1996): 298–321. Perhaps he is referring to the theory of the *spiritus visibilis* of Ibn-Al-Haytam (Alhazen), on which cf. *The History of Ophthalmology*, vol. 3, 63.

166 *De Anima* II:6 (418a7). In Greek: ἀλλ' ἑκάστη γε κρίνει περὶ τούτων, καὶ οὐκ ἀπατᾶται ὅτι χρῶμα οὐδ' ὅτι ψόφος, ἀλλὰ τί τὸ κεχρωσμένον ἢ ποῦ, ἢ τί τὸ ψοφοῦν ἢ ποῦ. The translation of the Greek text as well the commenbtray of Thomas Aquinas can be found here: http://dhspriory.org/thomas/DeAnima.htm#214 (accessed 3 May, 2018).

retinal membrane, or throughout the optic nerves, or in spirits, or in all of them clustered together?[167]

The Rabbi of Venice's main point is clearly formulated: "there is a great diversity between the appearance of objects and their true reality." When he first mentions the totality of the attempts to explain the process of vision, he returns to his premise of the dialectical confrontation with dogmatic philosophy, turning his attention to the deceitful source of knowledge that is the mirror, which is a prime example of the great difference between the appearance and the reality of objects.[168]

That Luzzatto discusses mirrors is not surprising, as mirror production was an important industry in Venice.[169] However, Luzzatto is still following the contours of the discussion on the senses and sight shaped by Sextus, who discusses mirrors in *Outlines* I:48 after presenting the argument of the first *topos* according to which the "same impressions are not produced by the same objects owing to the differences in animals."[170] Sextus introduces the example of the mirrors as follows:[171]

> Mirrors, too, owing to differences in their construction, represent the external objects at one time as very small—as when the mirror is concave—at another time as elongated and narrow—as when the mirror is convex. Some mirrors, too, show the head of the figure reflected at the bottom and the feet at the top. Since, then, some organs of sight actually protrude beyond the face owing to their convexity, while others are quite concave, and others again lie in a level plane, on this account also it is probable that their impressions differ, and that the same objects, as seen by dogs, fishes, lions, men and locusts, are neither equal in size nor similar in shape, but vary according to the image of each object created by the particular sight that receives the impression.

Luzzatto imports whole paragraphs from Sextus into the *Socrate:* Although mirrors are constructed on the basis of the same material, they reflect images in different ways depending on their shapes:[172]

> Furthermore, an evident lesson about this distortion of appearances is provided by mirrors, which are generally made of the same matter, but even a small difference in their form may consistently diversify the image reflected in them. Hence, we should consider that the images produced by the same object are [98] striking different forms of eyes, which are masses of various

---

167 *Socrate*, 97.
168 On the mirror, cf. Jurgis Baltrušaitis, *Essai sur une légende scientifique: Le miroir. Révélations, science-fiction et fallacies* (Paris: Elmayan, 1978), and Richard Gregory, *Mirrors in Mind* (London: Penguin, 1997).
169 Faye Tudor, "'All in him selfe as in a glass he sees.' Mirrors and Vision in the Renaissance," in *Renaissance Theories of Vision*, ed. John Hendrix and Charles H. Carman (Franham: Ashgate, 2010): 171–86.
170 *Outlines of Pyrrhonism*, I:40.
171 Cf. Diogenes, *Lives of the Philosophers* IX: 81, cf. *The Modes of Scepticism*, 173.
172 *Socrate*, 97: "[...] che se bene della istessa material construtti siano un poco do varietà che nella loro figura accade diversificano non poco l'imagini da essi riflesse."

matters. Therefore, they [i.e. the images] turn out to be reflected and consequently with a very different appearance from that of the object, as their origin and efficient, and also with strange dislocations and positions.

The reason for the difference in reflections cannot be in the object itself, because each reflects the same object; therefore, one has to infer that the perceived difference depends on the receiver, i.e. the eyes or the reflective surfaces of the mirrors. The images happen to meet with different shapes of eyes or are collected by different material. For that reason, they are refracted and take on an appearance and shape that differs from the original, with different effects, dislocations, and positions.[173] In this argument, Luzzatto apparently does not realise that the different refractions of the mirror are created by the mirror itself, which is surprising because this problem had already been discussed at length in medieval and humanistic literature;[174] it is difficult to assume that he was unaware of it. We have to bear in mind what the *Socrate*'s scope of discussion seeks to prove is the inconsistency of human knowledge which comes from the senses. The eye cannot ever be perfectly aware of reality because of its unreliability.

The mirror is an example of the unreliability of knowledge that does not affect the object but rather the source of vision itself. I admit that Luzzatto is not clear in his reasoning, but the use of the mirror cannot obscure the fact that he is speaking of vision and not of lenses for vision. Moreover, scientists of the seventeenth century don't address the "errors" of the mirror (*de erroribus speculorum*) but rather its fallacies (*de fallacia specula*), as Friedrich Risner's (1606)[175] and Ambrosius Rhodius's (1611)[176] compositions show. The change is in perspective: namely, the mirror does not produce "errors": it is a source of fallacies and deceits. The subject or passive object of such illusion is clearly the eye, as Luzzatto continues to maintain at the beginning of his treatise in defence of Socrates:[177]

> Therefore, everything that is perceptible only exists because our mind gives form and appearance to it. This complies perfectly with what our Protagoras used to utter: that man is the measure both of things [that are to the extent that they] appear to him in the world and also of those things which are not to the extent that they do not appear to him. The same happens to the objects that we apprehend: we wrongly consider our robes and coverings to be the source of that heat which, on the contrary, derives from ourselves and is merely reflected in them and sent back to us. Hence, we are used to believe perhaps mistakenly that those manifestations of exter-

---

[173] *Socrate*, 97–98: "[...] per il che l'imagini che dall'istesso oggetto prodotti sono, stimare dobbiamo che abbattendosi in varie figure di occhij, ammassati di diuerve materie, ci sortiscono retratti & per consequentemente di apparenza assai differente di quello è l'oggetto loro originario & efficiente, & con strani dislocamenti & positure."
[174] Cf. Jurgis Baltrušaitis, *Essa sur une légende scientifique*, 241–259.
[175] *Opticae libri quatuor ex voto Petri Rami novissimo per Fridericum Risnerum ejusdem in mathematicis adjutorem olim conscripti* (Cassellis: Wesselius, 1606).
[176] *Optica Ambrosii Rhodii [...] Cui additus est Tractatus De crepusculis* (Wittenberg: Seelfisch, 1611).
[177] *Socrate*, 14.

nal objects, we see on the external objects, are their true images, while in fact we are their original cause, since most of them come from us. Furthermore, the objects participate in producing them [i.e. images] by ejecting and sending them back to us, like mirrors that reflect the images of the object in front of them. However, the ejected simulacra differentiate and diversify one the other in accordance with the diversity of condition, figure, and composition of these mirrors. Thus, the suspension of judgment, which I considered extremely salutary and favourable to mankind, is now considered pernicious and harmful by others, particularly by my slanderers, since they and myself judge it with different disposition of mind.

But back to the mirror example: Luzzatto claims that the fallacy of the eyes can be proven by the fact that animals cannot perceive the fallacious beauty of visual arts (about all painting). In Luzzatto's words, they are incapable of perceiving the "charm of colours, symmetry, and beauty bodies" (*vaghezza di colori, simetria, & bellezza de' corpi*); this is to be seen as a consequence of the different manner in which their eyes are constructed and not a lack of inner sense ([...] *variando dal nostro, nella configuratione, situazione, qualità d'humori, membrane, e nervi, e non già per macamento di senso interno*).[178]

The difference between human and animal perception is of great disadvantage to the human being because, according to Luzzatto, animal perception, imitation, and reproduction of sound testify to their considerable perceptual abilities when compared to human musical performances. Evidence can be found in the nightingale, the ugly tarantula, "which is reputed to be capable of modulation of harmonic sound," as well as the blackbird and the parrot, which can perfectly learn human songs. According to Luzzatto, much more is required for perceiving, observing, and learning the harmony of sounds than just evaluating the charm of colours and bodily proportion. Even the common people perceive the last (*questi da più volgari e plebei ingegni sono osseruati*).

The Venetian Rabbi defends the superiority of music over the visual arts because the first requires much more learning and ability than the second. He is clearly comparing the perception and imitation of music with the perception of images, rather than with the reproduction of images, which is the task of painting and sculpture. For him, the near perfection of the auditory senses of animals proves that they possess an inner sense. The difference between animals and human beings rests only in their perception of images and not in the perception and imitation of sounds. This is a means for him to claim the superiority of animals' faculties of sight over those of

---

[178] *Socrate*, 98. The discussion of the topic of animal perception was en vogue in Luzzatto's time because of a general sceptical attitude towards human knowledge, as can be found in Descartes's speculation on mechanical clockworks (the automata). For a discussion of the "reason of the animal," see the very useful anthology of texts collected by Hans-Peter Schütt, *Die Vernuft der Tiere* (Frankfurt: Keip, 1990); and Richard Sorabji, *Animal Minds & Human Morals: The Origins of the Western Debate* (London: Duckworth, 1993). The topic is a desideratum for Judaic studies; for a first (theological) approach, cf. Andrew Linzey and Dan Cohn-Sherbok, *After Noah: Animals and the Liberation of Theology* (London: Mowbray, 1997).

humans because animals cannot be deceived by any illusion and fraud of painting, as we mere humans often are. Luzzatto attributes their greater ability to perceive the fiction of perspectives and fictive remote distances to the perfection of animals' visual faculties. To sustain his theory, Luzzatto speaks of a miracle, retelling the well-known episode of a bird, deceived by a painting, that wanted to peck a cluster of grapes.[179] Luzzatto believes that the "miracle" happened not because of the perfection of the picture, but because the natural perfection of the bird's inborn visual faculty was cancelled or suspended. For the "perfection of their organ defends them from such deceits" (*la perfezione del loro organo li difenda da tali fallacie*).[180]

To understand Luzzatto's argument, we have to remind the reader of the ancient, medieval, and humanist discussions regarding the property of the mirror/image (painting) and any animal's capacity or incapacity to cope with it. Starting from the observation that Luzzatto does not claim the mirror to be a source of fallacies, but rather the human eye, he cannot charge animals with being deceived by mirrors. It is not simply that animal vision is superior to humans, but because a mirror, being only an object, cannot deceive anyone. We can observe here an indirect criticism of magical uses and abuses of the mirror;[181] for example, the basilisk's stare can only be averted by a mirror.[182] To accept that the mirror can be a source of error or fallacy, he mentions artistic objects:

> What famous painter has ever represented an image so vivid as that [i.e. the image] which visible objects produce on polished and clear bodies, and yet ruled by simple Nature? What false contrast of light and dark may be compared with the mirroring and reflection [26] that appear on material mirrors? However, what increases our astonishment is the rapidity and promptness of their working: the image is represented on the mirror, which reproduces it properly according to the size and dimension of the object. If by chance the mirror breaks, dividing into minute fragments, in that instant the original, but smaller, simulacrum appears on each small shard and [it appears] with such symmetry, proportion and similarity that even the most expert painter with his instruments, wire grills, compasses and the expenditure of a long time, would never have reached the perfection of such an operation. Likewise, Nature is so sagacious in finding the centre of gravity of bodies that even the most speculative mechanic could never equal it [i.e. Nature]. Indeed, this one [i.e. Nature] instantaneously finds the centre of any body, even if is irregular, and this is something that the cleverest intellect can hardly achieve with laborious demonstrations.

The reader is obviously surprised that Luzzatto is returning to the concept of nature even as he qualifies himself a sceptic. In this aspect, he is following Sextus who "attacks such fundamental scientific concepts as time, space, motion, causation, but he

---

[179] This is an allusion to the story of Zeuxis and Parrhasios, see Pliny the Elder, *Natural History*, trans. John Bostock and H.T. Riley, http://www.perseus.tufts.edu/hopper/text?doc=Perseus:abo: phi,0978,001:35:36 (accessed 3 May, 2018), 65.
[180] *Socrate*, 99.
[181] On the use of mirrors in magic, see Baltrušaitis, *Essai sur une légende scientifique*, 181–214.
[182] Lucan, *Pharsalia* IX.

never attacks what was, for the Greek thinkers, the central notion of natural science, that of nature itself."[183] Perhaps this is because scepticism is not a system but consists of strategies to demolish dogmatic traditions with dialectic reasoning. Besides, the "nature" used in this quotation consists of facts; indeed, mathematical facts that contain "symmetry, proportion, [...] similarity," and gravity that cannot be demonstrated, according to Luzzatto. Facts are observable but the constitution of any science that tries to explain them is necessarily open to criticism.

Sceptical Attitude

Some centuries later, a descendant of the Luzzatto family, Samuel David Luzzatto, wrote some notes on his genealogical tree that referenced Simone Luzzatto's *Socrate*. There he tries to justify the sceptical tendencies of his ancestor, referring to the century of Descartes, to the crisis of Aristotelianism and, therefore, of the Scholastics, and the genesis of Ancient Greek philosophy. On Samuel's view, against the background of a sceptical approach to salutary beliefs (*salutari credenze*), Simone Luzzatto, erudite "philosopher and at the same time a religious man," considered it to be profitable to the faith and useful to society to lighten the uncertainty of human speculation. Samuel considered the *Socrate* to be an apologetic work designed to humiliate the temerity of false philosophers, supplying believers with an apologetic arsenal against their attackers.[184]

There is much truth in this. However, if the Rabbi of Venice did argue against the defects of knowledge gained through the senses and therefore of all knowledge based on them, he did not "absolve" his Socrates of the accusation of attacking authority. Perhaps he was aware that every method used against the human sciences can also be used against religion.

Luzzatto's book is a deconstruction *ante litteram* of the entire structure of empirical knowledge. He assumed that all knowledge tested by the intellect is a product of the senses, which are, of course, prone to error. Luzzatto's book is a sceptical approach to ancient and modern epistemology, not a treatise on theology. His intention, as Ruderman rightly stresses following Luzzatto's own words, is to subvert

---

183 *The Modes of Scepticism*, 75, with reference to *Outlines of Phyrronism* III and *Against the Mathematicians* IX–X.
184 Samuel David Luzzatto, *Autobiografia*, 7. The biographical and genealogical notices were translated into German and published in Vienna in 1847 by Isidor Busch, "Selbstbiographie des S.D. Luzzatto nebst vorangeschickten historischen und literarischen Nachrichten über die Familie Luzzatto seit dem XVI. Jahrhundert; aus dem noch ungedruckten italienischen Originale übersetzt," Kalender und Jahrbuch der Israeliten 6, trans. Davide Lotti (Crescini: 1847–1848), 95–116. The Italian perished in a flood, the translator Davide Lotti reports.

"human knowledge," adopting a mode of reflection that is "'tentative, sceptical, and doubting' rather than 'dogmatic and assertive.'"[185]

Sometime later, Spinoza used the same method for analysing "divine" knowledge, the theology of the Hebrew and Latin traditions. In the introduction to the "*benigno lettore*," Luzzatto is unmistakably clear: "Socrates confutes human, not inspired knowledge, infused by a superior mind."[186] It is difficult to know whether he was aware that the same sceptical attitude could be used when examining "divine" knowledge.[187] Although the distance from rational to theological scepticism is small, the existing difference between them should be maintained.[188]

If we compare the approach of Luzzatto with that of Moscato, we can maintain that the problem he is trying to resolve is very different from Moscato's division of the profane and holy sciences. While Moscato belittled the importance of the sciences, he did not totally reject them. The main sin of the sciences is in failing to search for agreement with the Torah, despite its claims being very similar to those of religion, in the sense that they seek to the perfection of God.

Luzzatto seems to reject *a priori* the authority of sciences, knowledge of the senses, and logical inference, instead advocating for systematic doubt. Only doubt can preserve humans from condemnation by the Agora, for the Agora seeks to preserve both the truth and accepted moral customs. Deviation is not completely desirable but is socially and philosophically necessary, albeit surely dangerous for the philosopher.

---

185 David B. Ruderman, "Science," 163.
186 *Socrate*, 1: "[...] confuta Socrate il sapere humano, non l'inspiratro, & infuso da mente superior."
187 I thank Warren Zev Harvey for his contribution to this section. He adds: "There may be a small contradiction here. Can 'every method' used against science also be used against religion, or is the 'existing difference' between the two worthy of being maintained?"
188 That is what Charles B. Schmitt, "The Rediscovery of Ancient Skepticism," in *The Skeptical Tradition*, ed. Myles Burnyeat (Berkley: The University of California Press, 1983): 225–251, also wants to stress: "Fideism—the position that faith alone provides the way to truth and that philosophical activity is of no avail—was a fairly common attitude among Renaissance skeptics" (Schmitt, 229). In the footnotes, he mentions two of examples of fideist scepticism, Giovanni Francesco Pico della Mirandola and Pedro de Valencia.

5 Sceptical Judaism: A Protestant Strategy

Parallel to the development of the Jewish tradition into a perennial philosophy and to its historicisation, a new and important phenomenon appeared in seventeenth-century Protestant universities: a concern with negating every philosophical characteristic of Jewish philosophy by means of attributing the classification of scepticism to Jewish philosophers. That is, the division between philosophy and the (alleged or believed) fundamental principles of Jewish wisdom and the emphasis on Jewish scepticism had a decisive starting point in the seventeenth century. Intriguingly, two different cultural areas brought this about: the previously examined Venetian Judaism, which was imbued with critical, sceptical, and libertine concepts in the first half of the century and the Protestant discussions of Johann Frischmuth and Jakob Friedrich Reimmann in Germany, which are the object of this chapter.

5.1 Negotiating the Principle of Contradiction: Johann Frischmuth on Rabbinic Dialectical Discussion

The principle of contradiction (αρχή τῆς ἀντιφάσεως) first appears in Aristotle's *Metaphysics* IV. Perhaps no other passage of Aristotelian philosophy is as controversially debated as the fundamental binary logical incompatibility between true and false, the foundation of the principle of contradiction (commonly called the principle or law of non-contradiction, PNC). Three formulations of it are given in the fourth chapter of the *Metaphysics:*[1]

> It is impossible for the same attribute at once to belong and not to belong to the same thing and in the same relation (τὸ γὰρ αὐτὸ ἅμα ὑπάρχειν τε καὶ μὴ ὑπάρχειν ἀδύνατον τῷ αὐτῷ καὶ κατὰ τὸ αὐτό);[2]
>
> It is impossible to hold (suppose) the same thing to be and not to be (ἀδύνατον γὰρ ὁντινοῦν ταὐτὸν ὑπολαμβάνειν εἶναι καὶ μὴ εἶναι);[3]
>
> Opposite assertions cannot be true at the same time (ἀδύνατον καὶ τἀναντία ὑπάρχειν ἅμα).[4]

---

[1] Here I am following Paula Gottlieb's argument in "Aristotle on Non-contradiction," *The Stanford Encyclopedia of Philosophy*, https://plato.stanford.edu/archives/sum2015/entries/aristotle-noncontradiction (accessed 3 May, 2018). The reader may find the literature on this topic there.
[2] Aristotle, *Metaphysics* IV:3 (1005b19–20), according to the Loeb Classical Library; Perseus: "It is impossible for the same thing to belong and not to belong at the same time to the same thing and in the same respect."
[3] Aristotle, *Metaphysics* IV:3 (1005b24; cf. 1005b29–30).
[4] Aristotle, *Metaphysics* IV:6 (1011b13–20).

The intention of Aristotle's formulations is to offer a fundamental proposition of ontological, psychological, and logical craft[5] in order to avoid an infinite recourse to the proof (*apodeixis*). Discussions of Aristotle's different formulations and their origin and logical consistency have been the object of many commentaries from antiquity to recent times.[6] It is not my intention to repeat, reformulate, or reinforce the valid and probable objections to the PNC or even to defend it against its opponents or detractors.[7] My purpose is only to introduce the reader to a seventeenth-century debate which originated in the Protestant University of Jena in Germany. The *apparent* intention of this debate was to present Jewish thought as an anti-Aristotelian tradition; its *real* purpose was to undermine the principle of the reception of the Dual Torah.

This discussion is imperative for the modern scholar not only because of its author's attempt to qualify a religion as an illogical system pretending to be true while contradicting the principle of non-contradiction, but also, and perhaps much more intriguingly, because of this attempt to judge Jewish scholars as blasphemous in their real or alleged attributions of logical contradictions to the first principle, i.e. God. We will first examine the primary cause of the discussion. Then, we will follow the attempts to resolve the question from a rabbinic point of view. Finally, we will attempt to discuss the diverse hypotheses of a fruitful discussion of or enquiry into the question of whether truth can be negotiable within the system of thought that defines it.

Casus disputandus: elu we-elu divre elohim ḥayyim

In 1658, Johann Frischmuth, professor of "Holy language" at the University of Jena in Germany, together with his student Johannes Leonart Will, presented and defended a *dissertatio*[8] on *Whether the Jews can Claim That the Same Thing Both can and cannot Exist at the Same Time* (*An Hebraei statuant idem posse esse et non esse*).[9] The booklet presents two arguments with the strategy of disavowing any connection between

---

5 Paula Gottlieb, "Aristotle on Non-contradiction," but cf. also the controversy about this formulation in Jean-Louis Hudry, "Aristotle on Non-Contradiction: Philosophers vs. Non-Philosophers," *Journal of Ancient Philosophy* 7 (2013): 51–74.
6 Cf. Enrico Berti, *Contraddizione e dialettica negli antichi e nei moderni* (Brescia: Morcelliana, 2015).
7 Cf. John Woods, "Dialectical Considerations on the Logic of Contradiction: Part I," *Logic Journal of the IGPL* 13 (2005): 231–260.
8 For the format of the *dissertatio*, cf. Giuseppe Veltri, "Academic Debates on the Jews in Wittenberg. The Protestant Literature on Rituals, the *Dissertationes* and the Writings of the Hebraists Theodor Dassow and Andreas Sennert," *European Journal of Jewish Studies* 6 (2012): 123–146.
9 Johann Frischmuth and Johannes L. Will, *De Loco Deut. XVII. v. 8. seqq. et quæ ad illum moveri solet, quæstione: An Ebræi Statuant, Idem Simul Posse Esse Et Non Esse, Exercitium Academicum, Præside Dn. M. Johanne Frischmuth, Lingg. Sacr. Prof. Publ. Famigeratissimo, & Facultatis Philosophicæ h.t. Decano spectabili, Publicè ventilandum exhibet M. Johannes Leonartus Will* (Jena: Krebsius, 1658) [PhD dissertation, Jena University, 1658].

Judaism and Aristotelianism: the foundation of rabbinical authority[10] and the Jewish principle of contradiction. In both cases, the rabbis, according to Frischmuth, are as impertinent and sacrilegious as to derive their own authority from God and—supreme blasphemy—to attribute to him the origin of two contradictory positions, or, in his own words, "If two rabbis contend amongst themselves and struggle, issuing contradictory sentences, it is nevertheless to be believed that both of them obtained their doctrine from Moses, each sentence being the word of the living God—which is a supreme blasphemy."[11]

The reader of Frischmuth's dissertation may be deceived by this formulation, believing that he is approaching a controversy of philosophical importance. On the contrary: Frischmuth is abusing a philosophical topic of Aristotelian logic to combat rabbinic authority based in the Oral Torah. Therefore, he begins with Deuteronomy 17:8, already quoted in the title of the *dissertatio,* where the main problem is the foundation of the Sanhedrin and the Torah as the supreme constitutional authorities, a court and a religious system as well as a political document, of the Jewish way of life,[12] interpreted in the light of Exodus 23:2, according to which the Halakhah follows the majority.[13]

Let us begin at the beginning. The blasphemy against God consists of attributing internally contradictory assertions because the Jews are controversially disputing (*contendant & pugnent*) the doctrine of Moses and hence basing their opposing authority against that of God himself (*credendum esse [...] utram sententiam verbum Dei viventis esse*). This rabbinic position indeed occurs in some texts, of which the most famous is a quotation from the Babylonian Talmud, *Eruvin* 13b, to which Frischmuth directly refers. It must be stated at the outset that his rendition does not come from the text of the Babylonian Talmud, but is a direct quotation from the anti-Christian *Sefer Niṣṣaḥon (Book of the Triumph)*[14] by Rabbi Yom Tov Lipmann Muehlhausen

---

10 Cf. Guido Bartolucci, "Jewish Thought vs. Lutheran Aristotelism: Johann Frischmuth (1619–1687) and Jewish Scepticism," *Yearbook of the Maimonides Centre for Advanced Studies* 2 (2017): 95–106.
11 *De Loco Deut. XVII,* (See Appendix II, 304): "Si duo Rabbini inter se contendant & pugnent, ac sermones contradicentes proferant, non minus credendum esse, utrumque suam doctrinam a Mose accepisse, immo (quae summa est blasphemia) utramque sententiam verbum Dei viventis esse."
12 On this topic, cf. Steven D. Fraade, "'If a Case is Too Baffling for You to Decide [...]' (Deut. 17:8–13): Between Constraining and Expanding Judicial Autonomy in the Temple Scroll and Early Rabbinic Scriptural Interpretation," in *Sibyls, Scriptures, and Scrolls: John Collins at Seventy,* Supplements to the *Journal for the Study of Judaism,* 175, ed. Joel S. Baden, Hindy Najman, and Eibert J. C. Tigchelaar (Leiden: Brill, 2016): 409–430.
13 Cf. Giuseppe Veltri, "The Limit of Scepticism and Tolerance," *Bollettino della Società Filosofica Italiana N.S.* 221 (2017): 37–55, especially 51–54.
14 Yom Tov Lipmann Muehlhausen, *Liber Nizachon Rabbi Lipmanni, conscriptis anno à Christo nato M. CCC. XCIX: diuq[ue] desideratus: nec ita pridem, fato singulari, è Judæorum manibus excussus. Oppositus Christianis, Sadducæis atque aliis. Editus typis academicis curante Theodori Hackspan [...] Accessit tractatus de usu librorum Rabbinicorum, prodromus apologiæ pro Christianis adversus Lipmannum triumphantem* (Nuremberg: Wolfgang Endter, 1644), 176 (§321); see Ḥaninah Ben-Menaḥem and

a philosopher and controversialist who lived in the fourteenth and fifteenth centuries:

> For three years, the House of Hillel and the House of Shammay debated. One said: "The Halakhah is in accordance with our opinion." The other objected: "The Halakhah is in accordance with our opinion." The voice of God rang out (and entered into the discussion), saying: "Both the one and the other are the word of the living God. The Halakhah, however, follows the words of the House of Hillel."[15]

Another text from the Babylonian Talmud, *Hagigah* 3b, is relevant to the question, according to Frischmuth, who follows Lippmann, because it describes a "rabbinic discussion" as a *perennially* controversial status: "'The masters of assemblies' (בעלי אסופות): these are the disciples of the wise, who sit in manifold assemblies and occupy themselves with the Torah, some pronouncing unclean and others pronouncing clean, some prohibiting and others permitting, some disqualifying and others declaring fit."[16] The Talmud gives a commentary on Kohelet 12:1, where the words of the wise are explained as goads, firmly fixed like "nails by the masters of assemblies." Frischmuth also adds the Talmudic comments that "they have been transmitted by one shepherd and one shepherd received them, one leader." He does not directly quote the version of the Talmudic discussion, which, according to the current version, reads:

> Should a man say: "How in these circumstances shall I learn Torah?" Therefore, the text says: "All of them are given from one Shepherd." One God gave them [the interpretations of the words/opinion]; one leader uttered them from the mouth of the Lord of all creation, blessed be He; for it is written: *And God spoke all these words* (Exodus 20:1).

This rendition is from the *Sefer Niṣṣaḥon*; however, "God" (*el*) is substituted with "Shepherd" in the sentence "All of them are given from one Shepherd. One Shepherd gave them," omitting "from the mouth of the Lord of all creation, blessed be He; for it is written: *And God spoke all these words*."

Lippmann adds his comment:

> That is a thing which is difficult to understand: the House of Shammay declared it as pure, the House of Hillel declared it as impure. How can it be possible that they are both the word of God? And how could Moshe—freedom be upon him—receive both of them from the Almighty? If he

---

Shimshon Eṭinger, eds., *Sugyot ba-mishpaṭ ha-'Ivri* vol. 1 (Hebrew) (Ra'ananah: ha-Universiṭah ha-Petuḥah, 2006), 148–150.
15 Muehlhausen, *Liber Nizachon*, 176 (§321). Cf. Johanan Frischmuth, *De Loco Deut. XVII, §15. §13* (See Appendix II, 357).
16 Herz's translation quoted in *The Babylonian Talmud: Translated into English with Notes, Glossary and Indices*, ed. Judah J. Slotki, Israel Brodie, and Isidore Epstein (London: Soncino Press, 1952).

received it pure, he could not receive it impure. If he received it impure, he could not receive it pure.[17]

With this quotation, the Protestant theologian wanted to emphasise that Jewish scholarship was conscious of the problem and made efforts to resolve the contradiction (*ad tollendam contradictionem*) because the principle of truth is of universal validity.

The whole discussion is tactically interesting because Frischmuth and his student present the reader with a melange of rabbinic texts in the original language with Latin translations interspersed with short commentaries, most of which are summaries of the rabbinic texts or insults to the Jews: liars, blasphemers, defenders of absurdities, etc. The tactic behind it is rhetorical, focussed on formulating, verifying with rabbinic texts, and then disseminating the idea that rabbinic and Jewish tradition is composed of nothing but contradiction. Seen from the rabbinic point of view, the message of the quoted texts implies that the entire dissertation is based on a syllogism: if two rabbinic schools have different *and contradictory* conclusions of capital importance, and if they have based their argumentation on the Torah of Moses, then their conclusions should be considered to have originated with the divine authority even when they are contradictory. I will now present the tactics and logic of rabbinic debate and the (ab)use that Frischmuth made of them.

Frischmuth's Tactics of Argumentation

Frischmuth analyses what a debate (*maḥloqet*) is, the value and persistence of this discussion, and the divine origin of the results of contradictory debates. All of these points are introduced and presented after rabbinic texts primarily taken from the treatise entitled *Pirqei Avot* and its later commentaries. *Pirqei Avot* is a rabbinic treatise, probably composed between the second century BCE and the second century CE,[18] that is unique in its genre because, although it belongs to the Mishnah, it mirrors a sapiential text with its religious, sapiential, and philosophical ideas rather than a typical Mishnaic halakhic composition. However, this text is fundamental to rabbinic identity because it presents the chain of tradition from Moses to the rabbinic period.

---

[17] See Johanan Frischmuth, *De Loco Deut. XVII*, §13 (See Appendix II, 317).
[18] The dating of rabbinic texts is a tremendous undertaking because of their nature as part of a literature of tradition, not of authors. Scholars consider the age of the Mishnah to be between the second century BCE and the second or third century CE.

Maḥloqet le-shem shamayim

Maḥloqet is a postbiblical term for division, controversy, contradictory dispute, or dissent. The reader of Talmudic passages would immediately acknowledge that the word was tantamount to ominous disunion. Because of the lack of a central authority capable of settling a dispute, *maḥloqet* was not synonymous with a peaceful dialectic discussion. Over the course of the centuries, it became a warning reminder of a violent episode in Talmudic times in which the students of the House of Shammay killed those of Hillel. This terrible anecdote is important for us because of the importance of both schools and their debates. According to the Babylonian Talmud, "They [House of Shammay] thrust a sword into the study house and declared: 'Whoever wants to enter may enter, but no one may leave!' And on that day Hillel sat in submission before Shammay, like one of the disciples, and it was as wretched for Israel as the day on which the [golden] calf was made."[19] More precisely, the Jerusalem Talmud reported, "It was taught in the name of Rabbi Yehoshua Oniya: The students of the House of Shammay stood below them and they began to slaughter the students of the House of Hillel. It was taught: Six of them ascended and the others stood over them with swords and lances."[20] The historical frame of this episode is not clear; however, it is certain that the discussion could have led to a violent altercation because of the vital topic they were discussing. As a contrast, we can recall a passage of the Jerusalem Talmud that reports a nostalgic time in which there had been no diversity of opinion, no *maḥloqet*, because of the existence of the Sanhedrin, which settled them.[21] Although the local Sanhedrin could be places of peaceful discussion and judgement, the passionate temperament and vital necessity of debating were and remain characteristic of Jewish religion and life.

The debates between the Houses or Schools of Hillel and Shammay were of a particular nature. Rabbinic literature considers them a kind of *maḥloqet*; this dispute, however, ended with an *aporia*, that is, it culminated in endless contradiction. The dispute between the Houses of Hillel and Shammay is endless because it is "for the sake of Heaven" (*le-shem shamayim*), as stated in Mishnah, *Avot* 5:17:

> All debates (*maḥloqet*) which are for the sake of Heaven will never cease to exist (סופה להתקיים); but one that is not in the name of Heaven will cease to exist. What [kind of] debate is for the sake of Heaven? Such as was the debate between Hillel and Shammay. What was an argument that was not for the sake of heaven? That of Korach and his congregation.

---

[19] Babylonian Talmud, *Shabbat* 17a; English translation by Daniel Roth, "The Ninth of Adar: The Day Constructive Conflict Turned Destructive," *Pardes* 4 (2013): 1–9.
[20] Jerusalem Talmud, *Shabbat* 1:4 (3c).
[21] Jerusalem Talmud, *Sanhedrin* 1:4 (19c): א"ר יוסי בראשונה לא היתה מחלוקת ישראל אלא סנהדרין של שבעים ואחד היתה יושבת בלשכת הגזית. On *maḥloqet*, cf. Moshe Sokol. "What Does a Jewish Text Mean? Theories on Elu ve-Elu Divrei Elohim Hayim in Rabbinic Literature," *Da'at* 32–33 (1994): 22–31 and Shaul Magid, "The Intolerance of Tolerance: Makhloket and Redemption in Early Hasidism," *Jewish Studies Quarterly* 8 (2001): 326–368.

What is a *maḥloqet?* Frischmuth quotes the Sephardic philosopher Isaac Abravanel, who wrote a commentary on the *Avot* during the fifteenth and sixteenth centuries.[22] According to Abravanel, a *maḥloqet* is not a play of dialectical value in order to overcome one's counterpart, but a negotiation during which the truth comes to light and secret things are revealed,[23] according to his own words: "(The *maḥloqet* is meant) for people to discuss, but not to prevail one against the other, although it is for the sake of Heaven, i.e. to let the truth come to light and to reveal the secret of the things which become known through the negotiation which is in the discussion."[24] Frischmuth did not understand the texts and translated מתוך המשא והמתן אשר במחלוקת as *id quod fiat interventu deliberationis in disceptatione* (to facilitate the decision in the discussion). It is absolutely true that discussion can contribute to resolving the question, but he missed the point of how this is reached. He misunderstood the important reference to negotiation as that which produces explanations and revelations of the secrets of the words. I do not know whether Abravanel was the first to compare the dialectic of discussion to a negotiation. However, Saadia Gaon had already compared the search for the truth of the senses to a test of genuine and counterfeit coins.[25]

However, similarly to every legal system, the idea of negotiation is a typical attitude in the rabbinic Halakhah. Also, on the *yom ha-din* (Day of Judgment) according to the Tosefta, *Sanhedrin* 13:3, the dead will be judged on every act of their lives: there will be the fully righteous, the fully evil, and those in-between, the *benonim* (equivalent) or *shequlim* (equipollent). Hence, in the Last Judgement, a situation of equipollence of evil/good and true/false can also exist and its result, if any, will be negotiated.

The idea of a negotiation of the truth is also present in Islamic philosophy, according to Dominique Raynaud.[26] He writes: "During the course of a controversy, truth is temporarily suspended and replaced by an exchange of arguments of uncer-

---

22 Isaac Abravanel, *Pirqei Avot. 'im perush* [...] *Mosheh Ben Maimon we-'im perush naḥalat Ya'aqov meha-sar ha-gadol rabbenu don Yiṣḥaq Abarbanel* (Hebrew) (New York: D. Silberman, 1952–1953), 357.
23 Georg Ursinus, בית הישיבה והמדרש *Seu Antiquitates Hebraicæ Scholastico-Academicæ. In Quibus Scholarum & Academiarum Judaicarum historia tam intra quam extra Scripturam, Forma earundem, Docentium & Discentium officia, Ritus, Dimissio è Schola, Promotio, Promotionum Tituli, Distincti Professorum Ordines & Facultates, Methodus Disputandi, Studia, Statuta, Privilegia & Stipendia continuo, ubi fieri potuit, S. Scripturæ & monumentorum Rabbinicorum concentu eruta leguntur* (Copenhagen: Lieben, 1702), 287.
24 לקנטר ולא להתגבר זה על זה כי אם לשום שמים ר"ל להוציא האמת לאור ולגלות מצפוני הדברים אשר יודעו מתוך המשא והמתן אשר במחלוקת ; cf. n. 14 and n. 23 above and Johanan Frischmuth, *De Loco Deut. XVII*, §14 (See Appendix II, 318).
25 Cf. Giuseppe Veltri, "Testing Genuine and Counterfeit Coins: The Subject's Error in Saadya's Argument of True Knowledge against Scepticism" (in preparation).
26 Dominique Raynaud, "Al-Samarqandī. Un précurseur de l'analyse des controversies scientifiques," *Al-Mukhatabat* 7 (2013): 8–25, now in Dominique Raynaud, *Scientific Controversies: A Socio-Historical Perspective on the Advancement of Science* (New Brunswick: Transaction Publishers, 2015): 163–182.

tain statute."²⁷ His point of departure is the Persian savant Shams al-Dīn Al-Samarqandī. He wrote some books on logic, mathematics, and astronomy and four treatises on the rules to be followed in the conduct of a scholarly controversy, of which only three are extant: *Risāla fī adāb al-baḥth* (*Epistle on the Rules and Etiquettes of Debate*), *Qustās al-afkār* (*The Weighing of Ideas*), and *al-Muʿtaqadāt* (*The Convictions*), all composed between 1291 and 1302. This is not the right place to explain the rules of rhetoric and dialectical debate which he settled and developed out of his knowledge of law and jurisprudence (*uṣūl al-fiqh* and *furūʿ*). Yet, Al-Samarqandī's contribution to the dialectic and rhetoric of the debate is his careful analysis of the settlement of controversies; he introduces the innovation of the "signs of defeat" (*dalāʾil al-inqiṭāʿ*), the indication of the moment when one "of the parties to the debate has [...] emerged as the victor or the vanquished."²⁸ The signs are: inconsistency (the conclusion is not proportional to the premises or is self-contradictory); *reductio ad absurdum*; silence; distinction (necessary for the chain of reasoning); incapacity (to respond to a question); digression (a break in the continuity of reasoning); commensurability (non-conformity to the case); deviation (a response to a different question); appeal to the crowd (appealing to the listeners, signifying a lack of arguments); or stubbornness (refutation of objections).

The expression "sign of defeat" is a rhetorical tool for referring to a negotiation which ends in a result, expected at a certain point when the adversary shows signs of weakness. We have a similar situation in the game of chess, which, according to the seventeenth-century philosopher Simone Luzzatto, is a symbol or metaphor of controversy and fundamental to the understanding of philosophical (sceptical) debates:

> Hence, I likewise started to suspect that as human beings we are indeed not endowed with sufficient organs and faculties to apprehend and acknowledge the truth. Besides, the early bases and foundations from which the edifice of human knowledge rises are indeed not fixed and stable, but arbitrary and laid at our whim, as is usually the case with games, especially with chess, where similarly, while deductions and consequences are necessary, the first positions are indeed contingent and voluntary.²⁹

The game is over when the "signs of defeat" are visible, unchallengeable as a consequence of the debate. According to Al-Samarqandī, they are valid only for controversies concerning philosophy, logic, astronomy, and mathematics. However, what is the purpose of controversies of vital religious importance? Is silence sufficient reason to end a discussion, for example? Or a controversial point of view? The thesis of a legal negotiation cannot obscure the fact that this Islamic philosophical movement is affected by the same tendency present in the debate on the first principle of contradiction: to demonstrate the validity of a principle which cannot be invalidated.

---

27 Raynaud, *Scientific Controversies*, 164.
28 Ibid., 175–176.
29 *Socrate*, 23–24.

That is the reason why the contradiction of the Halakhah disputation will be settled in the end. However, when is the end?

End or Persistence of a Discussion (sofah lehitqayyem)?

Negotiation is not the end of the discussion, and that is the problem. Frischmuth quotes the Jewish exegete 'Ovadyah of Bertinoro, who states that "he who can discuss exists and has not perished." This is a reference to Korach's debate in the Bible, also quoted from *Pirqei Avot*, because it was not *le-shem shamayim* (for the sake of Heaven). Korach was the leader of a rebellion against Moses in Numbers 16. He and his 249 co-conspirators were punished by fire from heaven. According to the rabbinic exegesis, Korach had a *maḥloqet* with Moses for private reasons; therefore, he was destroyed, according to both the Bible and 'Ovadyah.

Obadiah also transmits the tradition according to which *sofah* (the end) is not the end but the "intended purpose" (*takhlit*) of the discussion, namely, to reach the truth via debate (*maḥloqet*). The word *sof* (*finis*, end) became the "purpose" of finding the truth, which is for the sake of Heaven, as in the case of Hillel and Shammay.[30] The *maḥloqet* in the case of Korach was not *le-shem shamayim*, but rather an intention to dominate (*serarah*), being a desire to overcome (*ahavat ha-niṣṣaḥon*).

Word of the Living God?

The question remains unsolved, according to Frischmuth, because the question of why true and false should return to the living God (*elu we-elu divre elohim hayyim*) is unresolved. Frischmuth's quoting of Abravanel on *Pirqei Avot* 5:17 confirms that it is *only* by debating that one can establish which opinion is true and which is false. The truth can be established *only* by analysing the positions of both houses; therefore, the words of both houses are the word of the living God.

Here Frischmuth quotes Lipmann, who quotes[31] the anonymous *Sefer Ḥayyim*, which states that intention is the decisive grounds for determining that the schools of both Hillel and Shammay are acting for the sake of Heaven (*le-shem shamayim*). However, Frischmuth objected to the idea that good will (*bona intentio*) was adequate reason to qualify them with such a splendid title (*Ecquid vero bona intentio conferre postet ad id, ut illa tam splendido titulo insigniantur?*). Of course not: only conformity to the truth accords with the divine will. Nobody affirms, so Frischmuth

---

30 אני שמעתי פרוש סופה תכליתה המבוקש מעניינה והמחלוקת שהיא לשם שמים התכלית והסוף המבוקש מאותה מחלוקת, וזה מתקיים כמ"ש מתוך הויכוח מתברר האמת (פרק ה משנה ו בפרוש שם).

I am not sure that Obadiah is deconstructing the text, as Dov Landau puts it (See Appendix II, 319).

31 Yom Tov Lipmann Muehlhausen, *Liber Nizachon*, 289 (See Appendix II, 319).

says, that God's will is the contradiction of licit and illicit, pure and impure, unless he convinces himself that there is a known authority figure, like the Jews, who state such "absurdity." Yet Lipmann, the author most quoted by Frischmuth, states that the controversial point is to be found in the explanation and not in the body of the commandment. And so we have the real enemy of the Protestant theologian: the Oral Torah, the explanation of the written text, and, therefore, the authority of the rabbinic schools.

This is not the right place to tease out the differences between the Oral Torah as an unwritten teaching (like, perhaps, Plato's) in contrast the written text (e.g. the dogmas of Greek philosophy). Frischmuth stigmatises the arch-enemy of the Protestant Reformation, the oral authoritative tradition, as the source of every evil in (the Church's) history. False and true, the dichotomy cannot reside in the Written Torah and cannot be in God: it is only within the alleged authority of the Jews and their absurd commentaries.

The Jewish Sceptical Attitude

There are many contradictory statements in the Jewish tradition, beginning with the book of Kohelet and continuing throughout rabbinic literature. Frischmuth quotes abundant material from the Talmud, the Midrash, and contemporary scholarly literature, such as the much-quoted Ashkenazic Lipmann Muehlhausen and Sephardic Isaac Abravanel. Yet he only quotes from authors and works that tend to confirm his sceptical attitude, leaving out the considerable number of treatises of other opinions on Aristotelian logic quoted, translated, and commented on by medieval Jewish authors. A century later, in 1766, the scholar Johann Jakob Baur published an examination of the Jewish concern with philosophy, *A Stricture of Jewish Philosophy* (*Strictura quaedam ex Philosophia Hebraeorum*), a chapter of which is devoted to logic (*Strictura quaedam ex logica*).[32] He argues that nothing has endured from the ancient Jewish preoccupation with logic and that rabbinic academies were only using rules of hermeneutics that were based on logic such as *argumentum a maiore ad minus*, *analogia*, etc. Against Frischmuth's position, he quotes Maimonides,[33] who states that impossible things are excluded from the power of God (*Res impossibiles sive contradictoria ab ipsa potentia Dei O.M. excludi monet*), or, according to Friedlander's translation of this passage:

> We have thus shown that according to each one of the different theories there are things which are impossible, whose existence cannot be admitted, and whose creation is excluded from the

---

[32] Johann J. Baur, *Stricturae Quaedam Ex Philosophia Hebraeorum, Maxime Recentiorum Cum Moderna Philosophandi Ratione Conformi. Speciatim Ex Logica Atque Metaphysica* (Tübingen: Schramm, 1766).
[33] *Moreh Nevukhim* III: 15, Baur, *Stricturae*, XXXIII.

power of God, and the assumption that God does not change their nature does not imply weakness in God, or a limit to His power. Consequently, things impossible remain impossible, and do not depend on the action of an agent. It is now clear that a difference of opinion exists only as to the question to which of the two classes a thing belongs; whether to the class of the impossible, or to that of the possible.

Frischmuth claims that the negation of principle is not only a philosophical position, but also a typical characteristic of the Jewish temperament (*Sed nunc alia adhuc adducenda sunt, ex quibus patescet, hactenus Iudaeis nihil nos tribuisse, quod ab illorum indole sit alienum*).[34] The reader cannot avoid inferring that the Protestant theologian is looking for an argument for disqualifying Jewish philosophy, as such making it appear to possess a natural attitude towards contradiction. In attributing a sceptical attitude to Jews, he is carrying on Protestant theology's policy of negating any relationship of the Jewish tradition to philosophy, a project initiated with the Reformation and developed throughout the seventeenth and eighteenth centuries.

Some Remarks on PNC and the Rabbinic Mind

The logic of rabbinic discussion is based on dogma, like the dogma of PNC: The Principle of the Reception of Torah (PRT):

PNC: either false or true   PRT: either received or not

Neither is demonstrable. The debate on the plausibility of PNC or PRT is not proof of the validity of either. The discussion will last forever, according to the rabbinic mind, because nobody can claim to resolve the *aporia* of a written and oral Torah that is on earth and no longer in Heaven.

God (G) gave the written and the oral Torah (WT & OT), i.e. the text and its logical/interpretational rules and tradition, at Sinai (legislative moment). He therefore provided every tool for solving every problem. If Rabbi Hillel (RH) and Rabbi Shammay (RS) reached opposite conclusions (C1 and -C1) on the same problem (P), then there are three possible explanations for the opposition, the first two of which were developed by Saadiah Gaon in another context.

The opposition is because of RH and RS: this is excluded because they are not acting for themselves, but *le-shem shamayim* (for the sake of Heaven). They do not have any personal reason for a conflict of interest. They are not incapable of deciding on or are ignorant of OT & WT: this possibility is excluded because, according to the rabbinic mind, both the schools of RH and RS and the fundament of rabbinic authority are excellent. The contradiction is to be included in OT & WT, i.e. in the work of the lawgivers.

---

34 Cf. Johanan Frischmuth, *De Loco Deut*, XVII, §13 (See Appendix II, 316).

The everlasting debate is, therefore, to be interpreted as an everlasting *aporia*, the impossibility of finding a definitive solution to the problem. The Jewish scholars made a great effort to find a solution to the *aporia* of the everlasting debating between the rabbinic schools. 'Ovadyah Sforno interpreted *sofah lehitqayyem* as "the purpose of the truth will be reached," in contrast to the philological and philosophical arguments. However, *sofah lehitqayyem* really means "at its end (the discussion) will persist." The discussion is not a premise of a veritable conclusion, of which there can only be one—the truth—but, rather, the discussion will still continue at its end. The negotiation is only a temporary pause in the sequence of life. This would at least explain why both contradictory positions are "words of the living God." The God of the Jews vividly interferes in the debate, but only the majority can offer a temporary solution to the everyday dilemmas; "temporary" means that the debate will also be everlasting.

5.2 The "Sceptic" Solomon: Halle's Protestant Vision

Some years later in 1704,[35] an anonymous article was published in Halle in issue VIII of *Observationes selectae*, with the title "Could it be that Solomon was a Sceptic?" (*An Salomon fuerit Scepticus*)? As Martin Mulsow has shown, the author of this text was the Lutheran theologian and philosopher Jakob Friedrich Reimmann,[36] who, protected by the anonymity of the journal of Halle, experimented with "unorthodox ideas."

At the beginning of his article, the author provides a summary:

§ I. Ridiculum est ex omnibus Patriarchis Hebraeorum facere Philosophos.
§ II. Ac licet concesseris fuisse tales, dubium est, an fuerint Dogmatici.
§ III. Probabile esse, eosdem fuisse Scepticos docet exemplum Jobi.
§ IV. Nec obstat quicquam, quo minus dicamus Salomonem fuisse Ephecticum.
§ V. Diversa sane fuit ejus sapientia a nostra hodierna si spectemus causa efficientem.
§ VI. Item si consideremus materiam ejus in qua et circa quam.
§ VII. Porro si respiciamus formam.
§ VIII. Ac tandem finem.
§ IX. Tota autem quanta quanta fuit, fuisse videtur Sceptica.
§ X. Nolunt id quidem Dogmatici et inprimis nuperrimus Medicinae mentis Scriptor.
§ XI. Sed quinque committit παροράματα.
§ XII. Excutitur primum ejus σφάλμα, quo putat Philosophiam Scepticam obstare verae sapientiae et hominis sapientis officio.
§ XIII. Secundum σφάλμα quo arbitratur Scepticos impie et praepostere philosophari.
§ XIV. Item eosdem esse Atheos, virtutis irrisores et omnis verae religionis inhabiles.
§ XV. Tertium σφάλμα quo scribit, eos Philosophorum et Theologorum nomine indignos esse, qui

---

[35] Jakob F. Reimmann, "An Salomon fuerit Scepticus?" *Observationes selectae ad rem litterariam spectantes* 8 (1704): 327–367.
[36] Martin Mulsow, "Eclecticism or Skepticism? A Problem of the Early Enlightenment," *Journal of the History of Ideas* 58, no. 3 (1997): 465–477, here 466, footnote 5.

Salomonis doctrinam ἐν ἀκαθαληψία reponant.
§ XVI. *Quartum σφάλμα quo ait, se principium Salomonaeum, nos scire nihil, in Ecclesiaste reperire non potuisse.*
§ XVII. *Quintum σφάλμα quo putat, ex Nihilo Scepticorum, nihil derivari posse.*
§ XVIII. *Conclusio de commodis Philosophiae Scepticae.*

The author's intention is clear: to deny the philosophical characterisation of a biblical figure, or, in his own words: "It is ridiculous to make philosophers of all the Hebrew Patriarchs" (*ridiculum est ex omnibus Patriarchi Hebraeorum facere philosophos*). Because, for Reimmann, "Philosophers" implies a "dogmatic" tendency. The ironic tone of this claim cannot be ignored: the antediluvian patriarch had no more idea of philosophy in its later sense than of chess or the art of making periwigs (I).[37] But if they were philosophers, adds Reimmann, we should ask whether they were dogmatists or sceptics[38] or something else, for the same Moses became Cartesian, Aristotelian, Atomistic, etc. (II).[39] Reimmann adds that a "taste"[40] of the biblical texts we have makes the figure of Job as a prototype of scepticism because of Job's enquiries into the origin of evil, whether God is to be considered good, his negation of the presence of wisdom and knowledge on earth (very similar to *nil sciri*), etc. (III). He concentrates his attention on Job, considering him as an Ephectic (ἐφεκτικός, from ἐπέχειν)[41] who, as a sceptical Pyrrhonian, ends his enquiry with the *epoché*, the suspension of judgment.

Paraphrasing Kohelet 1:17, he writes that the Solomon of Ecclesiastes is obviously a *scepticus* because he applied his mind not only to known the wisdom (of the sceptics) but also to recognising the madness and the folly of the Dogmatists (IV).[42] The following points are interesting because the author researched the wisdom of Solomon according to what it could not be, and what it really is (κατ'ἄρσιν and κατὰ θέσιν, the rhetorical categories of negation and affirmation).

---

37 "Sane Patriarchae antediluviani ad unum omnes seu velint, seu nolint ipsis sunt Philosophi, licet in βιογραφία ipsorum, Philosophiae non magis quam ludi scachici, vel artis struendi capillaturam (Parruqven-macher-Kunst) fiat mentio." (Reimmann, *An Salomon*, 329).
38 "Nam licet omnes, qui historiam Philosophicam contexuere adhuc, eosdem fecerint Dogmaticos; tamen recogitandum est, hoc factum esse a Dogmaticis, adeoque exinde non consequi revera fuisse tales." (Reimmann, *An Salomon*, 330).
39 "Plane sicut experientia edocti sumus, Mosen jam Cartesianum, jam Aristotelicum, mox Atomisticum et Eclecticum factum esse, prout lectorem huic vel isti haeresi addictum indeptus fuerit." (Reimmann, *An Salomon*, 331).
40 The author derives the word *sapientia* (wisdom) from *sapor* (taste).
41 "Interim si fas est dicere quod sentio, non possum non aperto ore confiteri, me eos omnes habere pro Ephecticis. Etenim ut a JOBO faciamus differendi primordium, qui omnium scriptorum Hebraeorum, quorum monumenta ad nosmet pervenerunt, est antiquissimus, primusque qui problema istud Philosophicum; An et quare Deus viris bonis aliquid mali evenire patiatur?"
42 "Plane sicur Rex sapientissimus SALOMO c. I v. 17 scribit, se adjecisse animum non solum ad cognoscendam (Scepticorum) sapientiam (לדעת חכמה) sed etiam ad perspiciendam omnem (Dogmaticorum) insaniam et stoliditatem ודעת הוללות ושכלות Conf. cap. VII v. 26." (Reimmann, *An Salomon*, 334).

First, he returns to the Aristotelian teaching of the four causes—efficient (V), material (VI), formal (VII), and final (VIII)[43]—to conclude that the wisdom of Solomon is different from our (philo)*sophy* (IX).[44] It is not my aim here to analyse all the demonstrations of the *pars destruens* of the scholar from Halle because the main points are the paragraphs devoted to the scepticism of Solomon, which are the primary thesis of the pamphlet; the proposition that Solomon was not a dogmatic thinker is a thesis supported by all of the quoted texts.[45]

Paragraph X reveals a biographical feature that illuminates the circumstances of the composition of this articles and the reaction prior to its printing. Reimmann reports that he discussed his thesis on Solomon's Pyrrhonian identity with a *quidam medicinae mentis scriptor* (a certain author of the book *Medicinae mentis*) who, in his book published in the same year,[46] called Reimmann impious and perverted despite the fact that his conversation with Reimmann was private.[47] Riemann's opponent was Joachim Lange,[48] a professor at the University of Halle known for his aggressive pietism.[49] Reimmann was of the opinion that the first character of wisdom is peace: that is, a primary commitment to peace and tolerance for others, especially when they are dissenting.[50]

In 1710, six years after the publication of his article, the author experienced another criticism of his thesis by Reinhard Heinrich Roll,[51] who analysed Reimmann's arguments thoroughly. Drawing on the history of scepticism, the concept of wisdom, and Budde's history of Jewish philosophy, Roll was of the opinion that wisdom is not

---

[43] "Causa efficientis, materialis, formalis, et finalis." (Reimmann, An Salomon, 334).
[44] "Interim cum ex jam dictis sole meridiano liquidius appareat, Philosophiam Salomonis a nostra qua causam efficientem, materiam formam et finem esse diversam." (Reimmann, An Salomon, 334).
[45] "Apparet autem ex ejus scriptis dilucidissime, eam non fuisse dogmaticam." (Reimmann, An Salomon, 342)
[46] "Sed et nuper quidam MEDICINAE MENTIS Scriptor Part. V c. 1 §13, 393 pro sapientia hujus Regis dogmatica ita pugnavit, ut impios eos praeposterosque Philosophos appellitaverit, qui Salomonem fuisse Pyrhonium existimarent." (Reimmann, An Salomon, 342).
[47] "Et quia Auctori huic, quem alias ob pietatem et eruditionem magni facio, paneque ita rationem duco, eum non malo animo hunc paragraphum Historiae suae inseruisse; Ita colluluit hanc nostram sententiam, quam eidem privatim communicaveramus, publicere rejicere, eamque ceu impiam et praeposteram condemnare, fas erit, opinor, ad haec ejus dubia jam publice respondisse." (Reimmann, An Salomon, 344).
[48] Joachimi Langii, *Joachimi Langii medicina mentis qua praepostera philosophandi methodo ostensa ac rejecta, secundum sanioris philosophiae principia, aegrae mentis sanatio, ac sanatae usus in veri rectique investigatione ac communicatione, in gratiam traditur forum, qui per solidam eruditionem ad veram sapientiam contendunt* (Berlin: Orphanotropium, 1704).
[49] Cf. Rolf Dannenbaum, "Joachim Lange als Wortführer des Halleschen Pietismus gegen die Orthodoxie" (PhD dissertation, Göttingen University, 1951).
[50] "Cum enim vel ipso eodem teste Part.V c. IV §9 seqq. sapientiae character primarius sit pax, e qua deinceps ceu novae eruditionis notulae exsurgunt laetitia et TOLERANTIA seu studium pacis erga alios vel maxime dissentientes." (Reimmann, An Salomon, 344).
[51] Reinhard H. Roll, *Salomo A Scepticismi Crimine Contra Injustam Observatoris Halensis Imputationem* (Rostok: Weppling, 1710).

natural but supernatural and, therefore, rests beyond Reimmann's characterisation of it as scepticism.

However, according to Reimmann, Solomon (of Proverbs, the Song of Songs, and, of course, Kohelet) was by no means a philosopher of the *universalia*—that is, he was not a dogmatist—but of particular things under the sun, basing all things on experience instead of logical deductions and inferences. Reimmann's real intent is not primarily to characterise the biblical tradition of Solomon as sceptical; rather, he seeks to justify or support scepticism on the basis of biblical examples. Scepticism, then, is not only the foundation of the modern sciences: it originates from a new conception of divinity, one much more preoccupied with human life than with celestial dogmas.

Reimmann[52] dealt with the Jewish tradition and its theology and philosophy in various works, writing both in Latin and German. For example, he published a long and articulate treatise in German entitled *Versuch Einer Enleitung in die Historie der Theologie insgemein und Juedischen Theologie ins besondere* (Attempt at an Introduction to the History of Theology in General and Jewish Theology in Particular), which was published in Magdeburg in 1717.[53] However, his first attempt to deal with Jewish philosophy was made in the short tractate published in Halle. From the very beginning, he criticised the (ab)uses that several scholars had made of the Jewish philosophical tradition. He particularly underscored two aspects: 1) the Hebrew Patriarchs were often seen as dogmatic philosophers; and 2) their philosophy had been interpreted in as many ways as there were philosophical positions of their interpreters. For example, as I mentioned above, Reimmann notes that Moses was seen by some as a Cartesian philosopher, others, as an Aristotelian, and so on.

The first critique was probably addressed to Johan Franz Budde, who maintained that Jewish philosophy was based on the dogmatic Kabbalah, which had transmitted dogmas and theological and philosophical precepts throughout the centuries. Reimmann, therefore, distances himself from the previous tradition and lends a new shape to Jewish philosophy: the shape of scepticism. He maintains that, after Adam's fall, the human mind could no longer attain true knowledge of the world: only God could give men *vera sapientia*, true wisdom. By quoting passages from different books of the Old and the New Testament, Reimmann uses the Classical fideistic instruments of scepticism in order to demonstrate the weakness of the human mind. In this way, he seems to have adopted a traditional (conservative) attitude towards the new rationalistic philosophy of his day (such as that of Descartes and his followers).

---

[52] These two paragraphs are indebted to several conversations with Guido Bartolucci.
[53] Jakob F. Reimmann, *Versuch Einer Enleitung in die Historie der Theologie insgemein und Juedischen Theologie ins besondere* (Magdeburg: Christoph Seidel, 1717). On Reimmann, see Theodor Günther, *Jacob Friedrich Reimmann (1668–1743). Mühsal und Frucht* (Köln: 1974); Haim Mahlev, "Kabbalah as Philosophia Prennis? The Image of Judaism in the German Early Enlightenment: Three Studies," *Jewish Quarterly Review* 104, no. 2 (2014): 234–257.

Indeed, throughout the history of its (re)discovery during the early modern period, scepticism was often used as a tool against pagan philosophy, for example in the work of Giovanni Francesco Pico della Mirandola. Reimmann, however, had a different plan in mind.[54] As Martin Mulsow writes in one of the best contributions on this figure: "[Reimmann] viewed Pyrrhonic scepticism as offering significantly better possibilities for defeating the dogmatic philosophers than any other philosophical approach."[55] Reimmann argues that Solomon was the best example of this Jewish tradition, and he also adds that, because the Jewish king lived centuries before Pyrron, Solomon could be seen as the real founder of scepticism. The relationship between scepticism and the Jewish tradition, according to Reimmann's purpose, was to strengthen the main characteristic of that kind of Greek philosophy, that is, the acknowledgement of human ignorance and doubt. Reimmann uses fideistic garb in order to legitimise the sceptical strategy against dogmatism and traditional knowledge.

---

[54] Ralph Häfner, "Das Erkenntnisproblem in der Philologie," in *Philolopie und Erkenntnis. Beiträge zu Begriff und Problem frühneuzeitlicher Philologie*, ed. Ralph Häfner (Tübingen: Max Niemeyer Verlag, 2001): 93–128; *Skepsis, Providenz, Polyhistorie. Jakob Friedrich Reimmann (1668–1743)*, ed. Martin Mulsow and Helmut Zedelmaier (Tübingen: Max Niemeyer Verlag, 1998).
[55] Martin Mulsow, "Eclecticism or Skepticism?" 468.

Conclusion

Alienation and Philosophies

This enquiry into Jewish philosophy and scepticism has revealed how intriguing the question of philosophy is because it starts with a general conception of a body of work and ends with the question of whether that body of work exists at all. The task of this conclusion is not to summarise the results of this book—the reader has already encountered synopses at the beginnings of every part—but to suggest several opportunities for future research in the fields of philosophy, scepticism, and Judaism.

We will begin by clarifying what the alienation of philosophy may include and exclude if we speak about the history of the origins and development of Jewish philosophy, then we will occupy ourselves with the problems inherent to philosophies. At the end, I will present scepticism in general and Jewish scepticism in particular as dialectic "strategies."

The Nature of Alienation

Wisdom as *philo/sophia* and philosophy are two historically and theoretically different things. The love for wisdom and philosophy are not synonymous. Etymologically, σοφία means "cleverness or skill in handicraft and art" (Liddell-Scott); in philosophical texts, however, it is to be translated as "teaching and wisdom." But what is wisdom? Wisdom is the *synolon*, the essence and existence, of *epistēmē* and *technē*; it includes both traditions of these knowledges as well as a commitment to them. We could summarise it as the sciences and education; it is both the heritage of every people and their mediation. During the cultural exchange between ancient cultures the problem of commonality arose, especially in the case when something that was a result of *epistēmē* and *technē* was considered a "discovery" for human beings. Such times included the "discovery" of the alphabet, monarchy, democracy, architecture, agriculture, etc.; namely, findings that justify declarations about the superiority of one culture and civilisation over those of their neighbours. The claim of the "first discoverer" is a problem of political and economic supremacy as well as identity.

Theoretical explanations for the convergent evolution of cultures are hence political acts of an apologetic nature and attempts at validating identity and originality. Put as a theoretical principle, the unity and unicity of all sciences and wisdom, a prerequisite connected with one's own divinities and *Weltanschauung*, and the pervasive nature of imperial Greek and Greco-Roman cultures lead to the conclusion that the doctrine of the Greek "theft of wisdom" was the "natural" response to the fact the Greeks had stolen all or at least some of their ostensible discoveries in every branch of human life.

Speaking of the old tradition of "theft of the wisdom," it will astonish some readers that I have used the word "alienation" in the title of my book, a concept that clearly possesses the watermark of a modern Hegelian and Marxist matrix. However, alienation derives from the word *alienus*—"foreigner," that which does not belong to us. The term is used in this sense by Arnaldo Momigliano in his *Alien Wisdom* (1975), which examines the relationship between the Greeks and those ethnic groups considered by the Greeks to be "barbarian." Momigliano concerns himself with the phenomenon of osmosis between so-called "Hellenistic" culture and the peoples conquered by them (or at least by their weapons). Following the same logic, in the first chapter of this book I examined the phenomenon of "plagiarism," the Jews' accusation that the Greeks plagiarised their most fundamental concepts by first alienating them (the Jews) and then copying ideas and principles from the Torah.

A second meaning of the word "alienation" is directly connected with juridical language: it denotes the conferring of a good or resource on another person, occasioned when property changes hands. In the law, this means a voluntary transfer and reception (even there is a legal obligation involved) from one party to another.

In terms of Hegel's philosophical system, alienation represents the antithesis of the dialectic process. I will not linger here on the further connotations "alienation" has acquired since the days of German idealism. I would, in fact, distance myself from this usage, which emphasises the subject and undervalues the object itself, the thing that is "alienated." The logical process that conducts element A towards element C (A to C) subtends a factor B. It is this last factor (B) that is ceded (legally), or estranged (in the vocabulary that goes back to the elaborate theories of Marx and Engels), and thus would be subsumed by element C. In this context, "alienation" lies outside of these parameters and posits a concern with the reappropriation of something that was (believed to be) stolen from a subject (understood in the collective rather than individual sense) by other societies or groups or religions.

The historical process of alienation, understood in this last sense as an attributed or unattributed appropriation of another people's ideas, concepts, or philosophies, underscores the sense of the impoverishment of a specific culture when it is monopolised by others. In the history of Jewish philosophy, this phenomenon is connected to patristic literature and to the consequent vision of a *verus Israel christianus*, which casts Christians as the only audience for the Old Testament's prophecies. This is not a question of a juridical "ceding and transmitting ownership of goods to others" but one of dual heredity.

The concept of Perennial Philosophy, developed from the low Middle Ages through the modern age, having discarded its foundations in the mysticism and esotericism of Neoplatonism, Hermeticism, and Kabbalah, will continue to contribute to the impoverishment of wisdom through the process of passive alienation.

Regardless, at just the moment when the Kabbalah acquired a decisive role in Christianity, between the sixteenth and seventeenth centuries, a new tendency entered into the history of western thought, one that reduced the Jewish religion to a tradition of ceremonies. The impact of this tendency was to deny both ancient and modern Judaism any philosophical substance. Of the Torah of Moses there remained nothing other than its empirical side: only its external, ceremonial, and legal aspects were left.

In the nineteenth century, the age of Hegelian and Marxist philosophy, the concept of alienation arrived at a "turning point." The emancipation of the Jews, already problematic from the socio-political point of view, proved even more complex in the intellectual sphere. The attempt to redeem Jewish literature, philosophy, theology, and culture, was rejected en bloc by Protestantism. The unique alternative was to renounce the entire history of Judaism in favour of Christianity, accepting that the "Old Testament" was merely carrier of the "divination" of the New, and that the "strength" and "piety" of the divine was held only within the New Testament, as Friedrich Schleiermacher puts it.

Is it possible to apply this concept of alienation, in its multiform spectrum of meanings, to Jewish philosophy? In the process of alienation, according to the common understanding of the term, the subject that is alienated plays the principal role in the whole process; little significance is attributed to the object, that estranged part that never returns to the subject, even if the *Entäußerung* (alienation) is absorbed in the Hegelian manner by a synthesis that is not dialectically divisible.

My approach, grounded in the object of alienation rather than the subject, goes beyond the simple history of (alienated) ideas, establishing instead a philosophical analysis of the phenomenon of (Jewish) philosophy. I do this to assert Judaism's place in the larger history of philosophy, so that its contribution of an intrinsic logic of thought and a dialectical incentive is appreciated in modern philosophical discourse.

In following this line of thinking, we see that the alienated object acquires new forms, and, consequently, that emancipation from this process of reforming itself becomes an alienation. The attempts of the Jewish intellectual class towards cultural emancipation were always destined to fail: the dominant culture had not only alienated them from their own tradition, but had also reserved for them a redemption in the form of a Hegelian *Aufhebung* in which the age of Spirit is identified with the age of Christianity.

It is this author's conviction that the root of this strategy in German Judaism lies in a disposition that is sceptical in its method and in its conclusions, harkening back to the ancient and medieval Jewish world. The positing of a Jewish philosophy becomes in this way a critique of philosophy in general, particularly the philosophy that holds a claim to represent all of humanity. It is for this reason that alienation conducts individuals and peoples towards a radical scepticism, one that reflexively negates both the senses and logic.

The fecund critical tension between the pretext of universal philosophy and scepticism (moderate or radical)—the disposition to dig down for the roots of any ontology that claims to be eternal—is the axis of this book, one which at base aspires to leave traces rather than to delimit, draw borders around, establish, or reinforce any philosophical or cultural dogmatisms.

Alienation is the common process of borrowing, stealing, re-working, and re-naming everything in every religion, culture, and *Weltanschauung* that is in any contact with others. It is also a process of cross-pollination of cultures in contact. Can we reasonably speak of a general and particular philosophy, and, returning to the introduction of this book, is a Jewish philosophy possible? Is a process of alienation one of de-mythologisation or is there a reason why universal reason and particular *sophia* are often at odds?

Philosophies

The determinacy of universal reason tried to define the particular in its indeterminacy and to order it in its universal world. Or as Elliot R. Wolfson puts it, "I am committed to the proposition that the indeterminacy of the particular is always in the process of being determined by the determinacy of the universal, just as the determinacy of the universal is always in the process of being undetermined by the indeterminacy of the particular."[1] The logical paradox enunciated by Wolfson can be adapted to the very simple affirmation that the universal does exist when the particular is perceived as such. On the contrary, the particular is possible when the universal does at least logically exist and claims its status as such—e.g. given the definition of human beings is to infer that XY is human being if/in the case/when it suits to it. However, it is not absolutely convincing. For although without the particular there is no universal (induction), the opposite is not necessarily the case.

Applying the discussion of the particular and the universal to the debate on philosophy and philosophi(es), it is absolutely plausible that the development of a *Greek* philosophy was reputed to be general because it was understandable in the *Greek* language and those who had access to the language could understand it. Greek thinking made possible a philosophy which had the *claim* to be universal because (logically, linguistically) it was also comprehensible to a circle of people beyond the cultural/linguistic community of the Greek speaking people. The contrary is not possible, the formulation as follows is only true in the Platonic world of ideas: the conception/existence of a general supralunar (transcendent) philosophy made a particular *Greek* philosophy possible. Greek philosophy would be a concretisation of a general universal philosophy. In this case, we arrive at a vicious circle: Greek philosophy is universal because universal philosophy expresses itself in Greek language and culture.

The universality of a "philosophy" such as those of the Greeks or Germans requires not an internal procedure of self-definition and a claim to address the "uni-

---

[1] Elliot R. Wolfson, "Skepticism and the Philosopher's Keeping Faith," in *Jewish Philosophy for the Twenty-First Century. Personal Reflections*, ed. Aaron W. Hughes and Hava Tirosh-Samuelson (Leiden: Brill, 2014): 481–515.

versal" foundation of thought, but a long process that necessitates the translation and adaptation of its works in other cultures of majorities and minorities. Without the Latin and then the Arabic and Hebrew translation of Aristotle and Plato, "Greek" philosophy had no prospect of becoming a "general" philosophy in the modern world—i.e. a matrix philosophy capable of generating philosophies—and a language capable of creating languages and problems of common interest. The translation was not a "neutral" act, but, a *translatio sapientiae*, as Simone Luzzatto puts it ("the doctrines passed on to the Arab Nation following the decline of the Roman Empire") and then returned through Jewish intellectuals to the Latin word. The "passages" are not only a preservation of Ancient Greek thought and philosophy, but a reinterpretation and development within the translators' own categories, religions, and tradition. Only this path made Greek philosophy a paradigm for the Arabic, Jewish, and finally Latin world in the Middle Ages. Similar processes can be found in the early modern period, yet the occupation with philosophy experiences a turning point from metaphysical interest to gnoseologic concern at that time.

The very peculiar aspect of this debate is the moment in which Judaism became a particular philosophy. In this book I have concentrated on several aspects of the history of Jewish scepticism from the seventeenth century onwards, offering some contributions to the question of the universality and particularity of philosophy among Jewish intellectuals. While in the fifteenth and sixteenth centuries Judaism understood its own religious and philosophical tradition as constitutive of general philosophy, in the last decades of the sixteenth century and the seventeenth centuries the topic of the peculiarity of the Jewish religious tradition became prominent. It became perceived as a body of thought situated in intrinsic opposition to the sciences. The gnoseologic dilemma (to know or not to know) becomes the main question of the Jewish perception of human knowledge. The universality of Judaism is relegated only to the divine while human science became considered a product of mendacity, failure, and lies. The truth of revelation is incontrovertible because it is identified as existing beyond all scientific demonstrability. Revelation, which is the product of a particular mode of transmission, is universal because of its indemonstrable nature. Scepticism became a premise for absolute fideism. Yet, in order to question the truth of the human sciences, universities, *Yeshivot*, or academies, it was necessary to develop sceptical strategies within "universal" philosophy that could also apply to religious traditions (e.g. Spinoza). The fission between method and contents, or between sceptical strategies to be used only for human knowledge and dogmatic statements mounted through the chain of tradition, became a very modern trouble.

First among the secular assaults on the universality of Jewish religious tradition (Oral and Written Torah), which began in the epoch between the seventeenth and eighteenth centuries and which I discuss in the chapter on the historicisation of Jewish biblical tradition, was a discussion on the particularity of Jewish wisdom. According to Christian thinkers, Judaism does not belong to the system of Aristotelian logic or philosophy: scepticism is the door to consciousness of the particular seen from the perspective of the alleged general.

The problem of a Jewish philosophy on the basis of sceptical considerations of the value of reason is not new: if we start with the ancient and medieval period, the supremacy of Greek philosophy was considered a challenge to create new systems of thought and religion. The study of "other" philosophical conceptions and practices is not only opportune but also necessary in our world, which should be tantamount to communication and the perception of alterities. However, important aspects like the presence of alternative world views, the valorisation of nonconformist channels of perception, the inner philosophical perspective, the necessity of venturing beyond the dual logic of Aristotelian origin, the emphasis on practises beyond theories, are considerably underestimated, if perceived as philosophical entities of discourse at all. The Muslim scholar Al-Ghazālī transmits in his *Al-Munqidh min al-Dalāl* a tradition of the Apostle of God that "Every infant is born endowed with the *fiṭra* (فطرة): then his parents make him Jew or Christian or Magian." He adds, "Consequently I felt an inner urge to seek the true meaning of the original *fiṭra*, and the true meaning of the beliefs arising through slavish aping of parents and teachers."[2] According to the very influential Muslim thinker, a perusal of both the culture of the parents' religious communities and the personal search for an inner primordial nature (*fiṭra*) are key to a philosophical dialogue between cultures and movements in Western and Eastern civilisations. In another way: a plurality of approaches in the search for a common body of understanding is necessary.

To put it boldly, Jewish scepticism can be considered a "question mark" on the "Eurocentrism" of philosophical reason's claim to special access the universal dimension of critical reason. Paradoxically, philosophies of Judaism—as the translator of Julius Guttmann calls them—are expressions of alternative *Weltanschauungen* because they do *not* fit seamlessly into the worldview suggested by universal reason.

Sceptical Strategies

As seen in the above arguments, the main problem of Jewish thought and philosophy is how to define the preoccupation with philosophy as a general field from the perspective of a particular cultural group; Jewish thought and philosophy is between religion and language, between commitments to its own past and present and a preoccupation with an appropriate means of communication with others. This problem also belongs to the sceptical movement, a movement that is also difficult to define because of the inner, insoluble *aporia* of the word "limit," philologically connected with *definition*, to be understood as *delimitation*.

If, on the one hand, scepticism makes a forceful case for our knowledge being limited, on the other, it refuses every delimitation of "reality" and implication of au-

---

2 Al-Ghazālī, *Deliverance from Error, Al-Munqidh min al- Dalāl*, trans. Richard J. McCarthy (Boston: Twayne, 1980), 81.

thority, because it precludes other possibilities. Plato's Socrates, most notably, was called a subverter of laws and of the youth, primarily because he was a thinker who went beyond limits. There are two possible political consequences of a sceptical attitude: either it aims to avoid every constriction of society and to adopt a completely ataraxic attitude, or it accepts every possible and plausible solution without precluding anything. However, the "definition" of the research field of scepticism is more complicated.

Many scholars researching scepticism follow three very different objectives. The first objective is the study of the (critical) reception of ancient sceptical philosophy as the "sceptical tradition"—Academic scepticism and Pyrrhonism—where techniques and concepts were translated into other models and patterns of discourse. This entails an examination of the presence or absence of ancient scepticism during the Middle Ages and research into its early modern reception and further developments, as well as the emergence of modern and contemporary scepticism from the works of Descartes onwards.

The second objective, which is perhaps the most common in the philosophical community, is the application of methodical doubt at the beginning of every philosophical debate and treatise concerning all aspects of human life or, alternatively, an epistemological attitude which doubts the possibility of knowledge, or, more precisely, the perfect or almost-perfect, sufficient or almost-sufficient, and the possible or almost-possible reasons for certain knowledge. Although the history of philosophy is normally and generally considered to be part of philosophy, they are both in a controversial position because the second pretends to include the first, while the first claims to be perfectly autonomous as a philological, linguistic, and historical analysis of ideas and their development. In this controversy, no *ataraxia*, tranquillity, is given, granted, or even wanted.

The third crucial strand of enquiry is not narrowly defined, being sceptical in a more metaphorical and performative sense: it relates to sceptical strategies, concepts, and attitudes in areas not clearly defined as "philosophical," where doubts, criticism, and questions are expressed to effect the suspension of judgement. The educational and social reverberations of these strategies are what one could call sceptical in a wider sense. While the first and second objectives of scepticism are clearly and narrowly defined within the research community, the last is considered rather diffuse. Wrongly, I would say.

In his comprehensive article on medieval scepticism, Charles Bolyard asserts that scepticism is not hidden and forgotten in philosophical texts, or, to use his words: "Though medieval discussions of scepticism are often found buried within larger, formulaic discussions of theological topics, these treatments had influence beyond the academic circles within which they were originally created and considered."[3] This is a strange statement, as if there were a particular genre of sceptical

---

[3] Charles Bolyard, "Medieval Skepticism."

texts different from other treatments of philosophical matter which, as is well known, was incorporated primarily in commentaries, but also into theological treatises, exegetical dissertations, philological essays, religious poetry, etc. Scepticism is not a philosophical system, the object of commentaries. That is the reason why I speak of strategies rather than theories.

In his history of the concept of strategy, Lawrence Freedman[4] does not expressly address the question of scepticism, although he deals with philosophic dialectic strategies; he concentrates only on "Plato's strategic coup."[5] However, when dealing with Plato's attack against the sophists, Freedman emphasises the rhetorical dimension of Plato's review of prior philosophy which did accent the relativism of morality and a disinterest in truth, "suggesting that all that mattered was power".[6] Further, "tricks with language allowed the foolish and ignorant to appear wise and knowledgeable."[7] According to Freedman, the strategy of Plato was to discredit them by appealing to the universality and timeless nature of virtue against the alleged immorality of sophistry, "a choice between the ethical search for the truth on the one hand and the expedient construction of persuasive arguments as a form of trade on the other."[8]

Freedman reduces sceptical strategy to "the art of creating power," as he calls it, clearly influenced by the military arts, the object of his book. In my opinion, sceptical strategies are not intended to create power but, on the contrary, to weaken the creation of firm and fixed opinions. They are more or less formalised dialectical arguments[9] seeking to find weak points in the formulations of dogma, mostly ending either in the suspension of judgment or further enquiry. There are few winners in sceptical games, generally because of the equipollence of argumentations. The dialectic of sceptical argumentations pertains to the (im)possibility of reaching the truth, the (un)certainty of the responsibility of the individual, doubting everything subject to investigation etc. Strategy is a concept that can encircle scepticism at all because it is notoriously not a word which defines systems, not a theory, not an axiomatic principle, but an attitude towards an active life.

Two element are important in a strategy: to use the full arsenal of dialectical tools to weaken or even destroy the certainty of the adversary and to reckon with the possibility of an equipollence of arguments or even with the plausibility of a positive or negative result in the enquiry/dialectical struggle. Sceptical strategy is a bal-

---

4 Lawrence Freedman, *Strategy. A History* (Oxford: Oxford University Press, 2013). For the different meanings of the words see IX–XVI.
5 Lawrence Freedman, *Strategy*, 38–41; on Plato's strategy, see also 193 and 494.
6 Lawrence Freedman, *Strategy*, 39.
7 Ibid.
8 Ibid. See also the discussion on strategy and philosophy, or the philosophy of strategy, in Thomas C. Powell, "The Philosophy of Strategy," *Strategic Management Journal* 23 (2002): 873–880. I have not found any works on the idea that philosophy itself could (or should) be considered a strategy.
9 Cf. Katja M. Vogt, *Belief and Truth* 137 and 157.

ance between the arbitrariness of a fact, action, or thought/system of thoughts and the logical/mathematic consequences of them, as the chess metaphor below will seek to demonstrate.

Strategies and the Chess Metaphor

Strategy is an apt word for describing scepticism because it is notoriously not a word used to define systems, and scepticism is not a system, theory, or axiomatic principle, but an "attitude." This attitude implies some elements of language such as irony, contrast, contradictions, exaggeration, the disavowal of logical inferential argumentation, and enforcing arguments from common and particular experience, etc.[10] That is the reason why the sceptical seventeenth-century philosopher Simone Luzzatto speaks of a chess game, or, to use his words:[11]

> Some idle men promulgated other absurdities concerning this [i.e. original principles of the world], but it would be too inopportune now to attempt to summarize them. Yet by observing these arguments and controversies about the ancient principles of things, I began to have suspicions about the imbecility of human knowledge. According to the probable, I therefore argued that if the disagreements concerning the principles are so complex and numerous, then the difficulties in the development of the discourse will be even more inexplicable. Just like lines that go from the centre to the circumference, when they [i.e. the lines] are close to their origin, there is only a little distance between them, but as soon as they advance, they increasingly shift in different directions.
> Hence I likewise started to doubt that as human beings we are indeed not endowed with sufficient organs and faculties to apprehend and acknowledge the truth. Besides, the early bases and foundations from which rise the edifice of human knowledge are indeed not fixed and stable, but arbitrary and laid at our whim, as is usually the case with games, especially with chess, where similarly, while deductions and consequences are necessary, the first positions are indeed contingent and voluntary.[12]

The metaphor of chess is, of course, often used, and we know of some manuscripts from the eighteenth century that include diagrams of chessboards with inserted allegorical values

> The lady opens by advancing her pawn of Beauty two spaces, and the acteur counters with his pawn of Sweet thoughts. [...] She reinforces her first move by naively advancing her pawn of Sim-

---

10 Cf. Bill Rebiger, "Sceptical Strategies in Simone Luzzatto's Presentation of the Kabbalists in his *Discorso*," *Yearbook of the Maimonides Centre for Advanced Studies* 2 (2017): 51–69
11 *Socrate*, 22–23.
12 It is not surprising that Luzzatto refers to chess, a game highly beloved by the Jewish people of that time, especially because it was permitted on Saturdays. There is a very rich literature and bibliography about this topic, from the classic study of Moritz Steinschneider, *Schach bei den Juden: ein Beitrag zur Cultur- und Literaturgeschichte* (Berlin: Julius Springer, 1873) to Victor A. Keats's *Chess in Jewish History and Hebrew Literature* (Jerusalem: The Hebrew University Magnes Press, 1995).

plicity, which the acteur counters in symmetrical fashion with his pawn of Gazing. The lady's first of Beauty captures the man's pawn of Sweet Thoughts, thereby threatening the man's queen/pawn of Pleasure/Delight. The acteur counters again symmetrically by capturing Simplicity with Gazing and threatens her queen/pawn of Mannerism/Fair Seeming. She then takes his pawn of Delight and queen of Pleasure—a castration image if there ever was one—and the acteur becomes more concerned with losing his rook of Perseverance. As a result, he falters, commits an error in strategy: he preserves his rook rather than take her queen/pawn pair, and cannot recuperate, for perseverance does him no good now that she sees that he is bent on his own pleasure. From there, he goes on to lose. [13]

It is not my aim here to play a sceptical game with pawns, kings, bishops, rooks, and queens, nor would I like to engage with Wittgenstein's language-game theory, although I cannot deny that I am extremely tempted to do so. The moves of the chessboard would be more than a "primitive language," as Wittgenstein called his language-game. I would guess that the sceptical player would prefer a stalemate, which is very similar to the equipollence of sceptical memory. Let me sum up some elements which are important in order to make a game of sceptical interest out of the Jewish philosophical tradition.

The chess metaphor[14] helps us to understand the play of sceptical strategies, which are particularly evident in the ancient "school" of Sextus, but also in Cicero and Augustine; in the Middle Ages with Moses Maimonides, Ḥasdai Crescas, and Judah Halevi in Judaism, Al-Ghazālī in Islam, and John Buridan, Henry of Ghent, Duns Scotus, William of Ockham, and Nicholas of Autrecourt in Christianity; and in the early modern period Francisco Suarez, Juan Caramuel, and Simone Luzzatto. The game that is to be played includes a dialectical play between dogmatic concepts, such as, for example:

---

13 Daniel E. O'Sullivan, *Chess in the Middle Ages and Early Modern Age: A Fundamental Thought Paradigm of the Premodern World* (Berlin: De Gruyter, 2012), 218.
14 During the writing of this section, Warren Zev Harvey directed me to Ibn Ezra's poem: אֲשׁוֹרֵר שִׁיר בְּמִלְחָמָה עֲרוּכָה.

Authority
(Sources of) Knowledge
   Senses
   Science
   Nature

Logics & Dialectic
   Truth (criterion of)
   Certainty
   Dogma (Opinion)

Time (eternity)
Sceptical strategies/enquiry field such as
Enquiry
   Doubt
   Plausibility

Experience
   Contingency
   Time (absence of eternal validity)
   Convention

(anti-) Logical arguments, dialectic
   Paradoxes
   Contradiction
   Probable
   Deception
   Equipollence

Limits
   Relativism
   Agnosticism
   A-moralism

Results
   Suspension of Judgement
   Tolerance
   Enquiry
   Socratism

Playing the Sceptical Game

According to Sextus Empiricus, scepticism is not a philosophical system, but rather the ability to think and present arguments that lead to the acknowledgment of the limits of theories or beliefs, resulting in the suspension of judgment. Scepticism as a philosophical (and cultural) phenomenon offers both a critical theoretical reflection on the generation and representation of beliefs and knowledge and a practice of fragmenting philosophical discourse into its elements. Starting out with the assumption that scepticism means "enquiry" and that sceptics are merely "perpetual students" who always venture to doubt dogmatism and who continue to raise questions, our efforts should be centred on the paradox of a school in which the main object, the "enquiry," is at the same time the method and the aim of knowledge and research, which is merely and simply a sceptical paradox.

In the following I would like to summarise the topic touched upon in this book, outlining only the perspectives of sceptical enquiry and omitting the discussion the reader can already find in this book. The listing of the objects of sceptical occupation aims only at providing the width of the research field as well as some implications.

The senses are, of course, (the) sources of knowledge. The question of the reliability of knowledge and its sources primarily originated in the ancient and modern problem of the consistency of the senses and their impact on the intellect. Doubts about the reliability of the human sciences prompted controversial opinions. Uncertainty originated in the different prevailing opinions of the senses, objects, intellects, and knowledge and in the objects of discussion themselves. The analysis of the external and internal senses (common sense, imagination, and memory) induced ancient, medieval, and early modern sceptics to suspect their validity as sources of knowledge because of their being partially erroneous. The visual arts were a particularly strong focus of these questions, considered by some early modern philosophers as fallacious. Like visual perception, painting was seen as a construct for deceiving the intellectual capacity, which would be fooled by the beauty of an object. They claimed the superiority of animals because they were not affected by the illusion and fraud of visual art.

A privileged area of enquiry in the medieval and early modern pursuit of knowledge was the dichotomy between the sciences (medicine, astronomy, astrology, and magic) and revelation. While ancient scepticism is above all an enquiry into "dogmatic" issues of ancient philosophy, there was a shift in focus during the Renaissance and early modern period towards "errors" disseminated by the sciences (Sanchez, but also Moscato and Rabbi Löw of Prague): the humanities were prone to errors because they were produced by human experience and reflection, and consequently could not grasp the divine without communion with the divine intellect. This is an axiomatic but dogmatic position whose validity was generally taken for granted during the Middle Ages and early modern period. Historically, scientific knowledge was passed from generation to generation and regarded as a reflection of order in nature, while revelations regarding God came directly from Him.

Challenging the reliability of the sources of knowledge also involves a close study of ancient texts; in this way, the interpretation of language and linguistic features of these texts both leads to and causes philological scepticism. Assuming that revelation is one sort of authoritative and canonised text, there are many perpetual commentaries on the texts that use and implement (scientific, practical) knowledge. These commentaries also harbour criticism of acquired knowledge, e.g. the knowledge possessed in the sciences. It is a commonplace of philological research that textual criticism begins with doubts about the reliability of the (textual) tradition. Aside from specific aspects of textual transmission, medieval Jewish and Islamic schools developed critical concepts of language. The question of the reliability of texts, canons, and language is thus the first step in the sceptical approach to a tradition—which also influenced Christian, Jewish, and Islamic controversies—where claims of possible falsifications and questions of origin were discussed.

An often-underestimated aspect is the differentiated view of the so-called Jewish-Christian-Islamic (philosophical) controversies. Here, expressions of doubt about dogmas and the development of linguistic strategies that negotiate "otherness" on the basis of the reliability of authority, reason, and tradition are of vital importance. The questioning of the authority of a previous generation of scholars (as dogmatism) is considered a violation in Jewish, Christian, and Islamic traditions because it undermines their authority and thereby disrupts the chain of transmission of the "truth." However, it is only by distancing themselves from former generations that scholars can advance in their pursuit of knowledge and learning: tensions between adherence to tradition and advances in learning are expressed in the famous aphorism of dwarfs standing on the shoulders of giants, an image present in both Christian and Jewish scholarship.

The sceptic could be described as a "perpetual student" in relation to concepts such as education, criticism, learning, and teaching. The Jewish (sceptical) education has a long history that reaches back to the rabbinic period, further developing during the Arabic *adāb* period, and culminating during the humanist revival of ancient texts concerned with *paideia*. Eventually, as an important step towards the "condemnation" of the dominant authority of the Talmud and its tradition, the Enlightenment paved the way for a more universalist education, heading towards reason and the enhancement of criticism.

Scepticism has obviously been a recurrent theme in pedagogy and research into education, as it constitutes a field of tension between the teacher's view and the student's, encouraging the student to enquire sceptically into the nature of knowledge and authority. The frequently cited example of Plato's Socrates illustrates that education is far more than the investigation of (secular and sacred) knowledge, but that it is also crucial for observing the changes during the educational processes: understanding the formation of knowledge entails partial resistance against given authorities and a critical attitude towards unquestioned social rules. Despite the so-called crisis of authority in contemporary debates due to the focus on egalitarian partnership, and also in spite of the misunderstanding of scepticism as negative destruction, the critical and sceptical approach has remained an important reference within educational discourse, integrating sceptical methods and strategies for investigating the validity of claims of pedagogical propositions. Additionally, it is necessary to investigate how social norms and cultural practices shape different versions of scepticism and which hierarchical configurations and modes of self-examination are being addressed by these various methods.

Learning to "ask the right question" is the cardinal method of scepticism, while dialogue and dialectics are the literary implementations of this method. To put it very simply, dialogue in this proposal denotes the (real or fictive) literary form of written (and oral) philosophical or literary communication between two or more speakers, while dialectics is a method of arguing in order to create or resolve disagreement. By contrast, debate is a (real or fictive, mostly emotional) discussion of religious, philosophical, or literary questions usually directed at advancing or disproving the correctness or validity of the opponent's argument. It is obvious that dialogue, dialectics, and debate did not originate in sceptical schools, but that the former developed into a particular field within the latter. During a discussion, a student can rhetorically dilute an argument by dialectically expressing doubt about the teacher's statements. In some cases, the dialectics of dialogue are nothing but a monologue, in which the applied literary structure is intriguing, presenting a prolific rhetorical exercise.

Speaking of logical structure, sceptical strategies also imply irony, exaggeration, sarcasm, aporetic conclusions, and paradoxes. David Hume is very clear and concise in defining the question of sceptical paradox: "It may seem a very extravagant attempt of the sceptics to destroy reason by argument and ratiocination; yet is this the grand scope of all their enquiries and disputes."[15] Scepticism is inherently paradoxical because reason is scrutinised using reason itself (the basic paradox). Furthermore, "sceptic" literally means an "enquirer" whose main characteristic is that, in her or his eagerness to find the truth, she or he suspends all judgement about it. In consequence, the aim of enquiry becomes unattainable, since one can either enquire into what is known or encounter *aporia* (i.e. impasse in an enquiry), being faced with what cannot be known. In the first case, it is not necessary to enquire; in the second, it is impossible because one does not know what to look for and would not recognise it if one found it. This could appear as the negation of learning and teaching.

Yet ancient scepticism's questioning of everything was intended to promote the ethical aims of determining the right way to live (the ethical paradox). This becomes particularly evident among mystics, who accept revelation as a norm and as truth in-

---

[15] David Hume, *On Academical or Sceptical Philosophy*, part II, in http://www.bartleby.com/37/3/18.html (accessed 3 May, 2018).

fused into the human soul by the (Jewish, Christian, Muslim) divinity. The paradox rests in the assumption that human reason can be weakened by a reasonable argument and that revelation can be communicated without reason. Evoking a *ratio illuminata* through divinity or by adhering to a particular religion has been refused by sceptics as a solution to the paradox because of every religion's claim to absolute truth (see Al-Ghazālī, Yehoshua Lorki, etc.), which is impossible according to logical reasoning. Medieval anti-scepticism criticises a further paradox, namely the sceptic's criticism of knowledge relying on the senses by abating sensory perception (see Saadia's criticism of scepticism).

According to ancient scepticism, the aim of enquiry is the suspension of judgement in order to avoid any dogmatism; the result of this strategy is either silence or acting socially and morally in terms of what is probable or likely to be true. In the Jewish religious and philosophical tradition, the first dimension of silence is deeply anchored in the sphere of the sacred, not the sphere of cult and worship. It is a reaction to an event assumed to originate from the divine; for example, the imposed suspension of judgment ("Silence"!) in front of the unquestionably divine decision to give the Torah to Moses (and not to Rabbi Akiva). The decision to be silent began as a reaction to the divine and mysterious.

The rabbinic Babylonian tradition concerning the codes of religious law was also aware of a suspension of judgement in some cases; using the teyku-formula, the text presents some problems of halakhic norms to which there are no solutions because there were "two ways of looking at the matter either one of which may be correct and neither one of which can logically be favoured over the other."[16] The question of whether the Babylonian discussion is only an academic exercise or whether it is at the core of some halakhic problems cannot be answered with certainty; the rabbinic art of discussion leaves both solutions possible.

Silence resulting from a human reaction to the magnificence of the Godhead is also present in Maimonides.[17] The suspension of judgement in the ancient sceptical sense plays a role in Jewish philosophy during the early modern period; examples can be found in the writings of Yeḥiel of Pisa, Judah Moscato, and Baruch Spinoza.

Dialogical forms of scepticism are present not only in the Ancient period (e.g. Augustine's *Contra Academicos*), but also in Jewish philosophy during the Middle Ages (such as Judah Halevi's *Kuzari*). There are many passages in Francesco Petrarch's works, written during the fourteenth century, that use dialogue to explore doubts. Many examples can also be found in the sixteenth and seventeenth centuries as well. Debates are a specific form of dialogue which can be found in medieval disputations and in early modern public disagreements between Christians and Jews and between Christians, Jews, and Muslims. In these religious debates, it is the

---

[16] Louis Jacobs, *Teyku: The Unsolved Problem in the Babylonian Talmud* (London: Cornwall Books, 1981), 294.
[17] *Moreh Nevukhim* I:59.

task of the competitors to invalidate the veracity of their opponents' "truths" and to declare their own position as non-negotiable.

Moreover, dialogue, religious disputations, and debates, acquired a new significance in the early modern period. In contrast to the ancient and medieval dialogues where structures beyond time and space were the framework of universal debates, the Renaissance and early modern period turned to the specific, to "factual" places, historical times, and the "accidental." Thus, the veracity of the content by focussing on theatrically staged debates, now clearly presented as opinions, was weakened.

It is a well-known sceptical and stoic argument to describe man as a composition of various different "animals" that represent diverging and contrasting decisions, sentiments, actions, virtues, and vices. The Renaissance and early modern *literati*, influenced by the doctrine of Theophrastus' *Charakteres*, transferred this system to society, thereby challenging concepts such as free will. This well-known phenomenon led to the conclusion that the multi-layered structure of man might be the original drama, where the actors vividly impersonated philosophical and social ideas that were linked to concepts such as the arbitrariness of human individuality (see for example Juan Caramuel or Simone Luzzatto).

Where past scholarship was interested in emphasising the role of sceptical groups or individuals and their impact on society, as well as their alleged danger to the social order, recent research has increasingly focussed on sceptical challenges to hegemonic power structures and (state) religion (already a topic of Moses Mendelssohn). Here, Stuart Sim is worth quoting for his emphasis on the proposition "why we need more scepticism and doubt in the twenty-first century."[18] Sim envisages the problem of the entanglement between politics, the dominant culture, and (political) belief and argues for the need of a sceptical attitude as a privileged form of attacking authoritarianism in daily life. Although scepticism is commonly considered a negative attitude, it becomes a positive and necessary resistance to excessive power and the suppression of dissent.

In this way, the metaphor of a chess game is perfectly understandable. Sceptics against dogmatists is not a common game; rather, it is an attitude or strategy to life which may end either in an equipollence of arguments (stalemate), or, perhaps more often, in the checkmate that is a puzzling but simple proposition: we ultimately do not know what we know.

---

[18] Stuart Sim, *Empires of Belief. Why We Need More Scepticism and Doubt in the Twenty-First Century* (Edinburgh: Edinburgh University Press, 2006).

Appendix I

Johannes Frischmuth (1619–1687)
Guido Bartolucci

Johannes Frischmuth was born in Wertheim in 1619 and grew up in a bourgeois Lutheran family.[1] In 1636, he attended to the University of Altdorf, where he became particularly interested in religious matters and began to study oriental languages: Hebrew, Aramaic, Syriac, and Arabic. At this time, his professor was Theodoricus Hackspan, one of the great Hebraists of the period, who in 1649 published the Hebrew edition of *Sefer Niṣṣaḥon*, an anti-Christian treatise written by Rabbi Yom Tov Lipmann ben Solomon Muehlhausen at the end of the fourteenth century. Under the guidance of his professor, Frischmuth mainly focused on the study of rabbinic literature, in which he became a specialist. In 1645, he was called to the University of Jena, where he taught holy languages until his death in 1687. During his life, he published remarkable works devoted to investigating the relationship between the Bible and Jewish exegesis, particularly rabbinic interpretations. As his contemporaries have emphasised, Frischmuth's main task was to point out the dangers of rabbinic interpretation, especially for those scholars who considered it to be a faithful analysis of the divine text.[2]

He was influenced by Hackspan who published the Hebrew edition of the Sefer Niṣṣaḥon, a treatise on the use of Rabbinical literature in the theological debate of his time.[3] In fact, Hackspan used this anti-Christian text in order to show how important the interpretation of Jewish sources was, not just for traditional polemics against the Jews but also for the broader inter-confessional struggles of his time. His treatise, in fact, is full of references to the traditional Jewish interpretation of the Old Testament (especially of the Prophets) as well as to other religious confessions and heterodox religious movements, such as Calvinists, Catholics, and Socinians.

When Frischmuth moved to Jena, he began writing dissertations. Over the course of twenty years, he dedicated several works to the topic of the messiah, following the

---

[1] On Frischmuth's life cf. Johannes Simon Ponickau, *Oratio in memoriam et honorem viri celeberrimi Ioannis Frischmuthii professoris de Academia Ienensi optime meriti* (Jena: Golneriana, 1698); Gustav Moritz Redslob, "Johann Frischmuth," in *Allgemeine Deutsche Biographie* 8 (1878); Johann Zeumer, *Vitae professorum Theologiae, Iurisprudentiae, Medicinae et Philosophiae qui in illustri Academia Ienensi ab ipsius fundatione ad nostra usque tempora vixerunt et adhuc vivunt* (Jena: Johannes Felix Bielck, 1711): 101–104.
[2] Ponickau, *Oratio*, C2v.
[3] Theodoirco Hackspan, *De scriptorum Iudaicorum in Theologia usu vario et multiplici tractatus*, in *Liber Nizachon*, ed. Yom Tov Lipmann Muehlhausen, Editus typis Academicis, curante Theodorico Hackspan (Nuremberg: Wolfang Endter, 1644): 215–512.

model developed by Hackspan.⁴ In these dissertations, published between 1659 and 1678, Frischmuth analysed the rabbinical interpretation of traditional Christian messianic passages from the Old Testament. The German Hebraist did not only quote old Jewish sources like Ibn Ezra or David Kimchi, but also modern Jewish interpreters like as Isaac Abravanel, and contemporary Jewish scholars like Menasse ben Israel. As his teacher did before him, Frischmuth used the anti-Judaic messianic polemic as a tool to criticise Christian confessions and, in particular, Catholic and Calvinist scholars.

Frischmuth, however, did not focus his attacks on Judaism only within the narrow fence of theology. In 1653, he published a long treatise in which he analysed the right of kings in accordance with Deuteronomy 17.⁵ This work could easily be mistaken for a scholarly study on Jewish sources on monarchy; however, from the very beginning, the analysis of the sources on the Jewish kings was meant to be part of the larger debate on the monarchical institution, which began when the beheading of Charles I in 1649 marked the end of the English Revolution.⁶ Frischmuth's main purpose was to show that Jewish sources could not legitimise the superiority of other institutions, such as the Sanhedrin, over the king's authority. He harshly criticised Schickard, Selden, and Milton, who used rabbinic sources to support their claim that assemblies and magistrates had dominion over sovereign rulers. Frischmuth employs a very peculiar strategy to counter these claims: he demonstrates the inconsistency of Jewish interpretation by contrasting the sources adopted by his opponents with other Jewish authors, particularly Isaac Abravanel.⁷ Frischmuth's use of Jewish sources is always instrumental: even an author such as Abravanel, who took an open stance against the monarchical institution, becomes in Frischmuth's treatise a faith-

---

4 Johannes Frischmuth, *De primo quem in veri nominis messia Iudaei exigunt charactere dissertatio ex Esaiae XI, 1* (Jena: typis Samuelis Krebsii, 1666); Johannes Frischmuth, *De messia eiusque prodromo adversus Iudaeos triga disputationum* (Jena: 1661); Johannes Frischmuth, *De messia in sepulchro non reliquendo, nullique corruptioni obnoxio, super vaticinium Psalm. XVI, v. 10* (Jena: 1668).
5 Johannes Frischmuth, *De rege eligendo et deponendo discursus, ex Deuteronomio cap. XVII ac Ebraeorum commentariis Christianorum manibus haut ita tritis conscriptus* (Jena: Casper Frenschmied, 1653).
6 For the use of the Jewish sources in the debate on monarchy, see Eric Nelson, *The Hebrew Republic: Jewish Sources and the Transformation of European Political Thought* (Cambridge: Harvard University Press, 2010). The main works that participated in the debate on the Jewish king in this period were Wilhelm Schickard, *Mishpat haMelech, ius regum Hebraeorum a tenebris Rabbinicis erutum et Luci donatum* (Strasbourg: Lazarus Zetzner, 1625); Claude Saumaise, *Defensio regia pro Carolo I ad Serenissimum Magnae Britanniae regem Carolum II filium natu maiorem, heredem et successorem legitimum*, (s.l.: Sumptibus regis, 1649); John Milton, *Pro populo anglicano defensio contra Claudii anonymi, alias Salmasii defensionem regiam* (London: Typis du Gardianis, 1651); John Selden, *De Synedriis et Praefecturis iuridicis Veterum Ebraeorum libri tres* (London: Flesher, 1650–1655).
7 Isaac Abravanel was a Jewish author who was well known by Christian scholars in this period. However, we have yet to learn why; or, for that matter, for what reason his work was used against the rabbinical tradition.

ful ally against the enemies of monarchical absolutism.[8] In counterpoising various Jewish interpretations, Frischmuth seems to present the Jewish tradition as a realm in which opposing views could coexist together within the same passage. He thereby frames Judaism using a hermeneutical method that presents truth as beyond our reach. This implicit critique of Judaism in Frischmuth's work is linked to a much more general comparison of the Jewish political tradition with that of the Classical thought.

Frischmuth often quotes Hermann Conring's "*De republica Hebraeorum*," which was published as a *dissertatio* in 1648.[9] Conring, a German jurist and historian, wrote this work together with his student Martin Müller in order to criticise the Calvinist treatises on Jewish political institutions. He maintained that the Jewish tradition was unrelated to Aristotelian political thought because the Jewish constitutional model could not be included among the definitions Aristotle gave in his *Politics* (monarchy, aristocracy or democracy as it was above all a theocracy. Political power, Conring continued, was not managed by human beings but directly by God; therefore, the Jewish model could not be discussed within the framework of the current political debate.[10]

Frischmuth probably had Conring's account of the Jewish tradition combined with the idea that different and contradictory interpretations could coexist within the rabbinical tradition in mind when he published the dissertation *De loco Deuteronomio XVII v. 8 et seqq. et quae ad illum moveri solet questione: An Ebraei statuant,*

---

[8] Frischmuth, *De rege eligendo*, A2r–v: "Non placet haec interpretatio Abravaneli, cum aliis de causis tum maxime hisce. [...] His inquam rationibus motus Abravanel ipsi Maimonidi dicam scribere non veretur et examinatis aliorum quoque sententiis, novam expositionem molitur, eamque tam apte deducit, ut si Scaligero, Casaubono, Schickardo, Cunaeo aliisque oculis eam usurpare contigisset, haud dubie dicturi fuerint prae Maimonide eum inter Iudaeos ineptire desiisse." On the debate concerning monarchy in the Jewish tradition, especially in Maimonides and Abravanel, see David Polish, *Give Us a King: Legal-Religious Sources of Jewish Sovereignty* (Hoboken: Ktav, 1989).
[9] Conring, *De Republica Hebraeorum dissertatio*, (Helmaestadi: Henning Mueller, 1648). On his political interpretation see Valerio Marchetti, "Sulla degiudaizzazione della politica. In margine alla relazione di Horst Dreitzel," in *Aristotelismo politico e ragion di stato (Atti del convegno internazionale di Torino 11–12 Febbraio 1993)*, ed. Artemio Enzo Baldini (Florence: Olschki, 1995): 349–358, and Horst Dreitzel, *Absolutismus und ständische Verfassung in Deutschland: ein Beitrag zu Kontinuität und Diskontinuität der politischen Theorie in der frühen Neuzeit* (Mainz: Ph. von Zabern, 1992). On Conring's political thought, see Michael Stolleis, ed., *Hermann Conring: (1606–1681). Beiträge zu Leben und Werk* (Berlin: Duncker and Humblot, 1983); Costantin Fasolt, "Political Unity and Religious Diversity: Hermann Conring's Confessional Writings and the Preface to Aristotle's 'Politics' of 1637," in *Confessialisation in Europe, 1555–1700: Essays in Honor and Memory of Bodo Nischan*, eds. John M. Headley, Hans J. Hillerbrand, and Anthony J. Papalas (New York: Routledge, 2004): 319–345; Martin van Gelderen, "Aristotelians, Monarchomachs and Republicans: Sovereignty and respublica mixta in Dutch and German Political Thought, 1580–1650," in *Republicanism: A Shared European Heritage*, ed. Martin van Gelderen and Quentin Skinner (Cambridge: Cambridge University Press 2002): 195–217.
[10] Conring, *De Republica Hebraeorum dissertatio*, A4.

idem simul posse esse et non esse in 1658.[11] This treatise is different from all his other works, which are focused on political or theological issues: here he deals directly with a philosophical question, or, more precisely, with one of the main statements of Aristotelian philosophy, namely, the principle of non-contradiction. The dissertation begins with the assertion that the Jews used to pull the false out from the true, a statement that Frischmuth employs to demonstrate the untrustworthiness of rabbinic biblical exegesis.[12] At the heart of his reasoning is the passage in Deuteronomy 17 that discusses a judge's conduct when he is uncertain about a sentence. According to Deuteronomy, the judge ought to appeal to a higher authority chosen by God who would suggest the verdict to him and from whose decision the judge could not depart.[13] Starting from this passage, Frischmuth develops an account of the principle of authority in Jewish tradition by dividing his examination into two distinct parts: one mainly linked to the religious dispute and the other connected to philosophical speculation. The starting point of his analysis is the assertion that Jews hold the authority of their rabbis in such reverence that they are inclined to disregard the principle of non-contradiction even when faced with a clear and obvious reason to adopt it.[14]

To confirm his assumption, he quotes the works of two Lutheran scholars, the Helmstedt theologian Konrad Hornejus and the Jena philosopher Daniel Stahl, who stated that Jewish authority was founded on absurd principles.[15] Frischmuth makes use of the works of these two German scholars in order to link his analysis to the authority of Johannes Buxtorf and Martin Luther. The first author, Buxtorf, was one of the most important Hebraists of the sixteenth century. He wrote several works on Judaism, but he was best known for his anti-Jewish work *Synagoga Judaica*,

---

[11] Johannes Frischmuth, *De loco Deuteronomio XVII v. 8 et seqq. et quae ad illum moveri solet questione: An Ebraei statuant, idem simul posse esse et non esse exercitium academicum*, resp. Johannes Leonartus Will (Jena: Samuel Krebs, 1658).
[12] Frischmuth, *De loco Deuteronomio XVII*, A2r: "Ex ipsa veritate falsum eligere Ebraeos, saepenumero deprehendunt Christiani."
[13] Deut. 17:8–11: "If there arise a matter too hard for thee in judgment, between blood and blood, between plea and plea, and between stroke and stroke, being matters of controversy within thy gates: then shalt thou arise, and get thee up into the place which the Lord thy God shall choose. And thou shalt come unto the priests the Levites, and unto the judge that shall be in those days, and enquire; and they shall shew thee the sentence of judgment: And thou shalt do according to the sentence, which they of that place which the Lord shall choose shall shew thee; and thou shalt observe to do according to all that they inform thee: According to the sentence of the law which they shall teach thee, and according to the judgment which they shall tell thee, thou shalt do: thou shalt not decline from the sentence which they shall shew thee, to the right hand, nor to the left."
[14] Frischmuth, *De loco Deuteronomio XVII*, A2r: "Maxime vero omnium oculos in se convertunt Iudaei, dum dictamini rectae rationis haud obscure obniti et nimia doctorum suorum reverentia fascinati, illud in omni materia certissimum et irrefrenabile principium impossibile est idem simul esse et non esse, prorsus non agnoscere perhibentur."
[15] Konrad Hornejus, *De processu disputandi liber* (Frankfurt: Conrad Eifrid, 1633), 68–69; Daniel Stahl, *Regulae philosophicae sub titulis XXII comprensae* (London: F. Redmayne, 1672).

published in German in 1603 and then in Latin in 1604.[16] Frischmuth's engagement with Luther is centred on Luther's claim in his work on the Hebrew name of God (*Shem ha-mephorash*) that the Jews blindly believed in the authority of their rabbis regardless of the rationality of their words.[17]

By quoting Luther and Buxtorf, Frischmuth inserts his treatise into the Lutheran tradition of polemic writings against the Jews. The first part of his treatise is a development of Luther's (and Buxtorf's) claim about the authority of rabbis within Jewish communities. Frischmuth's first effort was not simply to attack Judaism, but to neutralise the Catholic interpretation of Deuteronomy 17. The Church of Rome had indeed legitimised the Pope's infallibility in judging religious matters precisely through its interpretation of role of the Sanhedrin.[18] The German Hebraist, on the other hand, maintains that Moses wanted to invest the Senate (that is, the Sanhedrin) only with the role of resolving those cases that were particularly difficult to judge.[19] Frischmuth thus attacks both Judaism and Catholicism; while the latter is condemned because of the claim of Pontifical primacy, the former is subjected to a more radical criticism, which he develops in the second part of his treatise.[20]

---

16 Frischmuth, *De loco Deuteronomio XVII*, A2v: "Nimirum si duo Rabbini inter se contendant et pugnent, ac sermones contradicentes proferant, non minus credendum esse utrumque suam doctrinam a Mose accepisse, immo (quae summa est blasphemia) utramque sententiam verbum Dei viventis esse." For the original quotation see Joannes Buxtorf, *Synagoga Judaica* (Basel: Ludovicus König, 1641), 61–64. On Buxtorf's life, see Stephen G. Burnett, *From Christian Hebraism to Jewish Studies: Johannes Buxtorf (1564–1629) and Hebrew Learning in the Seventeenth Century* (Leiden: Brill, 1996).
17 Frischmuth, *De loco Deuteronomio XVII*, A2v: "Beatus quoque Lutherus [...] Iudaeis exprobrat, quod Rabbinis dextram sinistram et sinistram dextram vocantibus credendum esse asserant." Cf. Martin Luther, *Vom Schemhamphoras: und vom Geschlecht Christi. Matthei am I. Capitel*, Wittenberg 1543, 8v: "Wie ists beschlossen [...] das alles was die Rabinen sagen, sol ein Jude gleuben, und nicht davon weichen. Dahersagen sie nu, Sie mussen iren Rabinen gleuben wenn die selben gleich sagten, die rechte hand were di lincte, und die lincte were di rechte, wie Purchetus schreibt." Luther took this idea from Porchetus de Salvaticis, *Victoria adversus impios Hebraeos*, (Paris: 1520). Luther's copy of Porchetus' work is now in Karlsruhe, Badische Landesbibliothek, RH (42B 297 RH). On Luther and Judaism, see Thomas Kaufmann, "Luther and the Jews," in *Jews, Judaism and the Reformation in Sixteenth-Century Germany*, ed. Dean P. Bell and Stephen G. Burnett (Leiden: Brill, 2006): 69–104.
18 Frischmuth, *De loco Deuteronomio XVII*, A3r: "Ad nauseam usque haec verba, quae tamen Ebraico textui minime respondent, urgere solent Pontificii demostraturi Romani Pontifici infallibilitatem."
19 Frischmuth, *De loco Deuteronomio XVII*, A3r–v: "Sane qui totum contextum sine praeiudicio perpendit, is animadvertit minime de religionis hic agi negotio, neque de causis, quae proprie videri possint sacerdotales, nedum ut Romani Pontificis in controversiis fidei infallibiliter definiendis confirmetur autoritas. Potius in eo occupatur legislator sapientissimus, ut doceat, iudici oppidano in causa ambigua et obscura haerenti [...] adeundum et consulendum esse Senatum illius loci, quem ad publicos conventus habendos Dominus elegerit et a quo ad alium appellare non liceat."
20 On this second part see Giuseppe Veltri, "Negotiating the Principle of (Non)-Contradiction: Johann Frischmuth on the Rabbinic Dialectic Discussion," in *Yearbook of the Maimonides Centre for Advanced Studies*, ed. Bill Rebiger (Berlin: De Gruyter, 2017): 107–119, as well as the last part of this book 297–309.

Frischmuth shifts his analysis from a controversial religious point of view to a philosophical one: he directly compares the principle of authority in the rabbinical tradition with Aristotelian thought by reaching far more extreme results. In doing so, he makes explicit something still hidden in his other works, namely, that Judaism is grounded on anti-Aristotelian principles of reasoning. Frischmuth's work is important for understanding the discussion of the Jewish tradition within the Lutheran world of the seventeenth century. As I have said, this work represents not an interpretation of Jewish philosophical thought, but rather an attack on anti-Aristotelian positions that were supported in that period both in- and outside the Reformation world. His work and his interpretation of Judaism has *always* had a political agenda linked to the cultural and political debate of his time.

Appendix II

Johann Frischmuth & Johann Leonhard Will[1]

De loco Deut. XVII v. 8 et seqq. et quae ad illum moveri solet, quaestione: an Ebraei statuant, idem simul posse esse et non esse, exercitium academicum

Jena, Krebsius, 1658

בהשי:

Quidlibet e quodlibet deducere et insuper habita *veritate connexionum*, quae teste Augustino lib. 2 *de Doct. Christiana* cap. 31 "non instituta sed animadversa est ab hominibus et notate," ex ipsa veritate falsum elicere Ebraeos, saepenumero deprehendunt Christiani.[2] Ex infiniti exemplis unicum hic adduxisse sufficiat, quod ex *Massechet* שבת cap.1 affert R. Abarbenel:

> כל דיין שדן דין אמת לאמתו אפילו שעה אחת כאלו נעשה שותף להקדוש ברוך הוא במעשה בראשית כתיב הכא וישב משה לשפוט את העם מן הבקר עד הערב וכתיב התם ויהי ערב ויהי בקר:
>
> Omnis Iudex, qui iudicat iudicium veritatis secundum veritatem suam vel unica bora, perinde se habet, ac si ipsi Deo in opere creationis cooperetur. Hic enim scriptum est (*Exod.* 18 v.13) et sedit Moses ad iudicandum populum a mane usque ad vesperam: et hic scriptum est (*Gen.* 1 v. 5) et fuit vespera et fuit mane.[3]

Ita Talmudistae modo hic, modo illic aliquid decerpunt, ubi vocum qualiscunque est similitudo, et inde talia colligunt, quae ne febricitanti quidem in mentem venire possint. Maxime vero omnium oculos in se convertunt Iudaei, dum dictamini rectae rationis haud obscure obniti, et nimia Doctorum suorum reverentia fascinati, illud in omni materia certissimum et irrefragabile principium, "impossibile est, idem simul esse et non esse," prorsus non agnoscere perhibentur. Quo ipso in quantam absurditatem incidant, iamdum ostenderunt viri celeberrimi, οἱ νῦν ἐν ἁγίοις, Conr. Horneius, aurei libelli *de Processu disputandi* cap. 5. et Daniel Stablius *Reg. I. Phil.* cuius verba ominino huc referenda duximus:

> Petrus Hurtadus de Mendoza *disp. Metaph.* 3. sect. 3. a nullo unquam homine id (principium) negatum fuisse scribit, sed Aristotelem suo more id alicui ex suo cerebro imposuisse, ut inde occasionem arriperet illius confirmandi. Atqui repertus est nostro seculo, qui non ipse tantum id negare non dubitavit, sed et orbi Christiano persuadere ausus fuit, veritati fidei id esse inim-

---

1 Trascription of the text by Valentina Decembrini.
2 Augustine, *De doctrina christiana*, 2, 121.
3 Magen Avot 1, 1.

icum. Scribit enim Sycophanta ille, qui falso se Christianum Israelitam nominat in libello quodam famoso, *assert. 3 contra Graverum:* axioma illud naturale, quod duae contradictoriae non possint simul esse verae, cum impossibile sit idem simul esse et non esse, neminem verum Chistianum posse agnoscere, imo nec debere. Eam nimirum fidem in populo Christiano esse voluit, qualis passim Iudaeis in Talmude, ut refert Buxtorfius in *Synag. Iud.* cap. 1 inculcatur: nimirum si duo Rabbini inter se contendant et pugnent, ac sermones contradicentes proferant, non minus credendum esse, utrumque suam doctrinam a Mose accepisse, immo (que summa est blasphemia) utramque sententiam verbum Dei viventis esse.[4]

Beatus quoque Lutherus Tom. 8 Germ. Ienens. fol. CXI Iudaeis exprobat, quod Rabbinis dextram sinistram et sinistram dextram vocantibus credendum esse asserant.[5] Unde me operae pretium facturum existimavi, si paulo accuratius in illorum mentem inquirerem, et vulgusne tantum, an et emunctiorum narium Ebraei tam crassum errent errorem, ex ipsorummet monumentis fusius ostenderem.

§2 Antequam vero in rem praesentem, quod dicitur, veniamus, facere non possumus, quin in loci istius, cuius occasione eiusmodi absurdam, et homine, nedum doctore, indignam assertionem probasse videntur, sensum verum et genuinum inquiramus. Extat vero is *Deut.* XVII v. 8 et secundum veritatem Ebraicam sic habet:

כִּי יִפָּלֵא מִמְּךָ דָבָר לַמִּשְׁפָּט בֵּין־דָּם לְדָם בֵּין־דִּין לְדִין וּבֵין נֶגַע לָנֶגַע דִּבְרֵי רִיבֹת בִּשְׁעָרֶיךָ וְקַמְתָּ וְעָלִיתָ אֶל־הַמָּקוֹם אֲשֶׁר יִבְחַר יְהוָה אֱלֹהֶיךָ בּוֹ: וּבָאתָ אֶל־הַכֹּהֲנִים הַלְוִיִּם וְאֶל־הַשֹּׁפֵט אֲשֶׁר יִהְיֶה בַּיָּמִים הָהֵם וְדָרַשְׁתָּ וְהִגִּידוּ לְךָ אֵת דְּבַר הַמִּשְׁפָּט: וְעָשִׂיתָ עַל־פִּי הַדָּבָר אֲשֶׁר יַגִּידוּ לְךָ מִן הַמָּקוֹם הַהוּא אֲשֶׁר יִבְחַר יְהוָה וְשָׁמַרְתָּ לַעֲשׂוֹת בְּכֹל אֲשֶׁר יוֹרוּךָ: עַל־פִּי הַתּוֹרָה אֲשֶׁר יוֹרוּךָ וְעַל־הַמִּשְׁפָּט אֲשֶׁר יֹאמְרוּ לְךָ תַּעֲשֶׂה לֹא תָסוּר מִן הַדָּבָר אֲשֶׁר יַגִּידוּ לְךָ יָמִין וּשְׂמֹאל: וְהָאִישׁ אֲשֶׁר יַעֲשֶׂה בְזָדוֹן לְבִלְתִּי שְׁמֹעַ אֶל־הַכֹּהֵן הָעֹמֵד לְשָׁרֶת שָׁם אֶת־יְהוָה אֱלֹהֶיךָ אוֹ אֶל־הַשֹּׁפֵט וּמֵת הָאִישׁ הַהוּא וּבִעַרְתָּ הָרָע מִיִּשְׂרָאֵל: וְכָל־הָעָם יִשְׁמְעוּ וְיִרָאוּ וְלֹא יְזִידוּן עוֹד:

Vulgatus interpres hunc in modum reddidit:

Si difficile et ambiguum apud te iudicium esse perspexeris inter sanguinem et sanguinem, inter iudicium et iudicium, inter plagam et plagam, verba contentionum in portis tuis, surges et ascendes ad locum, quem elegerit Dominus Deus tuus, et venies ad sacerdotes Levitas et ad iudicem, qui erit diebus illis, et quaeres et indicabunt tibi iudicii veritatem, et facies quaecunque dixerint, qui praesunt loco, quem elegerit Dominus, et docuerint te iuxta legem eius, sequerisque sententiam eorum, neque declinabis ad dextram neque ad sinistram. Qui autem superbierit nolens obedire sacerdotis imperio, qui eo tempore ministrat Domino Deo tuo; ex decreto iudicis

---

4 Conrad Horneius, *De processu disputandi liber* (Frankfurt: Conradi Eifridi, 1633), 68–69; Daniel Stahl, *Regulae philosophicae sub titulis XXII comprensae* (London: F. Redmayne, 1672). Ioannes Buxtorf, *Synagoga Iudaica* (Basel: Ludovicus König, 1641), 61–64.
5 Cf. Martin Luther, *Vom Schemhamphoras: und vom Geschlecht Christi. Matthei am I. Capitel* (Wittenberg: Erscheinungsjahr, 1543), 8v: "Wie ists beschlossen [...] das alles was die Rabinen sagen, sol ein Jude gleuben, und nicht davon weichen. Dahersagen sie nu, Sie mussen iren Rabinen gleuben wenn die selben gleich sagten, die rechte hand were di lincte, und die lincte were di rechte, wie Purchetus schreibt." Luther took this idea from Porchetus de Salvaticis, *Victoria adversus impios Hebraeos* (Paris: Aegidius Gourmont et Franciscus Regnault, 1520).

morietur homo ille et auseres malum de Israel, cunctusque populus audiens timebit, ut nullus deinde intumescat superbia.⁶

§3 Ad nauseam usque haec verba, quae tamen Ebraico textui minime respondent, urgere solent Pontificii demonstraturi Romani Pontificis infallibilitatem: quo nomine *Interrogationibus suis*, quas vocat, *Apologeticis*, eadem nuperrime praemisit Iesuitarum mordacissimus, Vitus Erbermannus, quem dignis modis ea propter excepit Vir summus, H. Conringius.⁷ Sane qui totum contextum sine praeiudicio perpendit, is animadvertit, minime de religionis hic agi negotio, neque de causis, quae proprie videri possint sacerdotales, nedum ut Romani Pontificis in controversiis fidei infallibiliter definiendis confirmetur autoritas. Potius in eo occupatur legislator sapientissimus, ut doceat, iudici oppidano in causa ambigua et obscura haerenti (hoc enim Graecus quoque innuisse videtur verbis: ἐὰν ἀδυνατήσῃ ἀπὸ σοῦ ῥῆμα ἐν κρίσει) adeundum et consulendum esse Senatum illius loci, quem ad publicos conventus habendos Dominus elegerit, et a quo ad alium appellare non liceat. Quem sensum cum *R. Abarbenel* sua explicatione confirmet, non gravabimur ipsius interpretamentum huc afferre. Ita vero fol. CCCLXVI col. 1 comment. in Pentateuchum loquitur:

> הפרשה לא תרבד עם בעלי דינים שיעשו זה כי אם עם השופטים שבעירים שזכר למעלה שאם יפלא ויסתר משכלם
> דבר בענין המשפט אם שיביא הספק ענין העדים שזכר או הוראת השעה או הוראת המקום או דבר הנחו' הדתיו'
> וכמו שמשפטים הכתובים בתורה וזה אם בין דם לדם רל שיתחדש הספק בין הדמים הטהורים לטמאים או בדיני
> נפשות בדם הנשפך בארץ שכל זה יקרא בין דם לרם או בין דין לדין שהוא בדיני ממונות בהבדלים אשר הן בין
> זכות והחובה או בין חנגעים אם לטוה' או לטמא או להסגיר אם יקרא נגע פצע וחבורה ודברי ריבות הם דיני
> נפשות ואפשר לפרש דברי ריבות שהוא הכלל ובכלל כל דברי ריבות שהיו בעריהם מאיזה מין שיהיו שאו יעלו
> השופטים ההם לירושלים וילכו לבית המקדש המקום אשר יבחר השם לפני הסנהדרין ולפני השופט שהוא הנשיא
> והראש אשר עליהם ושידרשו המשפט מאתם והם יגידו דבר המשפט ומה שיגידו הם ישמרו לעשות ולא יטו ימין
> ושמאל:

Sensus verborum est:

> Sectio haec non loquitur cum actore et reo, qui haec observare debeant, sed cum iudicibus, qui in urbibus eorum erant, quorum supra meminerat. Nempe si res captum illorum in iudicio superet; si vel ex parte testium, vel temporis, loci alteriusve rei ratione dubium exoriatur, quod suadere videatur, aliter de negotio esse iudicandum, quam iura recepta et praescripta legis postulent. Et huc spectant verba: inter sanguinem et sanguinem, q.d. si novum dubium emergat de sanguine mundo vel immundo, aut de iudiciis criminalibus, intelligendum est ob sanguinem effusum in regione. Omnia enim nomine sanguinis venire possunt. Vel inter causam et causam, quae intelligenda de iudiciis pecuniariis, an quis solvere teneatur nec ne. Aut inter plagas, mundusne sit dicendus an immundus: aut de lepra, an plaga, an vulnus, an tumor livens sit. Quando dicitur: Verba contentionum, itidem criminales causas respicit; fieri tamen potest, ut illa verba universaliter accipienda omnem notent causam, quae in portis illorum agi solebat, cuimodi illa

---

6 Deut. 17, 8.
7 Vit Erbermann, *Examen Examinis Conringiani, et repulsa peremptoria machinarum, quibus S. Romanae Apostolicae Cathedrae Infallibilitatem Helmstadienses Doctores hactenus arietando illustrarunt*, (Würzburg: Elia Michael Zinck, 1655), 83–84.

esset. Hisce talibus orientibus, iudices in civitatibus Hiersolymam ascendere, et ibi ad domum sanctuarii se conferre, locum nempe, quem Dominus elegerit coram Synedrio et iudice, qui erit princeps et caput illorum, et hos interrogare iubentur, qui sententiam sint laturi. Et quod hi iuris esse docuerint, id observandum esse ait, neque inde recedendum vel ad dextram vel sinistram.[8]

Ecquid haec faciunt ad privilegium ἀναμαρτησίας Pontificis Romani? Itane nihil in N.T. de illa habetur, ut ex V.T. praesidium petere fuerit necessum et illius Pontificis exemplo? At enim ne ipse quidem Pontifex V.T. unquam hac dote pollebat, quippe qui si eius particeps fuisset, in dubiis et difficilibus causis, quas ex lege et sua ipsius scientia resolvere non poterat, minime consulturus fuisset oraculum, *Num.* 27 v. 21 quod tamen ab ipso factum, largitur C. a *Lapide*.[9] Neque audiendus hic est Bellarminus, dum lib. 4 *de Spirit. Pontificis potestate* cap. 1 sic scribit:

> Est observandum, duas personas distingui, sacerdotis et iudicis, hoc est: Pontificis et Principis, et quidem Sacerdoti pronunciationem sententia, iudici Politico exequutionem demandari, id quod explicatur sequentibus verbis: Qui autem seperbierit, nolens obedire sacerdotis imperio, qui eo tempore ministrat Domino Deo, ex decreto iudicis morietur.[10]

Fallitur oppido Cardinalis, qui Vulgatum secutus textum non inspexit Ebraeum. Nihil quicquam in hoc de Sacerdotis imperio habetur, nihil de decreto iudicis: atque ita cum Ebraicae veritatis autoritas Bellarmino in os iacitur, apparet somnium esse, quod velut oraculum adduceratur. Quod vero Moses sacerdotum meminit et iudicis, id minime ita intelligi debet, ac si uno eodemque tempore utriusque in pronunciatione sententiae et eius exequutione distinctae fuerint functiones: sed ad temporum potius diversitatem referri debet. Quandoque enim Deus iudicem excitabat, cuiusmodi fuere Simson, Eli, Samuel etc. Interdum vero Senatus erat, sententiam dicere. Atque huc respicere legislatorem, patescit ex v. 12 ubi או "aut" particula disiuntiva occurrens monet, coniunctionem copulativam v. 9 ita quoque explicandam esse. Minime autem Pontificem dono infallibilitatis instruit, sed praecipit, ut Iudex minor vel privatus acquiescat sententia sacerdotum, qui cur in Senatum prae aliis lecti fuerint, R. Abarbanel his ostendit verbis:

> רוב סנהדרין היו מכהנים והלויים המשרתים את פני יהוה וזה היה לסבות מהן להיותם פנויים מבלי טורח ועמל הנחלות והקרקעות כי לא היה להם חלק ונחלה עם ישראל ולכן היו עוסקים תמיד בלמוד התורה ומשפטים והיו יותר מוכנים עלמוד בדבר המשפט וכמו שאמר יורו משפטיך ליעקב ותורתך לישראל וגו' ומהנה כי להיותם משרתי ה' וכהנים לאל עליון היתה חכמתם יתרה ויראת שמים בקרבם כפי עבודתם התמידית וכמו שכתוב שפתי כהן ישמרו דעת ותורה יבקש מפיהו כי מלאך יהוה צבאות הוא ומהם שלהיותם עובדים בבית המקדש היו נכנסים משם ללשכה והיה קרוב אליהם מאד דבר המשפט וכמו שאמר והאיש אשר יעשה בזדון לבלתי שמוע אל הכהן העומד לשרת שם וגו' ולכך אמרה תורה בענין הסנהדרין ובאת אל הכהנים הלויים ואל השופט אשר יהיה בימים ההם כי היו רוב הסנהדרין כהנים ולויים:

---

8 Itzrak Abarbanel, *Perush al ha-Torah*, (Jerusalem: Benei Arabel, 1964), 3, 158.
9 Cornelius a Lapide, *Commentaria in Pentateuchum Mosis*, (Paris: Renatus Giffart, 1621), 865–866.
10 Roberto Berllarmino, *Disputationes de controversiis Christianae fidei, adversus huius temporis haereticos*, (Cologne: Antonio and Arnold Hieratorum Fratrum, 1628), 209.

Synedrii bona pars constabat Sacerdotibus et Levitis, servientibus coram Domino, et hoc fiebat propterea, quod illi otio gaudebant, et haereditatis fundorumque cura minime distenti subinde in Lege et eius iuribus cognoscendis occupati erant. Erant quoque aptiores ad iudicia, quemadmodum dicitur (*Deut.* 21 v. 10) docebunt iudicia tua Iacob, et legem tuam Israel etc. Praeterea, quia Domino serviebant et Sacerdotes erant Dei altissimi, sapientia et Dei timore alios anteibant, quemadmodum dicitur, (*Mal.* 2 v. 7) labia sacerdotis custodient scientiam, et legem requirent ex ore eius, quia angelus Domini exercituum. Huc accedit, quod illi, cum in sanctuario servirent, inde in Synedrii conclave ingrediebantur, et iura eis norissima erant, quemadmodum dicitur (*Deut.* 17 v. 12) Et vir, qui egerit procaciter, noluerique audire sacerdotem, qui stat coram Domino Deo tuo, ut ibi ministret etc. Atque idcirco lex de Synedrio loquens sic ait: et veniet ad Sacerdotes Levitas, quia hi maximam Synedrii partem constituebant. [11]

§4 Equidem dono infallibilitatis praeditum Pontificem ius dixisse in V.T. praeterquam quod nec hic Scriptura nec alibi uspiam docet, ipsi Ebraei longe alium modum respondendi in usu quondam fuisse asseverant, quam Pontificii sibi imaginantur. Sic enim R. Moses Maimonides, *Hilkot* ממרים cap.

> כשהוה בית דין הגדול קיים לא היתה מחלוקת בישראל אלא כל דין שנולד בו ספק לאחד מישראל שואל לבית דין שבעירו אם ידעו אמרו לו אם לאו הרי השואל עם אותו בית דין או עם שלוחיו עולים לירושלים שואלין לבית דין שבהר הבית אם ידעו אמר ולו אם לאו הכל באין לבית דין שעל פתח העזרה אם ידעו אמרו להן ואם לאו הכל באין ללשכת לבית דין הגדול ושואלין אם היה הדבר שנולד בו הספק ידוע לכל אצל בית דין הגדול בין מפי הקבלה בין מפי חמדה שדנו בה אומרים מיד אם לא היה הדבר ברור אצל בית דין הגדול דנין בה בשעתן ונושאין ונותנין בדבר עד שיסכימו כולן או יעמדו למנין וילכו אחר הרוב ויאמרו לכל השואלין כן הלכה והולכים להן:

Quousque Synedrium magnum floruit, non fuit dissensio inter Israelitas. Si enim aliqua controversia exoriebatur alicui, suae civitatis Senatum consulere solebat, atque, si rem nosset, accipiebat responsum. Si secus, ille qui consulebat, cum illo Senatu vel legatis ipsius ascendebat Hierosolymam, et consulebat Synedrium, quod in monte templi erat, a quo si rem sciret, responsum accipiebant; sin secus, omnes ventitabant ad Synedrium, quod erat in porta atrii, a quo, si rem scirent, cognoscerent: sin secus, omnes accedebant ad conclave excisi lapidis, (vocant nonnulli Cameram augustam) ut consulerent Synedrium magnum. Si res, quae in controversiam veniebat, omnibus Synedrii assessoribus nota esset, sive secundum traditionem, sive secundum iudicandi modum, extemplo pronunciabant. Si vero rem minime haberent cognitam, suo tempore iudicabant, et tantisper ultro citroque conferebant, donec aut omnes consentirent, aut sententiis diversis maiorem consequerentur partem. Tum omnibus, qui responsum exspectabant, edicebant: Sic statutum est! Idque omnes recipiebant. [12]

Confer etiam *Massechet Sanhedrin* cap. 10. Atque ita, uti Caietanus quoque observat ex textu Scripturae, non ab uno sed a multis sacerdotibus, et iudice "describitur causae ambiguae definition," quam nemo impune reiicere poterat.[13] Quod si enim זקן ממרה sive "presbyter contumax" plurium sententiae refragari, et aliud quam communibus suffragiis decretum erat, procaciter executioni mandare non dubitasset, Hierosolymis eum (uti Maimonides sub finem cap. 3 *Hilkot Mamrim* docet)

---

[11] Abarbanel, *Perush Torah*, 3, 159.
[12] Moses Maimonides, *Mishne Torah*, *Mishpatim* (Jerusalem: Koren, 2017), 635.
[13] Thomas de Vio, *Commentarii illustres planeque insignes in quinque mosaicos libros* (Paris: Guillaume de Bossozel, 1539), 500.

עד הרגל משמרין וחונקין אותו ברגל שני וכל ישראל ישמעו ויראו מכלל שצריך הכרזה:

usque ad sestum custodiebant, quo eum strangulabant, quia dictum est, (*Deut.* 17 v. 13) et omnis Israel audiet et timebit. Ex quo concluditur, opus habere promulgatione.[14]

§5 Acquiescendum omnino fuisse Iudicibus minoribus sententia Synedrii, velut omnis ulterioris provocationis expertis, clare patescit cum ex poena, quam immorigero interminatur, tum mandato:

et facies quaecunque dixerint, et docuerint te iuxta legem, sequeris sententiam eorum, nec declinabis ad dexteram neque ad sinistram.[15]

Quae verba ex usu scripturae non nisi obedientiam significant. Longius igitur Veteres Iudaei in libro *Siphre* progressi sunt, quam par est, vel phrasis Ebraica admittit, dum sic loquuntur:

אפילו מראין על ימין שהוא שמאל ועל שמאל שהוא ימין שמע להם:

Etiamsi ostensa manu dextra, eam sinistram dicant, et sinistram dextram esse affirment, tu tamen eis obtemperes.[16]

Eadem in libro *Ialkut* quoque occurrentia fol. 284 col. 3 ad l. cit. duriuscula apparent, et ab ipsis Ebraeis diversimode explicantur.[17] R. Salomo com. ad loc. cit. nihil dissentiens a priscis ait:

אפילו אומר על ימין שהוא שמאל ועל שמאל שהוא ימין וכל שכן שאומר לך על ימין ימין ועל שמאל שמאל:

Etiamsi dixerit tibi de dextra, eam sinistram, et de sinistra eam dextram esse, quanto magis vero obtemperes dicenti, dexteram esse dexteram et sinistram sinistram.[18]

Paulo aliter R. Gerundensis:

אפילו תחשוב בלבבך שהם טועים והדבר פשוט בעיניך כאשר אתה יודע בין ימינך לשמאלו תעשה כמצותם:[19]

Etiamsi tibi persuaseris, eos errare, et in oculis tuis id tam evidens appareat, quam liquidam est discrimen inter dextram et sinistram, tamen facias oportet, quae illi praeceperint.

Etsi vero non idem plane sentire videtur R. Gerundensis cum R. Salomone, ait nihilominus R. Abarbenel, utrumque locutum esse

כפי מחשבת השואל ודעתו לא כפי האמת בעצמו כי ימין סנהדרין תמיד ימין והשמאל הוא תמיד שמאל:

---

14 Moses Maimonides, *Mishne Torah*, 644.
15 Deut. 17, 11.
16 *Siphre al dvarim*.
17 *Yalkut Shimoni*.
18 *Mikra'ot gedolot*, *ha-Ma'or*, (Jerusalem: Mekon ha-Ma'or, 1989–1991), 5, 320.
19 Ibid.

Secundum opinionem quaerentis, non quod revera se ita habeat: Synedrii enim dextram sempre dextram et sinitram eius sinistram esse.[20]

§6 Adhuc aliter veterum mentem explicat R. Nissim, ut Abarbenel l. cit. de ipso testatur his verbis:

ר״ן קבל הכתוב שהוא ימין ושמאל ודבריהם ז״ל על פי פשוטם אפילו יאמרו לך על ימין שהוא שמאל ועל שמאל שהוא ימין וגזר אמר שדברים כפשוטם ושלא דברה תורה והחכמים ז״ל כפי מחשבת השואל כי אם כפי אמתת הדין שיאמרו הסנהדרין בענין הדין על זולת אמתתו שהוא ימין בהיותו כפי האמת שמאל ועל שמאל כפי האמת יאמרו שהוא ימין אבל אמר שהתורה נהגה במצות כמו שנהג הטבע בדברים הטבעיים ששם כחות להתמדת מציאותו וטובתו והם על הרוב יתקנו המורכב ויתמידוהו עם היות שלפעמים על צד הזרות כבר ימשך מהכוחות ההם הפסד המורכב בענין בכח המושך ששם אותו הטבע להמשיך המזון הנאות אותו הטבע להמשיך המזון הנאות לאותו הנאות לאותו ימות עד״ז לפעמים הכח המושך ההוא ימשוך הדבר בלתי נאות ויתילדו ממנו חליאם ברב הזמן והטבע לזה לא ישגיח לפי שכוונתו תמיד על התקון הכללי ולא ישגיח על ההפסד המגיע על צד הזרות ועל המעט וכן היתה המצוה בסנהדרין שהשגיחה התורה על התקון לתקן ההפסד שהיה אפשר שיגיע בחלף הדעות והמחלוקות ושתעשה התורה תורות רבות ולתקן זה נתן ומסר הברעת הדור לחכמי הדור לפי שעל הרוב ימשך מזה תקון בשיהיה משפטם צודק כי שגיאות החכמים הגדולים מועטות וכל שכן היושבים לפני השם בסנהדרין ועם היות שעל המעט יאמרו על ימין שהוא שמאל לא חששה התורה להפסד ההוא המועט וראה לסבול אותו מצד התקון הכללי אשר בזה עוד ראה הרב לו תשובה אחרת בדבר והיא זה שימשך במה שיכריחו החכמים הפסד בנפש כלל גם שיאכל דבר טמא ואסור בחשבם שהוא מותר לפי שבתקון שימשך לנפש מהכנע למצות חכמים מורי התורה יסור הרע המעותר להתילד בנפש מהדבור האסור כמו שיקרה לאדם שיאכל דבר מזיק על דעת שהוא מועיל ולכן מחשבתו תפעל במאכל ההוא ויסור הזיקו ממנו:

Rabbi Nissim verba accepit proprie et literaliter. Nempe, etiamsi dixerint tibi de dextra, eam esse sinistram, et de sinistra eam esse dextram, et contendit, legem et sapientes l.m. non ex mente et opinione quaerentis esse locutos, sed ex sententia propria, quod Synedrium in iudiciis praeter veritatem de sinistra dicturum sit, eam dextram esse, et quae dextra revera est, eam sinistram esse. Sed ipsius sententia, cum lege et illius praeceptis ita fere comparatum est, ut se habet Natura et res naturales. In his enim sunt facultates, quae ad conservationem et existentiam illarum plerumque conducunt, etiamsi quandoque, contra quam fieri debet, composito exitium inde accersatur. Sic potentiae attractivae ea est natura, ut conveniens alimentum attrahat rei, ita ut cessante ea potentia, res ipsa pereat. Nihilominus illa facultas interdum aliquid attrahit, quod minime convenit et ex quo morbi sepe generantur. Sed Natura huc minime respicit, quippe cuius finis semper est, generale ordinare, neque ad corruptionem, quae raro fit et praeter intentionem, respicit. Consimilem in modum habet hoc praeceptum de Synedrio. Lex respexit ad ordinationem; qua damnum, quod ex diversis sententiis et dissensionibus oriri poterat, et quibus lex in multos sensus trahebatur, corrigeret. Hac fini Doctoribus illius temporis decidendi facultatem impertivit, quia plerumque ordo inde progignitur, nempe cum iura sunt clara. Errores doctorum virorum sunt exiles, quanto minores vero illorum, qui in Synedrio sedent coram Deo. Etiamsi quandoque dicant de dextra, quod sit sinistra, lex tamen tam exigui damni nullam habet rationem, sed illud tolerandum ducit intuitu generalioris ordinationis, quae hic invenitur. Adhuc aliam responsionem Rabbi Nissim sibi reperisse hic visus est. Nempe anima damnum patitur, dum cogunt sapientes, qui rem immundam atque adeo illicitam permittunt, arbitrantes licitam esse. Sed ab ordinationem quae ex praeponderatione praeceptorum Dd legem docentium, cessat malum, quod ex illicitare oriri poterat; perinde ac homini aliquid nocivum, quod comedit, et bonum esse arbitratur, non nocet, et ideo imaginatio facit, ut minime eo laedatur.[21]

---

20 Abarbanel, *Perush*, 3, 160.
21 Abarbanel, *Perush*, 3, 160–161.

§7 Quantum ex verbis allatis patescit, respicit *R. Nissim* ad id, quod in iudiciis usu venire solet. Ibi enim iudex, qui quod iuxtum et aequum sit, pronunciat, idque homines agere et in opus transferre compellat, ut plurimum rite iudicat: interdum tamen contingit, ut vel affectibus abreptus, vel alio modo praepeditus in iudicando sinistram dextram vocare videatur. Sed tum nihilominus partes litigantes parere tenentur, et nisi pareant, ad conservandam disciplinam et externam tranquillitatem in eos animadverti potest. Occurrunt sane in legibus quoque Romanis, quae huc collimant. Ulpianus enim l. *25ff. de statu hominum* ait: "Res iudicata pro veritate accipipitur."[22] Secundum Maecianum *l. 65 §2ff. ad S. Trebellianum:* "Dum praetor, cognita causa, per errorem vel etiam ambitiose iuberet, haereditatem ut ex fideicommisso restitui, etiam publice interest restitui, propter rerum iudicatarum autoritatem." Et *l. penult. ff. de Iustitia et Iure* Paulus ait: "Praetor quoque ius dicitur reddere, etiam cum inique decernit."[23] Caeterum tale quid Veteres Iudaeos voluisse innuere, prorsus non sit verisimile ob illas rationes, quas infra sumus adducturi. Neque unquam eum in modum, quo R. Nissim conatur, eos excusare vel duriora verba sic emollire quisquam est conatus. Unde R. Abarbenel ab eo non tantum facit divortium, sed his verbis explicationem eius impugnat:

> לא נחה בו דעתי לפי שעל הרוב ועל מעט אין ראוי שנאמין שימשך דבר רע מהמצות האלהיות ולא צוה השם ית'
> שיאמינו משאת שוא לא על המעט ולא על הרוב חלילה לרזׄל לכוין לדבר הזה ולא תסמוך התורה על פועל
> הדמיון בשומר המצות שיחשוב לטהור הטמא ולמותר האסור ולמועיל המזיק כי הנה תורת ה' צדק צדק תרדוף
> וה' אלהים אמת ותורתו אמת:

> Ipsius sententiae minime adscribo meam, quia non licet nobis credere, rem malam sive saepius sive rarius ex divinis praeceptis sequi. Neque etiam Deus praecepit, ut (*Thren.* 2. v. 14) mendacii oneribus credamus. Hoc ut sapientes nostri intenderint, id vero ab eis absit longissime. Porro nequaquam parest, ut ad phantasiae operationem legem exigas, ut observans praecepta cogitet rem immundam facere mundam, illicitam pronunciet licitam, et nocivum pro salubri habeat. Ecce enim Lex Domini praecipit (*Deut.* 16. v. 20) iustitiam iustitia sequeris. Et Deus est veritas, et lex ipsius est veritas. [24]

Quod Veteres illud, quod R. Nissim asseruit, nequaquam intenderint, id ut credamus, facile a nobis impetrare possumus. Neque simile illud, quod ex rebus naturalibus petit, huc satis quadrare videtur, cum legi humanae, nedum divinae, in eiusmodi casibus nihil prorsus possit imputari. Agnovit id ipsum Aristoteles, qui lib. V *Ethic.* cap. X sic loquitur:

> Τὸ ἁμάρτημα οὐκ ἐν τῷ νόμῳ, οὐδ'ἐν τῷ νομοθέτῃ, ἀλλ'ἐν τῇ Φύσει τοῦ πράγματός ἐστιν. εὐθὺς οὐδ'ἡ τῶν πρακτῶν ὕλη τοιαύτη ἐστί.

---

22 *Dig.* 50, 17.
23 *Dig.* 1, 1, 10.
24 Abarbanel, *Perush*, 161.

Peccatum non in lege, neque in legislatore, sed in rei natura est, statim enim rerum agendarum materia eiusmodi est. [25]

§8 Consequens igitur iam est, ut, quo maxime modo absurditatem amoliri velit R. Aberbenel, videamus. Ita vero ille:

הנראה בו אצלי באמת הענין הוא שמשפטי התורות הם כוללים ואי אפשר שימצאו בהם כל הדברים המקריים הפרטיים שיקרו בכל יום ומבואר הוא כי עם היות המשפטים הכוללים ההם צדיקים וישריש בעצמם כבר יקרה שיבא חדבר באופן שהמשפט הכולל לא יישירהו ולא יצדק עליו דרך משל כלל גדול אמרו בדיני ממונות המוציא מחברו עליו הראיה או הזקה אין אדם פורע תוך זמנו וכבר יקרה שתובע תובע דין אמת ואין לו ראיה או שפרע תוך זמן המויעד לו ואין רואה וכיוצא באלה הענינים ואז לא ימלט אם שישפוט השופט כפי משפט הפרטי ויעול ויחמוס כפי המשפט הכולל או שישפוט צדק כפי המשפט הכולל ויעול כפי האמת הפרטי:

Mihi res ita habere videtur. Legum rationes sunt generales, ac fieri non potest, ut omnes eventus vel casus, qui in singulos dies accidunt, in iis reperiantur. Constat etiam hoc, quod etsi legum rationes sint iusta; et secundum se recta; fiat tamen quandoque, ut illud ius generale huic casui singulari non queat accomodari. Ex. gr. in causa pecuniaria regula est, quae maximi fit: Actoris est probare, aut, Praesumptio est, statuto tempore aliquem non solvisse. Contingere potest, ut qui debitum exigit, iuste quidem id postulet, in probatione vero deficiat. Aut, ut quis statuto tempore solverit, nemine vidente, et sic in aliis exemplis. Tunc fieri non potest, quin iudex, si speciale ius observet, inique agat ratione generalioris iuris, si vero Ius generalius sequatur, ratione particularis veritatis inique aget. [26]

Ut haec illustret, in medium affert exemplum ex antiquo iure forensi, cuius rudera veteris Ebraeorum praxeos rationem suppeditare nonnulli censent. Ita vero ille:

Atque hoc se modo habet res in illo, quod legimus cap. היו בורקין (c. 5) *Massechet Sanhedrin*, quod testes interrogaverint in casu homicidii: Novistis ne illum? monuistisne illum? recepitne in se admonitionem? etc. occiditne ipsum eo temporis intervallo, quo quis alterum affari posset. Hoc omne enim necessarium est secundum Ius universale et determinatum, ut homo moriatur, nisi constet, eum propter factum, quod perpetravit, morti obnoxium esse. Iudices igitur iuxta ius clarum tradunt, non occidendum homicidam esse, nisi sint, qui testentur, eum occidisse, praevia item admonitione, et eo temporis intervallo, quo quis alium affari posset, et secundum omnes conditiones, quorum meminerunt. Coeterum si res hoc pacto protrahatur, futurum est, ut homicide multiplicentur, et Resp. pereat, quemadmodum idcirco Dd. nostri l.m. dixerunt capite אלו מציאות (cap. 2 *Massechet Bava Mezia*) non est Hierosolyma destructa, nisi quod secundum legem iudicarunt. q.d. iuxta veritatem universalem, et illam non accomodarunt tempori.

Florente Republica Ebraeorum, homicidam secundum legem Mosaicam eiusque; genuinam interpretationem occidi non potuisse, nisi septem observatis conditionibus, quas ridicule ex sacris probant Iudaei, eruditi iudicent, quam sit verisimile. Confer Notas Ioan. Coccei ad cap. V *Sanhedrin* p. 43 ubi eorum mentem latius explicat, et

---

25 Aristotle, *Ethics* 1137b, 5, 10, 4–5.
26 Abarbanel, *Perush*, 161.

nimium taediosum esse fatetur ostendere, quomodo singula ex scriptura probent.²⁷ Unde etiam patescit, quantum huic exemplo sit tribuendum.

§9 Sed reliqua quoque R. Abarbenelis verba audiemus:

> השי נתן בידם רשות ויכלת לישר את הנמוס התוריי ולתקנו כפי מה שיראה בעיניהם בענין החלקי ההוא ועל זה העני
> הזהיר שלא תסור מן הדבר אשר יגידו לך ימין ושמאל ר"ל כי על פי שיצאו משורת הדין הכולל ויקח הדבר
> לשמאלו או בהיות המשפט הצודק לשמאל יגזרו הדבר לימינו לא יסור מדבריהם כי מה שיגזרו הם בזה עם היותו
> כפי השרשים הכוללים על ימין שמאל ועל שמאל ימין הנה כפי האמת הפרטי וטבע ענין החלקי לא יאמרו אלא
> על ימין ימין ועל שמאל שמאל כי הוא מה שראו שיעשהו לא דבר אחר ובזה האופן כללה חכמה אלדית בתורתו
> כל חלקי האנשים וכל פרטי מעשיהם בכח הזה שמסר אל הסנהדרין הנה התבאר שלא יאמרו על ימין שהוא
> שמאל ועל שמאל שהוא ימין במה שיגידו סנהדרין מה שישמעו ויקבלו בקבלתם ולא גם על מה שפירשו על פי
> התורה כי בזה וכיוצא בו חלילה וחלילה להם מרשע שיאמרו על ימין שהוא שמאל ועל שמאל שהוא ימין לא כפי
> האמת גם לא כפי מחשבת השואל אבל אמרו זה על מה שיגזרו הם כפי צורך השעה כי הנה זהו בערך השרשים
> התורייים במשפטים הכוללים לזה יקרא ימין לשמאל ושמאל לימין:²⁸

Dedit Deus benedictus ipsis potestatem legem divinam ad particularia applicandi, prout rei natura exigere videretur. Hinc admonet, ne quis ausit ab illo, quod indicarint, recedere vel ad dextram vel sinistram. Quasi dicat: etiamsi extra lineam vel ordinem iudicii generalioris euntes, rem sinistra sui parte capiant, vel, cum ius certum et clarum ad sinistram positum est, rem ad dextram amplectantur, ab illorum verbis tamen non recedendum est. Etsi enim in illo, quod definiunt, iuxta fundamenta generalia, sinistrum dextrum, et dextrum sinistrum esse videatur: tamen secundum veritatem specialem, et naturam rei particularis non dicturi sunt, nisi dextram esse dextram et sinistram esse sinistram. Atque hoc est, quod facere debet, et non aliud quippiam. Atque hoc modo divina sapientia in lege sua comprehendit omnes homines et illorum actiones, dum hanc facultatem dedit Synedrio. Ecce ex his patescit, Synedrium, dum quae fando accepit, indicat, non dextra sinistram vocare et contra, neque etiam dum legis sensum genuinum profert. Absit ab eis, et iterum absit haec impietas, ut de dextra dicant, eam esse sinistram, et de sinistra eam esse dextram! neque secundum se et veritatem, neque secundum quaerentis opinionem, sed hoc affirmarunt de eo, quod urgente necessitatis casu decernitur. Hoc enim sit respectu legalium principiorum in rationibus generalioribus, ubi quod dextrum est, vocatur sinistrum, et quod sinistrum, dextrum vocatur.

§10 Hisce plane gemella docet R. Isaacus Arama fol. 139 comment. in *Pentateuchum* col. 2 et eadem explicatione, quam ex V *Ethic.* cap. 10 illustrat et corroborat, cum R. Abarbenele duriora Veterum verba mollire satagit.²⁹ Equidem infitias minime ibimus, Synedrium quondam Ebraeorum, etsi novi quid praecipere vel vetare ei minime concessum, imo plane interdictum erat, *Deut.* 4 v. 2 cap. 12 v. 32 ea tamen, quae in genere a Deo erant praescripta, ad speciales casus applicare, adeoque ex una lege multas sancire speciales, et ex circumstantiis, fine item et ratione legis de mente legislatoris iudicare potuisse; perinde ac apud Romanos in redditione iuris, quae fiebat per illius

---

27 *Duo tituli Thalmudici Sanhedrin et Maccoth* [...] *versa et annotationibus depromtis maximam partem ex Ebraeorum commentariis illustratta a Ioanne Coch Bremensi* (Amsterdam: Johan Janson, 1629), 43–44.
28 Abarbanel, *Perush*, 161.
29 Isaac ben Moses Arama, *Akeidas Ytzhak* (Venice: Bomberg, 1573), 139r–v.

applicationem ad factum, Praetores, cum animadvertebant, non pauca occurrere, in quibus vel mera ratio iuris cum aequitate naturali, quam potissimum intuebantur, pugnabat; vel aequitas evidens ratione iuris destituta erat, officio suo consentaneum putarunt, priori casu rigorem iuris civilis temperare et corrigere, posteriori, quod deerat, supplere, uti Magnif. Dn. Franzke, comment. in *Pandectas Tit. 2 de O.I* p. 32 loquitur.[30] Caeterum Ebraeos illo ex libro *Siphre* allato dicto hoc ipsum intendisse, et ad eiusmodi iuris ad factum applicationem tantum respexisse, haud immerito negamus. Arbitramur, eos, postquam Prophetae cessarunt, et locum tandem invenit oralis traditio, idcirco ita loquutos esse, ut eo maiorem fidem apud populum invenirent Magistrorum sententiae, et horum autoritas in immensum augeretur, quippe quorum responsiones, quantumvis rationis sensuumque iudicio repugnent, nihilominus velut sanctae recipiendae sint. Eiusmodi coecam obedientiam, qua Doctores suos nullis limitibus circumscripto obsequio colere debeant laici, Romana quoque exigit Ecclesia, quae Iudaicae in pluribus tam similis est, quam ovum ovo. Unde etiam Iosephus Voisin, annot. in *Pugionem* Martini Raimundi, inter utramque facta comparatione, de consensu illo Romanae Ecclesiae gratulatur, et pag. 12 in Sadducaeos invehitur, quod Veterum sanctas traditiones repudiarint.[31] Deprehendimus sane apud Pontifici Scriptores Iudaismum redolentes locutiones. Paulus Sarpius, lib. 2 p. 48 *Historiae Interdicti Veneti*, Patavii multa scripti cuiusdam exemplaria inventa fuisse affirmat, cuius regula decima tertia haec fuerit:

> Credendum Ecclesiae Hierarchica, etsi nigrum esse dixerit, quod oculis album videtur.[32]

Adde B.D. Calixti *Respons. Moguntinis Theol. oppositum*, ubi Pontificiorum de falsis credendis effata exhibet.[33] Greg. de Valentia Tom. 3 disp. I q. II Pancto v.

> quandoque potest contingere, ut quis teneatur conari ad eliciendum adsensum fidei supernaturalem circa id, cuius contrarium verum est.[34]

Et Franciscum Tolet. *Instructionis Sacerdotum* lib. 4 cap. 3

---

30 Georg Frantzke, *Commentarius in viginti et unum libros pandectarum iuris civilis priores* (Strassburg: Lazar Zetzner, 1644): 30.
31 Raimundus Martin, *Pugio fidei adversus Mauros et Iudaeos* (Leipzig: Friedrich Lanckis, 1687), 10–11.
32 Paolo Sarpi, *Interdicti Veneti Historia* (Cambridge: Thomas Bucke, John Brocke and Leonard Greene, 1626), 48.
33 Georg Calixt, *Responsi Maledicis Theologorum Moguntinorum Vindiciis oppositi. Pars altera, Infallibilitatem Romani Pontificis seorsim Excutiens* (Helmstad: Calixt, 1645).
34 Gregorio de Valencia, *Commentariorum Theologicorum tomus tertius* (Paris: Horatius Cardon, 1603), 342.

Si rusticus circa articulos credat suo episcopo proponenti aliquod dogma haereticum, meretur credendo, licet sit error, quia tenetur credere, donec constet esse contra Ecclesiam.³⁵

Quibus haud scio an Arabes illi accensendi sint, qui, teste Eduardo Pocokio pag. 267 *Not.* in Specim. Hist. Arab. docent, fieri posse, ut sint duo simul antistites in diversis terrae regionibus, quorum si alter alteri contrarium statuat, unterque tamen aequum rectumque; statuat, etiamsi sanguinem alterius fundi iusserit.³⁶ Sed haec obiter.

§11 Revera non tam ad sententias, quae in iudiciis sub ratione iusti feruntur, quam ad Doctorum quaevis sub ratione veri acceptanda placita Veteres spectasse, ex R. Lipmanno patescit num. 321 libri *Nizzachon*,³⁷ et R. Ioseph Albo, Hispanus haud obscure docet, cuius verba, lib. *Ikkarim* serm. 3 cap. 23 fol. 89 edit. Cracov. sic habent:

כוונתם בזה לומר כי לפי שכל אדם לחשוב מחשבות וליחס לעצמו ההתבוננות והסברה מדרכו וההשכל יותר מכל מה
שזולתו עד שתמצא כמה פתאים ויחשבו עצמם משכילים יותר מהם אמר הכתוב כי אף יראה לחולק שהחכמים
אומרים על ימין שהוא שמאל ועל שמאל שהוא ימין לא יזח מדבריהם לעולם אבל תהיה ההכרעה מסורה תמיד
אל רוב החכמים ואף אם אפשר שיהיה היחיד יותר חכם מכל אחד מהם ויהיה מסכים אל האמת מכלם
תהיה ההלכה בהכרעת הרוב ואין היחיד רשאי לעשות מעשה כדבריו כלל:

Mens illorum est: quandoquidem quisque solet sibi potius vendicare intellectum et sensum, quam aliis omnibus, ita ut tot simplices mulierculae et plebeii reperiantur, qui sapientes erroris insimulant, se ipsos vero illis sapientiores iudicant; idcirco ait scriptura, si vel maxime videatur dissentienti, quod sapientes dicant de dextra, quod sit sinistra, et de sinistra, quod dextra sit, nunquam tamen ab illorum verbis recedendum, sed multitudini Doctorum subinde traditam esse praeponderationem. Quin si fieri possit, ut unus aliis sapientior ad veritatem propius accedat, quam omnes reliqui, decisiva tamen sententia iuxta multitudinem erit, et uni illi non licet suo ipsius quidquam facere arbitrio. ³⁸

§12 Haec Albo, quem alias acerrimi iudicii Iudaeum, (uti Grotius *Annot. in cap. V Matth.* v. 20 eum appellat) Veterum sententiam latuisse haud est verisimile, de dicti illius sensu prodidit.³⁹ Ex recentioribus R. Moses Alschech audiatur, qui *Com. in Pentateuchum*, fol 209 col. 3 ad verba "iuxta legem" sic scribit:

עד כה דבר על מה שיפלא דבר למשפט והולכים שמה לסנהדרי גדולה שבמקדש לשאול את הדין ועתה נעתק לדבר
דרך כלל על כל דברי חכמים בכל דבר שהם מדברי סופרים:

---

35 Francois Tolet, *De instructione sacerdotum et peccatis mortalibus libri VIII* (Rouen: Jean Osmont, 1625), 612.
36 Gregor Abul Faraj, *Specimen Historiae Arabum sive de origine et moribus Arabum succincta narratio, opera et studio Eduardi Pocockii* (Oxford: H. Hall, 1650), 266–267.
37 Yom Tov Lipmann Muehlhausen, *Liber Nizachon, conscriptus anno a Christo nato MCCCXCIX diuque desideratus, nec ita pridem fato singulari e Iudaeorum manibus excussus, oppositus Christianis, Sadducaeis atque aliis. Editus typis Academicis, curante Theodorico Hackspan* (Nuremberg: Wolfang Endter, 1644), 176.
38 Joseph Albo, *Sefer 'Ikkarim* (Bratislava: Josef Schlesinger, 1853): 152r.
39 Hugo Grotius, *Annotationes in libros Evangeliorum* (Amsterdam: Blaev, 1641), 68–74.

> Hucusque locutus est de eo, quod in iudicio ambiguum postulat, ut Synedrium in Sanctuario adeant, quaesituri, quid iuris sit. Iam vero (v. 11) in genere de omnibus verbis Sapientum, et omni illo, quod e Scribarum decreto pendet, loquitur,[40]

ubi diserte fatetur, omnia Sapientum verba intelligi, a quibus non fit recedendum. Caeterum voces על פי התורה "iuxta legem" id minime significant. Quin si vel maxime cum Vatablo vertas: "iuxta institutionem, qua te instruxerunt," simpliciter et absque limitatione accipi neutiquam debent; sed uti alias in scripturis locutiones universales ex natura subiectae materiae et rei aequitate restringendae sunt; ita haec quoque cum conditione intelligenda veniunt, si id, quod praeceperint, honestum piumque sit, et praeceptis divinis minime adversum.[41] Alioquin enim, ut assensum praebeat falsa proferenti, aut illicitum quid iubenti obtemperet, nemo tenebitur. Hinc recte Carthusianus ad *Deut.* 17

> Dicit Glossa Ebraica, ut refert Lyra, etiamsi dixerint tibi, quod dextra tua sit sinistra, vel e converso, talis sententia est tenenda. Quod reprobat Lyra, quia sententia nullius hominis, cuiuscunque sit auctoritatis, si manifeste contineat falsitatem sive errorem, servanda est. Quae reprobatio vera est, si Glossa illa Ebraica dicere velit, quod talis sentetia sit tenenda, ita ut mente ei consentiatur, tanquam verae et iustae. Si autem vult dicere, quod est tenenda ita, quod poena aut damnum sententiae debeat patienter tolerari ab innocente, quia non potest ad altiorem iudicem in hoc mundo habere recursum, potest salvari.[42]

§13 Voluisse eos illimitatum obsequium Doctoribus praestandum verbis supra adductis praecipere, tanto minus dubitandum, quo frequentius in illorum libris similia dicta occurrunt, quae arrogantiam et imputendiam Doctorum produnt. In *Talmud Massechet Berachot*, cap. 1 fol. 3 diserte:

> חביבין דברי סופרים מדברי תורה
>
> dilectiora sunt verba Scribarum prae verbis legis.[43]

Et *Massechet Sanhedrin* c. X §3

> חומרם דברי סופרים מדברי תורה
>
> Gravius peccatur circa verba Scribarum, quam verba Legis.[44]

Et in *Medrasch Mischle* pag. mihi 1 col. 3

---

40 Moshe Alshekh, *Sefer Torath Moshe, Dvarim*, (Warsaw: 1861), 34.
41 *Biblia sacra, hebraice, graece and latine. Latina interpretatio duplex est, altera vetus, latera nova, cum annotationibus Francisci Vatabli* (Paris: Santandrea, 1586), 422.
42 Calixt, *Responsi*, Lr–v. The references to Vatable and to Dyonisius Carthus come from Calixt's work.
43 Talmud Yerushalmi, *Berkahot* 1:4.
44 Talmud Bavli, *Sanhedrin*.

אפילו שיחת חולין שלהם שקול כנגד כל התורה

etiam profanus illorum (Doctorum) sermo toti legi est aequiparandus.⁴⁵

Haec et alia complura hodieque apud illos obvia mentem illorum explicant, et simul comprobant, quam iustas causas in terris agens Salvator noster habuerit, cum multis modis verbi divini recta intelligentia corrupta erat et depravata, ipsos filios Levi, aliorum purgatores, purgandi, uti *Malach.* 3 v. 3⁴⁶ de ipso erat praedictum, et populum Iudaicum, ut sibi a fermento Pharisaeorum *Luc.* 12 v. 1⁴⁷ hoc est, personatis eorum moribus et sincerae doctrinae incrustatione caverent, commonendi, quibus tamen alias in Mosis Cathedra sedentibus obtemperandum docebat, *Matth.* 23 v. 3: "Πάντα," inquiens, "ὅσα ἂν εἴπωσιν ὑμῖν τηρεῖν, τηρεῖτε καί ποιεῖτε."⁴⁸ Quorum verborum cum optimus interpres esse nobis videatur iudiciosissimus H. Grotius, eum hic omnino audiendum arbitramur. In lege Mosis, inquit,

> sicut multa erant praecepta, ita in illis praeceptis multa erant, de quorum sensu ambigi poterat. In iis explicandis operam non malam navabant οἱ νομικοί, gnari linguae et historiae veteris, sine quarum cognitione legis pleraque recte intelligi nequibant. In his ergo Christus eos vult audiri a plebe, et eorum interpretationes, quanquam forte in duriorem partem inclinantes, recipi: quod extendi etiam potest ad rigidiores determinationes rerum in lege generaliter praeceptarum, quae sine determinatione aliqua expediri non poterant. Nam in his talibus debebat aliquid esse certi iuris, quod obtineri non poterat, nisi interpretum autoritate. Caeterum id non eo pertinet, ut si quid docerent, manifestis praeceptis, ipsique pietati contrarium, ut de Corbona parentibus praeferenda, sequendi essent duces coeci. Sed neque obligare cuiusquam conscientiam Christus voluit iis praeceptis, quae plane extra interpretandi officiu extraque legem ipsam οἱ νομικοί comminiscebantur, praesertim si ea praecepta superstructa essent falsae ac inani persuasioni, quale erat praeceptum de manibus abluendis, eo fine, ne manus contactu inquinatae animum inquinarent. Illud ergo, ὅσα ἂν εἴπωσιν ὑμῖν τηρεῖν, intelligendum ex connexu superiorum, quicquid iure Cathedrae, sive ut legis interpretes vobis faciendum dictaverint.⁴⁹

Hastenus Grotius.

§13. Sed nunc alia adhuc adducenda sunt, ex quibus patescet, hactenus Iudaeis nihil nos tribuisse, quod ab illorum indole sit alienum. In *Talmud, Massecheth Erubin*, cap. 1 fol. 13 sic legimus:

ג' שנים נחלקו בית שמאי ובית הלל הללו אומרים הלכה כמותינו והללו אומרים הלכה כמותינו יצאה בת קול ואמרה
להם אלו ואלו דברי אלהים חיים הן והלכה כדברי בית הלל:

---

45 *Midrash Mishlei*, 1: 6.
46 Mal. 3: 3.
47 Lc. 12: 1.
48 Mt. 23: 3.
49 Grotius, *Annotationes*, 381–382.

Tribus annis disceptarunt domus Schammai et domus Hillel. Hi dixerunt: decisio est iuxta nos: illi vero dixerunt: iusta nos est decisio. Exivit vox coelestis: quae ex utraque parte proferuntur, sunt verba Dei viventis, sed decisio ex iuxta domum Hillelis. [50]

Celebres apud Iudaeos fere Doctores Schammai et Hillel, qui tempore Imperatoris Augusti et Herodis vixisse feruntur, et fere perpetuo sibi invicem contradixerunt: nihilominus tamen utriusque verba Dei viventis esse perhibentur. Similiter *Massecheth Chagiga*, cap.1 ad locum *Eccles.* 12 v.11 scribunt:

בעלי אסופות אלו תלמידי חכמים שיושבים אסופות אסופות ועוסקין בתורה הללו מטמאים והללו מטהרים הללו אוסרים והללו מתירין הללו פוסלין והללו מכשירין:

Per autores congregationum intelliguntur discipuli sapientum, qui sedent congregati et in lege student. Hi rem immundam, illi mundam pronunciant. Hi prohibitam, illi licitam docent. Hi pro illegitima habent, illi pro legitima. [51]

Et subiungunt:

נתנו מרועה אחד רועה אחד נתנם ומפרנס אחד

ab uno pastore ea tradita sunt et unus pastor et Dux ea dedit.[52]

Non diffitetur R. Lipmannus, paradoxa haec videri, unde num. 321 ait:

הנה הדבר קשה להרגיש בית שמאי מטהרין ובית שמאי מטמאין איככה אפשר לקיים שניהם שיהיו דברי אלקים ואיך קבל מרעה מעת הגבורה שניהם אם קבל טהור לא קבל טמא ואם קבל שמא לא קבל טהור:

Ecce res intellectu difficilis est! Discipuli Schammai pronuntiant rem mundam, Hillelis vero immundam. Ecquomodo fieri potest, ut utriusque sententia stabiliatur et verba Dei viventis sint? Et quomodo Moses recepit utrumque; Si accepit eam mundam esse, minime accepit, immundam esse, et si immundam esse accepit, minime munda accepit.[53]

Haec rectae rationi satis consentanea sunt, quibus principii illius universalis veritatem agnovisse videtur, sed quidnam afferant Iudaei ad tollendam contradictionem, quae in illis verbis occurrit, paulo post visuri sumus.

§14 In *Pirke Aboth* cap. 5 haec verba leguntur:

כל מחלוקת שהיא לשום שמים סופה להתקיים ושאינו לשום שמים אין סופה להתקיים איזו היא מחלוקת שהוא לשום שמים זו מחלוקת הלל ושמאי ושאינה לשום שמים זו מחלוקת קרח ועדתו:

---

50 Talmud Bavli, *Eruvin*, 13b.
51 Talmud Bavli, *Hagigah*, 3b.
52 Ibid.
53 Lipmann Muehlhausen, *Liber Nizachon*, 176.

Omnis disputationis, quae propter Deum sit, finis est, ut stabiliatur: quae vero non est propter Deum, illius finis non ut, ut stabiliatur. Ecquae vero est disputatio propter Deum? Est Hillelis et Schammai. Quae vero non est propter Deum? illa est Korachi et eius coetus. [54]

Si scire aves, quid intelligant Iudaei per disceptationem, quae est propter Deum, R. *Abarbenel* comment. ad l. cit. docet talem intelligi, quae non sit instituta,

לקנטר ולא להתגבר זה על זה כי אם להוציא האמת לאור ולגלות מצפוני הדברים אשר יודעו מתוך המשא והמתן אשר במחלוקת:

ut alter alterum vexet, vel ei praevaleat, sed veritatem in lucem producat, et rerum abscondita revelet, id quod fiat interventu deliberationis in disceptatione.[55]

Sed et verborum סופה להתקיים "finis eius est, ut stabiliatur", explicationem audiamus oportet. R. Obadias de Bartenora geminam adducit. I. nonnulli sensum aiunt esse,

אנשי מחלוקת ההיא מת מתקיימים ואינם אובדין

illi, qui sic disceptant, subsistunt et non pereunt.[56]

Secundo ait:

שמעתי פירוש סופה תכליתה המבוקש מעניינה המהלוקת שהיא לשם שמים התכלית והסוף המבוקש מאותו מחלוקת להשיג האמת וזה מתקיים כמו שאמרו מתוך הוכוח יתברר האמת וכמו שנתברר במחלוקת הלל ושמאי שהלכה כבית הלל ומחלוקת שאינה לשום שמים תכלית הנרצה בה היא בקשת השררה ואהבת הנצחון וזה סוף אינו מתקיים כמו שמצינו במחלוקת קרח ועדתו:

Audivi explicationem, qua τὸ סופה notat finem, qui intenditur. Et hoc modo disceptationis, quae fit propter Deum, finis est veritatem apprehendere, et haec stabilitur, quemadmodum dicere solent; per disputationem veritas elucescit, veluti hoc patescit ex disceptatione Hillelis et Schammai, quod secundum Hillel sit statuendum. Illius vero, quae propter Deum non est, finis est studium dominandi et amor victoriae, quae minime stabilitur, uti in Korachi et coetus ipsius dissensione deprehendimus.[57]

§15 Quod si verborum illorum, quae ex *Pirke Aboth* paulo ante sunt allata, hic sit sensus: Disputationis inter Hillelis et Schammai discipulos institutae finem esse veritatis inquisitionem, eum quidem nemo ibit infitias, sed qua fronte affirmant: utriusque sententiam, quarum una alteram falsitatis arguit, simul veram et verba Dei viventis esse? R. Abarbenel l. cit. haesitare ipsemet videtur his verbis:

מאחר שכל בעלי מחלוקת אפילו שיהיה לשום שמים מאמריהם סותרים זה לזה ויחלקו בין האמת והשקר הני יתחייב שאם אחד דעתו אמת הדעת האחד יהיה כזב ואיך יאמר ששום מחלקת יתקיים שקרי לא יתקיים כי אם משתי הדעות אי אפשר שיתקיים כלו:

---

54 *Pirke Abot*, 5, 16.
55 Isaac Abrabanel, *Perush Pirke Aboth* (Ashkelon: 2013), 341.
56 *Mishnaiot Seder Neziqim* (Venice: 1548), 70v.
57 Ibid.

Quandoquidem omnium disputantium sermo, etiam illorum, qui propter Deum disputant, alteri contradicit, et inter veritatem et falsitatem versatur, ideo necessario inde sequitur, si una vera sit sententia, alteram esse falsam. Ecquomodo igitur ait, propter disputationem illam stabiliri, cum tamen fieri nullo modo possit, ut tota stabiliatur.[58]

§16 Caeterum etsi caeteris rectius videtur sentire *R. Abarbenel,* revera tamen in eodem cum reliquis haeret luto, dum utriusque verba a veritate stabiliri perhibet, sic enim loquitur:

התכלית הטוב ההוא שהמה מסכימים עליו הוא האמת המשותף המקיים דברי שניהם וזה היה סבה לשיזכרו שניהם בשוה בכל מקום ונושאים ונותנים עליהם מה טעמא דבית שמאי מה טעמא דבית הלל וכדומ' וכמו שאמרו על חכמי התלמוד וכתותיהם הללו מטהרין והללו מטמאין הללו פוסלין והללו מכשרין ואלו ואלו דברי אלהים חיים.

Finis bonus erat, in quo illi conveniebant, nempe Veritas coiungens et stabiliens verba utriusque. Atque haec causa est, quamobrem ubique una eademque ratione mentionem utriusque facientes deliberent; ecquae ratio est domus Schammai? acquae ratio est domus Hillelis? etc. Quemadmodum etiam dixerunt de doctoribus Talmudicis. Hi rem mundam pronunciant, illi immundam. Hi profanam, illi rectam aestimant; Et utraque verba sunt Dei viventis.[59]

Ita veteres sensisse R. Abarbenel affirmat, qui finem bonum veritatis nempe studium efficere posse haudquaquam negat, ut diversae quamlibet et pugnantes sententiae "verba Dei viventis" vocari queant. Idem etiam asserit autor libri החיים cap. 5 dum ait:

אף על גב דלכאורה נראה שאינה לשם שמים שהרי אי אפשר שיהיו דברי שניהם אמת אפילו הכי אמרינן הואיל וכוונתת לעם שמים הרי אלו ואלו דברי אלהים חיים.

Licet prima fronte videatur, ac si non sit propter Deum suscepta disputatio, cum impossibile sit, ut utriusque verba vera sint: nihilominus dicimus, quandoquidem intentio eorum in Deum fertut utriusque verba esse Dei viventis.[60]

§17 Eo Doctorum suorum reverentia abripit Ebraeos, ut falsa quoque illorum effata "verba Dei viventis" vocare nulli dubitent. Ecquid vero bona intentio conferre potest ad id, ut illa tam splendido titulo insigniantur? Sane, ut subiecti qualitas ad veritatem nihil facit, quippe quae duntaxat ab obiecto dependet, ita nullo modo fieri potest, ut Doctorum quamlibet finem bonum spectantium sententiae "verba Dei viventis" appellentur, nisi veritati sint conformes et cum Dei voluntate conveniant. Iam vero Deum velle, ut unum idemque simul "licitum" sit et "illicitum, mundum et immundum," nemo dixerit, nisi qui sibi quidlibet fingendi potestatem datam esse persuadet, veluti solent Iudaei. Seducti hi videntur inde quod saepius ab utroque disputante ad suae sententiae confirmationem afferri vident scripturae dicta, vel "verba Dei viventis." Sed hic meminisse deberent, quod R. Lipmannus ipsemet largitur,

לעולם לא ימצא פלוגתא בגוף המצוה כי אם בפירושו

---

58 Abrabanel, *Perush*, 344.
59 Ibid.
60 Lipmann Muehlhausen, *Liber Nizachon*, 289.

In aeternum non controverti de ipso praecepto, sed eius explicatione.[61]

Cum vero duae plane diversae, seque invicem falsi arguentes, afferuntur explicationes, clare patescit utramque non posse simul pro "verbis Dei viventis" haberi, nisi dicere velimus, idem simul posse esse et non esse.

§18 Scholiastes Talmudicus ad cap. 1 *Massechet Erubin* fol. 80 En Isr. loquitur:

שאלו רבנו צרפת ז״ל היאך אפשר שיהיה שניהם דברי אלהים חיים וזה אוסר וזה מתיר ותרצו כי כשעלה משה למרום
לקבל תורה נראה לו על כל דבר ודבר מ׳ט פנים לאיסור ותשעה וארבעים פנים להיתר שאל להקב״ה על זה ואמר שיהא
זה מסור לחכמי ישראל שבכל דור ודור ויהיה ההכרעה כמותם ונכון הוא לפי הדרש ובדרך האמת יש טעם וסוד דבר:

Quaesiverunt ex Doctore nostro Zarpath l. m. ecquomodo fieri possit, ut verba utriusque sint Dei viventis, cum hic licitum aliquid esse perhibet, ille illicitum? Ad hoc respondit: Cum Moses ascendebat in montem, ut acciperet legem, ostendi sunt ipsi novem et quadraginta modi unamquamque rem illicitam pronunciandi, et totidem modi licitam dicendi. Deum benedictum super hac re consulens hoc tulit responsi: tradendum hoc esse sapientibus Israelis quocunque tempore futuris, ut sit praeponderatio iuxta eos. Atque hoc recte se, habet ratione sensus mystici et revera huis rei subest mysterium.[62]

§19 Ut apud plebem haec paradoxa fidem invenirent, eis ex mendacio color quaerendus fuit, nempe ipsum Mosen legislatorem divinitus primum ita edoctum, Israelitarum Magistris postea eadem oretenus tradidisse. Neque ad איסור והיתר "interdictum et licitum" tantum, sed multo longius progressi ad totam legem restringunt. Rabbi enim Lipmannus lib. *Nizzachon* num. 321 sic scribit:

נראה שהש״י נתן התורה ושלש עשרה מדות לדרוש בהם התורה כל חכם וחכם לפי השגת דעתו ובלבד שיעסוק ויעיין
בכל כחו בלי ההתרשלות ואם יראה לסנהדרין על פי התורה והמדות שדבר אחד הוא טהור יהיה טהור ואם יעמוד
הסנהדרין אחריני ויראה להם שעל פי התורה והמדות אותו דבר טמא יהיה טמא כי הוא השי שנתן לנו התורה תלה
אותו ברעת חכמים לפי ראות עיניהם:

Videtur Deus legem eiusdemque modos tredecim unicuique Doctori pro scientiae suae modulo dedisse tantum ut diligenter studeat et meditetur. Quod si igitur Synedrio iuxta legem et modos visa fuerit res aliqua munda, erit munda, si vero aliud deinceps Synedrium succedat, et arbitretur secundum legem eiusque modos, rem illam esse immundam, talis quoque erit; quia Deus, qui legem nobis dedit, illam suspendit e mente sapientum, prout videlicet ipsis fuerit visum.[63]

Quin hoc in sacris literis confirmari affirmat, נאמר מציון, inquiens,

על זה תצא תורה ר״ל תצא דבר תורה היום שלא יצאת אתמול זה שאמר הכתוב ושאבתם מים ממעייני הישועה
ותי׳ אולפן חדשה לאפוקי מן הכופרים המפרשים על חדוש ישו שהרי אמר ושאבתם מים בששון ואין לנו עצבון בחדוש
תורתו אלא על חדוש תלמידי חכמים נאמר:

---

61 Cf. Lipmann Muehlhausen, *Liber Nizachon*.
62 Talmud Bavli, *Eruvin*, 3b.
63 Cf. Lipmann Muehlhausen, *Liber Nizachon*.

Hoc ipsum indicant verba (*Es.* 2 v. 3) ex Zion egredietur lex, q.d. aliquid legis egredietur, quod heri non est egressum. Similiter de hoc loquitur textus (*Esai.* 12 v. 3) haurietis aquas cum exaltatione e puteis salutis, quem Ionathan interpretatur: doctrinam novam, ad excludendum abnegantes, qui de novitate Iesu accipiunt. Ecce enim ait: haurietis aquas cum laetitia, sed nobis lex ipsius est dolori. Loquitur igitur de novitate discipulorum sapientum. [64]

§20 Haec, quae blasphemo ore eructat recutitus, insignitae illius caecitatis et amentiae, qua populum suum immorigerum se percussurum Deus est minatus *Deut.* 28 v. 28 sunt documenta. Sane veram et genuinam scripturas explicandi et intelligendi rationem se amisisse, vix alia ratione testatius reddere potuisset Lipmannus, quam Esaiae dictis tam absurdum sensum affigendo. Tredecim illos modos legis explicandae, quod inter preces matutinas, perinde ac si essent oratio, recitare solent Iudaei, Mosi referunt acceptos. Hinc R. Lipmannus lib. cit. num. 63

לא לחנם מרֵעה בהר סני היה ארבעים יום וארבעים לילה כי אם ללמוד פירושי התורה ומצות ודקדוקיהן:

Non frustra Moses Doctor noster in monte Sinai 40 diebus et totidem noctibus perseveravit, sed ut legis illius explicationes discerent, praecepta, eorumque subtilitates. [65]

Caeterum ut illi modi partim dialecticae sunt argumentationes a minore ad maius, a maiore ad minus; partim eiusmodi ratiocinandi rationes, quas a nemine alio usurpatas ad explicationem scripturae adhibere nequeas; ita nulla apparet causa, cur Mosi eos in monte Sinai dator affirment, maxime cum iis utendo, ea ex scripturis cruant, quae a mente Spiritus Sancti sint alienissima.

§21 Dum Deum a mente Sapientum legem suspendisse perhibet R. Lipmannus, respicit ad locum *Exod.* 23 v. 2 ubi verba לנפות אחרי רבים cum priscis Ebraeis et recentioribus, Aben-Esra, R. Salomone et aliis affirmative explicanda censet, quali in quavis oborta controversia plurium sententia praevalere debeat, et uti loco cit. loquitur Lipmannus:

תורה נתנה לפי הסכמת הרבים

Lex data sit iuxta consensum plurium[66]

quem tanti faciendum esse sibi persuadet, ut ne "vocem coelestem" quidem, quam בת קול vocant, ei quicquam derogare posse, scribat. Sed uti Cl. Hottingerus, Univ. Heidelbergensis decus, *Analect. diss.* 2 p. 90 bene monet, τὸ ῥητὸν, *Exod.* 23 "longe alium sensum ibi postulat,"[67] Rabbi quidem Aben Esra l. cit. sic scribit:

חז״ל פירשו כי מזה נלמוד כי הלכה כרבים ומה שהעתיקו הוא האמת ואחר שהכתוב אמר לא תהיה אחרי הרבים לרעות מזה נלמוד כי אם יהיו הרבים לטובה שהיא מצוה ללכת אחריהם:

---

64 Cf. Lipmann Muehlhausen, *Liber Nizachon*.
65 Cf. Lipmann Muehlhausen, *Liber Nizachon*, 40.
66 Cf. Lipmann Muehlhausen, *Liber Nizachon*.
67 Cf. Johan Heinrich Hottinger, *Analecta historico-theologica*, (s.l.: Johan Jacob Bodmer, 1652), 90.

Doctores l.m. explicarunt quod inde discamus, secundum multitudinem sentiendum esse. Et hoc, quod inde collegerunt, verum est. Quandoquidem enim Scriptura ait (v. 2) non declinandum esse post multos ad mala, propterea exinde discimus, si illi ad bonum respiciant, teneri nos, ut illos sequamur. [68]

Quilibet vero praeiudicio non occupatus sentit, ex textu id minime sequi, quippe qui,

כדמות שאלה ותוכחה לעורכי הדינים והמליצים כאומר הטוב בעיניך שגם אתה תהיה אחרי הרבים להטות את הדין הטענותיך:

Quasi interrogatione aliqua et reprehensione rabulas forenses alloquitur, hunc in modum: numquid et tibi visum est multos sequi ad pervertendum iudicium? [69]

uti Rabbi Abarbenel ad l. cit. commentatur.

§22 Ut adhuc clarius patescat, quantus Iudaeorum, postquam veram religionem et pietatem ad inanes et commentitios ritus traduxerunt, sit stupor, et quam vere huius absurditatis accusentur, quod statuant, "idem simul posse esse et non esse," aliud exemplum in medium proferemus. Vaticinii Iacobi Patriarchae, *Gen.* 49 v. 10 "Non recedet sceptrum de Iuda" etc.[70] non sine insigni verborum detorsione hunc sensum esse ait R. Lipmannus, num. 286

לבסוף יבוא משיח ולא יתבטל המלוכה עולמית

Tandem veniet Messias et non cessabit regnum in aeternum.[71]

Sed idem vocem שבט explicandam esse dicit פשוטו לפי המלכות על de "regno secundum sensum literalem," sui minime oblitus num. 46 ita loquitur:

שבט האמור כאן אינו לשון מטה ומלוכה אלא לשון רדוי ושעבוד מלשון כי יכה איש את עבדו או את אמתו בשבט וגו' ומחוקק האמור כאן לא אפרש לשון סופרים ותלמידי חכמים אלא לשון מרדע וייסורין מלשון במחוקק ובמשענותם והבי פירוש רדוי וייפירין לא יסורו לגמרי בלי חזרה מיורה עד כי יבא שילה.

Voce שבט, quae hic occurrit, non significatur scipio vel regnum, sed dominium et subiectio, quo sensu sumitur (*Exod.* 21 v. 20) in verbis; cum percusserint quispiam servum suum vel ancillam suam בשבט virga etc. Neque vocem מחוקק quae hic occurrit, de Scribis vel Sapientum discipulis accipio, sed de stimulo et castigatione, uti (*Num.* 21 v. 18) במחוקק ובמשענותם ut hic sensus emergat: castigationes a Iuda prorsus et ita, ut non redeant, non sunt recessurae, donec veniat Schilo.[72]

Secundum *Lipmannum* igitur unum simplex vocabulum שבט, uno eodemque loco semel duntaxat prolatum, diversis et contrariis significationibus exponendum nota-

---

68 Mikra'ot gedolot, *ha-Ma'or*, vol. 2, 564. (Ex. 23: 2).
69 Abrabanel, *Perush*, 2, 215.
70 Gn 49: 10.
71 Lipmann Muehlhausen, *Liber Nizachon*, 157.
72 Lipmann Muehlhausen, *Liber Nizachon*, 28.

bit "regnum" et non notabit "regnum," sed "afflictions." עד significabit "in aeternum," et notabit "aeternum," sed "donec," nempe tunc, cum reliqua verba Iudaeo patrocinabuntur. Et haec omnia nec violenta sunt Lipmanno, nec absurda, quia, ut num. 46 iterum loquitur

התורה סובלת סמה פירושים ואלו ואלו דברי אלהים חיים

lex multas expositiones admittit, et omnes sunt verba Dei viventis.[73]

§23 Ita Lipmannus ad ἀντιφατικὰ prolapsus scripturae verba pro libitu torquet et pervertit, omnibus legitimae interpretationis mediis neglectis, quae tamen alii Iudaei non penitus spernunt, sed bene monent,

נדרש המקרא לפניו ולאחוריו

Scripturam ex antecedentibus et consequentibus exponendam esse.[74]

Scire vero debuisset recutitus, unius loci sensum literalem non nisi unicum esse, quem autor intendit, et licet unum idemque vocabulum "absolute, in se ac nude" consideratum plura saepius significet: "respective" tamen et "determinate," prout in iusta oratione cum aliis vocibus copulatur, nonnisi unum quid, idque certum significare posse, dum contextu ad illud coarctatur, et restringitur. Scopus item autoris, et alia bonae interpretationis adminicula docent, qua significatione vocabulum loquens accipiat. Quae praesenti loco attendantur, proclive fuerit observare, τό שבט non significare "afflictionem": quia Iacobo decretum non erat infortunium praedicere Iudae, sed "praerogativam," qua reliquos fratres esset superaturus, quam Chaldaei quoque interpretes omnes pridem observarunt, vocem שבט reddentes per שולטן "dominatorem" vel מלכין "reges" et מחוקק per ספרא "scribam" vel legisperitum. Ut de "calamitatibus et afflictionibus" voces illae fumantur, neque contextus suadet, nec locus *Num.* 21 v. 18 Lipmanno allatus evincit, vocem מחוקק pro iis sumi. Fatente ipsomet R. Abarbenele

משה אדונינו מחוקק שנ' כשם חלקת מחוקק צפון:

Moses Dominus noster legislator ibi intelligitur, quia dictum est (*Deut.* 33 v. 21) quia pars ibi legislatoris tecti.[75]

Caeterum uti verbis Scripturae sensum inferre malunt Iudaei, quam eruere, ita fieri nequit, quin in scriptura coecutiant, id quod de seipsis asserere haud verentur. In *Medrasch Tillim,* מזמור קמ֗ה haec leguntur

---

73 Lipmann Muehlhausen, *Liber Nizachon,* 28.
74 Lipmann Muehlhausen, *Liber Nizachon.*
75 *Midrash Tehillim* 146, 4.

מי הן עורים הדורות האלו שהולכות בתורה כעורים שנאמר נגשה בעורים קיר כלם קורין ואין יודעין מה הן קורין שונין ואין יודעין מה הן שונין אבל לעתיד לבא אז תפקחנה עיני עורים:

Qui sunt illi coeci? illae generationes, quae in lege versantur instar coecorum (*Esai.* 59 v. 10) palpavimus sicut coeci parietem. Omnes legunt et nesciunt, quid legant, discunt, neque tamen quid discant, sciunt. Sed futurum aliquando est, ut oculi (*Es.* 35 v. 5) coecorum aperiantur. [76]

Hoc fiat: במהרה בימינו

FINIS

---

[76] *Midrash Tehillim.*

Bibliography

Abba Mari of Lunel. *Sefer Minḥat Qena'ot*. Pressburg: A. von Schmid, 1838.
Adelman, Howard Tzvi. "Leon Modena and Sarra Copia Sullam and l'Accademia degli Incogniti." In *Venezia, gli Ebrei e l'Europa (1516–2016)*, edited by Donatella Calabi, 284–286. Venice: Marsilio, 2016.
Adelman, Howard Tzvi. "Sara Copia Sullam." *Jewish Women: A Comprehensive Historical Encyclopedia*. Jewish Women's Archive. http://www.j-italy.org/libraries/sarra-copia-sullam/ (accessed 2 March 2015).
Adler, Israel. "The Rise of Art Music in the Italian Ghetto: The Influence of Segregation on Jewish Musical Praxis." In *Jewish Medieval and Renaissance Studies*, edited by Alexander Altmann, 321–364. Cambridge: Harvard University Press, 1967.
Adriaenssen, Han T. *Representation and Scepticism from Aquinas to Descartes*. Cambridge: Cambridge University Press, 2017.
Alberti, Leon Battista. *On Painting and on Sculpture*. Edited and translated by Cecil Grayson. London: Phaidon, 1972.
Albo, Joseph. *Sefer ha-'Ikkarim. Book of Principles*, 4 vols. Edited by Isaac Husik. Philadelphia: The Jewish Publication Society of America, 1946.
Albrecht, Christian. *Schleiermachers Theorie der Frömmigkeit. Ihr wissenschaftlicher Ort und ihr systematischer Gehalt in den Reden, in der Glaubenslehre und in der Dialektik*. Berlin: De Gruyter, 2011.
Al-Ghazālī. *Deliverance from Error, Al-Munqidh min al- Dalāl*, trans. Richard J. McCarthy. Boston: Twayne, 1980.
Algra, Keimpe. "Aristotle and the Aristotelian Tradition." *Phronesis* 50, no. 3 (2005): 250–261.
Allen, James. "Academic Probabilism and Stoic Epistemology." *Classical Quarterly* 44 (1994): 85–113.
Allen, James. *Pyrrhonism and Medicine*. In *The Cambridge Companion to Ancient Scepticism*, edited by Richard Bett, 232–248. Cambridge: Cambridge University Press, 2010.
Alpert, Michael. *Crypto-Judaism and the Spanish Inquisition*. New York: Palgrave, 2001.
Altmann, Alexander. "Eternality of Punishment: A Theological Controversy within the Amsterdam Rabbinate in the Thirties of the 17th Century." *Proceedings of the American Academy of Jewish Research* 40 (1972): 1–88.
Altmann, Alexander. *Moses Mendelssohn: A Biographical Study*. Tuscaloosa: University of Alabama Press, 1973.
Altmann, Alexander. "Zur Auseinandersetzung mit der 'dialektischen Theologie.'" *Monatsschrift für Geschichte und Wissenschaft des Judentums* 79 (1935): 345–361.
Altrocchi, Rudolph. "The Calumny of Apelles in the Literature of the Quattrocento." *Modern Language Association* 36, no. 3 (1921): 454–491.
Anderson, William H. U. "What is Skepticism and Can It Be Found in the Hebrew Bible?" *Scandinavian Journal of the Old Testament* 13, no. 2 (1999): 225–257.
Andreatta, Michela. *Il trattato sui dogmi ebraici (Sefer ha-'Iqqarim) di Yosef Albo. Il codice miniato dell'Accademia dei Concordi di Rovigo*. Treviso: Antilia, 2003.
Annas, Julia, and Jonathan Barnes. *Outlines of Scepticism*. Cambridge: Cambridge University Press, 2000.
Annas, Julia, and Jonathan Barnes. *The Modes of Scepticism: Ancient Texts and Modern Interpretations*. Cambridge: Cambridge University Press, 1997.
Anonymous. "Die jüdischen Zeremonialgesetze." *Jeschurun* [old series] 2 (1854–1855): 70–76.
Appelbaum, Robert. *Literature and Utopian Politics in Seventeenth-Century England*. Cambridge: Cambridge University Press, 2002.

Arkush, Allan. *Moses Mendelssohn and the Enlightenment*. Albany: State University of New York Press, 1994.

Arnim, Hans von. *Stoicorum veterum fragmenta*. Leipzig: Bibliotheca Teubneriana, 1903–1905.

Assmann, Jan. *Weisheit und Mysterium: das Bild der Griechen von Ägypten*. Munich: C.H. Beck Verlag, 2000.

Aughterson, Kate. *The English Renaissance: An Anthology of Sources and Documents*. London: Routledge, 1998.

Augustinus. *Contra Academicos, De beata vita, De ordine*. Edited and translated by Therese Fuhrer and Simone Adam. Berlin: De Gruyter, 2017.

Awerbuch, Marianne. "Über Juden und Judentum zwischen Humanismus und Reformation. Zum Verständnis der Motivation von Reuchlins Kampf für das jüdische Schrifttum." In *Reuchlin und die Juden*, edited by Arno Herzig and Julius H. Schoeps, 189–200. Sigmaringen: Jan Thorbecke, 1993.

Azinfar, Fatemeh C. *Atheism in the Medieval Islamic and European World: The Influence of Persian and Arabic Ideas of Doubt and Skepticism on Medieval European Literary Thought*, Bethesda: Ibex Publishers, 2008.

Bacon, Francis. *Of the Wisdom of the Ancients*. In *The Works of Francis Bacon*, edited by James Spedding, Robert Leslie Ellis and Douglas Denon Heath, 701–764. London: Longman, 1857–1870.

Bacon, Francis. *The Essays or Counsels, Civil and Moral*. Edited by Brian Vickers. Oxford: Oxford University Press, 1999.

Bacon, Francis. *The Works of Francis Bacon*. London: Adamant Media, 2000.

Baden, Joel S., Hindy Najman, and Eibert J. C. Tigchelaar. *Sibyls, Scriptures, and Scrolls: John Collins at Seventy, Supplements to the Journal for the Study of Judaism 175*. Leiden: Brill, 2016.

Baer, Yitzhak. "The Disputations of R. Yeḥiel and R. Moses ben Naḥman" [Hebrew]. *Tarbiz* 2 (1930–1931): 172–187.

Baffioni, Carmela. "Per l'ipotesi di un influsso della scepsi sulla filosofia islamica." In *Lo scetticismo antico, Atti del Convegno organizzato dal Centro di Studi del pensiero antico del CNR, Roma 5–8 Nov. 1980*, vol. 1, edited by Gabriele Giannantoni, 417–434. Napoli: Bibliopolis, 1981.

Bailey, Alan. *Sextus Empiricus and Pyrrhonean Scepticism*. Oxford: Oxford University Press, 2002.

Baltrušaitis, Jurgis. *Essai sur une légende scientifique: le miroir. Révélations, science-fiction et fallacies*. Paris: Elmayan, 1978.

Bamberger, Fritz. "Julius Guttmann: Philosopher of Judaism." *Leo Baeck Institute Year Book* 5 (1950): 3–34.

Bar-Kochva, Bezalel. *The Image of the Jews in Greek Literature: The Hellenistic Period*. California Scholarship Online, 2012. http://california.universitypressscholarship.com/view/10.1525/california/9780520253360.001.0001/upso-9780520253360 (accessed 3 May, 2018).

Baron, Hans. "Querelle of Ancients and Moderns." In *Renaissance Essays*, edited by Paul Kristeller and Philip W. Weiner, 95–114. New York: Harper and Row, 1968.

Barr, James. *The Semantics of Biblical Language*. Oxford: Oxford University Press, 1961.

Barthélemy, Dominique. *Études d'histoire du texte de l'Ancien Testament, Éditions universitaires*. Göttingen: Vandenhoeck and Ruprecht, 1978.

Barthélemy, Dominique. "L'Ancien Testament a mûri à Alexandrie." *Theologische Zeitschrift* 21 (1965): 238–370.

Bartolucci, Guido. "Il De Christiana religione di Marsilio Ficino e le 'prime traduzioni' di Flavio Mitridate," *Rinascimento* II s., 46 (2007): 345–355.

Bartolucci, Guido. *Vera religio: Marsilio Ficino e la tradizione ebraica*. Turin: Claudiana, 2017.

Bassani, Giorgio. *Il giardino dei Finzi Contini*. Turin: Einaudi, 1962.

Batnitzky, Leora. *How Judaism Became a Religion: An Introduction to Modern Jewish Thought.* Princeton: Princeton University Press, 2011.

Battagia, Michele. *Delle accademie Veneziane: Dissertazione storica,* Venezia: Orlandelli, 1826.

Baur, Johann Jakob. *Stricturae Quaedam Ex Philosophia Hebraeorum, Maxime Recentiorum Cum Moderna Philosophandi Ratione Conformi. Speciatim Ex Logica Atque Metaphysica,* Tübingen: Schramm, 1766.

Becker, Adam H. *Sources for the Study of the School of Nisibis,* Liverpool: Liverpool University Press, 2008.

Bellis, Delphine. "*Nos in Diem Vivimus:* Gassendi's Probabilism and Academic Philosophy from Day to Day." In *Academic Scepticism in the Development of Early Modern Philosophy,* edited by Plinio Junqueira Smith and Sébastien Charles, 125–152. New York: Springer, 2016.

Ben-Menaḥem, Ḥaninah. *Sugyot ba-mishpaṭ ha-'Ivri.* Ra'ananah: ha-Universiṭah ha-Petuḥah, 2006.

Ben-Sasson, Haim H. "Jewish-Christian Disputation in the Setting of Humanism and Reformation in the German Empire." *Harvard Theological Revue* 59 (1966): 369–390.

Berger, Natalia. "Doctors in the House." *Hadassah* 79 (1999): n.p.

Bergmann, Judah. *Jüdische Apologetik im neutestamentlichen Zeitalter.* Berlin: Reimer, 1908.

Bergmann, Judah. "Sokrates in der jüdischen Literatur." *Monatsschrift zur Geschichte und Wissenschaft des Judentums* 80 (1936): 3–13.

Berliner, Abraham. *Targum Onkelos: Einleitung und Register.* Frankfurt: Kauffmann, 1884.

Berti, Enrico. *Contraddizione e dialettica negli antichi e nei moderni.* Brescia: Morcelliana, 2015.

Biagioli, Mario. *Galileo Courtier. The Practice of Science in the Culture of Absolutism.* Chicago, London: The University of Chicago Press, 1993.

Bianchi, Luca. "Continuity and Change in the Aristotelian Tradition." In *The Cambridge Companion to Renaissance Humanism,* edited by James Hankins, 49–71. Cambridge: Cambridge University Press, 2007.

Bientenbard, Hans. *Der Tosefta-Traktat Sota. Hebräischer Text mit kritischem Apparat, Übersetzung und Kommentar.* Berlin: Lang, 1985.

Bientenbard, Hans. *Die Mischna. Seder 3, Naschim, Traktat 6, Sota (Die des Ehebruchs Verdächtige). Übersetzung, Erklärungen, textkritischer Anhang.* Berlin: Töpelmann, 1956.

Bickerman, Elias J. *The Jewish Historian Demetrios. Studies in Jewish and Christian History.* Leiden: Brill, 1980.

Bickerman, Elias J. *The Jews in the Greek Age.* Cambridge: Harvard University Press, 1988.

Blackburn, Simon. *The Oxford Dictionary of Philosophy,* Oxford: Oxford University Press, 1996.

Bloch, René. *Moses und der Mythos. Die Auseinandersetzung mit der griechischen Mythologie bei jüdisch-hellenistischen Autoren.* Leiden: Brill, 2011.

Bloch, René. *Orpheus als Lehrer des Musaios, Moses als Lehrer des Orpheus.* In *Antike Mythen. Medien, Transformationen und Konstruktionen,* edited by Ueli Dill and Christine Walde, 65–82. Berlin: de Gruyter, 2009.

Boccato, Carla. "Lettere di Ansaldo Ceba, genovese, a Sara Copio Sullam, poetessa del ghetto di Venezia." *Rassegna mensile di Israel* 40 (1974): 169–191.

Boccato, Carla. "Sara Copia Sullam: La poetessa del ghetto di Venezia: episodi della sua vita in un manoscritto del secolo xvii." *Italia* 6 (1987): 104–218.

Bodin, Jean. *Colloquium heptaplomeres de rerum sublimium arcanis abditis e codicibus manuscriptis bibliothecae academicae gissensis cum varia lectione aliorum apographorum nunc primum typis describendum.* Edited by Ludwig Noack Schwerin. Paris: F.G. Baerensprung, 1857.

Boeckh, August. *Encyklopädie und Methodologie der philologischen Wissenschaften.* Leipzig: B.G. Teubner, 1877.

Bolyard, Charles. "Medieval Skepticism." *The Stanford Encyclopedia of Philosophy.* http://plato.stanford.edu/archives/spr2013/entries/skepticism-medieval/ (accessed 3 May, 2018).

Bomhoff, Hartmut. *Abraham Geiger: Durch Wissen zum Glauben. Through Reason to Faith: Reform and the Science of Judaism*. Berlin: Hentrich und Hentrich Verlag, 2015.
Bonfil, Robert. "La produzione esegetica di 'O. Servadio Sforno." In *La lettura ebraica delle Scritture*, edited by Sergio. J. Sierra, 261–277. Bologna: Edizioni Dehoniane, 1995.
Bonfil, Robert. "The Historian's Perception of the Jews in the Italian Renaissance. Towards a Reappraisal." *Revue des Études Juives CXLIII* (1984): 59–82.
Bonfil, Robert. "Torat ha-nefesh ve-ha-qedushah be-mishnat R. 'Ovadyah Sforno." *Eshel Beer-Sheva, Studies in Jewish Thought* 1 (1976): 200–257.
Bonifaccio, Baldassarre. *Amata, tragedia di Baldassare Bonifaccio*. Venice: appresso Antonio Pinelli, 1622.
Bonifaccio, Baldassarre. *Lettere poetiche di Baldassare Bonifaccio, per difesa, e dichiaratione della sua Tragedia*. Venice: appresso Antonio Pinelli, 1622.
Bonifaccio, Baldassarre. *Risposta al Manifesto della Signora Sara Copia del Signor Baldassare Bonifaccio*. Venice: appresso Antonio Pinelli, 1621.
Botwinick, Aryeh. *Participation and Tacit Knowledge in Plato, Machiavelli and Hobbes*. Lanham: University Press of America, 1986.
Botwinick, Aryeh. *Skepticism*, Philadelphia: Temple University Press, 2010.
Botwinick, Aryeh. *Skepticism and Political Participation*. Philadelphia: Temple University Press, 1990.
Botwinick, Aryeh. *Skepticism, Belief, and the Modern: Maimonides to Nietzsche*. Ithaca: Cornell University Press, 1997.
Boyarin, Daniel. *Socrates and the Fat Rabbis*. Chicago: University of Chicago Press, 2009.
Boyle, Robert. *New Experiments and Observations Touching Cold*. London: Crook, 1665.
Bradshaw, Graham. *Shakespeare's Scepticism*. Brighton: Harvester Press, 1987.
Braude, William G. "Maimonides' Attitude towards Midrash." In *Studies in Jewish Bibliography, History and Literature in Honor of I. E. Kiev*, edited by Charles Berlin, 75–82. New York: Ktav, 1971.
Brittain, Charles. *Philo of Larissa: The Last of the Academic Sceptics*. Oxford: Oxford University Press, 2001.
Browne, Thomas. *Religio Medici: Hydriotaphia: And, the Garden of Cyrus*. Edited by Rossel H. Robbins. Oxford: Oxford University, 1972.
Bruno, Giordano. *Degli eroici furore*. Paris: Baio, 1585.
Brusoni, Girolamo, and Giovanni Francesco Loredan. *Le glorie de gli incogniti o vero gli huomini illustri dell'Accademia de' Signori incogniti di Venetia*. Venice: Francesco Valuasense, 1647.
Buber, Solomon, ed. *Aggadah Bereshit*, 2 vol. Vilnius: Romm, 1925.
Buber, Solomon, ed. *Midrash Tanḥuma*, 2 vol. Vilnius: Romm, 1885.
Buddeus, Johann Franz. *Io. Francisci Bvddei [...] introductio ad historiam philosophiae Ebraeorum. accedit dissertatio de haeresi Valentiniana. Editio nova eaque multis accessionibus auctior*. Halae Saxonum: Orphanotropheum, 1720.
Buitenwerf, Rieuwerd. *Book III of the Sibylline Oracles and Its Social Setting*, Leiden: Brill, 2003.
Burckhardt, Jacob. *Die Kultur der Renaissance in Italien*. Leipzig: Seemann, 1869.
Burckhardt, Jacob. *Die Kultur der Renaissance in Italien, mit einem Geleitwort von Wilhelm von Bode*. Berlin: Knaur Nachf, 1928.
Burckhardt, Jacob. *The Civilization of the Renaissance in Italy*. Vienna: Phaidon Press, 1937.
Burnett, Stephen G. "Distorted Mirrors: Antonius Margaritha, Johann Buxtorf and Christian Ethnographies of the Jews." *Sixteenth Century Journal* 25 (1994): 275–287.
Burrows, Mark S. "Christianity in the Roman Forum." *Vigiliae Christianae* 42 (1987): 209–235.
Busi, Giulio, Simonetta M. Bondoni, and Saverio Campanini, eds. *The Great Parchment: Flavius Mithridates' Latin Translation, the Hebrew Text, and an English Version, The Kabbalistic Library of Giovanni Pico della Mirandola*. Turin: Nino Aragno Editore, 2004.

Calabi, Francesca, ed. *Lettera di Aristea*. Milan: Biblioteca universale Rizzoli, 1995.
Campanini, Saverio. "Talmud, Philosophy, Kabbalah: A Passage from Pico della Mirandola's Apologia and its sources." In *The Words of a Wise Man's Mouth Are Gracious. Festschrift for Günter Stemberger on the Occasion of His 65th Birthday*, edited by Mauro Perani, 429–447. Berlin: De Gruyter, 2005.
Campanini, Saverio. "Un intellettuale ebreo del Rinascimento: 'Ovadyah Sforno a Bologna e i suoi rapporti con i Christiani." In *Verso l'epilogo di una convivenza: Gli ebrei a Bologna nel XVI secolol*, edited by Maria G. Muzzarelli, 98–128. Florence: La Giuntina, 1996.
Carandini, Silvia. *Teatro e spettacolo nel Seicento*. Rome: Laterza, 1990.
Carben, Victor von. *Hierinne wirt gelesen, wie Her Victor von Carben, Welicher eyn Rabi der Iude gewest ist zu Christlichem glawb komen*. Cologne: 1510.
Carben, Victor von. *Opus Aureum ac Novum* in *quo Omnes Judæorum Errores Manifestantur*. Cologne: 1509.
Carminati, Clizia. "Loredan Giovan Francesco." In *Dizionario Biografico degli Italiani*, 761–770. Rome: Istituto dell'Enciclopedia Italiana, 2005.
Carlebach, Elisheva. *Divided Souls: Converts from Judaism in Germany 1500–1750*. New Haven: Yale University Press, 2001.
Casas, Bartolomé de las. *Historia de las Indias, edición preparada por la Fundación 'Instituto Bartolomé de las Casas,' de los Dominicos de Andalucía*. Madrid: Alianza Editorial, 1994.
Casoni, Giovanni. *La Peste Di Venezia Nel 1630 Origine Della Erezione Del Tempio A S. Maria Della Salute*. Venice: Tipografia Di Alvisopoli, 1830.
Casselli, Stephen B. "The Threefold Division of the Law in the Thought of Aquinas." *Westminster Theological Journal* 61 (1999): 175–207.
Cassirer, Ernst. *Das Erkenntnisproblem in der Philosophie und Wissenschaft der neueren Zeit*, vol. 1. Darmstadt: Wissenschaftliche Buchgesellschaft, 1994.
Cassirer, Ernst. *Individuum und Kosmos in der Philosophie der Renaissance*. Darmstadt: Wissenschaftliche Buchgesellschaft, 1987.
Castagnoli, Luca. *Ancient Self-Refutation. The Logic and History of the Self-Refutation Argument from Democritus to Augustine*. New York: Cambridge University Press, 2010.
Catapano, Giovanni. "Quale scetticismo viene criticato da Agostino nel Contra Academicos?" *Quaestio* 6 (2006): 1–13.
Cave, Roy C., and Herbert H. Coulson. *A Source Book for Medieval Economic History*. Milwaukee: The Bruce Publishing Company, 1936.
Cave, Terence. *Pré-histoires: textes troublés au seuil de la modernité*. Genève: Droz, 1999.
Cebà, Ansaldo. *La Regina Ether*. Genua: Pavoni, 1615.
Celada Ballanti, Roberto. *La parabola dei tre anelli: Migrazioni e metamorfosi di un racconto tra Oriente e Occidente*. Rome: Edizioni di Storia e Letteratura, 2017.
Cervarius Tubero, Ludovicus. *De Turcarum origine, moribus et rebus gestis*. Florentiae: apud Antonium Patauinium, 1590.
Champier, Symphorian. *Symphoriani Champerii De Quadruplici vita. Theologia Asclepii, Hermetis Trismegisti discipuli cum commentariis eiusdem domini Simphoriani, Lugdunum*. 1507.
Champier, Symphorian. *Symphoriani Champerii De Triplici disciplina, cuius partes sunt: philosophia naturalis, medicina, theologia, moralis philosophia integrantes quadruvium ugdunum*. 1507.
Charles, Robert H. *The Apocrypha and Pseudepigrapha of the Old Testament*. Oxford: The Clarendon Press, 1913.
Charles, Sébastien. Smith Plínio J. *Scepticism in the Eighteenth Century: Enlightenment, Lumières, Aufklärung*, Dordrecht: Springer 2013.
Chayes, Evelien. "Language of Words and Images in the Rime degli Academici occulti 1568: Reflections of the Pre-Conceptual?" In *Language and Cultural Change. Aspects of the Study*

and Use of Language in the Later Middle Ages and the Renaissance, edited by Lodi Nauta, 149–171. Leuven: Peeters, 2006.

Chazan, Robert. Barcelona and Beyond. The Disputation of 1263 and its Aftermath. Berkeley: University of California Press, 1992.

Chazan, Robert. "From Friar Paul to Friar Raymond: The Development of Innovative Missionizing Argumentation." Harvard Theological Review 76 (1983): 289–306.

Chazan, Robert. "In the Wake of the Disputation." Hebrew Union College Annual LXI (1990): 185–201.

Chazan, Robert. Medieval Stereotypes and Modern Antisemitism. Berkeley: University of California Press, 1997.

Chazan, Robert. "The Barcelona 'Disputation' of 1263: Christian Missionizing and Jewish Response." Speculum 52 (1977): 824–842.

Chazan, Robert. "The Condemnation of the Talmud Reconsidered (1239–1248)." Proceedings of the American Academy of Jewish Research 45 (1988): 11–30.

Chisholm, Roderick M. "Sextus Empiricus and Modern Empiricism." Philosophy of Science 8, no. 3 (1941): 371–384.

Cicero. On Academic Scepticism, trans. Charles Brittain. Indianapolis: Hackett, 2006.

Cohen, Hermann. Die Religion der Vernunft aus den Quellen des Judentums. Leipzig: Fock, 1919.

Cohen, Hermann. Jüdische Schriften, vol. 2. Edited by Bruno Strauss. Berlin: Schwetschke, 1924.

Cohen, Jeremy. The Friars and the Jews. The Evolution of Medieval Anti-Judaism. Ithaca: Cornell University Press, 1982.

Cohen, Mark R. "Leone da Modena's Riti: A Seventeenth Century Plea for Social Toleration of Jews." In Essential Papers on Jewish Culture in Renaissance and Baroque Italy, edited by David B. Ruderman, 429–473. New York: New York University Press, 1992.

Cohen, Mark R. The Autobiography of a Seventeenth-Century Venetian Rabbi. Princeton: Princeton University Press, 1988.

Cohen, Martin A. "Reflections on the Text and Context of the Disputation of Barcelona." Hebrew Union College Annual 35 (1964): 157–192.

Colson, Francis H. Philo: In Ten Volumes, Cambridge: Harvard University Press, 1932.

Copenhaver, Brian P. "Lefèvre d'Etaples, Symphorien Champier, and the Secret Names of God." Journal of the Warburg and Courtauld Studies 40 (1977): 189–211.

Copenhaver, Brian P. "Pico risorto: cabbalà e dignità dell'uomo nell'Italia post-unitaria." In Giovanni Pico e la Cabbalà, edited by Fabrizio Lelli, 1–18. Florence: Olschki, 2014.

Corbin, Henry. History of Islamic Philosophy. London: Kegan Paul International, 1993.

Corpus Christianorum Series Latina. Turnhout: Brepols, 1954.

Cozzi, Gaetano. Giustizia "contaminata," Vicende giudiziarie di nobili ed ebrei nella Venezia del Seicento. Venice: Marsilio, 1996.

Cozzi, Gaetano. "Società veneziana, società ebraica." In Gli Ebrei e Venezia secoli XIV–XVIII, 333–374. Milan: Edizioni di Comunità, 1987.

Creizenach, Michael. "Grundlehren des israelitischen Glaubens." In Wissenschaftliche Zeitschrift für jüdische Theologie. Frankfurt: J. D. Gauerländer, 1835.

Crenshaw, James L. "The Birth of Skepticism in Ancient Israel." In The Divine Helmsman. Studies on God's Control of Human Events. Presented to Lou H. Silberman, edited by James L. Crenshaw and Samuel Sandmel, 1–19. New York: KTAV Publishing House 1980.

Crocco, Antonio. Gioacchino da Fiore. Naples: Empireo, 1960.

Cusa, Nicholas of. Opera Omnia. Edited by Ernst Hoffmann and Raymond Klibansky. Hamburg: Felix Meiner, 1932–2006.

d'Ancona, Alessandro. Origini del teatro italiano: Libri tre con due appendici sulla rappresentazione drammatica del contado toscano e sul teatro mantovano nel sec. XVI. Turin: Ermanno Loescher, 1891.

Dahlstrom, Daniel. "Moses Mendelssohn." *Stanford Enyclopedia of Philosophy.* https://plato.stanford.edu/archives/fall2008/entries/mendelssohn/ (accessed 3 May, 2018).
Dannenbaum, Rolf. "Joachim Lange als Wortführer des Halleschen Pietismus gegen die Orthodoxie." PhD dissertation, Göttingen, 1951.
Davis, Joseph. "The Ten Questions of Eliezer Eilburg and the Problem of Jewish unbelief in the 16th Century." *The Jewish Quarterly Review* XCI, no. 3–4 (2001): 293–336.
Denis, Albert-Marie. *Fragmenta pseudepigraphorum quae supersunt graeca.* Leiden: Brill, 1970.
Deonna, Waldemar. *Le Symbolisme de l'oeil, Ecole francaise d'Athènes.* Paris: Broccard, 1965.
de' Rossi, Azaria. *Sefer Me'or 'Enayim.* Edited by David Cassel. Vilnus: Romm, 1884–1886.
de' Rossi, Azaria. *The Light of the Eyes.* Edited by Joanna Weinberg. New Haven: Yale University Press, 2001.
Deutsch, Yaacov. *Judaism in Christian Eyes: Ethnographic Descriptions of Jews and Judaism in Early Modern Europe.* Oxford: Oxford University Press, 2012.
Deutsch, Yaacov. "Representations of Jews in Sixteenth-Century Germany." In *Jews, Judaism, and the Reformation,* edited by Dean P. Bell and Stephen G. Burnett, 347–356. Leiden: Brill, 2016.
Dickason, Olive Patricia. *The Myth of the Savage, and the Beginnings of French Colonialism in the Americas.* Edmonton: University of Alberta Press, 1997.
Diemling, Maria. "Anthonius Margaritha on 'Whole Jewish Faith': A Sixteenth-Century Convert from Judaism and his Depiction of the Jewish Religion." In *Jews, Judaism, and the Reformation,* edited by Dean P. Bell and Stephen G. Burnett, 303–333. Leiden: Brill, 2016.
Diemling, Maria."'Christliche Ethnographien' über Juden und Judentum in der Frühen Neuzeit." PhD dissertation, University of Vienna, 1999.
Dodds, Eric R. "Numenius and Ammonius." In *Les Sources de Plotin.* Geneva: Foundation Hardt, Vandœuvres, 1960.
Doggett, Rachel. *New World of Wonders. European Images of the Americas 1492–1700.* Seattle: University of Washington Press, 1992.
Dörrie, Henrich. *Der hellenistische Rahmen des kaiserzeitlichen Platonismus.* Stuttgart-Bad Cannstatt: Fromann, 1990.
Doyle, John P. *Francisco de Vitoria OP. On Homicide, and Commentary on Thomas Aquinas: Summa Theologiae 2a 2a–e 64.* Milwaukee: Marquette University Press, 1997.
Edwards, Mark J. "'Atticizing Moses?' Numenius, the Fathers and the Jews." *Vigiliae Christianae* 44 (1990): 64–75.
Efros, Israel. "Saadia's Theory of Knowledge." *The Jewish Quarterly Review* 33, no. 2 (1942): 133–170.
Ehrlich, Dror. "A Reassessment of Natural Law in Rabbi Joseph Albo's 'Book of Principles.'" *Hebraic Political Studies* 1 (2006): 413–439.
Eisenstadt, Shmuel N. *Jewish Civilization: The Jewish Historical Experience in a Comparative Perspective.* New York: State University of New York Press, 1992.
Eisenstein-Barzilay, Isaac. *Between Reason and Faith. Anti-Rationalism in Italian Jewish Thought 1250–1650.* Paris: The Hague, 1967.
Eisenstein-Barzilay, Isaac. "John Toland's Borrowings from Simone Luzzatto: Luzzatto's Discourse on the Jews of Venice (1638) the Major Source of Toland's Writing on the Naturalization of the Jews in Great Britain and Ireland (1714)." *Jewish Social Studies* 31 (1969): 75–81.
Eisenstein-Barzilay, Isaac. "The Ideology of the Berlin Haskalah." *Proceedings of the American Academy of Jewish Research* 25 (1956): 1–37.
Ellis, A. I. "Some Notes." The Classical Review 23 (1909): 246–247.
Elukin, Jonathan M. "Maimonides and the Rise and Fall of the Sabians: Explaining Mosaic Laws and the Limits of Scholarship." *Journal of the History of Ideas* 63 (2002): 619–637.

Engel, Michael. *Elijah Del Medigo and Paduan Aristotelianism investigating the Human Intellect.* London: Bloomsbury, 2017.

Ess, Josef van. *Die Er- kenntnislehre des ʿAḍudaddīn Al-Īcī. Übersetzung und Kommentar des ersten Buches seiner Mawāqif.* Frankfort: Universität Frankfurt Habilitations-Schrift, 1964.

Ess, Josef van. "Skepticism in Islamic Religious Thought." *Al-Abhath* 21 (1968): 1–17.

Euler, Walter A. "Una religio in rituum varietate. Der Beitrag des Nikolaus von Kues zur Theologie der Religionen." *Jahrbuch für Religionswissenschaft und Theologie der Religionen* 3 (1995): 67–82.

Euler, Walter A. "Una religio in rituum varietate. Die Begegnung der Religionen bei Nikolaus von Kues." *Zeitschrift für Missionswissenschaft und Religionswissenschaft* 85 (2001): 243–257.

Eusebius. *Evangelicae Praeparationes. Liber* XVI, vol. 3. Edited by Edwin Hamilton Gifford Oxford: Ex typographia academica, 1903.

Evans, Craig A. *Matthew. New Cambridge Bible Commentary.* Cambridge: Cambridge University Press, 2012.

Faino, Marco. "A Ghost Academy between Venice and Brescia: Philosophical Scepticism and Religious Heterodoxy in the Accademia dei Dubbiosi." In *The Italian Academies 1525–1700. Networks of Culture, Innovation and Dissent,* edited by Jane E. Everson, Denis V. Reidy, and Lisa Sampson, 102–115. Cambridge: Legenda, 2016.

Faino, Marco. "Fortunato Martinengo, Girolamo Ruscelli e l'Accademia dei Dubbiosi tra Brescia e Venezia." In *Girolamo Ruscelli dall'accademia alla corte alla tipografia. Atti del Convegno internazionale di studi, Viterbo, 6–8 Ottobre 2011,* vol. 2, edited by Paolo Marini and Paolo Procaccioli, 455–519. Manziana: Vecchiarelli, 2012.

Falaquera, Shem-Tov ibn. *Iggeret ha-wikuaḥ: Dialog zwischen einem Orthodoxen und einem Philosophen.* Edited by Adolf Jellinek. Vienna: 1875; reprinted in Jerusalem: n.p., 1970.

Falaquera, Shem-Tov ibn. *Sefer ha-Maʻa lot.* Edited by Ludwig Venetianer. Berlin: Verlag von S. Calvary &. Co., 1894.

Faleck, David. "Immovable Giants? Rabbinical Approaches to Science and Jewish Law," *Kedma* 3 (2007): n.p.

Faur, José. "Sanchez' critique of Authoritas: Converso Skepticism and the Emergence of Radical Hermeneutics." In *The Return to Scripture in Judaism and Christianity. Essays in Postcritical Scriptural Interpretation,* edited by Peter Ochs, 256–277. New York: Paulist Press, 1993.

Feest, Christian. "Mexico and South America in the European Wunderkammer." In *The Origins of Museums: The Cabinet of Curiosities in Sixteenth- and Seventeenth-Century Europe,* edited by Oliver Impey and Arthur Macgregor, 237–244. Oxford: Clarendon Press, 1985.

Feil, Ernst. *Religio. Forschungen zur Kirchen- und Dogmengeschichte.* Göttingen: Vandenhoeck & Ruprecht, 1986–2012.

Feingold, Aaron J. "The Marriage of Science and Ethics: Three Jewish Physicians of the Renaissance," In *Jews and Medicine. Religion, Culture, Science: based on the exhibit at the Beth Hatefusoth,* edited by Natalia Berger, 89–111. Philadelphia: The Jewish Publication Society, 1995.

Feingold, Aaron J. *Three Jewish Physicians of the Renaissance: The Marriage of Science and Ethics.* New York: American Friends of Beth Hatefutsoth, 1994.

Feldman, Louis H. "The Orthodoxy of the Jews in Hellenistic Egypt." *Jewish Social Studies* 22 (1969): 215–237.

Feldman, Louis H. "Torah and Secular Culture: Challenge and Response in the Hellenistic Period." *Tradition* 23 (1988): 26–40.

Feldman, Louis H., and John R. Levison. *Josephus' Contra Apionem. Studies in its Character and Context with a Latin Concordance to the Portion Missing in Greek.* Leiden: Brill, 1996.

Fensham, Charles. "Malediction and Benediction an Ancient Near Eastern Vassal-Treatises and the Old Testament." *Zeitschrift für die Alttestamentliche Wissen-schaft* 74 (1962): 1–9.

Finkel, Ephraim. "R. Obadja Sforno als Exeget." Inaugurialdissertation, Universität Tübingen. Breslau: Theodor Schatzky, 1896.

Firenzuola, Agnolo. "*Opere.*" Edited by Delmo Maestri. Turin: UTET, 1977.

Firmin-Didot, Ambroise. *Alde Manuce et l'hellénisme à Venise.* Paris, A. Firmin-Didot, 1875.

Fishbane, Michael. *Biblical Interpretation in Ancient Israel.* Oxford: Clarendon, 1985.

Floridi, Luciano. "The Diffusion of Sextus Empiricus's Works in the Renaissance." *Journal of the History of Ideas* 56, no. 1 (1995): 63–85.

Floridi, Luciano. "The Rediscovery and Posthumous Influence of Scepticism." In *The Cambridge Companion to Ancient Scepticism,* edited by Richard Bett, 264–287. Cambridge: Cambridge University Press, 2010.

Foresti Jacob Filippo *De plurimis claris scelectisque mulieribus opus prope divinum novissime congestum.* Ferrara: 1497.

Fortis, Umberto. *La "Bella Ebrea." Sara Copio Sullam poetessa nel ghetto di Venezia del '600.* Turin: Silvio Zamorani Editore, 2003.

Fraenkel-Goldschmidt, Hava. "On the Perephery of Jewish Society: Jewish Converts to Christianity in Germany During the Reformation" [Hebrew]. In *Culture and Society in Medieval Jewry,* edited by Menahem Ben Sasson, Robert Bonfil, and Joseph R. Hacker, 623–654. Jerusalem: Magnes, 1989.

Franck, Daniel H. and Oliver Leaman, eds. *The Cambridge Companion to Medieval Jewish Philosophy.* Cambridge: Cambridge University Press, 2003.

Françon, Marcel. "Petrarch, Disciple of Heraclitus." *Speculum* 11 (1936): 265–271.

Frede, Michael. "The Sceptic's Beliefs." In *The Original Sceptics: A Controversy,* edited by Myles Burnyeat and Michael Frede, 1–24. Indianapolis: Hackett, 1997.

Freedman, Lawrence. *Strategy. A History.* Oxford: Oxford University Press, 2013.

Freudenthal, Gideon. "Maimon's Subversion of Kant's Critique of Pure Reason. There are No Synthetic a priori Judgements in Physics." Berlin: Max-Planck-Institut für Wissenschaftsgeschichte, 2001.

Freudenthal, Gideon. *Salomon Maimon. Rational Dogmatist, Empirical Skeptic. Critical Assessments.* Dordrecht: Kluwer, 2003.

Freudenthal, Gideon. "The Remedy to Linguistic Skepticism. Judaism as a Language of Action." *Naharaim—Zeitschrift für deutsch-jüdische Literatur und Kulturgeschichte* 4, no. 1 (2011): 67–76.

Friedenwald, Harry. "Two Jewish Physicians of the Sixteenth Century. The Doctor, Amatus Lusitanus, the Patient, Azariah dei Rossi." In *The Jews and Medicine. Essays,* vol. 2, edited by Harry Friedenwald, 391–403. Baltimore: Johns Hopkins Press, 1944.

Frischmuth, Johann, and Johannes L. Will. *De Loco Deut. XVII. v. 8. seqq. et quæ ad illum moveri solet, quæstione: An Ebræi Statuant, Idem Simul Posse Esse Et Non Esse, Exercitium Academicum, Præside Dn. M. Johanne Frischmuth, Lingg. Sacr. Prof. Publ. Famigeratissimo, & Facultatis Philosophicæ h.t. Decano spectabili, Publicè ventilandum exhibet M. Johannes Leonartus Will.* Jena: Krebsius, 1658.

Fritsch, Matthias J. "Ansätze zur Religionsphilosophie bei Sigismund von Storchenau." *Verbum. Analecta Neolatina* 1 (1999): 105–116.

Front, Dov. "The Expurgation of the Books of Amatus Lusitanus: Censorship and the Bibliography of the Individual Book." *Book Collector* 47 (1998): 520–536.

Fuhrer, Therese. "Das Kriterium der Wahrheit in Augustins Contra Academicos." *Vigiliae Christianae* 46 (1992): 257–275.

Gabriel, Markus. "The Art of Skepticism and the Skepticism of Art." *Philosophy Today* 53/1 (2009): 58–69.

Gagarin, Michael and David Cohen, eds. *The Cambridge Companion to Ancient Greek Law.* Cambridge: Cambridge University Press, 2005.

Gager, John G. *Moses in Greco-Roman Paganism*. Nashville: Abingdon Press, 1972.

Galatino, Pietro. *Opus toti christianae Reipublicae maxime utile, de arcanis catholicae ueritatis, contra obstinatissimam Iudaeoru[m] nostrae tempestatis p[er]fidiam: ex Talmud, aliisq[ue] hebraicis libris nuper excerptum: & quadruplici linguarum genere eleganter congestum*. Suncinus: Orthonae Maris, 1518.

Galilei, Galileo. *Dialogo sopra i due massimi sistemi del mondo*. Edited by Fabio Attori. Milan: Sansoni, 2001.

Galilei, Galileo. *The Assayer*. In *Discoveries and Opinions of Galileo*, edited by Stillman Drake. 229–280. New York: Anchor, 1957.

Galilei, Galileo. *Sidereus Nuncius, or, The Sidereal Messenger*. Chicago: The University of Chicago Press, 1989.

Galilei, Galileo. *Two New Sciences*, trans. Stillman Drake. Madison: University of Wisconsin Press, 1974.

Gaon, Sa'adia. *The Book of Doctrines and Beliefs*. Indianapolis: Hackett, 2002.

Garin, Eugenio. *Filosofi italiani del Quattrocento*. Florence: Istituto nazionale di studi sul Rinascimento, 1942.

Garin, Eugenio. *L'uomo del Rinascimento*. Bari: Laterza, 1988.

Geiger, Abraham. *Judaism and Islam. A Prize Essay. Translated from the German by a Member of the Ladies League in Aid of the Delhi Mission*. Madras: M.D.C.S.P.C.K. Press, 1898.

Geiger, Abraham. *Wissenschaftliche Zeitschrift für Jüdische Theologie* 1. Frankfurt: J. D. Gauerländer, 1835.

Geiger, Abraham. *Wissenschaftliche Zeitschrift für Jüdische Theologie* 2. Frankfurt: J. D. Gauerländer, 1836.

Geiger, Ludwig. "Zunz im Verkehr mit Behörden und Hochgestellten." *Monatsschrift für Geschichte und Wissenschaft des Judentums* 60 (1916): 258–259.

Genebrard, Gilbert. *R. Iosephi, R. Davidis Kimhi, et alius cuiusdam Hebraei anonymi argumenta, quibus nonnulos fidei Christianae articulos oppugnant*. Parisiis: Martinus Iuvenis, 1566.

Genot-Bismuth, Jacqueline. "Philosophie et Poétique dans l'oeuvre d'Immanuel de Rom." PhD dissertation, University of Paris, 1977.

Georgijevic, Bartholomaeus. *De Turcarum moribus epitome*. Lyon: J. Tornaesius, 1555.

Gerber, Christine. *Ein Bild des Judentums für Nichtjuden von Flavius Josephus: Untersuchungen zu seiner Schrift "Contra Apionem."* Leiden: Brill, 1997.

Giannantoni, Gabriele. "Les perspectives de la recherche sur Socrate." In *Socrate et les Socratiques*, edited by Gilbert Romeyer Dherbey and Jean-Baptiste Gourinat 1–19. Paris: Vrin, 2001.

Gilbert, Felix. *Machiavelli and Guicciardini*. Princeton: Princeton University Press, 1965.

Gilson, Etienne. "Les 'Philosophantes.'" *Archives d'Histoire doctrinale et littéraire du Moyen Âge* 19 (1952): 135–140.

Gimma, Giacinto. *Idea della storia della Italia letterata*. Napoli: Felice Mosca, 1723.

Giuliani, Giambattista. *Le opere latine: Reintegrate nel testo con nuovi commenti*. Florence: Le Monnier, 1882.

Glatzer, Nahum N. *Leopold Zunz: Jude, Deutscher, Europäer, ein jüdisches Gelehrtenschicksal des 19. Jahrhunderts in Briefen an Freunde, herausgegeben und eingeleitet von Nahum N. Glatzer*. Tübingen: Mohr, 1964.

Goethe, Johann W. *Gedenkausgabe der Werke, Briefe und Gespräche* Vol. 2. Edited by Ernst Beutler. Zurich: Artemis, 1948–1954.

Goldenberg, Robert. "The Jewish Sabbath in the Roman World up to the Time of Constantine the Great." In *Aufstieg und Niedergang der römischen Welt*, vol. 2, 19.1, edited by Wolfgang Haase, 414–447. Berlin: De Gruyter, 1979.

Goldstein, Jonathan. *Jewish Acceptance and Rejection of Hellenism*. In *Jewish and Christian Self-Definition*, vol. 2, *Aspects of Judaism in the Graeco-Roman Period*, edited by Ed Parish Sanders, 64–87. Philadelphia: Fortress Press, 1981.

Goody, Jack. "A Kernel of Doubt." *The Journal of the Royal Anthropological Institute* 2, no. 4 (1996): 667–681.

Gossett, Thomas F. *Race. The History of an Idea in America*. Oxford: Oxford University Press, 1997.

Gottlieb, Paula. "Aristotle on Non-Contradiction." *The Stanford Encyclopedia of Philosophy*. https://plato.stanford.edu/archives/sum2015/entries/aristotle-noncontradiction (accessed 3 May, 2018).

Graetz, Heinrich. *Geschichte der Juden von den ältesten Zeiten bis auf die Gegenwart*, vol. 10. Leipzig: Leiner, 1897.

Grafton, Anthony. "On the Scholarship of Politian and its Context." *Journal of the Warburg and Courtauld Institutes* 40 (1977): 150–188.

Grafton, Anthony. "Juden und Griechen bei Friedrich August Wolf." In *Friedrich August Wolf: Studien, Dokumente, Bibliographie*, edited by Reinhard Markner and Giuseppe Veltri, , 9–31. Stuttgart: Franz Steiner, 1999.

Grant, Robert. "The Cohortatio of Pseudo-Justin." *Harvard Theological Review* 51 (1958): 128–134.

Greenstein, Jack M. "On Alberto's 'Sign': Vision and Composition in Quattrocento Painting." *The Art Bulletin* 79 (1997): 669–698.

Gregory, Richard. *Mirrors in Mind*. London: Penguin, 1997.

Grigore, Mihai-D. "Humanism and its Humanitas: The Transition from Humanitas Christiana to Humanitas Politica in the Political Writings of Erasmus." In *Humanity. A History of European Concepts in Practice from the Sixteenth Century to the Present*, edited by Fabian Klose and Mirjam Thulin, 73–90. Göttingen: Vandenhoeck & Ruprecht, 2016.

Gross, Benno. "Faith and Trust In the Maharal's Teaching" [Hebrew]. *Sinai* 101 (1988): 138–147.

Guidi, Angela. *Amour et Sagesse. Les Dialogues d'amour de Juda Abravanel dans la tradition salomonienne*. Leiden, Boston: Brill, 2011.

Guidi, Angela. "Sapienza salomonica e sapere pagano: tradizione ebraica e neoplatonismo nei Dialoghi d'amore di Leone Ebreo." *Revue des Études Juives* 165 (2006): 313–330.

Gunneweg, Antonius H. J. "Zur Interpretation der Bücher Ezra-Nehemia. Zugleich ein Beitrag zur Methode der Exegese." *Vetus Testamentum Supplement* 32 (1981): 146–161.

Gurwirth, Eliezer. "Amatus Lusitanus and the Location of Sixteenth Century Cultures." In *Cultural Intermediaries. Jewish Intellectual in Early Modern Italy*, edited by David Ruderman and Giuseppe Veltri, 216–238. Philadelphia: Pennsylvania University Press, 2004.

Guttmann, Jacob. *Die Scholastik des dreizehnten Jahrhunderts in ihren Beziehungen zum Judenthum und zur jüdischen Literatur*. Breslau: Marcus, 1902.

Guttmann, Julius. "Der Gottesbegriff Kants," PhD dissertation, University of Breslau, 1903.

Guttmann, Julius. *Kants Gottesbegriff in seiner positiven Entwicklung*. Berlin: Reuther & Reichard, 1906.

Guttmann, Julius. *Philosophie des Judentums*. Munich: Reinhardt-Verlag, 1933.

Gutwirth, Eliezer. "The 'Stranger's Wisdom: Translation and Otherness in Fifteenth-Century Iberia." *Portuguese Studies* 13 (1997): 130–142.

Guyer, Forster E. "The Dwarf on the Giant's Shoulders." *Modern Language Notes* 45 (1930): 398–402.

Hadas, Moses, ed. *Aristeas to Philocrates*. New York: Harper and Brothers, 1962.

Hadas, Moses. *Hellenistic Culture. Fusion and Diffusion*. New York: Columbia University Press, 1959.

Hadas, Moses. "Plato in Hellenistic Fusion." *Journal of the History of Ideas* 19 (1958): 3–13.

Halevi, Judah. *Sefer ha-Kuzari: Das Buch Kusari des Jehuda ha-Levi*. Edited by David Cassel. Leipzig: F. Voigt, 1869.

Halevi, Leor. "The Theologian's Doubts: Natural Philosophy and the Skeptical Games of Ghazali." *Journal of the History of Ideas* 63, no. 1 (2002): 19–39.

Hanke, Lewis. *The Spanish Struggle for Justice in the Conquest of America.* Philadelphia: University of Pennsylvania Press, 1949.

Harding, Brian. "Skepticism, Illumination and Christianity in Augustine's Contra Academicos." *Augustinian Studies* 34, no. 2 (2003): 197–212.

Harding, Sandra G. *Is Science Multicultural? Postcolonialisms, Feminisms, and Epistemologies.* Bloomington: Indiana University Press, 1998.

Harnack, Adolf von. *Sokrates und die alte Kirche. Rede beim Antritt des Rectorates gehalten in der Aula der Königlichen Friedrich-Wilhelms-Universität am 15. October 1900.* Berlin: Buchdruckerei von Gustav Schade, 1900.

Harrison, Peter. "Fixing the Meaning of Scripture: The Renaissance Bible and the Origins of Modernity Bond University." *Faculty of Humanities and Social Sciences Humanities & Social Sciences papers.* Bond University Year 2002. http://epublications.bond.edu.au/cgi/view content.cgi?article=1065&context=hss_pubs (accessed 3 May, 2018).

Hartwig, Dick. *Im vollen Licht der Geschichte: die Wissenschaft des Judentums und die Anfänge der kritischen Koranforschung.* Würzburg: Ergon-Verlag 2008.

Harvey, Steven. *Falaquera's* Epistle of the Debate: *An Introduction to Jewish Philosophy.* Cambridge: Harvard University Press, 1987.

Harvey, Steven. "Shem Tov Ibn Falaquera." *The Stanford Encyclopedia of Philosophy* http://plato.stanford.edu/archives/fall2014/entries/falaquera/ (accessed 3 May, 2018).

Harvey, Warren Zev. "Maimonides' first Commandment, Physics, and Doubt." In *Hazon Nahum, Studies in Jewish Law, Thought, and History Presented to Dr. Norman Lamm*, edited by Yaakov Elman and Jeffrey S. Gurock, 149–162. New York: Michael Scharf Publication Trust of the Yeshiva University Press; Hoboken: Ktav, 1997.

Hasse, Dag N. "Aufstieg und Niedergang des Averroismus in der Renaissance: Niccolò Tignosi, Agostino Nifo, Francesco Vimercato." In *"Herbst des Mittelalters?" Fragen zur Bewertung des 14. und 15. Jahrhundert*, edited by Jan A. Aertsen and Martin Pickavé, 447–473. Berlin: De Gruyter, 2004.

Hasse, Dag N. "The Social Conditions of the Arabic-(Hebrew-)Latin Translation Movements in Medieval Spain and in the Renaissance." In *Wissen über Grenzen: arabisches Wissen und lateinisches Mittelalter*, edited by Andreas Speer and Lydia Wegener, 68–87. Berlin: De Gruyter, 2006.

Haase, Karl A. von. *Libri symbolici Ecclesiae Evangelicae, sive Concordia.* Leipzig: Johannes Suehring, 1827.

Hayoun, Maurice R., Ora Limor, and Guy G. Stroumsa, eds. *Contra Iudaeos. Ancient and Medieval Polemics between Christians and Jews.* Tübingen: Mohr, 1995.

Heck, Paul L. "*Skepticism in Classical Islam: Moments of Confusion. Culture and Civilization in the Middle East.*" Hoboken: Taylor and Francis, 2013.

Hegel, Georg W. F. *Werke in zwanzig Bänden 16. Vorlesungen über die Philosophie der Religion*, 3rd ed. Frankfurt: Suhrkamp, 1995.

Helm, Jürgen. "Die Galenrezeption in Philipp Melanchthons *De Anima* (1540/1552)." *Medizinhistorisches Journal* 31 (1996): 298–321.

Hengel, Martin. *Aspekte der Hellenisierung des Judentums in vorchristlicher Zeit.* Stuttgart: KBW Verlag, 1976.

Hengel, Martin. *Judentum und Hellenismus.* Tübingen: Mohr, 1969.

Henkes, Harold E., and Claudia Zrenner. *History of Ophthalmology: Sub auspiciis Academiae Ophthalmologicae Internationalis.* Dodrecht: Kluwer Academic Publishers, 1990.

Heschel, Abraham J. "The Quest for Certainty in Saadia's Philosophy." *The Jewish Quarterly Review* 33, no. 3 (1943): 265–313.

Hezser, Cathrine. *Jewish Literacy in Roman Palestine*. Tübingen: Mohr, 2001.
Hillier, Chad. "The Rationalism of Jewish Law in Moses Mendelssohn." *Canadian Theological Review* 2, no. 1 (2013): 87–106.
Hirschberg, Julius. *The History of Ophthalmology*, vol. 1. Bonn: Wayenborgh, 1985.
Hodgson, Peter C. *Hegel: Lectures on the Philosophy of Religion. The Lectures of 1827*. Oxford: Oxford University Press, 2006.
Holladay, Carl R. *Fragments from Hellenistic Jewish Authors*. Chico: Society of Biblical Literature, 1983.
Homolka, Walter. "Jüdische Theologie. Zur Institutionalisierung eines Faches im Haus der Wissenschaft." *Theologische Literaturzeitung* 140 (2015): 164–180.
Hood, John Y.B. *Aquinas and the Jews*. Philadelphia: University of Pennsylvania Press, 1995.
Hoover, Jon. *Ibn Taymiyya's Theodicy of Perpetual Optimism*, Leiden, Boston: Brill, 2007, 129–130.
Horace, *Odes and Epodes*. Edited and translated by Paul Shorey and Gordon J. Laing. Chicago: Benj. H. Sanborn & Co., 1919.
Horovitz, Saul. *Der Einfluss der griechischen Skepsis auf die Entwicklung der Philosophie bei den Arabern*. Breslau: Th. Schatzky, 1915.
Horovitz, Saul. *Über den Einfluss der griechischen Philosophie auf die Entwicklung des Kalam*. Breslau: Th. Schatzky, 1909.
Horovitz, Saul. "Über die Bekanntschaft Saadias mit der griechischen Skepsis." In *Judaica. Festschrift zu Hermann Cohens siebzigstem Geburtstage*, edited by Ismar Elbogen, Benzion Kellermann, and Eugen Mittwoch, 235–252. Berlin: Bruno Cassirer, 1912.
Howland, Jacob. *Plato and the Talmud*, Cambridge: Cambridge University Press, 2011.
Hudry, Jean-Louis. "Aristotle on Non-Contradiction: Philosophers vs. Non-Philosophers." *Journal of Ancient Philosophy* 7 (2013): 51–74.
Hume, David. *Essays, Moral and Political*. Edinburgh: R. Fleming & A. Alison, 1741.
Hume, David. *The Philosophical Works: Essays, Moral, Political and Literary*. Edited by Thomas H. Green and Thomas H. Grose. London: Longmans, Green and Company, 1882.
Huser, Konrad. *Tractatus de imposturis et ceremoniis Iudaeorum nostri temporis, antea quidem ab authore Germanice editus: nunc vero in gratiam Reipublicae Christianae Latine redditus a Conrado Husero Tigurino*. Basileae: Per Petrum Pernam, 1575.
Iamblicus, *Les Mystères d'Egypte*, trans. Édouard Des Places. Paris: Les Belles Lettres, 1989.
Idel, Moshe. "Jewish Kabbalah and Platonism in the Middle Ages and Renaissance." In *Neoplatonism and Jewish Thought*, edited by Lenn E. Goodman, 319–351. Albany: State University of New York Press, 1992.
Idel, Moshe. *Kabbalah: New Perspectives*. New Haven: Yale University Press, 1988.
Idel, Moshe. "The Journey to Paradise: The Jewish Transformation of a Greek Mythological Motif." *Jerusalem Studies in Jewish Folklore* 2 (1982): 7–17.
Impey, Oliver, and Arthur MacGregor. *The Origins of Museums: The Cabinet of Curiosities in Sixteenth- and Seventeenth-Century Europe*. Oxford: Clarendon Press, 1985.
Irwin, Jay "Hamilton, Music, and the Doctrine of Adiaphora in Orthodox Lutheran Theology." *Sixteenth Century Journal* 14 (1983): 157–172.
Israel, Jonathan I. *Radical Enlightenment. Philosophy and the Making of Modernity 1650–1750*. Oxford: Oxford University Press, 2001.
Israel, Menasseh ben. *To His Highnesse the Lord Protector of the Common-Wealth of England, Scotland, and Ireland. The Humble Addresses of Menasseh Ben Israel, a Divine, and Doctor of Dhysick, in Behalfe of the Jewish Nation*. 1655. Ann Arbor, Michigan: University of Michigan, Digital Library Production Service, 2011.
Israel, Menasseh ben. *Vindiciae Judaeorum, Or a Letter in Answer to Certain Questions Propounded by a Noble and Learned Gentleman, Touching the Reproaches Cast on the Nation*

of the Jevves: Wherein all Objections are Candidly, and Yet Fully Cleared. Amsterdam: R. D., 1656.

Ivry, Alfred. "Remnants of Jewish Averroism in the Renaissance." In *Jewish Thought in the Sixteenth Century*, edited by Bernard D. Cooperman, 243–265. Cambridge: Harvard University Press, 1983.

Jacobs, Louis. *Teyku: The Unsolved Problem in the Babylonian Talmud*. London: Cornwall Books, 1981.

Jaquette, James L. *Discerning what Counts: The Function of the Adiaphora Topos in Paul's Letters*. Atlanta: Scholars' Press, 1995.

Jeauneau, Edouard. "'Nani gigantum humeris insidentes': Essai d'interpretation de Bernard de Chartres." *Vivarium* 5 (1967): 79–99.

Johansen, T.K. *Aristotle on the Sense-Organs*. Cambridge: Cambridge University Press, 1998.

Kasher, Asa, and Shlomo Biderman. "Why was Baruch de Spinoza excommunicated?" In *Sceptics, Millenarians and Jews*, edited by David S. Katz and Jonathan I. Israel 98–141. Brill: Leiden, 1990.

Katz, Jacob. *Exclusiveness and Tolerance. Studies in Jewish-Gentile Relations in Medieval and Modern Times*. Oxford: Oxford University Press, 1961.

Kimmelman, Burt. "Visionary Science in Purgatorio XVII and Paradiso XXX." *Comitatus* 26 (1995): 53–74.

King, Peter. "Mediaeval Thought-Experiments: The Metamethodology of Mediaeval Science." In *Thought-Experiments in Science and Philosophy*, edited by Gerry Massey and Tamara Horowitz, 43–64. New York: Rowman & Littlefield, 1991.

Kirn, Hans-Martin. *Das Bild vom Juden im Deutschland des frühen 16. Jahrhunderts dargestellt an den Schriften Johannes Pfefferkorns*. Tübingen: Mohr, 1989.

Klee, Heinrich. *Katholische Dogmatik*, 2nd ed. Mainz: Kirchheim Schott & Thielmann, 1840.

Klein, Peter. "Skepticism." *The Stanford Encyclopedia of Philosophy*. http://plato.stanford.edu/archives/sum2013/entries/skepticism/ (accessed 3 May, 2018).

Klein, Wolf P. *Am Anfang war das Wort*. Berlin: Akademie-Verlag, 1992.

Kleinecke, Ulrike. "Theologien des Judentums im jüdisch-amerikanischen Diskurs des 20. Jahrhunderts." *Pardes* 20 (2014): 117–131.

Kleingünther, Adolf. *Protos heuretes: Untersuchungen zur Geschichte einer Fragestellung*. Leipzig: Dieterich, 1933.

Knoch-Mund, Gaby. *Disputationsliteratur als Instrument antijüdischer Polemik. Leben und Werk des Marcus Lombardus, eines Grenzgängers zwischen Judentum und Christentum im Zeitalter des deutschen Humanismus*. Basel: Tübingen, 1997.

Koch, Klaus. "Ezra and the Origins of Judaism." *Journal of Semitic Studies* 19 (1974): 173–197.

Kohlers, Kaufmann. *Grundriss einer systematischen Theologie des Judentums auf geschichtlicher Grundlage*. Leipzig: Fock, 1910.

Koltun-Fromm, Ken. "Abraham Geiger—kulturwissenschaftliche Reflexionen." In *Jüdische Existenz in der Moderne: Abraham Geiger und die Wissenschaft des Judentums*, edited by Christian Wiese, Walter Homolka, and Thomas Brechenmacher. Berlin: De Gryuter, 2013.

Köpf, Ulrich. *Die Anfänge der theologischen Wissenschaftstheorie im 13. Jahrhundert*. Tübingen: Mohr, 1974.

Korvela, Paul-Erik. "The Machiavellian Reformation. An Essay in Political Theory." PhD dissertation, University of Jyvaskyla, 2016.

Kouremenos, Theokritos. *The Proportions in Aristotle's Phys. 7.5*. Stuttgart: Steiner, 2002.

Kraus, Hans-Joachim. *Die biblische Theologie. Ihre Geschichte und Problematik*. Neukirchen-Vluyn: Neukirchener Verlag, 1970.

Kristeller, Paul O. "Der Gelehrte und sein Publikum im Mittelalter und in der Renaissance." In *Medium aevum vivum. Festschrift Walter Bulst*, edited by Hans Robert Jauss and Dieter Schaller, 212–230. Heidelberg: Winter, 1960.

Krochmalnik, Daniel. "Das Zeremoniell als Zeichensprache. Moses Mendelssohns Apologie des Judentums im Rahmen der aufklärerischen Semitiok." In *Fremde Vernunft. Zeichen und Interpretation*, edited by Joseph Simon and Werner Stegmaier, 238–235. Frankfurt: Suhrkamp, 1998.

Krochmalnik, Daniel. "Mendelssohns Begriff 'Zeremonialgesetz' und der europäische Antizeremonialismus. Eine begriffsgeschichtliche Untersuchung." In *Recht und Sprache in der deutschen Aufklärung*, edited by Ulrich Kronauer and Jörn Garber, 128–160. Tübingen: Niemeyer, 2001.

Krümmel, Achim. "Mosellanus, Petrus (Peter Schade)." *Biographisch-bibliographisches Kirchenlexikon* VI (1993): 169–171.

Kudla, Hubertus. *Lexikon der lateinischen Zitate. 3500 Originale mit Übersetzungen und Belegstellen*. Munich: Beck, 2007.

Kuhn, Thomas. *The Structure of Scientific Revolutions*. Chicago: University of Chicago Press, 1962.

Laertius, Diogenes. *Lives of Eminent Philosophers*. Edited by Robert D. Hicks. Cambridge: Harvard University Press, 1979.

Laertius, Diogenes. *Vitae Philosophorum*. Stutgardiae: Teubner 1999.

Lagerlund, Henrik. *Rethinking the History of Skepticism. The Missing Medieval Background*. Leiden: Brill, 2010.

Lammenranta, Markus. "The Role of Disagreement in Pyrrhonian and Cartesian Skepticism." In *Disagreement and Skepticism*, edited by Diego E. Machuca, 46–65. New York: Routledge, 2012.

Lanata, Giuliana. *Medicina magica e religione popolare in Grecia fino all'età di Ippocrate*. Rome: Edizioni dell'Ateneo, 1967.

Lange, Joachim. *Joachimi Langii medicina mentis qua praepostera philosophandi methodo ostensa ac rejecta, secundum sanioris philosophiae principia, aegrae mentis sanatio, ac sanatae usus in veri rectique investigatione ac communicatione, in gratiam traditur forum, qui per solidam eruditionem ad veram sapientiam contendant*. Berlin: Orphanotropium, 1704.

Lange, Nicholas de. *Origen and the Jews. Studies in Jewish-Christian Relations in Third-Century Palestine*. Cambridge: Cambridge University Press, 1976.

Lauresen, John C. "Escepticismo y política." *Revista de Estudios Políticos* 144 (2009): 123–142.

Laursen, John C. "Pedro De Valencia's Academica and Scepticism in Late Renaissance Spain." In *Renaissance Scepticisms*, edited by Nicola Panichi and José Maia Neto, 111–124. Dordrecht: Springer, 2009.

Lauresen, John C. "Skepticism, Unconvincing Anti-Skepticism, and Politics." In *Scepticisme et modernité*, edited by Marc André Bernier and Sébastien Charles, 167–188. Saint-Étienne: Publications de l'Université de Saint-Étienne, 2005.

Laursen, John C. *The Politics of Skepticism in the Ancients, Montaigne, Hume, and Kant*. Leiden: Brill, 1992.

Lebram, Jürgen C.H. "Der Idealstaat der Juden." In *Josephus-Studien. Untersuchungen zu Josephus, dem antiken Judentum und dem Neuen Testament, Otto Michel zum 70. Geburtstag gewidmet*, edited by Otto Betz, Klaus Haacker, and Martin Hengel, 233–253. Göttingen: Vandenhoeck & Ruprecht, 1974.

Lee, Bernon. "Towards a Rhetoric of Contradiction in the Book of Ecclesiastes." PhD dissertation, University of Calgary, 1997.

Leftley, Sharon A. "A Millenarian Thought in Renaissance Rome with Special Reference to Pietro Galatino (c. 1464–c. 1540) and Egidio da Viterbo (c. 1469–1532)." PhD dissertation, University of Bristol, 1995.

Leibowitz, Yeshyahi and Michael Shashar. *Gespräche über Gott und die Welt*. Frankfurt: Insel Verlag, 1990.
Leon, Judah Messer. *Sefer Nofet Ṣufim. The Book of the Honeycomb's Flow. A Critical Edition and Translation*. Edited and translated by Isaac Rabinowitz. Ithaca: Cornell University Press, 1983.
Leone, Ebreo. "A Complaint Against Time" [Hebrew]. In *Anthologie der Hebräischen Dichtung in Italien*, edited by Jefim Schirmann, 217–222. Berlin: Schocken Verlag, 1934.
Leone, Ebreo. *Dialoghi d'amore: Hebräische Gedichte*. Edited by Carl Gebhardt. Heidelberg: Curis Societatis Spinozanae, 1929.
Leone, Ebreo. *Leone Ebreo (Giuda Abarbanel). Dialoghi d'Amore*. Edited by Santino Caramella. Bari: Laterza, 1929.
Leone, Modena. *Historia de riti Hebraici. Vita, & osseruanza de gl'Hebrei di questi tempi*. Venice: Benedetto Miloco, 1678.
Leone, Modena. *Les Juifs présentés aux chrétiens. Cérémonies et coutumes qui s'observent aujourd'hui parmi le Juifs*. Edited by Jacques Le Bruns and Guy G. Stroumsa. Paris: Les Belles Lettres, 1998.
Leone, Modena. *Magen wa-Ḥerev (Clipeus et gladius: tractatus antichristianus)*. Edited by Shlomo Simonsohn. Jerusalem: Mekitse Nirdamim, 1960.
Levenstein, Anna. "Songs for the First Hebrew Play *Tsahut bedihuta dekidushin* by Leone de' Sommy (1527–1592)." PhD dissertation, Case Western Reserve University, 2006.
Lévy, Carlo. "La conversion du scepticisme chez Philon d'Alexandrie," In *Philo of Alexandria and Post-Aristotelian Philosophy*, edited by Francesca Alesse, 103–120. Boston: Brill, 2008.
Lévy, Carlo. "Le concept de doxa des Stoïciens à Philon d'Alexandrie. Essai d'étude diachronique." In *Passions and perceptions. Studies in Hellenistic Philosophy of Mind. Proceedings of the Fifth Symposium Hellenisticum*, edited by Jacques Brunschwig and Martha C. Nussbaum, 250–284. Cambridge: Cambridge University Press, 1993.
Lévy, Carlo. "Le scepticisme de Philon d'Alexandrie, une influence de la Nouvelle Académie?" In *Hellenica et Judaica. Hommage à V. Nikiprowetzky*, edited by André Caquot, Mireille Hadas-Lebel, and Jean Riaud, 29–41. Leuven: Brill, 1986.
Lewis, John. *Adrien Turnebe (1512–1565): A Humanist Observed*. Geneva: Droz, 1998.
Lewy, Hans. "Aristotle and the Jewish Sage According to Clearchus of Soli." *The Harvard Theological Review* 31 (1938): 205–235.
Lieberman, Saul. *Hellenism in Jewish Palestine. Studies in the Literary Transmission, Beliefs and Manners of Palestine in the I Century BCE–IV Century CE*. New York: Jewish Theological Seminary of America, 1962.
Lightfoot, Jane L. *The Sibylline Oracles. With Introduction, Translation, and Commentary on the First and Second Books*. Oxford: Oxford University Press, 2007.
Lindberg, David C. *Sciences in the Middle Ages*. Chicago: University of Chicago Press, 1978.
Lindberg, David C. *Theories of Vision from al-Kindi to Kepler*. Chicago: University of Chicago Press, 1967.
Linzey, Andrew, and Dan Cohn-Sherbok. *After Noah: Animals and the Liberation of Theology*. London: Mowbray, 1997.
Lipmann Muhlhausen, Yom-Tov. *Liber Nizachon Rabbi Lipmanni*. Edited by Theodor Hackspan. Nuremberg: Wolfgang Endter,1644.
Löbl, Rudolf. *Technē: Untersuchungen zur Bedeutung dieses Worts in der Zeit von Homer bis Aristoteles*. Würzburg: Königshausen & Neumann, 2003.
Lom, Petr. *Scepticism, Eclecticism and the Enlightenment. An Inquiry into the Political Philosophy of Denis Diderot*. San Domenico: European University Institute, 1998.
Lucian of Samosata. *The Works of Lucian of Samosata*, trans. Henry W. Fowler and Francis G. Fowler. Oxford: The Clarendon Press, 1905.

Lufft, Johann K. *De Rebecca Polona Eruditarum in Gente Judaica Foeminarum Rariori Exemplo Preside Gustavo Georgio Zeltner.* Altdorfii: Iod. Guil. Kohlemsii, Universit. Typogr., 1719.

Luther, Martin. *Commentary on the Epistle to the Galatians (1535).* Grand Rapids: Zondervan Publishing House, 1949.

Luther, Martin. *D. Martin Luthers Werke. Krirtische Gesamtausgabe.* Weimar: Hermann Böhlaus Nachfolger 1914.

Luzzatto, Samuel David. *Autobiografia di S.D. Luzzatto preceduta da alcune notizie storico-letterarie sulla famiglia Luzzato a datare dal secolo decimosesto.* Padova: Crescini, 1878.

Luzzatto, Samuel David. "Selbstbiographie des S.D. Luzzatto nebst vorangeschickten historischen und literarischen Nachrichten über die Familie Luzzatto seit dem XVI. Jahrhundert; aus dem noch ungedruckten italienischen Originale übersetzt." *Kalender und Jahrbuch der Israeliten* 6 (1847–1848): 95–116.

Luzzatto, Simone. *Discorso circa il stato de gl'Hebrei et in particolare dimoranti nell'inclita Città di Venetia.* Venice: Calleoni, 1638.

Luzzatto, Simone. *Scritti politici e filosofici di un ebreo scettico nella Venezia del Seicento.* Introduced, commented, and edited by Giuseppe Veltri in cooperation with Anna Lissa and Paola Ferruta. Milan: Bompiani, 2013.

Luzzatto, Simone. *Socrates or on the Human Knowledge (1651). A Sceptical Essay by Simone Luzzatto Venetian Jew, Bilingual Edition.* Edited, translated, and commented by Giuseppe Veltri and Michela Torbidoni. Berlin: De Gruyter, 2018.

Luzzatto, Simone. *Socrate, ovvero, Dell'humano sapere: esercitio seriogiocoso.* Venice: Appresso il Tomasini, 1651.

Maccoby, Haim. *Judaism on Trial. Jewish-Christian Disputations in the Middle Age. With a New Introduction.* Oxford: The Littman Library of Jewish Civilization, 1993.

Machuca, Diego E. "Bibliography on Skepticism." https://sites.google.com/site/diegomachuca/blbliography-on-skepticism (accessed 3 May, 2018).

Magid, Shaul. "The Intolerance of Tolerance: Makhloket and Redemption in Early Hasidism." *Jewish Studies Quarterly* 8 (2001): 326–368.

Mahoney, Michael S. "Sketching Science in the Seventeenth Century." http://www.princeton.edu/~hos/mike/articles/whysketch/whysketch.html (accessed 3 May, 2018).

Maier, Johann. *Jüdische Auseinandersetzung mit dem Christentum in der Antike.* Darmstadt: Buchgesellschaft, 1982.

Maier, Johann. *Kriegsrecht und Friedensordnung in jüdischer Tradition.* Stuttgart: Kohlhammer, 2000.

Maimonides, Moses. *The Guide for the Perplexed*, trans. Moritz Friedländer. London: George Routledge & Sons 1904.

Malfitano, Stefano. "The Ways of Skepticism: An Arabic-Islamic Detour? Notes on Ibn Taymiyyah's Rebuttal of Logic and the Developments of Ancient Skepsis." https://www.academia.edu/1564827/The_Ways_of_Skepticism_an_Arabic-Islamic_Detour (accessed 3 May, 2018).

Marchesi, Angelo. *Una religio in rituum varietate. Il pensiero ecumenico di Nicola Cusano.* Parma: Zara 1986.

Marchetti, Valerio. "The Lutheran Discovery of Karaite Hermeneutics." In *Una manna buona per Mantova. Man tov le-Man Tovah. Studi in onore di Vittore Colorni per il suo 92° compleanno*, edited by Mauro Perani, 433–459. Florence: Olshki, 2004.

Marcus, Ralf. *Philo Quaestions and Answers in Genesis.* Cambridge: Harvard University Press, 1953, reprinted 1993.

Marenbon, John *Later Medieval Philosophy (1150–1350). An Introduction.* London: Routledge, 1991.

Margaritha, Antonius. *Der ganz Jüdisch Glaub mit sampt ainer gründtlichen und warhafften anzaygunge aller Satzungen, Ceremonien, Gebetten, haymliche und offentliche Gebreuch.* Augsburg: Heinrich Steyner, 1530.

Marti, Mario. *Poeti giocosi del tempo di Dante.* Milan: Rizzoli, 1956.

Mason, Steve. "Of Audience and Meaning. Reading Josephus' *Bellum Judaicum* in the Context of a Flavian Audience." In *Josephus and Jewish History in Flavian Rome and Beyond*, edited by Joseph Sievers and Gaia Lembi, 71–100. Leiden: Brill, 2005.

Mattioli, Pietro Andrea. *Commentarii, in libros sex Pedacii Dioscoridis Anazarbei, de medica materia. Adiectis quam plurimis plantarum & animalium imaginibus eodem authore.* Venice: Vincenzo Valgrisi, 1554.

Mattioli, Pietro Andrea. *Compendium de plantis omnibus, una cum earum iconibus, de quibus scripsit suis in commentariis in Dioscoridem editis: in eorum studiosorum commodum, atque usum; qui plantis conquirendis, ac indagandis student.* Venice: Valgrisius, 1571.

Mattioli, Pietro Andrea. *Di Pedacio Dioscoride Anazarbeo libri cinque della historia, & materia medicinale tradotti in lingua uolgare italiana da M. Pietro Andrea Matthiolo Sanese medico. Con amplissimi discorsi, et comenti, et dottissime annotationi, et censure del medesimo interprete. Da cui potra ciascuno facilmente acquistare la uera cognitione de' semplici non solamente scritti da Dioscoride, ma da altri antichi, & moderni scrittori, & massimamente da Galeno. La cui dottrina intorno à tale facultà tutta fedelmente interpretata si ritroua posta ne' proprij luoghi. Con due tauole alphabetiche da poter con prestezza ritrouare cio che ui si cerca [...].* Venice: Niccolo Bascarini, 1544.

Mattioli, Pietro Andrea. *Il Dioscoride con gli suoi discorsi aggiuntovi il sesto libro degli antidoti contra tutti i veleni.* Venice, 1544.

Maurus, Hrabanus. "De Universo Libri Viginti Duo, Praefatio Ad Ludovicum Regem Invictissimum Franciae." *Patrologia Latina* vol. 111. Paris: J. P. Migne, 1852.

Mayer, Thomas F. "Starkey and Melanchthon on Adiaphora: A Critique of W. Gordon Zeeveld." *Sixteenth Century Journal* 11, no. 1 (1980): 3–49.

Maylender, Michele. *Storia delle accademie d'Italia.* Bologna-Rocca S. Casciano: L. Cappelli Edit. Tip., 1926–1927.

McClelland, John S. *A History of Western Political Thought.* London: Routledge, 1998.

McGinn, Bernard. *L'abate calabrese. Gioacchino da Fiore nella storia del pensiero occidentale.* Genoa: Marietti, 1990.

McKeon, Michael. "Literary and Graphic Images of Intimacy in Seventeenth and Eighteenth-Century England." *Interfaces* 28 (2008): 95–114.

Meineck, Friedrich. *Machiavellism; The Doctrine of Raison D'Etat and its Place in Modern History.* New Haven: Yale University Press, 1957.

Melamed, Abraham. *Dat: From Law to Religion: A History of a Formative Term* [Hebrew]. Tel Aviv: ha-Kibbutz ha-me'uḥad, 2014.

Melamed, Abraham. *On the Shoulders of Giants: A History of the Debate between Moderns and Ancients in Medieval and Early Modern Jewish Thought* [Hebrew]. Ramat Gan: Bar-Ilan University, 2003.

Melamed, Abraham. *The Myth of the Jewish Origins of Science and Philosophy.* Jerusalem: Magnes Press, 2010.

Mendelssohn, Moses. *Gesammelte Schriften. Jubiläumsausgabe*, vol. 8. Edited by Alexander Altmann. Stuttgart: Frommann-Holzboog, 1983.

Mendelssohn, Moses. *Menasseh ben Israel's Mission to Oliver Cromwell: Being a Reprint of the Pamphlets Published by Menasseh ben Israel to Promote the Re-Admission of the Jews to England, 1649–1656.* Edited by Lucien Wolf. London: Macmillan & Co., 1901.

Merino, Luis D. "Philological Aspects in the Research of the Targums." In *Panel Session: Bible Studies and the Ancient Near East. Proceedings of the Ninth World Congress of Jewish*

Studies (Jerusalem: 1985), edited by Moshe H. Goshen-Gottstein, 87–97. Jerusalem: World Union of Jewish Studies, 1988.

Merton, Robert K. *On the Shoulders of Giants. A Shandean Postscript*. New York: Free Press, 1965.

Meyer, Kirstine. "Zur Geschichte der Antiperistatis." *Annalen der Naturphilosophie* 3 (1903): 413–441.

Meyer, Thomas. "Die Einheit von Wissenschaft und Religion. Die Herausforderung einer Wissenschaft des Judentums." In *Die "Wissenschaft des Judentums." Eine Bestandaufnahme*, edited by Thomeas Meyer and Andreas Kilcher, 159–175. Wilhelm Fink: Paderborn, 2015.

Meyer, Thomas. *Vom Ende der Emanzipation. Jüdische Philosophie und Theologie nach 1933*. Göttingen: Vandenhoeck & Ruprecht, 2008.

Migas, Avraham ibn. *Kevod Elohim: Constantinople 1585*. Jerusalem: Jewish National & University Library Press, 1976

Mihai, Mihaela. "Apology." *Internet Encyclopedia of Philosophy*. http://www.iep.utm.edu/apology/ (accessed 3 May, 2018).

Mihaly, Eugene. "A Rabbinic Defence of the Election of Israel." *Hebrew Union College Annual* 35 (1964): 103–143.

Miletto, Gianfranco. "Die Bibel als Handbuch der Kriegskunst nach der Interpretation Abraham ben David Portaleones." In *An der Schwelle zur Moderne. Juden in der Renaissance*, edited by Giuseppe Veltri and Annette Winkelmann, 78–89. Leiden: Brill, 2003.

Miletto, Gianfranco. "The Teaching Program of David ben Abraham and His Son Abraham Provenzali in the Historical-Cultural Context of the Time." In *Cultural Intermediaries. Jewish Intellectual in Early Modern Italy*, edited by David Ruderman and Giuseppe Veltri, 127–148. Philadelphia: Pennsylvania University Press, 2004.

Miletto, Gianfranco. "Tradition and Innovation: Religion, Science and Jewish Culture between the 16th and 17th Centuries." In *Religious Confession and the Sciences in the 16th Century*, edited by Jürgen Helm and Annette Winkelmann, 99–107. Leiden: Brill, 2001.

Mirandola, Giovanni Pico della. *Opera Omnia*. Basilae: per Henricum Petri, 1557.

Mirandola, Giovanni Pico della. *Oratio De hominis dignitate*. Edited by Eugenio Garin. Pordenone: Edizioni Studio Tesi, 1994.

Mirandola, Giovanni Pico della. *Über die Würde des Menschen*. Edited by August Buck. Hamburg: Meiner, 1990.

Momigliano, Arnaldo. *Alien Wisdom. The Limits of Hellenization*. Cambridge: Cambridge University Press, 1975.

Momigliano, Arnaldo. "Ancient History and the Antiquarian." *Journal of the Warburg and Courtauld Institutes* 13 (1950): 67–106.

Momigliano, Arnaldo. *Pagine ebraiche*. Turin: Einaudi, 1987.

Montaigne, Michel de. *Apologie de Raymond Sebond*. Edited by Paul Mathias. Paris: Flammarion, 1999.

Moore, George F. *Judaism in the First Centuries of the Christian Era*, vol. 2. Cambridge: Harvard University Press, 1927.

Moreau, Pierre-François. *Le stoïcisme au XVIe et au XVIIe siècle: le retour des philosophies antiques à l'Age classique*. Paris: A. Michel, 1999.

Morosini, Giulio. *Via della fede mostrata a'gli Ebrei, da Giulio Morosini Venetiano Scrittor della Biblioteca Vaticana nella Lingua Ebraica, e Lettor della medesima nel Collegio de Propaganda Fide*. Rome: Stamparia della Sacra. Cong. de Prop. Fide, 1683.

Moscato, Judah. *Judah Moscato's Sermons*. Edited by Gianfranco Miletto and Giuseppe Veltri. Boston, Leiden: Brill, 2011.

Mosellanus, Petrus. *Oratio de variarum linguarum cognitione paranda Petro Mosellano Protogense authore Lipsiae in magna eruditorum corona pronunciata*. Lipsiae: Valentini Schumann, 1518.

Mulsow, Martin. "Eclecticism or Skepticism? A Problem of the Early Enlightenment." *Journal of the History of Ideas* 58, no. 3 (1997): 465–477.

Mulsow, Martin. "Skepticism and Conversion to Judaism. The Case of Aaron d'Antan." In *Secret Conversions to Judaism in Early Modern Europe*, edited by Martin Mulsow and Richard H. Popkin, 123–182. Leiden: Brill, 2004.

Murray, Oswyne. "Peri basileias: Studies in the Justification of Monarchic Power in the Hellenistic World." PhD dissertation, Oxford University, 1971.

Myers, David N. "Philosophy and Kabbalah in Wissenschaft des Judentums: Rethinking the Narrative of Neglect." *Studia Judaica (Cluj-Napoca)* 16 (2008): 56–71.

Najm, Sami M. "The Place and Function of Doubt in the Philosophies of Descartes and Al-Ghazali." *Philosophy East and West* 16, no. 3–4 (1966): 133–141.

Nauta, Lodi. "Lorenzo Valla and Quattrocento Scepticism." *Vivarium. A Journal for Medieval and Early-Modern Philosophy and Intellectual Life* 44, no. 2–3 (2006): 375–395.

Nelson, Robert. *Visuality Before and Beyond the Renaissance. Seeing as Others Saw*. Cambridge: Cambridge University Press, 2000.

Newman, Louis I. *Jewish Influence on Christian Reform Movements*. New York: Columbia University Press, 1925.

Niewöhner, Friedrich. "Anmerkungen zum Begriff eines 'jüdischen Humanismus.'" *Archiv. für Begriffsgeschichte* 34 (1991): 214–224.

Nikiprowetzky, Valentin. *La troisième Sibylle*. Paris: Mouton, 1970.

Nodet, Étienne. "Editing the Bible: Alexandria or Babylon?" In *The Bible and Hellenism. Greek Influence on Jewish and Early Christian Literature*, edited by Thomas L. Thompson and Philippe Wajdenbaum, 36–55. Durham: Acumen, 2014.

Norton, David F. *David Hume: Common-Sense Moralist, Sceptical Metaphysician*. Princeton: Princeton University Press, 1982.

Obiwulu, Aloysius. *Tractatus de Legibus in 13th Century Scholasticism. A Critical Study of Law in Summa Frati Alexandri, Albertus Magnus and Thomas Aquinas*. Münster: Lit Verlag 2003.

Orlinsky, Harry M. "The Septuagint as Holy Writ and the Philosophy of the Translators." *Hebrew Union College Annual* 46 (1975): 110–113.

Osten-Sacken, Peter von der. *Martin Luther und die Juden: Neu untersucht anhand von Anton Margarithas "Der gantz Jüdisch glaub" (1530/31)*. Stuttgart: Kohlhammer, 2002.

O'Sullivan, Daniel E. "Changing the Rules in and of Medieval Chess Allegories." In *Chess in the Middle Ages and Early Modern Age: A Fundamental Thought Paradigm of the Premodern World*, edited by Daniel E. O'Sullivan, 199–220. Berlin: De Gruyter, 2012.

Otto, Johann Karl Theodor von. *Corpus apologetarum christianorum saeculi secundi. Iustini Philosophi et Martyris Opera quae feruntur omnia*. Ienae: G. Fischer, 1879.

Overduin, Floris. *Nicander of Colophon's Theriaca. A Literary Commentary*. Leiden: Brill, 2015.

Overfield, James H. "A New Look at the Reuchlin Affair." *Studies in Medieval and Renaissance History VIII* (1971): 165–207.

Oviedo, Gonzalo Fernandez de. *Historia general y natural de las Indias, Islas y Tierra Firme del Mar Oceano*, 4 vols., edited by José Amador de los Rios. Madrid: Real Academia de la Historia, 1851–1855.

Paganino, Santes. *Biblia: habes in hoc libro prudens lector utriusq[ue] instrumenti nouam tranlatione[m] / aeditam à reverendo sacre theologiae doctore Sancte Pagnino Luc[c]esi concionatore apostolico praedicatorii ordinis, necnon & librum de interpretamentis hebraicorum, arameorum graecorumq[ue] nominum, sacris in litteris contentorum in quo iuxta idioma cuiusq[ue] linguae, propriae ponuntur interpretationes, deriuationes ac eor[um] compositiones adamussim disquiruntur, citantur loca, & codicu[m] latinoru[m] varietates subnotantur, & corrupta ac deprauata propriae restitu[n]tur scriptioni, acce[n]tus quo[que] per impositas virgulas com[m]ostrant singulis in capitibus quot sint versus in hebraeis*

codicibus, rece[n]setur ut pauca sint desideranda: [...] abbreuiationem librorum historialium veteris instrumenti & erratorum castigationes quas. Lyon: Antoine du Ry, Francesco Turchi, Dominique Bertus, and Jacques Giunta, 1528.
Panichi, Nicola. "Montaigne and Plutarch: A Scepticism that Conquers the Mind." In *Renaissance Scepticisms*, edited by Nicola Panichi and José Maia Neto, 183–212. Dordrecht: Springer, 2009.
Panizza, Letizia A. "Lorenzo Valla's *De Vero Falsoque Bono:* Lactantius and Oratorical Scepticism." *Journal of the Warburg and Courtauld Institutes* 41 (1978): 76–107.
Parente, Fausto. "La Chiesa e il 'Talmud.' L'atteggiamento della Chiesa e del mondo cristiano nei confronti del 'Talmud' e degli altri scritti rabbinici, con particolare riguardo all'Italia tra XV e XVI secolo." In *Storia d'Italia. Gli Ebrei in Italia*, vol. 11: *Dall'alto Medievo all'età dei ghetti*, edited by Corrado Vivanti, 521–564.Turin: Einaudi, 1996.
Parry, Richard. *"Episteme* and *Techne." The Stanford Encyclopedia of Philosophy.* https://plato.stanford.edu/archives/fall2014/entries/episteme-techne/ (accessed 3 May, 2018).
Pasnau, Robert. *After Certainty: A History of Our Epistemic Ideals and Illusions.* Oxford: Oxford University Press, 2017.
Pastine, Dino. *Juan Caramuel: Probabilismo ed Enciclopedia*. Florence: Nuova Italia, 1975.
Patrologiae Cursus Completus, Series Latina. Parigi: 1844–1865.
Patsch, Hermann. "Friedrich August Wolf und Friedrich Ast: Die Hermeneutik als Appendix der Philologie." In *Klassiker der Hermeneutik*, edited by Ulrich Nassen, 76–107. Paderborn: Schöningh, 1982.
Pédech, Paul. *Historiens, compagnons d'Alexandre: Callisthène, Onésicrite, Nèarque, Ptolémée, Aristobule*. Paris: Les Belles Lettres, 2011.
Pederson, Jill. "The Academia Leonardi Vinci: Visualizing Dialectic in Renaissance Milan 1480–1499." PhD dissertation, The Johns Hopkins University, 2008.
Pépin, Jean. "Le 'challenge' Homère-Moïse aux premiers siècles Chrétiens." *Revue des sciences religieuses* 29 (1955): 105–122.
Perani, Mauro. *Gugliemo Raimondo Moncada alias Flavio Mitridate. Un ebreo converso siciliano. Atti del Convegno Internazionale Caltabellotta (Agrigento) 23–24 Ottobre 2004*. Palermo: Officina di Studi Medievali, 2008.
Perin, Casey. *The Demands of Reason: An Essay on Pyrrhonian Scepticism*. Oxford: Oxford University Press, 2010.
Perrone, Benigno F. "Pietro Colonna Galatino, O.F.M. (1465–1540). In un testo di Mariologia francescana condotto con metodo 'filologico-cabbalistico.'" *Studi Francescani LXXX* (1983): 127–164.
Perush 'al ha-Torah. Venice: Bomberg, 1523.
Philo of Alexandria. *Quod omnis probus liber sit*. Edited by Madeleine Petit. Paris: Édition du Cerf, 1974.
Pfefferkorn, Johann. *Ich heyß ain büchlein der iuden peicht. In allen orten vindt man mich leicht. Vil newer meren seind mir wol bekannt*. Cologne: Johannes Landen, 1508.
Pfefferkorn, Johann. *Libellus de judaica confessione sive sabbato afflictionis*. Nuremberg: Jo. Weyssenburger, 1508.
Pickavé, Martin. "Henry of Ghent and John Duns Scotus on Skepticism and the Possibility of Naturally Acquired Knowledge." In *Rethinking the History of Skepticism: The Missing Medieval Background,* edited by Henrik Lagerlund, 61–96. Leiden: Brill, 2010.
Pintard, René. *Le libertinage érudit dans la première moitié du xviie siècle*. Genève: Editions Slatkine, 2000.
Pissavin, Paolo. *Le Meraviglie del Probabile: Juan Caramuel, 1606–1682*, Vigevano: Assessorato alla Cultura, 1990.

Plater, Felix. *De corporibus humani structura et usu.* Basel: 1583.
Plato. *Plato in Twelve Volumes*, trans. Harold N. Fowler. Cambridge: Harvard University Press, 1925.
Plassmann, Thomas. "Pietro Colonna Galatino." *Catholic Encyclopaedia*. New York: Robert Appleton Company, 1909. http://www.newadvent.org/cathen/06340a.htm (accessed 3 May, 2018).
Plaut, W. Gunther. *The Rise of Reform Judaism.* New York: World Union for Progressive Judaism, 1963.
Plutarch. *Plutarch's Morals. Translated from the Greek by Several Hands. Corrected and Revised by William W. Goodwin, with an Introduction by Ralph W. Emerson.* 5 vol. Boston: Little, Brown, and Co., 1878.
Po-chia Hsia, Ronnie. "Christian Ethnographies of Jews in Early Modern Germany." In *The Expulsion of the Jews: 1492 and After*, edited by Raymond B. Waddington and Arthur H. Williamson, 223–235. New York: Garland, 1994.
Polito, Roberto *The Skeptical Road: Aenesidemus' Appropriation of Heraclitus.* Leiden: Brill, 2004.
Popkin, Richard H. "Amos Funkenstein and the History of Scepticism." In *Thinking Impossibilities. The Intellectual Legacy of Amos Funkenstein*, edited by Robert S. Westman and David Biale, 281–288. Toronto: Toronto University Press, 2008.
Popkin, Richard H. "Prophecy and Skepticism in the Sixteenth and Seventeenth Century," *British Journal for the History of Philosophy* 4, no. 1 (1996): 1–20.
Popkin, Richard H. *Scepticism in the Enlightenment.* Dordrecht: Kluwer 1997.
Popkin Richard H. *The History of Scepticism from Erasmus to Spinoza.* Berkeley: University of California Press, 1979.
Popkin, Richard H. *The History of Scepticism from Savonarola to Bayle.* Oxford: Oxford University Press 2003.
Popkin, Richard H. "The Sceptical Crisis and the Rise of Modern Philosophy: I–III." *Review of Metaphysics* 7, no. 1 (1953): 132–151.
Popkin, Richard H., and Arie Johan fun Vanderjagt. *Scepticism and Irreligion in the Seventeenth and Eighteenth Centuries.* Leiden: Brill, 1993.
Popkin, Richard H., and Charles B. Schmitt. *Scepticism from the Renaissance to the Enlightenment.* Wiesbaden: Harrassowitz 1987.
Portaleone, Avraham. *Shilṭe ha-Gibborim.* Mantua: Elieser d'Italia, 1612.
Prantl, Herr von. "Leonardo da Vinci in philosophischer Beziehung." *Sitzungsberichte der königlichen bayerischen Akademie der Wissenschaften zu München. Philosophisch-philologische Classe. Jahrgang 1885.* Munich: Akademische Buchdruckerei, 1886.
Prosman, A.A.A. (Ad). "Nietsches's 'The Antichirst': An Anti-Christian and Anti-Jewish Document." In *Strangers and Pilgrims on Earth: Essays in Honour of Abraham Van de Beek*, edited by Eduardus van der Borght, and Paul van Geest, 147–160. Leiden: Brill, 2012.
Puech, Henri-Charles. "Numénius d' Apamée et les théologies orientales au second siècle." *Annuaire de l'institut de philologie et d'histoire orientales* 2 (1934): 745–778.
Pullan, Brian. *Gli Ebrei d'Europa e l'Inquisizione a Venezia dal 1550 al 1670.* Rome: Il Veltro, 1985.
Quenstedt, Johannes Andrea. *Sepultura veterum sive Tractatus de antiquis ritibus sepulchralibus graecorum, romanorum, judaeorum & christianorum, [...] studio & opera Johannis Andreae Quenstedt.* Wittebergae: Sumptib. Haered. D. Tobiae Mevii & Elerdi Schumacheri, typis haered. Melchioris Oelschlegelii, 1660.
Radosav, Maria L. "The Metaphor of the Book. The Hebrew Book and its Perception in the Jewish Communities of North Transylvania." In *Essays in Honor of Moshe Idel*, 243–252. Cluj-Napoca: Editura Provopress, 2008.

Ramus, Petrus. *Opticae libri quatuor ex voto Petri Rami novissimo per Fridericum Risnerum ejusdem in mathematicis adjutorem olim conscripti.* Cassellis: Wesselius, 1606.

Rauschenbach, Sina. *Joseph Albo: Jüdische Philosophie und christliche Kontroverstheologie in der Frühen Neuzeit.* Leiden, Boston: Brill, 2002.

Ravid, Benjamin. "'Money Lending in Seventeenth-Century Jewish Vernacular Apologetica." In *Jewish Thought in the Seventeenth Century*, edited by Isadore Twersky and Bernard Septimus, 257–283. Cambridge: Harvard University Press, 1987.

Ravisius, Johannes. *De memorabilibus et claris mulieribus: aliquot diversorum scriptorium opera.* Paris: Simon de Colines, 1521.

Raynaud, Dominique. "Al-Samarqandī. Un précurseur de l'analyse des controversies scientifiques." *Al-Mukhatabat* 7 (2013): 8–25.

Raynaud, Dominique. *Scientific Controversies: A Socio-Historical Perspective on the Advancement of Science.* New Brunswick: Transaction, 2015.

Rebiger, Bill. "Sceptical Strategies in Simone Luzzatto's Presentation of the Kabbalists in his Discorso." *Yearbook of the Maimonides Centre for Advanced Studies* 2 (2017): 51–69.

Reimmann, Jakob F. "An Salomo fuerit Scepticus?" *Observationes selectae ad rem litterariam spectantes* 8 (1704): 327–367.

Reines, Alvin J. "Skepsis and Skepticism." In *Encyclopaedia Judaica*, vol. 18, edited by Michael Berenbaum and Fred Skolnik, 657–658. Detroit: Macmillan, 2010.

Redslob, Gustav M. "Hartmann, Anton Theodor." *Allgemeine Deutsche Biographie* 10 (1879): 680–681.

Rhode, Ambrosius. *Optica Ambrosii Rhodii [...] Cui additus est Tractatus De crepvsculis.* Wittenberg: Seelfisch, 1611.

Riel, Gerd van, and Pierre Destree. *Ancient Perspectives on Aristotles de Anima.* Leuven: Leuven University Press, 2009.

Ridings, Daniel. "The Attic Moses: The Dependency Theme in Some Early Christian Writers." PhD dissertation, University of Gothenburg, 1994.

Rijk, Lambert Marie de. *Aristotle: Semantics and Ontology.* Philosophia Antiqua 91, no. 1. Leiden: Brill, 2002.

Rinaldi, Giancarlo. *Biblia Gentium. Primo contributo per un indice delle citazioni, dei riferimenti e delle allusioni alla Bibbia negli autori pagani, greci e latini, di età imperial.* Rome: Libreria Sacre Scritture, 1989.

Roberts, Kate Louise, ed. *Hoyt's New Cyclopedia of Practical Quotations.* New York: Funk & Wagnalls, 1922.

Roll, Reinhard H. *Salomo A Scepticismi Crimine Contra Injustam Observatoris Halensis Imputationem.* Rostok: Weppling, 1710.

Rollston, Christopher A. *Writing and Literacy in the World of Ancient Israel: Epigraphic Evidence from the Iron Age.* Leiden: Brill, 2010.

Romano, Immanuel. *Mahberot Immanuel ha-Romi.* Edited by Abraham M. Haberman. Tel Aviv: 1946.

Rosand, Ellen. *Opera in Seventeenth-Century Venice: The Creation of a Genre.* Berkeley: University of California Press, 1991.

Rosenmeyer, Thomas G. *Senecan Drama and Stoic Cosmology.* Berkeley: University of California Press, 1989.

Rosenthal, Judah M. "The Talmud on Trial." *Jewish Quarterly Review* 47 (1956–1957): 58–76 and 145–169.

Ross, Tamar. "The Miracle as an Added Dimension in the Thought of the Maharal of Prague" [Hebrew]. *Daat* 17 (1986): 81–96.

Rotenstreich, Nathan. "The Problem of the 'Critique of Judgment' and Solomon Maimon's Scepticism." In *Harry A. Wolfson Jubilee Volume on the Occasion of His Seventy-Fifth*

Birthday, edited by Saul Lieberman, 677–702. Jerusalem: American Academy for Jewish Research, 1965.
Roth, Cecil. "L'accademia musicale del ghetto veneziano." *Rivista mensile d'Israele* 3 (1928): 160–162.
Roth, Cecil. "Léon de Modène, ses Riti ebraici et le Saint Office de Venise." *Revue des Études Juives* 7 (1929): 83–88.
Roth, Cecil. "Leone da Modena and the Christian Hebraists of His Age." *Jewish Studies in Memory of Israel Abrahams*, 384–401. New York: Press of the Jewish Institute of Religion, 1927.
Roth, Daniel. "The Ninth of Adar: The Day Constructive Conflict Turned Destructive." *Pardes* 4 (2013): 2–18
Roth, Norman. "The 'Theft of Philosophy' by the Greeks from the Jews." *Classical Folia* 32 (1978): 53–67.
Rubarth, Scott M. *Bryn Mawr Classical Review*, http://ccat.sas.upenn.edu/bmcr/1999/1999-09-24.html (accessed 3 May, 2018).
Ruderman, David B. "Science and Skepticism. Simone Luzzatto on Perceiving the Natural World." In *Jewish Thought and Scientific Discovery in Early Modern Europe*, edited by David B. Rudermann, 153–184. New Haven, London: Yale University Press, 1995.
Ruderman, David B. *The World of a Renaissance Jew. The Life and Thought of Abraham ben Mordecai Farissol*. Cincinnati: Hebrew Union College Press, 1981.
Rusconi, Roberto. *Gioacchino da Fiore tra Bernardo di Clairvaux e Innocenzo III*. Rome: Viella, 2001.
Sabunde, Raymundus de. *Theologia naturalis, sive liber creaturarum*. Strassburg: Martin Flach, 1496.
Salatowsky, Sascha. *De Anima. Die Rezeption der aristotelischen Psychologie im 16. und 17. Jahrhundert*. Amsterdam: Grüner Publishing Company, 2006.
Sánchez, Francisco. *Quod Nihil Scitur. Dass nichts gewusst wird*. Edited by Kaspar Howald. Hamburg: Felix Meiner, 2007.
Sánchez, Francisco. *That Nothing is Known*. Cambridge: Cambridge University Press, 1988.
Sanchez Nogales, Jose Luis. *Camino del hombre a Dios: la teología natural de R. Sibiuda*. Granada: Facultad de Teología, 1995.
Saperstein, Marc. "Problematizing the Bible in Late Medieval Jewish Exegesis." In *With Reverence for the Word: Medieval Scriptural Exegesis in Judaism, Christianity, and Islam*, edited by Jane Dammen McAuliffe, Barry D. Walfish, and Joseph W. Goering, 133–156. New York: Oxford University Press, 2003.
Schaeder, Hans H. *Esra der Schreiber*. Tübingen: Mohr, 1930.
Schäfer, Peter. "Israel und die Völker der Welt: Zur Auslegung von Mekhilta de Rabbi Yishma'el, baïodesh Yitro 5." *FJB4* (1976): 32–62.
Schäfer, Peter. *Studien zur Geschichte und Theologie des rabbinischen Judentums*. Leiden: Brill, 1978.
Scheftelowitz, Isidor. *Alt-palästinensischer Bauernglaube in religionsvergleichender Beleuchtung*. Hannover: Lafaire, 1925.
Schleiermacher, Friedrich. "Zweite(n) Sendschreiben über die Glaubenslehre an Dr. Lücke." *Theologische Studien und Kritiken* 2 (1829) 497.
Schleiner, Winfried. *Medical Ethics in the Renaissance*. Washington, D.C.: Georgetown University Press, 1995.
Schmidt-Biggemann, Wilhelm. *Philosophia Perennis. Historical Outlines of Western Spirituality in Ancient, Medieval and Early Modern Thought*. Dordrecht: Springer, 2004.
Schmidt-Biggemann, Wilhelm. *Philosophia Perennis. Historische Umrisse abendländischer Spiritualität in Antike, Mittelalter und Früher Neuzeit*. Frankfurt: Suhrkamp, 1998.

Schmitt, Charles B. "The Rediscovery of Ancient Skepticism in Modern Times." In *The Skeptical Tradition*, edited by Myles Burnyeat, 225–251. Berkeley: University of California Press, 1983.

Schoeps, Hans J. "Kritischer Idealismus und jüdische Theologie." *Monatsschrift für Geschichte und Wissenschaft des Judentums* 82 (1938): 73–85.

Schoeps, Julius. "Der Reuchlin-Pfefferkorn-Streit in der jüdischen Historiographie des 19. und 20. Jahrhunderts." In *Reuchlin und die Juden*, edited by Arno Herzig and Julius H. Schoeps, 203–212. Sigmaringen: Jan Thorbecke, 1993.

Schofield, Malcolm. *Plato and the Talmud*. Cambridge: Cambridge University Press, 1989.

Schreckenberg, Hans. *Die christlichen Adversus-Judaeos-Texte (11.–13. Jh.)*. Frankfurt: Lang, 1991.

Schürer, Emil. *The History of the Jewish People in the Age of Jesus Christ*. vol. 3, pt. 1. Edited by Geza Vermes, Emil Shürer, and Fergus Millar. Edinburgh: T. & Clark, 1986.

Schwab, Andreas. *Thales von Milet in der frühen christlichen Literatur: Darstellungen seiner Figur und seiner Ideen in den griechischen und lateinischen Textzeugnissen christlicher Autoren der Kaiserzeit und Spätantike*. Berlin: De Gruyter, 2011.

Schwartz, Daniel R. "The Priests in Ep. Arist. 310." *Journal of Biblical Literature* 97 (1978): 567–571.

Schmitz, Wolfgang. *Die Überlieferung deutscher Texte im Kölner Buchdruck des 15. und 16. Jahrhunderts*. Köln: Habilitationsschrift,1990.

Schütt, Hans-Peter. *Die Vernunft der Tiere*. Frankfurt: Keip, 1990.

Scott, James B. *The Spanish Origin of International Law. Francisco de Vitoria and his Law of Nations*. Oxford: The Clarendon Press, 1934.

Secret, François. *Les Kabbalistes Chrétiens de la Renaissance*. Paris: Dunod, 1964.

Secret, François. "Un texte mal connu de Simon Luzzato sur la cabbale." *Revue des Études Juives* 118 (1959/1960): 121–128.

Segesvary, Victor. *L'Islam et la reforme: Étude sur l'attitude des reformateurs Zurichois envers l'Islam 1510–1550*. La Haye: Mikes International, 2005.

Sennert, Andrea. *Exercitationes philologicarum Heptas altera: quarum I. De Div. Nom. Elohim. add: Mantissa de Jehovah; II. De Masorah; III. De Cabbalah; IV. De Musica Ebræor.; V. De Scholis, studiis, &c. &c. eorundem.; VI. De Mendis Codicum Apographorum V. Intr. Ebr. hodiernor.; VII. De Sceptro Judah, &c. ex Genes. c. XLIX. comm. 10, Cui additur Hierographicum Sinaicum Kircher &c. &c.* Wittenberg: Joh. Sigismundi Ziegenbeins, 1678.

Septimus, Bernard. "Biblical Religion and Political Rationality in Simone Luzzatto, Maimonides and Spinoza." In *Jewish Thought in the Seventeenth Century*, edited by Isadore Twersky and Bernard Septimus, 399–434. Cambridge: Harvard University Press, 1987.

Sextus Empiricus. *Outlines of Scepticism*. Edited by Julia Annas and Jonathan Barnes. Cambridge: Cambridge University Press, 2000.

Sezgin, Fuat. *Greek Philosophy and the Arabs: Texts and Studies*. Frankfurt: Institute for the History of Arabic-Islamic Science, 2000.

Sforno, 'Ovadyah. *Kitvei Rabbi 'Ovadyah Sforno*. Edited by Ze'ev Gottlieb. Jerusalem: Mosad ha-Rav Kuk, 1983.

Sforno, 'Ovadyah. *Lumen Gentium*. Bologna: apud Giaccarelli, 1547.

Sforno, 'Ovadyah. *Or 'Ammim*. Bologna: 1537.

Shaw, Duncan. *The History and Philosophy of Judaism: Or, A Critical and Philosophical Analysis of the Jewish Religion. From which is Offered a Vindication of its Genius, Origin, and Authority, and of the Connection with the Christian, against the Objections and Misrepresentations of Modern Infidels*. Edinburgh: C. Eliott, 1787.

Shear, Adam. *The Kuzari and the Shaping of Jewish Identity, 1167–1900*. Cambridge: Cambridge University Press, 2008.

Shell, Marc. *Money, Language, and Thought: Literary and Philosophic Economies from the Medieval to the Modern Era*. Baltimore, London: John Hopkins University Press, 1982.

Shepard, Sanford. "The Background of Uriel Da Costa's Heresy: Marranism, Skepticism, Karaism." *Judaism* 20 (1971): 341–350.

Siegel, Rudolph E. *Galen's System of Physiology and Medicine. An Analysis of his Doctrines and Observations on Bloodflow, Respiration, Humors and Internal diseases.* Urbana: University of Illinois Press, 1993.

Sim, Stuart. *Empires of Belief. Why We Need More Scepticism and Doubt in the Twenty-First Century.* Edinburgh: Edinburgh University Press, 2006.

Simon, Ernst. "Goethe und der religiöse Humanismus." In *Brücken. Gesammelte Aufsätze (mit einem Geleitwort von Martin Buber)*, edited by Ernst Simon, 220–245. Heidelberg: Schneider, 1965.

Simon, Gérard. *Le regard, l'être et l'apparence dans l'Optique de l'Antiquité.* Paris: Edition du Seuil, 1988.

Simon, Marcel. "La Bible dans les premières controverses entre Juifs et Chrétiens." In *Le monde grec ancien et la Bible*, edited by Claude Mondésert, 107–127. Paris: Beauchesne, 1985.

Simon, Marcel. *Verus Israel. Étude sur les relations entre Chrétiens et Juifs dans l'empire romain (135–425).* Paris: Boccard, 1964.

Siniscalco, Paolo. "Caratteri espressivi ed estetici della profezia vetero-testamentaria secondo la *Cohortatio ad Graecos*." *Studi Storico-Religiosi* 4 (1980): 29–44.

Sirat, Colette. *A History of Jewish Philosophy in the Middle Ages*, Cambridge: Cambridge University Press, 1985.

Slotki, Judah J., Israel Brodie, and Isidore Epstein, eds. *The Babylonian Talmud: Translated into English with Notes, Glossary and Endices.* London: Soncino Press, 1952.

Smalley, Beryl. "William of Auvergne, John de la Rochelle, and Thomas Aquinas on the Old Law." In *St. Thomas Aquinas Commemorative Studies*, vol. 2, edited by Armand Mauer, 11–71. Toronto: Pontifical Institute of Medieval Studies, 1974.

Smith, Frank D. "The Reuchlin Controversy." *Journal of Progressive Judaism* 4 (1995): 77–88.

Smith, William, William Wayte, and G. E. Marindin, eds. *A Dictionary of Greek and Roman Antiquities.* London: John Murray, 1890.

Snow, Charles P. *The Two Cultures and the Scientific Revolution.* Cambridge: University Press, 1959.

Sokol, Moshe. "What Does a Jewish Text Mean? Theories on Elu ve-Elu Divrei Elohim Hayim in Rabbinic Literature." *Da'at* 32–33 (1994): 22–31.

Sokoloff, Michael. *A Dictionary of Jewish Babylonian Aramaic of the Talmudic and Geonic periods.* Baltimore: Johns Hopkins University Press; Ramat-Gan: Bar-Ilan University Press, 2002.

Sorabji, Richard. *Animal Minds & Human Morals: The Origins of the Western Debate.* London: Duckworth, 1993.

Soto Posada, Gonzalo. "La muerte del escepticismo o san Augustín y los académicos." *Estudios de Filosofía* 26 (2002): 277–292.

Spencer, John. *De legibus hebraeorum ritualibus earumque rationibus libri quatuor. Praemittitur Christ. Matth. Pfaffii, Dissertatio praeliminaris qua de vita Spenceri, de libri pretio & erroribus quoque disseritur. Autoresque, qui contra Spencerum scripsere, enarrantur.* The Hague: Arnold Leers, 1686.

Spencer, John. *De legibus hebraeorum ritualibus et earum rationibus. Libri tres.* Cambridge: Richard Chiswel, 1685.

Spinelli, Emidio. "L'esperienza scettica: Sesto Empirico fra metodologia scientifica e scelte etiche." *Quaestio* 4 (2004): 25–43.

Spinelli, Emidio. *Questioni scettiche. Letture introduttive al pirronismo antico.* Rome: Lithos, 2005.

Spinelli, Emidio. "Sextus Empiricus." In *Dictionnaire des philosophes antiques*, vol. 6, edited by Richard Goulet, 265–300. Paris: CNRS éditions, 2016.

Spinelli, Emidio. "Stoic Utopia Reconsidered: Pyrrhonism, Ethics, and Politics." In *Philosophy and Political Power in Antiquity*, edited by Cinzia Arruzza and Dmitri Nikulin, 148–163. Brill: Leiden, 2016.

Spinelli, Emidio, and Mario de Caro. *Una vicenda filosofica*. Rome: Carocci, 2007.

Spinoza, Baruch. *The Collected Works of Spinoza*. Edited and translated by Edwin Curley. Princeton: Princeton University Press, 1985.

Stanistreet, Paul. *Hume's Scepticism and the Science of Human Nature*. Aldershot: Ashgate, 2002.

Stein, Nathanael. "Causal Necessity in Aristotle." *British Journal for the History of Philosophy* 20 (2012): 855–879.

Stern, Josef. *The Matter and Form of Maimonides' Guide*. Cambridge: Harvard University Press, 2013.

Stern, Menahem. *Greek and Latin Authors on Jews and Judaism*. Jerusalem: Magnes, 1974.

Storchen, Sigismund von. *Die Philosophie der Religion*. Augsburg: Veith, 1773–1789.

Strauss, Eduard. "Eine jüdische Theologie?" *Der Morgen* 8 (1932): 312–314.

Strauss, Leo. "The Law of Reason in the Kuzari." *Proceedings of the American Academy of Jewish Research* 3 (1943): 47–96.

Strebel, Georgius Sigismundus. *Decas selecta positionum philologicarum de antiquis antiquis Judaeorum ritibus et moribus, unde quamplurimis ssae. locis lux aliqua affunditur August Pfeiffer*. Wittenberg: Henckel, 1664.

Stroumsa, Guy G. *A New Science: The Discovery of Religion in the Age of Reason*. Cambridge: Harvard University Press, 2010.

Sturtevant, William C. "Does Anthropology Need Museums?" *Proceedings of the Biological Society of Washington* 82 (1969): 619–650.

Sullam, Sara Copio. *Manifesto Di Sarra Copia Svlam Hebrea: Nel quale è da lei riprouata, e detestata l'opinione negante l'immortalltá deli' Anima falsamente attribuitale dal Sig. Baldassare Bonifaccio*. Venice: Pinelli, 1621.

Sylla, Edith D. "Mendelssohn, Wolff, and Bernoulli on Probability." In *Moses Mendelssohn's Metaphysics and Aesthetics*, edited by Reinier Munk, 41–64. Dordrecht: Springer, 2011.

Tcherikover, Victor. "Jewish Apologetic Literature Reconsidered." *Eos* 48 (1956): 169–193.

Teicher, Jacob "Il principio 'Veritas filia temporis' presso Azaria de' Rossi." *Rendiconti della reale Accademia Nazionale dei Lincei. Classe Morali, Storiche e Filologiche* ser. 6, IX (1933): 268–275.

Thraede, Klaus. "Erfinder." *Reallexikon für Antike und Christentum* 5 (1962): 1191–1278.

Tissard, François. *Dialogus: Prothymopatris kai Phronimos […] De Judaeorum ritibus compendium. Tabula elementorum Hebraicorum. Documenta ut debeant illa elementa proferri ac legi. Ut Hebraei numeros signant. Oratio dominica Hebraicis characteribus impressa. Genealogia beatae Mariae: una cum aliis plusculis eisdem characteribus impressioni mandata. Iesus Nazarenus Rex Iudaeorum Latine, Graece et Hebraice. Grammatica Hebraica succincte tradita. Tabula elementorum Graecorum cum diphtongis et pronunciandi regulis et pluribus Graecis orationibus et Hyppocratis iusiurando. Abbrevationes Graece. Ut Graeci numeros signant amplissima descriptio. Operoso huic opusculo extremam imposuit manum Egidius Gourmontius integerrimus ac fidelissimus primus duce Francisco Tissardo Graecarum et Hebraearum litterarum*. Parrhisiis impressor, 1508.

Toland, John. *Reasons for Naturalizing the Jews in Great Britain and Ireland, on the same foot with all other Nations. Containing also, a defence of the Jews against all vulgar prejudices in all countries*. London: J. Roberts, 1714. Jerusalem: Hebrew University Department of Jewish History, 1963.

Tomim, Julius. "Socrates and the Laws of Athens." http://www.juliustomin.org/images/SOCRATES_AND_THE_LAWS_OF_ATHENS.pdf (accessed 3 May, 2018).

Torbidoni, Michela. "Il metodo del dubbio nel Socrate." In *Filosofo e Rabbino nella Venezia del Seicento. Studi su Simone Luzzatto (1583–ca.1663). Con un'appendice di documenti inediti dall'Archivio di Stato*, edited by Giuseppe Veltri, 183–245. Rome: Aracne, 2015.

Tracy, James D. *Erasmus of the Low Countries*. Berkeley: University of California Press, 1996.

Tramontano, Raffaele. *La lettera di Aristea a Filocrate*. Naples: Ufficio succursale della Civiltà cattolica, 1931.

Tribble, Evelyn. *Margins and Marginality: The Printed Page in Early Modern England*. Charlottesville: University Press of Virginia, 1993.

Trivellato, Francesca. "Jews and Early Modern Economy." In *The Cambridge History of Judaism. Volume 7: The Early Modern World, 1500–1815*, edited by Jonathan Karp and Adam Sutcliffe, 139–167. Cambridge: Cambridge University Press, 2018.

Troiani, Lucio. *Commento storico al Contro Apione di Giuseppe*. Pisa: Giardini, 1977.

Tucker George H., "To Louvain and Antwerp, and Beyond; The Contrasting Itineraries of Diogo Pires (Didacus Pyrrhus Lusitanus, 1517–1599) and Joao Rodrigues de Castelo Branco (Amatus Lusitanus, 1511–1568)." In *The Expulsion of the Jews and Their Emigration to the Southern Low Countries (15th–16th C.)*, edited by Luc Dequecker and Werner Verbene, 83–113. Leuven: Leuven University Press, 1998.

Tudor, Faye. "'All in him selfe as in a glass he sees.' Mirrors and Vision in the Renaissance." In *Renaissance Theories of Vision*, ed. John Hendrix and Charles H. Carman, 171–186. Franham: Ashgate, 2010.

Turkī, Abdel M. *Théologiens et juristes de l'Espagne musulmane: Aspects polémiques*. Paris: Maisonneuve et Larose, 1982.

Urbach, Ephraim E. "Halakha we-nevu'a." *Tarbiz* 18 (1946–1947): 1–27.

Urbach, Ephraim E. *The Sages. Their Concepts and Beliefs*. Jerusalem: The Hebrew University Magnes Press, 1979.

Ursinus, Georg. בית הישיבה והמדרש *Seu Antiquitates Hebraicæ Scholastico-Academicæ. In Quibus Scholarum & Academiarum Judaicarum historia tam intra quam extra Scripturam, Forma earundem, Docentium & Discentium officia, Ritus, Dimissio è Schola, Promotio, Promotionum Tituli, Distincti Professorum Ordines & Facultates, Methodus Disputandi, Studia, Statuta, Privilegia & Stipendia continuo, ubi fieri potuit, S. Scripturæ & monumentorum Rabbinicorum concentu eruta leguntur*. Copenhagen: Lieben, 1702.

Vecce, Carlo. "I Dialoghi d'amore di Leone Ebreo: incontri di culture nella storia di un libro del Rinascimento." In *Autour du livre italien ancien en Normandie*, edited by Silvia Fabrizio-Costa, 321–331. Berlin: Peter Lang, 2011.

Veltri, Giuseppe. "Academic Debates on the Jews in Wittenberg. The Protestant Literature on Rituals, the Dissertationes and the Writings of the Hebraists Theodor Dassow and Andreas Sennert." *European Journal of Jewish Studies* 6 (2012): 123–146.

Veltri, Giuseppe. "Altertumswissenschaft und Wissenschaft des Judentums: Leopold Zunz und seine Lehrer F. A. Wolf und A. Boeckh." In *Friedrich August Wolf. Studien, Texte, Bibliographie*, edited by Reinhart Markner and Giuseppe Veltri, 32–47. Göttingen: Steiner, 1999.

Veltri, Giuseppe. *A Mirror of Rabbinic Hermeneutics. Studies in Religion, Magic and Language Theory in Ancient Judaism*. Berlin: De Gruyter, 2015.

Veltri, Giuseppe. "Canone, Scrittura e contesto immanente in alcuni testi del I secolo." *Laurentianum* 30 (1989): 17–24.

Veltri, Giuseppe. "Dalla tesi giudeo-ellenistica del 'plagio' dei Greci al concetto rabbinico del verus Israel: Disputa sull'appartenenza della sofia." *Revista Catalana de Teologia* 17 (1992): 85–104.

Veltri, Giuseppe. "'Dannare l'universale per il particolare?' Colpa individuale e pena collettiva nel pensiero di Rabbi Simone Luzzatto." *Rassegna Mensile d'Israele* LXXVII, 1–2 (2012): 65–81.

Veltri, Giuseppe. *Dialectic and Doubt. Hellenistic, Rabbinic, and Jewish Medieval Sceptic Strategies*, working title, forthcoming, 2019.

Veltri, Giuseppe. "Die humanistischen Wurzeln der 'jüdischen Philosophie': Zur Konzeption einer konfessionellen Ontologie und Genealogie des Wissens." In *Die philosophische Aktualität der jüdischen Tradition*, edited by Werner Stegmaier, 264–272. Frankfurt: Suhrkamp 2000.

Veltri, Giuseppe. "Economic and Social Arguments and the Doctrine of the Antiperistasis in Simone Luzzatto's Political Thought: Venetian Reverberations of Francis Bacon's Philosophy." *Frühneuzeit-Info* 23 (2011): 23–32.

Veltri, Giuseppe. *Eine Tora für den König Talmai. Untersuchungen zum Übersetzungsverständnis in der jüdisch-hellenistischen und rabbinischen Literatur*. Tübingen: Mohr, 1994.

Veltri, Giuseppe. "Freche Schüler vs. gescheite Rabbinen. Die Kunst des Lernens im antiken Judentum." In *Meister und Schüler in Geschichte und Gegenwart: Von Religionen der Antike bis zur modernen Esoterik*, edited by Almut-Barbara Renger, 135–145. Göttingen: V&R Unipress, 2012.

Veltri, Giuseppe. *Friedrich August Wolf: Studien, Dokumente, Bibliographie*. Edited by Reinhard Markner and Giuseppe Veltri. Stuttgart: Franz Steiner, 1999.

Veltri, Giuseppe. *Gegenwart der Tradition: Studien zur jüdischen Literatur und Kulturgeschichte*. Leiden: Brill, 2002.

Veltri, Giuseppe. "Jewish Studies at German Universities in the Early Modern Period: The 'Dissertationes' at the University of Wittenberg." *European Journal of Jewish Studies* 5 (2011): n.p.

Veltri, Giuseppe. "Jüdische Einstellung zu den Wissenschaften im 16. und 17. Jahrhundert: Das Prinzip der praktisch-empirischen Anwendbarkeit." In *Judentum zwischen Tradition und Moderne*, edited by Gerd Biegel and Michael Graetz, 149–159. Heidelberg: C. Winter, 2002.

Veltri, Giuseppe. "La dimensione politico-filosofica dei *caeremonialia hebraeorum*: Baruk Spinoza e Simone Luzzatto." *Materia Giudaica* 13 (2008): 81–90.

Veltri, Giuseppe. *Language of Conformity & Dissent. The Imaginative Grammar of Jewish Intellectuals in the Nineteenth and Twentieth Centuries*. Boston: Academic Studies Press, 2013.

Veltri, Giuseppe. *Libraries, Translations, and "Canonic" Texts. The Septuagint, Aquila, and Ben Sira, in Jewish and Christian Tradition*. Leiden: Brill, 2006.

Veltri, Giuseppe. "Maharal against Azaria de' Rossi: The Other Side of Skepticism." In *Rabbinic Theology and Jewish Intellectual History. The Great Rabbi Loew of Prague*, edited by Meir Seidel, 65–76. Oxford: Routledge, 2012.

Veltri, Giuseppe. *Renaissance Philosophy in Jewish Garb: Foundations and Challenges in Judaism on the Eve of Modernity*. Leiden: Brill, 2009.

Veltri, Giuseppe. "Science and Religious Hermeneutics: The 'Philosophy' of Rabbi Loew of Prague." In *Religious Confession and the Sciences in the Sixteenth Century*, edited by Jürgen Helm and Annette Winkelmann, 119–135. Leiden: Brill, 2001.

Veltri, Giuseppe. "Testing Genuine and Counterfeit Coins: The Subject's Error in Saadya's Argument of True Knowledge against Scepticism." In preparation.

Veltri, Giuseppe. "The Humanist Sense of History and the Jewish Idea of Tradition: Azaria de' Rossi's Critique of Philo Alexandrinus." *Jewish Studies Quarterly* 2 (1995): 372–93.

Veltri, Giuseppe. "The Limit of Scepticism and Tolerance." *Bollettino della Società Filosofica Italiana N.S.* 221 (2017): 37–55.

Veltri, Giuseppe. "'Tochter der Zeit'—Zur Geschichte der Jüdischen Theologie in Deutschland." *Potsdamer Neueste Nachrichten*. 30 November, 2014. http://www.pnn.de/potsdam/913674 (accessed 3 May, 2018).

Veltri, Giuseppe. "Über die Anwendung christlicher Terminologie auf die rabbinische Tradition: Einige Anmerkungen zum Fall Suksession." In *Sukzession in Religionen. Autorisierung,*

Legitimierung, Wissenstransfer, ed. Almut-Barbara Renger and Markus Witte, 221–230. Berlin: De Gruyter, 2017.

Veltri, Giuseppe. "Von der 'philosophia giudaica seu ebraeorum' zur 'jüdischen Philosophie': (Ver)wandlungen eines Begriffes im Kontext der Kabbala Denudata." *Morgen-Glantz: Zeitschrift der Christian Knorr von Rosenroth-Gesellschaft 16* (2006): 323–341.

Veltri, Giuseppe. "Zur jüdischen und christlichen Wertung der Aggada." *Frankfurter Judaistische Beiträge* 22 (1995): 61–75.

Veltri, Giuseppe, and Annette Winkelmann. "'[…] daß er in Rabbinischer und in der Talmudischen Litteratur ziemlich bewandert ist.' Leopold Zunz und die Universität Halle–Wittenberg." In *Jüdische Bildung und Kultur in Sachsen–Anhalt von der Aufklärung bis zum Nationalsozialismus*, edited by Giuseppe Veltri and Christian Wiese. Berlin: Metropol Verlag, 2008, 239–260.

Veltri, Giuseppe, and Evelyn Chayes, *Oltre le Mura del Ghetto: Accademie, Scetticismo e Tolleranza nella Venezia Barocca*. Palermo: New Digital Frontiers, 2016.

Veltri, Giuseppe, and Gianfranco Miletto. "'[…] per esser buon Catolico Cristian, è necessario esser perfettamente Ebreo.' Difesa inedita del senatore veneziano Loredan in favore degli ebrei nel 1659/60, basata sul 'Discorso' di Simone Luzzatto." *Henoch* 26/2 (2014): 307–327.

Veltri, Giuseppe, Patrick Koch, and Gerold Necker. "Die versuchte Wiederaufnahme des jüdischen Freimaurers Ephraim J. Hirschfeld in den Orden der Asiatischen Brüder: Ein geheimer Rapport." *Judaica* 68, no. 2 (2012): 129–155.

Venetianer, Ludwig. *Asaf Judaeus. Der älteste medizinische Schriftsteller in hebräischer Sprache*. Strasbourg: Karl J. Trübner, 1916–1917.

Vinci, Leonardo da. *Scritti letterari di Leonardo da Vinci*. Edited by Augusto Marinoni. Milan: Rizzoli, 1974.

Victoria, Franciscus de. *De Indis recenter inventis et de jure belli Hispanorum in barbaros. Relectiones: Vorlesungen über die kürzlich entdeckten Inder und das Recht der Spanier zum Kriege gegen die Barbaren 1539*. Edited by Walter Schätzel. Tübingen: Mohr, 1952.

Viroli, Maurizio. *Machiavelli's God*. Princeton: Princeton University Press, 2010.

Viterbo, Ariel. "La mitzwàh di studiare le scienze nell'opera di Rav Simchah (Simone) Luzzatto." *Segulat Israel* 4 (1997): 54–67.

Viterbo, Ariel. "Socrate nel ghetto: lo scetticismo mascherato di Simone Luzzatto." *Studi Veneziani* 38 (1999): 79–128.

Vocabolario degli accademici della Crusca. Venice: 1612.

Vogt, Katja M. "Ancient Skepticism." *The Stanford Encyclopedia of Philosophy*. http://plato.stanford.edu/archives/win2011/entries/skepticism-ancient/ (accessed 3 May, 2018).

Vogt, Katja M. *Belief and Truth: A Skeptic Reading of Plato*. New York: Oxford University Press, 2012.

Wacholder, Ben Zion. *Eupolemos. A Study of Judaeo-Greek Literature*. Cincinnati: Hebrew Union College, Jewish Institute of Religion, 1974.

Walker, Daniel R. *Ancient Theology: Studies in Christian Platonism from the Fifteenth to the Eighteenth Century*. London: Duckworth, 1972.

Walter, Nicholas. *Der Thoraausleger Aristobulos. Untersuchungen zu seinen Fragmenten und zu pseudoepigraphischen Resten der jüdisch-hellenistischen Literatur*. Berlin: Akademie-Verlag, 1964.

Walter, Nicholas. *Unterweisung in lehrhafter Form. Das Buch Baruch. Der Brief Jeremias. Testament Abrahams. Fragmente jüdisch-hellenistischer Exegeten: Aristobulos, Demetrios, Aristeas* in *Jüdische Schriften aus hellenistisch-römischer Zeit*. Edited by Werner G. Kümmel. Gütersloh: Gütersloher Verl.-Haus Mohn, 1975.

Weinberg, Joanna. "Azaria de' Rossi: Towards a Reappraisal of the Last Years of his Life." *Annali della Scuola Normale di Pisa VIII* (1978): 493–511.

Wendland, Paul, ed. *Aristeas ad Philocratem epistola*. Leipzig: Teubner, 1900.
Wendland, Paul. "Zur ältesten Geschichte der Bibel in der Kirche." *Zeitschrift für alttestamentliche Wissenschaft* 1 (1900): 65–66.
Wengst, Klaus. *Didache (Apostellehre), Barnabasbrief, Zweiter Klemensbrief, Schrift an Diognet*. Schriften des Urchristentums 2. Munich: Kösel, 1984.
Westerkamp, Dirk. *Die philonische Unterscheidung. Aufklärung, Orientalismus und Kostruktion der Philosophie*. Munich: Fink, 2009.
Westerkamp, Dirk. "The Philonic Distinction: German Enlightenment Historiography of Jewish Thought." *History and Theory* 47 (2008): 533–559.
Wewers, Gerd A. *Geheimnis und Geheimhaltung im rabbinischen Judentum*. Berlin: De Gruyter, 1975.
Whittaker, John. "Moses Atticizing." *Phoenix* 21 (1967): 196–201.
Whittaker, John. *Studies in Platonism and Patristic Thought*. London: Variorum, 1984.
Wiener, Max. "Begriff und Aufgabe der jüdischen Theologie." *Monatsschrift für Geschichte und Wissenschaft des Judentums* 77 (1933): 3–16.
Wiese, Christian. *Jüdische Existenz in der Moderne: Abraham Geiger und die Wissenschaft des Judentums*. Berlin: De Gruyter, 2012.
Wirth, Rudolf. *De Festis Judaeorum et Ethnicorum, hoc est de origine, progressu, ceremoniis et ritibus festorum dierum Christianorum*. Leipzig: Jakob d. J. Apel, 1593.
Wirth, Rudolf. *De origine progressu ceremoniis et ritibus festorum dierum Judaeorum, Graecorum, Romanorum et Turcarum*. Tiguri: Wolphius, 1593.
Wolf, Friedrich A. *Encyclopädie der Philologie: Nach dessen Vorlesungen im Winterhalbjahre von 1789–1799*. Edited by S. M. Stockmann. Leipzig: Expedition des europäischen Aufsehers, 1831.
Wolf, Friedrich A. *Vorlesungen über die Alterthumswissenschaft*. Leipzig: JD. Gürtler, 1839.
Wolfes, Matthias. "Schleiermacher und das Judentum. Aspekte der antijudaistischen Motivgeschichte im deutschen Kulturprotestantismus." *Aschkenas* 14 (2007): 485–510.
Wolfson, Harry A. *Philo*. Cambridge: Harvard University Press, 1962.
Wolfson, Harry A. *Repercussion of the Kalam in Jewish Philosophy*. Cambridge: Harvard University Press, 1979.
Wolfson, Elliot R. "Skepticism and the Philosopher's Keeping Faith." In *Jewish Philosophy for the Twenty-First Century. Personal Reflections*, edited by Hava Tirosh-Samuelson and Aaron W. Hughes, 481–515. Leiden: Brill, 2014.
Woolf, Jeffrey R. "Between Diffidence and Initiative: Ashkenazic Legal Decision-Making in the Late Middle Ages (1350–1500)." *Journal of Jewish Studies* 52 (2001): 85–97.
Woods, John. "Dialectical Considerations on the Logic of Contradiction: Part I." *Logic Journal of the IGPL* 13 (2005): 231–260.
Yuval, Israel J. *"Two Nations in Your Womb." Perceptions of Jews and Christians*. Tel Aviv: Am Oved, 2001.
Zamir, Syed R. "Descartes and Al-Ghazali: Doubt, Certitude and Light." *Islamic Studies* 49, no. 2 (2010): 219–251.
Zerba, Michelle. *Doubt and Scepticism in Antiquity and Renaissance*. New York: Cambridge University Press, 2012.
Zonta, Mauro. "Aristotle's *De anima* and *De generatione et corruptione* in the Medieval Hebrew Tradition." In *Studies in the History of Culture and Science. A Tribute to Gad Freudenthal*, edited by Resianne Fontaine, Ruth Glasner, Reimund Leicht, and Giuseppe Veltri, 91–101. Leiden: Brill, 2011.
Zonta, Mauro. *Hebrew Scholasticism in the Fifteenth Century: A History and Source Book*. Dordrecht: Springer, 2006.
Zonta, Mauro. *La filosofia antica nel Medioevo ebraico*. Brescia: Paideia, 1996.

Zonta, Mauro. *La filosofia ebraica medievale: storia e testi*. Rome: Laterza, 2002.
Zonta, Mauro. "The Autumn of Medieval Jewish Philosophy." In *Herbst des Mittelalters? Fragen zur Bewertung des 14. und 15. Jahrhunderts*, edited by Jan A. Aertsen and Martin Pickave, 474–492. Berlin: De Gruyter, 2004.
Zunz, Leopold. "De Schem-Tobh Palkeira, imprimis de ejusdem libro, qui inscribitur Sepher-hamaaloth." PhD dissertation, University of Halle, 1821.
Zunz, Leopold. *Die gottesdienstlichen Vorträge der Juden, historisch entwickelt. Ein Beitrag zur Alterthumskunde und biblischen Kritik, zur Literatur- und Religionsgeschichte*. Berlin: Asher, 1832.
Zunz, Leopold. *Gesammelte Schriften*. Berlin: Curatorium der "Zunzstiftung," 1875.

Index

Abba Mari of Lunel 40
– *Sefer Yareaḥ* 40
Abraham of Benevento 161
Abravanel, Isaac 62
Academy, 45, 70, 105, 108, 155, 159, 160, 184, 186–189, 191–197, 200, 202, 207, 209, 244, 248
– Academy of Delphos 237
– Accademia degli Impediti 192
– Accademia degli Incogniti 143, 197, 209, 238
– Accademia degli Invaghiti 191
– Accademia dei Dubbiosi 143, 187f.
– Accademia Pontaniana 190
– Middle academy 146
– Neoaccademia Aldina 191
– New academy 213
– Philosophical academy 38, 190
– Platonic academy 20, 38, 146
adiaphora 50f.
Aggadah 31, 169f., 172, 175–177
– poetic parable 169
Agnosticism 291
Aguilar (d'), Moses Raphael 207
ahistorical 38
Alatino, Moses 161
Alberti, Giovanni 195
Alberti, Leon Battista 255
– *De pictura* 255
Albert the Great 71
Albo, Joseph 72f., 106, 113, 169, 182, 316
– *Sefer ha-'Ikkarim* 72, 182
Alexandrine Judaism, Hellenism XX, 3, 6f., 9, 11, 16, 17, 27f., 37
Al-Fârâbî, Abû Nasr Muhammad ibn Muhammad ibn Tarkhân ibn Uzalagh 139f., 162
Al-Ghazālī, Abū Ḥāmid Muḥammad ibn Muḥammad al-Ghazālī 148, 286, 290, 295
– *Al-Munqidh min al-Dalāl* 286
Al-Haytham, (ibn), Hasan 148–149
– *Al-Shukūk 'alā Baṭlamyūs* 149
– *Kitāb al-Manāẓir* 149
alienation 3, 145, 281–284
– Entäußerung 283
Al-Samarqandī, Shams al-Dīn 271f.
Amatus Lusitanus (Castelo Branco de, João Rodriguez) 43–46, 45f., 57, 69
Ambrogini, Angelo (Poliziano) 230

Anaxagoras 14, 228, 246
Anaximenes 245
anthropology 58, 60, 62f., 80
antiperistasis 96–99, 184, 217
apodeixis (proof) 266
Apollinaris 52
Apolline Temple 237
apology, apologetic 3, 5, 7–9, 14–16, 20–22, 37–40, 44, 56, 78, 84, 111, 116, 135, 136, 154, 170, 184, 193, 207, 213–215, 220, 230, 238, 243, 249, 263, 281
– apologetic holism XX
– apologetic literature 16, 47
– apologetic method 44
aporia 146, 156, 270, 275f., 286, 294
Aquinas, Thomas 61, 70–73, 88, 107, 139, 148, 200, 225, 240, 258
– *In psalmos Davidis* 200
– *Summa Quaestio* 71
– *Summa Theologica* 71, 107, 225
Aramaic 17, 37, 48, 135, 189, 297
arcana mundi 67
argument 6, 8, 10, 14, 19, 32, 38, 45, 62, 73, 79–82, 84, 86f., 93, 96, 98, 100, 102, 112, 116, 136, 139, 144, 148f., 152–154, 157, 159, 165f., 168f., 173, 178, 181f., 184, 190, 197, 199f., 203–206, 208f., 211, 214–218, 220, 227, 231, 238, 244, 246, 253, 258–260, 262, 265f., 270–272, 275f., 279, 286, 288f., 291f., 294–296
Aristobulus 10–12
Aristotle, Aristotelism 18, 20, 36, 40, 71, 92, 97f., 107, 118, 160–162, 188, 199, 201–203, 220, 224, 229, 244, 246f., 254f., 265–267, 285, 299, 312
– Arabic Aristotelianism 160
– Latin Aristotelianism 160
– corpus Aristotelicum 161
– *Ethica Nichomachea* 92
– *Metaphysics* 202, 265
– *Physics* 97, 99
– Peripatetic 38, 40, 96, 98f., 147, 149, 153, 158, 160f., 163, 188, 201–203, 224f., 230f., 247, 253, 258, 265–267, 274, 277–279, 285f., 299f., 302
Artapanus 10, 14, 18f.
Assmann, Jan XIII, 23
Ashkenazi, Eliezer 62

assimilation 151, 180, 219
Aufhebung 283
Augustinus, Aurelius 38 f., 51, 70, 71, 139 f.,147, 149, 290, 295
- Contra Academicos 147 f., 295
- De beata vita 147
- De ordine 147
authority 9, 16, 22, 27, 45, 57, 68, 81, 108, 111, 127, 130, 136, 138, 144, 148, 150, 154, 158 f., 162, 167–169, 175, 184 f., 187 f., 208, 232, 236 f., 240, 242, 244, 263 f., 267, 269 f., 274 f., 287, 291, 293 f., 298, 300–302
Averroes, 'Abū l-Walīd Muḥammad Ibn 'Aḥmad Ibn Rushd 107, 139, 158, 160–163, 240, 254
- Epitome of the De Anima 162
- GC De Anima 161
- GC Physicorum 161
- MC Categories 160
- MC De Interpretatione 160
- MC Isagoge 160
- MC Physicorum 161
- MC Posterior Analytics 161
- MC Prior Analytics 160

Bacon, Francis 98–100, 150, 181, 184, 216 f., 221–223, 225–227, 231
- De Augumentis Scentiarum 100
- De Sapienta Veterum 99
- Essays 43, 48, 112, 129, 155, 171 f., 217, 221, 225, 288, 299
- Novum Organum 98
Balmes (de), Abraham 161
- De intellectu et intellegibili 162
- Epitome of the De Anima 162
Bandeco, Daniel 119
- Monachusve Carmelita 119
- Pythagoras utrum fuerit Judaeus 119
barbarian 16 f., 20, 35 f., 216–218, 282
Barca (de la), Calderon 239, 247
beauty 17, 58, 61, 194, 204 f., 207, 232, 261, 289 f., 292
- feminine beauty 205
belief 3, 6 f., 15, 28, 30, 32, 37, 50, 54, 58, 67, 69, 74, 77 f., 85 f., 89, 91, 95–97, 100, 105, 119, 127, 150 f., 154, 157, 159, 166 f., 209, 216, 231, 251, 263, 286, 288, 292, 296
- principles of belief 50

Bene (del), David 73, 86, 207, 259, 324, 326
- Kissot le-vet David 207
Benjamin, Walter XIX, 187, 226, 256
Berardelli, Alessandro 195, 197
- Rime del Signor Numidio Paluzzi 197
Bernard of Clairvaux 24
Beroaldo, Filippo 52
Bessarione, Basilio 187
Bible, Hebrew Bible 3, 9, 11 f., 17 f., 21, 22, 30–32, 43, 48, 52, 67, 76, 79, 80, 115, 119, 122, 123, 152 f., 165 f., 175 f, 200, 236, 249, 273, 297
- Biblia 17 f., 19 f., 52 f.
- Septuagint 20, 21, 52
- Scriptures 8, 22, 86, 114, 115 f., 117, 173, 175, 239
Biblioteca Marciana 187
blasphemy 81, 102, 267
Bloch, Ernst XIX, 10, 14
Blois (de), Pierre 24
Bodin, Jean 73 f.
- Colloquium heptaplomeres 73
Boeckh, August 111, 121, 124 f., 134
- Encyclopädie und Methodologie 125
Bomberg, Heerz 40, 103, 314
Bonifaccio, Baldassarre 195–203, 205
- Dell'immortalità dell'anima 196, 202
- Risposta al Manifesto della Signora Sara Copia 200
Borsch, Johann Jacob 118 f.
- Dissertatio historica de peregrinationibus Pythagora 118
Boyle, Robert 97
- New experiments and observations touching cold 97
Bramante, Donato 183
- Heraclitus flens: Democritus ridens 183
Browne, Thomas 98
- Religio Medici 98
Bruno, Giordano 99, 137, 153
- Degli eroici furori 99
Brusoni, Girolamo (Giovanni Francesco Loredan) 61, 148, 178, 188, 193, 197, 280
- Le glorie de gli incogniti 188
Budde, Johann Franz 115 f., 119
- Introductio ad Historiam Philosophiae Ebraeorum 116, 119
Buridan, John 148, 157, 290
Burkhardt, Jacob 58

Buxtorf, Johannes   76, 84, 300 f., 304
– *Synagoga Judaica*   76, 84, 300 f.

Caerimonialia, ceremonial   63, 67, 71–77,
   81–88, 101–103, 136, 242, 244, 282
– ceremonial Laws   63, 69, 71–73, 82–83,
   88,100 f., 101, 103, 112
– ceremonial rites   XXI 63, 67, 71–77, 82, 83,
   88, 101–103, 113, 223, 266
– civil code (*iudicialia*)   71, 73, 74
– Luzzatto on *caerimonialia*   84–87, 91–96
– Mendelssohn on *caerimonialia*   89, 101–104
– custom 8, 26, 27, 63, 67, 69, 70, 74–76, 78,
   79, 82, 83, 87, 88, 90, 91, 95, 100, 112, 136,
   182, 186, 211, 217, 218, 221, 222, 229, 231–
   233, 244, 247, 249, 264
Calonymos ben David (Calonimo Calo)   161
– *Libellus seu epistola de connexione intellectus
   abstracti cum homine*   161
Camozza, Giovanni Battista   230
Caramuel Lobkowitz, Juan   240, 247, 249
Carbin (von), Victor   74, 76
– *De vita et moribus Iudaeorum*   74
– *Hierinne wirt gelesen, wie Her Victor von Carben, Wellcher eyn Rabi der Iude gewest ist zu
   Christlichem glawb komen*   74
– *Opus Aureum ac Novurn*   74
Casas (de las), Bartolomé   78
– *Historia de las India*   78
Casaubon, Isaac   230
Cassier, Ernst   58
category   71, 89, 104, 133, 144, 165, 214, 224 f.
cause   62, 85, 90–93, 95–99, 158, 170, 173 f.,
   221, 224, 232, 261, 266, 278, 293
– causa causarum (sibbat ha-sibbot)   62, 93,
   170, 173, 175
– efficient cause   276, 278
– final cause   278
– formal cause   278
– material cause   278
– sibba qeruva   62
Cebà, Ansaldo   194–197, 230
– *La Rheina Esther*   194
certainty   152–154, 157 f., 175, 213, 238, 288,
   291, 295
Chaldean, Chaldaic 6, 17, 37, 39, 43, 48, 135,
   189, 326
Champier, Symphorian   41
– *Simphoriani Champerii De Triplici disciplina*
   41

– *Symphoriani Champerii De quadruplici vita*
   41
Christiani, Fray Pablo   163, 169, 267, 300, 303,
   316
Chrysippus   217, 228
Cicero, Marcus Tulius   18, 38, 147, 290
– *Academica*   11, 73, 150
– *De finibus bonorum et malorum*   18
– *De Republica*   18, 299
– *Tusculanae disputationes*   18
Clearchus   13, 18
Clement of Alexandria   10 f., 19
– *Protrepticus*   7
– *Stromata*   7, 10, 19
Cohen, Hermann   45, 83, 137 f., 153, 192
– *Die Religion der Vernunft aus den Quellen des
   Judentums*   138
commandment 25, 63, 72, 74, 82, 96, 102 f.,
   112, 165 f., 236, 274
– *Mitzvoth*   127, 241 f.
commensurability   272
community   6, 9, 27 f., 33, 35–37, 47, 50, 62,
   74, 109, 121, 128 f., 131, 159, 166, 208 f.,
   218, 221, 236, 284, 287
– intellectual community   57
condemnation   29 f., 32, 45, 123, 242, 264,
   293
conjunction   162, 174, 180 f., 224
contingency   71, 208, 291
controversy   32, 44, 48, 82, 100, 154, 168,
   169, 175, 189, 197 f., 216 f., 267, 270–272,
   274, 287, 289, 293, 300
– debate   43, 45, 50, 51, 56, 60, 63, 79, 82,
   84, 88, 100, 105, 113 f., 118, 139, 143, 144,
   146, 150–154, 158, 167, 188, 189, 197, 207–
   208, 235, 237, 254, 255, 258, 266, 268–270,
   272, 273, 275, 276, 284, 285, 287, 294–299,
   302
– dispute   7, 40, 44 f., 72, 74 f., 82, 84, 88,
   127 f., 169, 170, 197, 98, 202, 203, 246, 2740,
   294, 300
– maḥloqet   269–271, 273
– querelle   4, 9, 43, 172
– wikuḥim   44 f.
convention   186, 216, 291
conversion   102, 147, 155, 187, 194, 199, 206,
   220

Copio Sullam, Sara   144, 188, 194, 205f., 208f., 230
- *Manifesto di Sarra Copia Sulam Hebrea* 195f., 205
- *Satire Sarreidi*   197
cosmopolitan   60
Costa (da), Uriel   155, 190, 198, 207
- *Exame das tradições farisaicas*   207
- *Sobre a mordalidade da alma do homem*   207
Cratander, Andreas   230
Cratylus   245–247
creation   3, 11f., 41, 59, 62, 67, 86, 88, 90, 114, 121, 124, 127, 130, 132, 146, 159, 163f., 173–175, 182, 188, 190, 196, 221, 233, 268, 274, 288
- Christian creation   59
Cremonini, Cesare   188, 197
Crescas, Ḥasdai   106, 153, 155, 177, 290
crisis   67f., 105, 136, 158, 162, 263, 294
Criticism 42, 46, 83, 88, 94–99, 107, 116f., 123, 125, 130, 134f., 152, 154, 170, 212, 216, 221, 223, 227, 236f., 240, 262f., 278, 287, 293, 295, 301
- criticism of rabbinical literature   170
- linguistic criticism   155
- rational criticism   155
- religious criticism   155
cult   56, 67, 74, 77, 83–85, 88, 90f., 124, 172, 295
culture, cultural   3, 5–7, 9, 14–16, 18, 20–22, 28, 30, 33, 37, 39, 45f., 57, 59f., 68f., 74, 77, 83, 92, 105–109, 120, 124, 127, 133–136, 143f., 146, 148f., 151, 156, 158–161, 175f., 178, 185–191, 198, 218, 237, 240, 242–244, 250f., 265, 281–286, 292, 294, 296, 302
- absence of culture   16, 36, 37, 151
- cultural autonomy   37
- cultural dialogue   185
- cultural memory   XIII
Curtius Rufus   224
- *Historia Alexandri Magni*   224

Dante Alighieri   107
- *Divina Commedia (Hell)*   239
- *Quaestio de aqua et terra*   107
debate (dispute)   7, 9, 14, 22, 37, 40, 42f., 44, 45, 50f., 56, 60, 63, 72, 74, 79, 82, 84, 88, 100, 105, 113, 118, 127,

deception   252, 258, 291
deconstruction   263
defeat   272
Demetrius of Phalerum   26
Democritus   18, 148, 221, 245, 256
demonstration   81, 178, 262, 278
- pars destruens   278
Demostenes   13
- *Contra Eubuliden*   13
- *Contra Stephanum*   13
Derrida, Jacques   XIX
Descartes, Réné   148, 150, 158, 261, 263, 280, 287
deviation   79, 211, 264, 272
dialectic, dialectical   5, 23, 143, 147, 157, 165, 183, 185, 194, 197, 205, 208, 236f., 242, 259, 263, 265f., 271f., 281, 283, 288, 290f., 294
- dialectic argumentation   157, 194, 214
- dialectic discussion   215, 270, 301
- dialectic process   282
dialogic   93, 148
Diaspora   28, 212, 221
Didymus   52
digression   272
Diodorus Siculus   18, 23
Diogenes Laertius   147
- *Vitae philosophorum*   147
disagreement   234, 246, 253, 289, 294f.
discourse   5, 25, 70, 115–117, 132, 186, 214, 227, 245, 250, 283, 287, 289
- importune discourse   248, 249
- discover (first), Protos Heuretes 3, 14, 18, 20, 21, 24, 281
dissertatio   19, 44, 56, 74, 77, 109, 116, 118f., 127, 138, 152, 170, 183, 192, 224, 235, 266f., 269, 278, 298–300
distinction   22f., 33, 62, 68, 71, 84f., 93, 105, 110, 115, 134, 149, 182, 230, 272
dogma, dogmatic   50, 68, 84, 86f., 89, 91, 100, 103f., 129, 132, 136, 139, 143f., 150, 156, 158, 168, 185, 187, 197, 208f., 213–218, 220, 223, 259, 263f., 274f., 277–280, 285, 288, 290–293, 315
- dogmatic belief   100, 103, 208
- dogmatic formulation   157, 288
- dogmatic system   151
- dogmatisation   68, 136
- new dogma   133–139
Donin, Nicholas   169

doubt 11, 20, 47f., 92, 95, 110f., 116f., 133, 143, 147–149, 151–157, 165–169, 173f., 179, 181, 187f., 191, 198, 200, 206–208, 221, 236, 242, 246, 248, 252, 258, 264, 280, 287, 289, 291–296
- Cartesian doubt 148
- doubt and perplexity 165
- *dubium* 117, 143, 165, 276, 278, 306
- methodological doubt 150, 157
Duns Scotus, Johannes 107, 148, 157, 183, 290
- *De primo principio* 107 f.

education 6, 99, 122, 131f., 134, 137, 156, 188f., 236, 240, 281, 293
- astrology (astronomy) 171, 292
- astronomy 50, 125, 160, 172, 178f., 272, 292
- humanistic education 133
- theological education 131
- arithmetic 22, 160, 178f., 179
- geometry 22, 172, 178f.; *figura figurarum* (geometrical figure) 175
- music 37, 51, 160, 178f., 188, 192–194, 239, 261
- ratio studiorum 159
- Trivium 160, 189
- Quadrivium 160, 189
eidola 256
Eliezer of Eilburg 155
Empedocles 97, 245
enquiry XXI, 90, 114, 125, 148, 156f., 188, 233, 246, 266, 277, 281, 287f., 291f., 294f.
Epicureanism 38
episteme 5, 37, 39, 281
- science of knowledge 5
- *scientia* 5
epistemology 4, 42f., 117, 139, 146, 150, 158, 263
epoché, ephectic 214, 277
equipollence 208, 214f., 271, 288, 290f., 296
esoteric, esotericism 6, 22f., 25, 33–36, 41, 53, 58, 107, 177, 282
- philosophical esotericism 36
- scientific esotericism 36
ethic 45–47, 113, 133, 137, 178, 234, 312, 314
- *Sittenlehre* 137
ethnography 74, 77
- polemical ethnography 77

Euclid 255
- *Optics* 149, 255, 257
Eupolemus 14
Eusebius of Caesarea 10, 11, 19, 252
- *Historia Ecclesiastica* 10
- *Praeparatio Evangelica* 7, 10f., 19, 56
exegesis, exegete 16, 28, 31, 62, 70, 94, 123f., 130, 165, 173, 273, 297, 300
exercise 107, 188, 198, 236, 238, 243f., 294f.
experience 23, 36, 49, 58, 98, 109, 120, 136, 215–218, 220, 245, 279, 285, 289, 291f.
Ezra 25–27, 70, 106, 290, 298

faith 45f., 51, 70, 75f., 81f., 86, 91f., 100, 118, 127, 132, 149, 157, 159, 174, 177, 206, 208, 212, 223, 229, 240, 242, 249, 263f., 284
Farisol, Avraham 48 f., 75
- *Magen Avrhahm* 48f.
Ficino, Marsilio 41f., 67, 90
fideism 264, 285
Figo, 'Azaryah ben Efrayim 249f.
- *Sefer Binah le-'Ittim* 249f.
Finzi, Moses 161, 194
Fire 4, 179, 183, 193, 206, 251, 273
- pure fire 256
Fonseca (de), Isaac Aboab 207
Foucault, Michel XIII
- *Archeology of Knowledge* XIII
freedom 50f., 53f., 57, 59f., 120, 128, 144, 150, 185f., 225, 232, 236f., 268
- human freedom 60
Freher, Marquard 230

Galatino, Pietro 43–45, 47–49, 57
- *Opus toti christianae Reipublicae maxime utile* 43, 48, 49
Galen 41, 98, 222f., 257f., 258f.,
- *De placitis Hippocratis et Platonis* 98
Galilei, Galileo 175, 250, 252
- *Dialogo sopra I due massimi sistemi del mondo* 252
- *Il Saggiatore*
- *Sidereus Nuncius* 250
Gassendi, Pierre 213, 217, 221, 242
- *De logicae fine* 213
- *Opera* 8, 77, 106, 118, 164, 181, 188, 199f., 212f., 217, 241, 304, 315, 318
- *Sintagma* 213

Geiger, Abraham   120, 127–132
– *Der Kampf christlicher Theologen*   128 f.
– *Die Gründung einer jüdisch-theologischen Facultät Was hat Mohammed aus dem Judenthume aufgenommen?*   130 f., 131 f.
Gentiles   15, 30, 36, 62, 70, 78, 81 f., 86, 96, 100, 172, 176, 199 f.
Georgijevic, Bartholomeus   78
– *De Turcarum moribus epitome*   78
Gerolamo, Aleandro   191
Gersonides (ben), Levi   165, 180
– *Sefer Milḥamot ha-Shem*   180
ghetto   74, 77, 84, 105, 120, 125, 144, 184–186, 192, 194 f., 197, 209 f., 221, 230, 237, 241
Gimma, Giacinto   186 f.
Giolito de Ferrara   188
Giovanni Pico della Mirandola   42, 60, 61, 63, 70, 106 f., 114, 116, 162
– *Oratio De hominis dignitate*   60
Giovanni Francesco Pico della Mirandola   264 f., 280
Glatzer, Nahum N   121 f.
gnoseology   53, 158
God, Deus, Creator, Father   7–12, 16 f., 17, 19, 22–27, 29–33, 35, 37, 41, 46, 48, 50, 54, 56, 59 f., 62, 69, 71 f., 72, 82 f., 85–88, 92, 95 f., 100–102, 108, 114, 117, 121, 129, 136 f., 152, 154, 164, 167, 169, 171–173, 176, 180–182, 184, 190, 195, 199 f., 202, 205 f., 218–221, 223, 225, 229, 232 f., 236 f., 246, 249, 264, 266–268, 273–277, 279, 286, 293, 299–301, 304, 306, 312, 314, 323 f.
– God is a body   219
– son of God   31, 48, 60, 83
– voice of God (Stimme Gottes)   11 f., 12, 268, 298
– words of God   11 f., 122
Goethe (von), Johann Wolfgang   59, 128
Gonzaga, Cesare   192
Gonzaga, Federico   192
Gorgias   246
Government   11, 30, 82, 211, 214, 221, 225, 226, 234–237
Grimani, Bartolo (Bartolomeo)   210 f.

Halakhah, Jewish Law   VIII, 11–12, 15, 17, 22 f., 25–30, 50, 69–74, 77 f., 80–88, 90, 101–104, 112, 127, 128, 130, 132, 136, 165, 172, 176, 193, 211, 223, 236, 267, 268, 269, 273, 295, 300 f.
Halevi, Judah   243
– *Sefer ha-Kuzari*   38 f., 70, 178, 180
Haskalah XXI,   150–151
heavens   82, 93, 100, 127, 163, 169, 171, 201 f., 202, 205, 232, 270 f., 273, 275
– celestial bodies   164, 174, 199, 250
– orbit   67, 174
– sun   98, 173 f., 201, 221, 250 f., 279
Hegel, Georg Wilhelm Friedrich   68, 111, 136, 282
Hermes Trismegistus   10, 41
– *Corpus Hermeticum*   6
– hermetic traditon   6, 48, 163, 282
Hermippus of Smyrna   18
Henry of Ghent   148, 157, 183, 290
Heraclitus   13, 178, 182 f., 245, 250
Heresy, Heretical   28, 46, 49, 50, 52, 54, 76, 79, 114 f., 115, 155, 157, 159, 171, 198, 206, 241 f.
historicisation   43, 67, 113, 132 f., 139, 156, 265, 285
Holy Spirit   62
Homer   5, 9, 12, 14, 229
Hoogstraten (van), Jacob   44
Horace   5, 195, 232, 239
– *Epistolae*   5
– *Odes*   232, 239
Horman, William   224
Horowitz, Saul   98, 137
Hrabanus, Maurus   53
– *De universo*   53
Humanism, humanis, humanitas   6, 38, 45, 58–61, 67, 90, 107, 149 f., 160, 175, 183, 186
– homo christianus   61, 63
– homo iudaicus   63
– homo novus   62
– homo universalis   58
– Renaissance man   58
– studium humanitatis (humanitas)   61, 90
humanity   17, 58, 70, 79, 85, 90 f., 95, 130, 184, 223, 283
humankind   60, 63
human essence   204
Humboldt (von), Alexander   59, 121, 124
Hume, David   111 f., 150, 234, 294
– *Of Superstition and Enthusiasm*   112
– *On Academical or Sceptical Philosophy*   294

Huser, Konrad (Lombardus Marcus) 76
– *Tractatus de imposturis et ceremoniis Iudaeorum* 76

Iamblichus 10, 60
– *De Mysteriis Aegyptiorum* 10
– *Protreptikos* 60
Ibn Gabirol, Shlomo XIX
Idealism, idealist 58, 60, 282
identity 9, 16, 28, 31f., 34, 57, 69, 87f., 105, 107, 109f., 137, 151, 178, 201, 212, 215, 278, 281
– Jewish identity 34, 88, 109
– Rabbinic identity 269
– Scientific identity 34
idolatrous 50, 76, 79, 171
immortality 102, 164, 180, 197, 199, 203, 207f.
– immortality of the intellect 199
impresa 226, 237
incapacity 236, 262, 272
inconsistency 152, 260, 272, 298
individual 5, 41, 46, 53, 57f., 60–62, 72, 99, 134, 150, 157–159, 164, 172, 194, 201, 203f., 208, 215, 224, 228, 231, 236, 282f., 288, 296
– individual being 58
– individual essence 201
– individual judgement 57
– individual perception 158
– Rational individual 53
inquisition, inquisitor 44, 55, 94, 157, 186–188, 198, 206, 244, 321
intellect 62, 94, 103, 161f., 179–181, 198, 200, 218, 245f., 262f., 292
– active intellect 162, 188, 204
– agent intellect 180, 188
– passive intellect 204
Isaac (ben), Zeraḥyah ben She'alti'el Ḥen 72, 102, 105, 113, 160f., 187, 207, 219, 223, 249, 271, 274, 298, 314, 320
Isocrates 18
– *Busiris* 18
Israel (ben), Menasseh 9, 21f., 25f., 28–33, 45, 51, 60, 62, 71f., 83, 88, 101f., 105, 109, 150, 152f., 173f., 192, 194, 198, 207f., 241, 249, 268, 270, 298, 305, 307f.
– *Nishmat Ḥayyim* 207
– *To His Highnesse the Lord Protector of the Common-wealth of England* 101f.

– *Vindiciae Iudaeorum* 101
Israeli, Isaac XIX
Isserles, Moses 62
– *Torat ha-'ola* 62
Iudecus, Nicolaus 191
Iulianus 18
– *Misopogon* 18

Jerome 52f., 69, 71
– *Contra Rufinum* 52
Jewish influx 53
Joachim of Fiore 54
Joël, Manuel 137
John of La Rochelle 71
Josephus 13–16, 18, 20, 107
– *Contra Apionem* 13–15, 18
– *Prōtos Heuretēs* 3, 14, 24
judgement 49–53, 57f., 148, 151, 189, 219, 237, 245f., 248, 253f., 270f., 287, 291, 294f.
Jüdische Philosophie 67, 72, 106, 109f., 131
Justinian 9
– *Novella* 9

Kabbalah 40, 45, 69f., 105f., 113–119, 163, 218f., 241, 279, 282
– Christian kabbalah 116
– Kabbalistic emanation 41
– Philosophy and kabbalah 113
Kalam 137, 153
Kaloskagathos 5
Kant, Immanuel 136, 138, 151, 234
Karaite Judaism 87
Kittel, Gerhard 134
– *Theologisches Wörterbuch zum Alten Testament*; 134
knowledge 4–6, 12, 18f., 24, 28, 33, 35, 38–40, 42f., 46f., 49, 51, 56f., 62, 67, 69, 90, 93–96, 103, 106f., 110f., 117, 122, 125, 133–136, 146, 149, 151–154, 165–168, 170–172, 174, 176f., 179–184, 186, 203, 206, 213, 233–237, 239–242, 244–249, 252f., 259f., 263f., 271f., 277, 279–281, 286f., 291–293, 295
– divine knowledge 3, 5, 117, 242
– experiential knowledge 49
– external knowledge 24
– human knowledge 43, 93, 95, 110f., 176f., 181, 184, 238f., 242, 244, 246, 248f., 260f., 264, 272, 285, 289

- internal knowledge 24
- non-human knowledge 176
- origin of knowledge 3, 21
- postcolonial system of knowledge 151

Lactantius, Lucius Caecilius Firmianus 7, 9, 89, 159
- *Institutiones Divinae* 7, 89
Lambertesco, Ottavio 193
Lando, Ortensio 188
- *Quattro libri de dubbi con le solutioni a ciascun dubbio accommodate* 188
Lange, Joachim 32, 123, 278
language 5, 21, 28–30, 37, 39f., 47f., 67, 69, 75, 84, 86, 89, 92, 119, 123, 127f., 130, 133–135, 139, 155f., 171f., 175, 183f., 186, 200, 207, 214, 217, 232, 237, 241, 243, 269, 282, 284–286, 288–290, 293, 297
- holy language 266, 297
- primitive language 290
- vir bilinguis 133
- vir trilinguis 133
Lascaris, Janus 191
law 3, 6f., 6, 7, 15, 17, 25–30, 35f., 50, 69–74, 78., 80–88, 90, 95, 143, 179, 187, 189, 207, 211, 218, 223, 236, 237, 247, 272, 282, 287
- law of reason 70, 81
- natural law 71–73, 78–81, 112, 247
- ritual law 82, 87
legitimacy 6, 9, 87, 215
- messianic legitimacy 215
Leibowitz, Yeshayahu 60
Leone Ebreo 40, 47, 105, 190
- *Dialoghi d'amore* 40, 190
- *Telunah 'al ha-zman* 190
Lessing, Gotthold Ephraim 92
- *Nathan the Wise* 92
libertinism 188
limit 17, 29, 57, 77, 80, 174, 242, 251, 267, 275, 286f., 291f.
- fines XIV
- limes XIV
Lipmann, Yom Tov ben Solomon Muehlhausen 121, 267, 273f., 297, 316, 319, 322–326
- *Sefer Niṣṣaḥon* 267f., 297
literature 3f., 10f., 18, 21f., 24–28, 37, 44f., 47, 59, 61, 68, 70, 75, 87, 101, 110, 113, 119f., 123, 125, 129, 132, 134f., 137, 139, 143, 145, 148, 150, 156, 169, 179, 186, 194, 198f., 211, 225f., 232, 235f., 239f., 243f., 260, 265f., 269f., 274, 282f., 289, 297
- canonical literature 144
- rabbinical literature 25, 28f., 121, 123, 169, 174, 297
liturgy 83, 112
Livy 222
- Ab urbe condita 222
locus communis 4, 183, 242
logic 3, 5, 9, 21, 39f., 42, 49, 86f., 97, 121, 148f., 158, 160–162, 173, 184, 201f., 212–216, 222, 248f., 266f., 269, 272, 274f., 282f., 285f., 291
- anti logic 158
- contradiction, contradictory 17, 53, 76, 134, 139, 152, 173, 181, 213, 215, 232, 234f., 237, 253, 257f., 264–267, 269f., 272–276, 289, 291, 299, 301, 320
- principle of contradiction 253, 265, 267, 272
- principle of non-contradiction 231, 266, 300
- reductio ad absurdum 272
logos 20, 134, 245, 247
logos hellenicos 16
Löw, Yehudah (Maharal) 49f., 50, 54f., 62, 105, 113, 144, 167–177, 292
- *Be'er ha-Golah* 170, 176f.
Lucan 229, 262
- *Pharsalia* 229, 262
Luther, Martin 53, 75f., 82f., 240, 300f., 304
- *Commentary on the Epistle to the Galatians* 82
Luzzatto, Samuel David 241, 263
Luzzatto, Simone XIX, 60, 77, 83f., 84–88, 89f., 90–97, 99f., 102, 106–109, 138, 143f., 150, 155–157, 167f., 168, 182, 184f., 185, 189, 209–215, 217–228, 230–234, 237–252, 254–264, 272, 285, 289f., 296
- Rabbi of Venice 84, 87, 91, 100, 144, 209, 225, 259, 263
- *Discorso circa il stato degli Hebrei* 77, 84–87, 90–93, 96, 100, 106, 108, 109, 167, 168, 189, 209–214, 217, 220, 221, 223–231, 238, 239, 243, 246, 247, 249, 250
- *Socrate overo dell'humano sapere* 90, 92–96, 107, 108, 155 168, 184, 189, 214–264
Lyotard, Jean-François 137

Machiavelli, Niccolò   95, 149, 216, 224f.
magic, magical   4, 105, 163, 196, 262, 292
– *magush*   152
Maimonides, Moseh ben Maimonide   35–37, 50, 71f., 77, 105f., 109, 113, 117, 138f., 146, 154, 156, 164–166, 169f., 176–178, 240, 249, 267, 274, 289f., 295, 299, 301, 307f.
– *Mishneh Torah*   50, 154
– *Moreh Nevukhim (Guide of the Perplexed)*   35, 36 f., 40, 71, 169, 170, 174f., 295f.
– *Sefer Shoftim*   138
Maimon, Salomon   35, 151, 155, 271
malicious genius   151
Mantino, Jacob   161
Manutius, Aldus   191
Margaritha, Antonius   75f., 82
– *Der gantz Jüdisch glaub*   75f.
Martinengo, Fortunato   187
Martin, Raimund   9f., 16, 45, 59, 74, 78, 121, 155, 161, 183, 276, 280, 299, 315
– *Pugio Fidei*   45, 315
Marx, Karl   282
Mathematic   101, 125, 172, 178–180, 194, 213, 240, 249, 272, 289
– language of mathematic   175
matter   3, 15f., 21, 33, 36, 48, 50, 54, 63, 67, 73, 82, 86, 95, 114, 125, 127, 130, 134, 154, 163f., 168, 171, 180, 182, 189, 199, 201–204, 213, 216, 237, 239f., 242, 247, 259f., 288, 295, 297f., 300f.
– eternity of the matter   202
Mattioli, Pietro Andrea   46
medicus prudens   47, 58
Medigo (del), Elijah   161f.
Megasthenes   13, 18, 20
Mélanchthon, Philippe   50, 51, 258f.
Melissus   245
memory   17, 23f., 28, 54, 83, 123, 166, 290, 292, 299
Mendelssohn, Moses   88f., 96, 100–103, 105, 121, 151, 202, 244, 296
– *Jerusalem oder über religiöse Macht und Judentum*   101
– *Morgenstunden oder Vorlesungen über das Daseyn Gottes*   101
– *Phädon oder über die Unsterblichkeit der Seele*   101
– *Über die Frage was heißt aufklären* 101
Messer Leon, Judah   160
– *GC Physicorum*   161
– *MC Categories*   160
– *MC De Interpretatione*   160
– *MC Isagoge*   160
– *MC Physicorum*   161
– *MC Posterior Analytics*   161
– *MC Prior Analytics*   160
– *Sefer Nofet Ṣufim*   160
metaphysic   139, 150, 151, 153f., 154,158, 162, 178–181, 202, 216, 265
– divine philosophy   178, 181
– first philosophy   178, 181
method   4f., 8, 26, 34, 40, 43f., 49–51, 55, 70, 115, 125, 131, 137, 146, 148, 150f., 157, 160, 163, 165, 171f., 214–216, 248, 252, 263f., 283, 285, 292, 294, 299
Migas (ibn), Avraham   138
– *Kevod Elohim*   138
miracle   93, 103, 115, 174, 262
Modena, Leone   49, 77, 83, 192–195, 197, 207, 209
– *Historia de riti Hebraici*   83
– *Magen wa-Ḥerev*   49
Molino, Francesco   238
money, usury   52, 83, 92, 222, 223, 225–227
Montaigne (de), Michel   78, 80, 99, 149f., 217, 234, 241f.
– *Apologie de Raymond Sebon*   99
– *Essays De l'éxperience*   217
moral, moralism, morality   35, 44, 57, 71f., 79, 82, 88, 90, 93, 95, 99f., 112, 128, 144, 159, 166, 187f., 201, 216–218, 222, 225, 227f., 261, 264, 288
– a-moralism   291
– moralism   291
– moral value   176
– natural morality   85, 90f., 218
Morel, Frédéric   230
More, Thomas   226
– *Utopia*   226, 234
Morosini, Giulio   192f.
– *Via della fede*   192f.
Mortera, Saul Levi   207
Moscato, Judah   168, 177–184, 213, 264, 292, 295,
– *Nefuṣot Yehudah Qol Yehudah*   178
Mosellanus, Petrus   47
Moses, Musaeus   3, 5–8, 10–14, 18f., 27, 29–31, 35f., 40, 44, 56, 82, 88, 102f., 108, 112, 117, 267, 269, 273, 277, 279, 283,

290, 295, 301, 303, 306–308, 314, 316, 319, 322, 324, 327
– Orpheus 10 f., 246
Muhammad al-Shahrastānī 38
mythos 14, 20
– demythologization 67, 68, 132, 133–139

Nachmanides, Moses ben Nachman 169
narratio (historia) 10, 46, 55 f., 73, 79, 91, 95, 121 f., 217, 241 f., 271, 277 f., 299, 315, 318
nations 21, 30–32, 34, 36, 45, 78, 95, 102, 110, 133, 163, 165, 187, 235
– condemnation of the nations 29, 30
– homicide 36, 73, 80, 313
– nations of the world 9, 28–32, 36
nature 12 f., 18, 23, 62, 67, 71 f., 75, 78, 80 f., 85, 90, 95, 97 f., 100, 102–104, 108, 110, 116, 124, 129, 136, 144 f., 150, 154, 157, 161, 173, 179 f., 182 f., 188, 195, 202 f., 209, 211, 214–216, 218–220, 224 f., 227–229, 232 f., 239, 253, 256, 258, 262 f., 269 f., 275, 281, 285 f., 288, 291, 293
necessity (*necessitas*) 25, 40, 61, 129–131, 154, 212, 214, 220, 223–225, 227, 270, 286
Nehemia 25
Nicholas of Autrecourt 148 f., 157, 290
Nicola of Cusa 41, 79, 90, 177, 212
– *Cribatio alchorani* 79
– *De conjecturis* 79
– *De docta ignorantia* 177
– *De pace fidei* 212
Nietzsche, Friedrich Wilhelm XIII, 154
Genealogy of Morals XIII
Nola (da), Ambrogio Leone 190
Numenius of Apamea 19

obligation 39, 57, 85 f., 90 f., 168, 192, 224, 282
ontology 58–63, 117
– confessional ontology 59
– religious ontology 58
opinion 18, 35 f., 41, 43, 51–54, 59, 72, 77, 82, 86 f., 93, 95, 102, 108, 111, 114, 127, 135, 143, 152, 154, 157, 159, 167–170, 175, 181–183, 186, 188, 191, 195 f., 198 f., 205, 208, 213, 217 f., 221, 226, 228, 231, 234–236, 242, 245–248, 255–258, 268, 270, 273–275, 278 f., 288, 291 f., 296, 310, 314
– false opinion 95, 244

– individual opinion 54
optic 257, 259
oracle 9 f., 132, 229
– Chaldean oracle 6
– Sibylline oracle 9, 10 f.
Origen of Alexandria 7
– *Contra Celsum* 7 f.,
orthodoxy 16, 50, 54, 156, 198, 206
Oviedo Gonzalo (de), Fernandez 79
– *Historia general y natural de las Indias* 79 f.

pagan 7, 16 f., 19 f., 27 f., 30, 36, 57, 70, 82, 85, 100, 170, 280
Pagnini, Santes 52
pain 61, 222, 228 f.
panegyric 16, 23
paradox 20, 234, 284, 291 f., 294 f.
PaRDeS 173
Parmenides 245
patriarch 132, 277, 279
Persio 8
– *Saturae* 8
Petrarch, Francesco 183, 295
Petronius 8
– *Satyricon* 8
Pfefferkorn, Johann 44, 74–76
– *Ich heyß ain büchlein der iuden peicht* 74
– *Libellus de judaica confessione sive sabbato afflictionis* 74
Philo of Alexandria 10, 16, 20, 41, 48, 51, 107 f., 123, 135, 147
– *De Confusione Linguarum* 13
– *De Vita Mosis* 17, 123
– *Legum allegoriae* 13
– *Quaestiones in Genesim* 13
– *Quis divinarum rerum heres sit* 13
– *Quod omnis probus liber sit* 12 f.
– *Specialibus Legibus* 12, 85
philosophia naturalis 41, 78
philosophia perennis (perennial philosophy) 6, 8, 68, 90, 115 f., 118, 135, 156
philosophoumena 200
physic 97, 99, 151, 153, 161 f., 165, 178, 199, 249
piety 128 f., 283
Pius V, Pope 47
plagia, plagiarism 3, 7, 11–18, 20 f., 33 f., 48, 197, 282

Plato, Platonism   7f., 10–12, 14f., 18f., 19,
    23–25, 40f., 93, 97, 101, 117f., 147–149,
    157, 163, 201, 218–220, 226, 228, 237,
    245f., 248, 256, 265, 274, 285, 287f., 293
– *Apology*   15f., 78, 136, 170, 214f., 236f., 243
– *Crito*   236, 255
– *Epinomis*   18
– *Hippias*   93–95, 248
– *Phaedrus*   22, 24f.
– *Timaeus*   97, 256
– Neoplatonism 19, 20, 40f., 60, 153, 178, 179,
    190, 282
plausibility   38f., 213, 215, 275, 288, 291
pleasure   95, 152, 195, 228f., 235f., 290
Pliny the Elder   262
– *Epistulae*   93, 195, 239
– *Naturalis Historia*   85
Plotinus   42, 54
Plutarch   100, 150
– *Moralia*   71, 100
politic, political   5, 10, 17, 21f., 26–28, 30f.,
    37, 39, 59, 67, 71f., 74, 77, 81, 87f., 90,
    94f., 100, 102, 105, 112f., 123, 128, 132,
    139, 144, 149f., 158f., 184–186, 209, 211–
    215, 217, 220–227, 231, 234–236, 241,
    243f., 247, 249, 251, 267, 281, 283, 287,
    296, 298–300, 302
– political humanity   90
Poliziano(Angelo Ambrogini)   230
– *Caratteri*   8, 230
Polibius   95
– *Histories*   95
Pomponazzi, Pietro   188
Pontano, Giovanni   190
Porphyry   19
Portaleone, Avraham   53f., 249
– *Shilṭe ha-Gibborim*   53f.
Postcolonial Studies   151
premise   9, 18, 38, 40, 55f., 61, 69, 78, 99,
    103f., 116, 120, 132–134, 139, 178, 208,
    234, 245–247, 259, 272, 276, 285
probable   213, 217, 237, 240, 246–248, 259,
    266, 289, 291, 295
proof   14, 32, 40, 42, 72, 80, 130, 167, 170,
    175, 177, 204, 210, 215, 239, 242, 266, 275
Properzio   52
prophecy   8, 15, 36, 38, 62, 96, 138, 171
proselytism   30, 86, 223
Prospero, Mandosio   195
Protagoras   245, 260

protestant, protestantism   43, 50f., 69, 76f.,
    82, 84, 87f., 112f., 118, 125, 132, 136, 144,
    152, 156, 175, 198, 265f., 269, 274–276,
    283
Pseudo-Iustinus   7
– *Cohortatio ad Graecos*   7f.
punishment   81, 86, 95, 102, 170, 174, 176,
    207
purpose   17, 68, 70, 75f., 80, 83, 88, 95, 114,
    117, 124, 164, 180f., 195, 197, 221, 229,
    239, 266, 272f., 276, 280, 298
– *sofah*   273, 276
– *takhlit*   273
Pyrrhonism, Pyrrhonian (Pyrrhon)   90, 146,
    149, 219f., 224, 234, 253, 277f., 287
Pythagoras   11f., 14, 18f., 118f., 244, 246, 255

Quenstedt, Johannes Andrea   77
– *Sepultura veterum sive tractatus de antiquis
    ritibus*   77
Quintilianus, Marcus Fabius   18
– *Institutio Oratoria*   18
Quṭb ad-Dīn Maḥmūd ibn Masʿūd aš-Šīrāzī   38

Rabbis, rabbinic   25, 28f., 40, 48–50, 54f.,
    60, 62, 69f., 72, 87, 89f., 102, 107–109,
    113, 117, 119, 127, 130f., 144, 147f., 150,
    152, 154, 156, 159f., 163, 168f., 173f.,
    176f., 179, 184f., 188, 192f., 195, 208,
    212f., 215, 217, 220f., 230f., 234–236,
    242f., 250, 261, 265–271, 273–276,
    292f., 295, 297f., 300f., 310f., 323–325
– rabbinical Judaism   9, 32–38
– ḥakhamim   32
– sages   18f., 28f., 32, 36, 41, 52, 72, 167,
    168, 170–174, 176, 177, 180
Ramus, Petrus   260
– *Opticae libri quatuor*   260
reader   24, 27, 37, 49–54, 57, 59, 62, 87, 92,
    94f., 98, 110, 116f., 120, 123, 129f., 136,
    143, 145f., 163f., 168, 172f., 176, 179, 184,
    192, 194, 196, 205, 216f., 223, 227, 229–
    232, 234, 237–239, 241, 243, 252, 254,
    262, 265–267, 269f., 275, 281f., 292
– illuminated reader   50
– *lector prudens*   42, 51–53, 57, 58, 247
– *qoreh maskil*   51
Realkritik   124, 130
reason, rational   9, 18, 22, 26f., 37f., 41, 53f.,
    60, 71, 73, 80f., 84–86, 89, 91, 93, 95f.,

100, 102–104, 107, 112 f., 123 f., 127, 135, 138, 143 f., 151, 153, 155 f., 158, 168 f., 173 f., 184, 186, 188, 193, 198 f., 202, 206, 209, 211, 214, 216, 223 f., 236–238, 240, 242–250, 258, 260 f., 264, 272 f., 275, 283 f., 286–289, 293–295, 298, 300
– human reason   96, 168, 238, 242, 295
Recanati, Menaḥem   40
Reformation (Protestant)   43, 44 f., 50 f., 69, 74 f., 76 f., 77, 82, 84, 87 f., 109, 112, 112 f., 118, 122 f., 125, 132, 136, 144, 150, 152, 156, 158, 175, 194,198, 224, 238, 265 f., 269, 274–276, 301 f.
Reimann, Jakob Friedrich   143,265, 276
– *An Salomo fuerit Scepticus?*   276
relativism   218, 288, 291
religion   5, 8, 10, 34, 37, 45, 55 f., 58 f., 63, 67–70, 76, 78 f., 83, 85–87, 89–93, 95 f., 100–105, 109, 112, 120, 128 f., 132, 135–139, 144, 152, 157 f., 174, 184, 188, 205, 208–211, 214 f., 223, 236, 242, 249 f., 263 f., 266, 282, 284–286, 295 f., 325
– confession 50, 59, 63, 86 f., 132, 136, 159, 208, 250, 297 f.
– authority and religion   108
– Jewish philosophy of religion   135, 139, 143
– Jewish religion   8, 67–69, 75, 85, 88–91, 100, 105, 111 f., 139, 157, 202 f., 211, 270, 282
– natural religion   70
– Philosophy and religion   20, 92, 139
– practical religion   96
– pragmatic religion   96
– *Religionsphilosophie* (Philosophy of religion)   68, 135–137
– rituus varietate 90
– true religion   8, 67, 69, 89 f., 92–94, 96, 207
– universal religion   86
– Irreligion   155
Republic   46, 74, 210, 222, 226, 229, 243, 298
– Republic of Venice (Serenissima)   144, 187, 222, 225
– *res publica*   221
response   14, 16 f., 29, 39, 45, 47, 53, 62, 83, 128, 139, 151 f., 196, 200, 203, 206, 223, 227, 272, 281
Reuchlin, Johannes   44 f., 47, 57, 69 f., 74, 114, 116

revelation   8, 13, 15, 29, 40, 45, 49, 56, 71, 78, 86 f., 89, 93, 95, 103, 107–109, 130, 136, 138, 168, 172 f., 175–177, 184, 223, 238, 240, 242, 249, 271, 285, 292–295
reward 102, 221, 235 f., 248
– remuneration   144
– doctrine of remuneration   144
rhetoric, rhetorical   6, 53, 107, 130, 143, 160, 181, 205–206, 215, 230, 236, 243, 269, 272, 278, 288, 294
Rhode, Ambrosius   260
– *Optica Ambrosii Rhodii*   260
Risner, Friedrich   260
Roll, Reinhard Heinrich   143, 278 f.
Rosenroth (von), Christian Knorr   106, 116 f.
– *Cabbala Denudata* 106 f., 116–117
Rossi (de'), Bonaiuto (Azaria de' Rossi)   24, 41, 43, 47, 49, 51, 54–57, 62, 113, 144, 167–170, 172, 175–177,
– *Sefer Me'or 'Enayim*   41

Saadia Gaon   167, 208, 271, 275
– *Sefer Emunot we-de'ot*   167
Sabunde (de), Raymundus   78
– *Theologia naturalis*   78, 136
Sánchez, Francisco   150, 155
– *Quod Nihil Scitur*   150
Sannazzaro, Iacopo   190
Santa Fe (de), Geronimo   169
scepticism, sceptic, sceptical   4, 37, 38, 43, 58, 62, 68, 78, 90, 93, 95, 103, 106, 108, 136, 139, 143–159, 162, 167 f., 176 f., 182–184, 186–188, 197, 207, 209, 212–222, 224, 227, 232–237, 240–243, 245 f., 247, 248 f., 253, 259, 261–265, 267, 272, 274–277, 279 f., 283, 285–296
– academic scepticism   147, 213, 287
– anti scepticism   147, 148, 295
– epistemological scepticism   236
– Jewish scepticism   143, 146 f., 151, 153–157, 265, 267, 281, 285 f.
– radical scepticism   249, 283
– skepsis   146–149, 151–155, 158, 168, 183, 221, 234, 241, 253, 264, 276, 280, 284, 287
– *skeptische Geistesströmung*   153
– sceptical nature   144
– sceptical vein   158
– tropoi   147, 217, 219 f.
Schiller, Friedrich   59

Schleiermacher, Friedrich 128 f., 134–136, 283
- *Zweite(n) Sendschreiben über die Glaubenslehre an Dr. Lücke* 128
Schleiner, Winfried 47
scholar 4, 16, 32, 43, 50 f., 53, 57–59, 67 f., 70, 74, 77 f., 89 f., 105, 108, 115, 118 f., 121, 130–135, 137, 144, 146 f., 149, 153 f., 157–159, 161–163, 165 f., 168–172, 174, 177, 192, 195, 213 f., 234–236, 240, 249, 253, 266, 269, 274, 276, 278 f., 287, 293, 297 f., 300
- Christian scholar 3, 47, 69 f., 72, 76, 79, 84, 298
- Jewish scholar 3
- Muslim scholar 38, 154, 286
- Protestant scholar XXII
Scholastic, Scholasticism 70, 71, 93, 107, 158–162, 165, 240, 263
- Hebrew Scholasticism 160, 163, 165
- quaestio disputata 163, 165, 186 f, 200, 206
Science 3, 5 f., 10, 21, 35–40, 44 f., 47, 50, 55, 57, 62, 89, 92, 98, 108–110, 122–125, 128–132, 137, 139, 148, 150 f., 155, 158, 160 f., 167 f., 170–173, 175–184, 188, 213, 215, 217, 234, 236 f., 241 f., 248–252, 254, 256 f., 259, 263 f., 271, 279, 281, 285, 291–293
- divine science 182
- ethical science 179
- mathematical science 178–180
- metaphysical science 3, 6, 35, 150
- physical science 179
- science of Judaism (*Wissenschaft des Judentums*) 122, 124, 127, 129, 131 f.
- secret Jewish science 45
Scot, Michael 161
sect 6–8, 22, 208, 303
- Pythagorean sect 248
sefirah 218–220
Seneca, Lucius Annaeus 93, 150, 227–229
- *Epistulae morales ad Lucilium* 227
Sennert, Andrea 113 f., 266
- *Exercitationes philologicarum Heptas altera* 114
senses 60, 67, 94, 162, 168, 173, 182, 204, 218, 246, 252–254, 259–261, 263 f., 271, 283, 291 f., 295
Sepharad, Sephardic 36, 154, 157, 271, 274

Sextus Empiricus 38, 147, 149, 157, 215–220, 292
- *Against the Mathematicians* 263
- *Against the Professor* 216
- *Outlines of Pyrrhonism* 147, 149, 157, 216, 218 f., 253 f.
- empiricism 38, 147, 149, 157, 214–220, 292
Sforno, 'Ovadyah 143, 158, 162–167, 276
- *Lumen Gentium* 163, 165
- *Or 'Ammim* 163, 165
Shakespeare, William 99, 150, 239
- *The Merchant of Venice* 225
Shaw, Duncan 111
- *The History and Philosophy of Judaism* 111
shelemah 72
Shem-Tov ibn Falaquera 39 f., 40
- *Iggeret ha-wikuaḥ* 40
- *Sefer ha-Ma'a lot* 39
significance 4, 27, 31, 54, 88, 100, 113, 135, 169, 173, 175, 216, 243, 283, 296
- natural significance 216
silence 24, 148, 208, 244, 248, 272, 295
Silva (da), Samuel 207
- *Tratado da immortalidade da alma* 207
Simplicius 220
- *Commentary on Categories* 220
Simulacra 255–257, 261
sin 7 f., 35, 73, 79–82, 98 f., 103, 115, 174, 177, 199, 202, 205, 226–228, 233, 264, 301, 305, 308, 318, 325
- original sin 54, 57, 199, 202, 205
Socrates (philosopher) 5, 11–13, 22 f., 93–95, 148, 150, 201, 213 f., 226–229, 234, 236–240, 242–248, 250, 252, 260, 263 f., 287, 293
- socratism 291
Solomon 4, 17, 30 f., 92, 155, 181–183, 199, 228, 276–280, 297
Solution 139, 150, 156, 165, 199, 206, 245, 276, 287, 295
Sommi (de'), Leone 191–193
Soncino, Gershom 43, 127, 268
soul 61, 77, 83, 86, 93, 131, 161 f., 164 f., 180, 191, 194, 196, 199, 202–208, 228–230, 239, 256, 295
- animal soul 227
- immortality of the soul 101, 144, 157 f., 161–163, 188, 195–200, 202 f., 206–208
- intellective soul 180
- perfection 61, 164, 166, 181, 264

Spencer, John 77
– *De legibus Hebraeorum* 77
Spinoza, Baruch XIX, 87f., 96, 103, 105, 108, 116, 118, 150, 184, 203, 207, 221, 242, 249, 264, 285, 295
– *Tractatus* 49, 71, 199, 260, 267, 297
stalemate 290, 296
Stampa, Gaspara 187
steam 178–181, 183
Stimme Gottes 11, 12, 298
– *Bat Qol* 169
Stobaeus, Johannes 228, 250
Stoicism, Stoic 14, 38, 51, 96, 100, 146, 150, 217–221, 227f., 234, 250, 296
Storchenau (von), Sigismund 136
Strabo 8, 253
– *Geographica* 8
strategy XXI, 27, 143–145, 154, 215, 218, 220, 223f., 227, 265f., 280, 283, 288–290, 295f., 298
– chess game 289, 296
– conversion strategy 155
– dialectic strategy 194–212
– tactic 144, 216, 269
Strebel, Georgius Sigimundus 77
– *De antiquis Judaeorum Ritibus* 77
stubbornness 272
summa 7, 71, 73, 163, 267, 301, 304
superstition 69, 89–96, 112

Tacitus, Publio Cornelius 69, 217, 229
– *Historiae* 217
Tales 245, 276f.
Techne, craft 5, 68, 130, 206, 266
Telesio, Bernardino 216
– *De natura rerum* 98
Tertullian 6–8, 14f., 21
– *Apologeticum* 6–8, 15
teyku-formula 295
theatre 6, 94, 186f., 194, 230, 232, 239, 247
– theatrical figures 232
theatrum mundi 94, 230, 239f.
theocracy 299
theodicy 129, 137, 144, 149, 164
– Gottesidee 137
theology XIX, 15, 41, 51, 61, 67, 78, 82, 103–105, 113, 117f., 124, 126, 129–131, 133, 135–137, 139, 148, 152, 156, 168, 178, 180, 207, 249, 261, 263f., 279, 283, 298
– Christian theology XIX, 61, 68, 87, 129, 139

– Jewish theology 68, 120, 125, 127, 129–132, 279
negative theology 15, 41, 51, 61, 67, 78, 82, 103–105, 113, 117f., 124, 126, 129–131, 133, 135–137, 139, 148, 152, 156, 168, 178, 180, 207, 249, 261, 263f., 279, 283, 298
– Neoplatonic theology XIX
– positive theology 129
– *prisca theologia* 41
– Protestant theology 81, 116, 118, 132, 143, 175, 275
– *teologi filosofanti* (*philosophantes*) 107, 108f.
– theologians 6, 107f., 122, 128f., 156, 167
– theological discourse 186
– theology of Maimonides 154
– *via negativa* 154
Theophrastus 150, 229f., 296
– *De Causis Plantarum* 97
theoretic, theoretical 40, 57, 87, 143, 154, 221, 237, 281, 292
Theuth 22f.
Thucydides 239
– *History of the Peloponnesian War* 239
time 3, 8, 17, 25f., 34, 36f., 40, 43, 46–50, 53f., 56f., 59, 62, 68, 72, 74, 76, 78, 82, 87, 90, 93f., 100, 105, 109–111, 115, 118, 120, 123, 130, 132, 134f., 138, 147, 150, 154, 157, 160, 163, 168, 171, 174, 181–183, 185, 188, 190–192, 194, 196f., 199–204, 206–208, 213, 220–222, 227, 229–231, 234, 238–244, 246, 248, 252, 259, 261–263, 265f., 270, 281, 285, 289, 291f., 296f., 302
Tissard François 75–76
– *Dialogus* 70, 75
– *Prothymopatris kai Phronimos* 75
Toland, John 87, 102, 209
– *Reasons for Naturalizing the Jews in Great Britain and Ireland* 102, 209
tolerance 45, 55, 58f., 62, 143, 236, 267, 270, 278, 291
Torah 3, 5f., 9, 11, 13, 16f., 19–22, 25–36, 39f., 62f., 71f., 84, 88, 105, 108, 112, 127, 143f., 152, 166f., 178, 180f., 188, 211, 249f., 264, 266–269, 274f., 282f., 285, 295, 306–308
– appropriation of the Torah 3, 8, 9, 30–34, 35, 45, 143
– Greek Torah 20, 26f.

– Jewish and Christian Torah 36
– Miqra' 22
– Mosaic Torah 41
– Moses Torah 82, 102, 108, 112, 283, 295, 319, 327
– reception of Torah 275
– rite of the Torah 88
– secret of the Torah 35
– written and oral Torah 3, 144, 168, 236, 275
tradition 3, 5–9, 14–17, 20–22, 24f., 27–31, 33–36, 39, 41, 43, 45, 47–51, 53f., 56–58, 68–70, 72, 83, 86, 88f., 93, 96, 98, 105, 112f., 115, 117, 124f., 136, 143–146, 152, 155–163, 165, 169, 171, 173, 175, 177f., 185, 188, 190, 209, 219, 223–225, 250, 263f., 266, 269, 273–275, 279, 281–283, 285–287, 290, 293, 295, 298f., 301f., 308, 315
– ancient tradition 16, 20, 55, 168
– chain of tradition 38, 172, 269, 285
– Christian tradition 8, 16, 36, 51f., 200
– classical-pedagogic tradition 137
– collective tradition 53
– exegetical tradition 53, 234
– Hebrew tradition 48, 51, 161
– hermeneutical tradition 9
– intellectual tradition 105
– Jewish-Hellenistic tradition 15, 47
– Jewish tradition 4, 9, 14, 18–20, 22, 44f., 49, 51, 57, 67, 69, 87, 89, 104, 106, 112, 116, 122–124, 132, 134, 143, 151, 170, 189, 191, 236, 249, 265, 269, 274f., 279f., 299f., 302
– literary tradition 57, 67
– Midrashic tradition 28
– mystical tradition 69f.
– postbiblical tradition 112
– primeval tradition 67, 90
– rabbinic tradition 76
– textual tradition 52
– tradition as Religion 89
– written and oral tradition 103, 105
translation, translator 3, 6, 8, 10f., 16–18, 20–22, 25–27, 31–33, 35, 39, 46–48, 56, 70, 72f., 75f., 81, 84, 93, 99–101, 108, 113, 117, 136, 149, 157, 160f., 163, 165–167, 170, 177–179, 182, 190f., 194, 216, 219, 226f., 230–232, 249f., 256, 258, 263, 268–270, 274, 285f.
truth (veritas) 7, 9, 15, 29, 36, 41, 45, 48–50, 53–55, 57f., 62, 67, 95, 102f., 108, 117, 132, 138, 148, 150, 157f., 162, 166–168, 170, 172–173, 175–179, 181f., 217, 223, 231–234, 240, 242, 246–248, 250, 263f., 266, 269, 271–273, 276, 285, 288f., 291, 293–296, 299, 303–316, 321–322
– discovery of truth 50
– divine truth 103
– ethical-religious truth 57
– nude truth 220, 230
– veracity 20, 118, 167, 296
Tubero, Ludovicus Cervarius 78
– *De Turcarum origine, moribus et rebus gestis* 78

University, school 5, 6, 10, 13, 17–19, 23, 32, 36, 39f., 44–47, 62, 69, 71, 73f., 76f., 79f., 83, 88f., 92–95, 97f., 99, 101, 106, 108f., 111, 120f., 122, 127f.,131, 133–136, 138, 146–157, 159, 160, 162, 165, 169, 170, 172f., 175, 178, 187–190, 192, 209, 213–216, 219, 221f., 224–226, 228, 235, 236, 237f., 240, 241, 243, 249–254, 256–258, 264, 266, 269, 270, 273–276, 278, 285, 288f., 290, 296–299
Protestant University XXII
utility 56, 103, 223f.

Valencia (de), Pedro 150, 264, 315
Valla, Lorenzo 159
– *Donatio Constantini* 159
value 9, 30, 71, 74, 82, 86, 88, 129, 144, 172, 175f., 195, 211, 221, 269, 271, 286, 289
Vega (de), Lope 239
Ventimiglia, Angelico Aprosio 195
verus Israel 9, 32–34, 282
vestigia trinitatis 42
Victoria (de), Franciscus 78, 301, 304, 321
– *De Indis* 78, 80f.
Vinci (da), Leonardo 183, 225
vir perfectus 58
virtue 58, 63, 71, 92, 99, 176, 205, 212, 220, 227–229, 237, 255f., 288, 296
– vulgar 95, 102, 228, 231, 233

Weltanschauung XXI, 44, 125, 156, 281, 284, 286
will 3f., 6, 9, 15, 23, 25, 28, 30f., 34, 37, 39, 43, 47, 50f., 53–55, 58–63, 67–69, 78, 81, 87, 89f., 92, 94, 98, 101f., 104, 108, 111f., 116, 120, 123, 126, 128, 130–132,

139, 143–146, 151f., 154–156, 158, 164, 166, 168, 171f., 178, 180–182, 188f., 199f., 202, 204, 209, 213–215, 220–223, 226f., 229–231, 233–237, 240, 246–248, 257, 266, 269–271, 273–276, 281f., 289, 300, 303
- divine will   86, 103, 127, 273
- free will   86, 164, 296
William of Moerbeke   71
William of Ockham   148, 157, 216, 290
Will, Johannes Leonart (Frischmuth, Johann) 3f., 6, 9, 15, 23, 25, 28, 30f., 34, 37, 39, 43, 47, 50f., 53–55, 58–63, 67–69, 78, 81, 87, 89f., 92, 94, 98, 101f., 104, 108, 111f., 116, 120, 123, 126, 128, 130–132, 139, 143–146, 151f., 154–156, 158, 164, 166, 168, 171f., 178, 180–182, 188f., 199f., 202, 204, 209, 213–215, 220–223, 226f., 229–231, 233–237, 240, 246–248, 257, 265–271, 273–276, 281f., 289, 297–303
- An Hebraei statuant idem posse esse et non esse   266
- De Loco Deut. XVII   267–269, 271, 275, 299–303
Wirth, Rudolf (Hospinian, Rudolf)   76
- De Festis Judaeorum et Ethnicorum   76
- De origine progressu ceremoniis   76
wisdom   XXI, 3, 6f., 10, 16–18, 20, 22–24, 28f., 33, 35f., 39f., 42f., 54, 56–58, 62, 67, 90, 93f., 99, 106, 110, 113, 116–119, 132, 135, 143, 145, 156, 172f., 177, 181, 183, 191, 213, 229, 233–236, 246, 249, 277–279, 281f.
- alienated wisdom   XIV, 3
- *ascosa sapientia* (hidden wisdom)   135
- genealogy of wisdom   3, 21f., 39, 133, 143
- Greek wisdom   36f.
- Jewish wisdom   9, 35f., 38, 40, 43, 67, 110f., 113, 265, 285

- lost wisdom   38
- love for wisdom   281
- primordial wisdom   6, 43, 47, 57
- *sophia*   XX, 3, 6, 7, 9, 15, 19, 33, 281, 284
- *sapientia capta*   VIII, XX
- Torah and Rabbinical wisdom   62
- *translatio sapientiae*   35, 107, 285
- written and oral wisdom   21
Wissenschaft des Judentums (Science of Judaism)   67–69, 105, 109–111, 113, 119f., 122, 125, 127, 129, 131f., 137, 139, 155, 189
Wittgenstein, Ludwig   XIX, 290
Wolf, Friedrich A.   41, 101, 111, 121, 124f., 129f., 133–135
- *Encyclopädie der Philologie*   133
- *Vorlesungen über die Alterthumswissenschaft*   124f., 135f.
worship   71f., 76, 79, 128, 295
Wunderkammer   80

Xenophon   5, 244f.

Yehudah of Prague (Marahal)   49, 144
Yeḥiel of Pisa   295
Yeshivah   188–189, 285
Yosef (ben), Yeḥi'el   49, 72, 167, 169, 187

Zabarella, Jacopo   188
Zeno of Cittum   13, 250
Zunz, Leopold   67, 105, 106, 109–111, 113–115, 119, 120–125, 130, 132, 135, 189
- *De Schem-Tobh Palkeira, imprimis de ejusdem libro*   109
- *Die gottesdienstlichen Vorträge der Juden*   120
- *Die jüdische Litteratur*   122
- *Etwas über die rabbinische Litteratur*   109f., 121–126

www.ingramcontent.com/pod-product-compliance
Lightning Source LLC
Chambersburg PA
CBHW081823230426
43668CB00017B/2357